Surveying the Social Sciences

COMPILED BY:

Katherine Humber
University of Maryland

PEARSON

ISBN 10: 1-256-55289-5
ISBN 13: 978-1-256-55289-5

Table of Contents

$\mathcal{H}$istorical Roots of Social Science

Natural scientists tell us that the world has been around for some 6 billion years and that living things have been around for at least 3 billion. We will go back, however, only about 2,600 years, when Western philosophy began on the fringes of ancient Greece (some theorists hold that the Greeks responded to ideas from Eastern civilizations, but there are limits to even our broad sweep). The Greeks came to realize that their ancient account of how the world was created and administered—by an enormous collection of gods, or pantheon—was not the only possible explanation. They are credited with being the first to establish rational theory, independent of theological creed; to grasp rational concepts and use them as a way of looking at reality and seeing logical connections; and to be empirical and antimystical. Two great Greek thinkers of the third and fourth centuries B.C., Plato and Aristotle, are responsible for establishing a basis for knowledge as we know it and deal with it today.

The philosophical debates of the Greek period were in many ways the same ones that go on today, explaining how, when all things change, things must also be simultaneously unchanging; otherwise, something would have to be created out of nothing—a logical impossibility. These ideas would later develop into modern physics, including the laws of thermodynamics and the proposition that matter can neither be created nor destroyed—merely transformed. The Greeks also considered many of the issues that later became the social sciences; for example, they considered the role of the state (political science), the way minds interact with society (psychology), and individuals' interaction within the market (economics). Thus, the history of the social sciences begins with the Greeks. The history, however, is not continuous.

Much of the Greek contribution to knowledge would have been lost (who knows what other contributions actually have been lost?) were it not for its preservation by Eastern civilizations. On their forays into the East during the Crusades (the religious wars from 1095 to 1272 in which Christians in Europe attempted to capture Christianity's traditional territory in the Middle East), Europeans became reacquainted with the learning of the ancient Greeks, and they brought back the body of ancient Greek learning to Europe, where it was generally available by the twelfth century. These ideas spread slowly throughout Europe over the next three hundred years, and by the middle of the fifteenth century, rediscovery of Greek civilization in Europe was widespread. Because the period from about 1453 (the fall of Constantinople) to the end of the seventeenth century was characterized by the rebirth and proliferation of ancient knowledge, it became known as the **Renaissance** (a French word meaning "rebirth").

The Renaissance must have been a wonderful time for scholars. The totality of knowledge was still comprehensible by the human mind. An ideal in the Renaissance was that an educated person could know everything and exercise all skills and social graces. A true Renaissance man was willing to take on all comers on any issue.

As the store of knowledge grew, it became harder and harder to know everything, and so people began to specialize. A natural division opened, one between the humanities (the study of literature, music, and art) and physics. The physics part of this division was not refined enough, and soon physics was broken up into empirical studies (which developed into the various natural sciences) and metaphysics (nonempirical studies that developed into philosophy).

The Renaissance was preceded by the **Middle Ages** (a period from roughly A.D. 476, and the end of the Roman Empire, to A.D. 1453, the defeat of Christian religious armies in Constantinople by the Islamic Turks). In the Middle Ages, religion was so central to life that the study of religion was taken for granted, and it tied together all the other fields of study. For example, painters painted religious pictures, musicians wrote religious music, and the study of literature was the study of the Bible and its commentators. Questions that today seem the obvious ones, such as, Why are people divided into classes? and Why are the poor poor? were simply not asked. Things were the way they were because that was God's will. Once one knew God's will, the issue was how to carry it out. For example, medieval scholars believed in a "just" price and that collecting interest on savings was immoral. They taught those principles and condemned those who did not follow their teachings.

As the Renaissance dawned and continued, that religious tie provoked tension as scholars in the various fields of study came to conclusions different from the church's doctrines, beginning a long conflict between religious learning and beliefs and so-called rationalist learning and beliefs.

The tension between religious explanations and rationalist explanations was (and still is) inevitable. The rationalist approach places human reason above faith. In a rationalist approach, one looks for logical connections and is continually asking the question, Can you prove it? This meant that somehow the rationalists had to figure out what it meant to prove something. A religious approach places faith above reason. A religious explanation had no need to prove anything: Explanations were accepted on faith.

Throughout the Renaissance, rationalism more and more replaced religion as the organizing principle of knowledge, and as it did, the various fields of knowledge became divided along rationalist lines. The humanities still reflected religious issues; the rationalist revolution came much later to the humanities. To the degree that they were considered, most of the issues we now classify under social science were studied as part of history. History was part of literature and the humanities. It was simply a documentation of what had happened—it never asked *why* something happened. To ask why meant failure to accept God's will. Thus, it was primarily from philosophy, not history, that most of the social sciences emerged.

The natural sciences and philosophy divided along modes of inquiry and answers to the question, Can you prove it? The study of philosophy itself evolved into a variety of fields, such as logic, morals, and epistemology (the study of knowledge).

The Enlightenment

The **Enlightenment** is the period in which rationalism definitely replaced religion as the organizing principle of knowledge. The Enlightenment began between A.D. 1650 and A.D. 1700 and continued for about one hundred years. It is in this period that the development of the social sciences took hold and flourished.

By the time of the Enlightenment, it had become evident that to know everything—to be a Renaissance scholar—was impossible. Not only was it impossible to know everything, but it was also impossible to know everything about just one subject—say, all of physics or all of philosophy. Individuals began to specialize their study. For instance, chemistry and astronomy were separated from physics.

As philosophers delved into their subject, they further divided philosophy into parts. One part was metaphilosophy, the study of issues that most scholars agreed were not empirically testable. One such issue was: Because God is all-powerful, can he create a rock so heavy he cannot move it? The other division of philosophy dealt with issues that could, in principle at least, be empirically tested. For instance: What type of political organization of society is preferable? It is from the second division that the social sciences evolved. (They were called sciences because they were in principle meant to be empirically testable.)

The Enlightenment spawned social science because the Enlightenment rejected the assumption that the classical world of the Greeks and the Romans was perfect. In the Enlightenment (roughly the whole of the eighteenth century), there was a general belief that civilization had improved and so too should the thinking about civilization. Moreover, in the seventeenth century, just preceding the Enlightenment, there was continual turmoil—a long drawn-out war between France and England and a religious conflict between Catholics and Protestants about how to interpret God's will. That fight broke down the religious explanations and made people very much aware of social problems. Which of the two explanations, Catholic or Protestant, was right? Why were they fighting? What could be done about it? The social sciences developed as individuals attempted to explain those social problems and suggest what could be done to solve them.

Although the existence of social problems that require solutions may seem obvious to you, it was not always so obvious. This view is the product of the Enlightenment, which established the "three humiliations" of human beings. These are:

1. The earth is not the center of the universe.
2. Humans are creatures of nature like other animals.
3. Our reasoning ability is subject to passions and subconscious desires.

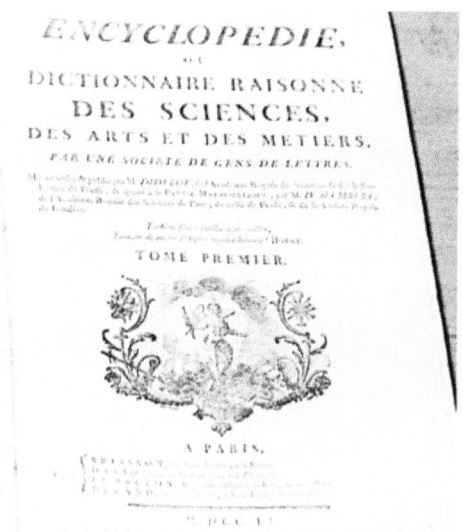

Frontispiece from Diderot's Encyclopédie, *written during the Enlightenment.*

Before we experienced these humiliations, thinkers could rely on an order they believed was established by God. Social problems were set up by God and were to be accepted or endured. Only after the beginning of the Enlightenment did people begin to believe that society and culture are themselves products of history and the evolution of culture—that they had changed and would continue to change.

As is often the case, the change in viewpoint had a paradoxical counterpoint, and human beings' "humiliation" was accompanied by a belief in human beings' power. If society could change, then the change could be, at least to some extent, guided and directed by human beings.

Since its conception, social science has entwined these two aspects. Sometimes it is simply trying to understand, and it accepts our limited powers and our place in the cosmos, and at other times it is trying to change society.

From Philosophy to Social Science

The evolution of philosophy into the social sciences can be seen in France, where philosophers joined to produce an encyclopedia, edited by Denis Diderot and Jean d'Alembert, which appeared over a span of several years in the mid-1700s. The full title of this encyclopedia proclaimed it to be a rational dictionary of science, art, and industry. Unlike earlier compilations, it contained systematic articles on man, society, and method, and a number of the first definitions of the social sciences can be traced to this mammoth work.

There are many ways to look at social problems, and as scholars began considering human beings in reference to their social environment, the diversity soon became apparent. The history of each of the social sciences becomes hopelessly tangled with that of each of the others at this point. In the Enlightenment, scholars were debating one another and ideas were quickly evolving. To capture even a flavor of the interaction and debate leads to a formidable morass, hardly conducive to a social science course. So we will stop our consideration here.

Some Important Terms

Enlightenment
Middle Ages
Renaissance

Social Science and Its Methods

After reading this chapter, you should be able to:

- Define social science and explain why it is important
- List the various social sciences
- State the nine steps that make up the scientific method
- Discuss some reasonable approaches to problems in social science
- Differentiate the historical method from the case method and the comparative method
- Distinguish educated common sense from common sense
- Explain why a good scientist is always open to new ways of looking at issues

Theories should be as simple as possible, but not more so.

—Albert Einstein

On September 11, 2001, eighteen men boarded airplanes with the intent of crashing them into the World Trade Center, the Pentagon, and the White House or Capitol. They succeeded with three of the planes, causing enormous destruction. The fourth plane crashed, but thanks to passengers who discovered the highjackers' plans and attacked the highjackers, the destruction of the White House or Capitol was prevented. What forces drove the highjackers to undertake such action? What forces led the passengers to organize together to thwart them? What might have prevented the highjackings? Such questions fall under the purview of **social science**—the scientific study of social, cultural, psychological, economic, and political forces that guide individuals in their actions.

Formal social science is relatively new. Nevertheless, a vast amount of information has been accumulated concerning the social life of human beings. This information has been used in building a system of knowledge about the nature, growth, and functioning of human societies. Social science is the name given to that system of knowledge.

All knowledge is (1) knowledge of human beings, including their culture and products, and (2) knowledge of natural environment. Human culture has been changing, and knowledge about it has been gradually accumulating ever since the far distant time when humans first assumed their distinctively human character. But until rather recent times, this knowledge was not scientific in the modern sense. **Scientific knowledge** is knowledge that has been systematically gathered, classified, related, and interpreted. It is concerned with learning the concepts and applying those concepts to particulars, rather than just learning a vast amount of information.

Primitive peoples acquired much of their knowledge unconsciously, just as we today still begin the use of our native language and acquire many of the basic elements in our culture unconsciously. For the most part, they accepted the world as they found it, and if any

From Chapter 1 of *Social Science: An Introduction to the Study of Society,* 14/e. Elgin F. Hunt. David C. Colander. Copyright © 2011 by Pearson Education. Published by Allyn & Bacon. All rights reserved.

Social Science versus the Soaps

Faced with the events that affect our lives, we have two options: We can lose ourselves in a parody of reality, such as becoming experts on the soaps (is Laura really sleeping with John's wife's brother?), or we can try to understand those events—what actually happens. Some educators, following the philosophy of Plato, try to argue the moral superiority of the latter: Better to be an unhappy learned person than a happy fool. Others find that unconvincing. Following Jeremy Bentham, the social philosopher, they prefer happiness. The problem they have with the soaps is that soaps don't make you happy; soaps quickly become boring. You soon play out the options in your head and, often, create far better scenarios than the television writer. It's a bit like tic tac toe: one move (if you know what you are doing), and the game is done. Pinochle is somewhat more interesting, and the good TV shows approach the complexity of pinochle. But here again, after seven or eight cards have been played, the possibilities soon become evident. Chess is a step above this, with its infinite number of possibilities. But still, after twenty or so moves (and often fewer), good chess players can anticipate the outcome and choose to call a draw, resign, or declare victory.

Quite frankly, soaps, tic tac toe, pinochle, and chess are not for this author. I prefer a far more complicated game—one in which I'm both a player and a pawn. That game could be called the game of life, or it could be called the game of society. It is played by some 7.8 billion people, each having a wide variety of possible moves that range from shooting up a playground full of schoolchildren to trying to travel farther into outer space, construct faster computers, or improve humans by modifying their genes. The players in the game of society are divided into two types: male and female. These two types have certain drives, and desires, and certain rules that are passed on to them, either through their genes or through society's mores.

The ultimate goal of the game is often unclear, although its day-to-day objects can be said to consist of continuing to play the game and to keep the game itself alive. What winning or losing the game might be is clouded. Probably, if we commit suicide, we are losers. If we make a million dollars, are admired by our acquaintances for it, and are happy, we are probably winners. Many people even question whether we are playing the game of our own free will or whether we are merely the pawns of a god who has predetermined all our actions.

This game is far more diverse and interesting than other games. The possibilities are endless and the challenge immediate. It has elements of danger, like Russian roulette (if we really *do* goof, we *will* blow ourselves up). And it has its peaceful moments. But what makes it the most interesting game of all is that we are both the players and the played, at times moving ourselves as we make stupid or foolish choices and contrive sophisticated or imaginative solutions, and at other times watching other players as they make their choices and contrive their solutions. *Trying to understand this game is what social science is all about.* And the reason I am a social scientist instead of a TV fan is that I watch society and try to understand what makes society work. It's a whole lot more challenging and fun than watching the soaps. Moreover, unlike the soaps, watching society has a purpose—if we can understand society, we might be able to make it better.

Social science has fascinated enormous numbers of people, and a whole set of ponderings about the game has already developed. These ponderings concern the nature, growth, and functioning of human societies. This text introduces you to the past ponderings of social scientists.

explanations seemed called for, they invented supernatural ones. Some primitive peoples believed that every stream, tree, and rock contained a spirit that controlled its behavior.

In modern times, our emphasis is on the search for scientific knowledge. We have divided human knowledge into a number of areas and fields, and every science represents the systematic collection and study of data in one of these areas, which can be grouped roughly into two major fields—social science and natural science. Each of these fields is subdivided into a number of specialized sciences or disciplines to facilitate more intensive study and deeper understanding. Social science is the field of human knowledge that deals with all aspects of the group life of human beings. **Natural science** is concerned with the natural environment in which human beings exist. It includes such sciences as physics and chemistry, which deal with the laws of matter, motion, space, mass, and energy; it also includes the **biological sciences,** which deal with living things. The third field of study is the **humanities,** which deals with literature, music, art, and philosophy. The humanities are closely related to social science in that both deal with humans and their culture. Social science, however, is most concerned with those basic elements of culture that determine the general patterns of human behavior. The humanities deal with special aspects of human culture and are primarily concerned with our attempts to express spiritual and esthetic values and to discover the meaning of life. Whereas the social sciences study issues in a systematic, scientific way, the focus of the humanities is more on the emotions and feelings themselves than on the system employed to sharpen that focus.

The importance of social science goes far beyond the specific social sciences. It is social science thinking that underlies much of the law as well as our understanding of international relations and government. All these fields are the natural byproducts of social science inquiry. Thus, a knowledge of social science is necessary for anyone trying to understand current world events.

Social Science

No field of study is more important to human beings than the social sciences. To understand society is to learn not only the conditions that limit our lives but also the opportunities open to us for improving the human condition. Increasing our knowledge of human society is as important as learning more about mathematics, physics, chemistry, or engineering, for unless we can develop societies in which human beings can live happy, meaningful, and satisfying lives, we cannot reap the benefits from learning how to make better automobiles and skyscrapers, traveling in space, or constructing faster computers. Albert Einstein summed it up: "Politics is more difficult than physics and the world is more likely to die from bad politics than from bad physics."

Because all expressions of human culture are related and interdependent, to gain a real understanding of human society we must have some knowledge of all its major aspects. If we concentrate on some phases and neglect others, we will have a distorted picture. But social science today is such a vast complex that no one student can hope to master all of it. Thus, social science itself has been broken up into anthropology, sociology, history, geography, economics, political science, and psychology. (The boxes in this chapter provide a brief introduction to each of these disciplines.)

This list of social science disciplines is both too broad and too narrow. It is too broad because parts of the fields of history, geography, and psychology should not be included as social sciences. For instance, parts of history and geography belong in the humanities, and parts of psychology belong in the natural sciences. The list is too narrow because new social sciences are emerging, such as cognitive science and sociobiology, that incorporate new findings and new ways of looking at reality. (See box on The Evolving Social Sciences.)

Because all knowledge is interrelated, there are inevitable problems in defining and cataloging the social sciences. Often, it is difficult to know where one social science ends and another begins. Not only are the individual social sciences interrelated, but the social sciences as a whole body are also related to the natural sciences and the humanities. The strains of the old song, "The hip bone's connected to the thigh bone,..." are appropriate to the social sciences. To understand history, it is helpful, even necessary, to understand geography; to understand economics, it is necessary to understand psychology. Similar arguments can be made for all of the social sciences.

One of the difficulties in presenting definitions and descriptions of the various social sciences is that social scientists themselves don't agree on what it is they do, or should be doing. In preparing this chapter, we met with groups of social scientists specializing in specific fields and asked them to explain what it was that distinguished their field from others.

The Evolving Social Sciences

The themes of this text are evolution and change. Thus, it would be surprising if the divisions among the social sciences that currently exist still remain ten years from now. Indeed, with the development of new technology and technological advances in the physical sciences, the distinction among the various sciences is blurring and new sciences are developing. As these fields develop, the boundaries of the various social sciences change.

Interaction among the various social sciences is creating new fields, such as economic psychology, psychological economics, and sociopolitical anthropology. In economics and political science, too, a group of economists is calling for the reintegration of these two fields into political economy, and some schools do have departments of political economy.

Change is also occurring in the natural sciences, and there is interaction between the natural and social sciences. New developments in genetic theory have caused many to believe it is time for a new social science, called cognitive science, which combines psychology, linguistics, philosophy, social anthropology, and molecular biology. Although it is still in the process of formation, a tentative definition of **cognitive science** is the study of how the mind identifies problems and how it solves those problems. For instance, there are more ways to write the letter *s* than there are people who know how to write that letter (all people who write plus the printing press and computer software and innumerable typefaces designed for them). Let us identify the problem as how to recognize the letter *s* when we see it. We know the result of the exercise: Everyone who knows how to read can instantly recognize most renditions of the letter *s* (the handwriting of a few college students and some physicians excepted). But we do not currently know *how* we do it. Or, how do you know the face of your roommate from the face of your mother, from the face of the letter carrier, from the face of Brad Pitt? There has been speculation about how the mind works for almost as long as there have been minds, theories, and even experiments, but few specific riddles have been conclusively solved.

Whether these upstart disciplines take hold remains to be seen, but that some change will take place is certain.

There was little agreement among specialists in a particular social science, let alone among all social scientists. A cynic once said, "Economics is what economists do." If we replaced "economics" and "economists" with any of the other social sciences and its practitioners, we would have as good a definition as possible. Unfortunately, it would not be very helpful to those who do not know what social scientists do.

One important difference among the individual social scientists did come out of these discussions: Even when two social scientists are considering the same issue, because their training is different they focus on different aspects of that problem. Geographers fixate on spaces and spatial relativities, economists on market incentives, and political scientists on group decision making. Thus, although we might not be able to define, unambiguously, the domains of the various social sciences, you will get a sense of the various approaches as we consider issues from various perspectives throughout the text.

The study of social science is more than the study of the individual social sciences. Although it is true that to be a good social scientist you must know each of those components, you must also know how they interrelate. By specializing too early, many social scientists can lose sight of the interrelationships that are so essential to understanding modern problems. That's why it's necessary to have a course covering all the social sciences. In fact, it wouldn't surprise me if one day a news story such as the one in the box on the next page appeared.

To understand how and when social science broke up, you must study the past. Imagine for a moment that you're a student in 1062, in the Italian city of Bologna, site of one of the first major universities in the Western world. The university has no buildings; it consists merely of a few professors and students. There is no tuition fee. At the end of a professor's lecture, if you like it, you pay. And if you don't like it, the professor finds himself without students and without money. If we go back still earlier, say to Greece in the

𝒰nified Social Systems Theory Derived

Dateline 2050. Researchers today announced the development of a unified theory of the social sciences. The new theory, which had its early foundations in the work of Ludwig von Bertalanffy, is the equivalent in social science of the unified field theory in physics, which tied together the various forces of nature into a general theory. The formulation of the unified field theory in 2020 solved the problem that stymied earlier physicists such as Albert Einstein. It intensified the efforts of social scientists to develop their own unified theory. The theory, which is also called a unified social systems theory, ties together the various social sciences that in the nineteenth and twentieth centuries diverged into anthropology, sociology, history, geography, economics, political science, and psychology. The theory combines the work on complex systems begun by John von Neumann in the late 1940s and early 1950s with game theory, also begun by von Neumann, to form a coherent whole, and captures many of the interrelationships that were previously lost in the fragmentation or divisions of social science. That work was extended in the complexity revolution in science that came into its own in the early 2000s. By combining these theories with recent advances in the separate social sciences, the resulting new unified social science theory provides new insights into how society works.

When asked what set her on this path, the social scientist who developed the theory said it was the experience in her first social science class, in which she used the classic Hunt and Colander text, *Social Science*. In that class, with the aid of the insights her teacher provided, the scientist grasped the first inklings of how these various theories might be put together, setting the stage for her later achievement.

sixth century B.C., we can see the philosopher Socrates walking around the streets of Athens, arguing with his companions. He asks them questions, and then other questions, leading these people to reason the way he wants them to reason (this became known as the *Socratic method*).

Times have changed since then; universities sprang up throughout the world and created colleges within the universities. Oxford, one of the first universities, now has thirty colleges associated with it, and the development and formalization of educational institutions has changed the roles of both students and faculty. As knowledge accumulated, it became more and more difficult for one person to learn, let alone retain, it all. In the sixteenth century, one could still aspire to know all there was to know, and the definition of the Renaissance man (people were even more sexist then than they are now) was one who was expected to know about everything.

Unfortunately, at least for someone who wants to know everything, the amount of information continues to grow exponentially while the size of the brain has grown only slightly. The way to deal with the problem is not to try to know everything about everything. Today we must specialize. That is why social science separated from the natural sciences and why social science, in turn, has been broken down into various subfields, such as anthropology and sociology.

There are advantages and disadvantages to specialization, and many social problems today are dealt with by teams of various social scientists. Each brings his or her specialty to the table. For example, one of the authors is an economist but works on projects with geographers, sociologists, anthropologists, political scientists, and psychologists. More and more interdisciplinary majors are being created; one of the authors of this text teaches in both the economics department and the international politics and economics department at his school. Interdisciplinary graduate schools of public policy have grown enormously. In these programs, students study all the social sciences while specializing in one. Figure 1 provides a graphic overview of the evolution of knowledge and the present social sciences. (The appendix at the end of this chapter expands on the ideas in this diagram.)

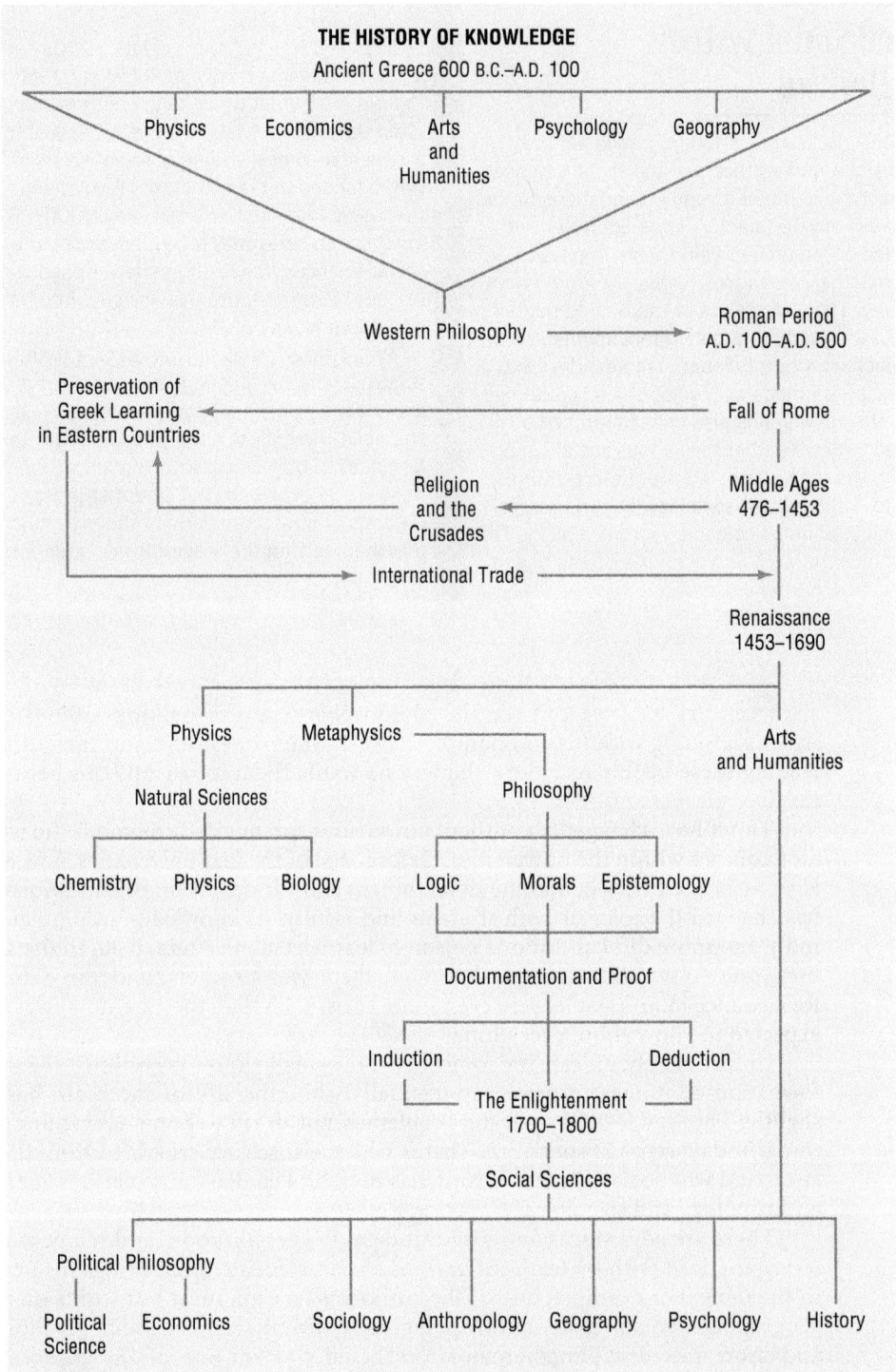

Figure 1

Knowledge at a glance. The development of knowledge in messy, but assuming that a picture is worth a thousand words, we offer this sketch of the development of knowledge. Maybe it's worth five hundred words.

*A*nthropology

Anthropology is the study of the relationship between biological traits and socially acquired characteristics. Sometimes called the study of humans, it consists of two broad fields:

1. Physical anthropology
2. Cultural anthropology

Some of the concerns of physical anthropology are:

■ Influence of evolution of natural environment on the physical characteristics of humans

■ Human evolution: how modern *homo sapiens* evolved from earlier species

Some of the concerns of cultural anthropology are:

■ Archaeology, or the remains of extinct civilizations that left no written records

■ Organization of preliterate societies

■ Characteristics of subgroups or subcultures within contemporary society

Among the topics that interest anthropologists are excavation of formerly inhabited sites, fossils, the gene pool, technology and artifacts, linguistics, values, and kinship.

Social Science as a System of Rules

Today the amount of knowledge is increasing faster than ever. How, then, can a unified social science theory ever be formulated? The answer is found in abstraction and the ability to discover rules or relationships (rather than simply facts) and rules relating rules to other rules.

To understand the importance of knowing rules, think back to grade school when you learned addition. You didn't memorize the sum of 127 and 1,448. Instead you learned an algorithm (a fancy name for a rule) about adding (7 + 8 = 15; write down the 5 and carry the 1...). Then you had to memorize only a few relationships. By changing the number system from a base ten system to a binary system (0 and 1 are the only numbers), you cut substantially the amount of memorization (all you need to know is 0 + 0 = 0; 0 + 1 = 1; and 1 + 1 = 10) and you could apply the same rule again and again, adding all possible numbers (an insight that played an important role in the development of the computer). Knowing the rules saved you from enormous amounts of memorization, but nonetheless gave you access to a large amount of information.

Another way to look at the problem is to think of the library. If you have a small library, you can know nearly everything in it, but once your library gets larger, you will quickly find that having more books makes it harder to know what's in there. However, if you put in place a filing system, such as the Dewey decimal system or the Library of Congress system, you can access the books through a filing system. The rules of the filing system give you the key to great amounts of information, just as the rules of addition, subtraction, or algebra do. General rules, once learned, can be applied to large numbers of particulars. The higher you go (rules about rules about rules), the more you can know with less memorization.[1]

All this is relevant to social science and the 2050 dateline because social science, too, is held together by rules or relationships. If there is to be a unified social science theory, it will be because some student started thinking about rules and how the rules of the various social sciences can fit together. If you understand the general concepts, you can apply them in a variety of circumstances. Thus the future "unified social scientists" will not necessarily know all the facts of a particular social science. Each of the specialties will retain its identity and will likely become even more specialized. But as that specialization occurs, it creates the need for a new specialization that concentrates on tying together the various component parts of social science. The new unified social scientists will know the general rules of the individual social sciences and the rules of how one social science interacts with another, but they will not know all the specific facts of any one of them.

The preceding argument is a heavy one to throw at you in the first pages of a textbook because it asks you not only to know the lessons of the individual social sciences, but also to

---

[1]It was an architect, Ludwig Mies van der Rohe, who compressed such exposition into a famous statement, "Less is more."

Sociology

Sociology is the systematic study of relationships among people. Sociologists assume that behavior is influenced by people's social, political, occupational, and intellectual groupings and by the particular settings in which they find themselves at one time or another. Sociologists differ in their approach. Their three major choices are:

1. Functionalism
2. Conflict
3. Interactionism

Sociology's vast subject matter can be identified as a study of people:

- Where they collect
- How they socialize and organize
- Whom they include in and exclude from their groups
- What they do to their environment
- When they confront formulas for control, such as politics, law, finance, religion, education, and social pressures
- Why they change

Geography

Geography is the study of the natural environment and how it influences social and cultural development. Some of the concerns of geography are:

- Ecology
- Climate
- Resources
- Accessibility
- Demography

Geography has practical applications manifest in:

- Maps
- Trade patterns
- Industrial and agricultural decisions
- Settlement of population
- Aggression and acquisition

go beyond and strive for an understanding of their synthesis. Going beyond is ultimately what learning is all about and what makes it so challenging. We would like to be able to say that we can guide you to a unified social science theory, but the truth is that all we can do is give you a boost and encouragement. After surveying the social sciences, you can decide in which one, if any, you want to specialize; whether you should work toward tying them all together; or whether you should bag the whole approach and go into a premed program.

The Scientific Method and Its Application

The **scientific method** is a set of rules about how to establish rules. The use of the scientific method is perhaps the most important tool you can have in studying social science because it enables you not only to learn the lessons of the individual social sciences, but also to go beyond and strive for an understanding of their synthesis.

Conditions Favorable to Scientific Inquiry. Scientific inquiry is possible only in a society in which certain attitudes are developed or tolerated. Successful scientific investigation requires from the investigator not only intelligence but certain mental attitudes as well. One of these is curiosity, which makes people ask two questions: Why? and How? Another is skepticism, which makes people reexamine past explanations and reevaluate past evidence. To reexamine and reevaluate, investigators need objectivity, which enables them to seek impartially for the truth, to make every effort not to allow personal preconceptions, prejudices, or desires to color the observed facts or influence the interpretation of those facts. When these three attitudes—curiosity, skepticism, and objectivity— come together, scientific inquiry can flourish.

In preliterate tribal societies, the obstacles to the development of scientific methods of inquiry are very great. Such societies are much more bound by custom and tradition than are modern societies. The traditional way of doing things is regarded as the only right way. Moreover, any serious deviation from established procedures is likely to be regarded as a danger to the group.

We cannot classify Europe in the Middle Ages as either preliterate or tribal. Nevertheless, respect for tradition, for ancient authorities, and for religious

History

History is the study of past events. It is a social science in the sense that it is a systematic attempt to learn about and verify past events and to relate them to one another and to the present. Every event has a historical context within which we commonly say the event must be studied. The subject matter of history is everything that has already happened. The study of history involves:

- Identifying
- Classifying
- Arranging
- Patterning

The fruits of the study of history are:

- Imposition of order
- Appreciation of variety
- Possibilities of prediction
- Realization of limitation

dictates was so strong then that the growth of a scientific spirit was stunted. The free development of modern science had to wait until such events as the Crusades, the Renaissance, the great voyages of discovery, and the Reformation had loosened the hold of tradition.

Nature of the Scientific Method.   Modern science is based on the assumption that this is an orderly universe, ruled by the law of cause and effect. Any given set of circumstances always produces the same result. If seemingly identical situations have different results, they were not really alike; some significant difference existed and was overlooked. Further investigation should disclose what this difference was.

Science offers no final explanations of the universe and its phenomena. Time, space, matter, energy—existence itself—are mysteries the ultimate nature of which are probably forever beyond the grasp of the human search. But an accepted scientific theory may be regarded as an explanation, up to a certain point, of a scientific law.

Scientific investigation is seldom simple. Each field of knowledge has its special problems, and investigators must always adjust their methods to the peculiarities of the situation they are dealing with. A method of investigation that is of great importance in some fields is the setting up and carrying out of controlled experiments.

The Experimental Method and Its Limitations.   The **experimental method** is a method of separating out causal factors. It consists of running an experiment many times with only one variant. If the results of the experiments are different, that one variant is most likely the cause.[2] In chemistry, physics, and biology, such controlled experiments play an important role in discovering facts and testing hypotheses. In these sciences, an investigator can create a situation in which all the significant factors that bear on a problem can be controlled.

But there are limits to the use of the experimental method when a scientist cannot control the situations that are significant for the solution of problems. In the social sciences, very little use can be made of the method of controlled experiment except in dealing with certain relationships that involve rather small groups, because the investigator cannot control the situations. For example, one way to prove or disprove the proposition that high tariffs bring prosperity would be to apply very heavy duties to all goods entering the United States for a considerable period of time, while holding constant all other factors affecting business activity. If a sustained increase in prosperity followed, we would then have substantial evidence to support the thesis that high tariffs are a cause of prosperity. No investigator, let us say an economist, can control the country's tariff policy; and even if she could, while the high tariff was in effect many other social changes would be taking place, such as strikes, the establishment of new industries, and perhaps even wars. Some of these other changes would doubtless have much more influence on the state of national prosperity than

---

[2]But it is always possible that some other factor was not "held constant." If you remember chemistry experiments in high school, you know how hard it is to keep all other things constant.

The Saga of Hans, the Thinking Horse

The scientific method can be seen in the saga of Hans, the Thinking Horse. Around 1900, according to reports published in a Berlin, Germany, newspaper, there was a horse that was good at math, and when his owner asked him math questions, the horse could answer by tapping out the correct number with one of his front hooves. People who witnessed the horse's ability were puzzled, and they called in a number of social scientists to investigate the phenomenon. To their amazement, they found that not only could Clever Hans, as he was known, add and subtract when his owner asked him—he could also calculate square roots. The social scientists were convinced that, against all odds, they had indeed been shown a thinking horse.

Another social scientist, though, a skeptical young psychologist by the name of Oskar Pfungst, had a different idea. He retested Hans, asking a set of questions to which Pfungst himself did not know the answers. He discovered that although Hans succeeded on nearly every question if the questioner knew the answer, the horse failed nearly every question when the questioner did not know the answer. A social scientist's skepticism had shown that Hans could not really reason, even though it seemed as if he could. This true story demonstrates the important trait of skepticism. The scientific community declared that Hans was just a horse.

But a quality those scientists did not show was imagination. Even though Hans could not think and reason, he had an amazing ability: He could almost read minds. When it came to people who knew the answers to the questions they were asking, he could monitor changes in his questioners' posture, their breathing, their facial expressions, and their inflections and speech patterns. He could interpret the signals they were sending and then provide the responses they wanted. This is an ability that some humans have—although generally to a lesser degree than Hans—and it is an ability that can supplement thinking. Yet it was only at the end of the twentieth century that comparative psychologists showed the imagination to start analyzing this kind of ability in detail.

The lack of imagination exhibited by some scientists in the past limited the scope of the scientific programs they followed. A good scientist must have both skepticism and imagination.

would the high tariff and would make it impossible to separate out the effects of the high tariff from the effects of all these other events.

Most problems of interest to social scientists involve very large groups of people, often society as a whole. Controlled experiments cannot be used to solve such problems. When, however, social scientists can solve a problem by working with small groups, they may be able to make a limited use of the experimental method if the people involved will cooperate. Also, they can study **natural experiments,** which occur when two similar areas or entities choose different policies, and the effects of the different policies can be systematically studied. With natural experiments, researchers do not get perfect control, but they get some.

In the future, with further advances in computer technology, social scientists will study policy issues using virtual social systems in which a computer model of numerous interacting individuals creates a virtual system that can analogue what occurs in the real world. Because of the complexity of social systems, such virtual systems remain a hope for the future, not a reality.

Social experiments are sometimes called experiments, but, unless they have a "control" that followed a different path and hence can be studied as a natural experiment, they are not what we mean by experiment. A social experiment is simply the introduction and "trying out" of new social policies. For example, Oregon's change in the financing of health insurance or Florida's experiments with vouchers for financing education might be called social experiments. The distinction involves the ability to have a control and to be able to replicate the experiment. The less the control, and the less the ability to repeat the experiment, the less sure we are of the results.

Methodology and the Social Sciences

Because it is so difficult to experiment in social science, some people have insisted that it is not science. Except for the prestige carried by the word, whether we call the study of society

Economics

Economics is the study of the ways in which men and women make a living, the most pressing problem most human beings face. It considers the social organization through which people satisfy their wants for scarce goods and services. Its subject matter is often summarized as:

- Production
- Distribution
- Consumption

Some of the topics it includes are:

- Supply and demand
- Monetary and fiscal policy
- Costs
- Inflation
- Unemployment

Economics seeks to explain, guide, and predict social arrangements by which we satisfy economic wants.

Political Science

Political science is the study of social arrangements to maintain peace and order within a given society. It deals with government, and its interests are:

- Politics
- Laws
- Administration
- Theory of the nature and functions of the state
- International relations

It has both a philosophical and a practical base. It examines the theory of systems of government, but it also studies actual practices by which government:

- Taxes
- Prohibits
- Regulates
- Protects
- Provides services

a science is not important. It is merely a question of definition. If we mean by *science* the natural sciences only, then social science is not true science. If we mean by science only the so-called exact sciences, then again social science is not included. If, however, we use the term *science* broadly, to include all systematic attempts to expand knowledge by applying the scientific method, then social science must definitely be included in the scientific family. What is really important is that social scientists have discovered many significant relationships that are sufficiently dependable to add greatly to our understanding of social behavior and to serve as useful guides in dealing with some social problems.

There has been much debate about the correct methodology to be used in social science. Thomas Kuhn, a famous philosopher of science, defined a **paradigm** as a scientific theory and the core of beliefs that surround it. He argued that scientific progression occurs by paradigm shifts in which, for a long time, scientists will resist change and hold on to an old theory even as evidence mounts up against it, and even when another theory better fits the data. Eventually, however, the evidence in favor of the new theory is so great that suddenly scientists shift their thinking. The process can be likened to the way a drop of water forms on a faucet. It grows larger and larger until it falls. A good example in the sciences is Einstein's relativity theory in physics, which was initially scoffed at but was later adopted because it was consistent with a wider range of physical phenomena than was the earlier gravitational theory of Sir Isaac Newton.

Social scientists have discussed at great length whether Kuhn's theory of paradigm shift is appropriate for the social sciences. If it is, it gives legitimacy to competing theories. If it is not, then the generally accepted theory can be considered the best. The issue has never been resolved, but our understanding of the relevance of theories has advanced.

Imre Lakatos, another famous philosopher of science, has extended Kuhn's arguments by saying that in social science there are generally many competing theories, each being extended through competing **research programs,** or groups of scientists working on a particular problem. For example, in psychology there are the behaviorists and the Freudians. In sociology there are functionalists, conflict theorists, and interactionists. We could cite different theories within each social science. Advocates of each of the paradigms compete for researchers. The group of researchers most successful in competing for followers is the one most likely to grow.

*P*sychology

Psychology deals with the mind and personality of the individual. It is a social science because humans are social creatures. It focuses on the individual and physical processes, such as:

- Biological structure
- Development and maturation

Of the various branches of psychology, the most relevant to social science is social psychology. Social psychology is the study of the individual's behavior as it influences and is influenced by the behavior of others. Some specific topics that interest psychologists and social psychologists are:

- Socialization
- Environment and heredity
- Adjustment and maladjustment

These social scientists deal with natural phenomena such as emotion, memory, perception, and intelligence.

Other philosophers of science go further. Some, like Paul Feurabend, argue that all methodology is limiting and that the correct methodology is no methodology. Still others argue that sociological issues, such as what is likely to advance a scientist's career, rather than the truth of a theory determine what the scientist believes.

In this text, we emphasize the competition among various theories. By doing so, we hope to show how, in social science, controversy plays an important role in the development of our knowledge.

Probably the best way to understand the scientific method is to consider a couple of examples that do *not* follow the scientific method. For instance, consider astrology or numerology. These pseudostudies hold that by analyzing the alignment of the stars or the position of certain numbers, individuals can discover or predict events that will affect them. However, the accuracy of the discoveries or the reliability of the predictions has never been satisfactorily demonstrated to most social scientists. Even though we might turn to our horoscopes and say, "Aha! That seems to fit my character or my experience," if we critically consider these predictions, often we see that the statements are so broad that they can be applied more or less appropriately to a wide range of happenings or possibilities. This is not to say that the social sciences always avoid that. Economics, for instance, often comes up with predictions from large, highly sophisticated mathematical models (called *econometric models*), and some of these predictions are no better for steering a course than back-of-the-envelope estimates.

A good social scientist generally takes an agnostic (not believing but also not disbelieving) position about claims until they can be tested and retested. Consider, for example, parapsychology, which argues that people can transmit certain information independently of all conventional forms of communication. Shirley MacLaine's best-selling book *Out on a Limb* convinced many people that the claim of parapsychology is true. Most social scientists remain unconvinced. They hold that, to date, the theories have not been sufficiently demonstrated. In stating that these theories have not been tested, a good social scientist is not dogmatic. It is possible that we social scientists become so tied to our way of looking at the world that we are unable to consider the possibilities of other ways. Who is to say that the tests we accept as conclusive are the "right" tests? Or that our training hasn't biased the tests?

Ultimately, however, we must make a working judgment about what is and what isn't an acceptable test, and social scientists' methodology is an expression of that working judgment. It should, however, be presented as a working judgment, not as a set of definitive criteria of what is true and what is false. That's why, generally, good social scientists remain agnostic over a wide range of issues that they just don't have time to investigate. Thus, in many ways, what you will get out of a study of social science and an understanding of its methods is a healthy understanding of the limitations of your powers to know.

The Methods of Social Science

The basic procedures of the scientific method are as important in social science as in physical science. Social scientists must observe carefully, classify and analyze their facts, make generalizations, and attempt to develop and test hypotheses to explain their generalizations. Their problem, however, is often more difficult than that of physical scientists. The facts gathered by the social scientist—for example, those concerning the cultures of different peoples—have similarities, but each fact may also be unique in significant respects. Facts of this kind are difficult to classify and interpret. Further, as we have already noted, the generalizations or laws that the social scientist can make are likely to be less definite and certain than those of the physical scientist.

The difficulty of discovering relatively exact laws that govern social life results from several circumstances. First, the things of greatest importance in our social life—satisfactions, social progress, democracy—are not really measurable. Second, society is extremely complex. It is difficult and usually impossible to find and evaluate all the many causes of a given situation, though often we can discover the factors that were most important in bringing it about. Third, in every social situation there is the human element. Frequently, the course of social events depends on the reaction of a few individuals who are leaders, and, except in routine situations, we can seldom predict individual behavior with complete certainty.

If the social scientist finally does succeed in finding uniformities or "laws" of social behavior and in setting up hypotheses to explain them, there is still another difficulty—namely, that investigators can seldom employ controlled experiments to test their hypotheses. To a considerable extent, the social scientist must substitute careful observation and the mental process of abstraction for experiments. The investigator abstracts from a given situation some one factor in order to consider what effect it would have if acting alone. To do this, the investigator imagines that any other factors present remain constant or inert and asks, for example, a question such as: If other factors affecting economic life remained constant, what would be the economic effect of raising tariff rates on imports?

A social scientist with a thorough knowledge of a situation may correctly calculate the effect of a given causal factor by assuming that all other things remain equal. However, to reach correct conclusions by this method, the investigator must be both competent and painstaking. Even then, the dangers of error are great. If anything, there is more need for competence in the social scientist than in the physical scientist. The theories of a physical scientist often can be proved right or wrong by experiments, but this is seldom true of those of the social scientist. An unfortunate result is that it is easier in social science than in physical science to be needlessly vague, to perpetuate errors, and to cover up incompetence.

Social scientists also have more difficulty than physical scientists in being objective. Because they deal

"I'm a social scientist, Michael. That means I can't explain electricity or anything like that, but if you ever want to know about people. I'm your man."

with human beings and are human themselves, social scientists find it hard to put aside their own likes and dislikes, their sympathies, prejudices, and frustrations. As a result, they sometimes fall into the trap of trying to justify their own hopes, beliefs, or biases instead of seeking to discover the truth. We should always be on guard against those who pose as social scientists but who, in fact, substitute propaganda and charisma for objectivity and competence.

This does not mean that social science is any less scientific than the natural sciences, or that it is less objective. It simply means that social scientists must be continually on guard against such traps and must be as clear and objective as possible.

The differences between physical science and social science lead to slightly different structures of research. Although there is no ideal structure, a reasonable approach to a problem in social science is the following:

1. Observe.
2. Define the problem.
3. Review the literature. (Become familiar with what others have observed.)
4. Observe some more.
5. Develop a theoretical framework and formulate a hypothesis.
6. Choose the research design.
7. Collect the necessary data.
8. Analyze the results.
9. Draw conclusions.

Using this outline as a rough guide, and recognizing that the specific project and each specific social science determine the exact nature of the methodology to be used, you have a reasonably good method of attack.

Observing.   Notice that social science begins with observation. Social science is about the real world, and the best way to know about the real world is to observe it.

Defining the problem.   Of the various research steps listed, this one is probably the most important. If you've carefully defined your terms, you can save an enormous amount of energy. Put simply, if you don't know what you're doing, no matter how well you do it, you're not going to end up with much. The topic might be chosen for a variety of reasons, perhaps because it raises issues of fundamental social science importance, perhaps because it has suddenly become a focus of controversy, or perhaps because research funds have become available to investigate it.

Reviewing the literature.   Knowledge of the relevant literature is essential because it provides background, suggests approaches, indicates what has already been covered and what hasn't, and saves you from redoing what has already been done. It is a way of using other people's observations.

Observing some more.   After you have defined your problem and reviewed the literature, your observation will be sharper. You will know more precisely what you are looking for and how to look for it.

Developing a theoretical framework and formulating a hypothesis.   Make a statement predicting your results and then clarify what each of the terms in the statement means within the framework of your research. Suppose your hypothesis is: "High price increases sales of fashionable magazines." You should specify how high is high, and compared to what specific price is the price stated to be high; how much of an increase is significant over the circulation the magazine enjoyed at the lower price; what sales are included (newsstand, subscription, or both); and what is "fashionable." Different researchers may define the same term differently, which is one of the reasons why the same research subject can produce different results.

Choosing a research design. Pick a means of gathering data—a survey, an experiment, an observational study, use of existing sources, or a combination. Weigh this choice carefully because your plan is the crux of the research process.

Collecting the necessary data. Data are what one collects from careful observation. Your conclusions will be only as good as your data, so take great care in collecting and, especially, in recording your data. If you can't document what you've done, you might as well not have done it.

Analyzing the results. When all the data are in, classify facts, identify trends, recognize relationships, and tabulate the information so that it can be accurately analyzed and interpreted. A given set of facts may be interpreted two different ways by two different analysts, so give your analysis careful, objective attention. After this step has been taken, your hypothesis can then be confirmed, rejected, or modified.

Drawing conclusions. Now you can prepare a report, summarizing the steps you've followed and discussing what you've found. A good report will relate your conclusions to the existing body of research, suggest where current assumptions may be modified because of new evidence, and possibly identify unanswered questions for further study.

These steps differ slightly from those used by a natural scientist, but only slightly—the primary difference comes in testing a hypothesis. In some natural sciences, it is possible to conduct controlled experiments in which the same experiment can be repeated again and again under highly regulated conditions. In the social sciences, such controlled experiments are more difficult to construct.

The line between social science and natural science is not fixed. In some natural sciences, perfectly controlled experiments are impossible. In cosmological physics, for example, one can't create the universe again and again. Thus, one must speculate about a hypothesis, draw conclusions from that hypothesis, and see whether the conclusions match what one observes in the universe. Alternatively, in the social science of psychology, certain controlled experiments are possible—for example, individuals can be given specific stimuli under specific conditions again and again. Thus, the difference between the way one deals with the natural sciences and the way one deals with the social sciences can be blurry.

Let's take an example of the use of the social science method—Joseph Holz's study of the implications of teen pregnancy. First, he studied all the writing on teen pregnancy. Then he set up the following hypothesis: Teen motherhood causes the mothers to be economically and socially worse off than they otherwise would have been. To test this hypothesis, he used data that had been collected over many years tracking the lives of teenage women. From that he extracted two groups—a set of teenagers who had become pregnant and borne the child and a set of teenagers who had become pregnant but had miscarried. He then compared their economic and social positions when they were in their mid-thirties. If teen motherhood caused the mother to be worse off, then the teens who had borne their babies should have been in a worse position than those who miscarried. They weren't. He found no significant difference between the two groups: Both were low income, significantly dependent on welfare benefits, and had completed the same number of years of school. The initial hypothesis was false. Teen pregnancy did not make mothers worse off; it was simply a symptom of a larger set of problems. This larger set of problems was so severe that whether mothers had borne a child in their teens made little difference to their economic and social positions.

Holz's findings were published as the government was conducting a costly campaign against teen motherhood, and his conclusions were unpopular with both liberals and conservatives. Liberals did not like them because his study suggested that much of the family planning advice and sex education developed by liberals was of little help in improving these women's lives. Conservatives didn't like them because his study implied that more substantive changes than simply eliminating teen motherhood were needed to improve these women's lives and break the cycle of poverty. But good social science methodology is not about pleasing anybody—it is about understanding social issues and social problems.

Although Holz's experiment was not fully controlled, it was as close as one could come to a controlled experiment in the social sciences. It selected similar groups to compare in such a way that no obvious reason existed as to why these two groups should differ.

Social Science Approaches to Problems

As you review the literature about various social science studies, you will see that social scientists can use many different approaches and methods as they study problems. We first consider alternative approaches; then we consider alternative methods.

Alternative Approaches.   The approach one takes when analyzing a problem reflects one's worldview—the lens through which one sees the world. Four approaches that social scientists use are the functionalist theory approach, the exchange theory approach, the conflict theory approach, and the symbolic interaction theory approach.

The functionalist theory approach.   This approach emphasizes the interconnectedness of social life and the difficulty of affecting only one part of society with a policy. Followers of the **functionalist theory approach** are hesitant to make social judgments because all aspects of society have certain functions.

The exchange theory approach.   Closely related to the functionalist approach, the **exchange theory approach** emphasizes the voluntary exchanges of individuals as reflecting individuals' choices. Thus, the structure of society reflects individuals' desires. The exchange theory approach lens is one of relative harmony in society, sometimes upset by dysfunctional elements.

The conflict theory approach.   The **conflict theory approach** sees far less harmony than the exchange theory approach. Followers of this approach see social behavior in terms of conflict and tension among competing groups or classes. Whereas the exchange theory approach sees individuals' voluntary choices, the conflict theory approach sees force and power directing individual actions.

The symbolic interaction theory approach.   The **symbolic interaction theory approach** sees individuals as deriving meaning from the symbols they learn from. Followers of this approach see reality as reflecting less what people do and more what they think and feel. Their motives and perceptions, rather than actions, are emphasized.

These approaches are not necessarily independent of one another. Some social scientists use a combination of approaches to study problems, while some use one at one time and another at another time.

Alternative Methods.   In addition to using different approaches, social scientists also use different methods. These include the historical method, the case method, and the comparative and cross-cultural methods.

The historical method.   Because most social developments—such as the government of the United States—have unique characteristics, in order to understand them as fully as possible the social scientist must rely heavily on a study of their historical background. We can never understand completely how any historical situation came to exist, because there are limits to our historical knowledge and causes become increasingly complex and uncertain as we trace them further into the past. We can, however, make both historical events and present social situations much more intelligibly by using the **historical method**—tracing the principal past developments that seem to have been directly significant in bringing about a social situation. To trace these past developments, a historian will use many of the same methods as other social scientists such as collecting birth and marriage certificates and classifying those data.

It has been noted that history never really repeats itself. Nevertheless, present and past situations often have such striking similarities that a knowledge of the past can give us insights into present situations and sometimes into future trends.

The case method.   Writers on the methodology of social research have devoted a great deal of attention to the case method—its characteristics, its variations, the uses it can serve, its advantages, and its limitations. Here we only describe its basic nature. The **case method** involves making a detailed examination and analysis of a particular issue or problem situation. This can involve a case study of a single person such as that by a psychologist of his client, a single area or town such as a sociologist's study of why a town changes, or even a study of whole countries such as an economist's when comparing various countries.

A case study can be intended to discover how to bring about desirable changes in a particular problem situation: for example, to find the most effective ways of upgrading or rehabilitating a slum area. More often, the chief purpose of a case study is to throw light on many similar situations that exist in a society. The hope is that an understanding of one or a few cases will illuminate the others and thus aid in solving the social problems they present. The case or cases selected should be typical of the group they purport to represent.

The preceding requirement can be a limiting factor in the usefulness of the case method. Suppose we wanted to make a study of the class structure of U.S. society as a whole. Obviously, it would be easier to select as cases for study several relatively small and isolated cities in various sections of the country. But it is questionable whether these would give us a true picture of the country as a whole, because today a great proportion of our people live in large metropolitan areas where the class structure is likely to be much more complex than in smaller and more isolated communities. However, to study and describe in detail the class structure of such an area may be prohibitively difficult and expensive, and therefore impractical.

The comparative and cross-cultural methods.   The **comparative method** was formerly often employed in the hope of discovering evolutionary sequences in the development of human institutions—that is, patterns of social development or progress that would be universal. For example, it was sometimes assumed that definite stages existed in the development of governmental institutions, and it was thought that these stages could be discovered by comparing a society at one level of development with some other society at a different level. Today, this attempt to find patterns of social evolution that can be applied to all societies has been largely abandoned.

However, comparison of different societies still plays an important role in anthropological studies through what is called the **cross-cultural method.** This method consists of making detailed studies of the culture patterns of a number of societies for the purpose of comparing the different ways in which their people meet similar needs. These studies sometimes show surprising similarities in the cultural traits of widely separated peoples who appear to have had no direct or indirect contacts with one another.

Comparison of the characteristics of different societies involves problems. At times, it is difficult to decide whether two or more societies are independent or should be treated as one. Or consider definitions: If we are comparing the family institution in different societies, we must define *family* broadly enough to cover cultural variations yet specifically enough to make comparisons meaningful. Sociologists do not always agree on just what a family is. Again, if we are comparing unemployment in urban-industrial societies, we must agree on what we mean by *unemployment.* For example, in the early 1980s, the unemployment rate in Mexico, computed by U.S. standards, was approximately 30 percent. Mexican economists, however, argued that this figure was meaningless because Mexican work habits and culture were different from those in the United States. Much of what was measured as unemployment, they said, was actually individuals working at home and not earning money in the marketplace. Thus, although they had nonmarket jobs, they had been counted as unemployed.

Common Sense in the Social Sciences

Probably the most important lesson to remember when conducting any research is that you should use what might be called an educated common sense. You can understand the analytic argument for common sense by considering the mind as a supercomputer storing enormous amounts of information, not all of which may lie at the surface of recall. This holds true even with the vast increase in computer power. Processing speeds of computers double every eighteen months, according to Moore's Law. That increase has made it possible to do enormous things even with home computers. However, compared with the capabilities of the human mind, even the most powerful computer counts by using its fingers and toes. The mind processes trillions of pieces of information in millinanoseconds (we don't know what they are either, but we do know they are very small). When the results of the models and the minds diverge, it seems reasonable to rely on the more powerful computer—the mind. It makes sense to do so, however, only if the best information has been input into the mind. Common sense is not sufficient; we must use educated common sense.

To see the difference between common sense and *educated* common sense, consider the problem: Does the earth circle the sun or does the sun circle the earth? Uneducated common sense tells us that the sun circles the earth, and that commonsense conclusion became built into society and society's view of itself throughout the Middle Ages. To believe otherwise was heresy. In 1540, Copernicus tried to fit that commonsense view with observations that classical Greeks had made of the heavens. As he went about this task, he discovered that he could get a good fit of the data with the theory only if he assumed the earth moved around the sun. His was an **educated common sense**—rational thought based on observation and the best information available. It was that kind of educated common sense that ultimately led to the scientific method. As specialization makes us focus on narrower and narrower issues, it is important to keep in the back of our minds that scientific analysis has made us look at only part of the problem and that we must also use our educated common sense to interpret the results reasonably.

The Use of Statistics

Whenever possible, social scientists rely on quantitative data—data that can be reduced to numbers—but often quantitative data are not available, so social scientists must rely on qualitative data such as interviews or heuristic summaries of information in the literature. When using qualitative data, it is much more difficult to draw specific inferences from the data, because the "facts" one finds depend on how one interprets the qualitative data. One way to partially overcome such "interpretive problems" is the "Delphic method" in which another specialist in the field reviews your interpretation and then you modify your interpretation in response if you see fit, explaining your reasons for accepting or rejecting the suggested modifications. Another way is to translate the qualitative data into quantitative data, creating "proxies" (stand-ins) for any missing quantitative data, although that often simply hides the interpretative issues rather than eliminating them.

If quantitative data are available, social scientists rely on **statistical analysis**—information in numerical form that has been assembled and classified—to provide the social scientist with the information needed to understand social relationships and processes. Statistics do not enable us to measure directly such basic social values as good citizenship, happiness, or welfare, but they are useful in measuring other factors that underlie social life, such as the size of the population of a country, or the number of families whose incomes fall below some level that we set as the minimum for decent and healthful living. Statistical relationships also give us insights into social problems. If we find that the proportion of males in juvenile detention centers who come from broken homes is substantially greater than the proportion of males in the population at large who come from such homes, this suggests that broken homes may be an important factor contributing to juvenile delinquency. But statistics must always be interpreted with care, for it can be easy to read into them conclusions they do not justify. Also, it is sometimes possible to manipulate them so that they appear to show what we want them to show.

Although statistics measure the results of social activity and highlight trends, they have other useful functions: testing theories and discovering relationships. For example, *correlation* is the relationship between two sets of data. A high correlation between sets of data means that if an element in one set rises, its corresponding element in the other set is also likely to rise. Other statistics determine how sure we are of a relationship. We do not discuss these statistics because an introductory social science course is not the place to learn them, but it *is* the place to learn that such techniques of testing relationships exist, and they may be worth your while to study at some point in the future.

If we are going to use statistics, we must have data. Data are the raw numbers describing an event, occurrence, or situation. Social scientists' data come from measuring and counting all occurrences of a particular happening. For example, we might find, "In 2007, there were x number of murders and y number of suicides." One way to get data is to conduct a **survey,** a method whereby data are collected from individuals or institutions by means of questionnaires or interviews. For instance, we might conduct a survey in which selected people are questioned or polled on such matters as their incomes, their beliefs on certain issues, or the political candidate for whom they intend to vote. Figure 2 gives an example of such a survey. Statistics can tell us how large a portion of a group must be surveyed before we can be reasonably sure that the results will reflect the views of the entire group. Such techniques are used extensively in surveys such as the Gallup or Harris public opinion polls.

The use of statistics has been greatly facilitated, and therefore greatly expanded, by the computer. The computer has made it possible to record, arrange, and rearrange voluminous information quickly and analytically. Today, enormous amounts of data and other resources are available to anyone with a computer or other access to the Internet.

With the expansion of social data and the enormous increase in computing power, it is increasingly possible for social scientists to look for relationships in the data alone, rather than to be guided in that search by theories. Using highly sophisticated statistical techniques, social scientists analyze data, looking for patterns. After they find a pattern, they fit that pattern to a theory. For example, social scientists Stephen Levitt and John Donohue searched the data and found a relationship between the passage of the abortion rights law in the United States and a decrease in crime in later periods. Based on this evidence, they argued that because abortion reduced the number of unwanted children, those children who were born had more guidance, and that it was the law making abortion legal, not any change in law enforcement or increase in the number of inmates

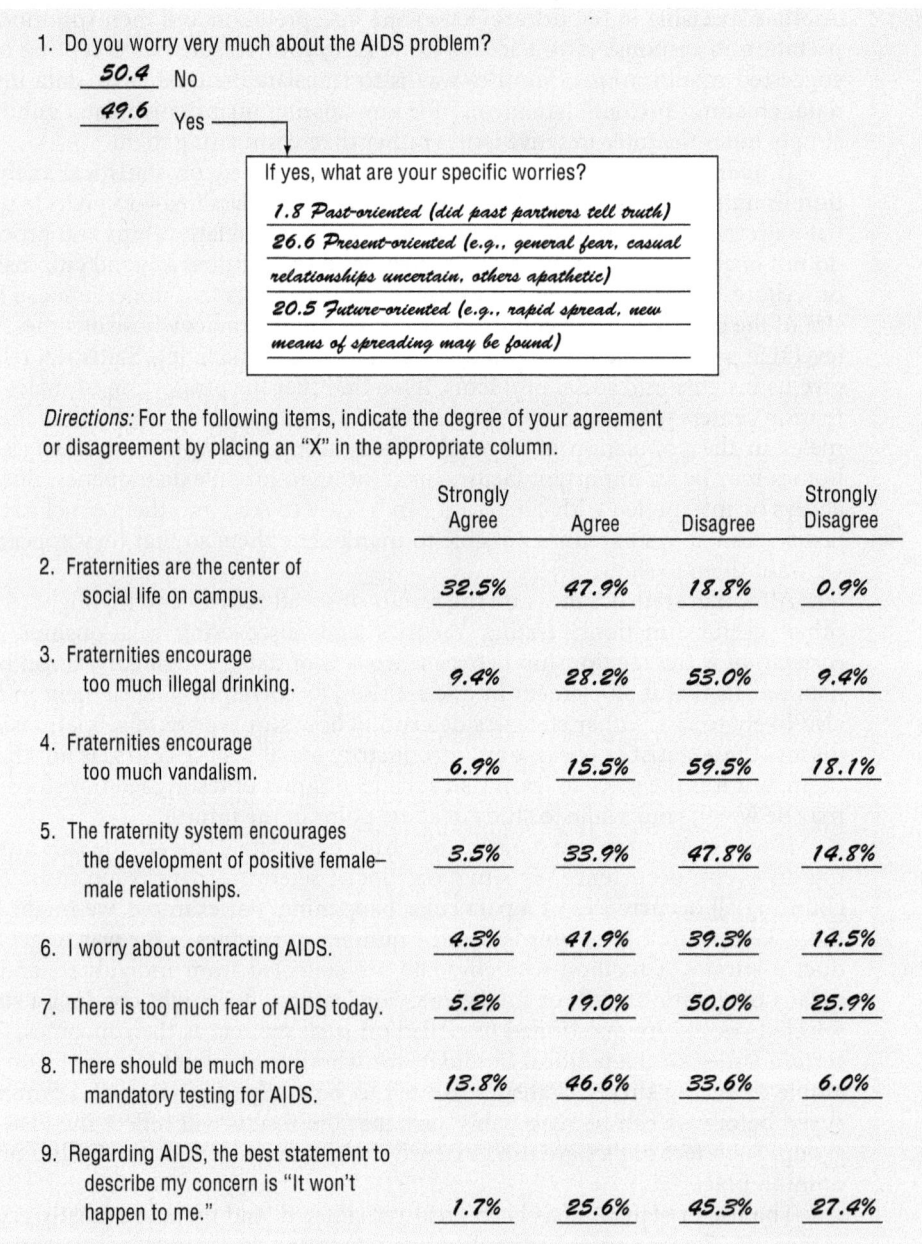

1. Do you worry very much about the AIDS problem?

_50.4_ No

_49.6_ Yes

> If yes, what are your specific worries?
>
> _1.8 Past-oriented (did past partners tell truth)_
> _26.6 Present-oriented (e.g., general fear, casual relationships uncertain, others apathetic)_
> _20.5 Future-oriented (e.g., rapid spread, new means of spreading may be found)_

Directions: For the following items, indicate the degree of your agreement or disagreement by placing an "X" in the appropriate column.

	Strongly Agree	Agree	Disagree	Strongly Disagree
2. Fraternities are the center of social life on campus.	_32.5%_	_47.9%_	_18.8%_	_0.9%_
3. Fraternities encourage too much illegal drinking.	_9.4%_	_28.2%_	_53.0%_	_9.4%_
4. Fraternities encourage too much vandalism.	_6.9%_	_15.5%_	_59.5%_	_18.1%_
5. The fraternity system encourages the development of positive female–male relationships.	_3.5%_	_33.9%_	_47.8%_	_14.8%_
6. I worry about contracting AIDS.	_4.3%_	_41.9%_	_39.3%_	_14.5%_
7. There is too much fear of AIDS today.	_5.2%_	_19.0%_	_50.0%_	_25.9%_
8. There should be much more mandatory testing for AIDS.	_13.8%_	_46.6%_	_33.6%_	_6.0%_
9. Regarding AIDS, the best statement to describe my concern is "It won't happen to me."	_1.7%_	_25.6%_	_45.3%_	_27.4%_

Figure 2

One of the best ways by which social scientists collect information is through a survey. This is one page of a fourteen-page survey conducted by college students for their sociology class. Because of time pressures in that particular survey, they were unable to perform an extensive analysis of their data. For this reason, they urged caution in the use and interpretation of the information.

jailed, that was mostly responsible for the decrease in crime rates that the United States experienced in the 1990s.

Whenever making such claims, social scientists should be very careful not to confuse **correlation**—the simultaneous movement of two variables—with **causation**—in which change in one variable brings about change in the other variable. The difference can be seen in the following example. When it is expected to rain, more people carry umbrellas, so umbrella usage and rain are correlated. But the fact that people carry umbrellas does not cause it to rain, or so most of us believe.

The Interdisciplinary Approach

Modern industrial societies and their problems are becoming increasingly complex, and because no one person today can master all the social sciences, growing emphasis is placed on the interdisciplinary approach to many social problems. The **interdisciplinary approach** means that a group of social scientists with different specialties will work together on a certain problem, not all of whose aspects any one of the group fully understands. For some problems, such as those surrounding pollution, it may be necessary to call in, say, a physical scientist, a geologist, and an engineer. But in facing all of these problems, the need for educated people who have a broad sense of problems and interrelationships—who understand the need for a unified social science—is also becoming more and more evident.

Though few social relationships can be reduced to exact and invariable laws, human beings in large groups everywhere show great likenesses of behavior when conditions are really similar. Thus, there is reason to believe that we can, through systematic study and research, greatly increase our understanding of the nature and development of human societies, and to hope that the attitudes fostered by the interdisciplinary approach itself and the knowledge to which it leads us can ultimately result in greater tolerance and cooperation among diverse groups and among nations.

Social Science and Society

Some people believe that the social sciences are lagging behind the natural sciences. They maintain that not only does social science have no exact laws, but that it has also failed to eliminate great social evils such as racial discrimination, crime, poverty, and war. They imply that social scientists have failed to accomplish what might reasonably have been expected of them. However, such critics are usually unaware of the real nature of social science and of its special problems and basic limitations. For example, they forget that the solution to a social problem requires not only knowledge but also the ability to influence people. Even if social scientists discover the procedures that should be followed to achieve social improvement, they are seldom in a position to control social action. For that matter, even dictators find that there are limits to their power to change society.

Agreeing on Policy

One of the great problems in a democracy is getting the majority of people to reach substantial agreement on the major policies that should be followed to create a better society. Social scientists can aid in bringing about this agreement by helping people to understand the issues, the difficulties involved, and the possible steps to a solution. If we express social objectives in sufficiently general terms, agreement is not so hard to obtain. Most people would like to have a heaven on earth characterized by peace and goodwill, with freedom, justice, security, health, and happiness for all. But when it comes to drawing up a blueprint for reaching these objectives, disagreements and obstacles become apparent. Social scientists themselves are not always in complete agreement on what our specific social goals should be or on how we can best work toward them.

In any case, the function of social science and of those who practice it is not primarily to determine social objectives. Its major function is to discover how our objectives can be achieved. The determination of the goals themselves—our social values—is not a scientific problem but one having to do with our likes and dislikes, our esthetic concepts, our moral standards, and our philosophical and religious beliefs.

Values, Terminology, and Rhetoric

This chapter began with a quotation from Albert Einstein who said that "theories should be as simple as possible, but not more so." The same thing could be said about ideas and the expression of those ideas. Unfortunately, specialists have an incentive to develop a terminology that is anything but simple and that often obscures rather than clarifies. One of the many social science teachers who has written us about this text (and in doing so, these teachers have played an important role in its development) described a history conference she attended where "we were treated to such goodies" as

> The sociopolitical internecine amortizations of agronomous proletarization, if solely counterproductive of Jurassic multi-dimensional interstitial extrapolated Augustinian and Aristotelian epistemological diagrammetric middle-sector dichotomies, as measured in the context of paradigmatic vestigiae (though challenged none too effectively, if I am not remiss in saying so, by Freylinghausen's hypothesis delivered at the University of Bordeaux in April 1896) are existentially and polaristically categorized by Nordlinger's Metternichian thermodynamics as tangentially interrelated with studies promulgated by Darffenstangenovich on a scale of one to twenty factored to the 24th power.

Although she may have used a bit of literary license in transcribing the conference proceedings, her point is well taken. She was attending a conference on her specialty, yet she didn't understand what was being said. It happens all the time, not only to students, but to teachers as well. Although there may be valuable ideas in what many specialists have to say, we can't profit from them if we can't understand them, or if we must spend hours translating them.

In his wonderful book, *The Sociological Imagination,* C. W. Mills made precisely this point. He argued that in many social sciences, "high theory" is top-heavy with jargon. As an example, he interpreted sociologist Talcott Parsons's terminology: He reduced it by 80 to 90 percent and at the same time made it more intelligible. Mills wasn't making the point that Parsons's insights weren't good ones; to the contrary, Mills believed that Parsons was a brilliant sociologist. But Parsons's language obscured his brilliant ideas.

Another characteristic of language is that it embodies value judgments and preserves ways of looking at problems. A good social scientist recognizes this and is always open to dealing with reality by alternative modes of expression and new ways of looking at issues.

Conclusion

If this chapter has succeeded in its intended purpose, it should have given you a sense of what it means to be a social scientist. As you saw, the social sciences are evolving: They interact and they move among the humanities, the natural sciences, and the individual social sciences depending on who is working with them. They are fluid, not static, and that fluidity will present problems to anyone who attempts too fixed a definition of any of them.

The ability to handle the fluid definitions, to recognize the shadows as well as the objects without flinching, is an important characteristic that good social scientists exhibit—one which, if learned, will serve you well as you study this text and play the game of life.

Key Points

- Social science is the name given to our knowledge about the nature, growth, and functioning of human society.
- The scientific method is a set of rules about how to establish rules.
- A good social scientist generally takes a wait-and-see position about claims until they are tested and retested.
- A reasonable approach to a problem in social science is to observe, define the problem, review the literature, observe some more, develop a theoretical framework and formulate a hypothesis, choose the research design, collect the necessary data, analyze the results, and draw conclusions.
- Three typical methods in social science are the historical method, the case method, and the comparative method.
- It is important to use educated common sense in the social sciences.
- A good social scientist is always open to new ways of looking at issues.

Some Important Terms

anthropology
biological science
case method
causation
cognitive science
comparative method
conflict theory approach
correlation
cross-cultural method
economics
educated common sense
exchange theory approach

experimental method
functionalist theory
    approach
geography
historical method
history
humanities
interdisciplinary approach
natural experiments
natural science
paradigm
political science

psychology
research program
scientific knowledge
scientific method
social science
sociology
statistical analysis
survey
symbolic interaction theory
    approach

Questions for Review and Discussion

1. What is scientific knowledge? How does it differ from knowledge acquired "unconsciously"?
2. Distinguish among the three major fields of human knowledge. What is the emphasis of each?
3. Name the principal social sciences and define the field with which each deals.
4. Why would it have been difficult to carry on scientific investigation in primitive societies or even in the Middle Ages?
5. What is the scientific method?
6. What basic assumption underlies the use of the scientific method?
7. What is the experimental method?
8. Why is it difficult to formulate precise laws in the field of social science?
9. Are there any advantages to having competing research programs?
10. In what sense is social science scientific?
11. Why is it often impossible to study social problems by means of the experimental method?

12. Explain the ways in which the problems of social science differ from those of the exact natural sciences.
13. What are the advantages of the interdisciplinary approach to the study of many social problems?
14. Social science has been broken down into specialties. Why is it a problem to put them back together through a unified theory?
15. What new social science fields do you think will be important ten years from now? Why do you think so?

Internet Questions

1. Using an Internet search engine directory (for example, http://dir.google.com or http://dir.yahoo.com), look at the lists of topics included under Social Science or Society. How many fields are listed? What fields would you add (or delete) in a list of your own?
2. The website www.buildfreedom.com/content/scientific_method.shtml uses an abbreviated version of the scientific method to solve the social problem of dating. Use this process to "solve" another everyday problem.
3. Go to www.wikipedia.org and choose one of the branches listed under Social Sciences. What are the subdisciplines or branches listed under your choice?
4. Take the survey about alcohol use at www.alcoholscreening.org. After taking the survey, look at the feedback you are given based on your answers. What can the results for this survey be used for?
5. Go to www.ncpa.org/pi/crime/pd08599g.html and read the discussion about Donohue and Levitt's study of abortion and crime rates mentioned in the text. What are some of the alternative arguments that critics use to explain why the crime rate has decreased?

For Further Study

Greene, Brian, *The Fabric of the Cosmos*, New York: Knopf, 2004.

Hecht, Jennifer Michael, *Doubt: A History: The Great Doubters and Their Legacy of Innovation*, San Francisco: Harper, 2004.

Mills, C. Wright, *The Sociological Imagination*, New York: Oxford University Press, 1959.

Repcheck, Jack, *Copernicus' Secret: How the Scientific Revolution Began*, New York: Simon & Schuster, 2009.

Slater, Lauren, *Opening Skinner's Box: Great Psychological Experiments of the Twentieth Century*, New York: Norton, 2004.

Tilly, Charles, *Why*, Princeton, NJ: Princeton University Press, 2006.

Wilson, Edward O., *Consilience: The Unity of Knowledge*, New York: Knopf, 1998.

WWW   Anthropology Resources on the Internet www.anthropologie.net

WWW   Economic History Services http://eh.net/

WWW   Encyclopedia of Psychology www.psychology.org (accessed June 16, 2009)

WWW   Political Resources on the Net www.politicalresources.net

WWW   Social Science Research Council www.ssrc.org

WWW   Sociological Resources on the Internet www.socioweb.com

WWW   Virtual Library in Economics www.helsinki.fi/WebEc

WWW   Virtual Library in Sociology http://socserv.mcmaster.ca/w3virtsoclib

Anthropology

Dr. Raymond B. Hames

Introduction to Anthropology

From Chapter 1 of *Anthropology: A Global Perspective*, Seventh Edition. Raymond Scupin, Christopher R. DeCorse. Copyright © 2012 by Pearson Education, Inc. All rights reserved.

Chapter Questions

■ **What** is unique about the field of anthropology as compared with other disciplines?

■ **How** does the field of anthropology bridge both the sciences and the humanities?

■ **Why** should students study anthropology?

((•—[Listen to the **Chapter Audio** on **myanthrolab.com**

Anthropologist Morton Fried once pointed out the similarities between the space travel described in science fiction and the field of anthropology (1977). He noted that when Neil Armstrong became the first human to set foot on the moon in July 1969, his step constituted first contact. To space travelers created by science fiction writers, *first contact* refers to the first meeting between humans and extraterrestrial beings. To anthropologists, the phrase refers to initial encounters between peoples of different societies. For thousands of years, peoples throughout the world have had first contacts with each other. As we shall see in this chapter, the field of anthropology includes four major subdisciplines that seek to understand different aspects of humanity in much the same way that future space travelers might investigate extraterrestrials. Anthropologists draw upon a variety of field methods, techniques, and approaches to conduct their investigations, which have two major goals: to understand the *uniqueness and diversity* of human behavior and human societies around the world and to discover the *fundamental similarities* that link human beings throughout the world in both the past and the present. To accomplish these goals, anthropologists undertake systematic case studies of people living in particular locations, in the past and present, and use comparative techniques to assess the similarities and differences among societies.

Using these goals as a springboard, anthropology has forged distinctive objectives and propelled research that has broadened our understanding of humanity, from the beginnings of human societies to the present. This chapter introduces the distinctive approaches used in anthropology to achieve these goals.

Anthropology: The Four Subfields

The word *anthropology* is derived from the Greek words *anthropo*, meaning "human beings" or "humankind," and *logia*, translated as "knowledge of" or "the study of." Thus, we can define **anthropology** as the systematic study of humankind. This definition in itself, however, does not distinguish anthropology from other disciplines. After all, historians, psychologists, economists, sociologists, and scholars in many other fields systematically study humankind in one way or another. Anthropology stands apart because it combines four subfields, or subdisciplines, that bridge the natural sciences, the social sciences, and the humanities. These four subfields—physical anthropology, archaeology, linguistic anthropology, and cultural anthropology or ethnology—constitute a broad approach to the study of humanity the world over, both past and present. Figure 1 shows these subfields and the various specializations that make up each one. A discussion of these subdisciplines and some of the key specializations in each follows.

The subfields of anthropology initially emerged in Western society in an attempt to understand non-Western peoples. When Europeans began exploring and colonizing the world in the fifteenth century, they encountered native peoples in the Americas, Africa, the Middle East, and Asia. European travelers, missionaries, and government officials described these non-Western cultures, providing a record of their physical appearances, customs, and beliefs. By the nineteenth century, anthropology had developed into the primary discipline and science for understanding these non-Western societies and cultures. The major questions that these nineteenth-century anthropologists sought to answer dealt with the basic differences and similarities of human societies and cultures and with the physical variation found in peoples throughout the world. Today, anthropologists do not solely focus their attention on non-Western cultures, and they are just as likely to examine cultural practices in an urban setting in the United States as to conduct fieldwork in some far-off place. However, anthropologists continue to grapple with the basic questions of human diversity and similarities through systematic research within the four subfields described below.

Physical Anthropology

Physical anthropology is the branch of anthropology concerned with humans as a biological species. As such, it is the subfield most closely related to the natural sciences. Physical anthropologists conduct research in two major areas: human evolution and modern human variation. The investigation of human evolution presents one of the most tantalizing areas of anthropological study. Research has now traced the African origins of humanity

Hominid skull in burial.

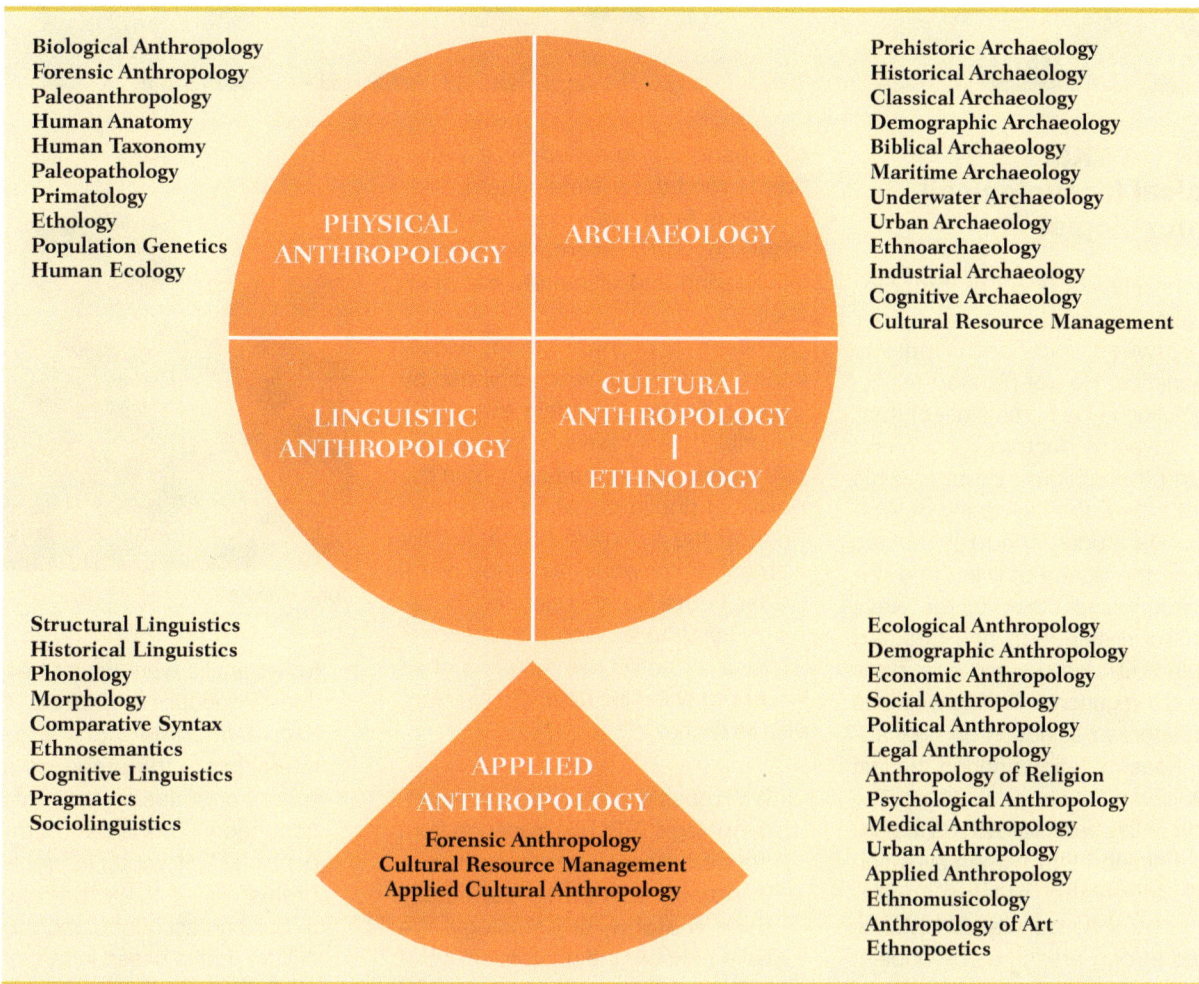

Figure 1 The four core subfields of anthropology and applied anthropology. Also included are some of the various specializations within each of the subfields, which are discussed in this text. Many of these specializations overlap with one another in the actual studies carried out by anthropologists.

back over 6 million years. Fieldwork in other world areas has traced the expansion of early human ancestors throughout the world. Much of the evidence for human origins consists of **fossils**, the fragmentary remains of bones and living materials preserved from earlier periods. The study of human evolution through analysis of fossils is called **paleoanthropology** (the prefix *paleo* means "old" or "prehistoric"). Paleoanthropologists use a variety of scientific techniques to date, classify, and compare fossil bones to determine the links between modern humans and their biological ancestors. These paleoanthropologists may work closely with archaeologists when studying ancient tools and activity areas to learn about the behavior of early human ancestors.

Other physical anthropologists explore

human evolution through **primatology**, the study of primates. **Primates** are mammals that belong to the same overall biological classification as humans and, therefore, share similar physical characteristics and a close evolutionary relationship with us. Many primatologists observe primates such as chimpanzees, gorillas, gibbons, and orangutans in their natural habitats to ascertain the similarities and differences between these other primates and humans. These observations of living primates may provide insight into the behaviors of early human ancestors.

Another group of physical anthropologists focuses their research on the range of physical variation within and among different modern human populations. These anthropologists study human variation by measuring physical characteristics—such as body size, variation in blood types, or differences in skin color—or various genetic traits. Their research aims at explaining *why* such variation occurs, as well as documenting the differences in human populations. Skeletal structure is also the focus of anthropological research. Human *osteology* is the particular area of specialization within

31

Anthropologists at Work

JOHN HAWKS:
Physical (or Biological) Anthropologist

John Hawks is an anthropologist who works on the border between paleoanthropology and genetics. He got his start teaching evolution in his home state of Kansas, followed by doctoral training and teaching in Michigan, Utah, and his current home, the University of Wisconsin. He studies the relationships between the genes of living and ancient people, to discover the ways that natural selection has affected them. In 2007, Hawks and coworkers scanned the genome, finding evidence for widespread selection on new advantageous mutations during the last 40,000 years (Hawks et al. 2007). The breadth of this selection across the genome indicated that human evolution actually accelerated, as larger populations and new agricultural subsistence exerted strong pressures on ancient people. Far from slowing down our evolution, culture had created new opportunities for adaptive change in the human population.

Now, Hawks is busy examining the Neandertal genome. The availability of genetic evidence from ancient bones has transformed the way we study these ancient people. By comparing Neandertal genes with humans and chimpanzees, it will become possible to expand our knowledge of evolution beyond the skeletal record, finding signs from the immune system, digestion, and pigmentation, to traits like hearing and ultimately, the brain itself.

Hawks is probably most widely known for his blog, which is visited by several thousand readers every day. Describing new research from an expert's perspective, he has shown the power of public outreach as an element of the scientific process. This element of his work has made him a leader in the "open science" movement, trying to expand public accessibility to scientific research and open access to scientific data. On his blog, Hawks writes:

What does it mean to be a paleoanthropologist? To use evidence from the fossil record, we must be trained in human anatomy—especially *bone* anatomy, or osteology. We have to know the anatomical comparisons between humans and other primates, and the way these anatomies relate to habitual behaviors. The social and ecological behaviors of primates vary extensively in response to their unique ecological circumstances. Understanding the relationship of anatomy, behavior, and environment gives us a way to interpret ancient fossils and place them in their environmental context.

John Hawks

My scientific work hasn't been limited to genetics and fossils. Lately, I have become more and more interested in the problems of cultural transmission and information theory. This is part of my "first principles" approach to problems in prehistory—I think that we have to build an account of the origins of culture that is based in the simplest rules of information transfer.

Hawks welcomes everyone who is interested in human evolution based on a scientific approach to go to his blog at http://johnhawks.net/weblog/hawks/hawks.html.

✳ Explore the Concept on myanthrolab.com

physical anthropology dealing with the study of the human skeleton. Such studies have wide-ranging applications, from the identification of murder victims from fragmentary skeletal remains to the design of ergonomic airplane cockpits. Physical anthropologists are also interested in evaluating how disparate physical characteristics reflect evolutionary adaptations to different environmental conditions, thus shedding light on why human populations vary.

Physical anthropologists have also shed light on general questions about humanity such as the propensity of violence in human societies. Physical anthropologist Philip Walker has conducted in-depth research on human skeletal materials from various periods of prehistory that attempts to answer general questions about the prevalence of violence in past societies (2001). Walker finds that human skeletal remains with traumatic injuries such as embedded flint arrow points in the vertebrate or cut marks on cranial skulls and other archaeological materials from the past suggest that both violence and cannibalism has been pervasive since the beginning of human prehistory. Although the prehistoric data indicates that there were periods of peace, Walker's data based on an enormous amount of skeletal data indicates that warfare and violence were frequent (2001:590). The data indicates that the frequency of prehistoric human violence is associated with climatic changes in the past that resulted in crop failures or other scarcities (2001:591). Thus, the research in physical anthropology has provided deep insights into the patterns of human violence that help us understand our condition in the contemporary era.

An increasingly important area of research for some physical anthropologists is *genetics*, the study of the biological "blueprints" that dictate the inheritance of physical characteristics. Genetics research examines a wide variety of questions. It has, for example, been important in identifying the genetic sources of some diseases, such as sickle cell anemia, cystic fibrosis, and Tay-Sachs disease. A new example of genetic research on a modern population is that conducted by physical anthropologist Cynthia Beall in the Himalayan Mountains of Tibet. Beall and her team did detailed genealogical and historical interviews with thousands of women between the ages of 20 and 60 who had moved and were adapting to new environmental conditions at the altitude of 4,000 meters at low oxygen levels. Ruling out such factors as age, illness, and smoking, the team found that one group of these women had blood oxygen levels that were 10 percent higher than normal. Beall and her team found that the children of these women were much more likely to survive to the age of 15 or older; the group's average for childhood death was .04. In contrast, the low-oxygen group of women had an average of 2.5 children die during childhood. Thus, Beall and her team found that the gene or genes that determine high-oxygen blood count for women gave survival and adaptive capacities in this high mountain altitude (Beall, Song, Elston, and Goldstein 2004). This anthropological research has demonstrated a case of natural selection and human evolution that is occurring presently within a particular environment.

Genetics has also become an increasingly important complement to paleoanthropological research. Through the study of the genetic makeup of modern humans, physical anthropologists have been working on calculating the genetic distance among modern humans, thus providing a means of inferring rates of evolution and the evolutionary relationships within the species. An important project run by genetic paleoanthropologist Spencer Wells is helping to illuminate the migrations of humans throughout the world. Wells is the director of the Genographic Project, sponsored by the National Geographic Society and IBM.

Although anthropologists study the distinctive features of different cultures, they also recognize the fundamental similarities among people throughout the world.

The Genographic Project is gathering samples of DNA from populations throughout the world to trace human evolution. Wells is a pioneer in this form of genetic paleoanthropology. He has developed an international network of leading anthropologists in genetics, linguistics, archaeology, paleoanthropology, and cultural anthropology to assist in this project. Labs analyzing DNA have been established in different regions of the world by the Genographic Project. As DNA is transmitted from parents to offspring, most of the genetic material is recombined and mutated. However, some mutated DNA remains fairly stable over the course of generations. This stable mutated DNA can serve as "genetic markers" that are passed on to each generation and create populations with distinctive sets of DNA. These genetic markers can serve to distinguish ancient lineages of DNA. By following the pathways of these genetic markers, genetic paleoanthropologists such as Wells can blend archaeology, prehistoric, and linguistic data with paleoanthropological data to trace human evolution.

The Genographic Project traces both mitochondrial DNA (passed from mother to offspring in long lineages of maternal descent) and the Y chromosome (passed from father to son). These data have helped provide independent evidence for the African origins of the modern human species and human ancestors. This evidence will be discussed in later chapters on the evolution of modern humans. Individuals can join the project and submit samples of their own DNA to trace their genetic linkage to ancient populations at www.nationalgeographic.com/ Genographic.

Archaeology

Archaeology, the branch of anthropology that examines the material traces of past societies, informs us about the culture of those societies—the shared way of life of a group of people that includes their values, beliefs, and norms. However, as we will see below some archaeologists do research in contemporary societies. **Artifacts**, the material products of former societies, provide clues to the past. Some archaeological sites reveal spectacular jewelry like that found by the movie character Indiana Jones or the treasures of a pharaoh's tomb. Most artifacts, however, are not so spectacular. Despite the popular image of archaeology as an adventurous, even romantic pursuit, it usually consists of methodical, time-consuming, and—sometimes—somewhat tedious research. Archaeologists often spend hours sorting through ancient trash piles, or **middens**, to discover how members of past societies ate their meals, what tools they used in their households and in their work, and what beliefs gave meaning to their lives. They collect and carefully analyze the broken fragments of pottery, stone, glass, and other materials. It may take them months or even years to fully complete the study of an excavation. Unlike fictional archaeologists, who experience glorified adventures, real-world archaeologists thrive on the intellectually challenging adventure of systematic, scientific research that enlarges our understanding of the past.

Archaeologists have examined sites the world over, from campsites of the earliest humans to modern landfills. Some archaeologists investigate past societies whose history is primarily told by the archaeological record. Known as *prehistoric archaeologists*, they study the artifacts of groups such as the ancient inhabitants of

Eric Isselée/Shutterstock.com

Europe and the first humans to arrive in the Americas. Because these researchers have no written documents or oral traditions to help interpret the sites they examine and the artifacts they recover, the archaeological record provides the primary source of information for their interpretations of the past. *Historical archaeologists*, on the other hand, work with historians in investigating the artifacts of societies of the more recent past. For example, some historical archaeologists have probed the remains of plantations in the southern United States to gain an understanding of the lifestyles of enslaved Africans and slave owners during the nineteenth century. Other archaeologists, called *classical archaeologists*, conduct research on ancient civilizations such as in Egypt, Greece, and Rome.

There are many more areas of specialization within archaeology that reflect the geographic area, topic, or time period on which the archaeologist works (see Figure 1). One more contemporary development in the field of archaeology is called ethnoarchaeology. **Ethnoarchaeology** is the study of material artifacts of the past along with the observation of modern peoples who have knowledge of the use and symbolic meaning of those artifacts. Frances Hayashida has been conducting ethnoarchaeological research in the coastal areas of Peru regarding the production and consumption of ancient maize beer called *chicha* and this tradition carried on in modern breweries (2008). This ethnoarchaeological research involves the study of the contemporary *chicha* production along with the investigation of how prehistoric indigenous peoples were providing inputs of labor, raw materials, and the different technologies in their development of breweries in different areas of coastal Peru. This ethnoarchaeological research involves in-depth observations and interviews with modern peoples in order to understand what has been retained from the past regarding *chicha* production.

There are many other fields of archaeology as indicated in Figure 1. For example, some specializations in archaeology include industrial archaeologists, biblical archaeologists, medieval and postmedieval archaeologists, and Islamic archaeologists. Underwater archaeologists work on a variety of places and time periods throughout the world; they are distinguished from other archaeologists by the distinctive equipment, methods, and procedures needed to excavate underwater.

One new interesting approach used in archaeology employs the GIS (Geographical Information Systems),

Archaeologist digging at a site.

a tool that was adopted by geologists and environmental scientists as well as physical anthropologists. Archaeologists can use the GIS systems linked to satellites to help locate specific transportation routes used by peoples and their animals in the past as well as many other patterns (Tripcevich 2010).

In another novel approach, still other archaeologists have turned their attention to the very recent past. For example, in 1972, William L. Rathje began a study of modern garbage as an assignment for the students in his introductory anthropology class. Even he was surprised at the number of people who took an interest in the findings. A careful study of garbage provides insights about modern society that cannot be ferreted out in any other way. Whereas questionnaires and interviews depend upon the cooperation and interpretation of respondents, garbage provides an unbiased physical record of human activity. Rathje's "garbology project" is still in progress and, combined with information from respondents, offers a unique look at patterns of waste management, consumption, and alcohol use in contemporary U.S. society (Rathje and Ritenbaugh 1984).

Linguistic Anthropology

Linguistics, the study of language, has a long history that dovetails with the discipline of philosophy, but is also one of the integral subfields of anthropology. **Linguistic anthropology** focuses on the relationship between language and culture, how language is used within society, and how the human brain acquires and uses language. Linguistic anthropologists seek to discover the ways in which languages are different from one another, as well as how they are similar to one another. Two wide-ranging areas of research in linguistic anthropology are structural linguistics and historical linguistics.

Structural linguistics explores how language works. Structural linguists compare grammatical patterns or other linguistic elements to learn how contemporary languages mirror and differ from one another. Structural linguistics has also uncovered some intriguing relationships between language and thought patterns among different groups of people. Do people who speak different languages with different grammatical structures think and perceive the world differently from each other? Do native Chinese speakers think or view the world and life experiences differently from native English speakers? Structural linguists are attempting to answer this type of question.

Linguistic anthropologists also examine the connections between language and social behavior in different cultures. This specialty is called **sociolinguistics**. Sociolinguists are interested both in how language is used to define social groups and in how belonging to particular groups leads to specialized kinds of language use. In Thailand, for example, there are thirteen forms of the pronoun *I*. One form is used with equals, other forms come into play with people of higher status, and some forms are used when males address females (Scupin 1988).

Another area of research that has interested linguistic anthropologists is historical linguistics. **Historical linguistics** concentrates on the comparison and classification of different languages to discern the historical links among languages. By examining and analyzing grammatical structures and sounds of languages, researchers are able to discover rules for how languages change over time, as well as which languages are related to one another historically. This type of historical linguistic research is particularly useful in tracing the migration routes of various societies through time, confirming archaeological and paleoanthropological data gathered independently. For example, through historical linguistic research, anthropologists have corroborated the Asian origins of many Native American populations.

Cultural Anthropology or Ethnology

Cultural anthropology or **ethnology** is the subfield of anthropology that examines various contemporary societies and cultures throughout the world. Cultural anthropologists do research in all parts of the world, from the tropical rainforests of the Democratic Republic of the Congo and Brazil to the Arctic regions of Canada, from the deserts of the Middle East to the urban areas of China. Until recently, most cultural anthropologists conducted research on non-Western or remote cultures in Africa, Asia, the Middle East, Latin America, and the Pacific Islands and on the Native American populations in the United States. Today, however, many cultural anthropologists have turned to research on their own cultures in order to gain a better understanding of their institutions and cultural values.

Anthropologists at Work

KELLEY HAYS-GILPIN: Archaeologist

Conservation of the past, the deciphering of gender in the archaeological record, and the meaning of rock art are just a few of the intriguing topics that Kelley Hays-Gilpin has addressed in more than two decades of research. Hays-Gilpin is an archaeologist with a research focus on the prehistoric American Southwest, particularly the history and archaeology of the Pueblo peoples. Like many modern archaeologists, her career has included work in both cultural resource management and university teaching. She completed her doctoral work focusing on early decorated ceramics in the Four Corners region in the Southwest and then, began her career with the Navajo Nation Archaeology Department in Flagstaff, Arizona. Hays-Gilpin worked on collections salvaged from archaeological sites destroyed by development projects or threatened by construction. Currently, she teaches archaeology, ceramic analysis, and rock art courses at Northern

Arizona University in Flagstaff, located just hours from the Petrified Forest National Park and her favorite rock art sites.

Although concerned with the interpretation of past technology and adept at ceramic classification, Hays-Gilpin has consistently sought to push the interpretation of archaeological data to extract deeper meaning than archaeologists usually propose. Beginning with her doctoral work, she became increasingly interested in the study of ideology, symbols, and gender in the archaeological record. Through the comparative study of pottery, textiles, and rock art, she used ancient art as a means of understanding cultural continuity and change. This research furthered her understanding of modern Native American perceptions of and concerns about the past. For Hays-Gilpin, the significance of ancient objects to contemporary indigenous people—having conversations about ancestors and making connections between the past and present—is of crucial importance. It is about being able to glean messages from the

Kelley Hays-Gilpin at the Museum of Northern Arizona front entrance, Photo by Michele Mountain, © 2006 Museum of Northern Arizona

Kelley Hays-Gilpin

past that help us live better lives in the present, including such matters as how to grow food in the desert and how to help others understand and appreciate their heritage.

Hays-Gilpin co-authored an interdisciplinary study of *Prehistoric Sandals from Northeastern Arizona: The Earl H. Morris and Ann Axtell Morris Research*, which was published in 1998. It draws on the research of

Cultural anthropologists (sometimes the terms *sociocultural anthropologist* and *ethnographer* are used interchangeably with *cultural anthropologist*) use a unique research strategy in conducting their fieldwork in different settings. This research strategy is referred to as **participant observation** because cultural anthropologists learn the language and culture of the group being studied by participating in the group's daily activities. Through this intensive participation, they become deeply familiar with the group and can understand and explain the society and culture of the group as insiders.

The results of the fieldwork of the cultural anthropologist are written up as an **ethnography**, a description of a culture within a society. A typical ethnography reports on the environmental setting, economic patterns, social organization, political system, and religious rituals and beliefs of the society under study. This description of a society is based on what anthropologists call

Michael Doolittle/The Image Works

A linguistic anthropologist interviewing a woman from a different culture.

ethnographic data. The gathering of ethnographic data in a systematic manner is the specific research goal of the cultural anthropologist. Technically, **ethnologist** refers to anthropologists who focus on the cross-cultural

three generations of women engaged in the study of essentially the same group of archaeological materials from sites in northeastern Arizona. While it provides a detailed examination of a particular collection, the study also affords insight into changing perceptions of archaeological interpretation. Also published in 1998 was Hays-Gilpin's co-edited volume, the Routledge *Reader in Gender Archaeology*, which helped establish the legitimacy of gendered approaches to the study of the archaeological record.

For archaeologists, rock art— paintings and engravings—provides a unique source of information, offering clues to prehistoric subsistence, ideology, and religion. Yet the interpretation of these prehistoric creations is challenging, and they have often received less attention than they deserve. Hays-Gilpin's *Ambiguous Images: Gender and Rock Art* (2004), which won the Society for American Archaeology's 2005 book prize, provides a significant contribution to the relatively unexplored field of gender in rock art. Hays-Gilpin demonstrates that rock art is one of

the best lines of evidence available to understand the ritual practices, gender roles, and ideological constructs of prehistoric peoples.

In addition to her current academic position, Hays-Gilpin holds the Edward Bridge Danson Chair of Anthropology at the Museum of Northern Arizona, where she is director of the Hopi Iconography Project. This project, a collaborative effort between the museum and the Hopi Tribe's cultural preservation office, explores Hopi cultural continuity over centuries, if not millennia, through pottery, rock art, mural painting, baskets, and textiles. More important, the project is exploring ways in which Hopi traditions can help shape a sustainable future for Hopi communities through subsistence farming, craft production, public health programs, and cultural revitalization.

For Hays-Gilpin, the study of archaeology must emphasize teamwork and reward team players. She feels that archaeologists are not in competition with one another, but rather in competition with the forces

that are destroying the archaeological record faster than it can be studied. Her research and career epitomize this approach to archaeology. Hays-Gilpin advocates monitoring and reporting on sites that have been threatened with destruction, and she continues work on many collections that have resided in museums for as much as century. Her work has led her to collaborate with a network of archaeologists, cultural anthropologists, art historians, linguistic anthropologists, and Hopi artists. Her interdisciplinary approach to the past exemplifies modern archaeology's holistic and inclusive requirements—quite a contrast to its more narrowly specialized traditions. With this new approach, Hays-Gilpin has helped to redefine the discipline of archaeology.

❋ Explore the **Concept** on **myanthrolab.com**

---

aspects of the various ethnographic studies done by the cultural anthropologists. Ethnologists analyze the data that are produced by the individual ethnographic studies to produce cross-cultural generalizations about humanity and cultures.

Applied Anthropology

The four subfields of anthropology (physical anthropology, archaeology, linguistic anthropology, and cultural anthropology) are well established. However, some scholars recognize a fifth subdiscipline. **Applied anthropology** is the use of anthropological data from the other subfields to address modern problems and concerns. These problems may be environmental, technological, economic, social, political, or cultural. Anthropologists have played an increasing role in the development of government policies and legislation, the planning of development projects, and the implementation of marketing strategies. Although anthropologists are typically trained

in one of the major subfields, an increasing number are finding employment outside of universities and museums. Although many anthropologists see at least some aspects of their work as applied, it is the application of anthropological data that is the central part of some researches' careers. Indeed, approximately half of the people with doctorates in anthropology currently find careers outside of academic institutions.

Each of the four major subfields of anthropology has applied aspects. Physical anthropologists, for example, sometimes play a crucial role in police investigations, using their knowledge of the human body to reconstruct the appearance of murder victims on the basis of fragmentary skeletal remains or helping police determine the mechanisms of death. Archaeologists deal with the impact of development on the archaeological record, working to document or preserve archaeological sites threatened by the construction of housing, roads, and dam projects. Some linguistic anthropologists work with government agencies and indigenous peoples to document

Anthropologists at Work

BAMBI B. SCHIEFFELIN: Linguistic Anthropologist

As an undergraduate at Columbia University, Blin was drawn to two fields: anthropology and comparative literature. After spending a summer on a field trip to rural Bolivia and a year in the southern highlands of Papua New Guinea, Schieffelin decided to pursue a doctorate in anthropology, with a specialty in linguistic anthropology. She combined the fields of developmental psychology, linguistics, and anthropology, which prepared her for fieldwork among the Kaluli people in Papua New Guinea. After completing her Ph.D. degree, Schieffelin spent a year teaching anthropology at the University of California at Berkeley and also teaching linguistics at Stanford University. Since 1986, she has been teaching at New York University in the Department of Anthropology.

Schieffelin's work focuses on language use and socialization. She studies how language is acquired by children and how language is used in various social contexts. She has collaborated with Elinor Ochs to develop innovative approaches to understanding how language use is influenced by socialization. Together they have edited several volumes, including *Language Socialization across Cultures* (1987). In addition, Schieffelin has developed these topics in her own book, *The Give and Take of Everyday Life: Language Socialization of Kaluli Children* (1990).

Through their research on children's language socialization, Schieffelin and Ochs contributed to a cross-cultural understanding of this process. Until the early 1970s, most of the theories on language and socialization had been drawn from psychological research on middle-class Americans. Schieffelin and Ochs focused instead on language and socialization among many different societies. They emphasized the importance of cultural practices in shaping verbal activities. For example, prior to their research, it was assumed that "baby talk" was the same all over the world. They found, however, that "baby talk" is not universal and is linked to ideas that people have about children.

In her ethnographic research, Schieffelin tape-records and transcribes everyday social interactions in different speech communities. She has carried out research in Papua New Guinea since 1967, focusing not only on language socialization, but also on language change and the introduction of literacy into a nonliterate society. In addition to this work in a relatively traditional society, Schieffelin has worked in a number of urban speech communities in the United States, where linguistic diversity is apparent on every street corner. Her research in Philadelphia among Sino-Vietnamese people focused on language socialization and literacy, and her studies of Haitians in New York analyzed language socialization and code-switching practices.

As a linguistic anthropologist, Schieffelin tries to integrate two perspectives. First, she focuses on how the study of language use can lead to insights into how culture is transmitted from generation to generation in everyday social interactions. Second, she analyzes the ways in which language expresses social relationships and cultural meanings across different social and political contexts. Recently, Schieffelin has been engaged in research on how language relates to Bible translation and conversion to Christianity in Papua New Guinea. She does research on how translations of parables and speech activities change the meaning of concepts of place and the body in the Christian missionization process among

Bambi Schieffelin

the native peoples such as the Bosavi. In addition, Schieffelin has been examining speech activities and language use on commercials on YouTube and icanhascheezburger.com and the use of texting by teenagers. This piqued the interest of many undergraduates who began to explore the techniques used by linguistic anthropologists for exploring new types of media. Schieffelin's work represents the most current developments in linguistic anthropology today.

Linguistic anthropologists have broadened their vision of places in which to investigate language use—including the legal, medical, scientific, educational, and political arenas—as these contexts are critical to understanding how power is acquired and distributed. They are also studying all varieties of literacy, including television, radio, and the Internet providing new perspectives on these new forms of global communication.

❋ Explore the Concept on myanthrolab.com

disappearing languages or work in business to help develop marketing strategies. Cultural anthropologists, such as A. Peter Castro (see "Anthropologists at Work: A. Peter Castro: Applied Anthropologist"), have played a key role in the planning of government programs so that they take peoples' cultural beliefs and needs into consideration.

Holistic Anthropology, Interdisciplinary Research, and the Global Perspective

By its very nature, anthropology is an interdisciplinary, holistic field. Most anthropologists receive some training in each of four subfields of anthropology. However, because of the huge amount of research undertaken in these different subfields—more than three hundred journals and hundreds of books are published every year—no one individual can keep abreast of all the developments across the discipline. Consequently, anthropologists usually specialize in one of the four subfields. Nevertheless, most anthropologists are firmly committed to a **holistic** approach to understanding humankind—a broad, comprehensive account that draws on all four subfields under the umbrella of anthropology. This holistic approach involves the analysis of biological, environmental, psychological, economic, historical, social, and cultural conditions of humanity. In other words, anthropologists study the physical characteristics of humans, including their genetic endowment, as well as their prehistoric, historical, and social and cultural environments. Through collaborative studies among the various specialists in the four subfields, anthropologists can ask broadly framed questions about humanity.

Anthropology does not limit itself to its own four subfields to realize its research agenda. Although it stands as a distinct discipline, anthropology has strong links to other social sciences. Cultural anthropology or ethnology, for instance, is closely related to sociology. In the past, cultural anthropologists examined the traditional societies of the world, whereas sociologists focused on modern societies. Today, cultural anthropologists and sociologists explore many of the same societies using similar research approaches. For example, both rely on statistical and nonstatistical data whenever appropriate in their studies of different types of societies.

Cultural anthropology also overlaps the fields of psychology, economics, and political science. Cultural anthropologists draw on psychology when they assess the behavior of people in other societies. Psychological questions bearing on perception, learning, and motivation all figure in ethnographic fieldwork. Additionally, cultural anthropologists or ethnologists probe the economic and political behavior and thought of people in various societies, using these data for comparative purposes.

Finally, anthropology dovetails considerably with the field of history, which, like anthropology, encompasses a broad range of events. Every human event that has ever taken place in the world is a potential topic for both historians and anthropologists. Historians describe and explain human events that have occurred throughout the world; anthropologists place their biological, archaeological, linguistic, and ethnographic data in the context of these historical developments.

Through the four subfields and the interdisciplinary approach, anthropologists have emphasized a *global perspective*. The global perspective enables anthropologists to consider the biological, environmental, psychological, economic, historical, social, and cultural conditions of humans at all times and in all places. Anthropologists do not limit themselves to understanding a particular society or set of societies, but attempt to go beyond specific or local conditions and demonstrate the interconnections among societies throughout the world. This global perspective is used throughout this text to show how anthropologists situate their findings in the interconnecting worldwide context.

Anthropological Explanations

A fundamental question faced by anthropologists is how to evaluate the particular social, cultural, or biological data they gather. Human knowledge is rooted in personal experience, as well as in the beliefs, traditions, and norms maintained by the societies in which people live. This includes such knowledge as assumptions about putting on warm clothing in cold weather and bringing an umbrella if it is going to rain, for example. Yet, it also includes notions about how food should be prepared, what constitutes "appropriate" behavior, and what the appropriate social and cultural roles are for men and women.

Religion constitutes another source of human knowledge. Religious beliefs and faith are most often derived from sacred texts, such as the Bible, Qur'an, and Talmud, but they are also based on intuitions, dreams, visions, and extrasensory perceptions. Most religious beliefs are cast in highly personal terms and, like personal knowledge, span a wide and diverse range. People who do not accept these culturally coded assumptions may be perceived as different, abnormal, or nonconformist by other members of their society. Yet, ethnographic and cross-cultural research in anthropology demonstrates that such culturally constituted knowledge is not as general as we might think. This research indicates that as humans, we are not born with this knowledge. Such knowledge tends to vary both among different societies and among different groups within the same society.

Popular perceptions about other cultures have often been based on ethnocentric attitudes. **Ethnocentrism** is the practice of judging another society by the values and standards of one's own society. To some degree, ethnocentrism is a universal phenomenon. As humans learn

Anthropologists at Work

SCOTT ATRAN:
Cultural Anthropologist

Born in 1952 in New York City, Scott Atran went to Columbia University as a Westinghouse mathematics scholar. At a student demonstration against the Vietnam conflict in 1970, he met the famous anthropologist Margaret Mead and she invited him to work as her assistant at the American Museum of National History. In 1970, Atran also traveled to the Middle East for the first time, conducting fieldwork in Palestinian villages. As a graduate student in 1974, Atran organized a famous debate at the Abbaye de Royaumont in France on the nature of universals in human thought and society, with the participation of some well-known scholars such as the linguist Noam Chomsky, the psychologist Jean Piaget, the anthropologists Claude Lévi-Strauss and Gregory Bateson, and the biologists François Jacob and Jacques Monod, which many consider a milestone in the development of the field known as cognitive science.

Atran continued observing societies as he traveled overland from Portugal to China, via Afghanistan and Pakistan. Landing again in the Middle East, he conducted ethnographic research on kinship and social ties, land tenure, and political economy among the Druze, a religious group in Israel and Lebanon. Later, Atran became a pioneer in the study of the foundations of biological thinking in Western science and other Native American Indian groups such as the Itzá Maya in Mexico. This research became the basis of his well-known books *Cognitive Foundations of Natural History: Towards an Anthropology of Science* and *The Native Mind and the Cultural Construction of Nature*, and *Plants of the Peten Itzá Maya*, which illustrate how people throughout the world classified biological species of plants and animals in very similar ways.

Later, Atran began an investigation of the cognitive and evolutionary foundations of religion, which resulted in his widely acclaimed book *In Gods We Trust: The Evolutionary Landscape of Religion* published by Oxford Press. In this book Atran, explores the psychological foundations of religion and how it has become a universal feature of all human societies. Currently, his most recent work is on the characteristics associated with suicide bombers and political and religious terrorism in different areas of the world. Atran has been funded by the National Science Foundation and other agencies to study the phenomena of terrorism and this has included fieldwork and interviews with imprisoned Al Qaeda members and their supporters in Europe, the Middle East, Central and Southeast Asia, and North Africa. His recent book *Talking to the Enemy: Faith, Brotherhood and the (Un)Making of Terrorists* is based on this long-term research. In March, 2010 Atran testified before the Senate Armed Services Subcommittee on Emerging Threats and Capabilities today on "Pathways to and from Violent Extremism: The Case for Science-Based Field Research." His testimony can be seen at http://www.edge.org/3rd_culture/atran10/atran10_index.html.

Atran has taught at Cambridge University, Hebrew University in Jerusalem, and the École des hautes études in Paris. He is currently a research director in anthropology at the Centre national de la recherche scientifique (The Center for Scientific Research) based in Paris and is a member of the Jean Nicod Institute at the École normale supérieure. He is also visiting professor of psychology and public policy at the University of Michigan, presidential scholar in sociology at the John Jay College of Criminal Justice in New York City, and co-founder of ARTIS Research and Risk Modeling. Atran's broadly interdisciplinary scientific studies on human reasoning processes and cultural management of the environment, and on religion and terrorism, have been featured around the world in science publications, such as *Science, Nature, Proceedings of the National Academy of Sciences USA,*

Scott Atran

and *Brain and Behavioral Sciences*, as well as the popular press, including features stories with BBC television and radio, National Public Radio, *The Wall Street Journal*, and *Newsweek*. He has been the subject of a cover story in the *New York Times Magazine* ("Darwin's God," 2007) and has written numerous op-eds for the *New York Times*.

Atran has teamed up with psychologists and political scientists, including Douglas Medin and Robert Axelrod, to experiment extensively on the ways scientists and ordinary people categorize and reason about nature, on the cognitive and evolutionary psychology of religion, and on the role of sacred values in political and cultural conflict. Based on recent fieldwork, he has testified before the U.S. Congress and has repeatedly briefed National Security Council staff at the White House on paths to violent extremism among youth in Southeast and South Asia, the Middle East, North Africa, and Europe. Atran has utilized his knowledge and research as a cultural anthropologist to help understand some of the basic questions of human life and also to contribute to solving some of our current problems with globally-sponsored political and religious terrorism.

✳ **Explore** the **Concept** on **myanthrolab.com**

the basic values, beliefs, and norms of their society, they tend to think of their own culture as preferable, and as what is normal, while ranking other cultures as less desirable. Members of a society may be so committed to their own cultural traditions that they cannot conceive of any other way of life. They often view other cultural traditions as strange or alien, perhaps even inferior, crazy, or immoral.

Such deeply ingrained perceptions are difficult to escape, even for anthropologists. Nineteenth-century anthropologists, for example, often reinforced ethnocentric beliefs about other societies. The twentieth century saw the co-opting of anthropological data to serve specific political and social ends. As the twentieth century progressed, however, anthropologists increasingly began to recognize the biases that prevented the interpretation of other cultures in more valid, systematic ways.

The Scientific Method

Given the preceding concerns, it is critical to understand how anthropological interpretations are evaluated. In contrast to personal knowledge and religious faith, anthropological knowledge is not based on traditional wisdom or revelations. Rather, anthropologists employ the **scientific method**, a system of logic used to evaluate data derived from systematic observation. Researchers rely upon the scientific method to investigate both the natural and the social worlds because the approach allows them to make claims about knowledge and to verify those claims with systematic, logical reasoning. Through critical thinking and skeptical thought, scientists strive to suspend judgment about any claim for knowledge until it has been verified.

Testability and *verifiability* lie at the core of the scientific method. There are two ways of developing testable propositions: the inductive method and the deductive method. In the **inductive method**, the scientist first makes observations and collects data (see Figure 2). Many of the data collected are referred to as variables. A **variable** is any piece of data that changes from case to case. For example, a person's height, weight, age, and sex all constitute variables. Researchers use the observations about different variables to develop hypotheses about the data. A **hypothesis** is a testable proposition concerning the relationship between particular sets of variables in the collected data. The practice of testing hypotheses is the major focus of the scientific method, as scientists test one another's hypotheses to confirm or refute them. If a hypothesis is found to be valid, it may be woven together with other hypotheses into a more general theory. **Theories** are statements that explain hypotheses and observations about natural or social phenomena. Because of their explanatory nature, theories often encompass a variety of hypotheses and observations. One of the most comprehensive theories in anthropology is the theory of evolution. This theory helps explain a diversity of hypotheses about biological

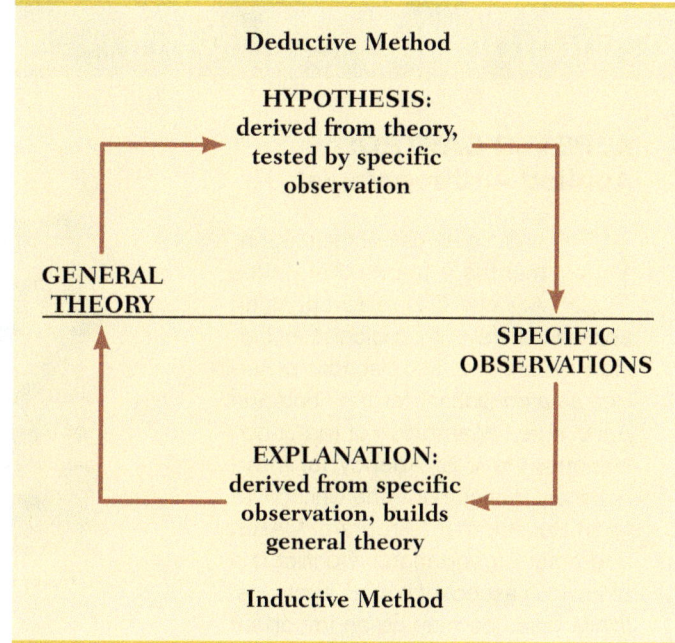

Figure 2 Deductive and inductive research methods

and natural phenomena, as well as discoveries by paleoanthropologists and geneticists.

In contrast to the inductive method, the **deductive method** of scientific research begins with a general theory from which scientists develop testable hypotheses. Data are then collected to evaluate these hypotheses. Initial hypotheses are sometimes referred to as "guesstimates" because they may be based on guesswork by the scientist. These hypotheses are tested through experimentation and replication. As with the inductive method, scientists test and retest hypotheses and theories to ensure the reliability of observations made.

Through these methods, researchers do not arrive at absolute truths. Theories may be invalidated or falsified by contradictory observations. Yet, even if numerous observations and hypotheses suggest that a particular theory is true, the theory always remains open to further testing and evaluation. The systematic evaluation of hypotheses and theories enables scientists to state their conclusions with a certainty that cannot be applied to personal and culturally construed knowledge.

Despite the thoroughness and verification that characterize the research, anthropological explanations have limitations. Anthropologists must grapple with the myriad of complex, interwoven variables that influence human society and biological processes. The complexities of the phenomena being studied make it difficult to assess all of the potential variables, and disagreements about interpretations are common. Consequently, conclusions are frequently presented as tentative and hypothetical. The point here, however, is not that progress is impossible. Anthropological evidence can be verified or discarded by making assumptions explicit and weeding out

Anthropologists at Work

A. PETER CASTRO:
Applied Anthropologist

Conflict over use of the environment is a theme that unites A. Peter Castro's work as an applied cultural anthropologist, including his more than two decades of service as a consultant for the Food and Agriculture Organization of the United Nations, the U.S. Agency for International Development, the United Nations Development Program, CARE, and other organizations. Conflict is a ubiquitous aspect of human existence. While disputes may be an important means for people to assert their rights, interests, and needs, conflicts can escalate into violence that threatens both lives and livelihoods. Castro has used his perspective, skills, and knowledge as a cultural anthropologist to address issues related to understanding and dealing with environmental conflicts in participatory and peaceful ways. Besides his ongoing work as a consultant, he incorporates conflict issues into his classes in the Anthropology Department of the Maxwell School of Citizenship and Public Affairs at Syracuse University, where he is an associate professor.

Castro's interest in environmental conflicts reflects his rural California

A. Peter Castro with a man and woman in Ethiopia

Courtesy of A. H. Peter Castro

upbringing, where farm worker unionization struggles, debates about offshore oil development, and conflicts over housing and commercial expansion were everyday occurrences. He credits his professors at the University of California, Santa Barbara, where he obtained his undergraduate and graduate degrees, with giving him the inspiration and the training to use cultural anthropology to address pressing social and environmental issues. As an undergraduate, Castro was a research assistant on a number of applied anthropology projects. In classes and through long discussions outside of class, he learned invaluable lessons from various professors about

issues in health care and agricultural programs and about the importance of linking local, national, and global dimensions of human and environmental crises. Castro's Ph.D. advisor, David Brokensha, has a distinguished record as an applied anthropologist and was instrumental in providing opportunities for Castro to develop contacts in international agencies. Brokensha was one of the founders of the Institute for Development Anthropology, a nonprofit research and educational organization dedicated to applying anthropological theories and methods to improving the condition of the world's poor.

Castro's early work as an applied anthropologist for international

contradictory, subjective knowledge. Poor hypotheses are rejected and replaced by better explanations. Explanations can be made stronger by drawing on independent lines of evidence to support and evaluate theories. This process makes the scientific method much more effective than other means of acquiring knowledge.

Anthropology and the Humanities

The scientific method is not the only means used by anthropologists to study different societies and cultures. Anthropologists also employ a more humanistic-interpretive approach as they study cultures. Think of this analogy. When botanists examine a flower, they attempt to understand the different components of the plant within a scientific framework; they analyze the biochemical and

physical aspects of the flower. However, when painters, poets, or novelists perceive a flower, they understand the plant from an aesthetic standpoint. They might interpret the flower as a symbolic phenomenon that represents nature. The scientist and the humanist use different approaches and perspectives when examining the natural world. Anthropologists employ a humanistic-interpretive approach in many circumstances.

James Peacock uses another type of analogy to discuss the difference between the scientific and the humanistic-interpretive approaches in anthropology (1986). Peacock draws from the field of photography to construct his analogy. He discusses the "harsh light" of the rigor of scientific analysis, used to study the biological and material conditions of a society, versus the "soft focus" used when interpreting the symbols, art, literature,

organizations focused on practical aspects of planning, managing, and evaluating community forestry programs and projects. Although conflict between communities and public forest administrators often helped propel the rise of such programs and projects, conflict itself was not initially seen by officials and technical officers as a topic of concern. Nonetheless, Castro found that, whether carrying out applied ethnographic fieldwork on deforestation in Kenya for the U.S. Agency for International Development or preparing a literature-based review of indigenous forest management practices for the Food and Agriculture Organization, one needed to take such issues into account. For example, it was apparent that conservation efforts in Kenya could not be understood without relating them to long struggles involving different rural groups, government agencies, commercial interests, and other stakeholders. In addition, Castro discovered through ethnographic interviews and archival research that conflicting interests had sometimes negotiated agreements calling for locally based management or collaborative activities that still had relevance today (for example, see Castro's book *Facing Kirinyaga: A Social History of Forest Commons in Southern Mount Kenya*, 1995). Castro's concern with integrating historical analysis, as well as conflict analysis, into international development planning is illustrated in his edited collection of articles on the theme "Historical Consciousness and Development Planning" in the interdisciplinary journal *World Development* (1998).

The importance of dealing with environmental conflicts became starkly clear when Castro was asked by the United Nations Development Program (UNDP) in 1992 to serve as team leader for the midterm evaluation of Bangladesh's Social Forestry Project, a countrywide effort being implemented at a cost of $46 million. The project was supposed to create the capacity for Bangladesh's Forestry Department to engage in community-oriented training, tree planting, and resource protection. While the project had many accomplishments, it also had severe problems in many areas due to lack of public participation (see Castro and Nielsen 2005). Sadly, a project meant to address some long-standing conflicts sometimes served to intensify them. The evaluation mission identified these issues, but because the UNDP could not compel changes, it terminated the project early in some tribal areas where conflict was becoming particularly intense.

Castro has been working as a consultant for the Forestry Department of the Food and Agriculture Organization of the United Nations (FAO), writing and editing a number of publications aimed at providing information and practical training on natural resource conflict management. He co-edited a useful book with Antonio Engel called *Negotiation and Mediation Techniques for Natural Resource Management* in 2007. This book has been used widely by applied anthropologists and others in development work and can be found at ftp://ftp.fao.org/docrep/fao/010/ai052e/ai052e00.pdf. In 2009, Castro participated in a United Nations University of Peace conference in Sudan and wrote a paper about conflict management in the Darfur area. The paper can be downloaded at http://www.africa.upeace.org/documents/environment_files.pdf. Currently, Castro is co-editing a book *Climate Change and Threatened Communities* with David Brokensha and Dan Taylor. Castro's work as an applied anthropologist has been recognized throughout the world.

✳ **Explore** the **Concept** on
myanthrolab.com

religion, or music of different societies. Peacock concludes that both the "harsh light" and the "soft focus" are vital ingredients of the anthropological perspective.

Cultural anthropologists utilize the humanistic-interpretive method as they conduct ethnographic research. However, archaeologists also try to employ these same methods when examining artifacts from ancient societies. When cultural anthropologists or archaeologists examine various practices and institutions in different societies, they often find that an outsider cannot easily comprehend these phenomena. In order to comprehend these different practices and institutions, cultural anthropologists or archaeologists often have to interpret these phenomena, just as one might interpret a literary, poetic, or religious text. Cultural beliefs and practices may not be easily translatable from one society to another. Cultural anthropologists or archaeologists frequently find practices and institutions that have meaning and significance only within a specific language and culture. Cultural anthropologists or archaeologists endeavor to understand cultural practices or institutions that may have rich, deep, localized meaning within the society being examined, but that are not easily converted into transcultural or cross-cultural meaning.

Thus, in addition to its interconnections with the natural and social sciences, the discipline of anthropology is aligned with the humanistic fields of inquiry. This is particularly true with respect to the field of cultural anthropology, as these researchers are involved in the study of different contemporary cultures. When participating in the life and experience of people in various societies, ethnographers must confront a multitude of different behaviors and values that may have to be translated and interpreted. As mentioned above, archaeologists also confront this type of problem when studying past cultures and civilizations from different regions of the world. Similar issues confront linguistic anthropologists as they translate and understand various languages.

Many anthropologists explore the creative cultural dimensions of humanity, such as myth, folklore, poetry, art, music, and mythology. **Ethnopoetics** is the study of poetry and how it relates to the experiences of people in different societies; for example, a provocative study of the poetry of a nomadic tribe of Bedouins in the Middle East has yielded new insights into the concepts of honor and shame in this society (Abu-Lughod 1987). Another related field, **ethnomusicology**, is devoted to the study of musical traditions in various societies throughout the world. Ethnomusicologists record and analyze music and the traditions that give rise to musical expression, exploring similarities and differences in musical performance and composition. Ethnomusicologist Dale Olsen completed a fascinating study of Japanese music in South America. There are Japanese minority populations in the countries of Peru, Brazil, Argentina, Paraguay, and Bolivia. Olsen has studied the musical forms, both popular and classical, of these Japanese minorities and how they reflect the maintenance of ethnicity and culture in South America (2004). Other anthropologists study the art of particular societies, such as pottery styles among Native American groups.

Studies of fine art conducted by anthropologists have contributed to a more richly hued, global portrait of humankind. Artistic traditions spring up in all societies, and anthropologists have shed light on the music, myths, poetry, literature, and art of non-Western and other remote peoples. As a result, we now have a keener appreciation of the diverse creative abilities exhibited by humans throughout the world. As anthropologists analyze these humanistic and artistic traditions, they broaden our understanding of the economic, social, political, and religious conditions that prevail within these societies.

One fundamental difference exists between the scientific and the humanistic-interpretive aspects of anthropology. This difference pertains to the amount of progress one can achieve within these two different but complementary enterprises. Science has produced a cumulative increase in its knowledge base through its methodology. Thus, in the fields of astronomy, physics, chemistry, biology, and anthropology, there has been significant progress in the accumulation of

knowledge; we know much more about these fields of science than our ancestors knew in the fifteenth or nineteenth century. As a result of scientific discoveries and developments, the scientific knowledge in these areas has definitely become more effective in offering explanations regarding the natural and social world. Anthropologists today have a much better understanding of human behavior and culture than did anthropologists in the nineteenth century. Through the use of the scientific method, anthropology has been able to make strides in assessing human behavior and cultural developments.

In contrast, one cannot discuss the progress in the humanities in the same manner. Myth, literature, music, and poetry have not progressed in the way that scientific explanations have. One certainly cannot say that the literature or music of the twenty-first century has progressed beyond that of Sophocles', Shakespeare's, Dante's, Bach's, or Beethoven's time period. As we shall see, the various humanistic endeavors involving beliefs, myths, and artistic expression in small-scale and ancient civilizations are extremely sophisticated and symbolically complex, and one cannot assess modern societies as "superior" or more "progressive" in those domains.

The essence of anthropology consists of understanding and explaining human behavior and culture with endeavors monopolized by no single approach. Such an enlarged perspective within anthropology requires peaceful coexistence between scientism and humanism, despite their differences. In a recent discussion of this issue within anthropology, Anne Campbell and Patricia Rice suggest that many anthropologists do not agree with one another's assumptions from either a humanistic or a scientific perspective because of their philosophical commitments to one or the other area (Campbell and Rice 2003). However, anthropologists

Ethnomusicologists study the musical traditions of different societies. This photo shows a group from North India playing traditional musical instruments. .

recognize these differences among themselves, and this is helpful, to a great degree, in making progress in our field because we continue to criticize and challenge one another's assumptions and orientations, which results in better understanding of both the scientific explanations and the humanistic understandings within our field.

What we are going to find in this textbook is that the many great syntheses of anthropological knowledge require the fusion of both the scientific and the humanistic perspectives. When the archaeologist studies the precision and beauty embodied in the 4,500-year-old pyramids of the Egyptian civilization, he (or she) finds that their inspiration came partly from the mathematics of numbers considered sacred and divine and partly from the emulation of nature. Both scientific and humanistic approaches enable anthropologists to study the sacred and the mundane aspects of nature and culture. When anthropologists combine the scientific and humanistic approaches, they can discover what is transcultural and universal and what is unique to specific societies. This is the major goal of anthropological research to determine the similarity and differences of humans in the past and the present.

Why Study Anthropology?

Many students today question the practical benefits of their educational experience. Hence, you might ask, "Why study anthropology?" First, anthropology contributes to a general liberal arts education, which helps students develop intellectually and personally, as well as professionally. Numerous studies indicate that a well-rounded education contributes to a person's success in any chosen career, and because of its broad interdisciplinary nature, anthropology is especially well suited to this purpose.

Critical Thinking and Global Awareness

In the context of a liberal arts education, anthropology and anthropological research cultivate critical thinking skills. As we noted earlier, the scientific method relies on constant evaluation of, and critical thinking about, data collected in the field. By being exposed to the cultures and lifestyles of unfamiliar societies, students may adopt a more critical and analytical stance toward conditions in their own society. Critical thinking skills enhance the reasoning abilities of students wherever life takes them.

Anthropology also creates an expanding global awareness and an appreciation for cultures other than our own. In this age of rapid communication, worldwide travel, and increasing economic interconnections, young people preparing for careers in the twenty-first century must recognize and show sensitivity toward the cultural differences among peoples, while understanding the fundamental similarities that make us all distinctly human. In this age of cultural diversity and increasing internationalization, sustaining this dual perception of underlying similar human

characteristics and outward cultural differences has both practical and moral benefits. Nationalistic, ethnic, and racial bigotry are rife today in many parts of the world, yet our continuing survival and happiness depend upon greater mutual understanding. Anthropology promotes a cross-cultural perspective that allows us to see ourselves as part of one human family in the midst of tremendous diversity. Our society needs not just citizens of some local region or group but also, and more importantly, world citizens who can work cooperatively in an inescapably multicultural and multinational world to solve our most pressing problems of bigotry, poverty, and violence.

In addition, an anthropology course gives students a chance to delve into a discipline whose roots lie in both the sciences and the humanities. As we have seen, anthropology brings to bear rigorous scientific methods and models in examining the causes of human evolution, behavior, and social relationships. But anthropologists also try to achieve a humanistic understanding of other societies in all their rich cultural complexity. Anthropology casts a wide net, seeking an understanding of ancient and contemporary peoples, biological and societal developments, and human diversity and similarities throughout the world.

Viewing life from the anthropological perspective, students will also gain a greater understanding of their personal lives in the context of the long period of human evolution and development. In learning about behavior patterns and cultural values in distant societies, students question and acquire new insights into their own behavior. Thus, anthropology nurtures personal enlightenment and self-awareness, which are fundamental goals of education.

While these general goals are laudable, the study of anthropology also offers more pragmatic applications (Omohundro 1998). As seen in the discussion of applied anthropology, all of the traditional subfields of anthropology have areas of study with direct relevance to modern life. Many students have found it useful to combine an anthropology minor or major with another major. For example, given the increasingly multicultural and international focus of today's world, students preparing for careers in business, management, marketing, or public service may find it advantageous to have some anthropology courses on their résumés. The concepts and knowledge gleaned from anthropology may enable students to find practical applications for dealing with issues of cultural and ethnic diversity and multiculturalism on a daily basis. Similarly, policy makers in federal, state, and local governments may find it useful to have an understanding of historic preservation issues and cultural resource management concerns. In education, various aspects of anthropology—including the study of evolution, the human past, and non-European cultures and the interpretation of cultural and social phenomena—are increasingly being integrated into elementary and secondary school curricula. Education majors preparing for the classroom can draw on their background in anthropology to provide a more insightful context for some of these issues.

Summary

Anthropology consists of four subfields: physical anthropology, archaeology, linguistic anthropology, and cultural anthropology or ethnology. Each of these subfields uses distinctive methods to examine humanity in the past and in all areas of the world today. Physical anthropologists investigate human evolution and the physical variation of human populations across many geographical regions. Archaeologists study the past by analyzing artifacts (material remains) of past societies. Linguistic anthropologists focus their studies on languages, seeking out historical relationships among languages, pursuing clues to the evolution of particular languages, and comparing one language with another to determine differences and similarities. Cultural anthropologists conduct fieldwork in various societies to examine people's lifestyles. They describe these societies in written studies, called ethnographies which highlight behavior and thought patterns characteristic of the people studied. In examining societies, cultural anthropologists use systematic research methods and strategies, primarily participant observation, which involves participating in the daily activities of the people they are studying.

Anthropologists draw on the scientific method to investigate humanity, while recognizing the limitations of science in grasping the subtleties of human affairs. Yet, anthropology is also a humanistic discipline that focuses on such cultural elements as art, music, and religion. By bridging the sciences and the humanities, anthropology enables us to look at humanity's biological and cultural heritage with a broad perspective.

For students, anthropology creates a global awareness and a deep appreciation of humanity past and present. By evaluating anthropological data, students develop critical thinking skills. And the process of anthropological inquiry—exploring other cultures and comparing them to one's own—sheds light on one's personal situation as a human being in a particular time and place.

Questions to Think About

1. As an anthropologist on a starship in the twenty-first century, you are a specialist in "first contact" situations. Briefly describe your goals and methods.

2. As an anthropologist, you find out about the existence of a group of humans in the Amazon rainforest that have never been contacted. How would you use the four subfields of anthropology to investigate this human community?

3. How do anthropologists utilize the scientific method in their studies? What are the limitations of the scientific method in anthropological studies?

4. You are talking with a friend who asks, "Why would anyone want to study anthropology? What practical benefits can be gained from taking a course in anthropology?" How would you answer your friend?

5. What is the holistic approach, and how is it related to anthropology and its four subfields, as well as to other disciplines?

Key Terms

anthropology	ethnography	hypothesis	primatology
applied anthropology	ethnologist	inductive method	scientific method
archaeology	ethnology	linguistic anthropology	sociolinguistics
artifacts	ethnomusicology	linguistics	structural linguistics
cultural anthropology	ethnopoetics	middens	theories
deductive method	fossils	paleoanthropology	variable
ethnoarchaeology	historical linguistics	participant observation	
ethnocentrism	holistic	primates	

For further information about topics covered in this chapter, go to MyAnthroLab at www.myanthrolab.com and access the following readings in MyAnthroLibrary:

Terence E. Hays, *From Ethnographer to Comparativist and Back Again.*

Katharine Milton, *The Evolution of a Physical Anthropologist.*

Richard E. Blanton, *Archaeologist at Work.*

Evolution

James L. Amos/Photo Researchers, Inc.

Evolution

Chapter Questions

- **How** do other cosmologies of human origins differ from the scientific view of evolution?

- **In what** ways does Darwin's view of evolution differ from Lamarck's?

- **How** does natural selection work?

- **What** were Mendel's contributions to our understanding of heredity?

- **In what** ways has molecular genetics broadened our insights into evolution?

- **How** do mutations affect the evolutionary process?

- **How** does the new view of punctuated equilibrium help us understand evolution?

- **What** are the basic weaknesses of the creationist or intelligent design approach to evolution?

((•─ **Listen** to the **Chapter Audio** on **myanthrolab.com**

One of the challenges of physical anthropology is to provide insights into the origins of humankind. The fossil record preserves evidence of past life on Earth, tracing a progression of simple one-celled organisms to increasingly diverse forms. How did these different forms of life emerge and new species arise? The biological explanations for this change are the focus of this chapter.

Theories concerning the evolution of life date back to the ancient Greeks, but it was only during the nineteenth century that the first comprehensive theories of evolution were developed. They were made possible through discoveries in many different areas. The acceptance of evolutionary theory is based on research in many fields. Indeed, the value of evolutionary theory is its utility as a consistent explanation for a wide variety of phenomena. Before examining the scientific basis for our understanding of evolution, it is useful to consider other explanations of human origins.

Cosmologies and Human Origins

The most profound human questions are the ones that perplex us the most. Who are we? Where did we come from? Why are we here? What is our place in the universe? These questions have been shared by many people throughout history. Most cultures have developed explanations that provide answers to these fundamental questions. **Cosmologies** are conceptual frameworks that present the universe (the *cosmos*) as an orderly system. They often include answers to these basic questions about the place of humankind in the universe and about human origins, usually considered the most sacred of all cosmological conceptions.

Cosmologies account for the ways in which supernatural beings or forces formed human beings and the planet we live on. These beliefs are transmitted from generation to generation through ritual, education, laws, art, and language. For example, the Navajo people of the southwestern United States believe that the Holy People, supernatural and sacred, lived below ground in twelve lower worlds. A massive underground flood forced the Holy People to crawl through a hollow reed to the surface of the Earth, where they created the universe. A deity named Changing Woman gave birth to the Hero Twins, called Monster Slayer and Child of the Waters. Human mortals, called Earth Surface People, emerged, and First Man and First Woman were formed from the ears of white and yellow corn.

In the tradition of Taoism, male and female principles known as *yin* and *yang* are the spiritual and material sources for the origins of humans and other living forms. Yin is considered the passive, negative, feminine force or principle in the universe, the source of cold and darkness, whereas yang is the active, positive, masculine force or principle, the source of heat and light. Taoists believe that the interaction of these two opposite principles brought forth the universe and all living forms out of chaos. These examples illustrate just two of the highly varied origin traditions held by different people around the world.

Western Traditions of Origin

In the Western tradition, the ancient Greeks had various mythological explanations for human origins. One early view was that Prometheus fashioned humans out of water and earth. Another had Zeus ordering Pyrrha, the inventor of fire, to throw stones behind his back, which in turn became men and women. Later Greek views considered biological evolution. The Greek philosopher Thales of Miletus (c. 636–546 B.C.) attempted to understand the origin and the existence of the world without reference mythology. He argued that life originated in the sea and that humans initially were fishlike, eventually moving onto dry land and evolving into mammals. The most important cosmological tradition affecting Western views of creation is recounted in the biblical Book of Genesis, which is found in Greek texts dating back to the third century B.C. This Judaic tradition describes how God created the cosmos. It begins with "In the beginning God created the heaven and the earth" and describes how creation took six days during which light, heaven, Earth, vegetation, Sun, Moon, stars, birds, fish, animals, and humans originated. Yahweh, the Creator, made man, Adam, from "dust" and placed him in the Garden of

This painting by Michelangelo in the Sistine Chapel represents the idea of spiritual creation, the dominant worldview in Western cosmology for centuries.

Erich Lessing/Art Resource, NY

Eden. Woman, Eve, was created from Adam's rib. Later, as Christianity spread throughout Europe, this tradition became the dominant cosmological explanation of human origins.

In Europe before the Renaissance, the Judeo-Christian view of creation provided the only framework for understanding humanity's position in the universe. The versions of creation discussed in the biblical text fostered a specific concept of time: a linear, non-repetitive, unique historical framework that began with divine creation. These events were chronicled in the Bible; there was no concept of an ancient past stretching far back in time before human memory. This view led some theologians to attempt to calculate the precise age of the Earth on the basis of information in the Bible, such as references to births and deaths and the number of generations. One of the best known of these calculations was done by Archbishop James Ussher of Ireland (1581–1665). By calculating the number of generations mentioned in the Bible, Ussher dated the beginning of the universe to the year 4004 B.C. Thus, according to Bishop Ussher's estimate, the Earth was approximately 6,000 years old.

The biblical account of creation led to a static, fixed view of plant and animal species and the age of the Earth. Because the Bible recounted the creation of the world and everything on it in six days, medieval theologians reasoned that the various species of plants and animals must be fixed in nature. God had created plant and animal species to fit perfectly within specific environments and did not intend for them to change. They had been unaltered since the time of the divine creation, and no new species had emerged. This idea regarding the permanence of species influenced the thinking of many early scholars and theologians.

The Scientific Revolution

In Europe during the Renaissance (after c. 1450 A.D.), scientific discoveries began to challenge conceptions about both the age of the Earth and humanity's relationship to the rest of the universe. Copernicus and Galileo presented the then novel idea that the Earth was not circled by the celestial bodies, but rather just one of several planets revolving around the Sun. As this idea became accepted, humans could no longer view themselves and their planet as the center of the universe, which had been the traditional belief. This shift in cosmological thinking set the stage for entirely new views of humanity's links to the rest of the natural world. New developments in the geological sciences began to radically revise the estimates of the age of the Earth, which contradicted a literal reading of the biblical account of creation. These and other scientific discoveries in astronomy, biology, chemistry, physics, and mathematics dramatically transformed Western thought, including ideas about humankind (Henry 2002)

Among the most dramatic ideas to result from the scientific revolution was the scientific theory of evolution, which sees plant and animal species originating through a gradual process of development from earlier forms. Although it is not intended to contradict cosmologies, it is based on a different kind of knowledge. Cosmological explanations frequently involve divine or supernatural forces that are, by their nature, impossible for human beings to observe. We accept them and believe in them, on the basis of faith. Scientific theories of evolution, in contrast, are derived from the belief that the universe operates according to regular processes that can be observed. The scientific method is not a rigid framework that provides indisputable answers. Instead, scientific theories are propositions that can be evaluated by future testing and observation. Acceptance of the theory of evolution is based on observations in many areas of geology, paleontology, and biology.

Catastrophism versus Uniformitarianism

The pre-Renaissance view of a static universe and of an Earth a few thousand years old with unchanging species posed problems for early geologists and naturalists (a term used at that time to refer to biologists), who were beginning to study thick layers of stone and gravel deposits containing the fossilized remains of forms of life not represented in living species. How long had it taken to form these thick deposits of soil and stone? How old were the remains of the strange creatures represented in the fossil remains? The geological record did not seem to fit within the time frame that a literal reading of the biblical account of creation allowed.

As evidence for the great antiquity of the Earth and evidence for many extinct animal species accumulated, some scholars proposed theories that attempted to reconcile the geological and fossil records with the biblical account of Genesis. One interpretation was presented by Georges Chrétien Léopold Frédéric Dagobert Cuvier (1769–1832), a French naturalist who is sometimes called the father of zoology (Rudwick 1997). Georges Cuvier, as he is more commonly known, studied the fossil record, including the remains of extinct, prehistoric elephant-like animals called *mammoths* in the vicinity of Paris. He also noted the successive replacement of fossil species through time. However, he saw species as fixed and unchanging. He proposed the geological theory known as **catastrophism**, which reasoned that the Earth had been created and destroyed multiple times. The extinct species represented in the fossil record had disappeared through a series of catastrophes of divine origin. Some species of animals might survive these events, just as the account of creation in the Book of Genesis recounted that animals collected by Noah and taken aboard the ark survived the biblical flood. The new species of animals that appeared in the following layers represented a new creation event. Catastrophism became the best-known geological explanation consistent with the literal interpretation of the biblical account of creation.

Other geologists challenged catastrophism and the rigidity of nature through scientific studies. They noted evidence that suggested the Earth changed through gradual, natural processes that were still observable. This view, which provided the basis for later geological interpretations, became known as **uniformitarianism** (Repcheck 2003). One of the first proponents of this perspective was the French naturalist and keeper of the king's gardens, Georges-Louis Leclerc, the Comte de Buffon (1707–1788). In 1774, Buffon theorized that the Earth changed through gradual, natural processes that were still observable. He proposed that rivers had created canyons, waves had changed shorelines, and other forces had transformed the features of the Earth. After being criticized by theologians, Buffon attempted to coordinate his views with biblical beliefs. He suggested that the six days of creation described in the Bible should not be interpreted literally. Buffon suggested that these passages actually refer to six *epochs* representing a gradual period of creation rather than 24-hour days. Each epoch consisted of thousands of years in which the Earth and different species of life were transformed. Although Buffon's interpretation allowed more time for geological changes in the Earth's past, there was no geological evidence for the six epochs of gradual creation.

As information on the geological record accumulated, the uniformitarian view eventually became the mainstream position in geology. In 1795, James Hutton, in his landmark book *Theory of the Earth*, explained how natural processes of erosion and deposition of sediments had formed the various geological strata of the Earth. Hutton observed that these natural processes must have taken thousands of years. In his book, he estimated that the Earth was at least several million years old. In 1833, the English scholar Charles Lyell (1797–1875), noted by some as the father of modern geology, reinforced the uniformitarian view. In his *Principles of Geology*, Lyell discussed natural processes, such as volcanoes, earthquakes, glaciers, erosion, and decomposition that shaped the geological landscape. More importantly, in a readable and comprehensive way, he observed that these processes were still observable and had been constant—uniform—over time. He also argued that scientists could deduce the age of the Earth from the rate at which sediments are deposited and by measuring the thickness of rocks. Through these measurements, Lyell also concluded that the Earth was millions of years old.

Modern geologists have a far better understanding of geological processes and much more sophisticated means of dating the Earth. As will be discussed later, the age of the Earth is now estimated to be billions, rather than millions, of years, divided into five major ages and many other periods and epochs. Although many of the views of Buffon, Hutton, and Lyell have been superseded, they were historically important in challenging the traditional views of a static universe with fixed species. Their fundamental points concerning the consistent and ongoing natural processes that have shaped the geological landscape have been reaffirmed by modern research. The uniformitarian view thus set the stage for an entirely new way of envisioning the universe, the Earth, and the living forms on the planet.

Theories of Evolution

The scientific revolution also led to changing perspectives regarding the origin of species and humankind's place in nature. There were discoveries of archaeological remains and contacts with the non-Western populations that were unmentioned in any written records including the Bible and Classical Greek and Roman writings. Where did the Native American Indians come from? Were they one of the lost tribes of Israel referred to in the Bible, or were they created separately and without souls, as some sixteenth-century scholars suggested (Adovasio and Page, 2002, 5)? Antiquarians—as collectors of artifacts and curiosities of the past were sometimes called—of the eighteenth and nineteenth centuries increasingly began to recognize archaeological materials that predated written history. The relative ages of both fossils and archaeological materials could be dated by their stratigraphic positions, suggesting periods older than the historically known Greek and Roman civilizations. There were also many discoveries of fossil remains clearly unlike any living species. Scholars, including many clergy, documented systematic change through time in the fossil species represented (see discussion of faunal succession in Chapter 2). How were these finds to be explained? Scholars started to question the fixity of species and a literal interpretation of the biblical account of creation. They suggested that plants and animals had evolved through natural processes.

Evolution refers to the process of change in the genetic makeup of a species over time. It is used to explain the emergence of new species. Evolutionary theory holds that existing species of plants and animals have emerged over millions of years from simple organisms. Although the theory of evolution is usually associated with Charles Darwin, the idea that modern plants and animals could change was posited by a number of scholars prior to the mid-1800s. Georges-Louis Leclerc, the Comte de Buffon (1707–1788), who had argued that the Earth changed through gradual, natural processes, also underscored the changing nature of species and their ability to adapt to local environmental conditions.

Erasmus Darwin (1731–1802), an eighteenth-century physician and Charles Darwin's grandfather, also suggested evolutionary concepts. However, none of these early theorists suggested a unified theory that *explained* evolution. They proposed no reasonable mechanism for evolution and, consequently, most people could not accept these ideas.

A more comprehensive early theory that attempted to explain evolution was posited by a French chemist and biologist, Jean-Baptiste Pierre Antoine de Monet, Chevalier de Lamarck (1744–1829). Lamarck proposed that species could change as a result of dynamic interactions with their environment. As a result of changing environmental conditions, behavioral patterns of a species would alter, increasing or decreasing the use of some physical structures. As a result of these changing physical needs, the *besoin* (the force for change within organisms) would be directed to these areas, modifying the appropriate structures and enabling the animal to adapt to their new environmental circumstances. In other words, if a particular animal needed specialized organs to help in adaptation, these organs would evolve accordingly. In turn, because the characteristics made the animal better suited to its environment, these new structures would be passed on to their offspring (Mayr 1982).

The most famous example used by Lamarck was the long necks of giraffes. He suggested that this distinctive feature evolved when a short-necked ancestor took to browsing on the leaves of trees instead of on grass. Lamarck speculated that the ancestral giraffe, in reaching up, stretched its neck. The force for change was directed to the giraffe's neck, and it was increased in length. This physical characteristic was passed on to the giraffe's offspring. The offspring of this ancestral giraffe stretched still further. As this process repeated itself from generation to generation, the present long neck of the giraffe was eventually achieved.

Because evolution takes place as a result of physical characteristics acquired in the course of a creature's lifetime, Lamarck's theory is referred to as the *inheritance of acquired characteristics* or *use-disuse theory*. Variations of Lamarck's view of inheritance were used by many nineteenth-century scientists to explain how physical characteristics originated and were passed on. Today, however, this theory is rejected for several reasons. First, Lamarck overestimated the ability of a plant or an animal to adapt or change to meet new environmental conditions. In addition, we now know that physical traits acquired during an organism's lifetime cannot be inherited by the organism's offspring. In order for traits to be passed on, they must be encoded in genetic information contained within the sex cells (see discussion below). For example, a weightlifter's musculature, an acquired characteristic, will not be passed on to his or her children. Nevertheless, Lamarck's ideas illustrate early theories that attempted to explain evolutionary change. His work is notable in proposing a unified theory of how evolution takes place and also because of the emphasis it placed on the interaction between organisms and their environments.

Darwin, Wallace, and Natural Selection

Two individuals strongly influenced by the scientific revolution were Charles Robert Darwin (1809–1882) and Alfred Russel Wallace (1823–1913), nineteenth-century British naturalists. Through their careful observations and their identification of a plausible mechanism for evolutionary change, they transformed perspectives of the origin of species. Impressed by the variation in living species and their interaction with the environment, Darwin and Wallace independently developed an explanation of why this variation occurs and the basic mechanism of evolution. This mechanism is known as **natural selection**, which can be defined as genetic change in a population resulting from differential reproductive success. This is now recognized as one of the four principal evolutionary processes.

Beginning in 1831, Darwin traveled for five years on a British ship, the HMS *Beagle,* on a voyage around the world. During this journey, he collected numerous plant and animal species from many different environments. In the 1840s and 1850s, Wallace observed

The HMS *Beagle*, a British ship that took Darwin to many regions of the world.

different species of plants and animals during an expedition to the Amazon and later continued his observations in Southeast Asia and on the islands off Malaysia. Darwin and Wallace arrived at the theory of natural selection independently, but Darwin went on to present a thorough and completely documented statement of the theory in his book *On the Origin of Species*, published in 1859. The volume's full title gives a fair idea of its focus: *On the Origin of Species by Means of Natural Selection, or the Preservation of Favored Races in the Struggle for Life.*

In their theory of natural selection, Darwin and Wallace emphasized the enormous variation that exists in all plant and animal species. They combined this observation with those of Thomas Malthus (1766–1834), a nineteenth-century English clergyman and political economist whose work focused on human populations. Malthus was concerned with population growth and the constraints that limited food supplies had on population size. Darwin and Wallace realized that similar pressures operate in nature. Living creatures produce more offspring than can generally be expected to survive and reproduce. For the thousands of tadpoles that hatch from eggs, few live to maturity. Similarly, only a small number of the seeds from a maple tree germinate and grow into trees. In recognizing the validity of this fact, Darwin and Wallace realized that there would be *selection* in which organisms survived. What factors would determine their survival?

Variation within species and reproductive success are the basis of natural selection. Darwin and Wallace reasoned that certain individuals in a species may be born with particular characteristics or traits that make them better able to survive. For example, certain seeds in a plant species may naturally produce more seeds than others, or some frogs in a single population may have coloring that blends in with the environment better than others, making them less likely to be

Charles Darwin (1809–1882).

53

eaten by predators. With these advantageous characteristics, certain species are more likely to reproduce and, subsequently, pass on these traits to their offspring. Darwin and Wallace called this process *natural selection* because nature, or the demands of the environment, actually determines which individuals (or which traits) survive. This process, repeated countless times over millions of years, is the means by which species change or evolve over time.

Examples of Natural Selection

One problem Darwin faced in writing *On the Origin of Species* was a lack of well-documented examples of natural selection at work. Most major changes in nature take place over thousands or millions of years. As a result, the process of natural selection is often too slow to be documented in a researcher's lifetime. However, when animals or plants are exposed to rapid changes in their environment, we can actually observe natural selection in action.

A classic case of natural selection is illustrated by the finches of the Galapagos Islands, located about 500 miles off the coast of South America. These birds were studied by Charles Darwin when he visited the islands during his travels on the HMS *Beagle*. Volcanic in origin and cut off from the South American mainland, the Galapagos have a diversity of species related to, but distinct from, those of South America. Darwin was struck by how the geographic isolation of a small population could expose its members to new environmental conditions where different adaptive features might be favored. Darwin described the variation in the Islands' finches: In general, the birds have rather dull plumage and are quite similar, except in the size and shape of

Alfred Russell Wallace.

their beaks—a feature that is closely related to the ways in which the birds obtain their food. Some species of finch, for example, have short, thick beaks that they use to eat seeds, buds, and fruits, while others have long, straight beaks and subsist primarily on nectar from flowers.

The finches of the island of Daphne Major in Galapagos were the focus of a long-term research project by Peter and Rosemary Grant, beginning in 1973 (Grant 1999; Weiner 1994). The island is small enough to allow researchers to intensively study the island's flora and fauna and provide an unambiguous demonstration of natural selection in operation. The Grants and their students focused on two species of finch—the medium ground finch and the cactus finch. Over time, every finch on the island was captured, carefully measured and weighed, and also tagged so that each bird could be identified in the field. The diet of the birds was documented and the availability of food resources charted.

A dramatic change in the finches' food resources occurred between mid-1976 and early 1978 as a result of a drought. The lack of rainfall led to a decrease in the food supplies favored by smaller-beaked finches. The remaining food consisted of larger, harder seeds that were difficult for finches with small beaks to break open. On the other hand, finches with larger, heavier beaks were able to more easily crack and extract food from hard-shelled seeds. Not surprisingly, many of the finches with smaller beaks died of starvation during the drought.

The variation in beak size is a good illustration of how natural selection may act on different species, but it also illustrates the significance of variation within individual species. Of the more than 1,000 medium ground finches found on the island at the beginning of the Grants' study, only 180 remained after the drought. Notably, the finches that survived had a larger average beak size than that of the population prior to the drought. As beak size is an inherited characteristic, the new generations of birds born after the drought also had a larger average beak size. This case study illustrates how natural selection can eliminate maladaptive traits from a population and select for features that help ensure survival and, ultimately, reproductive success for some members of a species. Many modern scientists believe that new species emerge when small populations become isolated from the parent group and encounter new selective pressures that may favor different characteristics.

Natural selection is currently viewed as one of four major guiding forces in the evolution of species. It enabled Darwin to explain the mechanisms of biological evolution, and it remains a powerful explanation for the development of living species of plants and

The finches of the Galapagos Islands provide an excellent example of natural selection at work. The beaks of the various species of finch are used for exploiting different kinds of foods. If environmental conditions suddenly change, some characteristics may be more favored than others.

animals. Before turning to the other three processes that guide evolution, we will consider the way traits are passed on from one generation to the next.

Principles of Inheritance

Darwin contributed to the modern understanding of biological evolution by thoroughly documenting the *variation* of living forms and by identifying the key process of natural selection. Like most nineteenth-century scientists, however, he did not understand *heredity*, or how specific traits are passed on from one generation to the next. Darwin reasoned that during the reproductive process, the parental substances are mixed to produce new traits in the parents' offspring. These conclusions were based in part on his experiments with plants and animals, in which he had observed that the offspring often had characteristics from both parents. Darwin was unclear about how these traits were transmitted, but he reasoned that

as with a metal alloys, such as bronze, which is a mixture of tin and copper, the traits of an offspring represented a blending of parental substances. Today, we know that inherited characteristics are not a mixture of parental substances, such as with the mixing of fluids or metal alloys. Rather, traits are passed from parents to offspring in individual "particles" or packages—what we now refer to as genes.

Mendel and Modern Genetics

Modern understanding of heredity emerged through the studies of an Austrian monk named Gregor Johann Mendel (1822–1884). During the 1860s, Mendel began a series of breeding experiments with pea plants that revolutionized biological thought. Although his findings were not recognized until the twentieth century, Mendel laid the groundwork for what is today known as the science of *genetics*, the biological subfield that deals with heredity. In compiling his rules of heredity, Mendel discredited earlier theories of inheritance. He was the first to conclusively demonstrate that traits are inherited in discrete packages of information that were not mixed during reproduction. The principles he laid out as a result of this work are useful in understanding inheritance in humans, as well as all other biological organisms.

Mendel's most important experiments involved the crossbreeding of pea plants. In order to discern patterns of inheritance, Mendel focused on traits that could each be expressed in only one of two ways. Height and seed color are two examples: He studied plants that were either tall *or* dwarf or plants that produced either green *or* yellow peas. He initially focused his experiments on one characteristic or trait at a time, carefully cross-pollinating *purebred* plants, plants that were similar with regard to one of his traits. Mendel crossed purebred tall pea plants with purebred dwarf, or short plants. In this way, he was able to study the number and variety of *hybrids*, the offspring resulting from tall and dwarf plants. He could then evaluate the proportion of characteristics found in successive generations. Mendel drew several important conclusions from these experiments.

The photos of different dogs exhibit the wide variation in physical characteristics that may be found within the same species.

Source: Courtesy of (from left) C. R. DeCorse, Margaret Antonini, Joyce Perkins.

Gregor Mendel (1822–1884).

Mendel's Principle of Segregation

By following the results of cross-pollination through several generations, Mendel discovered a distinct pattern of reproduction. The first generation of hybrid plants—that is, plants produced by parents having purebred tall and purebred dwarf characteristics—were all tall. However, when he crossbred these hybrid plants, the next generation contained both tall and dwarf plants. Thus, the dwarf variety that seemed to disappear in the first generation of hybrids reappeared in the second generation (see Figure 1).

Significantly, the ratio of tall to dwarf plants in the second hybrid generation was always approximately three-to-one (three tall plants to one dwarf plant). Mendel conducted similar experiments focusing on other characteristics and obtained similar results. This led Mendel to reject the earlier notions of inheritance, such as blending. None of the pea plants exhibited mixed characteristics: all of the plants were either tall or short; all of the peas were either green or yellow.

The fact that the three-to-one ratio reappeared consistently convinced Mendel that the key to heredity lay deep within the pea plant seeds. Mendel correctly concluded that the particles responsible for passing traits from parents to offspring occurred in pairs, each offspring receiving half of a pair from each parent. During fertilization, the particles of heredity, what we now call genes, from each parent are combined. The observation that units of heredity (or genes) occur in pairs and that offspring receive half of a pair from each parent is the basis of the *principle of segregation*, Mendel's first principle of inheritance.

Dominant and Recessive Traits

Mendel also observed that certain traits prevailed over others. He labeled the prevailing traits **dominant**. In contrast, he labeled as **recessive** those traits that were unexpressed in one generation but expressed in following generations. In pea plants, he found that tall was dominant and dwarf was recessive.

Figure 1 illustrates why recessive traits can disappear in one generation and appear in the next. In the first generation, a purebred tall plant and a purebred dwarf plant are crossbred. The pairs of genetic information in the purebred tall plants only contain genetic material for tallness (*TT*), and the purebred dwarf plants only contain information for the dwarf trait (*tt*). When these purebred plants are crossbred, the offspring receive genetic material from each parent (*Tt*). Only the tall trait appears in the offspring because tall is the dominant trait and the dwarf characteristic is recessive. However, when these hybrid plants are crossbred, the recessive trait reappears. As Figure 1 illustrates, the crossing of two hybrid parents (*Tt*) produces four possible combinations: one *TT*, two *Tt*, and one *tt*. The single offspring that only has the tall characteristic (*TT*) as well as those that inherited both tall and dwarf characteristics (*Tt*) appear tall, the dwarf characteristic being recessive. The offspring that inherit two recessive particles (*tt*) exhibit the recessive trait. This accounts for the 3:1 ratio that Mendel observed in the offspring of two hybrid plants. Mendel concluded that the particle containing the recessive trait, which is masked by the dominant trait in one generation, can reappear if it occurs in both parents. Mendel's theory explained how hybrid parents expressing only the dominant trait could produce offspring exhibiting the recessive trait. Purebred parents could pass on only the dominant or recessive trait, whereas hybrid parents could pass on either one.

The alternate forms of the same genes, such as "tall" or "dwarf," are referred to as **alleles**. When an organism has two of the same kinds of alleles, it is referred to as **homozygous** for that gene. Thus, homozygous tall plants are *TT* (purebred dominant for tallness), whereas homozygous dwarf plants are *tt* (purebred recessive for shortness). In contrast, when an organism has two different alleles, it is **heterozygous** for

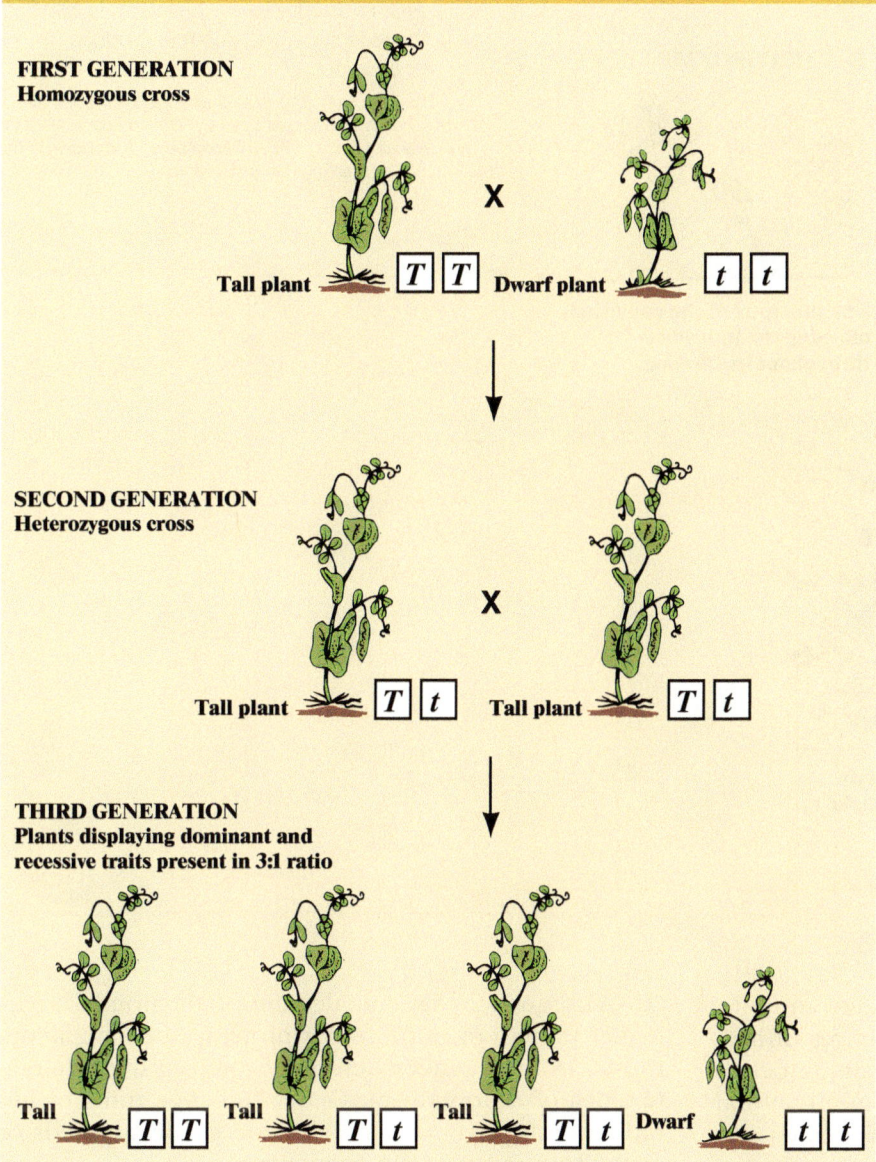

FIRST GENERATION
Homozygous cross

Tall plant [T] [T]   X   Dwarf plant [t] [t]

SECOND GENERATION
Heterozygous cross

Tall plant [T] [t]   X   Tall plant [T] [t]

THIRD GENERATION
Plants displaying dominant and recessive traits present in 3:1 ratio

Tall [T] [T]   Tall [T] [t]   Tall [T] [t]   Dwarf [t] [t]

Figure 1 In one of his experiments, Mendel crossbred plants that were purebred (homozygous) for particular traits, as illustrated here by the tall and dwarf pea plants. As tallness is a dominant trait, all the offspring of this cross were tall. In the third generation, however, the recessive traits reappear, or segregate.

Principle of Independent Assortment

The preceding experiments all focused on one physical trait. In subsequent studies, Mendel investigated the outcomes of fertilization between pea plants that differed in two ways, such as in both plant height and color of the pea, in order to evaluate whether the two characteristics were linked. As in the previous experiments, the offspring of purebred (homozygous) parents exhibited only the dominant characteristics. When Mendel cross-fertilized these hybrids, however, the offspring displayed the characteristics present in the purebred generation in a ratio of 9:3:3:1, as illustrated in Figure 3.

This experiment indicated that no two traits are always passed on together. Mendel concluded that during the reproductive process, the particles determining different traits separate from one another and then *recombine* to create variation in the next generation. Thus, in the experiments by Mendel discussed above, plants produced peas that were yellow and round, yellow and wrinkled, green and wrinkled, and green and round. Mendel referred to the fact that individual traits (such as height or color) occur independently of one another as the *principle of independent assortment*.

Molecular Genetics

Mendel's principles of segregation and independent assortment and the concepts of recessive and dominant traits are still viewed as key mechanisms of heredity. However, because Mendel did not have the advanced technology needed to investigate cellular biology, he did not know the inner workings of the units of inheritance. Modern scientists have a better understanding than did Mendel of the dynamics of heredity at the cellular level.

that gene. Thus, the *Tt* hybrids are heterozygous plants, possessing both tall and dwarf alleles. When a heterozygous plant expresses only characteristics of one allele such as tallness, that allele is dominant. The allele whose expression is masked in a heterozygote (for example, shortness) is a recessive allele. Thus, two organisms with different allele combinations for a particular trait may have the same outward appearance: *TT* and *Tt* pea plants will appear the same.

Biologists distinguish between the genetic constitution and the outward appearance of an organism. The actual genetic makeup of an organism is referred to as its **genotype**; the external, observable characteristics of that organism that are shaped in part by both the organism's genetic makeup and unique life history, are called its **phenotype**. Genotype and phenotype are illustrated in Figure 2.

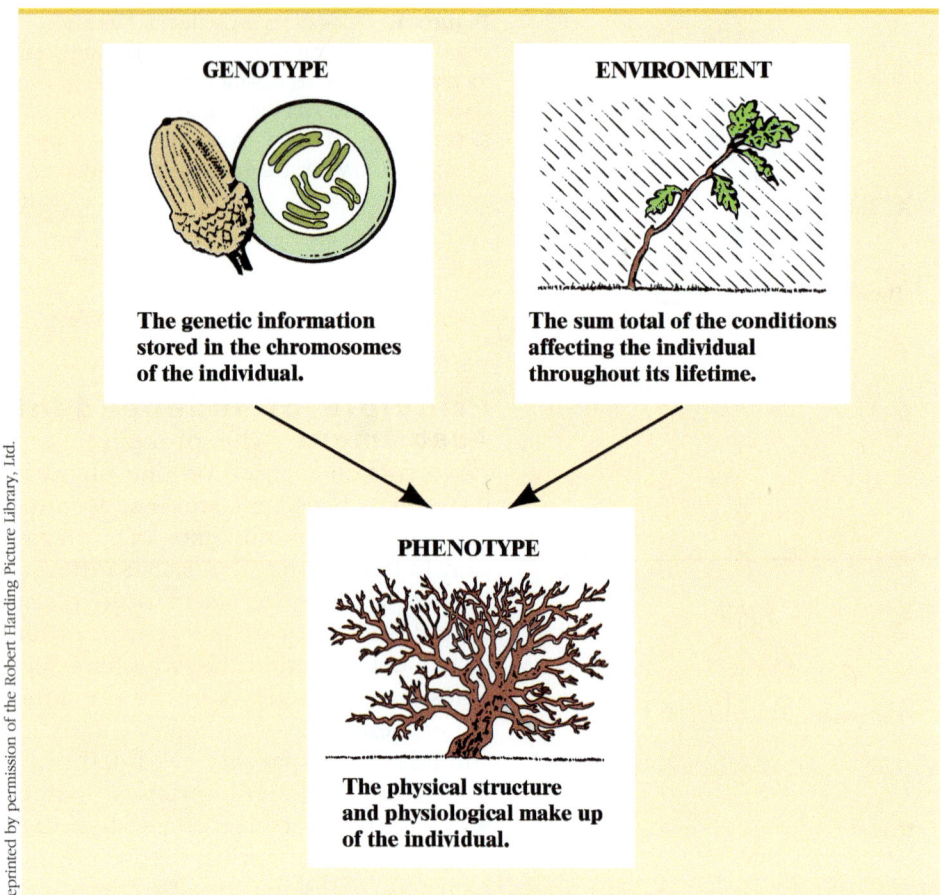

GENOTYPE

The genetic information stored in the chromosomes of the individual.

ENVIRONMENT

The sum total of the conditions affecting the individual throughout its lifetime.

PHENOTYPE

The physical structure and physiological make up of the individual.

Figure 2 The genotype interacts with the external environment to produce the phenotype.

Source: From *The Illustrated Origin of Species* by Charles Darwin, abridged by Richard Leakey (Rainbird/ Faber & Faber, 1979). Reprinted by permission of the Robert Harding Picture Library.

Cells and Genes Heredity is encoded in cells, which are the building blocks of all living things. Bacteria and amoebas are examples of single-celled organisms, but plants and animals are multicellular life-forms made up of billions of cells. Humans and other animals have two different forms of cells: **somatic cells** (body cells) and **gametes** (sex cells). Somatic cells make up the basic structural components of the body, including the soft tissues, bones, and organs. The gametes, on the other hand, are specifically involved in reproduction, and they do not form structural components of the body. Gametes occur in two forms: the *ova* or female egg cells and *sperm*, the male sex cells. The sole purpose of a sex cell is to unite with another sex cell and form a **zygote**, a cell formed by the combination of a male and female sex cell that has the potential of developing into a new organism.

Both somatic cells and gametes contain the units of heredity that constitute an organism's genetic blueprint (though only the gametes have the potential to pass this genetic information on to the next generation). We now know Mendel's particles or units of inheritance as *genes*. For the purposes of this discussion, a **gene** can be considered a deoxyribonucleic acid

(DNA) sequence that encodes the production of a particular protein or portion of a protein. In combination, these DNA sequences determine the physical characteristics of an organism. Genes, discrete units of hereditary information, may be made up of hundreds or even thousands of DNA sequences.

The Role of DNA Molecules of **deoxyribonucleic acid** (DNA) are the secret of a cell's genetic blueprint. The DNA molecule looks like a spiral ladder or, more poetically, like a *double helix* (Figure 4). The sides of the ladder consist of sugar (deoxyribose) and phosphate, and the rungs are made up of four nitrogen bases: adenine, thymine, guanine, and cytosine. The DNA bases are arranged in sequences of three, called *codons*. These sequences determine the assembly of different amino acids. For example, the combination and arrangement of the bases guanine, thymine, and cytosine encode the amino acid glutamine. *Amino acids* are chemicals joined together in chains to produce different proteins—chemical compounds that are fundamental to the makeup and running of the body's cells. There are twenty different kinds of amino acids that

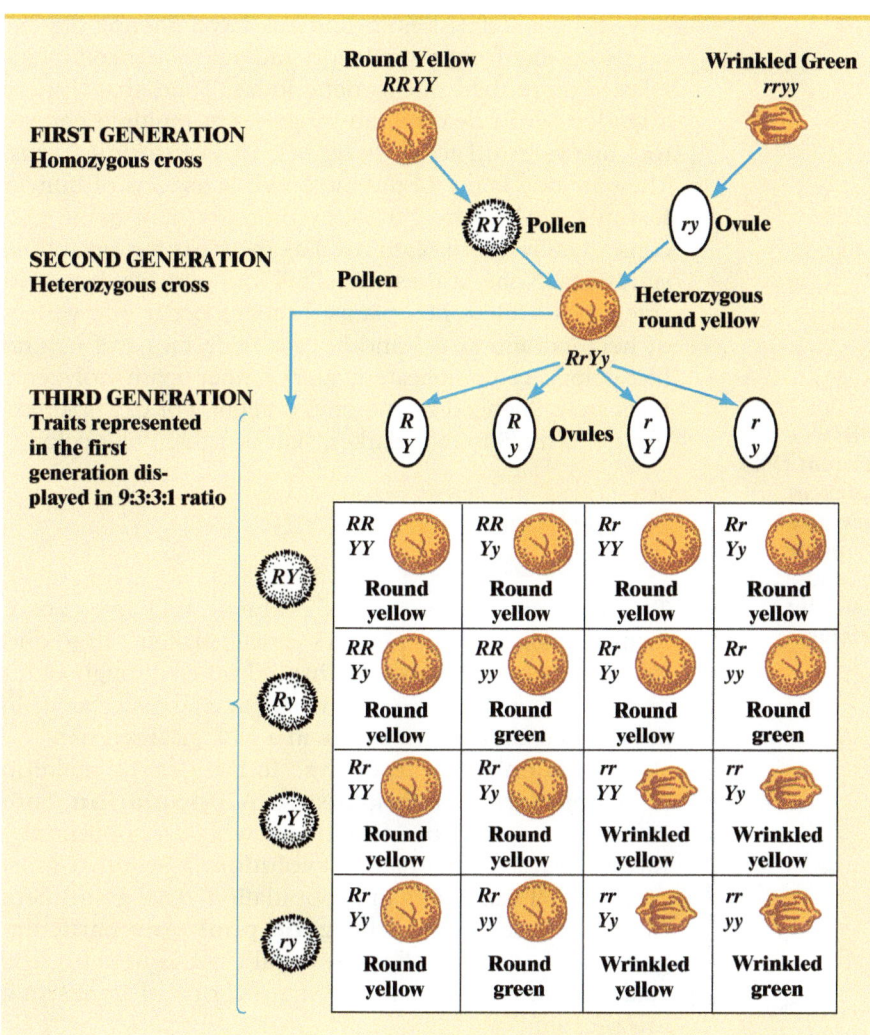

Figure 3 This diagram, referred to as an extended Punnett square, demonstrates the principle of independent assortment discovered by Mendel. When two heterozygous pea plants are cross-fertilized, the alleles that determine two different traits sort independently of each other, creating the phenotypic ratio of 9:3:3:1.

can, in differing combinations and amounts, produce millions of different proteins basic to life.

Mitosis and Meiosis At certain times, cells divide forming new cells. Gametes and somatic cells divide in different ways, a fact that is very significant in terms of their differing roles. Strands of DNA containing heredity information are contained in each living cell, but while both kinds of cells contain an organism's genetic code, only the gametes provide a means of passing this information on to an offspring through reproduction. Normally, the DNA molecules exist as single, uncoiled, thread-like strands within each cell. The minute DNA threads contained within each human somatic cell are estimated to be as much as six feet long. During cell division the DNA becomes tightly coiled and forms discrete structures called *chromosomes*. The single DNA threads replicate by forming a double strand, one strand being an exact copy of the original. Each species has a specific number of chromosomes that make up their somatic cells. Humans

have twenty-three pairs of chromosomes or forty-six chromosomes in all.

When somatic cells divide to produce new cells—a process biologists call **mitosis**—they replicate themselves to produce identical cells. Somatic cells have complete pairs of chromosomes. Mitosis is simply a process for making identical cells within a single individual. In contrast, sex cells, or gametes, are produced through the process of **meiosis**—two successive cell divisions that produce cells with only *half* the number of chromosomes (twenty-three in the case of humans). Meiosis reduces the amount of genetic material to half to prepare for sexual reproduction. During fertilization when two sex cells are joined together, they reproduce a new organism with a complete complement of chromosomes (forty-six in humans).

The process of meiosis is very important in terms of evolution because it necessitates genetic recombination. Offspring of sexually reproducing species are not identical copies of their parents, but rather unique individuals that have received contributions of genetic material from each

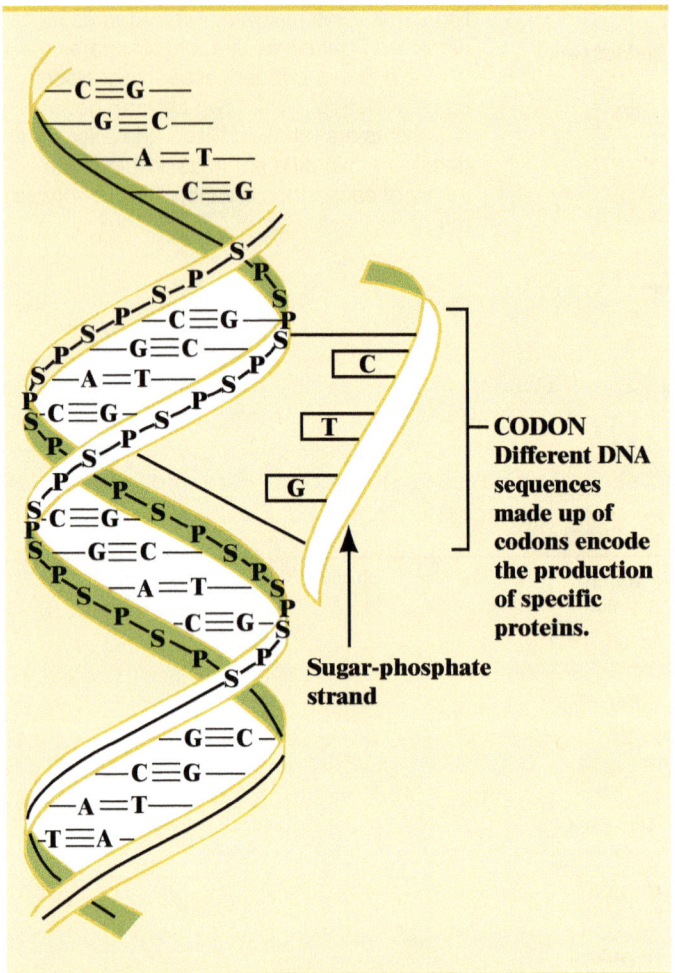

Figure 4 This illustration shows the chemical structure of DNA. The DNA molecule forms a spiral ladder of sugar (S) and phosphate (P) linked by four nitrogen bases: adenine (A), guanine (G), thymine (T), and cytosine (C).

parent. It is during meiosis and sexual reproduction that Mendel's principles of segregation and independent assortment operate. This reshuffling of genetic material does not change allele frequencies by itself. It ensures, however, that the entire range of traits present in a species is produced and can subsequently be acted on by evolutionary forces.

Polygenic Inheritance Mendel's experiments with pea plants discussed above focused on the investigation of physical traits that were controlled by alleles at one genetic locus and had phenotypic expressions that were distinct: Plants were either tall or dwarf; the peas either green or yellow. There were no plants of varying height or of mixed green and yellow color. Today these are called *Mendelian traits* or *traits of simple inheritance*. More than 4,500 human traits are inherited in this manner. The A, B, and O blood types in humans are an example; individuals have one or another of these blood groups; they do not have a mixture.

While some human characteristics are inherited as discrete traits, the majority are passed on in a more complicated fashion. In contrast to Mendelian traits, many physical characteristics in humans have phenotypic expressions that form a gradation and are influenced by alleles at more than one genetic locus. Traits that display a graded series determined by genes at multiple genetic loci are referred to as *polygenic* or *continuous traits*. They include many of the most visible aspects of human features, such as height, skin color, and hair color, and consequently, were often used as the basis for racial classifications. None of these traits fall into perfectly bounded categories. Unlike pea plants, humans occur in a variety of heights (and sizes) and have a wide range of natural hair colors. To complicate matters further, many polygenic traits are influenced by the environment. For example, exposure to the Sun may darken skin or lighten hair color.

Population Genetics and Evolution

To understand the process of evolution fully, we cannot focus on individuals. A person's genetic makeup, fixed during conception, remains with that individual throughout his or her lifetime. Although people mature and may change in appearance, they do not *evolve* in a biological sense.

Evolution refers to change in the genetic makeup of a *population* of organisms. A **population** here refers to a group of individuals who can potentially interbreed. To understand evolution, a scientist must consider all the genes in a population. This assortment of genes is known as the **gene pool**. Any particular gene pool consists of different allele frequencies, the relative amounts of the alternate forms of genes that are present.

In terms of genetics, evolution can be defined as the process of change in allele frequencies between one generation and the next. Alternation of the gene pool of a population is influenced by four evolutionary processes, one of which, natural selection, has already been discussed in relation to the work of Charles Darwin and Alfred Wallace. The other three processes are mutation, gene flow, and genetic drift.

Mutations

Mutations are alterations of genetic material at the cellular level. They can occur spontaneously during the cell replication process, or they can be induced by environmental factors such as radiation. Although we frequently think of mutations as harmful, they introduce variation into the gene pool and may create new, advantageous characteristics. Mutation serves as the primary force behind evolution because it is the *only* source of new genetic variation. The other evolutionary processes act on the genetic variation introduced through mutation. Maladaptive characteristics introduced by mutation are quickly eliminated by natural selection.

The role of mutation was only recognized during this century with better understanding of molecular genetics. Most mutations occur in the somatic cells of organisms. These types of mutations are not heritable. When the organism dies, the mutation dies with it. Some mutations, however, alter the DNA in reproductive cells. In this case, even change in a single DNA base, or a *point mutation*, may produce observable phenotypic change, for example, differences in blood chemistry. A mutation occurring in this instance will be passed on to the offspring.

Generally, the rates of mutations are relatively stable. If we make the conservative estimate that humans have approximately 20,000 to 25,000 genes with hundreds of DNA bases, then each of us clearly holds the potential for carrying new mutant genes. When the size of human population is considered, it is evident that the mutation process provides a large source of variability. It would, however, be unlikely for evolution to occur solely as a result of mutation. The rate of mutation of a particular trait within a specific population as a whole is likely to be relatively low—perhaps present only in one individual out of 10,000. Hence, mutation alone would be unlikely to effect great change in allele frequencies within the population. On the other hand, some mutations may have no adaptive consequences. Yet, if mutations are acted on by natural selection, they become a potentially important source of evolutionary change.

Gene Flow

Gene flow is the exchange of alleles between populations as a result of interbreeding. When this exchange occurs, new genetic material may be introduced, changing the allele frequencies in a population. The process of gene flow has affected most human societies. Migrants from one society enter a new region and intermarry with the local population. Through reproduction, they transmit new genes into the population. In this way, new mutations arising in one population can be transmitted to other members of the species.

In addition to providing a mechanism for introducing new genetic material, gene flow can act to decrease variation between populations. If two distinct populations continue to interbreed, they will become progressively similar genetically. Migration and connections between different populations have long been a feature of human societies and among early human ancestors. This genetic interconnectedness explains why new human species have not emerged: There has been sufficient gene flow between populations to prevent the creation of substantial genetic distance.

With the development of modern transportation, gene flow occurs on a worldwide scale. In this context, however, it is useful to remember that many cultural or social factors play a role in gene flow in human populations. Religious practices, socioeconomic status, and ethnicity may all influence the selection of mates.

Genetic Drift

Genetic drift is evolutionary change resulting from random sampling phenomena that eliminate or maintain certain alleles in a gene pool. It includes the influence of chance events that may affect evolutionary change that are in no way influenced by individuals' genetic makeup. For example, in any population, only a small sample of the potential array of genetic material is passed on from one generation to the next. Every human being produces hundreds of thousands of gametes, each representing a different genetic combination, yet people produce only a few offspring. The chance selection of genetic material that occurs during reproduction results in minor changes in allele frequencies from one generation to the next. Chance events, such as death by disease or accident, also bring about change in allele frequencies. For example, if only ten individuals within a population carry a particular genetic trait and all of them die as a result of accident or disease, this genetic characteristic will not be passed on to the next generation.

Because evolution occurs in populations, change resulting from genetic drift is influenced by the size of the population as well as the relative allele frequencies represented. In larger populations, random events, such as accidental deaths, are unlikely to have as significant an effect on the population's gene pool. In smaller populations, however, such events can substantially alter the genetic variation present. A particular kind of genetic drift, known as the **founder effect**, results when only a small number of individuals in a population pass on their genes to the following generation. Such a situation might result when a famine decimates a large group or when a small migrant population moves away and establishes a new settlement in an isolated area. In these instances, the founding members of the succeeding generation will have only a portion—a sample—of the full range of the genetic material that was present in the original population. Because early human ancestors and human populations lived in small bands of people, perhaps consisting of family groups, genetic drift was likely an important evolutionary force.

Natural Selection

Natural selection provides the key to evolution. It can be defined as genetic change in a population, as reflected in allele frequencies and as a result of differential reproductive success. The other evolutionary forces already discussed are important in creating variation in allele frequencies within and between populations, but they provide no direction—no means for a population to adapt to changing conditions. This direction is provided by natural selection.

As illustrated in the case of Darwin's finches on the Galapagos Islands, certain alleles (as expressed in particular physical traits such as long or short beaks) may be selected for by environmental factors. They may enable an organism to resist disease better, obtain food more efficiently, or avoid predators more effectively. Individuals with such advantages will, on average, be more successful in reproducing and will thereby pass on their genes to the next generation at higher rates.

Evolutionary "success" can be evaluated only in relative terms; if the environment changes, selection pressures also change. In the case of the finches, the larger- and smaller-beaked varieties were initially equally successful (or "fit"), but as food resources were depleted by drought, the individuals with heavier beaks were favored. This shift in allele frequencies in response to changing environmental conditions is called **adaptation**. Through evolution, species develop characteristics that allow them to survive and reproduce successfully in particular environmental settings. The specific environmental conditions to which a species is adapted is referred to as its **ecological niche**.

How Does Evolution Occur?

Although it is useful to discuss mutation, gene flow, genetic drift, and natural selection as distinct processes, they all interact to affect evolutionary change. Mutation provides the ultimate source of new genetic variants, whereas gene flow, genetic drift, and natural selection alter the frequency of the new allele. The key consideration is change in the genetic characteristics of a population from one generation to the next. Over time, this change may produce major differences among populations that were originally very similar.

To measure evolutionary change, researchers find it useful to evaluate evolutionary processes operating on a population by comparing allele frequencies for a particular trait to an idealized, mathematical model known as the **Hardy-Weinberg theory of genetic equilibrium**. This model, developed independently by G. H. Hardy and W. Weinberg, sets hypothetical conditions under which none of the evolutionary processes is acting and no evolution is taking place. The model makes several important assumptions. It presumes that no mutation is taking place (there are no new alleles); there is no gene flow (no migration or movement in or out of the population); no genetic drift (a large enough population is represented that there is no variation in allele frequencies due to sampling); and that natural selection is not operating on any of the alleles represented. The model also assumes that mating is randomized within the population so that all individuals have equal potential of mating with all other individuals of the opposite sex.

Given these assumptions, there will be no change in allele frequencies from one generation to the next. If examination of genotype frequencies within a population matches the idealized model, no evolution is taking place, and the population is said to be in Hardy-Weinberg equilibrium. If study suggests the genotype frequencies are not the same as the predicted model,

then we know that at least one of the assumptions must be incorrect. Further research can then be undertaken to identify what the source of evolutionary change is. In practice, determining which evolutionary processes are acting on a population is challenging. Different evolutionary processes may act against one another, giving the appearance that none is operating. Small amounts of change may also go unrecognized. Nevertheless, the Hardy-Weinberg theory provides a starting point for evaluating evolutionary change.

Speciation

One of the most interesting areas of research in evolutionary theory is how, why, and when new species arise. This is known as the study of **speciation**. Generally, biologists define a **species** as a group of organisms that have similar physical characteristics, can potentially interbreed with one another to produce fertile offspring, and who are reproductively isolated from other populations.

Phyletic Gradualism According to evolutionary theory, speciation occurs when there is an interruption in gene flow between populations that formerly were one species but became isolated by geographic barriers. In geographic isolation, these populations may reside in different types of environments, and natural selection, mutation, or genetic drift may lead to increasingly different allele frequencies. Eventually, through evolutionary change, these two populations become so different genetically that they are no longer the same species. Darwin hypothesized that speciation was a gradual process of evolution occurring very slowly as different populations became isolated. This view is called *gradualism*, or **phyletic gradualism**.

Punctuated Equilibrium Beginning in the early twentieth century, some scientists challenged the gradualistic interpretation of speciation, arguing that new

A characteristic of a species is that its members can successfully interbreed only with one another. The mule is the offspring of a female horse and a male donkey, two clearly distinct species. As mules are always sterile, however, the reproductive isolation of the two species is maintained.

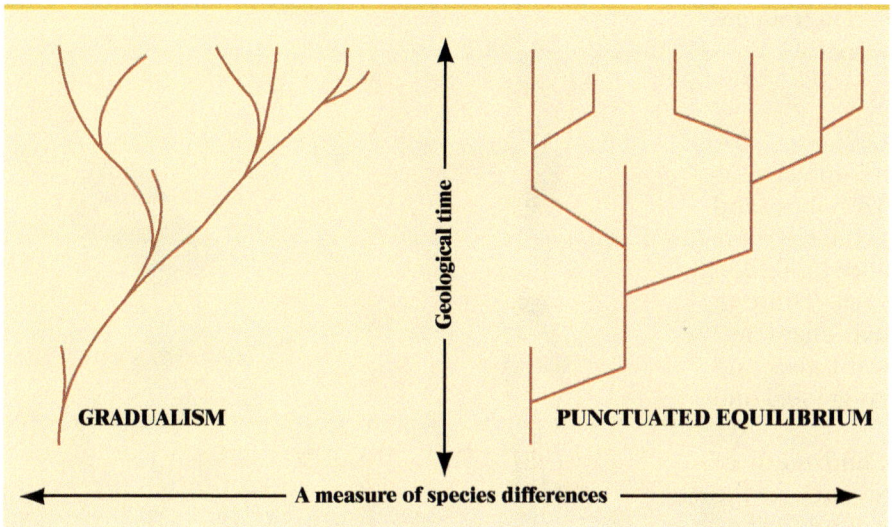

Figure 5 An illustration of two models of evolution. Gradualism implies a gradual, steady rate of speciation, while punctuated equilibrium suggests evolutionary change as a series of steps and starts. The two perspectives are not inconsistent with each other and the fossil record provides evidence of both.

GRADUALISM

PUNCTUATED EQUILIBRIUM

Geological time

A measure of species differences

species might appear rapidly. Paleontologists (fossil specialists) Stephen Jay Gould and Niles Eldredge (1972) proposed a theory known as **punctuated equilibrium**. When examining ancient fossil beds, paleontologists discovered that some plants or animals seemed to exhibit little change over millions of years. These creatures appeared to remain in a state of equilibrium with their habitats for long geological periods, which were interrupted by major changes, or punctuations, leading to rapid speciation.

Punctuated equilibrium and gradualism (see Figure 5) present extreme perspectives of the rate at which evolution occurs, but the two views are not incompatible. Indeed, neither Darwin or Gould and Eldredge suggested particular rates that were the same in all cases (Gingerich 1984). The fossil record provides examples of both cases (Bown and Rose 1987; Levinton 1988). The particular rate of change in a particular species depends on its specific adaptive features and the surrounding environmental conditions. Most paleontologists, biologists, and anthropologists hypothesize that both types of evolution have occurred under different circumstances during different geological epochs. As our understanding of the fossil record increases, we will be better able to specify when and where speciation and evolution occurred rapidly and when and where they occurred gradually.

Adaptive Radiation

Adaptive radiation is the rapid diversification and adaptation of an evolving population into new ecological niches. It provides a useful illustration of the evolutionary process and the factors that influence rates of evolutionary change. As we have seen, organisms have tremendous reproductive potential, yet this potential is generally limited by the availability of food, shelter, and space in the environment. Competition with other organisms and natural selection limit the number of offspring that live.

Eventually, organisms may utilize all the resources available in a particular ecological niche, making competition for food and other resources intense. Some individuals in a population may move into new environmental niches or explore new territories where resources are more available and chances for survival greater. In these new environments, with limited competition and abundant food, they may expand rapidly.

The creatures of the Galapagos Islands, discussed earlier with regard to Darwin's studies, provide an illustration of adaptive radiation. Located 500 miles off the coast of South America, the islands present an amazing diversity of flora and fauna. The islands species are similar to those found on the South American mainland where they originated. Yet, while similar, they are also distinct in many respects. Darwin reasoned that the island was initially colonized by a few representatives of the mainland species. The newly formed volcanic islands had no life-forms and the arriving, mainland colonists, unfettered by competition, quickly expanded in the new niche. Because the various environments of the islands were different from those of the mainland, the descendents of the original arrivals evolved traits favorable to the exploitation of the new conditions and, therefore, increased chances of reproductive success.

The adaptive radiation of many species is recorded in the fossil record. For example, at the beginning of the Mesozoic when reptiles first adapted to land environments, they were able to expand into a vast array of ecological niches with little competition. Environmental change may also create conditions favorable for the adaptive radiation of some species. Even natural disasters that lead to the extinction of many species may provide opportunity for others, as described in the box "Nemesis Theory." Such conditions favor species that have the ability to exploit the changing conditions, and this likely explains the expansion of the placental mammals at the beginning of the Cenozoic Age. Evolutionary processes acting on the expanding population may produce many new varieties and species adapted to ecological niches different from the parent population, ultimately leading to new species.

The Evolution of Life

Modern scientific findings indicate that the universe as we know it began to develop between 13 billion and 20 billion years ago. At approximately 4.6 billion years ago, the Sun and the Earth formed, and about a billion years later, the first life appeared in the sea. Through evolution, living forms developed adaptive characteristics, survived, and reproduced. Geological forces and environmental changes, bringing about both gradual and rapid changes, led to new forms of life.

From studying the fossilized bones and teeth of different creatures, paleontologists have tracked the evolution of living forms throughout the world. They document the fossil record according to geological time, which is divided into *eras*, which are subdivided into *periods*, which in turn are composed of *epochs*.

Analogy and Homology

How do paleontologists determine evolutionary relationships? Two useful concepts in discussing the divergence and differentiation of living forms are homology and analogy. **Homology** refers to traits that have resulted from a common evolutionary origin, though they may differ in form and function. For example, a human hand bears little resemblance to a whale's fin. Humans and whales live in very different environments, and the hand and fin perform in very different ways. Careful examination of human and whale skeletons, however, reveals many structural similarities that can be explained by a common, albeit distant, evolutionary relationship (see Figure 6). Thus, the hand and the fin are referred to as homologous. To understand the evolutionary relatedness of different species, researchers focus on homologous features.

Yet, not all features result from shared evolutionary origins. **Analogy** refers to similarities in organisms that have no evolutionary relationship. Analogous forms result from *convergent evolution*, the process by which two unrelated types of organisms develop similar physical characteristics. These resemblances emerge when unrelated organisms adapt to similar environmental niches. For example, hummingbirds and hummingmoths resemble each other physically and have common behavioral characteristics. However, they share no direct evolutionary descent.

Blood Chemistry and DNA

The majority of information on the evolution of life and human origin is provided by the information found in fossil records. In recent years, however, studies of the genetic makeup of living organisms have received increasing attention. It is striking to note that despite the tremendous diversity of life, the DNA codes for the production of proteins—with few exceptions—dictate the

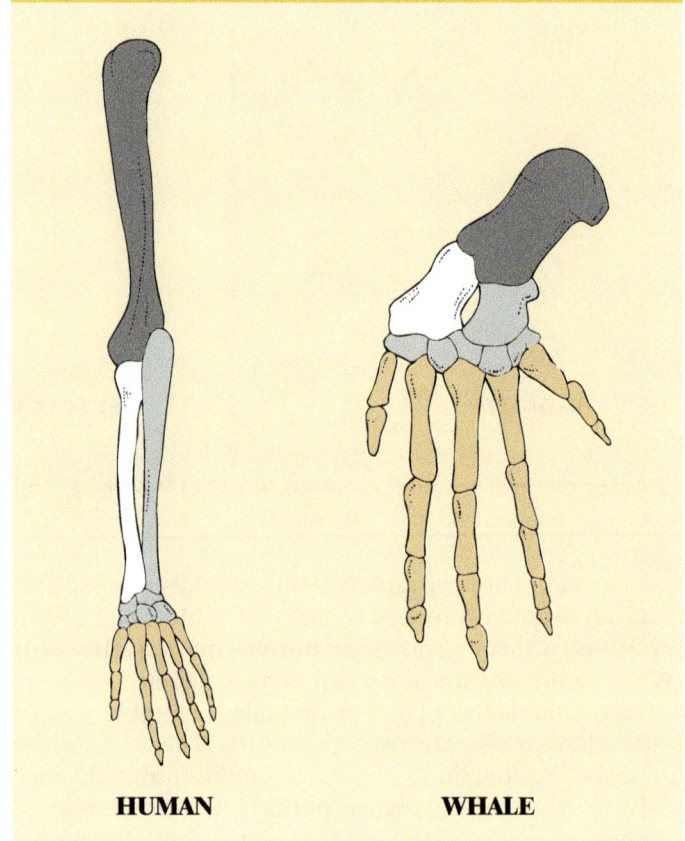

HUMAN   **WHALE**

Figure 6 The structural similarities between the human hand and the whale's fin are an example of homology: features that share a common evolutionary origin but which may differ in form and function.

joining of the same amino acids in all organisms, from the simplest one-celled plants and animals to humans. This semblance of genetic building blocks provides additional evidence for the common origin of all life.

Study of the differences and similarities in the arrangement of genetic material for living animals provides important insights into evolutionary relationships. Similarities in the DNA of different species indicate that they inherited genetic blueprints (with minor modifications) from a common ancestor. In most instances, this information has provided independent confirmation of conclusions about evolutionary relationships based on the study of skeletal characteristics and fossil remains. In some instances, however, physical characteristics may be confused because of convergent evolution. Study of genetic information and blood chemistry helps to avoid this confusion.

Genetic material of living animals has also been used to estimate when different species diverged. A technique known as *molecular dating* was developed by Vincent Sarich and Allan Wilson of the University of California, Berkeley (1967). The technique involves comparing amino acid sequences or, more recently, using what is called *DNA hybridization* to compare DNA material itself. As a result, Sarich and Wilson provided useful insights into the genetic relationship of humans to other species and estimates regarding when species may have separated.

Critical Perspectives

Planetary-Level Extinctions

Most scientists today accept that dramatic extinctions, followed by periods of relative stasis, occurred in the evolution of life. These punctuations, date long before the emergence of even the most distant human ancestors. Among the most notable are the Cretaceous-Tertiary extinction event of 65 million years ago that resulted in the disappearance of most species of dinosaurs, and an even more dramatic Permian-Triassic event that may have witnessed the extinction of most life on Earth around 251 million years ago. Estimates of similar events occurring in the Earth's past range from five major events to over twenty (Benton 2003; Raup and Sepkoski 1984; Raup 1999). In the case of the five major events, it is estimated that 50 to 90 percent of life on Earth became extinct. What could cause these dramatic events?

A variety of theories have been proposed, including the possible impact of large-scale volcanic activity, drop in sea levels, long terms stress on the ecosystem (from a variety of factors), and a gamma ray burst from a super nova (Macleod 2001). Increasing evidence, however, indicates that meteorite strikes may have been a major contributing factor in these extinctions. The evidence includes the presence of large concentrations of iridium in geological deposits dating to the Cretaceous-Tertiary boundary, the period of time that witnessed the extinction of the dinosaurs. Iridium is only found in extraterrestrial objects such as meteorites, asteroids, and comets. Evidence also includes craters,

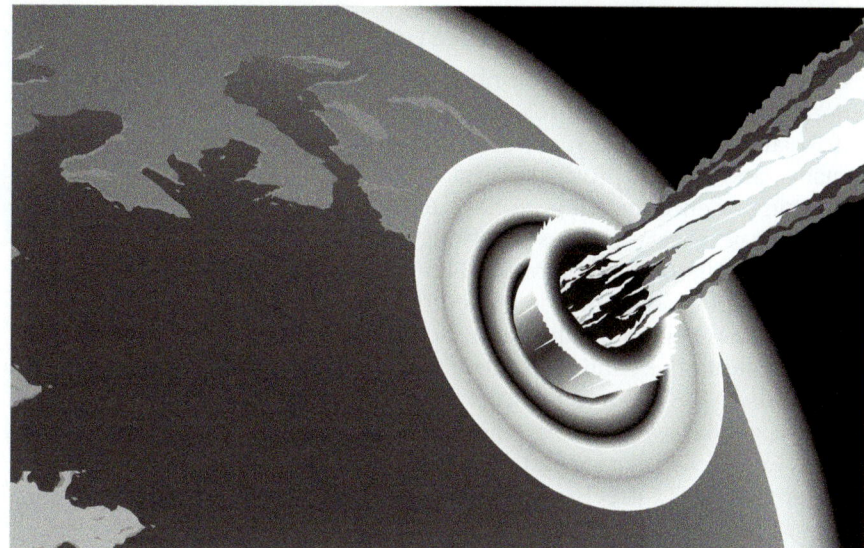

Meteor hitting the Earth.

such as the one found at the tip of the Yucatán Peninsula in the Gulf of Mexico. This crater is a mile wide and a mile deep and dates back 65 million years. A meteor strike large enough to cause such a crater would have thrown massive amounts of dust and debris into the atmosphere, shutting out the sun's radiation and warmth for more than two years. These months of darkness, similar to a "nuclear winter," would have been followed by soaring temperatures, polluted air, and dead seas. With the blockage of sunlight, photosynthesis would be suppressed, thereby choking off plant life, interrupting most of the Earth's food chains, and ultimately causing mass extinctions of millions of plant and animal species. The stories of science fiction novels and film thus may have some basis in reality.

While such planetary level events may played a dramatic and catastrophic role in the survival of some species, as Stephen Jay Gould (1985) pointed out, the disastrous conditions would also have created conditions conducive to new forms of life. Thus, although a meteorite impact may have resulted in the demise of the dinosaurs, it produced new environmental conditions that favored the adaptive radiation of creatures such as mammals. In other words, it set the stage for an explosion of new life-forms.

Points to Ponder

1. Discuss the evolutionary processes of natural selection, gene flow, and genetic drift in light of a planetary extinction-level event such as a meteor strike.

2. Evaluating theories of planetary-level extinctions involves multiple sources of evidence from numerous fields of study. Discuss these sources and evaluate their relative importance.

Molecular dating is based on two key assumptions: (1) molecular evolution proceeds at a fairly constant rate over time, and (2) the greater the similarity between animals in biochemical terms, the more likely it is that they share a close evolutionary relationship. Research based on these concepts has been applied to the interpretation of human evolution.

The reliability of this technique as a dating tool has been hotly debated. Many scientists challenge the assumption that molecular evolution is constant over time. Rather, they believe that variation in mutation rates and the disparate generation lengths of different species skew the measurements of the "molecular clock" (Lovejoy and Meindl 1972; Goodman, Baba and Darga 1983; Li and Tanimura

1987). Other researchers feel that the technique remains useful if the potential limitations are taken into consideration. Future work may help to resolve these issues.

Plate Tectonics and Continental Drift

In examining the evolution and distribution of living forms, it is important to consider the role of geological processes. The formation of natural features, such as continents, mountains, and oceans, provides an important mechanism for restricting or encouraging gene flow. **Plate tectonics** is the complex geological process that brings about the drift of continents. The outer shell of the Earth is made up of plates that are in constant motion caused by the movement of molten rocks deep within the Earth. According to scientific investigation, the continents move a few centimeters a year (Tarling 1985). Over millions of years, the continents have sometimes drifted together and then separated, a process known as **continental drift**.

Determining the precise location of different continents at specific geological time periods has helped scientists to understand evolutionary connections among different species of plants and animals. Scientists hypothesize that until about 200 million years ago, the Earth's landmass was one gigantic, interconnected continent that is referred to as *Pangaea*. During the Mesozoic era, Pangaea began to break apart, forming two supercontinents. The southern supercontinent, known as *Gondwana*, consisted of what are now South America, Africa, Antarctica, Australia, and India. The northern continent, consisting of North America, Greenland, Europe, and Asia, is known as *Laurasia* (see Figure 7).

Throughout the Mesozoic and Cenozoic eras, the supercontinents continued to move. South America separated from Africa; North America, Greenland, and Europe divided; and Africa joined with Eurasia. Forty million years ago, North America separated from Europe. By 20 million years ago, the continued fracturing and movements of the geological plates resulted in the gradual migration of the continents to their present locations.

Examination of continental drift has helped paleontologists and other scientists understand the distribution of different plant and animal species. For example, the same types of fossil reptiles have been recovered from Mesozoic deposits in North America and the Gobi Desert in Asia, a good indication that these landmasses were connected at that time. In contrast, the separation of South America from other continents during the Cenozoic era supports the fossil and biological evidence for the divergence of primates from Africa, Asia, and Europe and primates from the Americas.

The Paleontological Record

The Precambrian and Paleozoic Eras The fossil evidence shows that during the Precambrian, simple forms of life resembling modern bacteria including some

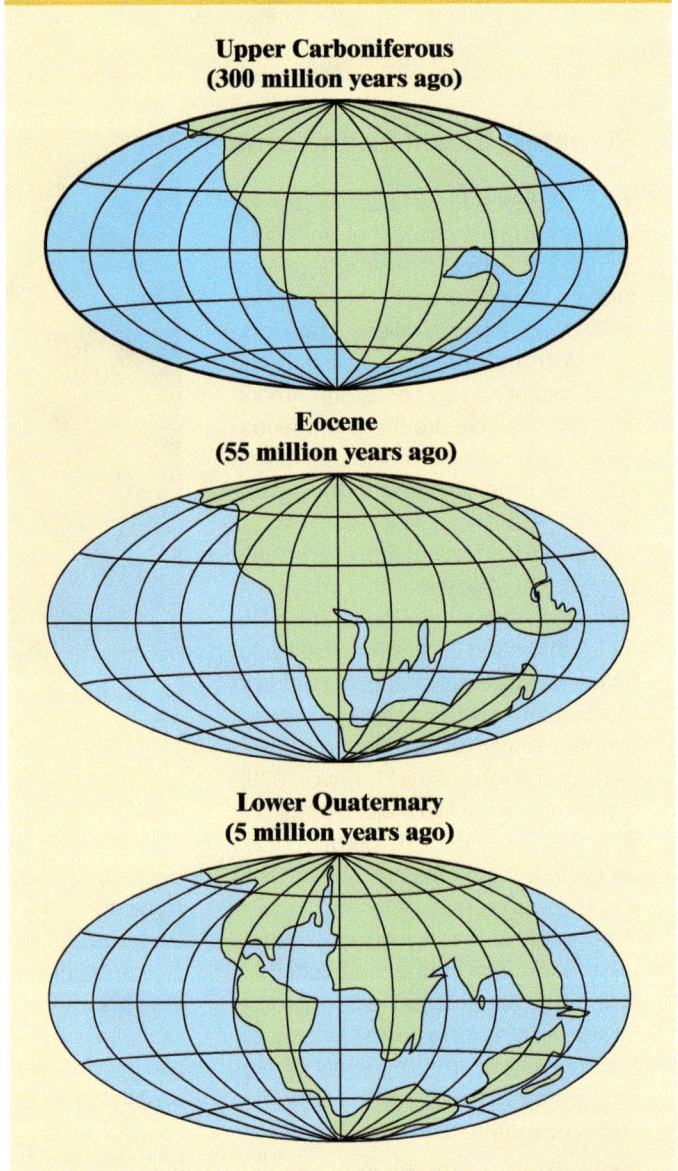

Figure 7 Understanding the geological process of continental drift—the movement of continents as a result of plate tectonics—helps paleontologists understand the distribution of fossil species.

species that may have been able to *photosynthesize*, had emerged. Apparently, the predominant organisms during this era were various kinds of algae (see Table 1). Beginning with the Paleozoic, which dates from 570 million to 248 million years ago, deposits of fossils became more abundant, enabling paleontologists to follow the adaptive radiation of jellyfish, worms, fish, amphibians, and early reptiles.

The Mesozoic Era The Mesozoic (248 million to 65 million years ago) marks the adaptive radiation of reptiles. This era is divided into the Triassic, Jurassic, and Cretaceous periods. The Mesozoic is known as the Age of Reptiles. Unlike earlier forms of life, reptiles could exist entirely outside the water. They were the first successful land animals and reigned as the dominant species in this

Table 1 A Record of Geological Time

Era	Period	Epoch	Millions of Years Ago	Geological Conditions and Evolutionary Development
Cenozoic (Age of Mammals)	Quaternary	Holocene	0.01	End of last Ice Age; warmer climate. Decline of woody plants; rise of herbaceous plants. Age of *Homo sapiens*.
		Pleistocene	2.0	Four Ice Ages; glaciers in Northern hemisphere; uplift of Sierras. Extinction of many large mammals and other species. Emergence of genus *Homo*.
	Tertiary	Pliocene	5	Uplift and mountain building; volcanoes; climate much cooler. Development of grasslands and flowering plants; decline of forests. Large carnivores; many grazing mammals; australopithecines appear.
		Miocene	23	Major continents in approximately their current locations; mountain formation. Climate drier, cooler. Flowering plants continue to diversify. Many forms of mammals; anthropoid primates flourish; earliest hominoid primates.
		Oligocene	38	Rise of Alps and Himalayas; most land low; volcanic activity in Rockies. Spread of forests and flowering plants; rise of monocotyledons. All present mammal families represented; anthropoid primates evolve.
		Eocene	55	Climate warmer. Gymnosperms and flowering plants dominant. Modern birds; first true primates appear.
		Paleocene	65	Climate mild to cool; continental seas disappear; North America and Europe still joined. Age of Mammals begins; likely emergence of the first primate ancestors.
Mesozoic (Age of Reptiles)	Cretaceous		144	Continents start to separate; formation of Rockies; swamps. Rise of flowering plants; gymnosperms decline. Dinosaurs peak, then become extinct; toothed birds become extinct; first modern birds; primitive mammals.
		Jurassic	213	Climate mild; continents low; inland seas; mountains form; continental drift continues. Gymnosperms common. Large, specialized dinosaurs; first toothed birds; insectivorous marsupials.
		Triassic	248	Many mountains and deserts form; continental drift begins. Gymnosperms.
Paleozoic (Age of Ancient Life)	Permian		286	Continents merge as Pangaea; glaciers; formation of Appalachians. Conifers diversify; cycads evolve. Modern insects appear; mammal-like reptiles; extinction of many Paleozoic invertebrates.
	Carboniferous		360	Lands low; great coal swamps; climate warm and humid, then cooler. Forests of ferns, club mosses, horsetails, and gymnosperms. First reptiles; spread of ancient amphibians; many insect forms; ancient sharks abundant.
	Devonian		408	Glaciers; inland seas. Terrestrial plants well established; first forests; gymnosperms and bryophytes appear. Age of Fishes; amphibians and wingless insects appear; many trilobites.
	Silurian		438	Continents mainly flat. Vascular plants appear; algae dominant in aquatic environment. Fish evolve; terrestrial arthropods.
	Ordovician		505	Sea covers continents; climate warm. Marine algae dominant; terrestrial plants appear. Invertebrates dominant; fish appear.
	Cambrian		570	Climate mild; lands low; oldest rocks with abundant fossils. Algae dominant in aquatic environment. Age of Marine Invertebrates; most modern phyla represented.
(Precambrian) Proterozoic			1,500	Planet cooled; glaciers; Earth's crust forms; mountains form. First multicellular forms of life appear; primitive algae and fungi, marine protozoans; marine invertebrates appear toward end of period.
Archean Origin of the Earth; Origin of the Universe			3.5 billion 4.6 billion 13 to 20 billion	Evidence of first prokaryotic cells.

Critical Perspectives

Creationism, Intelligent Design, and Evolution

Despite the increasing scientific evidence supporting evolution, not all segments of American and Western society have accepted the geological, genetic, and fossil data that are the basis of evolutionary theory (Petto and Godfrey 2007; Young and Largent 2007). Various versions of creation that rely on literal interpretations of the Bible are taught by some Christian, Jewish, and Islamic groups, as well as other religious denominations. For example, many members of the Old Order Amish accept an extreme literal reading of the biblical passage that refers to "four corners of the Earth held up by angels" and believe that the Earth is a two-dimensional flat plane. Members of the International Flat Earth Society have similar beliefs about a flat Earth (Scott 2004). These views reflect the ancient Hebrew description in the biblical passages referring to the Earth as a flat disk floating on water with the heavens held up by a dome (or firmament) with the Sun, Moon, and stars attached to it.

In the nineteenth century, some individuals attempted to reconcile a literal reading of the account of creation in Genesis 1:22 by translating the Hebrew term *day* as periods of time thousands or millions of years long, rather than 24-hour days (Sedley 2007). Some contemporary creationists' teachings expose similar views; they are sometimes referred to as "Day-Age" creationists. However, the vast majority of activists in the campaign against teaching evolution call themselves "Progressive Creationists." The Progressive Creationists accept the modern scientific view of the Big Bang and that the earth is billions of years old, but do not accept the theory of evolution. They believe that God not only created the Big Bang, but also created separate "kinds" of plants and animals with genetic variations that resulted in the development of contemporary species of living organisms.

A group of creationists that have actively campaigned against the teaching of evolution call themselves "Scientific Creationists," represented by the Institute for Creation Research. This group proposes a biblically based explanation for the origins of the universe and of life. They reject modern physics, chemistry, and geology concerning the age of the Earth. They argue that the entire universe was created within a period of six days, based on the account in Genesis 1:2. They believe that the universe was spontaneously created by divine fiat 6,000 to 10,000 years ago, challenging evidence for billions of years of geological history and fossil evidence. These creationists explain the existence of fossilized remains of ancient life by referring to a universal flood that covered the entire Earth for 40 days. Surviving creatures were saved by being taken aboard Noah's ark. Creatures that did not survive this flood, such as dinosaurs, became extinct. This creationist view is taught in some of the more fundamentalist denominations of Protestantism, Judaism, and Islam.

Scientific creationists read the texts and theories presented by biologists, geologists, and paleontologists and then present their arguments against the evolutionary views. They do very little, if any, direct biological or geological research to refute evolutionary hypotheses (Rennie 2002). Their arguments are based on biblical sources mixed with misinterpretations of scientific data and evolutionary hypotheses. The cosmological framework espoused by the scientific creationists is not based on any empirical findings. For example, scientists around the world find no physical evidence of a universal flood. Local floods did occur in the Near East and may be related to the story of Noah that appears in the Bible (and in earlier Babylonian texts). But to date, no evidence exists for a universal flood that had the potential to wipe out human populations worldwide or to cause the extinction of creatures such as dinosaurs (Isaak 2005).

A more recent form of creationism has been referred to as "Intelligent Design Creationism" (Gross and Forest 2004; Petto and Godfrey 2007). The historical roots of this conceptual stance go back to philosophers such as Plato and Aristotle in the Greek tradition, who suggested that a spiritual force structured the universe and society. These ideas were Christianized by Saint Thomas Aquinas (1225–1274) and European scholars during the medieval period. In the nineteenth century, theologian William Paley (1743–1805) argued that one could see proof of God's existence by examining the Earth and the remarkable adaptations of living organisms to their environments, using the famous analogy that if we found a watch, we would have to assume that there was a watchmaker—we can see God's plan as we observe the natural world (1803). Two contemporary theorists who support this position are LeHigh University's biochemist Michael Behe, author of *Darwin's Black Box* (1996), and philosopher and mathematician William Dembski, professor of science and theology at Southern Seminary in Louisville, author of the book *Intelligent Design* (1999).

Debates between intelligent design proponents and other researchers have been extensive and, at times, quite spirited (Rennie 2002; Shanks 2004; Shanks and Joplin 1999). Critics of intelligent design creationism note that Behe, Dembski, and their followers concede that microevolution and macroevolution has occurred, but contend that some biological phenomena and the complexity of life cannot be explained by modern science and that this complexity itself is proof that there must be an intelligent supernatural designer. Although most scientists would not rule out the possibility of supernatural creation, they do require evidence. In this respect, intelligent design has failed to provide a more compelling argument of human origins than evolutionary theory.

Given these diverse perspectives, is there any common ground between religious explanations of human origins and scientific theories? Surveys indicate that a surprising number of Americans assume that the creation-evolution controversy is based on a dichotomy between believers in God and secular atheists who are antireligious. This is incorrect. There are many varieties of both religious perspectives and evolutionary explanations, many of them compatible. Scientists and others who accept evolution are not necessarily atheists (Pennock 2003; Scott 2004). One major view of evolution is known as *theistic evolution*, which promotes the view that God creates through the evolutionary processes. Supporters of this perspective accept the modern scientific findings in astronomy, biology, genetics, and fossil and geological evidence, but see God as intervening in how evolution takes place. Theistic evolution is the official view accepted by the Roman Catholic Church; it was recently reiterated by Pope John Paul II in 1996. In this statement, John Paul II emphasized that evolution was not just "theory," but was based on an enormous amount of empirical evidence, or "facts." The Roman Catholic theological position is that although humans may indeed be descended from earlier forms of life, God created the human soul. Other contemporary mainstream Protestant, Jewish, Muslim, Hindu, and Buddhist scientists also accept theistic evolution. This position sees no conflict between religion and science and reflects a continuum between the creationist and evolutionary views.

Another view of evolution is sometimes referred to as *materialist evolutionism* or *philosophical materialism*. Scientists and philosophers who hold this view believe that the scientific evidence for evolution results in a proof of atheism. Charles Darwin recorded in his memoirs how he vacillated between muddled religious faith, atheism, and what he later accepted as agnosticism (the belief that one cannot know as humans whether God exists or not) (Desmond and Moore 1991). Survey polls demonstrate that most Americans believe materialist evolutionism is the dominant view among scientists, despite the fact that this is not the case. Because it challenges religious interpretations, it is one of the primary reasons why some fundamentalist religious-based groups have opposed the teaching of evolution in the public schools in the United States.

In actuality, there are scientists who accept theistic evolution or other spiritual views along with scientific theories. For example, one of the leading critics of intelligent design creationism is the practicing Roman Catholic biologist at Williams College, Kenneth Miller. Miller has authored a book called *Finding Darwin's God: A Scientist's Search for Common Ground between God and Evolution* (2000). In this book, Miller draws on biology, genetics, and evolutionary data to challenge intelligent design proponents' claims that the complexity of life demonstrates an intelligent designer. Paul Davies, a Protestant theologian and philosopher who authored the book *The Fifth Miracle* (2000) about faith and the evolution of life, is also critical of the intelligent design creationist model and relies on the empirical findings in science and evolution to refute their claims.

These individuals and other scientists accept theistic views of evolution, but emphasize that scientific understanding of the universe and life must be based on the methods of *naturalism*. This *methodological naturalism* requires the scientist to rely on "natural" or "materialist" (biological and physical) explanations rather than spiritual or theological explanations for examining the universe and evolution, *but it does not compel one to accept atheism*. In fact, many major philosophers and scientists, such as anthropologist Eugenie Scott (director of the National Center for Science Education) and the famed Albert Einstein, argued that one cannot prove or disprove the existence of God through the use of science. Methodological naturalism does not result in a conflict between faith and science. Rather, faith and science are viewed as two separate spheres and modes of understanding the world. This method of naturalism coincides with the teachings of the Roman Catholic position and many mainstream Protestant, Jewish, Muslim, Hindu, and Buddhist traditions.

Evolutionary explanations and other scientific theories often fail to satisfy our deep spiritual questions and moral concerns. While science can give us some basic answers about the universe and life, it cannot reveal spiritual insights. And yet, a scientific perspective does tend to leave us in a state of "spiritual awe" as described by Darwin in the famous closing passage of the *Origin of Species*: "There is grandeur in this view of life."

Points to Ponder

1. How can accounts of creation such as that found in Genesis 1:2 be evaluated empirically?

2. Have any of the scientific creationist claims convinced you of the falsity of evolution?

3. Do you think that faith and science are compatible when assessing the scientific record regarding evolution?

new environment. Many of the snakes, lizards, and turtles found in Mesozoic formations are similar to contemporary species. Of all the reptiles that lived during the Mesozoic, the dinosaurs are the most well known today. They included the giant carnivore (meat eater) *Tyrannosaurus*; larger, plant-eating creatures such as the *Brachiosaurus*; and numerous other species, both large and small.

Although reptiles were the dominant animals of the Mesozoic, paleontologists have found fossils of many other organisms from this same era. For example, bird fossils, some even showing the outlines of feathers, have been preserved from the Jurassic period. The paleontological record demonstrates beyond a doubt that a direct evolutionary relationship exists between reptiles and birds. One classic fossil example is *Archaeopteryx*, an animal about the size of a crow, with small wings, teeth, and a long, reptilian tail.

Mike Price/Shutterstock.com

Near the end of the Cretaceous period, many animals became extinct. Changing climatic conditions, competition from newly evolving mammals, and, possfibly, extraterrestrial episodes led to the demise of many reptile species, including the dinosaurs, as well as many other organisms.

The Cenozoic Era   The Cenozoic era (65 million years ago to the present), or the Age of Mammals, was characterized by the dominance and adaptive radiation of mammals. This era is divided into two periods, the Tertiary, which encompassed 63 million years, and the Quaternary, which covers the last 2 million years. During the Cenozoic, various species of mammals came to occupy every environmental niche. Some, such as whales and dolphins, adapted to the sea. Others, such as bats, took to the air. Most mammals, however, are land animals, including dogs, horses, rats, bears, rabbits, apes, and humans. One of the major evolutionary advantages that enabled mammals to radiate so rapidly was their reproductive efficiency. In contrast to reptiles, which lay eggs that are vulnerable to predators, most mammals retain their eggs internally within the female. The eggs are thus protected and nourished until they reach an advanced stage of growth. Consequently, a much higher percentage of the young survive into adulthood, when they can reproduce. It is the early Cenozoic period that witnessed the evolution of earliest primates, the order of which humans are part.

✓ Study and Review on myanthrolab.com

Summary

Following the scientific revolution in the West, various developments in the natural sciences, including geology and biology, led to new perspectives on the age of the Earth and humankind's origins. Geologists began to discover that the Earth had an ancient history, much longer than the few thousand years allowed by a literal reading of biblical chronology. In the nineteenth century, these new ideas influenced biologists Charles Darwin and Alfred Wallace, who were documenting the tremendous variation of plants and animals around the world. From their observations, they developed the theory of natural selection to explain how organisms evolved over time, adapting and reproducing successfully in particular environments.

Although Darwin and Wallace recognized the vast amount of variation in organisms in different environments, they lacked an adequate understanding of how characteristics were passed on from one generation to the next or, in other words, the principles of heredity. Through his experiments on pea plants, an Austrian monk, Gregor Mendel, discovered the essential principles of heredity. Mendel's insights regarding the transmission of dominant and recessive traits, segregation, and independent assortment have remained basic to our understanding of heredity.

Modern scientists have refined Mendel's insights on the study of inheritance. Today, biologists have a better understanding of cell biology and what is known as molecular genetics. Through studies of cells, biologists have unraveled some of the processes of inheritance. The DNA molecule found in the cell is the key factor in determining the traits that organisms inherit from their parents. It contains the chemical information that provides the coding for specific proteins that determine the physical characteristics of organisms.

Modern biologists study evolution in populations of organisms. They identify changes that mutation, gene flow, genetic drift, and natural selection create in the allele frequencies of populations. Changes in allele frequencies may enhance or limit the abilities of a population to adjust successfully to a specific environment.

Recently, paleontologists have challenged the gradualist form of evolution as proposed by early thinkers such as Darwin. They have found that species of organisms sometimes remain unchanged for millions of years, and then new species suddenly develop successfully in varied environments. Today, this punctuated equilibrium model of evolution complements the earlier gradualist model in explaining the proliferation of different species of organisms on the Earth.

Some people have not accepted the modern scientific theories regarding the development of the universe and living organisms. In particular, creation scientists have rejected the evolutionary concepts of modern biology. They propose that the Earth has a recent history dating back about 10,000 years, and they believe that different species of life were created spontaneously by divine fiat. The creationists do not conduct scientific studies to refute the modern explanations of evolution. Instead, they criticize scientific findings based on a distorted understanding of evolutionary processes and the scientific enterprise itself. Scientific creationists and intelligent design theorists do not offer scientific explanations but rather base their views on religious faith. As emphasized in Chapter 1, scientific knowledge takes a distinctively different form from that of religious knowledge. Hypothesis testing and acts of faith are radically different means of acquiring knowledge of the universe. To mix one form of knowledge with another, as the creationist scientists do, is to misunderstand this fundamental difference.

Questions to Think About

1. Compare the scientific contributions of Buffon, Cuvier, and Lyell. How did each attempt to provide a more scientific understanding of the past?

2. In your own words, explain what is meant by the terms *natural selection*, *adaptation*, and *evolution*. Create examples to illustrate the concepts.

3. What are the four mechanisms of evolution, and how do they operate to change gene frequencies in a population?

4. Is gene flow influenced by cultural factors such as religion, kinship, language, socioeconomic status, and ethnicity? If so, how? Give some examples.

5. Should contemporary models of human evolution be classified as "origin myths"? Why or why not?

6. What is intelligent design? How is it different from science? Should intelligent design be taught alongside the theory of evolution in public school science classrooms? Why or why not?

Key Terms

adaptation
adaptive radiation
alleles
analogy
catastrophism
continental drift
cosmologies
deoxyribonucleic acid (DNA)
dominant
ecological niche

evolution
founder effect
gametes
gene
gene flow
gene pool
genetic drift
genotype
Hardy-Weinberg theory
    of genetic equilibrium

heterozygous
homology
homozygous
meiosis
mitosis
mutations
natural selection
phenotype
phyletic gradualism
plate tectonics

population
punctuated equilibrium
recessive
somatic cells
speciation
species
uniformitarianism
zygote

Read the Original Source on myanthrolab.com

For further information about topics covered in this chapter, go to MyAnthroLab at www.myanthrolab.com and access the following readings in MyAnthroLibrary:

Ian Tattersall, *Paleoanthropology and Evolutionary Theory*.
Robert B. Eckhardt, *Evolutionary Genetics*.

Jon Bower Thailand/Alamy

Culture

From Chapter 10 of *Anthropology: A Global Perspective*, Seventh Edition. Raymond Scupin, Christopher R. DeCorse. Copyright © 2012 by Pearson Education, Inc. All rights reserved.

Chapter Questions

■ **What** are the basic characteristics of the term *culture* as discussed by anthropologists?

■ **What** are the basic components of culture?

■ **How** have anthropologists refined their understanding of culture today?

■ **How** does culture lead to both differences and similarities among people in widely separated societies?

((●─ **Listen** to the **Chapter Audio** on **myanthrolab.com**

The Characteristics of Culture

Culture is a fundamental concept within the discipline of anthropology. In everyday conversation many people use the word *culture* to refer to "high culture": Shakespeare's works, Beethoven's symphonies, Michelangelo's sculptures, gourmet cooking, imported wines, and so on. E. B. Tylor, the first professional anthropologist, proposed a definition of culture that includes all of human experience:

Culture … is that complex whole which includes knowledge, belief, arts, morals, law, custom, and any other capabilities and habits acquired by man as a member of society. (1871:1)

This view suggests that culture includes tools, weapons, fire, agriculture, animal domestication, metallurgy, writing, the steam engine, glasses, airplanes, computers, penicillin, nuclear power, rock and roll, video games, designer jeans, religion, political systems, subsistence patterns, science, sports, and social organizations. In Tylor's view, culture includes all aspects of human activity, from the fine arts to popular entertainment, from everyday behavior to the development of sophisticated technology. It contains the plans, rules, techniques, designs, and policies for living. Tylor was using the term *culture* as a general phenomenon for all of humanity that was different than our physical or biological characteristics.

This nineteenth-century definition of culture has some terminology that would not be acceptable to modern anthropologists. For example, it relies on the word *man* to refer to what we currently would refer to as *humanity*. In addition, nineteenth century theorists such as Tylor tended to think of "culture" as equivalent to "civilization," which implicitly suggested that there was an increase, accumulation, or growth in "culture" and "civilization" as societies progressed and evolved. This is not the meaning of culture that contemporary anthropologists maintain. As we will discuss, humans have had different languages, beliefs, values, dietary habits, and norms or "cultures" that are associated with various regions in the past as well as the present. Cultures are not evolving in some simplistic manner from early civilizations to modern civilizations as the nineteenth-century anthropologists believed.

Also, in the past, most anthropologists accepted a broad conception of culture as a shared way of life that included values, beliefs, and norms transmitted within a particular society from generation to generation. However, as we discuss later in this chapter, contemporary anthropologists have a much more refined view of the concept of culture.

Notice that Tylor's definition includes the word *society*. In general terms, society refers to a particular group of animals within a specific territory. In particular, it refers to the patterns of relationships among the animals within this definite territory. Biologists often refer to certain types of insects, herd animals, and social animals such as monkeys and apes as living in societies.

In the past, anthropologists attempted to make a simple distinction between society and culture. **Society** was said to consist of the patterns of relationships among people within a specified territory, and **culture** was viewed as the by-products of those relationships. This view of society as distinguishable from culture was derived from ethnographic studies of small-scale societies. In such societies, people within a specific territory were believed to share a common culture. However, contemporary anthropologists have found this notion of shared culture to be too simplistic and crude. For example, in most countries where modern anthropologists conduct ethnographic research, the societies are extremely complex and consist of distinctive groups that maintain different cultural traditions. Thus, this simple distinction between society and culture is too artificial for modern anthropologists. And even in small-scale societies, the conception that all these people share a collective "culture" is also too crude and simplistic. As we shall see in this chapter, this conception of a collectively shared culture often resulted in gross stereotypes of and vulgar generalizations about groups of people and their behavior.

Many anthropologists have adopted the hybrid term *sociocultural system*—a combination of the terms *society* (or *social*) and *culture*—to refer to what used to be called "society" or "culture." As we shall see in later chapters, many anthropologists use the term *sociocultural system* as the basic conceptual framework for analyzing ethnographic research.

Culture Is Learned

The unique capacity for culture in the human species depends upon learning. We do not inherit our culture through our genes in the way we inherit our physical characteristics. Instead, we obtain our culture through the process of enculturation. **Enculturation** is the process of social interaction through which people learn and acquire their culture. Humans acquire their culture both

Susan Hogue/Anthro-Photo

A pigeon being conditioned to behave in a specific manner. This is an example of situational learning.

Tom McHugh/Photo Researchers, Inc.

This photo shows a chimpanzee using a tool, a crumpled leaf, as a sponge for drinking water. The chimp learned this behavior by observing other chimps—an example of social learning.

consciously, through formal learning, and unconsciously, through informal interaction. Anthropologists distinguish among several types of learning. One type is known as **situational learning**, or trial-and-error learning, in which an organism adjusts its behavior on the basis of direct experience. In other words, a stimulus is presented in the environment, and the animal responds and receives reinforcement or feedback from the response, in the form of either a reward (pleasure) or a punishment (pain). Psychologists refer to this type of learning as conditioning.

Humans and many other animals, even single-celled organisms, learn situationally and modify their behavior in different situations. For example, dogs can learn a variety of tricks through rewards such as treats given after the completion of the trick. In some cases, human behavior can be modified through conditioning. Overeating, gambling, and smoking can sometimes be reduced through psychological techniques that involve rewarding new forms of behavior.

Another form of learning, called **social learning**, occurs when one organism observes another organism respond to a stimulus and then adds that response to its own collection of behaviors. Thus, the organism need not have the direct experience; it can observe how others behave and then imitate or avoid these behaviors (Rendell et al. 2010). Obviously, humans learn by observing classmates, teachers, parents, friends, and the media. Other social animals also learn in this manner. For example, wolves learn hunting strategies by observing pack members. Similarly, chimpanzees observe other chimps fashioning twigs with which to hunt termites and then imitate these behaviors. Recently, some primatologists and anthropologists have suggested that nonhuman primates have "culture" based upon how they learn socially from one another and have variations of behavior from one group to another (Sapolsky 2006; Laland et al. 2009). However, it appears that non-human animals including primates do not intentionally or deliberately teach one another as humans do (Tomasello et

al. 2005). In addition, as we will discuss below, these nonhuman primates do not appear to have a core aspect of what most anthropologists view as an important criteria for designating a "culture," and that is the ability to symbolize (Rossano 2010; Konner 2010).

Symbols and Symbolic Learning

The form of learning that is uniquely human and that provides the basis for the capacity for culture is known as symbolic learning. **Symbolic learning** is based on our linguistic capacity and ability to use and understand **symbols**, arbitrary meaningful units or models we use to represent reality. An example of the arbitrary aspects of symbolism would be the colors red, yellow, and green for traffic lights in the United States (Sahlins 1976). Traffic lights could be other colors in different societies, but in the United States, they take this arbitrary form. Sounds such as "cat," "dog," "tree," "one," "two," and "three" in English are symbolic and arbitrary because, as we know, the sounds that symbolize those words in languages such as Chinese, Navajo, or Russian can be completely different. However, linguistic anthropologists know that symbols do not just refer to items such as animals or numbers. Symbolic communication and language can be used to represent abstract ideas and values. Symbols are the conceptual devices that we use to communicate abstract ideas to one another. We communicate these symbols to one another through language. For example, children can learn to distinguish and name coins such as pennies, nickels, and quarters and to use this money as a symbolic medium of exchange. The symbols of money in the United States or other societies are embedded within a host of many other symbols. Symbols do not stand in isolation from one another; instead, they are interconnected within linguistic symbol systems that enable us to provide rules and meanings for objects, actions, and abstract thought processes. The linguistic capacity that we

A Chinese teacher is communicating ideas through calligraphy, an example of symbolic learning.

Lawrence Migdale/Photo Researchers Inc.

are born with gives us the unique ability to make and use symbolic distinctions.

Humans learn most of their behaviors and concepts through symbolic learning. We do not have to depend upon situational learning or observations of others to perceive and understand the world and one another. We have the uniquely human ability to abstract the essence of complex events and patterns, creating images through symbols and bestowing meaning on them.

Through the ability to symbolize, humans can learn and create meanings and transmit these meanings to one another effectively. Parents do not have to depend on direct experience to teach children. As children mature, they can learn abstract rules and concepts involving symbolic communication. When we study mathematics, we learn to manipulate abstract symbols. As you read this textbook, you are learning new ideas based on symbols transmitted to you through English words in ink on a page. Symbolic learning has almost infinite possibilities in terms of absorbing and using information in creative ways. Most of our learning as humans is based on this symbolic-learning process.

Symbols and Signs Symbols are arbitrary units of meaning, in contrast to **signs**, which are directly associated with concrete physical items or activities. Many nonhuman animals can learn signs. For example, a dog can learn to associate the ringing of a bell (a physical activity) with drinking water. Hence, both humans and other animals can learn signs and apply them to different sorts of activities or to concrete items.

Symbols are different from signs in that they are not directly associated with any concrete item or physical activity; they are much more abstract. A symbol's meaning is not always obvious. However, many symbols are powerful and often trigger behaviors or emotional states. For example, the designs and colors of the flags

of different countries represent symbolic associations with abstract ideas and concepts (see "Critical Perspectives: Key National Symbols"). In some flags, the color red may symbolize blood; in others, it may symbolize revolution. In many countries, the desecration of the national flag, itself a symbol, is considered a crime. When the symbols associated with particular abstract ideas and concepts that are related to the national destiny of a society are violated, powerful emotions may be aroused.

The ability to symbolize, to create symbols and bestow meaning on them, enhances our learning capacities as humans in comparison with other types of animals. Anthropologist Leslie White maintained that the most distinctive feature of being human is the ability to create symbols:

It is impossible for a dog, horse, or even an ape, to have any understanding of the meaning of the sign of the cross to a Christian, or of the fact that black (white among the Chinese) is the color of mourning. No chimpanzee or laboratory rat can appreciate the difference between Holy water and distilled water, or grasp the meaning of Tuesday, 3, or sin. (1971:23–24)

Symbols and Culture The human capacity for culture is based on our linguistic and cognitive ability to symbolize. Culture is transmitted from generation to generation through symbolic learning and language. Through the transmission of culture, we learn how to subsist, how to socialize, how to govern our society, and what gods to worship. Culture is the historical accumulation of symbolic knowledge that is shared by a society. This symbolic knowledge is transmitted through learning, and it can change rapidly from parents to children and from one generation to the next. Generally, however, people in societies go to great lengths to conserve their cultural and symbolic traditions. The persistence of cultural and symbolic traditions is as widespread as cultural change.

Culture Is Shared

Culture consists of the shared practices and understandings within a society. To some degree, culture is based on shared meanings that are to some extent "public" and thus, beyond the mind of any individual (Geertz 1973). Some of this culture exists before the birth of an individual into the society, and it may continue (in some form) beyond the death of any particular individual. These publicly shared meanings provide designs or recipes for surviving and contributing to the society. On the other hand, culture is also within the minds of individuals. For example, we mentioned that children learn the symbolic meanings of the different coins and bills that constitute money. The children figure out the meanings of money by observing practices and learning the various symbols that are public. However, children are not just passive assimilators of that cultural knowledge. Cognitive anthropologists such as Roy D'Andrade and Naomi Quinn emphasize **schemas**, or cultural models that are internalized by individuals and have an influence on decision making and behavior. They emphasize how culture is acquired by and modeled as schemas within individual minds and can motivate, shape, and transform the symbols and meanings (Quinn and Holland 1987; D'Andrade 1989, 1995).

Contemporary anthropologists recognize that cultural understandings are not shared equally by all members of a society (Fox and King 2002; Barth 2002; de Munck 2000). Even in small-scale societies, culture is shared differently by males and females or by young and old. Some individuals in these societies have a great deal of knowledge regarding agriculture, medical practices, or religious beliefs; those beliefs and that knowledge are not equally distributed. In our complex industrialized society, culture consists of a tremendous amount of information and knowledge regarding technology and other aspects of society. Different people learn different aspects of culture, such as repairing cars or television sets, understanding nuclear physics or federal tax regulations, or composing music. Hence, to some extent, culture varies from person to person, from subgroup to subgroup, from region to region, from age group to age group, and from gender to gender. Contemporary anthropologists also note how culture is "contested," referring to how people question and may fundamentally disagree and struggle over the specifics of culture. Yet despite this variation, some common cultural understandings allow members of society to adapt, to communicate, and to interact with one

Elen/Shutterstock.com

another. Without some of these common understandings, a society could not exist.

One recent anthropological understanding of culture is sometimes referred to as the epidemiological approach pioneered by Dan Sperber and his colleagues (Sperber 1996, Sperber and Hirschfeld 1999, Ross 2004). These anthropologists draw on the fields of cognitive science and cognitive psychology to discuss how culture propagates like a contagious disease from one person to another. Thus, religious beliefs, cooking recipes, folktales, and even scientific hypotheses are ideas or representations within the human mind that spread among people in a shared environment. Chains of communication propagate these beliefs or cultural representations within a population. As in the spread of a contagious disease, some representations take hold and are maintained in particular populations, while other beliefs or representations do not resonate with specific groups and become extinct. Also, some beliefs or representations spread and are retained more easily within a population because they are more easily acquired than other beliefs. For example, some folktales or religious narratives are easily maintained within a population in contrast to highly complex abstract mathematical formulae and narratives based on the findings within science. This epidemiological approach to culture is widely used by cognitive anthropologists to study how culture is transmitted and retained within populations.

Aspects of Culture

Within a broad and refined understanding, contemporary anthropologists have tried to isolate the key elements that constitute culture. Two of the most basic aspects of culture are material and nonmaterial culture.

Material culture consists of the physical products of human society (ranging from weapons to clothing styles), whereas **nonmaterial culture** refers to the intangible products of human society (values, beliefs, and norms). The earliest traces of material culture are stone tools associated with early hominids. They consist of a collection of very simple choppers, scrapers, and flakes. Modern material culture consists of all the physical objects that a contemporary society produces or retains from the past, such as tools, streets, buildings, homes, toys, medicines, and automobiles. Cultural anthropologists investigate the material culture of the societies they study, and they also examine the relationship between the material culture and the nonmaterial culture: the values, beliefs, and norms that represent the patterned ways of thinking and acting within a society. Archaeologists, meanwhile, are primarily concerned with interpreting past societies by studying their material remains.

Values

Values are the standards by which members of a society define what is good or bad, holy or unholy, beautiful or ugly. They are assumptions that are widely shared within

Critical Perspectives

Key National Symbols

Societies throughout the world have drawn upon important cultural symbols as a means of distinguishing their community from others. Some of these cultural symbols are secular or nonreligious in meaning, whereas others have religious connotations. Anthropologist Victor Turner (1967) described symbols as "multivocal," suggesting that they have multiple meanings for people within a society. He also said that symbols have the characteristic of "condensation," having the ability to unify many things and actions into a single formation.

National symbols such as flags have the potential for expressing deep-felt emotions in condensed forms. Flags, with their great public visibility, have been an extremely important symbolic medium of political communication throughout the centuries. In U.S. society, the flag is a key secular symbol reflecting deeply felt community ties. A number of legal battles have been waged over the so-called desecration of the U.S. flag. For example, members of the Jehovah's Witnesses religious sect refuse on principle to salute the flag, for which they have been prosecuted. Political protesters, such as those opposed to the Vietnam War in the 1960s, tried to dramatize their cause by burning the flag or otherwise defacing it. In the late 1980s, the issue found its way to the U.S. Supreme court, which ruled that a protester who had burned the flag at the 1988 Republican National Convention was merely expressing free speech. The court later ruled that a law protecting the flag from desecration was unconstitutional. This issue remains controversial for many U.S. citizens. There is a political movement to amend the U.S. Constitution to protect the flag.

Virgin of Guadalupe, Mexico.

Beren Patterson/Alamy

The 2010 controversy about the flying of the Confederate flag over the South Carolina statehouse also demonstrates the potency of symbols and the different meanings evoked by symbols for different people. Some white southerners view the Confederate flag as part of their cultural heritage, whereas many African Americans understand the flag as a symbol of slavery.

Various religious symbols have produced fundamental meanings and metaphors for many countries throughout the world. For example, the symbols associated with the Virgin Mary in Roman Catholicism have developed into national symbols of unity for some countries. In Mexico, the symbolism associated with the Virgin of Guadalupe has served to unify different ethnic communities (Wolf 1958; Kurtz 1982; Ingham 1986; Beatty 2006). After Spain had colonized the indigenous Indian communities of Mexico beginning in the sixteenth century, many of the Indians, such as the Aztecs, were converted to Roman Catholicism. According to Mexican tradition, the Virgin Mary appeared before a Christianized Indian, Juan Diego, in 1531 in the form of a brown-skinned Indian woman.

Tepeyac, the place where the apparition occurred, was the sacred site of an Aztec fertility goddess, Tonantzin, known as Our Lady Mother. Aztec cosmology contained many notions regarding the virgin births of deities. For example, Huitzilopochtli, the deity believed to have led the Aztecs to their home in Tenochtitlán, had been miraculously conceived by the Aztec mother goddess. Thus, Aztec religious beliefs regarding Tonantzin somewhat paralleled Catholic teachings about Mary.

During the Virgin's appearance, Tonantzin commanded Juan Diego to inform the bishop of Mexico that a shrine should be built at the spot. The Shrine of the Virgin of Guadalupe is today a huge church, or basilica. Over the altar, Juan Diego's cloak hangs, embossed with the image of a young, dark-skinned woman wearing an open crown and flowing gown, standing on a half-moon that symbolizes the Immaculate Conception.

The Virgin of Guadalupe became a potent symbol that has endured throughout generations, assuming different meanings for different social groups. To the Indians of Mexico, the Virgin embodies both Tonantzin and the newer Catholic beliefs and aspirations concerning eternal salvation. To the mestizos, people with mixed Spanish and Indian ancestry, she represents the supernatural mother who gave them a place in both the indigenous and the colonial worlds. To Mexicans in general, the Virgin represents the symbolic resolution of the many conflicts and problems that resulted from violent encounters between the Europeans and the local population (Kurtz 1982). The Guadalupe shrine has become one of the most important pilgrimage sites in Mexico. In 2002, the late Pope John Paul II made a trip to Mexico to canonize Juan Diego as a saint in the Roman Catholic Church. The Vatican's recognition of this important hybrid religious figure helped reinforce the importance of this national symbol for Mexico (Beatty 2006).

The Virgin Mary has also played an important symbolic role in a European country that has undergone major political and social transformations. Until recently, Poland was a socialist country under the indirect control of the former Soviet Union. Beginning in the 1980s, however, the Polish people, who were organized through a union-based political party known as Solidarity, began to challenge the Communist Party that ruled Poland. During Communist Party rule in Poland, religious symbolism and Roman Catholicism, deeply rooted in Polish history, were to some degree repressed by the government. One of the most important symbols of Polish Catholicism is a famous picture of the Virgin Mary in a Paulite monastery. According to Polish tradition, the picture, known as the Black Madonna of Czestochowa, was painted by St. Luke the Evangelist, one of the authors of the Christian New Testament, on a piece of cypress wood from the table used by Mary. After the picture was placed in the monastery, where it was revered by many Polish Catholics, a party of robbers raided the monastery for treasures in 1430 and slashed the image of the Madonna with a sword. Although painstakingly restored, the picture still bears the scars of that destruction, with sword slashes on the cheek of the Black Madonna.

As Poland was divided among different countries such as Sweden, Germany, Turkey, and Russia during various periods, the image of the Black Madonna served as a symbol of Polish religious and national unity. It became one of the most important pilgrimage sites for Polish Catholicism. Millions of pilgrims from Poland and other European countries made their way to the Czestochowa shrine every year to take part in various religious rites. When the Solidarity movement in Poland challenged the Commu-

nist Party during the 1980s, leaders such as Lech Walesa wore an image of the Black Madonna on their suit lapels. Pope John Paul II visited the Black Madonna shrine and placed a golden rose there to help resuscitate religiosity in Poland. Thus, the Black Madonna image served to unify Polish Catholics in their struggle against the antireligious stance of the Communist authorities. Other Madonna shrines in Spain and France provided symbols of nationalism and political-religious identity for Catholics in Europe (Bowen 2005).

National symbols, whether religious or secular, have played extremely important roles in mobilizing people and countries in times of transition and struggle. These national symbols reflect the deep feelings that tie peoples together in what some scholars have referred to as "imagined communities" (Anderson 1991). People share some basic key symbols with millions of people in an "imagined community" or nation regardless of whether they know one another as individual persons. Regardless of whether these communities are imagined or not, such symbols are key aspects of culture that are likely to be retained by societies worldwide in the twenty-first century.

Points to Ponder

1. What kinds of feelings and emotions do you have when you hear your national anthem played as you watch your flag?

2. Can you think of any other examples of national symbols that have played a role in world history or politics?

3. Are there any disadvantages of national symbols that have influenced various societies?

4. Could international symbols be developed that would draw all of humanity together?

the society. Values are a central aspect of the nonmaterial culture of a society and are important because they influence the behavior of the members of a society. The predominant values in the United States include individual achievement and success, efficiency, progress, material comfort, equality, freedom, science, rationality, nationalism, and democracy, along with many other assumptions (Williams 1970; Bellah et al. 1985, 2000). Although these values might seem normal to Americans, they are not accepted values in all societies. For instance, just as American society tends to emphasize individualism and self-reliance, other societies, such as the Old Order Amish in the United States, instead stress cooperation and community interest.

Beliefs

Beliefs held by the members of a society are another aspect of nonmaterial culture. Beliefs are cultural conventions that concern true or false assumptions, specific descriptions of the nature of the universe and humanity's place in it. Values are generalized notions of what is good and bad; beliefs are more specific and, in form at least, have more content. "Education is good" is a fundamental value in American society, whereas "Grading is the best way to evaluate students" is a belief that reflects assumptions about the most appropriate way to determine educational achievement.

Most people in a given society assume that their beliefs are rational and firmly grounded in common sense. Some beliefs may not necessarily be scientifically accepted. For example, our intuitive and commonsense understandings may lead us to conclude that the Earth is flat and stationary. When we look around us, the plane of the Earth looks flat, and we do not feel as if the Earth is rotating around the Sun. Yet, our cognitive intuitions and commonsense beliefs about these notions are contradicted by the knowledge gained by the scientific method.

Some anthropologists in the past have referred to the worldview of a particular society. A *worldview* was believed to consist of various beliefs about the nature of reality that provided a people with a more or less consistent orientation toward the world. Worldviews were viewed as guides to help people interpret and understand the reality surrounding them. Early anthropologists believed, for example, that the worldviews of the traditional Azande of East Africa and the traditional Navajos of the southwestern region of the United States included meaningful beliefs about witches (Evans-Pritchard 1937; Kluckhohn 1967). In these societies, witchcraft was believed to cause illnesses in some unfortunate individuals. On the other hand, in societies such as that of Canada, medical doctors diagnosed illnesses using the scientific method and believed illnesses were caused by viruses, bacteria, or other material forces. These early anthropologists maintained that such differing beliefs about illness reflected

the different worldviews of these societies. However, modern anthropologists remain very skeptical about these notions of worldviews shared by entire cultures. This notion suggested that cultures were very homogeneous. Presently, anthropologists concur that the concept of a people sharing a worldview is highly questionable. Instead, anthropologists discover a great deal of variation in cultural beliefs held within any society.

In particular circumstances within a society, some beliefs may be combined into an ideology. An **ideology** consists of cultural symbols and beliefs that reflect and support the interests of specific groups within society (Yengoyan 1986; Comaroff and Comaroff 1991:22). Particular groups promote ideologies for their own ends as a means of maintaining and justifying economic and political authority. Different economic and political systems—including capitalism, socialism, communism, democracy, and totalitarianism—are based on differing ideologies. For example, many political leaders in capitalist societies maintain the ideology that individuals should be rewarded monetarily based on their own self-interest. In contrast, leaders in socialist societies have adopted the ideology that the well-being of the community or society takes precedence over individual self-interest.

In some societies, especially complex societies with many different groups, an ideology may produce **cultural hegemony**, the ideological control by one dominant group over values, beliefs, and norms. For example, one dominant ethnic group may impose its cultural beliefs on subordinate groups. In the United States, the dominant ethnic group in the eighteenth and nineteenth centuries, white Anglo-Saxon Protestants, was able to impose its language, cultural beliefs, and practices on the Native Americans in U.S. society. In many areas of the world, minority groups often accept the ideologies of the economically and politically dominant groups through the process of cultural hegemony. Some anthropologists have noted that subordinate groups may accept the ideology of the dominant group even if it is to their disadvantage. Thus, for example, in the past some Native Americans or African Americans accepted the belief that white Americans were superior because they appeared to have many more opportunities to acquire wealth and political power than they did. Thus, the ideological culture of the dominant group becomes the "taken-for-granted" natural order and reality of the minority groups. In other cases of cultural hegemony, subordinate groups begin to resist the ideological foundations of the dominant group. For example, anthropologist Lila Abu-Lughod studied how Bedouin women of the Arab world resisted the imposition of the male-dominated ideologies in Egypt (1990).

Norms

Norms—a society's rules of right and wrong behavior—are another aspect of nonmaterial culture. Norms are

Luftikus/Shutterstock.com

shared rules or guidelines that define how people "ought" to behave under certain circumstances. Norms are generally connected to the values, beliefs, and ideologies of a society. For example, we have seen that in U.S. culture individualism is a basic value that is reflected in the prevailing worldview. It is not surprising, then, that U.S. society has many norms based upon the notion of individual initiative and responsibility. Individuals are admonished to work for their own self-interest and not to become a burden to their families or community. Older Americans, if self-sufficient, are not supposed to live with their children. Likewise, self-sufficient young adults beyond a certain age are not supposed to live with their parents. These individualistic norms reflect the values of U.S. society and contrast with norms existing in other societies. In many agricultural societies, it would be considered immoral to allow aging parents to live outside the family. In these societies, the family is a moral community that should not be separated. Rather than individualism, these norms emphasize communal responsibility within the family unit.

Folkways Norms guiding ordinary usages and conventions of everyday life are known as **folkways**. Members of a society frequently conform to folkways so readily that they are hardly aware these norms exist. For example, if a Chinese anthropologist were to ask an American why Americans eat with knives and forks, why Americans allow dating between single men and women without chaperones, or why American schoolchildren are not allowed to help one another on exams, he or she might get vague and uninformative answers, such as "Because that's the way it is done." or "It's the custom." or even "I don't know." Cultural anthropologists are accustomed to receiving these kinds of answers from the members of the society they are studying. These folkway

norms or standards of etiquette are so embedded in the society that they are not noticeable unless they are openly violated.

Folkways help ensure that social life proceeds smoothly by providing guidelines for an individual's behavior and expectations of other people's behavior. At the same time, folkways allow for some flexibility. Although most people conform to folkways most of the time, folkways are sometimes violated, but these violations are not severely punished. Thus, in U.S. society, people who eat with chopsticks rather than with knives and forks or who do not keep their lawns neatly mowed are not considered immoral or depraved, nor are they treated as criminals.

Mores **Mores** (pronounced MOR-ays) are much stronger norms than are folkways. Members of society believe that their mores are crucial for the maintenance of a decent and orderly way of life. People who violate mores are usually severely punished, although punishment for the violation of mores varies from society to society. It may take the form of ostracism, vicious gossip, public ridicule, exile, loss of one's job, physical beating, imprisonment, commitment to a mental asylum, or even execution. For example, in some Islamic societies such as Iran and Saudi Arabia, the manner in which a woman dresses in public is considered morally significant. If a woman violates the dress code in these societies, she may be arrested by religious police and detained. Government and religious regulations control how Saudi women have to dress. They have to wear the *abaya* (a full black cloak), the *hijab* (head scarf), and the *niqab* (face veil). As we shall see later in the text, in hunting-and-gathering societies, individuals who do not share goods or resources with others are often punished by gossip, ridicule, and occasionally ostracism.

Not all norms can be neatly categorized as either folkways or mores. Distinguishing between the two is especially difficult when dealing with societies other than our own. In reality, norms fall at various points on a continuum, depending upon the particular circumstances and the society under consideration. The prohibition of public nudity may be a strong norm in some societies, but it may be only a folkway or pattern of etiquette in others. Even within a society, rules of etiquette may come to have moral significance. For example, as discussed above, the proper form of dress for women in some societies is not just a matter of etiquette, but has moral or religious connotations.

Saudi women in government-prescribed clothing.

Values, beliefs, and norms are used by many social scientists when referring to nonmaterial culture. However, not all anthropologists agree that there are concise, clear-cut distinctions among these terms. The terms are used only to help us understand the complex symbolic aspects of nonmaterial culture.

Ideal versus Real Culture

When discussing values, beliefs, and norms, cultural anthropologists often distinguish between ideal culture and real culture. **Ideal culture** consists of what people say they do or should do, whereas **real culture** refers to their actual behaviors. Cultural anthropologists have discovered that the ideal culture frequently contrasts with people's actual behavior. For instance, a foreign anthropologist may learn that Americans cherish the value of equal opportunity, yet in observing Americans, the anthropologist might encounter many cases in which people from different economic, class, racial, ethnic, and religious backgrounds are treated in a highly unequal manner. In later chapters, we discuss how some societies are structured around kinship ties and principles of lineage such as patrilineal and matrilineal descent. Anthropologists often discover, however, that these kinship and descent principles are violated by the actual practices of people (Kuper 1988). Thus, in all societies, anthropologists find that there are differences between the ideal and real cultural practices of individuals.

Cultural Diversity

Throughout history, humans have expressed an interest in cultural diversity. People have recognized differences in values, norms, beliefs, and practices everywhere. Whenever different groups have come into contact with one another, people have compared and contrasted their respective cultural traditions. Societies often differentiated themselves from one another based on these variant cultural patterns. For example, one of the first Western historians, Herodotus, a Greek scholar of the fifth century B.C., wrote about the different forms of behavior and belief in societies such as that of Egypt. He described how the Egyptians behaved and thought differently from the Greeks.

Writings on the diversity of cultures have often been based on ethnocentric attitudes. *Ethnocentrism* is the practice of judging another society by the values and standards of one's own society. It appears that ethnocentrism is a universal phenomenon (D. Brown 2011). As humans learn the basic values, beliefs, and norms of their society, they tend to think of their own group and culture as preferable, ranking other cultures as less desirable. In fact, members of a society become so committed to particular cultural traditions that they cannot conceive of any other way of life. They often view other cultural traditions as strange, alien, inferior, crazy, or immoral.

The study of cultural diversity became one of the principal objectives of anthropology as it developed as a profession in the nineteenth century. But like earlier writers, nineteenth-century anthropologists often reinforced ethnocentric beliefs about other societies. In the twentieth century, however, anthropologists began to recognize that ethnocentrism prevents them from viewing other cultures in a scientific manner.

To combat the problem of ethnocentrism, twentieth-century anthropologists developed the concept of cultural relativism. **Cultural relativism** is the view that cultural traditions must be understood within the context of a particular society's responses to problems and opportunities. Cultural relativism is a method or procedure for explaining and interpreting other people's cultures. Because cultural traditions represent unique adaptations and symbolic systems for different societies, these traditions must be understood by anthropologists as objectively as possible. In order to do an ethnographic study, anthropologists must suspend their own judgments and examine the other society in terms of its history and culture. Cultural relativism offers anthropologists a means of investigating other societies without imposing ethnocentric assumptions. Cultural anthropologists attempt to understand the logic of the people they are studying. Perhaps that logic does not make sense from the anthropologists' perspective, but the task is to understand and explain the reasoning of the people studied.

Although cultural relativism provides a sound methodological basis for ethnographic research, it may involve some serious ethical problems. For example, many cultural anthropologists have found themselves in societies in which cultural practices may produce physical harm to people. How do cultural anthropologists refrain from making a value judgment about such harmful cultural practices as infanticide, child or spousal abuse, torture, or murder? This issue is an ever-present problem for anthropologists and deserves careful thought. Anthropologists do not argue that any practice or culture is as good or worthy as another. In fact, one of the major goals in anthropology is to improve conditions and enhance human rights for all people.

Food and Diversity

To understand the difference between human biological and cultural behaviors, we can simply observe the variety of ways in which different societies satisfy a basic biological drive such as hunger. Although humans are omnivorous animals with the ability to digest many types of plants and animals for nutrition, there are many differences in eating behaviors and food preferences throughout the world. Food is not just a source of nutrition and oral pleasure. It becomes an aesthetic experience, a mechanism of sharing, a center of celebration, and sometimes a statement about one's own ethnic, religious, and cultural identity (Appadurai 1981; Rozin 2010).

In general, American culture labels animals as either edible or inedible. Most Americans would be repulsed by the thought of eating insects and insect larvae, but many societies consider them to be delicacies. American culture also distinguishes between pets, which are not eaten, and farm animals, such as chickens, cows, and pigs, which can be eaten. In the United States, horses are considered pets, and there are no industries for raising them for human consumption. Yet, horsemeat is a regular part of the continental European diet. The French, Belgians, Dutch, Germans, Italians, Poles, and other Europeans consume significant quantities of horsemeat each year (Harris 1985).

Anthropologists explain differences in dietary preferences in different ways. For example, Mary Douglas offers an explanation of why the Jewish people have prohibitions against eating pork. She describes this prohibition in her book *Purity and Danger: An Analysis of the Concepts of Pollution and Taboo* (1966) by suggesting that all societies have symbolic classifications of certain objects or foods that are unclean, tabooed, polluted, or dirty, as well as those that are clean, pure, or undefiled. To illustrate her ideas regarding the classification of matter or foods, Douglas examined the ancient Israelites' classification of animals and taboos against eating certain animals such as pigs and shellfish, as described in Leviticus in the Bible. Douglas argues that like other humans, the ancient Israelites classify reality by placing things into distinguishable "mental boxes." However, some things do not fit neatly into distinguishable mental boxes. Some items are anomalous and ambiguous and fall between the basic categories that are used to define cultural reality. These anomalous items are usually treated as unclean, impure, unholy, polluting, or defiling.

In explaining how these processes influenced the classification of animals among the ancient Israelites, Douglas alludes to the descriptions in the first chapter of the Bible, Genesis, where God creates the animals with specific characteristics: birds with feathers are soaring in the sky; fish with scales and fins are swimming in the water; and creatures with four feet are walking, hopping, or jumping on the land. However, some animals did not easily fit into the cultural categories used for the classification of animals. Animals that combined elements of different realms were considered ambiguous, and therefore unclean or unholy. For example, terrestrial animals that move by "swarming upon the earth" such as insects were declared unclean and were prohibited from being eaten. Animals that have cloven hoofs and chew cud, such as sheep, goats, and cattle, were considered clean and could be eaten. However, pigs have cloven hoofs but do not chew cud and, therefore, failed to fit into the cultural classification of reality accepted by the ancient Israelites. Consequently, pigs were considered unclean and polluting and were prohibited in the ancient Israelite diet. Shellfish and eels were also unclean animals because they swim in the water but lack fins and scales. These anomalous creatures fell outside of the systematic classification of animals. Douglas maintains that the dietary laws of Leviticus represented an ideal construction of reality that represented God's plan of creation, which was based on perfection, order, and holiness. This became integral to the worldview of the ancient Israelites and affected their dietary preferences.

The late anthropologist Marvin Harris hypothesized that cultural dietary preferences frequently have an adaptive significance (1977, 1985). In seeking the origins of the pig taboo, Harris emphasized, as did Douglas, that among the ancient Israelites, pigs were viewed as abominable animals not suited for human consumption. Yet, many societies show no aversion to the consumption of pork. Pigs have been a primary source of protein and fat throughout China and Europe. In some societies in the Pacific Islands, pigs are so highly regarded they are treated as members of the family (but they are also eaten). One medical explanation for the dietary prohibition is that the pig is an unclean animal and that it carries diseases such as trichinosis, which is caused by a type of tapeworm. Harris, however, considered these explanations to be unsatisfactory. Regarding cleanliness, Harris acknowledged that because pigs cannot sweat, in hot, dry climates such as the Middle East they wallow in their excrement to keep cool. He noted, however, that other animals, such as goats and chickens, can also be dirty, but they are eaten. Similarly, Harris emphasized that many other animals, such as cows, which are widely consumed, also carry diseases.

Ultimately, Harris explained the origins of the pig taboo in Judaism (and later Islam) by analyzing the ecological conditions of the Middle East. He maintained that this dietary restriction represented a cultural innovation that

Connie Bransilver/Photo Researchers, Inc.

In some areas of the world, pigs are prized as food; in other cultures, it is forbidden to eat pork.

Anthropologist at Work

NANCY ROSENBERGER:
Gender, Food, Globalization, and Culture

After earning her university degree, Nancy Rosenberger traveled to northeastern Japan to teach English. She had majored in English and had never taken an anthropology or Japanese course in her life! While living in Japan, Rosenberger became fascinated with Japanese culture and language and wanted to study more. By chance, she read an article about the famous anthropologist Lévi-Strauss in a popular magazine by an anthropology professor named Aram Yengoyan. The global questions about culture and society which anthropologists ask intrigued her. Several years later, Rosenberger studied anthropological theory under Professor Yengoyan at the University of Michigan where she earned her doctorate in cultural anthropology.

Rosenberger's main topic of research has been Japan and the changing position of women. For her Ph.D. dissertation, she investigated middle-aged women and the way they expressed their dissatisfaction, not in words, but through bodily aches and pains which they labeled as menopausal problems. Since 1993, she has conducted a longitudinal study of 55 Japanese women who were single and between the ages of 25 and 35 when she first met them. Rosenberger has since followed these women into middle age. She was particularly interested in this cohort because they are highly affected by the globalization of media and individualized consumption in Japan, but they also learned post-war Japanese values emphasizing group responsibility. These women's personal decisions about delaying marriage and having one or no children have changed Japan in big ways, yet they deal with contradictions. Work and educational institutions have not changed so much, and Japanese women have had to compromise in order to maintain relationships with husbands, children, and parents. All of this research material contributed to Rosenberger's book, *Gambling with Virtue: Japanese Women and the Search for Self in a Changing Nation* (2001).

Rosenberger is currently working on a book called *Tales of Ambivalence*, which traces the ambiguous feelings

Nancy Rosenberger

that include both the resistance and compliance of the Japanese women in this longitudinal study. For comparative purposes, Rosenberger also did research in Korea and Thailand on young, single women and saw how similar global ideas combine with local values and situations. She discovered that in these countries women gain independence from global ideas and processes, but they still cope with entrenched gender inequality.

helped the societies of this region to adapt. About 1200 B.C., the ancient Israelites had settled in a woodland area that had not been cultivated. As they rapidly cut down trees to convert areas to irrigated agricultural land, they also severely restricted areas suitable for raising pigs on natural forage. Eventually, pigs had to be fed grains as supplements, which made them extremely costly and direct competitors with humans. Moreover, they required artificial shade and moisture to keep cool. In addition, pigs were not useful for pulling plows, producing milk, or providing hides or wool for clothing.

According to Harris, despite the increasing costs associated with pig raising, people were still tempted to raise them for nutritional reasons. He hypothesized that the pig taboo was established to inhibit this practice through religious authorities and texts that redefined the pig as an unclean animal. Neighbors of the ancient Israelites, such as the Egyptians, began to share the abhorrence of the pig. The pig taboo was later incorporated into the Islamic religious text, the Qur'an, so that today both Muslims and Jews are forbidden to eat pork.

Thus, according to Harris's hypothesis, in the hot, dry regions of the world where pigs are poorly adapted and extremely costly to raise, the meat of the pig came to be forbidden. He emphasized the practical considerations of pig raising, including the fact that they are hard to herd and are not grazing animals like goats, sheep, or cattle. In contrast, in the cooler, wetter areas of the world that are more appropriate for pig raising, such as China and New Guinea, pig taboos are unknown, and pigs are the prized foods in these regions.

Both Douglas and Harris offer insights into the development of the dietary preferences of Jews and Christians. While Douglas explores the important symbolic significance of these preferences, Harris examines the cost effectiveness and practical aspects of these food taboos. Anthropologists

In 2001, Rosenberger began applied research for a local Hunger Taskforce in Oregon. With her colleague, Joan Gross, she interviewed low-income people in two rural communities about questions of food security—whether they had enough nutritious and culturally appropriate food. In their study, Rosenberger and Gross found that people had enough food, but the food that they could afford through box stores and food banks was not very nutritious, especially if they were diabetic or obese. They also found that these people are victims of a globalized food system that produces much processed food, but takes the control of food production out of local hands. Rosenberger has continued to work on local food issues with an organization called Ten Rivers Food Web which encourages the production and distribution of local food across three counties, and links affluent and low-income people with local foods.

In 2005, Rosenberger took her new interest in food and culture to Uzbekistan on a Fulbright scholarship to study in Central Asia. She is presently writing a book on food, nationalism, and class, gender, and ethnic differences in Uz-

bekistan called *Seeking Food Rights: Nation, Inequality and Repression in Uzbekistan*. In this book, she explores the class, gender, and ethnic differences that emerge through food in Uzbekistan, even though leaders attempt to unite the nation through a national cuisine. Rosenberger has found that the Uzbek people are hospitable and proud of their identity; they want to share their national cuisine with plenty of meat. However, poor people, particularly those who live in the Uzbekistan countryside, cannot be full citizens in this way. Ironically, while globalization overwhelms much of the world, the leaders of Uzbekistan have tightened their borders to keep out globalized food. McDonald's is nonexistent in this country, but people do desire more food choices. In the main city in Uzbekistan, Rosenberger saw a hamburger shop set up in a park that advertised "Madonna's" on red sign with golden arches—an example of the creative mixtures that people construct from global culture.

Rosenberger's interest in food has also transferred back to Japan. She notes that the global world is one of risk, as is our food supply because it is produced and comes from all over the

world. Japan is highly dependent upon food imports, many from the United States, and increasingly from China. In 2007, when some Japanese became ill from poison pot stickers made in China, the local media went wild with accusations of "global food terror." Individual Japanese felt powerless and fears of their Chinese neighbors welled up over food. All of this made local Japanese food more popular, and profited a group of organic farmers with whom Rosenberger was doing research in Japan. These organic farmers live consciously in resistance to global capitalism, practice self-sufficiency to the fullest extent possible, and sell their food only in face-to-face relationships.

Rosenberger emphasizes that cultural anthropology has made for a fascinating career. Through it, she has talked in depth with many interesting people in a variety of countries and walks of life. She enjoys alerting students to both the inequalities in the world and the creativity that people bring in blending their local ways with global forces.

Explore the **Concept** on
myanthrolab.com

such as Harris and others have been studying dietary diversity, such as why some people prohibit the eating of beef, whereas other people have adopted it as an integral aspect of their diet. Food preferences illustrate how humans the world over have universal needs for protein, carbohydrates, minerals, and vitamins but obtain these nutrients in different ways, depending upon the dietary preferences established within their culture. Anthropologists Sidney Mintz and Christine DuBois have summarized how other anthropologists have studied food and eating habits around the world and how these developments are associated with ecological conditions, technological requirements, biological factors, but also with patterns of identity, gender, class differences, and ritual and religious beliefs (2002).

Anthropologists have continued to explore these numerous dimensions of food and eating habits in many different societies. For example, Daniel Fessler and C. D. Naverette looked at a broad cross-cultural sample of

food taboos (2003). They found that food taboos are overwhelmingly associated with meat and animal products compared to fruits or vegetables. Animal foods are viewed as much more dangerous than fruits and vegetables in respect to disease or death. The high cost of trial and error learning about which animal foods would be harmful would be counterproductive in any cultural tradition, thus food taboos associated with animals tend to become more pervasive than prohibitions against fruits or vegetables. Research on the cultural aspects of food is an important arena for contemporary anthropological research.

Dress Codes and Symbolism

Although some cultural differences may relate to the environmental adaptations of societies emphasized by some anthropologists, much more of our cultural diversity is a consequence of symbolic creations.

Symbols provide the basis of meaningful shared beliefs within a society. Because of our inherent cultural capacity, we tend to be meaning-seeking creatures. In addition to the satisfaction of biological needs, we have needs for meaning and significance in our personal and social lives.

The importance of symbols as a source of cultural diversity can be seen in the dress codes and hairstyles of different societies. In most situations, the symbolism of clothing and hairstyles communicates different messages, ranging from political beliefs to identification with specific ethnic or religious groups. The tartan of a Scottish clan, the black leather jacket and long hair of a motorcycle gang member in the United States, and the veil of an Islamic woman in Saudi Arabia all provide a symbolic vocabulary that creates cultural diversity.

Many examples of clothing styles can be used to illustrate how symbols contribute to cultural diversity. Consider, for instance, changing dress codes in the United States. During the 1960s, many young people wore jeans, sandals, and beads to symbolize their rebellion against what they conceived as the conformist inclinations of American society. By the 1980s, many of the same people were wearing three-piece "power suits" as they sought to advance up the corporate ladder.

An example of how hairstyles can create meaningful symbolic codes can be seen in a group known as the Rastafarians (sometimes known as Rastas or Rastaman) of Jamaica. The majority of the people of Jamaica are of African descent. During the eighteenth and nineteenth centuries, they were brought to Jamaica by European slave traders to work on plantations. The Rastafarians are a specific religious group that believes Haile Selassie (1892–1975), the former emperor of Ethiopia whose original name was Ras Tafari, was the black Messiah who appeared in the flesh for the redemption of all blacks exiled in the world of white oppression. Rastafarian religion fuses Old Testament teachings, Christian mysticism, and Afro-Jamaican religious beliefs. The Rastafarian movement originated as a consequence of harsh economic, political, and living conditions in the slums of Jamaica.

In the 1950s, during the early phase of the Rastafarian movement, some male members began to grow their hair in "locks" or "dreadlocks" to symbolize their religious and political commitments. This hairstyle became well known in Western society through reggae music and Rasta musicians such as the late Bob Marley. Rastafarians derive the symbolism of their dreadlock hairstyle from the Bible. They view the unshaven man as the natural man and invoke Samson as one of the most important figures in the Bible. Dreadlocks also reflect a dominant symbol within the Rastafarian movement—the lion—which is associated with Haile Selassie, one of whose titles was the "Conquering Lion of Judah." To simulate the spirit of the lion, some Rastas do not cut their hair, sometimes growing their locks 20 inches or more.

Bob Marley (1945–1981), a Rastafarian musician.

Daniel Lainé/Corbis

In addition, the dreadlock hairstyle has a deeper symbolic significance in Jamaican society, where hair was often referred to as an index of racial and social inequality. Fine, silky hair was considered "good," whereas woolly, kinky hair was frowned upon (Barrett 1977). The white person with fine, silky hair was considered higher on the social ladder than was the typical African descendant in Jamaica. Thus, the Rastafarian hairstyle is a defiant symbol of resistance to the cultural values and norms of Jamaican society.

Rastafarian dreadlocks and long beards symbolize savagery, wildness, danger, disorder, and degeneration. They send the message that Rastafarians are outside of Jamaican society. Many Jamaicans view the dreadlocks as unkempt, dangerous, and dirty, yet to the Rastafarians, dreadlocks symbolize power, liberation, and defiance. Through their hairstyle, they announce to society that they do not accept the values, beliefs, and norms of the majority of the people.

Thus, to a great extent, culture consists of a network of symbolic codes that enhance values, beliefs, worldviews, norms, and ideologies within a society. Humans go to great lengths to create symbols that provide meaning for individuals and groups. These symbolic meanings are a powerful source of cultural diversity. When anthropologists study these symbolic codes and meanings, they often draw upon the humanistic-interpretive approach to comprehend these phenomena.

Ethnicity

One important aspect of culture is the recognition of one's own group as distinct from another based on different values, beliefs, norms, and other characteristics. When referring to these differences, anthropologists use the terms *ethnic group* and *ethnicity*. **Ethnicity** is based upon perceived differences in ancestral origins or descent and upon shared historical and cultural heritage. An **ethnic group** is a collectivity of people who believe they share a common history, culture, or ancestry. For example, a small ethnic group known as the Old Order Amish maintains very strong ethnic boundary markers in U.S. society (Hostetler 1980; Kephart and Zellner 1994). Amish ethnicity originated in Switzerland during the sixteenth century. The Old Order Amish descended from a group of Anabaptists who split off with their own leadership during the Protestant Reformation. After this split, the Amish began to define themselves as different from other Anabaptists, Protestants, and Catholics, and they faced a great deal of persecution from the religious authorities (Kephart and Zellner 1994; Kraybill 2001). Eventually, the Amish fled to the United States in the 1700s, settling first in Lancaster, Pennsylvania. From there, they have grown in number and live in twenty different states in the United States. Today, the Amish population is about 227,000 with about 50,000 in Ohio, 40,000 in Pennsylvania, and smaller numbers in 17 different states. There are no longer any Amish living in Europe.

The Old Order Amish in the United States emphasize their ethnic difference through language by speaking a German dialect within their communities. The Amish dress in a traditional manner similar to that prescribed by the cultural codes of the 1600s. Men wear hats and have long beards; women have long hair, which is always covered by a hat in public. Based upon their interpretation of the Bible, the Amish strive to maintain a conservative, traditional way of life that does not allow the adoption of modern technology such as electricity, automobiles, or television. They do not allow their children to be educated beyond the eighth grade so that they are not exposed to modern U.S. culture. The Amish have an extremely emotional attachment to their ethnicity and culture. These sentiments are deeply rooted within Amish culture and are evident in their language, dress, and traditional style of life, which distinguish them from other North Americans.

We will discuss many different ethnic groups throughout the various chapters in this text, and in Chapter 23 we elaborate on how anthropologists have developed methods to investigate the complexities of ethnicity, ethnic groups, and ethnic movements around the world.

Cultural Universals

As previously discussed, early anthropologists emphasized the realities of cultural diversity in their research and writings. Some anthropologists, however, began to recognize that humans throughout the world share some fundamental behavioral characteristics. George Murdock, an anthropologist who devoted himself to cross-cultural analysis, compiled a lengthy list of cultural universals from hundreds of societies. **Cultural universals** are

An Amish family.

Godong Godong/Photolibrary.com

essential behavioral characteristics of societies, and they are found all over the world. Murdock's list of cultural universals can be seen in Table 1; it includes such basics as language, cooking, family, folklore, games, community organization, decorative art, education, ethics, mythology, food taboos, numerals, personal names, magic, religious rituals, puberty customs, toolmaking, and sexual restrictions. Although the specific content and practices of these universals may vary from society to society, the fact that these cultural universals exist underlies the essential reality that modern humans are of one biological family and one species.

In an influential book entitled *Human Universals* (1991), anthropologist Donald E. Brown suggests that in their quest to describe cultural diversity, many anthropologists have overlooked basic similarities in human behavior and culture. This has led to stereotypes and distortions about people in other societies, who are viewed as "exotic," "inscrutable," and "alien."

Following in Murdock's footsteps, Brown describes many human universals. In one imaginative chapter, Brown creates a group of people he refers to as the "Universal People," who have all the traits of any people in

Donald E. Brown.

any society throughout the world. The Universal People have language with a complex grammar to communicate and think abstractly; kinship terms and categories to distinguish relatives and age groupings; gender terms for male and female; facial expressions to show basic emotions; a concept of the self as subject and object; tools, shelter, and fire; patterns for childbirth and training; families and political groupings; conflict; etiquette; morality, religious beliefs, and worldviews; and dance, music, art, and other aesthetic standards. Brown's depiction of the Universal People clearly suggests that these and many other aspects of human behavior result from certain problems that threaten the physical and social survival of all societies. For a society to survive, it must have mechanisms to care for children, adapt to the physical environment, produce and

Table 1   Cultural Universals Described by Anthropologist George Murdock

age grading	faith healing	joking	pregnancy usages
athletics	family	kin groups	property rights
bodily adornments	feasting	kin terminology	propitiation of supernatural beings
calendar	fire making	language	puberty customs
community organization	folklore	magic	religious rituals
cooking	food taboos	marriage	residence rules
cooperative labor	funeral rites	mealtimes	sexual restrictions
cosmology	games	medicine	soul concepts
courtship	gestures	modesty	status differentiation
dancing	gift giving	mourning	toolmaking
decorative art	greetings	music	trade
division of labor	hairstyles	mythology	visiting
dream interpretation	hospitality	numerals	weaning
education	housing	obstetrics	weather control
ethics	hygiene	personal names	
ethnobotany	incest taboos	population policy	
etiquette	inheritance	postnatal care	

Source: Adapted from George Peter Murdock, "The Common Denominator of Cultures." In *The Science of Man in the World Crisis*, edited by Ralph Linton. Copyright © 1945 by Columbia University Press. Reproduced with permission of Columbia University Press in the format textbook via Copyright Clearance Center.

distribute goods and services, maintain order, and provide explanations of the natural and social environment. In addition, many universal behaviors result from fundamental biological characteristics common to all people.

Anthropologists have discovered that culture can be both diverse and universal. The challenge for anthropology is to understand the basis of both this diversity and this universality. To paraphrase the late anthropologist Clyde Kluckhohn: "Every human is like all other humans, some other humans, and no other human." The major objective of cultural anthropology is to investigate the validity of this statement.

Summary

Culture is a key concept in anthropology. Culture is learned and is transmitted from generation to generation in a society. Humans learn through direct experience (situational learning), observation (social learning), and symbols (symbolic learning). Symbols are arbitrary meanings that vary from society to society. Many anthropologists view symbolic learning as the major distinction between human and nonhuman animals.

Culture includes material and nonmaterial components. The material aspect of culture consists of tools, clothing, shelter, armaments, and other innovations that enable humans to adapt to their environments. The nonmaterial components of culture are values, beliefs, norms, and ideologies.

Different societies maintain different cultural and symbolic structures, creating the great variety and diversity of norms, values, worldviews, and behaviors. Cultural anthropologists have discovered that cultural items—ranging from dress to technology to sexual practices to dietary habits—are enormously diverse. Anthropologists also recognize that many patterns of human behavior are universal. The universal distribution of certain cultural traits suggests that humans everywhere have similar biological requirements and tendencies that influence behavior. Thus, anthropologists have been engaged in exploring both the diversity and the similarity of human cultures throughout the world.

Questions to Think About

1. How do anthropologists differentiate culture from nonhuman animal behavior?

2. As a college student, you have probably heard about cultural diversity or multiculturalism and the changing demographics in the United States. What is multiculturalism? Why is it important to understand this concept? Are there any dangers in implementing multicultural education programs?

3. Using an anthropological perspective, explain the statement "You are what you eat."

4. After reading the section on dress codes and symbolism, pick another example of a form of dress or hairstyle and explain what it symbolizes to the individuals involved.

5. Can you distinguish ethnic groups from each other in your own society? How do you make that distinction?

6. If you were to create the Universal People, how would they behave and organize themselves? What would they believe? And how might they act?

7. Interpret the statement, "Every human is like all other humans, some other humans, and no other human."

Key Terms

beliefs	ethnic group	mores	situational learning
cultural hegemony	ethnicity	nonmaterial culture	social learning
cultural relativism	folkways	norms	society
cultural universals	ideal culture	real culture	symbolic learning
culture	ideology	schemas	symbols
enculturation	material culture	signs	values

Read the Original Source on myanthrolab.com

For further information about topics covered in this chapter, go to MyAnthroLab at www.myanthrolab.com and access the following readings in MyAnthroLibrary:

Douglas Raybeck, *Do the Wrong Thing: Variation in Deviance.*

Jon D. Holtzman and Nancy Foner, *Nuer Journeys, Nuer Lives: Sudanese Refugees in Minnesota* (Part of the New Immigrants Series).

Johanna Lessinger and Nancy Foner, *From the Ganges to the Hudson: Indian Immigrants in New York City* (Part of the New Immigrants Series).

Rosemary Gartner Crime: *Variations across Cultures and Nations.*

Marc Howard Ross, *Ethnocentrism and Ethnic Conflict.*

Applied Anthropology

Hamilton Wright/Photo Researchers Inc.

Applied Anthropology

Chapter Questions

- **What** types of projects are conducted by applied anthropologists?

- **What** are the different roles of applied anthropologists in various projects?

- **What** type of research is identified with medical anthropology?

- **How** are archaeologists involved in applied anthropology?

- **How** have applied anthropologists become involved in human rights research?

((•—[**Listen** to the **Chapter Audio** on **myanthrolab.com**

Anthropologists conduct research in the four basic subfields of the discipline: physical anthropology, archaeology, linguistics, and ethnology. Within these fields, different specializations have emerged that allow for the gathering of data and the testing and evaluation of specific hypotheses regarding human societies and behavior. One of the most important developments in the field of anthropology has been the growth of **applied anthropology**, the use of anthropological data to offer practical solutions to modern problems and concerns. This chapter introduces some of the issues that have been addressed by applied anthropologists.

The Roles of the Applied Anthropologist

The popular, if not accurate, images of anthropologists vary from the adventurous explorer seeking out lost treasure to the absent-minded academic working away in the dusty halls of a university or museum. These perspectives do not provide a valid picture of the modern anthropologist. Anthropologists are increasingly engaged in a variety of activities that have direct relevance to the modern world. Rather than being confined to the halls of the university, an increasing number of anthropologists have become practitioners of anthropology.

Distinguishing applied anthropology from other anthropological pursuits in many respects presents a false dichotomy. Methodological and theoretical concerns are shared by all; the difference lies in perceptions of the practitioners' objectives, an arbitrary division based on the practicality of the intended outcomes. As Bronislaw Malinowski observed more than sixty years ago: "Unfortunately, there is still a strong but erroneous opinion in some circles that practical anthropology is fundamentally different from theoretical

or academic anthropology. The truth is that science begins with application....What is application in science and when does 'theory' become practical? When it first allows us a definite grip on empirical reality" (1945:5).

The work of many anthropologists can be seen as applied in some sense. In an overview of applied anthropology, Erve Chambers (1985) classified the different roles of applied anthropologists. Although he was primarily concerned with the applied aspects of cultural anthropology, his observations are equally relevant to the work of physical anthropologists and archaeologists. One role noted by Chambers is that of *representative*, in which the anthropologist becomes the spokesperson for the particular group being studied. Anthropologists at times have represented Native American communities in negotiations with state and federal authorities, mining companies, and development organizations. Anthropologists can also be seen as *facilitators*. In this capacity, anthropologists actively help bring about change or development in the community being researched. For example, they may take a proactive, participatory role in economic or social change to improve medical care, education, or public facilities. An alternative position is the *informant role*, in which the applied anthropologist transfers cultural knowledge obtained from anthropological research to the government or other agency that wants to promote change in a particular area. The U.S. government has employed anthropologists as on-site researchers to provide data on how local-level service clients and delivery agencies respond to government policy. Informally, many archaeologists and anthropologists become involved in local activities and educational programs that present anthropological findings to the public.

Yet another role of applied anthropologists is that of *analyst*. Rather than being just a provider of data, the practicing anthropologist sometimes becomes engaged in the actual formulation of policy. In archaeology, in particular, this has become an important area with the passage of the National Historic Preservation Act in 1966, the Native American Graves Repatriation Act of 1990, and other related legislation. These laws have afforded increased protection to some archaeological resources and mandated the consideration of archaeological resources in planning development. Archaeologists have increasingly found employment in federal, state, or local governments reviewing proposals for development and construction projects that impact cultural resources and archaeological sites. Another role Chambers identified is that of *mediator*, which involves the anthropologist as an intermediary among different interest groups that are participating in a development project. This may include private developers, government officials, and the people who will be affected by the project. As mediator, the anthropologist must try to reconcile differences among these groups, facilitating compromises that ideally will benefit all parties involved in the project. The following discussions highlight some of the applied work that physical anthropologists and archaeologists are engaged.

Physical Anthropology

As seen in the preceding chapters, physical anthropologists deal with the biological aspects of humans and human ancestors in the past and the present. Much of the basic information gathered consists of the measurement, observation, and explanation of various physical characteristics. Anthropometry, for example, concerns the measurement of human body parts, and osteometry is the measurement of skeletal elements. This information is basic to the interpretation of fossil hominids as well as human remains recovered from archaeological sites. However, some of this information has immediate relevance to the present. Such information may be used in combination with engineering data to design ergonomically efficient airplane cockpits, work environments, or equipment. Such data may also provide an important aid to police in murder investigations or the identification of disaster victims. Physical anthropological study of the causes of diseases, when combined with knowledge of cultural anthropology, offers important insight into perceptions of medical treatment in different cultural settings. Some of these examples of practicing anthropologists are considered in this section.

Forensic Anthropology

A fragmentary skeleton is accidentally found in a desolate part of the desert. Through a series of twists and turns, an enterprising detective pieces together clues to a twenty-year-old murder and brings a fugitive to justice. Such a scenario is the stuff of mystery novels, but real-life criminal investigations often do depend upon the identification of fragmentary skeletal remains. **Forensic anthropology** can be defined as the application of physical anthropological data to law. Physical anthropologists in this area of specialization are often called to assist police when unidentified human remains are found. Whereas medical doctors focus on the soft tissues, forensic anthropologists study the hard tissues—the skeletal remains (Isçan and Kennedy 1989; Reichs 1998; Steadman 2003). Analysis of such material would begin by reconstructing the skeleton and joining together the often fragmentary and broken remains. Missing pieces might be reconstructed or estimated. The materials are then carefully measured and compared to anthropological data. Such research can yield the sex, approximate age, height, and physical characteristics of an individual.

The skeleton also provides a record of medical problems, illnesses, and the overall health of a person. The bones may preserve information about a person's health at the time of death, as well as the living conditions and health problems the individual faced during his or her lifetime. For example, broken bones, although healed, still leave a trace on the skeleton. Arthritis, certain infections, dietary stress, and nutrition may also be in evidence. This kind of information may provide insight into living conditions in the distant human past, as, for example, when considering the consequences of domestication (see Chapter 8), but it also provides details that may be very helpful to the police in identifying victims. Unidentified skeletal remains from a white female, 5'4" to 5'6", 40 to 45 years of age, with a healed fracture of the left leg and traces of arthritis in the hands, would dramatically reduce the number of potential fits with reported missing persons files.

A specialized area within forensic anthropology deals specifically with the reconstruction of faces (Prag and Neave 1997). Using average skin depth, muscle patterns, and knowledge about the skeleton, the researcher can create an image of what a person looked like when alive. This interdisciplinary work draws on information from anatomy, facial surgery, pathology, dentistry, and the skills of an artist, as well as physical anthropology. Reconstruction of a face based solely on information provided by the skull may be done using a computer or may be sketched by an artist, but researchers also rely on a detailed model of a skull, which they then cover with clay. Muscles of clay are sculpted over the skull and covered with additional clay, which represents the overlying tissues. The thickness of the skin covering the skull is based on average thickness at different points of the skull, estimated for individuals of different ages, sexes, body builds, and ethnic groups. A final model is

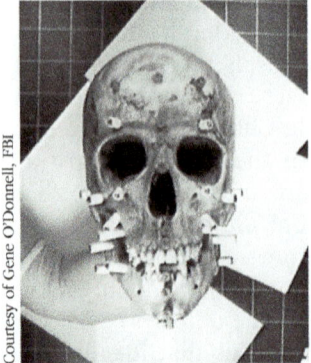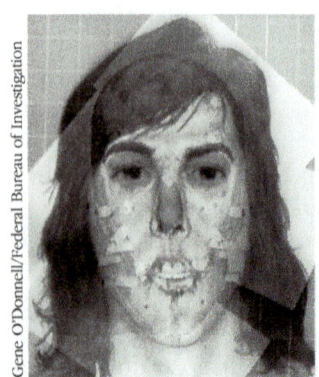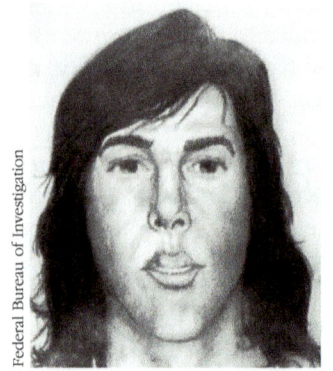

A specialized area of forensic anthropology deals with the reconstruction of facial features. The photographs illustrate (from left) the victim's skull, a reconstruction of the face, a sketch based on the reconstruction, and a photograph of how the victim actually appeared in life.

Source: Courtesy of Gene O'Donnell, FBI.

Anthropologists at Work

CLYDE COLLINS SNOW: Forensic Anthropologist

Clyde Collins Snow obtained a master's degree in zoology from Texas Technical University and planned to pursue a Ph.D. in physiology, but his career plans were interrupted by military service. While stationed at Lackland Air Force Base near San Antonio, he was introduced to the field of archaeology and became fascinated with the ancient artifacts discovered in the surrounding area.

After leaving the military, Snow attended the University of Arizona, where his zoological training and archaeology interests led him to a Ph.D. in physical anthropology. He became skilled at identifying old bones and artifacts. With his doctoral degree completed, he joined the Federal Aviation Administration as a consulting forensic anthropologist, providing technical assistance in the identification of victims of aircraft accidents. Snow also lent his expertise to the design of safety equipment to prevent injuries in aircraft accidents.

As word of Snow's extraordinary skill in forensic anthropology spread, he was called to consult on and provide expert testimony in many criminal cases. His testimony was crucial at the sensational murder trial of John Wayne Gacy, accused of murdering more than thirty teenagers in the Chicago area. Snow also collaborated with experts in the reinvestigation of President John F. Kennedy's assassination. These experts built a full-scale model of Kennedy's head to determine whether Lee Harvey Oswald could have inflicted all of

Dr. Clyde Snow

AP Photo/Victor Ruiz C

Kennedy's wounds. They did not uncover any scientific evidence to contradict the Warren Commission's conclusion that Oswald was the sole assassin.

More recently, Snow and his team have been recognized for their contributions to human rights issues. Snow served as a consultant to the Argentine government's National Commission on Disappeared Persons in its efforts to determine the fate of thousands of Argentineans who were abducted and murdered by military death squads between 1976 and 1983, when the country was under the rule of a military dictatorship. As a result of his investigations, Snow was asked to testify as an expert witness in the trial of the nine junta members who ruled Argentina during the period of military repression. He also assisted people in locating their dead relatives.

Snow stresses that in his human rights investigative work he is functioning as an expert, not necessarily as an advocate. He must maintain an objective standpoint in interpreting his findings. The evidence he finds may then be presented by lawyers (as advocates) in the interests of justice. Snow's human rights work is supported by various agencies, such as the American Association of Advanced Sciences, the Ford Foundation, the J. Roderick MacArthur Foundation, Amnesty International, Physicians for Human Rights, and Human Rights Watch (Mann and Holland 2004).

✳ **Explore** the **Concept** on
myanthrolab.com

prepared using plaster of Paris, which is colored and given hair. Although the final product may not be an exact portrait, the resemblance to the living individual has proven remarkable. Techniques such as these, whether using a pen and ink, a computer, or plaster models, help police put flesh on the bones and can be invaluable in investigations.

Forensic anthropology may also offer important clues about the circumstances of a person's death and the treatment of the body after death (Haglund and Sorg 1997). Damage or trauma to the bones may provide a primary indicator of the cause of death. For example, bullet wounds, stabbings, and blunt-force trauma may be identified in skeletal remains. Careful study of the skeleton may also indicate whether an individual was killed where the body was found or at another location and then, transported to the site. Forensic anthropologists may be able to determine whether the body was disturbed or transported after burial. Such information may be extremely important in determining the cause of death. As in the case of archaeological and paleontological investigations, the *context* of the findings is very important. Hence, physical anthropologists with archaeological training can help ensure that all of the remains are recovered.

Because the cause of death may be central to a murder investigation and trial, the forensic anthropologist is often called upon to testify as an expert witness. In such cases, the forensic anthropologist impartially presents his or her findings that may prove or disprove the identity or cause of death of the victim. The ultimate concern of the forensic anthropologist is not the outcome of the trial, but the evidence provided by the skeletal remains. The amount of information extracted from skeletal remains can be surprising. Many illustrations from actual criminal cases can be recounted (Stewart 1979; Rathbun and Buikstra 1984). For example, fractures of the hyoid or the thyroid, a small bone and ossified cartilage of the throat, may indicate strangulation. The location and kind of breaks may offer clues to the type of weapon used, as well as the position of the attacker relative to the victim. In the vein

of a Sherlock Holmes novel, it may actually be possible to determine that a fatal blow was struck from behind by a right-handed assailant.

Both archaeology and forensic anthropology played key roles in the John McRae case (Sauer et al. 2003). In 1997, police in northern Michigan were called when a farmworker uncovered human skeletal remains while excavating a refuse pit with a backhoe. On the basis of dental records, the police soon identified the victim as Randy Laufer, a 15-year-old boy who had disappeared 11 years previously. The boy had been last seen when he left school to visit a friend. The principal suspect in the case was the friend's father, John McRae, who had owned the land where the bones were recovered and who had been convicted of the murder of another young boy. At the time of their discovery, the bones were fragmentary and devoid of flesh. More significantly, they had not been recovered under ideal conditions. Archaeological investigations were carried out to recover any remaining bones, locate the original burial pit, and reconstruct the location of structures that had been on the property when McRae owned the property. Dr. Steven Symes, a leading authority on the interpretation of cut marks on bones, was consulted to evaluate cut marks found on the bone and determine the cause of death. Both the archaeological evidence and physical anthropological evidence proved crucial in bringing McRae to justice. Archaeological excavation established that the body

Excavation of the burial site of civilians who were killed by government troops at El Morote, El Salvador, during the country's civil war in the 1980s. Forensic anthropologists often play an important role in the identification of victims of natural disasters, airplane crashes, wars, and genocide.

had likely been buried no more than 15 feet from the front door of McRae's trailer, beneath a gravel driveway or just inside an adjacent barn. The skeletal evidence established Laufer's identity and also that he had been mutilated at the time of death. The osteological evidence indicated that the cuts and trauma to the bone did not result from their accidental excavation, but occurred at about the time of death. The boy had been stabbed or hacked in the left shoulder and between the neck and shoulder, and his body cut in half.

Forensic anthropologists have also played important roles in the identification of victims of natural disasters, airplane crashes, war, bombings, and genocide (Stewart 1970; Stover 1981, 1992; Snow et al. 1989; Snow and Bihurriet 1992; Steadman 2003). Many of the methods and techniques used by modern forensic anthropologists were needed during and after World War II to assist with the identification and repatriation of the remains of soldiers killed in battle. This remained an important role for forensic anthropologists during the Korean and Vietnam wars (Stewart 1979; Mann et al. 2003). In these cases, the physical remains recovered are matched against the life histories provided by medical and dental records. In some instances, the positive identification may be dependent on relatively minor variation in bony structures. The role of physical anthropologists in locating and identifying American soldiers killed or missing in action in Vietnam continues to this day. Forensic anthropologists and archaeologists have assisted in the documentation of human rights abuses and recovery of victims from mass graves in Argentina, Brazil, Croatia, El Salvador, Haiti, Iraq, Rwanda, and other world areas.

Konstantnin/Shutterstock.com

Medical Anthropology

Another subfield of anthropology, **medical anthropology**, represents the intersection of cultural anthropology with physical anthropology. Medical anthropologists may study disease, medicine, curing, and mental illness in a cross-cultural perspective. Some focus specifically on **epidemiology**, which examines the spread and distribution of diseases and how they are influenced by cultural patterns. For example, these anthropologists may be able to determine whether coronary (heart) disease or cancer is related to particular cultural or social dietary habits, such as the consumption of foods high in sodium or saturated fats. They also study cultural perceptions of illness and their treatment. These studies can often help health providers design more effective means for delivering health care and formulating health care policies (Schell and Denham 2003).

An illustration of medical anthropology is the work of Louis Golomb (1985), who conducted ethnographic research on curing practices in Thailand. Golomb did research on Buddhist and Muslim medical practitioners who rely on native spiritualistic beliefs to diagnose and cure diseases. These practices are based on earlier Hindu, magical, and animistic beliefs that had been syncretized with Buddhist and Muslim traditions. Practitioners draw on astrology, faith healing, massage, folk psychotherapy, exorcism, herbs, and charms and amulets to treat patients. The most traditional practitioners are curer-magicians, or shamans, who diagnose and treat every illness as an instance of spirit possession or spirit attack. Other practitioners are more skeptical of the supernatural causation of illness and diagnose health problems in reference to natural or organic causes. They frequently use herbal medicines to treat illnesses.

Golomb discovered that although Western-based scientific forms of medicine may be available, many Thais still rely on traditional practitioners. He found that even urban-educated elite, including those who had studied in the United States and other Western countries, adhered to both supernatural and scientific views. Golomb referred to this as *therapeutic pluralism*. He observed that patients do not rely on any single therapeutic approach, but rather use a combination of therapies that include elements of ritual, magic, and modern scientific medications. Parasites or germs are rarely seen as the only explanations of disease; a sick person may go to a clinic to receive medication to relieve symptoms, but may then seek out a traditional curer for a more complete treatment. Golomb emphasized that the multiplicity of alternative therapies encourages people to play an active role in preserving their health.

In Thailand, as in many other countries undergoing modernization and globalization, modern medical facilities have been established based upon the scientific treatment of disease. Golomb found that personnel in these facilities are critical of traditional medical practices. Nevertheless, he discovered that although the people in the villages often respect the modern doctor's ability to diagnose diseases and prescribe medications to relieve symptoms, in most cases they do not accept the scientific explanation of the disease. In addition, villagers feel that modern medical methods are brusque and impersonal, because doctors do not offer any psychological or spiritual consolation. Doctors also do not make house calls and rarely spend much time with patients. This impersonality in the doctor–patient relationship is also due to social status differences based on wealth, education, and power. Golomb found that many public health personnel expected deference from their rural clientele. For these reasons, many people preferred to rely on traditional curers.

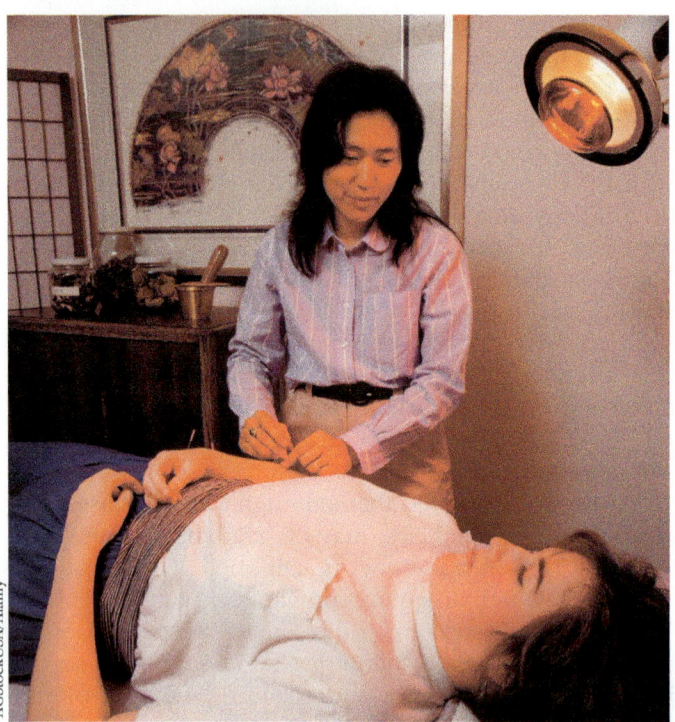

Medical anthropologists do studies to help improve basic health care delivery in countries around the world.

Through his study of traditional medical techniques and beliefs, Golomb isolated some of the strengths and weaknesses of modern medical treatment in Thailand. His work contributed to a better understanding of how to deliver health care services to rural and urban Thais. For example, the Thai Ministry of Public Health began to experiment with ways of coordinating the efforts of modern and traditional medical practitioners. Village midwives and traditional herbalists were called on to dispense modern medications and pass out information about nutrition and hygiene. Some Thai hospitals have established training sessions for traditional practitioners to learn modern medical techniques. Golomb's studies in medical anthropology offer a model for practical applications in the health field for other developing societies. This type of ethnographic study that combines globalization approaches with in-depth local cultural knowledge is an example of ongoing anthropological attempts to assist in solving practical problems for humanity.

Interventions in Substance Abuse

Another area of research and policy formulation for applied medical anthropologists is substance abuse, many of the causes of which may be explained by social and cultural factors. For example, Michael Agar (1973, 1974) did an in-depth study of heroin addicts based upon the addicts' description of U.S. society and its therapeutic agencies in particular. His research involved taking on the role of a patient himself so that he could participate in some of the problems that exist between patients and staff. From that perspective he was better able to understand the "junkie" worldview.

Through his research, Agar isolated problems in the treatment of heroin addiction. He found that when the drug methadone was administered by public health officials as a substitute for heroin, many heroin addicts not in treatment became addicted to methadone, which was sold on the streets by patients. This street methadone would often be combined with wine and pills to gain a "high." In some cases, street methadone began to rival heroin as the preferred drug, being less expensive than heroin, widely available, and in a form that could be taken orally rather than injected. By providing this information, Agar helped health officials monitor their programs more effectively.

In a more recent study, Philippe Bourgois spent three and a half years investigating the use of crack cocaine in Spanish Harlem in New York City. In his award-winning ethnography, *In Search of Respect: Selling Crack in El Barrio* (1996), Bourgois noted that policymakers and drug-enforcement officials minimize the influences of poverty and low status in dealing with crack addiction. Through his investigation of cultural norms and socio-economic conditions in Spanish Harlem, Bourgois demonstrated that crack dealers are struggling to earn money and status in the pursuit of the American dream. Despite the fact that many crack dealers have work experience, they find that many of the potential jobs in construction and factory work are reserved for non-Hispanics. In addition, unpleasant experiences in the job world lead many to perceive crack dealing as the most realistic route toward upward mobility. Most of the inner-city youths who deal crack are high school dropouts who do not regard entry-level, minimum-wage jobs as steps to better opportunities. In addition, they perceive the underground economy as an alternative to becoming subservient to the larger society. Crack dealing offers a sense of autonomy, position, and rapid short-term mobility.

Bourgois compared the use of crack to the feelings that people have in millenarian movements or other spiritual movements. As he observed:

Substance abuse in general, and crack in particular, offer the equivalent of a millenarian metamorphosis. Instantaneously, users are transformed from being unemployed, depressed high school dropouts, despised by the world—and secretly convinced that their failure is due to their own inherent stupidity, "racial laziness," and disorganization—into being a mass of heart-palpitating pleasure, followed only minutes later by a jaw-gnashing crash and wide-awake alertness that provides their life with concrete purpose: get more crack—fast! (1989b:11)

Bourgois's depictions of the culture and economy of crack dealers and users provided useful policy suggestions. He concluded that most accounts of crack addiction deflect attention away from the economic and social conditions of the inner city and that, by focusing on the increases of violence and terror associated with crack, U.S. society is

Andy Bullock/The Image Bank/Getty Images

Some applied anthropologists have been doing studies of drug addiction to assist agencies in the prevention of drug use.

absolved from responsibility for inner-city problems. He suggested that rather than use this "blame-the-victim" approach, officials and policymakers need to revise their attitudes and help develop programs that resolve the conditions that encourage crack use.

Applied Archaeology

One of the problems that humanity faces is how to safeguard the cultural heritage preserved in the archaeological record. Although archaeology may address questions of general interest to all of humanity, it is also important in promoting national heritage, cultural identity, and ethnic pride. Museums the world over offer displays documenting a diversity of local populations, regional histories, important events, and cultural traditions. The number of specialized museums focusing on particular peoples, regions, or historic periods has become increasingly important. Archaeologists must be concerned with the preservation of archaeological sites and the recovery of information from sites threatened with destruction, as well as the interpretation and presentation of their findings to the more general public.

Preservation of the past is a challenge to archaeologists, government officials, and the concerned public alike, as archaeological sites are being destroyed at an alarming rate. Archaeological materials naturally decay in the ground, and sites are constantly destroyed through geological processes, erosion, and animal burrowing. Yet, while natural processes contribute to the disappearance of archaeological sites, by far the greatest threat to the archaeological record is human activity. Construction projects such as dams, roads, buildings, and pipelines all disturb the ground and can destroy archaeological sites in the process. In many instances, archaeologists work only a few feet ahead of construction equipment, trying to salvage any information they can before a site disappears forever.

Some archaeological sites are intentionally destroyed by collectors searching for artifacts that have value in the antiquities market, such as arrowheads and pottery. Statues from ancient Egypt, Mayan terra cotta figurines, and Native American pottery may be worth thousands of dollars on the antiques market. To fulfill the demands, archaeological sites in many world areas are looted by pot hunters, who dig to retrieve artifacts for collectors, ignoring the traces of ancient housing, burials, and cooking hearths. Removed from their context, with no record of where they came from, such artifacts are of limited value to archaeologists. The rate of destruction of North American archaeological sites is such that some researchers have estimated that 98 percent of sites predating the year 2000 will be destroyed by the middle of the twenty-first century (Herscher 1989; Knudson 1989).

The rate at which archaeological sites are being destroyed is particularly distressing because the archaeological record is an irreplaceable, *nonrenewable* resource. That is, after sites are destroyed, they are gone forever, along with the unique information about the past that they contained. In many parts of the world, recognition of this fact has led to legislation aimed at protecting archaeological sites (see Table 1). The rational for this legislation is that the past has value to the present and, hence, should be protected and interpreted for the benefit of the public.

Preserving the Past

Recognition of the value and nonrenewable nature of archaeological resources is the first step in a planning process. Archaeological resources can then be systematically identified and evaluated. Steps can be taken to preserve them by limiting development or designing projects in a way that will preserve the resource. For example, the projected path of a new road might be moved to avoid an archaeological site or a building might be planned so that the foundations do not extend into a historic burial ground (see the photos of the African burial ground). Alternatively, if a site must be destroyed, effective planning can ensure that information about the site is recovered by archaeologists prior to its destruction.

Table 1 Major Federal Legislation for the Protection of Archaeological Resources in the United States

Antiquities Act of 1906	Protects sites on federal lands
Historic Sites Act of 1935	Provides authority for designating National Historic Landmarks and for archaeological surveys before destruction by development programs
National Historic Preservation Act of 1966 (amended 1976 and 1980)	Strengthens protection of sites on a National Register and integrates state and local agencies into a nationalprogram for site preservation
National Environmental Policy Act of 1969	Requires all federal agencies to specify the impact of development programs on cultural resources
Archaeological Resources Protection Act of 1979	Provides criminal and civil penalties for looting or damaging sites on public and Native American lands
Convention on Cultural Property of 1982	Authorizes U.S. participation in 1970 UNESCO conventions to prevent illegal international trade in cultural property
Cultural Property Act of 1983	Provides sanctions against U.S. import or export of illicit antiquities
Abandoned Shipwreck Act of 1988	Removes sunken ships of archaeological interest from marine salvage jurisdiction; provides protection under state jurisdiction
Native American Graves Protection and Repatriation Act of 1990 (NAGPRA)	Specifies return of Native American remains and cultural property to Native American groups by U.S. museums

Source: From *Discovering Our Past: A Brief Introduction to Archaeology* by Wendy Ashmore and Robert J. Sharer. Copyright ©2003 by Mayfield Publishing Company. Reprinted by permission of the publisher.

One of the most spectacular examples of salvage archaeology arose as a result of the construction of a dam across the Nile River at Aswan, Egypt, in the 1960s. The project offered many benefits, including water for irrigation and the generation of electricity. However, the rising water behind the dam threatened thousands of archaeological sites that had lain undisturbed and safely buried by desert sand for thousands of years. The Egyptian government appealed to the international community and archaeologists from around the world to mount projects to locate and excavate the threatened sites.

Among the sites that were to be flooded by the dam was the temple of Pharaoh Ramses II at Abu Simbel, a huge monument consisting of four colossal figures carved from a cliff face on the banks of the Nile River. With help from the United Nations Educational, Scientific, and Cultural Organization (UNESCO), the Egyptian government was able to cut the monument into more than a thousand pieces, some weighing as much as 33 tons, and reassemble them above the floodwaters. Today, the temple of Ramses can be seen completely restored only a few hundred feet from its original location. Numerous other archaeological sites threatened by the flooding of the Nile were partly salvaged or recorded. Unfortunately, countless other sites could not be located or even recorded before they were flooded.

The first legislation in the United States designed to protect historic sites was the Antiquities Act of 1906, which safeguarded archaeological sites on federal lands (see Table 1). Other, more recent legislation, such as the National Historic Preservation Act passed in 1966, has extended protection to sites threatened by projects that are funded or regulated by the government. The federal Abandoned Shipwreck Act of 1988 gives states jurisdiction over shipwreck sites. This legislation has had a dramatic impact on the number of archaeologists in the United States and has created a new area of specialization, generally referred to as **cultural resource management (CRM)**. Whereas most archaeologists had traditionally found employment teaching or working in museums, many are now working as applied archaeologists, evaluating, salvaging, and protecting archaeological resources that are threatened with destruction. Applied archaeologists conduct surveys before construction begins to determine if any sites will be affected. Government agencies such as the United States Forest Service have developed comprehensive programs to discover, record, protect, and interpret archaeological resources on their lands (Johnson and Schene 1987).

Unfortunately, current legislation in the United States leaves many archaeological resources unprotected. In many countries, excavated artifacts, even those located on privately owned land, become the property of the government. This is not the case in the United States. One example of the limitations of the existing legislation is provided by the case of Slack Farm, located near

Located just blocks from Wall Street in New York City, an eighteenth-century African burial ground was accidentally uncovered during construction of a federal office building in 1991. The 427 burials excavated at the site are testament to the enslaved Africans that made up the second largest slave population in colonial America. As many as 20,000 individuals may have been buried at the site. Following discovery, local community protests over the treatment and interpretation of the remains led to a delay in construction, modification of the construction plan, and the increased involvement of African-American researchers in the analysis of the finds.

Source: Courtesy of the General Services Administration.

Uniontown, Kentucky (Arden 1989). Archaeologists had long known that an undisturbed Native American site of the Late Mississippian period was located on the property. Dating roughly to between 1450 and 1650, the site was particularly important because it was the only surviving Mississippian site from the period of first contact with Europeans. The Slack family, who had owned the land for many years, protected the site and prevented people from digging (Arden 1989). When the property was sold in 1988, however, conditions changed. Anthropologist Brian Fagan described the results:

Ten pot hunters from Kentucky, Indiana, and Illinois paid the new owner of the land $10,000 for the right to "excavate" the site. They rented a tractor and began bulldozing their way through the village midden to reach graves. They pushed heaps of bones aside and dug through dwellings and potsherds, hearths, and stone tools associated with them. Along the way, they left detritus of their own—empty pop-top beer and soda cans—scattered on the ground alongside Late Mississippian pottery fragments. Today Slack Farm looks like a battlefield—a morass of crude shovel holes and gaping trenches. Broken human bones litter the ground, and fractured artifacts crunch underfoot. (1988:15)

The looting at the site was eventually stopped by the Kentucky State Police, using a state law that prohibits the desecration of human graves. Archaeologists went to the site attempting to salvage what information was

left, but there is no way of knowing how many artifacts were removed. The record of America's prehistoric past was irrevocably damaged.

Regrettably, the events at Slack Farm are not unique. Many states lack adequate legislation protecting archaeological sites on private land. For example, Arkansas had no laws protecting unmarked burial sites until 1991. As a result, Native American burial grounds were systematically mined for artifacts. In fact, one article written about the problem was titled "The Looting of Arkansas" (Harrington 1991a). Although Arkansas now has legislation prohibiting the unauthorized excavation of burial grounds, the professional archaeologists of the Arkansas Archaeological Survey face the impossible job of trying to locate and monitor all of the state's archaeological sites. This problem is not unique. Even on federal lands, the protection of sites is dependent on a relatively small number of park rangers and personnel to police large areas. Even in national parks, such as Mesa Verde or Yellowstone, archaeological sites are sometimes vandalized or looted for artifacts. Much of the success that there has been in protecting sites is largely due to the active involvement of amateur archaeologists and concerned citizens who bring archaeological remains to the attention of professionals.

The preservation of the past needs to be everyone's concern. Unfortunately, however well intended the legislation and efforts to provide protection for archaeological sites may be, they are rarely integrated into comprehensive management plans. For example, a particular county or city area might have a variety of sites and resources of historic significance identified using a variety of different criteria and presented in different lists and directories. These might include National Historic sites, designated through the National Historic Preservation office; state files of archaeological sites; data held by avocational archaeological organizations and clubs; and a variety of locations of historical importance identified by county or city historical societies. Other sites of potential historical significance might be identified through documentary research or oral traditions. Ideally, all of these sources of information should be integrated and used to plan development. Such comprehensive approaches to cultural resource management plans are rare rather than the norm.

Important strides have been taken in planning and coordinating efforts to identify and manage archaeological resources. Government agencies, including the National Park Service, the military, and various state agencies, have initiated plans to systematically identify and report sites on their properties. There have also been notable efforts to compile information at the county, state, and district levels. Such efforts are faced with imposing logistical concerns. For example, by the mid-1990s, over 180,000 historic and prehistoric archaeological sites had been identified in the American Southeast (including the states of Alabama, Arkansas, Florida, Georgia, Kentucky, Louisiana, Mississippi, North Carolina, South Carolina, and Tennessee). In addition, an estimated 10,000 new sites are discovered each year (Anderson and Horak 1995). A map of these resources reveals a great deal of variation in their concentration. On one hand, this diversity reflects the actual distribution of sites; on the other, it reflects the areas where archaeological research has and has not been undertaken. Incorporating the thousands of new site reports into the database requires substantial commitment of staff resources. What information should be recorded for each site? What computer resources are needed? The volume of information is difficult to process with available staff, and massive backlogs of reports waiting to be incorporated into the files often exist. Nevertheless, this kind of holistic perspective is needed to ensure effective site management and the compliance of developers with laws protecting archaeological sites. It also provides a holistic view of past land use that is of great use to archaeologists.

Cultural resource management is a worldwide concern, particularly in developing countries that often lack legislation and resources to protect archaeological sites, but simliar problems are faced in industrialized countries (Serageldin and Taboroff 1994; Schmidt and McIntosh 1996; Kankpeyeng and DeCorse 2004). On one hand, archaeological sites are looted for artifacts to be sold on the antiquities market. On the other hand, the priority given to development—including the construction of new housing, roads, and dams—often results in the destruction of archaeological sites. These facts are all the more troubling because some countries lack well-developed

archaeological traditions, and the archaeological past will be gone before anyone has the opportunity to study it. To address these concerns, UNESCO launched the "World Decade for Cultural Development" in 1988, which emphasized the need to consider cultural resource planning in development (Serageldin and Taboroff 1994).

Development and the management of archaeological resources can go hand in hand. While the material traces of the past—including archaeological resources, historic buildings, and cultural sites—may be important in promoting cultural heritage and national identity, many governments have also started to realize the potential economic worth of effective cultural resource management. Cultural tourism, arising out of the human fascination with the past, has become a major revenue source for some nations. The treatment of cultural heritage as a commodity is most obvious in Western Europe and the United States, but many countries in Asia, South America, and Mesoamerica have also capitalized on their cultural patrimony (e.g., Layton 1989; Ekechukwu 1990; Bruner 1996a, b).

A number of archaeologists throughout the world are using their skills to both preserve archaeological sites and improve the lives of modern inhabitants of the communities where the sites are located. In countries such as Guatemala, the location of a number of spectacular Mayan ruins, archaeologists are increasingly integrating economic development and environmental preservation into their research programs. The ancient Mayan sites pose special conservation concerns because of their size. For example, Chocolá, the focus of research by American archaeologist Jonathan Kaplan, has more than 60 mounds, large irrigation systems, and numerous monuments (Bawaya 2005). Information from the site has shed insight into the origins of Mayan civilization. Yet the farmers of modern Chocolá, descendants of the ancient Maya, face poverty and disease. In the face of such modern needs, the preservation of ancient monuments and the surrounding environment is of limited concern.

The past cannot be preserved without addressing the concerns of the present. To address these problems, Kaplan has established a trash removal service, worked with an environmental scientist to improve drinking water, and developed plans for museums that might attract tourists and so stimulate economic development. He is also working with the local government officials on a plan that would allow farmers to swap land of no archaeological value with areas that include Mayan ruins. At El Pilar, another Mayan site, archaeologist Anabel Ford not only does archaeological excavations, but also directs efforts to help conserve the archaeological sites and the surrounding forest. Straddling the Belize and Guatemalan border, the site of El Pilar is also one of the richest forest areas in the world. Ford hopes the archaeological field research and the data recorded on the tropical forest will heighten the awareness of local officials, tourism directors, and others in the region to improve conservation methods.

Another important series of archaeological projects in the Amazon area in South America has studied human impact on the environment. Archaeologists Thomas Neumann, Anna C. Roosevelt, Clark Erickson, and Peter Stahl, as well as anthropological botanist Charles R. Clement, discovered that the early Native American societies in this region not only had very large settlements—overturning earlier archaeological assessments that the Amazon did not support large civilizations—but contributed new methods that may help conserve this fragile environment (Mann 2002). These early civilizations had extensive agricultural systems that were crippled since the advent of European colonialism. Research may provide insight into how to restore the productivity of the land and more efficient land use in the future. Thus, applied archaeology can provide new knowledge that will enhance the conservation and preservation of different environments throughout the world. A broad holistic perspective involving teams of archaeologists and other scientists is needed to ensure effective site management and the compliance of developers with laws protecting archaeological sites. It also provides a holistic view of past land use that is of great use to archaeologists. Called "community" or "action" archaeology by some, engagement with local peoples' needs has become an increasing concern of archaeologists worldwide.

The Study of Garbage

The majority of archaeological research deals with the interpretation of past societies. Whether the focus is on the Stone Age inhabitants of Australia or the archaeology of nineteenth-century mining communities in the American West, the people being examined lived at a time somewhat removed from the present. There are, however, some archaeologists who are concerned with the study of the refuse of modern society and the application of archaeological methods and techniques to concerns of the present—and the future. The focus for these researchers is not the interpretation of past societies, but the immediate application of archaeological methods and techniques to the modern world. The topics examined range from the use of archaeological data in marketing strategies to the best methods for marking nuclear waste sites. Archaeologists who routinely examine artifacts thousands of years old can, for example, provide important perspectives of the suitability of different materials and burial strategies that can be used to bury nuclear waste (Kaplan and Mendel 1982).

One of the more interesting examples of this kind of applied archaeology is *Le Projet du Garbage*, or the Garbage Project, that grew out of an archaeological method and theory class at the University of Arizona in 1971 (Rathje and Ritenbaugh 1984; Rathje 1992). Archaeologists William L. Rathje and Fred Gorman were so intrigued by the results of the student projects that they established the Garbage Project the following year, and the project is still ongoing. The researchers gather trash from households with the help of the City of Tucson sanitation foremen, who tag the waste with identification numbers that allow the trash bags to be identified with specific census tracts within the city. The trash bags are not identified with particular households, and personal items and photographs are not examined. Over the years research has been broadened to the study of trash from other communities, including Milwaukee, Marin County, and Mexico City, and also to the excavation of modern landfills in Chicago, San Francisco, and Phoenix using archaeological methods.

The Garbage Project has provided a surprising amount of information on a diversity of topics. On one hand, the study provides data that are extremely useful in monitoring trash disposal programs. As Rathje observed, study of waste allows the effective evaluation of current conditions, the anticipation of changing directions in waste disposal, and, therefore, more effective planning and policy making (1984:10). Reviewing data on the project, Rathje noted a number of areas in which this archaeological research dispelled some common notions about trash disposal and landfills. Despite common perceptions, items such as fast-food packaging, polystyrene foam, and disposable diapers do not account for a substantial percentage of landfills. Rathje observed:

Of the 14 tons of garbage from nine municipal landfills that the Garbage Project has excavated and sorted in the past five years, there was less than a hundred pounds of fast-food packaging—that is, containers or wrappers for hamburgers, pizzas, chicken, fish and convenience-store sandwiches, as well as the accessories most of us deplore, such as cups, lids, straws, sauce containers, and so on. (Rathje 1992:115)

Hence, fast-food packaging makes up less than one-half of 1 percent of the weight of landfills. The percentage by volume is even lower. Rathje further noted that despite the burgeoning of materials made from plastic, the amount of plastic in landfills has remained fairly constant since the 1960s, or even decreased. The reason for this, he believes, is that while more things are made of plastic, many objects are now made with less plastic. A plastic milk bottle that weighed 120 grams in the 1960s weighs 65 grams today.

Rathje found that the real culprit in landfills remains plain old paper. A year's subscription to *The New York Times* is roughly equivalent to the volume of 18,660 crushed aluminum cans or 14,969 flattened Big Mac containers. While some predicted that computers would bring about a paperless office, the photocopier and millions of personal printers ensure that millions of pounds of paper are discarded each year: "Where the creation of paper waste is concerned, technology is proving to be not so much a contraceptive as a fertility drug" (Rathje 1992:116). He also observed that despite popular perception, much of the paper in landfills is not biodegrading.

Because of the limited amount of moisture, air, and biological activity in the middle of a landfill, much of the nation's newsprint is being preserved for posterity.

The Garbage Project has also provided information on a diversity of issues connected with food waste, marketing, and the disposal of hazardous materials. In these studies, archaeology has provided a unique perspective. Much of the available data on such topics has typically been provided by questionnaires, interviews, and data collection methods that rely on the cooperation of informants. The problem is that informants often present biased responses, consistently providing lower estimates of the alcohol, snack food, or hazardous waste that they dispose of than is actually the case. Archaeology, on the other hand, presents a fairly impartial material record. While there are sampling problems in archaeological data—some material may be sent down the garbage disposal and not preserved in a landfill—the material record can provide a fairly unambiguous record of some activities.

The Garbage Project has examined the discard of food and food waste for the U.S. Department of Agriculture; the recycling of paper and aluminum cans for the Environmental Protection Agency; studies of candy and snack food consumption for dental associations and manufacturers; and the impact of a new liquor store on alcohol consumption in a Los Angeles neighborhood.

Christopher R. DeCorse

Archaeological study of modern garbage has provided important insights into waste management procedures, marketing, food wastage, and recycling.

In the latter case, researchers conducted both interviews and garbage analysis before and after the liquor store opened. The interview data suggested no change in consumption patterns before and after the store's opening. Study of the trash, however, showed a marked increase in the discard of beer, wine, and liquor cans and bottles. Studies such as these have wide applications both for marketing and policy makers.

Who Owns the Past?

A critical issue for modern archaeologists and physical anthropologists is **cultural patrimony,** that is, who owns the human remains, artifacts, and associated cultural materials that are recovered in the course of research projects. Are they the property of the scientists who collected or excavated them? The descendants of the peoples discovered archaeologically? The owners of the land on which the materials were recovered? Or the public as a whole? Resolution of this issue has at times been contentious, and the position taken by anthropologists has not always been the best. Prior to the twentieth century, laws governing the deposition of antiquities were nonexistent or unclear at best, and the "owner" often became the person, institution, or country with the most money or the strongest political clout. Colonial governments amassed tremendous collections from their territories throughout the world; the spoils of war belonged to the victors. Such a position remained the norm until after the turn of the century. Rights of conquest were only outlawed by the Hague Convention of 1907 (Shaw 1986; Fagan 1992).

Prior to the twentieth century, there was also little or no legislation governing human remains. Researchers appropriated excavated skeletal material, medical samples, and even cadavers of the recently deceased (Blakely and Harrington 1997). Native American remains from archaeological sites were displayed to the public, despite the fact that some of the descendant communities found such displays inappropriate or sacrilegious. Scientific value was the underlying rational for ownership, though until the latter half of the twentieth century there was little discussion of this issue. As in the case of antiquities, value and ownership were vested in the politically stronger, whether a colonial government or the politically enfranchised within a country. Such remains had scientific value, and this was viewed as more important than the interests of other groups or cultural values.

Ironically, such views would seem to fly in the face of some of the basic tenets of modern anthropology, which underscore sensitivity and openness to other cultural perspectives and beliefs. In fact, archaeological resources and human remains at times do provide unique, irreplaceable information that cannot be obtained through any other source. Archaeologists and physical anthropologists have provided information extremely important in documenting the past of Native Americans and indigenous peoples throughout the world, at times serving to underscore their ties to the land and revealing cultural practices forgotten from memory. But what is the cost of such information if the treatment and methods of obtaining the artifacts and remains are abhorrent to the populations whose history is represented? Researchers of the present cannot afford to ignore the views and concerns of the focus of their research.

Recognition of the validity of different concerns and perspectives of cultural patrimony has not made resolution of debate easier. Artifacts now in museums were, in some instances, obtained hundreds of years ago in ways that were consistent with the moral and legal norms of that time (see the box "The Elgin Marbles"). Many antiquities have legitimately changed ownership numerous times. Not infrequently, information about the original origins may be unclear, and there are differences of opinion or uncertainty about the cultural associations of some artifacts or cultural remains. These issues aside, there remain fundamentally different perspectives about the role of the descendant population.

Native American Graves Protection and Repatriation Act

The most important legislation affecting the treatment and protection of archaeological and physical anthropological resources in the United States is the Native American Graves Protection and Repatriation Act (NAGPRA), passed on November 16, 1990 (McKeown 1998). This legislation is the most comprehensive of a series of recent laws dealing with the deposition of Native American burials and cultural properties. NAGPRA and related legislation require that federal institutions consult with the lineal descendants of Native American groups and Native Hawaiians prior to the initial excavation of Native American human remains and associated artifacts on federal or tribal lands. Under this legislation, federal agencies and institutions receiving federal funding are also required to **repatriate**—or return—human remains and cultural items in their collections at the request of the descendant populations of the relevant Native American group. NAGPRA also dictates criminal penalties for trade in Native American human remains and cultural properties.

The impact of NAGPRA has been profound, not only on the way in which many archaeological projects are conducted, but also on the way in which museums and institutions inventory, curate, and manage their collections. The law has, at times, placed very different worldviews in opposition. For many Native Americans, the past is intricately connected to the present, and the natural world—animals, rocks, and trees, as well as cultural objects—may have spiritual meaning (Rose et al. 1996). This perspective is fundamentally different from that of most museums, where both human remains and cultural artifacts are treated as nonliving entities, and the continuing spiritual links with the present are, at least at times, unrecognized. Museums are traditionally concerned with the collection

and exhibition of objects. Reburial or repatriation of collections is the antithesis of their mission. As one scholar noted: "No museum curator will gladly and happily relinquish anything which he has enjoyed having in his museum, of which he is proud, which he has developed an affection for, and which is one of the principal attractions of his museum" (Shaw 1986:46). In a similar vein, reburial and repatriation may conflict with researchers' desire for complete analysis and study. The intersection of these varied interests is highlighted by ongoing debate about the treatment of skeletal remains (Bruning 2006).

NAGPRA and repatriation also raise pragmatic concerns. Return of objects or remains is dependent on a complete and accurate inventory of all of a museum's holdings. Yet, often museums have amassed collections over many decades, and detailed information on all of their collections may not exist or be readily assessable. A case in point is the collection of the Peabody Museum of Archaeology and Ethnology at Harvard University. Founded in 1866, the Peabody has a massive collection from all over the world, including substantial Native American and ancient Mesoamerican holdings. In the 1970s and 1980s, before the passage of NAGPRA, the museum repatriated several burials, collections, and objects at the request of various constituencies. NAGPRA spurred the museum to complete a detailed inventory. They found that the estimated 7,000 human remains in the collections grew to an inventory of about 10,000, while the amount of archaeological objects grew from 800,000 to 8 million (Isaac 1995). Following NAGPRA guidelines, the Peabody sent out summaries of collections to the 756 recognized tribal groups in the United States. Determining the cultural affiliations, the relevant descendant communities, and the need for repatriation of all of these items is a daunting task.

Many museums have undertaken major inventories, revamped storage facilities, and hired additional staff specifically to deal with the issue of repatriation. Impending repatriation of collections and human remains has also spurred many institutions and researchers to reexamine old collections. Such study is necessary to ensure that the presumed age and cultural attribution of individual remains are correct. Of course, all of these concerns have serious budgetary considerations.

While NAGPRA has produced conflicts, it has also both vastly increased the tempo of work on skeletal collections and provided an avenue for new cooperation between Native Americans and researchers. Many of the collections now analyzed would not have been examined if not for NAGPRA. Native claims will in some instances necessitate additional research on poorly documented groups. Indeed, anthropological or archaeological research may be critical to assessing the association and ownership of cultural materials and human remains. On the other hand, anthropologists are given the opportunity to share their discoveries with those populations for whom the knowledge is most relevant.

Critical Perspectives

The Elgin Marbles

The story of the Parthenon sculptures—or Elgin marbles as they came to be called—is a twisted tale of the nineteenth-century quest for antiquities, international politics, and the complexities of cultural heritage. The Parthenon, perched on a hilltop overlooking Athens, is a striking symbol of both ancient Greece and the modern Greek nation-state. It was built by the Greek ruler Pericles to commemorate the Greek victory over the Persians at Plataea in 479 B.C. A temple to Athena, the patron goddess of Athens, the Parthenon was deemed by Pericles to be one of the most striking edifices in the city. The Parthenon is clearly the most impressive of the buildings in the Acropolis, the cluster of classical structures that cover Mount Athena. It is regarded by some to be one of the world's most perfect buildings. The Parthenon was distinguished by a full surrounding colonnade, and the exterior walls were decorated with a processional frieze. The pediments, or peaked eaves, in the east and west also had exquisitely detailed sculptures.

The structure has endured for millenia, and it has come to embody classical civilization to the world. In recent years, the Parthenon has been the focus of several restoration efforts that have stabilized the structure, removed more recent additions, and replaced some of the fallen masonry.

The Parthenon still overlooks Athens and it hopefully will for years to come. But while the Parthenon is an architectural treasure, today only traces of the magnificent art that once adorned it remain. Fragments its frieze and sculptures are scattered in museums around the world. The largest collection is in the British Museum in London, where large portions of the Parthenon's frieze are displayed in a specially designed room. To understand why statuary of such clear cultural significance to Greece is to be found in England, one has to go back to the early nineteenth century and the exploits of Thomas Bruce, the 7th Earl of Elgin (Jackson 1992). By the early nineteenth century, Britain was in the midst of a classical revival. The country's well-to-do traveled to Europe to visit the historic ruins of ancient Greece and Rome. The wealthier purchased statuary and antiquities for their estates. Patterns and illustrations from classical Greek and Roman motifs were reproduced and incorporated into architectural features, jewelry, and ceramic designs. Within this setting, Lord Elgin, a Scottish nobleman, set out to obtain sketches and casts of classical sculptures that might be used at his estate, then being built near the Firth of Forth.

In 1799, Elgin was appointed British ambassador to the Ottoman Empire, which extended over much of the eastern Mediterranean from Western Europe to Egypt. By the late eighteenth century, the Ottomans had ruled Greece for 350 years. A major military power and one-time master of the Mediterranean, the Ottomans have been viewed by historians in a variety of ways, but one thing is certain: They were not overly concerned with the glories of ancient Greece. During their rule the Parthenon was used as a mosque, then as an ammunition dump; also, various Turkish structures were built on the site. Much of the north colonnade was destroyed in the Venetian bombardment of 1687. Some of the Parthenon marble was ground to make lime, and bits of statuary were broken off (Jackson 1992). In 1800, one of the world's most perfect buildings was in a sorry state.

Elgin initially proposed that the British government finance a survey of the art of the Acropolis as a resource for British art. When this initiative was turned down, Elgin made his own plans and contracted laborers. Initially, his workers were to make copies of the Parthenon sculptures. In 1801, however, Britain defeated Napoleon's forces in Egypt, saving the Ottoman Empire. Coincidentally, Elgin soon obtained a permit from the Ottomans not only to copy and make molds of the Parthenon art, but also to "take away any pieces of stone with old inscriptions or sculptures thereon" (Jackson 1992:137). During 1801 and 1802, scaffolding was erected, and hundreds of laborers went to work on the Parthenon with blocks and tackles and marble saws. Some sculptures broke or crashed to the ground. Twenty-two ships conveyed the marbles, loaded in hundreds of crates, back to England.

The marbles hardly proved to be good fortune for Elgin. The expense of obtaining them ruined his credit, and he discarded the idea of installing them at his estate. Totaling all of his expenses, Elgin estimated that he had spent over £60,000. To recoup his costs, he began negotiations for sale of the marbles to the government for display in the British Museum. After long parliamentary debate, they

Applied Cultural Anthropology

Planning Change

Over the years, many applied cultural anthropologists have worked to help improve societies through planned change. To assist governments, private developers, or other agencies, applied anthropologists are hired because of their ethnographic studies of particular societies. Government and private agencies often employ applied anthropologists to prepare **social-impact studies**, research on the possible consequences that change will have on a community. Social-impact studies involve in-depth

Two young horsemen join a procession of sculpted figures on the Parthenon frieze. The marbles were taken from Greece in the early nineteenth century and are now on display in the British Museum, London.

were sold for £35,000 in 1816. More than half of this amount went to clear Elgin's debt.

Elgin's treatment of the Parthenon's marbles had its contemporary critics. Among the most vocal opponents was none other than the Romantic poet and celebrator of Greek art and culture, Lord Byron, who immortalized the story of the Elgin marbles in the poems "Childe Harold's Pilgrimage" and "Curse of Minerva." Disgusted by what he saw as the desecration of the Parthenon, Byron asked by what right Elgin had removed these treasures of national cultural significance.

Greece gained independence from Turkey in 1830, and the Parthenon became integrally tied to the new nation's identity. The first restoration efforts began soon after independence.

In the years since their installation in the British Museum, the ownership of the Parthenon's marbles and demands for their return have periodically been raised by Greeks and Britons alike, but to no avail. In the 1980s, then Greek Minister of Culture Melina Mercouri charged the British with vandalism and argued that the continued possession of the marbles by the British Museum was provocative. Although garnering substantial international support from ministers of culture from around the world, these efforts also proved unsuccessful.

In his defense of his actions, Elgin pointed to the poor conditions of the Parthenon and the ill treatment that the sculptures had received. If left in place they would surely have continued to deteriorate. Why not remove them and have them cared for and appreciated by those who could afford to preserve them? Despite criticism, Elgin believed he was saving the sculptures from the ravages of time and neglect. Time has proven Elgin at least somewhat correct. The Parthenon continues to present a complex and continuous preservation problem. Time has ravaged the remains of the sculptures that were not removed, and deterioration of the monument accelerated rather than diminished throughout the twentieth century. Stonework and architectural detail have been eaten away by erosion, pollution, and acid rain, as well as by early and poorly conceived restoration efforts. As recently as 1971, a UNESCO report stated that the building itself was so weakened that it was in danger of collapse. Recent supporters of retaining the Elgin marbles argue that the marbles were obtained honestly with the permission of the government then in power. Other ancient Greek treasures, such as the Venus de Milo (currently on display in the Louvre in Paris), have also been removed from the country. Are these to be returned as well? For the time being it seems that the Elgin marbles remain in London.

Points to Ponder

1. Do you feel Elgin was right or wrong to remove the marbles?
2. Should the Elgin marbles be returned to Greece? On what basis did you make your decision?
3. The conservation of the Parthenon and the preservation of the sculptures are valid concerns. How can these concerns be reconciled with the question of ownership?

interviews and ethnological studies in local communities to determine how various policies and developments will affect social life in those communities.

One well-known social-impact study was carried out by Thayer Scudder and Elizabeth Colson (1979; Glazier 1984) in the African country of Zambia. Scudder and Colson had conducted long-term ethnographic research for about thirty years in the Gwembe Valley in Zambia. In the mid-1950s, the Zambian government subsidized the development of a large-scale dam that would provide for more efficient agricultural activities and electrification. Because of the location of the dam, however, the people in the Gwembe Valley would be forced to relocate. Scudder and Colson used their knowledge from their long-term research and subsequent interviews to study the potential impact of this project on the community.

From their social-impact study, Scudder and Colson concluded that the forced relocation of this rural community would create extreme stresses that would result in people clinging to familiar traditions and institutions during the period of relocation. Scudder did social-impact studies of other societies in Africa experiencing forced relocation due to dams, highways, and other developments. These studies enabled Scudder and Colson to offer advice to the various African government officials, who could then assess the costs and benefits of resettling these populations and plan their development projects with consideration being given to the impact on the people involved.

Applied anthropologists often serve as consultants to government organizations, such as the Agency for International Development (AID), that formulate policies involving foreign aid. For example, anthropologist Patrick Fleuret (1988), a full-time employee of AID, studied the problems of farmers in Uganda after the downfall of Idi Amin in 1979. Fleuret and other AID anthropologists discovered that, on the heels of the political turmoil in Uganda, many of the peasants had retreated into subsistence production rather than participate in the market economy. They also found that subsistence production was affected by a technological problem—a scarcity of hoes for preparing the land for cultivation. In response, AID anthropologists helped design and implement a system to distribute hoes through local cooperative organizations.

This plan for the distribution of hoes reflects the development of new strategies on the part of AID and the facilitator role for applied anthropologists. Most of the development work sponsored by AID and applied anthropology in the 1950s and 1960s was aimed at large-scale development projects such as hydroelectric dams and other forms of mechanized agriculture and industrialism. Many of these large-scale projects, however, have resulted in unintended negative consequences. In the preceding chapter, we saw how the Green Revolution frequently led to increasing inequality and a mechanized agriculture system

that was expensive, inefficient, and inappropriate. Often these large-scale projects were devised in terms of the modernization views proposed by economists, such as Walt Rostow, and were designed to shift an underdeveloped country to industrialism very rapidly.

Most recently, AID and applied anthropologists have modified their policies on development projects in many less-developed countries. They now focus on projects that involve small-scale economic change with an emphasis on the development of appropriate technologies. Rather than relying on large-scale projects to have "trickle-down" influences on local populations, applied anthropologists have begun to focus more realistically on determining where basic needs must be fulfilled. After assessing the needs of the local population, the applied anthropologist can help facilitate change by helping people learn new skills.

One early project that placed applied anthropologists in decision-making and analytical roles was run by Allan Holmberg of Cornell University. In the 1950s and 1960s, Holmberg and Mario Vasquez, a Peruvian anthropologist, developed what is known as the Vicos Project in the Andean highlands. (Vicos is the name of a hacienda that was leased by Cornell in 1952 as part of a program to increase education and literacy, improve sanitation and health care, and teach new agricultural methods to the Andean Indians.) Prior to the Vicos Project, these Indians were peasant farmers who were not able to feed themselves. Their land on the hacienda was broken into small plots that were insufficient to raise potato crops. The South American Indians were indebted to the hacendado and were required to work on the hacendado's fields without pay to service their debts.

Although the applied anthropologists took on the role of a new patron to the Indians, the overall aim was to dissolve historic patterns of exploitation and to guide the

Applied anthropologists often act as consultants for native peoples who produce crafts in areas such as Latin America.

Peggy/Yoram Kahana/PhotoLibrary

Anthropologists at Work

JOHN McCREERY: Applying Anthropology in Japan

This chapter has some examples of anthropologists who work outside the academic setting. John McCreery is an anthropologist who has lived in Japan since 1980 and has developed a productive and fruitful career in the area of advertising. For a number of years, he worked as a copywriter and creative director for Hakuhodo Incorporated, Japan's second largest advertising agency. In 1984, he and his wife and business partner, Ruth McCreery, founded The Word Works, a supplier of translation, copywriting, and presentation support services to Japanese and other clients with operations in Japan. While earning his living as vice president and managing director of The Word Works, he is also a lecturer in the graduate program in Comparative Culture at Sophia University in Tokyo. There he teaches seminars on "The Making and Meaning of Advertising" and "Marketing in Japan." When asked how an anthropologist got into advertising, McCreery replied, "In Taiwan I studied magicians. In Japan I joined the guild."

As an undergraduate in the honors college at Michigan State University, McCreery studied philosophy and medieval history. In the summer after his junior year, a friend recommended that he take a course in East African Ethnography taught by anthropologist Marc Swartz. The course and the thought of doing research that involved travel to exotic places were fascinating. Another friend was studying Chinese, and noting that an anthropologist should have some experience with a non-Indo-European language, McCreery decided to study Chinese as well. One thing led to another, and he wound up in graduate school at Cornell University, doing a Ph.D. in anthropology and preparing to do research in Chinese anthropology. McCreery's first field research was in Puli, a market town in central Taiwan, where he and Ruth McCreery lived and worked from September 1969 to August 1971. He returned to Taiwan in 1976–1977, the summer of 1978, and again in 1983.

At Cornell University, McCreery studied with Victor Turner. In Taiwan, McCreery focused his ethnographic study on religious traditions and worked with a Taoist master, Tio Se-lian. Both Victor Turner and Tio Se-lian were teachers with a willingness to listen, a flair for the dramatic, a passion for detail, and a breadth of humanity that moved all those with whom they came in contact. They, and senior creative director Kimoto Kazuhiko, who shared these earlier mentors' traits and gave McCreery his job at Hakuhodo, are the models he tries to emulate in his work.

McCreery's essays on Chinese religion and ritual have appeared in *The Journal of Chinese Religions* and *American Ethnologist*. He is also the author of a book on Japanese consumer behavior, *Japanese Consumer Behavior: From Worker Bees to Wary Shoppers* (2000), which follows the current trends in postindustrial Japan

John McCreery

that have resulted in new consumption preferences and behaviors for the Japanese men, women, and young people. Currently, as an anthropologist he is involved in assessing new trends in the use of the Internet in respect to the spread of global media changes in Japan. McCreery and his wife, Ruth, who run their translating business in Japan, have completed a major comprehensive chapter evaluating the prehistory, language, history, and current cultural changes in Japan based upon state-of-the-art anthropological research in a textbook on the *Peoples and Cultures of Asia* (Scupin 2006). McCreery maintains his contact with other anthropologists through an Internet listserv, Anthro-list, which provides lively discussions on ethnographic and theoretical issues in the field. Anthropologists from many backgrounds participate on this listserv. As a student you may want to become involved in lurking or participating on this listserv yourself.

✳ **Explore** the **Concept** on **myanthrolab.com**

Indians toward self-sufficiency (Holmberg 1962; Chambers 1985). The Indians were paid for their labor and were also introduced to new varieties of potatoes, fertilizers, and pesticides. New crops such as leafy vegetables and foods such as eggs and fruit were introduced into their diet.

Through an educational program, the Indians became acquainted with forms of representative democratic organization. Developing more independence, they eventually overturned the traditional authority structure of the hacienda. In 1962, the Indians purchased the land of the hacienda from its former owners, which gave the Indians a measure of self-sufficiency. Overall, the Vicos Project led to basic improvements in housing, nutrition, clothing, and health conditions for the Indians. It also served as a model for similar projects in other parts of the world.

Involvement with indigenous communities is a long-term commitment of most applied anthropologists.

Today Vicos is still an independent, active Indian community. It is within a Peruvian national park that includes the Cordillera Blanca, and community members are participating in an ecotourism project. Three community representatives recently visited Cornell University and marched in the inauguration of the new university president. They came, in part, to discuss concerns about Vicos land and water rights going back to the 1950s. They also requested information on the boundary limits at the higher mountain elevations.

Problems sometimes arise between applied anthropologists and private developers or government officials. Many developers and governments want to induce modernization and social change as rapidly as possible with capital-intensive projects, hydroelectric dams, and manufacturing facilities. In many cases, anthropologists have recommended against these innovations because of their expense and inefficient use of labor resources and the heavy cost to communities. (For example, anthropologist Billie DeWalt argued that the majority of Mexicans were not receiving benefits from the adoption of mechanized agriculture that was being encouraged by the government.) Political officials, however, often ignore these recommendations because they are committed to programs that serve their political and personal interests. In these circumstances, applied anthropologists are often forced to take an advocacy approach, or the representative role, which means supporting the interests of the people who will be directly affected by policies and projects.

People within indigenous small-societies face difficulties as they confront globalization. Some anthropologists such as the late David Maybury-Lewis established Cultural Survival in 1972, which is actively engaged in trying to reduce the costs imposed by globalization on small-scale societies. Driven by trade deficits and gigantic foreign debts, many governments in developing countries want to extract as much wealth as possible from their national territories. Highway expansion, mining operations, giant hydroelectric projects, lumbering, mechanized agriculture, and other industrial developments all intrude on the traditional lifestyle and territory of small-scale societies. Applied anthropologists connected with groups such as Cultural Survival try to obtain input from the people themselves and help them represent their interests to the government or private developers.

Maybury-Lewis (1985) admitted that the advocacy role in anthropology is extremely difficult, requiring great sensitivity and complex moral and political judgments. Most recently, many small-scale societies and minority groups in developing countries are organizing themselves to represent their own interests. This has resulted in the diminished role of the applied anthropologist as advocate or representative. Generally, anthropologists are pleased when their role as advocates or representatives is diminished, because these roles are called for only when native people are dominated by forces from globalization that are beyond their control.

Applied Anthropology and Human Rights

Cultural Relativism and Human Rights

A recent development that has had wide-ranging consequences for applied anthropology and ethnographic research involves the ways in which anthropologists assess and respond to the values and norms of other societies. Recall our discussion of *cultural relativism*, the method used by anthropologists to understand another society through their own cultural values, beliefs, norms, and behaviors. In order to understand an indigenous culture, the anthropologist must strive to temporarily suspend judgment of that culture's practices (Maybury-Lewis 2002). Sometimes, anthropologists refer to this as *methodological relativism* (Brown 2008). While difficult, this procedure does help the anthropologist gain insights into that culture. However, some critics have charged that anthropologists (and other people) who adopt this position cannot (or will not) make value judgments concerning the values, norms, and practices of any society. If this is the case, then how can anthropologists encourage any conception of human rights that would be valid for all of humanity? Must anthropologists accept such practices as infanticide, caste and class inequalities, slavery, torture, and female subordination out of fear of forcing their own values on other people?

Relativism Reconsidered These criticisms have led some anthropologists to reevaluate the basic assumptions regarding cultural relativism. In his 1983 book *Culture and Morality: The Relativity of Values in Anthropology*, Elvin Hatch recounted the historical acceptance of the cultural-relativist view. As we saw in Chapter 13, this was the approach of Franz Boas, who challenged the unilineal-evolutionary models of nineteenth-century anthropologists like E. B. Tylor, with their underlying assumptions of Western cultural superiority. Boas's approach, with its emphasis on tolerance and equality, appealed to many liberal-minded Western scholars. For example, the earlier nineteenth-century ethnocentric and racist assumptions held within anthropology were used at the 1904 World's Fair in St. Louis to display other peoples as barbaric, uncivilized, and savage to the "civilized" citizens who viewed them. For example, "pygmies" from Central Africa were given machetes to show how they "beheaded" one another in their local regions and the Igorot tribal people of the Philippines were given a dog to cook and eat daily in front of the "civilized" citizens of the United States in order to portray them as inferior races and cultures (Breitbart 1997). Such displays of these peoples during that period both distorted their cultural practices and allowed *anthropologists* of the time to treat them in an inhumane and unethical manner; they also resulted in harmful practices toward these native peoples in different regions. Thus, the criticisms of these nineteenth-century racist and ethnocentric views and the endorsement of cultural relativism were an important human rights innovations by twentieth-century anthropologists. In addition, many Westerners were stunned by the horrific events of World War I and the devastation and massive casualties for people within Western societies that were supposedly morally and culturally superior to other non-Western societies. Cultural relativism appealed to many people in the West as a corrective to the earlier racist and ethnocentric views (Hatch 1983; Brown 2008).

However, belief in cultural relativism led to the acceptance by some early-twentieth-century anthropologists of moral or **ethical relativism**, the notion that we cannot impose the values or morality of one society on other societies. Ethical relativists argued that because anthropologists had not discovered any universal moral values, each society's values were valid with respect to that society's circumstances and conditions. No society could claim any superior position over another regarding ethics and morality.

As many philosophers and anthropologists have noted, the argument of ethical relativism is a circular one that itself assumes a particular moral position. It is, in fact, a moral theory that encourages people to be tolerant toward all cultural values, norms, and practices. Hatch notes that in the history of anthropology, many who accepted the premises of ethical relativism could not maintain these assumptions in light of their data. Ethical relativists would have to tolerate practices such as homicide, child abuse, human sacrifice, torture, warfare, racial discrimination, and even genocide. In fact, even anthropologists who held the ethical-relativist position in the early period of the twentieth century condemned many cultural practices. For example, Ruth Benedict condemned the practice of the Plains Indians to cut off the nose of an adulterous wife. Boas himself condemned racism, anti-Semitism, and other forms of bigotry. Thus, these anthropologists did not consistently adhere to the ethical-relativist paradigm.

The horrors associated with World War II eventually led most scholars to reject ethical relativism. The argument that Nazi Germany could not be condemned

Photo from the 1904 World's Fair in St. Louis showing "pygmies" beheading one another. This was never an aspect of "pygmy" culture.

because of its unique moral and ethical standards appeared ludicrous to most people. In the 1950s, some anthropologists such as Robert Redfield suggested that general standards of judgment could be applied to most societies. However, these anthropologists were reluctant to impose Western standards on prestate indigenous societies. In essence, they suggested a *double standard* in which they could criticize large-scale, industrial state societies but not prestate indigenous societies.

This double standard of morality poses problems, however. Can anthropologists make value judgments about homicide, child abuse, warfare, torture, rape, and other acts of violence in a small-scale society? Why should they adopt different standards in evaluating such behaviors in prestate indigenous societies as compared with industrial state societies? In both types of societies, human beings are harmed. Don't humans in all societies have equal value?

A Resolution to the Problem of Relativism

Is there a resolution to these philosophical and moral dilemmas? First, we need to distinguish between *cultural relativism* (or *methodological relativism*) and *ethical relativism*. In other words, to understand the values, the reasoning and logic, and the worldviews of another people does not mean to accept all of their practices and standards (Salmon 1997). Second, we need to realize that the culture of a society is not completely homogeneous or unified. Culture is distributed differentially within any society. People do not all share the same culture within any society. For example, men and women do not share the same "culture" in a society. Ethnographic experience tells anthropologists that there are always people who may not agree with the content of the moral and ethical values of a society. Treating cultures as "uniform united wholes" is a conceptual mistake. For one thing, it ignores the *power relationships* within a society. Elites within a society can maintain cultural hegemony or dominance and can use harmful practices against their own members to produce conformity. In some cases, governments use the concept of relativism to justify their repressive policies and deflect criticism of these practices by the international community. In Asia, many political leaders argue that their specific culture does not have the same notion of human rights that is accepted in Western society. Therefore, in China or Singapore, human rights may be restricted by political rulers who draw on their cultural tradition to invoke repressive and totalitarian political policies (Ong 2006; Brown 2008). Those who impose these harmful practices upon others may be the beneficiaries of those practices.

To get beyond the problem of ethical relativism, we ought to adopt a humanitarian standard that would be recognized by all people throughout the world. This standard would not be derived from any particular cultural values—such as the U.S. Declaration of Independence—but rather would involve the basic principle that every individual is entitled to a certain standard of "well-being."

For example, no individual ought to be subjected to bodily harm through violence or starvation.

Of course, we recognize certain problems with this solution. Perhaps, the key problem is that people in many societies accept—or at least appear to accept—behaviors that Westerners would condemn as inhumane. For example, what about the Aztec practice of human sacrifice? The Aztecs firmly believed that they would be destroyed if they did not sacrifice victims to the Sun deity. Would an outside group have been justified in condemning and abolishing this practice? A more recent case involves the West Irian tribe known as the Dani, who engaged in constant warfare with neighboring tribes. They believed that through revenge they had to placate the ghosts of their kin who had been killed in warfare because unavenged ghosts bring sickness and disaster to the tribe. Another way of placating the ghosts was to bring two or three young girls related to the deceased victim to the funeral site and chop two fingers off their hands. Until recently, all Dani women lost from two to six fingers in this way (Heider 1979; Bagish 1981). Apparently, these practices were accepted by many Dani males and females.

In some Islamic countries, women have been accused of sexual misconduct and then executed by male members in what are called "honor killings." The practice of honor killings, which victimizes women, has been defended in some of these societies as a means to restore harmony to the society. The males argue that the shedding of blood washes away the shame of sexual dishonor. There have been a number of "honor killings" among immigrant Middle Eastern families within the United States. In both Africa and the Middle East, young girls are subjected to female circumcision, a polite term for the removal of the clitoris and other areas of the vagina. These practices, referred to by most human rights advocates as female genital mutilation/cutting (FGM or FGC), range from the cutting out of the clitoris to a more severe practice known as Pharoanic infibulation, which involves stitching the cut labia to cover the vagina of the woman. One of the purposes of these procedures is to reduce the pleasure related to sexual intercourse and thereby, induce more fidelity from women in marriage. Chronic infections are a common result of this practice. Sexual intercourse is painful, and childbirth is much more difficult for many of these women. However, the cultural ideology may maintain that an uncircumcised woman is not respectable, and few families want to risk their daughter's chances of marriage by not having her circumcised (Fluehr-Lobban 2003). The right of males to discipline, hit, or beat their wives is often maintained in a male-dominated culture (Tapper and Tapper 1992–1993). Other examples of these types of practices, such as head-hunting, slavery, female subordination, torture, and unnecessarily dangerous child labor, also fall into this category. According to a universal humanitarian standard suggested here, all these practices could be condemned as harmful behaviors.

The Problem of Intervention

The condemnation of harmful cultural practices with reference to a universal standard is fairly easy. The abolition of such practices, however, is not. Anthropologists recommend that one should take a pragmatic approach in reducing these practices. Sometimes, intervention in the cultures in which practices such as genocide are occurring would be a moral imperative. This intervention would proceed not from the standpoint of specific Western values, but from the commonly recognized universal standards of humanitarianism.

Such intervention, however, must proceed cautiously and be based on a thorough knowledge of the society. Ethnographers must gather empirical knowledge, studying the history, local conditions, social life, and various institutions, and assess carefully whether the cultural practice is shown to clearly create pain and suffering for people. For example, in Thailand, many young women are incorporated into the prostitution and sex tourist industry to help increase their parents' income (Barmé 2002). This prostitution and sex tourist industry must be thoroughly understood within the historical, economic, and cultural context of Thai society prior to endorsing a human rights intervention that would abolish these practices. When such understanding is present, intervention should take place by engaging in a form of dialogue, rather than by preaching human rights in a monolithic manner to various people in the community. In a recent ethnographic study of the attempt to abolish FGM in the Darfur region of the Sudan, anthropologist Ellen Gruenbaum focused on seven different communities to investigate how the UN agencies, the nongovernment organizations, and other human rights agencies are influencing these practices (2004). Gruenbaum found that at times women were participating in the FGM practices such as the Pharoanic infibulation because they "perceived" them as a means of protection against rape and illicit premarital intercourse within their communities. Rape is often used in these communities as a means of warfare. Thus, the historical and cultural context of these practices needs to be investigated cautiously by anthropologists prior to advocating a rapid enforcement of human rights that may result in outright rejection of the dedicated human rights workers (Shweder 2003).

As is obvious, these suggestions are based on the highly idealistic standards of a universal humanitarianism. In many cases, intervention to stamp out a particular cultural practice may not be possible, and in some cases, it may cause even greater problems. Outside global intervention adversely affected such peoples as the Ju/'hoansi, Mbuti, Yanomamö, and Native Hawaiians. Communal riots, group violence, or social chaos may result from the dislocation of certain cultural practices. Thus, caution, understanding, and dialogue are critical to successful intervention. We need to be sensitive to cultural differences, but not allow them to produce severe harm to individuals within a society.

Universal Human Rights

The espousal of universally recognized standards to eradicate harmful practices is a worthwhile, albeit idealistic, goal. Since the time of the Enlightenment, Western societies have prided themselves on extending human rights. Many Western theorists emphasize that human rights have spread to other parts of the world through globalization, thus providing the catalyst for social change, reform, and political liberation. At the same time, as people from non-Western societies can testify, the West has also promoted intolerance, racism, and genocide. Western society has not always lived up to the ideals of its own tradition.

The Role of Applied Anthropology in Human Rights

Cultural anthropologists and applied anthropologists have a role in helping to define the universal standards for human rights in all societies. By systematically studying community standards, applied anthropologists can determine whether practices are harmful and then help provide solutions for reducing these harmful practices. This may involve consultation with local government officials and dialogue with members of the community to resolve the complex issues surrounding the identified harmful practices. The exchange of ideas across cultures through anthropological research is beginning to foster acceptance of the universal nature of some human rights regardless of cultural differences.

An illustration of this type of research and effort by applied anthropologists is the work of John Van Willigen and V. C. Channa (1991), who have done research on the harmful consequences of the dowry in India. India, like some other primarily agricultural societies, has the cultural institution known as the *dowry*, in which the bride's family gives a certain amount of cash or other goods to the groom's family upon marriage. Recently, the traditions of the dowry have led to increasing cases of what has been referred to as "dowry death" or "bride burning." Some husbands or their families have been dissatisfied with the amount of the dowry that the new wife brings into the family. Following marriage, the family of the groom begins to make additional demands for more money and goods from the wife's family. These demands result in harassment and abuse of the wife, culminating in murder. The woman is typically doused with kerosene and burned to death, hence the use of the term *bride burning*.

Dowry deaths have increased in recent years. In 1986, 1,319 cases were reported nationally in India. There are many other cases in which the evidence is more ambiguous, however, and the deaths of these women might be reported as kitchen accidents or suicides (Van Willigen and Channa 1991). In addition, the burdens imposed by the dowry tradition have led many pregnant women to pay for amniocentesis (a medical procedure to determine the health status of the fetus) as a means to determine the sex of the fetus. If the fetus is female, in many cases Indians have an abortion partly because of the increasing burden and expense of raising a daughter and developing a substantial dowry for her marriage. Thus, male children are preferred and female fetuses are selectively aborted.

Van Willigen, an American anthropologist, and Channa, an Indian anthropologist, studied the dowry problem together. They found that the national law established against the institution of the dowry (the Dowry Prohibition Act of 1961, amended in 1984 and 1986) is very tough. The law makes it illegal to give or take a dowry, but the law is ineffective in restraining the practice. In addition, a number of public education groups have been organized in India. Using slogans such as "Say No to Dowry," they have been advertising and campaigning against the dowry practices. Yet the problem continues to plague India.

After carefully studying the dowry practices of different regions and local areas of India, Van Willigen and Channa concluded that the increase in dowry deaths was partially the result of the rapid inflationary pressures of the Indian economy, as well as the demands of a consumer-oriented economy. Consumer price increases have resulted in increasing demands for more dowry money to buy consumer goods. It has become more and more difficult to save resources for a dowry for a daughter or sister that is substantial enough to satisfy the groom's family. Van Willigen and Channa found that aside from wealth, family "prestige" that comes with wealth expenditures is sought by the groom's family.

From the perspective of the bride's family, dowry payments provide for present consumption and future earning power for their daughter through acquiring a husband with better connections and future earning potential. In a developing society such as India, with extremely high unemployment and rapid inflation, the importance of investing in a husband with high future earning potential is emphasized. When asked why they give a dowry when their daughters are being married, people respond, "Because we love them." The decision by the groom's family to forgo the dowry would also be very difficult.

There appears to be a very positive commitment to the institution of the dowry in India. Most people have given and received a dowry. Thus, declaring dowry a crime technically makes many people criminals. Van Willigen and Channa recommended that to be effective, the antidowry practices must be displaced by other, less problematic practices and that the apparent causes of the practice must be attacked. Women's property rights must be examined so as to increase their economic access. Traditional Hindu cultural norms regarding inheritance, which give sons the right from birth to claim the so-called ancestral properties, must be reformed. At present, male descendants inherit property, but females must pay for marriage expenses and dowry gifts. Van Willigen

Critical Perspectives

Ethical Controversies in El Dorado

In 2000, an investigative journalist named Patrick Tierney had a book published called *Darkness in El Dorado: How Scientists and Journalists Devastated the Amazon*, in which he alleged that Chagnon and other anthropologists and scientists working among the Yanomamö had devastated their communities. Tierney's book accused Chagnon and geneticist James Neel of seriously disrupting the Yanomamö society and in some cases, increasing death rates among these people. Tierney alleged that Neel improperly used a measles vaccine among the Yanomamö, resulting in a measles epidemic that caused "hundreds, perhaps thousands of deaths." Tierney suggested that Neel did this in order to experiment in a natural laboratory, the isolated Yanomamö, and to observe an epidemic for scientific reasons. In other words, Tierney accused Neel and his accomplice Chagnon of carrying out a dangerous campaign among these people. He also claimed that Neel was conducting secret radiation experiments among the Yanomamö.

Darkness in El Dorado also indicted Chagnon for nefarious misdeeds in his role as an anthropologist. Tierney argued that Chagnon staged warfare and violence among the Yanomamö for filmmaker Timothy Asch in order to project an image of a warlike, violent people. In addition, Tierney argued that Chagnon fraudulently manipulated his analysis of warfare and violence among the Yanomamö to support his sociobiological views about how violence and aggression are adaptively advantageous for males. Tierney went on to allege that Chagnon himself is directly or indirectly responsible for the endemic warfare found among the Yanomamö. Tierney

suggested that by introducing trade items such as machetes, metal goods, and imported foods to these tribal people, Chagnon created conditions for competition among villages for these goods, and consequently this competition resulted in intergroup warfare and violence. Tierney argued that Chagnon perpetuated an image of the Yanomamö as a naturally violent and warlike people, and as a result of this stereotype, 40,000 gold miners invaded Yanomamö territory between 1980 and 1987. Additionally, he said that the military and government officials used violence against the Yanomamö to remove them from their land. Tierney also alleged that Chagnon colluded with some Venezuelan politicians to help them gain control of Yanomami land in return for illegal gold mining concessions to benefit himself and some other wealthy interests.

This book resulted in a widespread ethical scandal for anthropology that had international consequences for the field. A fascinating in-depth account of the science and ethical problems resulting from this scandal has been written by anthropologist Robert Borofsky (2005). Borofsky's book *Yanomami: The Fierce Controversy and What We Can Learn from It* is based on extensive research and on interviews and testimony from all sides of this controversy, including leaders of the Yanomamö people themselves.

Napoleon Chagnon earned his B.A., M.A., and Ph.D. degrees in anthropology at Michigan. After completing his Ph.D. in 1966, he joined the Department of Human Genetics at the University of Michigan Medical School and participated in a multidisciplinary study of the Yanomamö Indians of Venezuela and Brazil along with the geneticist James Neel. Chagnon returned to do fieldwork among the Yanomamö almost every year for thirty years beginning in 1964, enabling him to conduct a long-term, systematic study of change within this population. Chagnon's ethnographic

studies and the many educational films that he and colleague Timothy Asch have produced have made the Yanomamö well-known around the world.

In a book about his fieldwork, *Studying the Yanomamö* (1974), Chagnon describes both his analytical techniques and his immersion into Yanomamö society. Over the years, he has written dozens of books and hundreds of articles about Yanomamö society and culture. These books made him one of the most well-known anthropologists in the world. The books sold in the millions to anthropologists who used them in their courses.

Tierney's allegations about Chagnon and Neel created a well-publicized controversy that was carried internationally in leading newspapers, the Internet, and other media. The book led to a lot of investigations and soul-searching among anthropologists. Many anthropologists began to ask themselves if this book was going to unhinge their whole discipline. Immediately, the University of Michigan and the University of California at Santa Barbara (both of which helped sponsor Chagnon's research), as well as the National Academy of Sciences and the American Anthropological Association launched investigations into the possible malfeasance of Neel and Chagnon. Teams of researchers began to assess every one of the allegations that Tierney made and to follow up every claim and every footnote in his book.

The most serious allegation—that Neel had improperly introduced a measles vaccine that resulted in loss of life among the Yanomamö—has been thoroughly refuted by leading scientists who investigated Neel's medical documents concerning the vaccination process (Dreger 2011; Lancaster and Hames 2011). The co-developer of the actual measles vaccine, Dr. Samuel Katz, has stated that the vaccine was not virulent and thus, could not cause measles and that it had never done so in millions of applications. In addition, researchers found medical reports stating that Brazilian missionaries had caused the initial measles outbreak among the Yanomamö in November 1967, prior to the Chagnon–Neel expedition in 1968. Chagnon, Neel, and the medical team were actively trying to vaccinate the population to reduce the incidence of measles. Through investigation of Neel's field journals and daily logs, the allegation that he was using radiation experiments among the Yanomamö was also refuted.

Researchers also investigated Tierney's claims regarding Chagnon's misdeeds in his role as an anthropologist. Although Timothy Asch, the filmmaker, had died before the publication of Tierney's book, many of his assistants who had done research for and had helped edit the films on the Yanomamö insist that the films were not staged productions, but rather were authentic portrayals of the life of these people.

Tierney's claim that Chagnon was directly or indirectly responsible for the endemic warfare among these people has also been examined carefully. Archaeologists have exhumed an enormous amount of evidence of warfare in this region of the Amazon, going back at least 3,500 years. They have found that missionaries and other explorers had been publishing accounts of warfare among the Yanomamö since the sixteenth century. The Yanomamö describe themselves as *waitiri*, which Chagnon translated as "fierce and valiant." Chagnon changed the title of later editions of *The Yanomamö: The Fierce People* to *The Yanomamö*, saying that sometimes this word for "fierce" in Portuguese and Spanish may have resulted in some erroneous stereotypes.

Tierney's thesis that Chagnon's characterization of these people as fierce and violent resulted in the gold miners' attacks and invasions does not appear completely valid when examined historically. The treatment of indigenous Native American peoples by gold miners during the gold rushes in California and in the Black Hills of the Dakota region parallels the behavior of the gold miners in the Amazon. These gold miners often brutalized Native Americans. It did not take an anthropological description to motivate these misbehaviors, just as it did not take Chagnon's depictions to motivate gold miners, the military, and government officials to invade, attack, and attempt to take over Yanomamö land (Dreger 2011; Lancaster and Hames 2011).

As for the charge that Chagnon manipulated or "cooked" his data to support his sociobiological view that warlike, violent Yanomamö males were likely to have more wives and to be more reproductively successful, other anthropologists such as Clayton and Carole Robarchek have found a similar correlation in their ethnographic data on the Waorani Indians of Ecuador (1998). However, the Robarcheks interpret these data differently from Chagnon and offer a different hypothesis. Their data indicate that the longer a man lives, the more children he will have, and in that context, Waorani males will more frequently be associated with warfare and homicides. Thus, the number of a man's wives and offspring was a function of his longevity. This conclusion indicates that more research needs to be done on this ethnographic issue to provide more testable hypotheses.

One of the negative consequences of the publication of Tierney's book is that politicians, scholars, and journalists in various countries have been calling for a boycott of further anthropological and medical research on populations in their regions. Without assessing Tierney's claims, many countries have declared their populations "off limits" to anthropological research or medical care from outsiders (Gregor and Gross 2004). Surely, this will have negative effects on the indigenous peoples who will be invaded by gold miners, be infected by diseases from the outside, and experience the downside of globalization, without having their conditions ameliorated or improved by research and medical care.

The allegations in Tierney's book have been refuted with the completion of the final report of the American Anthropological Association (AAA) in 2001. As anthropologists were shaken worldwide by the publication of the allegations within Tierney's book, the AAA appointed a task force that assessed the ethics of anthropological research in light of the allegations in Tierney's book. The AAA emphasized that the Yanomamö are currently in a position of great danger, with exceptionally high rates of infant mortality, African river blindness, and malaria. Their land, livelihood, and lives are imperiled. The AAA also emphasized that it was not condemning or finding fault with or defending the past actions of Chagnon or others; rather, it was providing opportunities for all anthropologists to consider the ethics of several dimensions of the anthropological enterprise. In 2010, the blood samples collected by James Neel have been returned to the Yanomamö (Couzin-Frankel 2010).

As Robert Borofsky's book about the controversy indicates, *Darkness in El Dorado* did call attention to the dire plight of the Yanomamö and other indigenous people of the Amazon and has caused anthropologists to reflect deeply on the ways in which they conduct research. However, as the various investigations of the scientific and ethical controversy indicate, Tierney's book contains many unfounded, misrepresented, and sensationalistic accusations about the conduct of anthropology among the Yanomamö. These misrepresentations fail to live up to the ethics of responsible journalism even as they pretend to question the ethical conduct of anthropology.

As described in Borofsky's book on the controversy, most anthropologists today, as they look back on the early stages of Chagnon's research, would not conduct themselves in the

CONTINUED

same manner. Chastened by some of the postmodern critiques about fieldwork in anthropology (see Chapter 13), anthropologists today are much more sensitive to their own role and activities among the people they are studying. Presently, many of the native peoples have become educated, and some of them are actively engaged in ethnographic research themselves. Anthropologists today are active in obtaining informed consent from the people they are studying to avoid harmful research activity. In other words, the population being studied must have the right to approve the research project and withdraw from it if it is harmful to their interests (Couzin-Frankel 2010). Sometimes, this creates difficulties as anthropologists come across difficult ethical and political problems in their research locations. However, ethnographic research ought to be practiced in accord with the ethical principles espoused by the medical oath of the Hippocratic creed: "Do No Harm."

To be fair to Chagnon, over the years he developed many close ties and friendships among the Yanomamö and organized a Yanomamö survival fund to try to help protect these people from external forces that wanted to take their land (Dreger 2011; Lancaster and Hames 2011). If it was not for the thorough pioneering research on the Yanomamö by Chagnon, we would probably not be aware of the conditions and problems that these people face today. Ethnographic research and anthropological explanations and interpretations have to proceed, despite the negative publicity that they sometimes entail. On the other hand, anthropologists must be aware of some of the unintended results of their ethnographic research that can result in harm to the populations among which they reside. Without anthropologists, we are not going to be able to gain a comprehensive picture of humanity's diversity throughout the world. But obtaining that portrait inevitably offers ethical and political challenges for anthropologists who want to learn, but also help improve conditions for humanity across the world.

Points to Ponder

1. Can you think of any cases where popular portrayals of scientific research proved to be dramatically wrong?

2. Can ethnographic research be conducted without changing the circumstances of the people being studied?

3. How should contemporary anthropologists conduct their ethnographic fieldwork?

4. How do you weigh the moral claims versus the scientific research in this controversy?

and Channa assert that a gender-neutral inheritance law in which women and men receive equal shares ought to be established to help reduce the discrepancy between males and females in India.

In addition, Van Willigen and Channa recommended the establishment of universal marriage registration and licensing throughout India. This may enable the government to monitor dowry abuses so that antidowry legislation could be more effective. These anthropologists concluded that a broad program to increase the social and economic status of women, along with more rigorous control of marriage registration and licensing, would be more effective in solving the dowry death problem in Indian society.

The use of applied anthropology, based on collaboration among Western and non-Western anthropologists, government and military officials, economic consultants and advisors, and local and national government leaders, to help solve fundamental human rights issues represents a commendable strategy for applied anthropologists in the future. It is hoped that through better cross-cultural understanding, aided by ethnographic research, and through applied anthropology, universally recognized humanitarian standards will be widely adopted throughout the world. Many anthropologists are promoting advocacy anthropology, the use of anthropological knowledge to further human rights. Universal human rights would include the right to life and freedom from physical and psychological abuse,

Applied anthropologists use their research to help develop human rights for women in India and in other areas of the world.

including torture; freedom from arbitrary arrest and imprisonment; freedom from slavery and genocide; the right to nationality; freedom of movement and departure from one's country; the right to seek asylum in other countries because of persecution in one's own country; the rights to privacy, ownership of property, and freedom of speech, religion, and assembly; the right of self-determination; and the right to adequate food, shelter, health care, and education (Sponsel 1996). Obviously, not all these rights exist in any society at present. However, most people will probably agree that these rights ought to be part of any society's obligations to its people.

As people everywhere are brought closer together with the expansion of the global village, different societies will experience greater pressures to treat one another in sensitive and humane ways. We live in a world in which our destinies are tied to one another more closely than they have ever been. Yet, it is a world containing many different societies with varied norms and practices. Sometimes, this leads to mutual distrust and dangerous confrontations, such as the 9/11 tragedy in the United States.

Anthropologists may be able to play a role in helping to bring about mutual understanding of another's right to existence. Perhaps, through this understanding we may be able to develop a worldwide, **metaculture**, a global system emphasizing fundamental human rights, with a sense of political and global responsibility. This cross-cultural understanding and mutual respect for human rights may be the most important aspect of anthropological research today.

✓●⌐ **Study** and **Review** on **myanthrolab.com**

Summary

Applied anthropology is one of the specializations that has offered new opportunities for physical anthropologists, archaeologists, and ethnologists to serve as consultants to public and private agencies to help solve local and global human problems. Applied anthropologists cooperate with government officials and others in establishing economic development projects, health care systems, and substance abuse programs. They serve in a variety of roles, including representatives of indigenous groups, facilitators of change or development, or analysts, helping to bring about solutions to human problems.

Physical anthropologists help solve problems related to the design of physical environments for the human body. They also provide assistance in solving crimes using their knowledge in the growing field of forensic anthropology. A recent development in the field of archaeology is cultural resource management, or applied archaeology. Legislation passed by state and federal authorities in the United States requires the preservation of both prehistoric and historic materials. Applied archaeologists are involved in identifying important sites that may be endangered by development. They conduct surveys and excavations to preserve data that are important to understanding the cultural heritage of the United States. Cultural resource management offers new career opportunities for archaeologists in government agencies, universities, and consulting firms.

Early anthropologists who accepted the tenets of cultural relativism sometimes also embraced ethical relativism, the idea that a person should not make value judgments about other societies. Although most anthropologists reject ethical relativism, the issue of universal standards to evaluate values and harmful cultural practices is still problematic. Proposing universal standards to make value judgments and help reduce harmful cultural practices remains one of the most important tasks for applied anthropology and future ethnological research.

Questions to Think About

1. What is applied anthropology? Erve Chambers suggests that there are different roles that applied anthropologists play. Discuss each of these roles as they apply to present-day applied anthropological studies.

2. Forensic anthropology may offer information of critical importance in a police investigation. Consider the different types of information that can and cannot be provided.

3. What is medical anthropology? What are some of the types of things that medical anthropologists do?

4. What is cultural resource management? What resources are being evaluated and preserved?

5. Examine the concepts of cultural relativism and ethical relativism. Can an anthropologist be involved in applied anthropology and adhere to either of these principles or views? Are there any problems associated with an ethical relativist perspective?

6. Is it possible to understand the values and world-view of another culture and not accept all of their practices and standards? In other words, can one be a cultural relativist and not an ethical relativist at the same time?

7. Do you think it is possible to adopt a humanitarian standard that would be accepted by everyone in the world? What might this view entail?

8. Are there universal human rights?

Key Terms

applied anthropology

cultural patrimony

cultural resource management

epidemiology

ethical relativism

forensic anthropology

medical anthropology

metaculture

repatriate

social-impact studies

[●—[Read the Original Source on myanthrolab.com

For further information about topics covered in this chapter, go to MyAnthroLab at www.myanthrolab.com and access the following readings in MyAnthroLibrary:

Jonathan G. Andelson, *Building a Dream: International Communities in Anthropological and Historical Perspective*.
Alex Cohen and Paul Koegel, *Homelessness*.

Andrew W. Miracle, *A Shaman to Organizations*.
Paul C. Rosenblatt, *Human Rights Violations Across Cultures*.

Sociology

The Sociological Perspective

The Sociological Perspective

Bangladesh

E ven from the glow of the faded red-and-white exit sign, its faint light barely illuminating the upper bunk, I could see that the sheet was filthy. Resigned to another night of fitful sleep, I reluctantly crawled into bed. I kept my clothes on.

The next morning, I joined the long line of disheveled men leaning against the chain-link fence. Their faces were as downcast as their clothes were dirty. Not a glimmer of hope among them.

> I was determined. "I will experience what they experience," I kept telling myself.

No one spoke as the line slowly inched forward.

When my turn came, I was handed a cup of coffee, a white plastic spoon, and a bowl of semi-liquid that I couldn't identify. It didn't look like any food I had seen before. Nor did it taste like anything I had ever eaten.

My stomach fought the foul taste, every spoonful a battle. But I was determined. "I will experience what they experience," I kept telling myself. My stomach reluctantly gave in and accepted its morning nourishment.

The room was strangely silent. Hundreds of men were eating, each one immersed in his own private hell, his mind awash with disappointment, remorse, bitterness.

As I stared at the Styrofoam cup that held my coffee, grateful for at least this small pleasure, I noticed what looked like teeth marks. I shrugged off the thought, telling myself that my long weeks as a sociological observer of the homeless were finally getting to me. "It must be some sort of crease from handling," I concluded.

I joined the silent ranks of men turning in their bowls and cups. When I saw the man behind the counter swishing out Styrofoam cups in a washtub of murky water, I began to feel sick to my stomach. I knew then that the jagged marks on my cup really had come from another person's mouth.

How much longer did this research have to last? I felt a deep longing to return to my family—to a welcome world of clean sheets, healthy food, and "normal" conversations.

The Sociological Perspective

Why were these men so silent? Why did they receive such despicable treatment? What was I doing in that homeless shelter? After all, I hold a respectable, professional position, and I have a home and family.

Sociology offers a perspective, a view of the world. The *sociological perspective* (or imagination) opens a window onto unfamiliar worlds—and offers a fresh look at familiar ones. You will find yourself looking at your own world in a different light. As you view other worlds—or your own—the sociological perspective enables you to gain a new perception of social life. In fact, this is what many find appealing about sociology.

The sociological perspective has been a motivating force in my own life. Ever since I took my introductory course in sociology, I have been enchanted by the perspective that sociology offers. I have enjoyed both observing other groups and questioning my own assumptions about life. I sincerely hope the same happens to you.

Seeing the Broader Social Context

The **sociological perspective** stresses the social contexts in which people live. It examines how these contexts influence people's lives. At the center of the sociological perspective is the question of how groups influence people, especially how people are influenced by their **society**—a group of people who share a culture and a territory.

To find out why people do what they do, sociologists look at **social location,** the corners in life that people occupy because of where they are located in a society. Sociologists look at how jobs, income, education, gender, age, and race–ethnicity affect people's ideas and behavior. Consider, for example, how being identified with a group called *females* or with a group called *males* when you were growing up has shaped your ideas of who you are. Growing up as a female or a male has influenced not only how you feel about yourself but also your ideas of what you should attain in life and how you relate to others.

Sociologist C. Wright Mills (1959) put it this way: "The sociological imagination [perspective] enables us to grasp the connection between history and biography." By *history*, Mills meant that each society is located in a broad stream of events. This gives each society specific characteristics—such as its ideas about the proper roles of men and women. By *biography*, Mills referred to our experiences, which give us our orientations to life. In short, people don't do what they do because they inherited some internal mechanism, such as instincts. Rather, *external* influences—our experiences—become part of our thinking and motivation. In short, the society in which we grow up, and our particular location in that society, lie at the center of what we do and how we think.

Consider a newborn baby. As you know, if we were to take the baby away from its U.S. parents and place it with the Yanomamö Indians in the jungles of South America,

sociological perspective understanding human behavior by placing it within its broader social context

society people who share a culture and a territory

social location the group memberships that people have because of their location in history and society

Examining the broad social context in which people live is essential to the *sociological perspective*, for this context shapes our beliefs and attitudes and sets guidelines for what we do. From this photo of a Yanomamö man blowing yokoana, a hallucinogenic powder, up his nose, you can see how distinctive those guidelines are for the Yanomamö Indians who live on the border of Brazil and Venezuela. How has this Yanomamö man been influenced by his group? How have groups influenced *your* views and behavior?

©Victor Englebert/Time Life Pictures/Getty Images

when the child began to speak, his or her words would not be in English. You also know that the child would not think like an American. The child would not grow up wanting credit cards, for example, or a car, a cell phone, and an iPod. He or she would take his or her place in Yanomamö society—perhaps as a food gatherer or a hunter—and would not even know about the world left behind at birth. And, whether male or female, the child would grow up assuming that it is natural to want many children, not debating whether to have one, two, or three children.

If you have been thinking along with me—and I hope you have—you should be thinking about how *your* social groups have shaped *your* ideas and desires. The way you look at the world is the result of your exposure to specific human groups. I think you will enjoy the process of self-discovery that sociology offers.

The Global Context—and the Local

How life has changed! Our predecessors lived on isolated farms and in small towns. They grew their own food and made their own clothing. They bought only sugar, coffee, and a few other items that they couldn't produce. Beyond the borders of their small communities lay a world they perceived only dimly. The labels on our clothing (from Hong Kong to Italy), in contrast, as well as the many other imported products that have become part of our daily lives shout that our world has shrunk into a global village.

Even though we can pick up a telephone or use the Internet to communicate instantly with people anywhere on the planet, we continue to occupy our own little corners of life. Like those of our predecessors, our worlds, too, are marked by differences in family background, religion, gender, race–ethnicity, and social class. In these corners, we continue to learn distinctive ways of viewing the world.

One of the beautiful—and fascinating—aspects of sociology is that it enables us to look at both parts of our current reality: the changes that incorporate us into a global network *and* our unique experiences in our smaller corners of life. Each of these worlds is so vital to understanding who we are.

Origins of Sociology

Tradition Versus Science

Just how did sociology begin? In some ways, it is difficult to answer this question. Even ancient peoples tried to figure out social life. They, too, asked questions about why war exists, why some people become more powerful than others, and why some are rich, but others are poor. However, they often based their answers on superstition, myth, or even the position of the stars and did not *test* their assumptions.

Science, in contrast, requires theories that can be tested by research. Measured by this standard, sociology emerged about the middle of the 1800s, when social observers began to use scientific methods to test their ideas.

Sociology was born in social upheaval. The Industrial Revolution had just begun, and masses of people were moving to cities in search of work. This broke their ties to the land—and to a culture that had provided ready answers to the difficult questions of life. The cities greeted them with horrible working conditions: low pay; long hours; and dangerous work. Families lived on the edge of starvation, and children worked alongside the adults. Life no longer looked the same, and tradition, which had provided the answers to social life, no longer could be counted on.

Tradition suffered further blows. With the success of the American and French revolutions, new ideas swept out the old. As the idea that individuals possess inalienable rights caught fire, many traditional Western monarchies gave way to more democratic forms of government. This stimulated even new perspectives.

The French Revolution of 1789 not only overthrew the aristocracy but also upset the entire social order. This extensive change removed the past as a sure guide to the present. The events of this period stimulated Auguste Comte to analyze how societies change. His writings are often taken as the origin of sociology. This painting shows a crowd of women marching to Versailles to capture the royal family.

©Roger-Viollet/The Image Works

scientific method the use of objective systematic observations to test theories

positivism the application of the scientific approach to the social world

sociology the scientific study of society and human behavior

class conflict Marx's term for the struggle between capitalists and workers

bourgeoisie Marx's term for capitalists, those who own the means of production

Auguste Comte (1798–1857), who is credited as the founder of sociology, began to analyze the bases of the social order. Although he stressed that the *scientific method* should be applied to the study of society, he did not apply it himself.

About this time, the **scientific method**—using objective, systematic observations to test theories—was being tried out in chemistry and physics. This opened many secrets that had been concealed in nature. With traditional answers falling, the next step was to apply the scientific method to questions about social life. The result was the birth of sociology.

Auguste Comte and Positivism

Auguste Comte (1798–1857) suggested that we apply the scientific method to the social world, a process known as **positivism.** Reflecting on the upheavals of the French Revolution and on the changes he experienced when he moved to Paris from the small town in which he had grown up, Comte wondered what holds society together. He began to ask what creates social order, instead of anarchy or chaos, and why, once society becomes set on a particular course, what causes it to change.

Comte decided that the scientific method held the key to answering such questions. Just as the scientific method had revealed the law of gravity, so, too, it would uncover the laws that underlie society. Comte called this new science **sociology**—"the study of society" (from the Greek *logos,* "study of," and the Latin *socius,* "companion," or "being with others"). The purpose of this new science, he said, would be not only to discover social principles but also to apply them to social reform. Comte developed a grandiose view: Sociologists would reform the entire society, making it a better place to live.

Comte did not do what we today call research, and his conclusions have been abandoned. Nevertheless, his insistence that we must observe and classify human activities to uncover society's fundamental laws is well taken. Because he developed and coined the term *sociology,* Comte often is credited with being the founder of sociology.

Herbert Spencer and Social Darwinism

Herbert Spencer (1820–1903), who grew up in England, is sometimes called the second founder of sociology. Spencer's views were quite different. He said that sociology should *not* guide social reform. Societies are evolving, going from lower ("barbarian") to higher ("civilized") forms. As generations pass, a society's most capable and intelligent ("the fittest") members survive, while the less capable die out. These fittest members produce a more advanced society—unless misguided do-gooders get in the way and help the less fit (the lower classes) survive.

Spencer called this principle *the survival of the fittest.* Although Spencer coined this phrase, it usually is attributed to his contemporary, Charles Darwin, who proposed that organisms evolve over time as they adapt to their environment. Where Spencer referred to the evolution of societies, Darwin referred to the evolution of organisms. Because Darwin is better known, Spencer's idea is called *social Darwinism.* History is fickle, and if fame had gone the other way, we might be speaking of "biological Spencerism."

Like Comte, Spencer did armchair philosophy instead of conducting scientific studies, and his ideas, too, were discarded.

Karl Marx and Class Conflict

Karl Marx (1818–1883) not only influenced sociology but also left his mark on world history. Marx's influence has been so great that even the *Wall Street Journal,* that staunch advocate of capitalism, has called him one of the three greatest modern thinkers (the other two being Sigmund Freud and Albert Einstein).

Like Comte, Marx thought that people should try to change society. His proposal for change was radical: revolution. This got him thrown out of Germany, and he settled in England. Marx believed that the engine of human history is **class conflict.** Society is made up of two social classes, he said, and they are natural enemies: the **bourgeoisie** (boo-shwa-ZEE) (the *capitalists,* those who own the capital, land, factories, and machines) and the **proletariat** (the exploited workers). Eventually, the workers will unite and break their chains of bondage. The workers' revolution will be bloody, but it will usher in a classless society, one free of exploitation. People will work according to their abilities and receive goods and services according to their needs (Marx and Engels 1848/1967).

Marxism is not the same as communism. Although Marx proposed revolution as the way for workers to gain control of society, he did not develop the political system called *communism.* This is a later application of his ideas. Marx himself was disgusted when he heard debates about his analysis of social life. After listening to some of the positions attributed to him, he shook his head and said, "I am not a Marxist" (Dobriner 1969b:222; Gitlin 1997:89).

Emile Durkheim and Social Integration

The primary professional goal of Emile Durkheim (1858–1917), who grew up in France, was to get sociology recognized as a separate academic discipline (Coser 1977). Until Durkheim's time, sociology was viewed as part of history and economics. Durkheim achieved his goal in 1887 when the University of Bordeaux awarded him the world's first academic appointment in sociology.

Durkheim's second goal was to show how social forces affect people's behavior. To accomplish this, he conducted rigorous research. Comparing the suicide rates of several European countries, Durkheim (1897/1966) found that each country has a different suicide rate—and that these rates remain about the same year after year. He also found that different groups within a country have different suicide rates and that these, too, remain stable from year to year: Males are more likely than females to kill themselves, Protestants more likely than Catholics or Jews, and the unmarried more likely than the married. From these observations, Durkheim concluded that suicide is not what it appears—individuals here and there deciding to take their lives for personal reasons. Instead, *social factors underlie suicide,* which is why a group's rate remains fairly constant year after year.

Durkheim identified **social integration,** the degree to which people are tied to their social groups, as a key social factor in suicide. He concluded that people who have weaker social ties are more likely to commit suicide. This, he said, explains why Protestants, males, and the unmarried have higher suicide rates. This is how it works: Protestantism encourages greater freedom of thought and action; males are more independent than females; and the unmarried lack the ties that come with marriage. In other words, members of these groups have fewer of the social bonds that keep people from committing suicide. In Durkheim's term, they have less social integration.

Despite the many years that have passed since Durkheim did his research, the principle he uncovered still applies: People who are less socially integrated have higher rates of

Herbert Spencer (1820–1903), sometimes called the second founder of sociology, coined the term "survival of the fittest." Spencer thought that helping the poor was wrong, that this merely helped the "less fit" survive.

Karl Marx (1818–1883) believed that the roots of human misery lay in class conflict, the exploitation of workers by those who own the means of production. Social change, in the form of the overthrow of the capitalists by the workers (*proletariat*), was inevitable from Marx's perspective. Although Marx did not consider himself a sociologist, his ideas have influenced many sociologists, particularly conflict theorists.

proletariat Marx's term for the exploited class, the mass of workers who do not own the means of production

social integration the degree to which members of a group or a society feel united by shared values and other social bonds; also known as *social cohesion*

The French sociologist **Emile Durkheim** (1858–1917) contributed many important concepts to sociology. His comparison of the suicide rates of several counties revealed an underlying social factor: People are more likely to commit suicide if their ties to others in their communities are weak. Durkheim's identification of the key role of *social integration* in social life remains central to sociology today.

©Bettmann/Corbis

suicide. Even today, those same groups that Durkheim identified—Protestants, males, and the unmarried—are more likely to kill themselves.

Here is the principle that was central in Durkheim's research: *Human behavior cannot be understood only in terms of the individual; we must always examine the social forces that affect people's lives.* Suicide, for example, appears to be such an intensely individual act that psychologists should study it, not sociologists. As Durkheim stressed, however, if we look at human behavior only in reference to the individual, we miss its *social* basis. To see what Durkheim meant, look at Figure 1, which shows the methods by which African Americans and whites commit suicide. I'm sure you'll be struck by how similar their methods are. It might surprise you that the patterns are so consistent that we can predict, with high accuracy, that 29,000 whites and 2,000 African Americans will commit suicide this year. The patterns are so firm that we can also predict that of the 29,000 whites about 15,500 will use guns to kill themselves, and that of the 2,000 African Americans 60 to 70 will jump to their deaths. Since these patterns recur year after year, they indicate something far beyond individuals. They reflect conditions in society, such as the popularity and accessibility of guns. They also reflect conditions that we don't understand. Perhaps this course in sociology will pique a student's interest enough to investigate these patterns.

Max Weber and the Protestant Ethic

Max Weber (Mahx VAY-ber) (1864–1920), a German sociologist and a contemporary of Durkheim, also became a professor in the new academic discipline of sociology. With Durkheim and Marx, Weber is one of the three most influential of all sociologists, and you will come across his writings and theories in later chapters. For now, let's consider an issue Weber raised that remains controversial today.

Religion and the Origin of Capitalism. Weber disagreed with Marx's claim that economics is the central force in social change. That role, he said, belongs to religion. Here's how it works. Roman Catholics were taught that because they were church members they were on the road to heaven. This encouraged them to hold on to traditional ways of life. Protestants, in contrast, those of the Calvinist tradition, were told that they wouldn't know if they were saved until Judgment Day. Understandably, this teaching made them a little uncomfortable. Looking for "signs" that they were in God's will, the Calvinists concluded that financial success was a blessing, indicating that God was on their side. This motivated them to bring about this "sign" and receive spiritual comfort. They began to live frugal

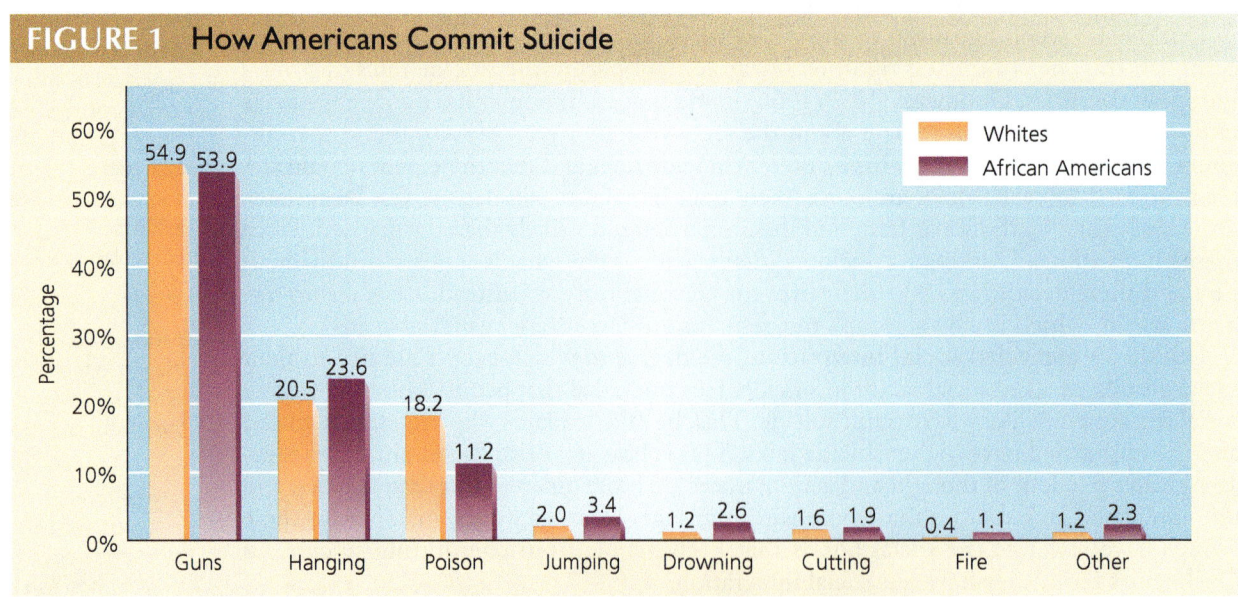

FIGURE 1 How Americans Commit Suicide

Legend: Whites, African Americans

Method	Whites	African Americans
Guns	54.9	53.9
Hanging	20.5	23.6
Poison	18.2	11.2
Jumping	2.0	3.4
Drowning	1.2	2.6
Cutting	1.6	1.9
Fire	0.4	1.1
Other	1.2	2.3

Note: These totals are the mean of years 2001–2005. ("Mean" is explained on page 23.)
Source: By the author. Based on Centers for Disease Control and Prevention 2007c, and earlier years.

lives, saving their money, and investing it in order to make even more. A surprising result of religious teaching, then, was the birth of capitalism, which transformed society.

Weber (1904/1958) called this self-denying approach to life the *Protestant ethic.* He termed the readiness to invest capital in order to make more money the *spirit of capitalism.* To test his theory, Weber compared the extent of capitalism in Roman Catholic and Protestant countries. In line with his theory, he found that capitalism was more likely to flourish in Protestant countries. Weber's conclusion that religion was the key factor in the rise of capitalism was controversial when he made it, and it continues to be debated today (Wade 2007).

Sociology in North America

Sexism and Early Female Sociologists

As you may have noticed, all the sociologists we have discussed are men. In the 1800s, sex roles were rigid, with women assigned the roles of wife and mother. In the classic German phrase, women were expected to devote themselves to the four K's: *Kirche, Küchen, Kinder, und Kleider* (the four C's in English: church, cooking, children, and clothes). To try to break out of this mold meant risking severe disapproval.

Few people, male or female, attained any education beyond basic reading and writing and a little math. Higher education, for the rare few who received it, was reserved primarily for men. Of the handful of women who did pursue higher education, some became prominent in early sociology. Marion Talbot, for example, was an associate editor of the *American Journal of Sociology* for thirty years, from its founding in 1895 to 1925. The influence of some early female sociologists went far beyond sociology. Grace Abbott became the first chief of the U.S. government's Children's Bureau, and Frances Perkins was the first woman to hold a cabinet position, serving twelve years as Secretary of Labor under President Franklin Roosevelt. Jane Addams was awarded the Nobel Prize for Peace, the only sociologist to win this acclaimed honor. Photos of some of these early sociologists are included in this chapter.

Many early female sociologists wrote extensively. Their writings—and matching social activism—were directed almost exclusively at social reform, such as ways to improve the working conditions of poorly paid workers, the need to integrate immigrants into society, and promotion of the anti-lynching movement. As sociology developed in North America, a debate arose about the proper purpose of sociology: Should it be social reform or objective analysis? At that time, the debate was won by those who held the university positions. These were men, and it was they who then wrote the history of sociology. Distancing themselves from the social reformers, they ignored the early female sociologists (Lengermann and Niebrugge 2007). Now that women have again become a voice in sociology—and have begun to rewrite its history—early female sociologists are again, as here, being acknowledged.

Harriet Martineau and Research on the United States

A good example is Harriet Martineau (1802–1876), who was born into a wealthy English family. When Martineau first began to analyze social life, she would hide her writing beneath her sewing when visitors arrived, for writing was considered "masculine" and sewing "feminine" (Gilman 1911:88). Martineau persisted in her interests, however, and she eventually studied social life in both Great Britain and the United States. In 1837, two or three decades before Durkheim and Weber were born, Martineau published *Society in America.* In this remarkable book, she analyzed this new nation's customs—family, race, gender, politics, and religion. Despite her insightful analysis of U.S. life, which is still worth reading today, Martineau's research met the same fate as that of other early female sociologists and, until recently, was ignored. Instead, she became known primarily for translating Comte's ideas into English.

Racism at the Time: W. E. B. Du Bois

Not only was sexism assumed to be normal during this early period of sociology, but so was racism, which made life difficult for African American professionals such as

The Granger Collection, New York

Max Weber (1864–1920) was another early sociologist who left a profound impression on sociology. He used crosscultural and historical materials to trace the causes of social change and to determine how social groups affect people's orientations to life.

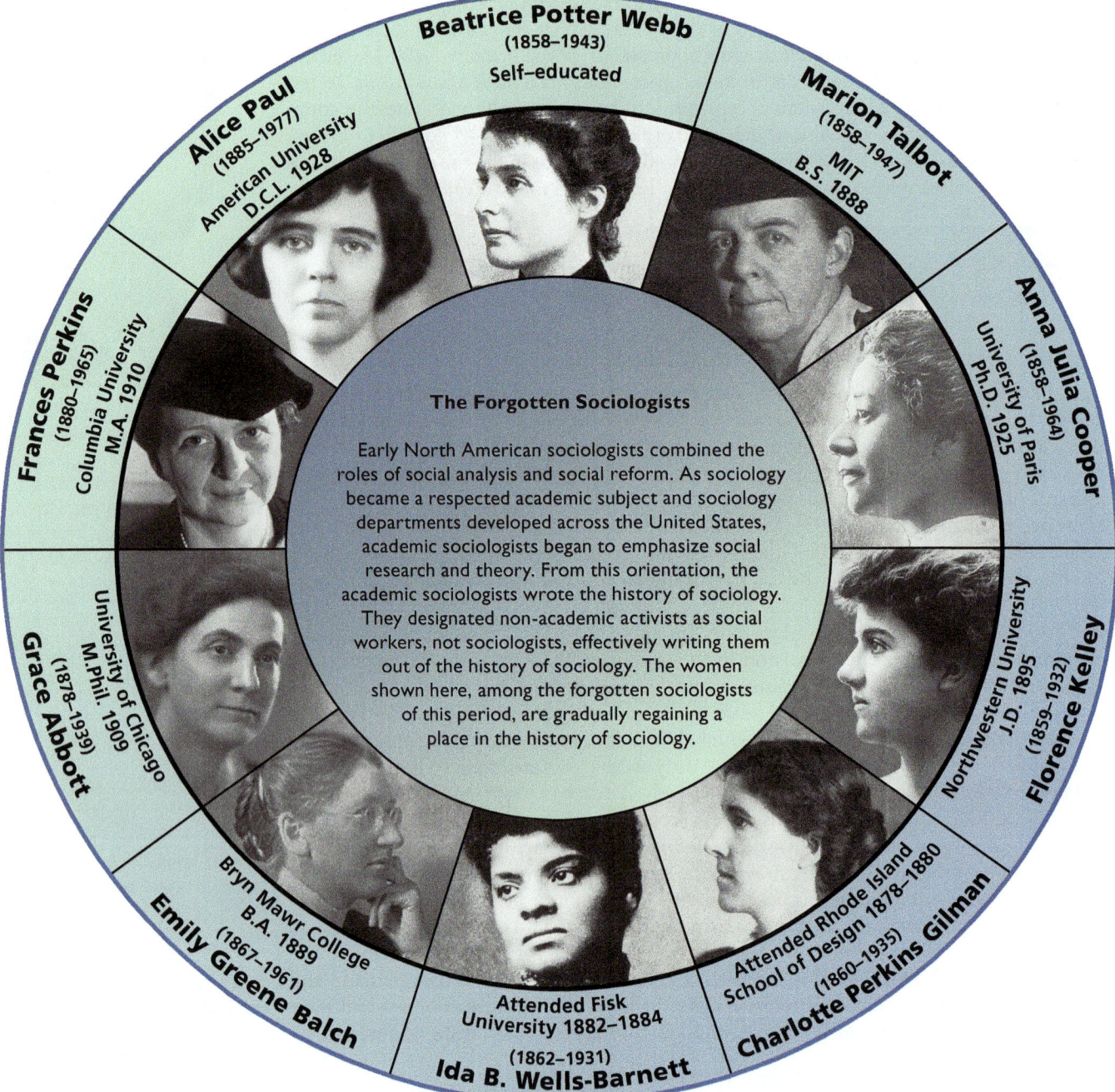

The Forgotten Sociologists

Early North American sociologists combined the roles of social analysis and social reform. As sociology became a respected academic subject and sociology departments developed across the United States, academic sociologists began to emphasize social research and theory. From this orientation, the academic sociologists wrote the history of sociology. They designated non-academic activists as social workers, not sociologists, effectively writing them out of the history of sociology. The women shown here, among the forgotten sociologists of this period, are gradually regaining a place in the history of sociology.

Beatrice Potter Webb
(1858–1943)
Self–educated

Alice Paul
(1885–1977)
American University
D.C.L. 1928

Marion Talbot
(1858–1947)
MIT
B.S. 1888

Frances Perkins
(1880–1965)
Columbia University
M.A. 1910

Anna Julia Cooper
(1858–1964)
University of Paris
Ph.D. 1925

Grace Abbott
(1878–1939)
University of Chicago
M.Phil. 1909

Florence Kelley
(1859–1932)
Northwestern University
J.D. 1895

Emily Greene Balch
(1867–1961)
Bryn Mawr College
B.A. 1889

Charlotte Perkins Gilman
(1860–1935)
Attended Rhode Island
School of Design 1878–1880

Ida B. Wells-Barnett
(1862–1931)
Attended Fisk
University 1882–1884

(Gilman): Hulton Archive/Getty Images; (Cooper): The Granger Collection, New York; (Wells-Barnett): R. Gates/Hulton Archive/Getty Images; (Kelley, Perkins & Paul): Bettmann/Corbis; (Webb): Mary Evans Picture Library/The Image Works; (Balch): Wellesley College Archives; (Abbott & Talbot): The University of Chicago Library Special Collections Research Center

W. E. B. Du Bois (1868–1963). Du Bois, who became the first African American to earn a doctorate at Harvard, also studied at the University of Berlin, where he attended lectures by Max Weber. In 1897, Du Bois went to Atlanta University, where he remained for most of his career. You can get a flavor of this period from the Down-to-Earth Sociology box on the next page.

It is difficult to grasp how racist society was at this time. As Du Bois passed a butcher shop in Georgia one day, he saw the fingers of a lynching victim displayed in the window (Aptheker 1990). When Du Bois went to national meetings of the American Sociological Society, restaurants and hotels would not allow him to eat or room with the white sociologists. How times have changed. Today, sociologists would not only boycott such establishments, but also refuse to hold meetings in that state. At that time, however, racism, like sexism, prevailed throughout society, rendering it mostly invisible to white sociologists.

Down-to-Earth Sociology

W. E. B. Du Bois: The Souls of Black Folk

Du Bois wrote more like an accomplished novelist than a sociologist. The following excerpt is from pages 66–68 of *The Souls of Black Folk* (1903). In this book, Du Bois analyzes changes that occurred in the social and economic conditions of African Americans during the thirty years following the Civil War.

For two summers, while he was a student at Fisk University, Du Bois taught in a segregated school housed in a log hut "way back in the hills" of rural Tennessee. The following excerpts help us understand conditions at that time.

In the 1800s, most people were so poor that they expended their life energies on just getting enough food, fuel, and clothing to survive. The average person died before reaching age 40. Formal education beyond the first several grades was a luxury. This photo depicts the conditions of the people Du Bois worked with.

It was a hot morning late in July when the school opened. I trembled when I heard the patter of little feet down the dusty road, and saw the growing row of dark solemn faces and bright eager eyes facing me. . . . There they sat, nearly thirty of them, on the rough benches, their faces shading from a pale cream to deep brown, the little feet bare and swinging, the eyes full of expectation, with here and there a twinkle of mischief, and the hands grasping Webster's blue-black spelling-book. I loved my school, and the fine faith the children had in the wisdom of their teacher was truly marvelous. We read and spelled together, wrote a little, picked flowers, sang, and listened to stories of the world beyond the hill. . . .

On Friday nights I often went home with some of the children—sometimes to Doc Burke's farm. He was a great, loud, thin Black, ever working, and trying to buy these seventy-five acres of hill and dale where he lived; but people said that he would surely fail and the "white folks would get it all." His wife was a magnificent Amazon, with saffron face and shiny hair, uncorseted and barefooted, and the children were strong and barefooted. They lived in a one-and-a-half-room cabin in the hollow of the farm near the spring. . . .

Often, to keep the peace, I must go where life was less lovely; for instance, 'Tildy's mother was incorrigibly dirty, Reuben's larder was limited seriously, and herds of untamed insects wandered over the Eddingses' beds. Best of all I loved to go to Josie's, and sit on the porch, eating peaches, while the mother bustled and talked: how Josie had bought the sewing-machine; how Josie worked at service in winter, but that four dollars a month was "mighty little" wages; how Josie longed to go away to school, but that it "looked liked" they never could get far

enough ahead to let her; how the crops failed and the well was yet unfinished; and, finally, how mean some of the white folks were.

For two summers I lived in this little world. . . . I have called my tiny community a world, and so its isolation made it; and yet there was among us but a half-awakened common consciousness, sprung from common joy and grief, at burial, birth, or wedding; from common hardship in poverty, poor land, and low wages, and, above all, from the sight of the Veil* that hung between us and Opportunity. All this caused us to think some thoughts together; but these, when ripe for speech, were spoken in various languages. Those whose eyes twenty-five and more years had seen "the glory of the coming of the Lord," saw in every present hindrance or help a dark fatalism bound to bring all things right in His own good time. The mass of those to whom slavery was a dim recollection of childhood found the world a puzzling thing: it asked little of them, and they answered with little, and yet it ridiculed their offering. Such a paradox they could not understand, and therefore sank into listless indifference, or shiftlessness, or reckless bravado.

*"The Veil" is shorthand for the Veil of Race, referring to how race colors all human relations. Du Bois' hope, as he put it, was that "sometime, somewhere, men will judge men by their souls and not by their skins" (p. 261).

W(illiam) **E**(dward) **B**(urghardt) **Du Bois** (1868–1963) spent his lifetime studying relations between African Americans and whites. Like many early North Americans sociologists, Du Bois combined the role of academic sociologist with that of social reformer. He was also the editor of *Crisis*, an influential journal of the time.

Du Bois did extensive research, for about twenty or so years publishing a book a year on black–white relations. He was also a social activist. Along with Jane Addams and others from Hull-House, Du Bois founded the National Association for the Advancement of Colored People (NAACP). Continuing to battle racism both as a sociologist and as a journalist, Du Bois eventually embraced revolutionary Marxism. He became such an outspoken critic of racism that for years the U.S. State Department, fearing he would criticize the United States, refused to issue him a passport (Du Bois 1968). At age 93, dismayed that so little improvement had been made in race relations, he moved to Ghana, where he died and is buried (Stark 1989).

Talcott Parsons and C. Wright Mills: Theory Versus Reform

Like Du Bois and Addams, many early North American sociologists worked toward the reform of society, but by the 1940s the emphasis had shifted to social theory. Talcott Parsons (1902–1979), for example, a major sociologist of this period, developed abstract models of society that influenced a generation of sociologists. Deploring Parsons' theoretical abstractions and the general dry analyses of this period, C. Wright Mills (1916–1962) urged sociologists to get back to social reform. He said that sociologists were missing the point, that our freedom was threatened by the coalescing interests of a group he called the *power elite*—the top leaders of business, politics, and the military. Shortly after Mills' death came the turbulent late 1960s and 1970s. This precedent-shaking era sparked interest in social activism, making Mills' ideas popular among a new generation of sociologists.

The Continuing Tension and Applied Sociology

As we have seen, two contradictory aims—analyzing society versus working toward its reform—have run through North American sociology since its founding. This tension is still with us. Some sociologists see their proper role as analyzing some aspect of society and publishing their findings in books and sociology journals. Others argue that sociologists have an obligation to use their expertise to try to help reform society, especially to help bring justice to the poor and oppressed.

As Figure 2 shows, somewhere between these extremes lies **applied sociology,** using sociology to solve problems. Applied sociology is not new, for as we've seen, sociologists founded the NAACP. Although today's applied sociologists lack the early sociologists' broad vision of social reform, their application of sociology is wide-ranging. Some work for business firms to solve problems in the workplace, while others investigate social problems such as pornography, rape, pollution, or the spread of AIDS. A new application of sociology is determining ways to disrupt terrorist groups (Sageman 2008).

Although applied sociology pleases many sociologists, it frustrates both those who want the emphasis to be on social reform and those who want it to be on objective analysis.

applied sociology the use of sociology to solve problems— from the micro level of family relationships to the macro level of global pollution

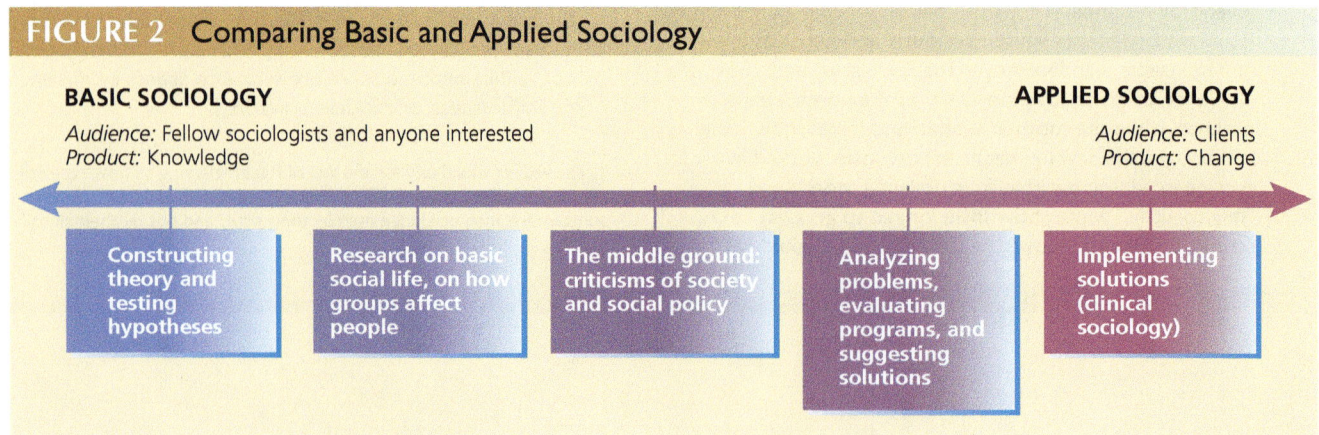

FIGURE 2 Comparing Basic and Applied Sociology

BASIC SOCIOLOGY
Audience: Fellow sociologists and anyone interested
Product: Knowledge

APPLIED SOCIOLOGY
Audience: Clients
Product: Change

| Constructing theory and testing hypotheses | Research on basic social life, on how groups affect people | The middle ground: criticisms of society and social policy | Analyzing problems, evaluating programs, and suggesting solutions | Implementing solutions (clinical sociology) |

Source: By the author. Based on DeMartini 1982.

Those who favor social reform point out that the application of sociology in some specific setting is far from an attempt to rebuild society. Those who want sociology's emphasis to be the discovery of objective knowledge say that when sociology is applied, it is no longer sociology. If, for example, sociologists use sociological principles to help teenagers escape from pimps, they say, what makes it sociology?

This contemporary debate on the purpose and use of sociology, with roots that go back a century or more, is likely to continue for another generation. At this point, let's consider how theory fits into sociology.

Theoretical Perspectives in Sociology

Facts never interpret themselves. To make sense out of life, we place our experiences (our "facts") into a framework of more-or-less related ideas. Sociologists do this, too, but they place their observations into a conceptual framework called a theory. A **theory** is a general statement about how some parts of the world fit together and how they work. It is an explanation of how two or more "facts" are related to one another.

Sociologists use three major theories: symbolic interactionism, functional analysis, and conflict theory. Let's look at each theory, first examining its main elements and then applying it to the U.S. divorce rate, to see why it is so high. As we do this, you will see how each theory, or perspective, provides a distinct interpretation of social life.

Symbolic Interactionism

The central idea of **symbolic interactionism** is that *symbols*—things to which we attach meaning—are the key to understanding how we view the world and communicate with one another. This perspective was brought to sociology by Charles Horton Cooley (1864–1929), William I. Thomas (1863–1947), and George Herbert Mead (1863–1931). Let's look at the main elements of this theory.

Symbols in Everyday Life. Without symbols, our social life would be no more sophisticated than that of animals. For example, without symbols we would have no aunts or uncles, employers or teachers—or even brothers and sisters. I know that this sounds strange, but it is symbols that define our relationships. There would still be reproduction, of course, but no symbols to tell us how we are related to whom. We would not know to whom we owe respect and obligations, or from whom we can expect privileges—the essence of human relationships.

I know it is vague to say that symbols tell you how you are related to others and how you should act toward them, so let's make this less abstract:

> Suppose that you have fallen head over heels in love. After what seems forever, it is the night before your wedding. As you are contemplating tomorrow's bliss, your mother comes to you in tears. Sobbing, she tells you that she had a child before you were born, a child that she gave up for adoption. Breaking down, she says that she has just discovered that the person you are going to marry is this child.

You can see how the symbol will change overnight—and your behavior, too!

The symbols of boyfriend and brother—or girlfriend and sister—are certainly different, and, as you know, each symbol requires rather different behavior. Not only do relationships depend on symbols, but so does society itself. Without symbols, we could not coordinate our actions with those of others. We could not make plans for a future day, time, and place. Unable to specify times, materials, sizes, or goals, we could not build bridges and highways. Without symbols, we would have no movies or musical instruments, no hospitals, no government, no religion. The class you are taking could not exist. On the positive side, there would be no war.

In Sum: Symbolic interactionists analyze how social life depends on the ways we define ourselves and others. They study face-to-face interaction, examining how people make sense out of life, how they determine their relationships.

theory a statement about how some parts of the world fit together and how they work; an explanation of how two or more facts are related to one another

symbolic interactionism a theoretical perspective in which society is viewed as composed of symbols that people use to establish meaning, develop their views of the world, and communicate with one another

FIGURE 3   U.S. Marriage, U.S. Divorce

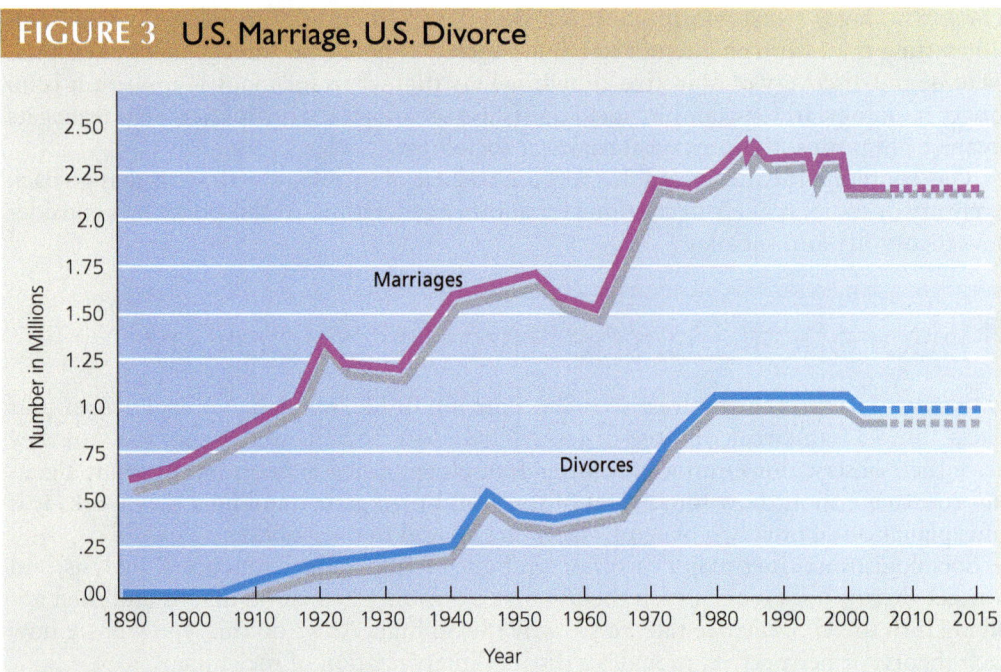

Source: By the author. Based on Statistical Abstract of the United States 1998: Table 92 and 2011: Table 129; earlier editions for earlier years; National Vital Statistics Reports, vol. 58, no. 25, NCHS, 2010. The broken lines are the author's estimates.

Applying Symbolic Interactionism.   Look at Figure 3, which shows U.S. marriages and divorces over time. Let's see how symbolic interactionists would use changing symbols to explain this figure. For background, you should understand that marriage used to be a *lifelong commitment.* A hundred years ago (and less) getting divorced was viewed as immoral, a flagrant disregard for public opinion, and the abandonment of adult responsibilities. Let's see what changed.

The meaning of marriage: By the 1930s, young people were coming to view marriage in a different way, a change that was reported by sociologists of the time. In 1933, William Ogburn observed that they were placing more emphasis on the personality of their potential mates. Then in 1945, Ernest Burgess and Harvey Locke noted that couples were expecting more affection, understanding, and compatibility in marriage. In addition, less and less people saw marriage as a lifelong commitment based on duty and obligation. As they began to view marriage as an arrangement based on attraction and feelings of intimacy, it became one that could be broken when feelings changed.

The meaning of divorce: As divorce became more common, its meaning changed. Rather than being a symbol of failure, divorce came to indicate freedom and new beginnings. Removing the stigma from divorce shattered a strong barrier that had prevented husbands and wives from breaking up.

Changed guidelines: Related symbols also changed—and none of these changes strengthened marriage. For example, traditional marriage had firm guidelines, and newlyweds knew what each was supposed to do regarding work, home, and children. In contrast, today's guidelines are vague, and couples must figure out how to divide up responsibilities. This can be a struggle, even a source of conflict, and many flounder. Although couples find it a relief not to have to conform to what they consider to be burdensome notions, those traditional expectations (or symbols) did provide a structure that made marriages last. Changing symbols weakened this structure, making marriage more fragile and divorce more common.

The meaning of parenthood: Parenthood and childhood also used to be quite different. Parents had little responsibility for their children beyond providing food, clothing, shelter, and moral guidance. And they needed to do this for only a short time, because children began to contribute to the support of the family early in life. Among many people, parenthood is still like this. In Colombia, for example, children of the poor often are expected to support themselves by the age of 8 or 10. In industrial societies, however, we assume that children are vulnerable beings who must depend on their parents for financial and emotional support for many years—often until they are well into their 20s. The greater responsibilities that we assign to parenthood place heavy burdens on today's couples and, with them, more strain on marriage.

The meaning of love: And we can't overlook the love symbol. As surprising as it may sound, to have love as the main reason for marriage weakens marriage. In some depth of our being, we expect "true love" to deliver constant emotional highs. This expectation sets people up for crushed hopes, as dissatisfactions in marriage are inevitable. When they come, spouses tend to blame one another for failing to deliver the expected satisfaction.

In Sum: Symbolic interactionists look at how changing ideas (or symbols) of love, marriage, relationships, parenthood, and divorce put pressure on married couples. No single change is *the* cause of our divorce rate, but, taken together, these changes provide a strong push toward divorce.

Functional Analysis

The central idea of **functional analysis** is that society is a whole unit, made up of interrelated parts that work together. Functional analysis (also known as *functionalism* and *structural functionalism*) is rooted in the origins of sociology. Auguste Comte and Herbert Spencer viewed society as a kind of living organism. Just as a person or animal has organs that function together, they wrote, so does society. And like an organism, if society is to function smoothly, its parts must work together in harmony.

Emile Durkheim also viewed society as being composed of many parts, each with its own function. When all the parts of society fulfill their functions, society is in a "normal" state. If they do not fulfill their functions, society is in an "abnormal" or "pathological" state. To understand society, then, functionalists say that we need to look at both *structure* (how the parts of a society fit together to make the whole) and *function* (what each part does, how it contributes to society).

Robert Merton and Functionalism. Robert Merton (1910–2003) dismissed the organic analogy, but he did maintain the essence of functionalism—the image of society as a whole composed of parts that work together. Merton used the term *functions* to refer to the beneficial consequences of people's actions: Functions help keep a group (society, social system) in balance. In contrast, *dysfunctions* are consequences that harm a society: They undermine a system's equilibrium.

Functions can be either manifest or latent. If an action is *intended* to help some part of a system, it is a *manifest function*. For example, suppose that government officials become concerned about our low rate of childbirth. Congress offers a $10,000 bonus for every child born to a married couple. The intention, or manifest function, of the bonus is to increase childbearing within the family unit. Merton pointed out that people's actions can also have *latent functions;* that is, they can have *unintended* consequences that help a system adjust. Let's suppose that the bonus works. As the birth rate jumps, so does the sale of diapers and baby furniture. Because the benefits to these businesses were not the intended consequences, they are latent functions of the bonus.

Of course, human actions can also hurt a system. Because such consequences usually are unintended, Merton called them *latent dysfunctions*. Let's assume that the government has failed to specify a "stopping point" with regard to its bonus system. To collect more bonuses, some people keep on having children. The more children they have, however, the more they need the next bonus to survive. Large families become common, and poverty increases. Welfare is reinstated, taxes jump, and the nation erupts in protest. Because these results were not intended and because they harmed the social system, they would be latent dysfunctions of the bonus program.

functional analysis a theoretical framework in which society is viewed as composed of various parts, each with a function that, when fulfilled, contributes to society's equilibrium; also known as *functionalism* and *structural functionalism*

In Sum: From the perspective of functional analysis, society is a functioning unit, with each part related to the whole. Whenever we examine a smaller part, we need to look for its functions and dysfunctions to see how it is related to the larger unit. This basic approach can be applied to any social group, whether an entire society, a college, or even a group as small as a family.

Applying Functional Analysis. Now let's apply functional analysis to the U.S. divorce rate. Functionalists stress that industrialization and urbanization undermined the traditional functions of the family. For example, before industrialization, the family formed an economic team. On the farm where most people lived, each family member had jobs or "chores" to do. The wife was in charge not only of household tasks but also of raising small animals, such as chickens. Milking cows, collecting eggs, and churning butter were also her responsibility—as were cooking, baking, canning, sewing, darning, washing, and cleaning. The daughters helped her. The husband was responsible for caring for large animals, such as horses and cattle, for planting and harvesting, and for maintaining buildings and tools. The sons helped him.

This certainly doesn't sound like life today! But what does it have to do with divorce? Simply put, the husband and wife depended on each other for survival—and there weren't many alternatives.

Other functions also bound family members to one another: educating the children, teaching them religion, providing home-based recreation, and caring for the sick and elderly. To further see how sharply family functions have changed, look at this example from the 1800s:

> **When Phil became sick, Ann, his wife, cooked for him, fed him, changed the bed linens, bathed him, read to him from the Bible, and gave him his medicine. (She did this in addition to doing the housework and taking care of their six children.) Phil was also surrounded by the children, who shouldered some of his chores while he was sick. When Phil died, the male relatives made the casket while Ann, her sisters, and mother washed and dressed the body. Phil was "laid out" in the front parlor (the formal living room), where friends, neighbors, and relatives paid their last respects. From there, friends moved his body to the church for the final message and then to the grave they themselves had dug.**

Sociologists who use the *functionalist perspective* stress how industrialization and urbanization undermined the traditional *functions* of the family. Before industrialization, members of the family worked together as an economic unit, as in this painting of Italian farm life by Francesco Bassano (1549–1592). As production moved away from the home, it took with it first the father and, more recently, the mother. One consequence is a major dysfunction, the weakening of family ties.

©Alexander Burkatovski/Corbis

In Sum: When the family loses functions, it becomes more fragile, and an increase in divorce is inevitable. Economic production is an excellent example of how the family has lost functions. No longer is making a living a cooperative, home-based effort, where husband and wife depend on one another for their interlocking contributions to a mutual endeavor. Husbands and wives today earn individual paychecks and increasingly function as separate components in an impersonal, multinational, and even global system. The fewer functions that family members share, the fewer are their "ties that bind"—and these ties are what help husbands and wives get through the problems they inevitably experience.

Conflict Theory

Conflict theory provides a third perspective on social life. Unlike the functionalists, who view society as a harmonious whole, with its parts working together, conflict theorists stress that society is composed of groups that are competing with one another for scarce resources. Although the surface may show alliances or cooperation, scratch that surface and you will find a struggle for power.

Karl Marx and Conflict Theory. Karl Marx, the founder of conflict theory, witnessed the Industrial Revolution that transformed Europe. He saw that peasants who had left the land to seek work in cities had to work for wages that barely provided enough to eat. Things were so bad that the average worker died at age 30, the average wealthy person at age 50 (Edgerton 1992:87). Shocked by this suffering and exploitation, Marx began to analyze society and history. As he did so, he developed **conflict theory.** He concluded that the key to human history is *class conflict.* In each society, some small group controls the means of production and exploits those who are not in control. In industrialized societies, the struggle is between the *bourgeoisie,* the small group of capitalists who own the means to produce wealth, and the *proletariat,* the mass of workers who are exploited by the bourgeoisie. The capitalists also control the legal and political system: If the workers rebel, the capitalists call on the power of the state to subdue them.

When Marx made his observations, capitalism was in its infancy and workers were at the mercy of their employers. Workers had none of what we take for granted today—minimum wages, eight-hour days, coffee breaks, five-day work weeks, paid vacations and holidays, medical benefits, sick leave, unemployment compensation, Social Security, and, for union workers, the right to strike. Marx's analysis reminds us that these benefits came not from generous hearts, but by workers forcing concessions from their employers.

Conflict Theory Today. Many sociologists extend conflict theory beyond the relationship of capitalists and workers. They examine how opposing interests permeate every layer of society—whether that be a small group, an organization, a community, or the entire society. For example, when police, teachers, and parents try to enforce conformity, this creates resentment and resistance. It is the same when a teenager tries to "change the rules" to gain more independence. There is, then, a constant struggle throughout society to determine who has authority or influence and how far that dominance goes (Turner 1978; Leeson 2006; Piven 2008).

Sociologist Lewis Coser (1913–2003) pointed out that conflict is most likely to develop among people who are in close relationships. These people have worked out ways to distribute power and privilege, responsibilities and rewards. Any change in this arrangement can lead to hurt feelings, resentment, and conflict. Even in intimate relationships, then, people are in a constant balancing act, with conflict lying uneasily just beneath the surface.

Feminists and Conflict Theory. Just as Marx examined conflict between capitalists and workers, many feminists analyze conflict between men and women. A primary focus is the historical, contemporary, and global inequalities of men and women—and how the traditional dominance by men can be overcome to bring about equality of the sexes. Feminists are not united by the conflict perspective, however. They tackle a variety of topics and use whatever theory applies.)

Applying Conflict Theory. To explain why the U.S. divorce rate is high, conflict theorists focus on how men's and women's relationships have changed. For millennia, men

conflict theory a theoretical framework in which society is viewed as composed of groups that are competing for scarce resources

macro level an examination of large-scale patterns of society

micro level an examination of small-scale patterns of society

social interaction what people do when they are in one another's presence

dominated women. Women had few alternatives other than to accept their exploitation. Then industrialization ushered in a new world, one in which women could meet their basic survival needs outside of marriage. Industrialization also fostered a culture in which females participate in social worlds beyond the home. With this new ability to refuse to bear burdens that earlier generations accepted as inevitable, today's women are likely to dissolve a marriage that becomes intolerable—or even unsatisfactory.

In Sum: The dominance of men over women was once considered natural and right. As women gained education and earnings, however, they first questioned and then rejected this assumption. As wives strove for more power and grew less inclined to put up with relationships that they defined as unfair, the divorce rate increased. From the conflict perspective, then, our high divorce rate does not mean that marriage has weakened, but, rather, that women are making headway in their historical struggle with men.

Putting the Theoretical Perspectives Together

Which of these theoretical perspectives is *the* right one? As you have seen, each produces a contrasting picture of divorce. The pictures that emerge are quite different from the commonsense understanding that two people are simply "incompatible." *Because each theory focuses on different features of social life, each provides a distinctive interpretation. Consequently, we need to use all three theoretical lenses to analyze human behavior. By combining the contributions of each, we gain a more comprehensive picture of social life.*

Levels of Analysis: Macro and Micro

A major difference among these three theoretical perspectives is their level of analysis. Functionalists and conflict theorists focus on the **macro level;** that is, they examine large-scale patterns of society. In contrast, symbolic interactionists usually focus on the **micro level,** on **social interaction**—what people do when they are in one another's presence. These levels are summarized in Table 1.

To make this distinction between micro and macro levels clearer, let's return to the example of the homeless, with which we opened this chapter. To study homeless people, symbolic interactionists would focus on the micro level. They would analyze what homeless people do when they are in shelters and on the streets. They would also analyze their

TABLE 1 Three Theoretical Perspectives in Sociology

Perspective	Usual Level of Analysis	Focus of Analysis	Key Terms	Applying the Perspective to the U.S. Divorce Rate
Symbolic Interactionism	Microsociological: examines small-scale patterns of social interaction	Face-to-face interaction, how people use symbols to create social life	Symbols Interaction Meanings Definitions	Industrialization and urbanization changed marital roles and led to a redefinition of love, marriage, children, and divorce.
Functional Analysis (also called functionalism and structural functionalism)	Macrosociological: examines large-scale patterns of society	Relationships among the parts of society; how these parts are functional (have beneficial consequences) or dysfunctional (have negative consequences)	Structure Functions (manifest and latent) Dysfunctions Equilibrium	As social change erodes the traditional functions of the family, family ties weaken, and the divorce rate increases.
Conflict Theory	Macrosociological: examines large-scale patterns of society	The struggle for scarce resources by groups in a society; how the elites use their power to control the weaker groups	Inequality Power Conflict Competition Exploitation	When men control economic life, the divorce rate is low because women find few alternatives to a bad marriage. The high divorce rate reflects a shift in the balance of power between men and women.

communications, both their talk and their **nonverbal interaction** (gestures, use of space, and so on). The observations I made at the beginning of this chapter about the silence in the homeless shelter, for example, would be of interest to symbolic interactionists.

This micro level, however, would not interest functionalists and conflict theorists. They would focus instead on the macro level. Functionalists would examine how changes in the parts of society have increased homelessness. They might look at how changes in the family (fewer children, more divorce) and economic conditions (fewer unskilled jobs, loss of jobs to workers overseas) cause homelessness among people who are unable to find jobs and who have no family to fall back on. For their part, conflict theorists would stress the struggle between social classes. They would be interested in how decisions by international elites on global production and trade affect the local job market, and along with it unemployment and homelessness.

nonverbal interaction
communication without words through gestures, use of space, silence, and so on

How Theory and Research Work Together

Theory cannot stand alone. As sociologist C. Wright Mills (1959) so forcefully argued, if theory isn't connected to research, it will be abstract and empty. It won't represent the way life really is. It is the same for research. Without theory, Mills said, research is also of little value; it is simply a collection of meaningless "facts."

Theory and research, then, go together like a hand and glove. Every theory must be tested, which requires research. And as sociologists do research, they often come up with surprising findings. Those findings must be explained, and for that, we need theory. As sociologists study social life, then, they combine research and theory.

Let's turn now to how sociologists do research.

Doing Sociological Research

Around the globe, people make assumptions about the way the world "is." Common sense, the things that "everyone knows are true," may or may not be true, however. It takes research to find out. Do you want to test your own common sense? Take the little quiz below.

Down-to-Earth Sociology
Enjoying a Sociology Quiz— Sociological Findings Versus Common Sense

Some findings of sociology support commonsense understandings of social life, and others contradict them. Can you tell the difference? To enjoy this quiz, complete *all* the questions before turning the page to check your answers.

1. **True/False** More U.S. students are killed in school shootings now than ten or fifteen years ago.
2. **True/False** The earnings of U.S. women have just about caught up with those of U.S. men.
3. **True/False** With life so rushed and more women working for wages, today's parents spend less time with their children than previous generations did.
4. **True/False** It is more dangerous to walk near topless bars than fast-food restaurants.
5. **True/False** Most rapists are mentally ill.
6. **True/False** A large percentage of terrorists are mentally ill.
7. **True/False** Most people on welfare are lazy and looking for a handout. They could work if they wanted to.
8. **True/False** Compared with women, men make more eye contact in face-to-face conversations.
9. **True/False** Couples who lived together before marriage are usually more satisfied with their marriage than couples who did not live together before marriage.
10. **True/False** Because bicyclists are more likely to wear helmets now than a few years ago, their rate of head injuries has dropped.

Down-to-Earth Sociology

Sociological Findings Versus Common Sense—Answers to the Sociology Quiz

1. **False.** More students were shot to death at U.S. schools in the early 1990s than now (National School Safety Center 2009).
2. **False.** Over the years, the wage gap has narrowed, but only slightly. On average, full-time working women earn less than 70 percent of what full-time working men earn. This low figure is actually an improvement over earlier years.
3. **False.** Today's parents actually spend more time with their children (Bianchi et al. 2006).
4. **False.** The crime rate outside fast-food restaurants is considerably higher. The likely reason for this is that topless bars hire private security and parking lot attendants (Linz et al. 2004).
5. **False.** Sociologists compared the psychological profiles of prisoners convicted of rape and prisoners convicted of other crimes. Their profiles were similar. Like robbery, rape is a learned behavior (Scully and Marolla 1984/2005).
6. **False.** Extensive testing of Islamic terrorists shows that they actually tend to score more "normal" on psychological tests than most "normal" people. As a group, they are in better mental health than the rest of the population (Sageman 2008b:64).
7. **False.** Most people on welfare are children, elderly, sick, mentally or physically handicapped, or young mothers with few skills. Less than 2 percent fit the stereotype of an able-bodied man.
8. **False.** Women make considerably more eye contact (Henley et al. 1985).
9. **False.** The opposite is true. Among other reasons, couples who cohabit before marriage are usually less committed to one another—and a key to marital success is a strong commitment (Dush et al. 2003; Osborne et al. 2007).
10. **False.** Bicyclists today are more likely to wear helmets, but their rate of head injuries is higher. Apparently, they take more risks because the helmets make them feel safer (Barnes 2001).

FIGURE 4 The Research Model

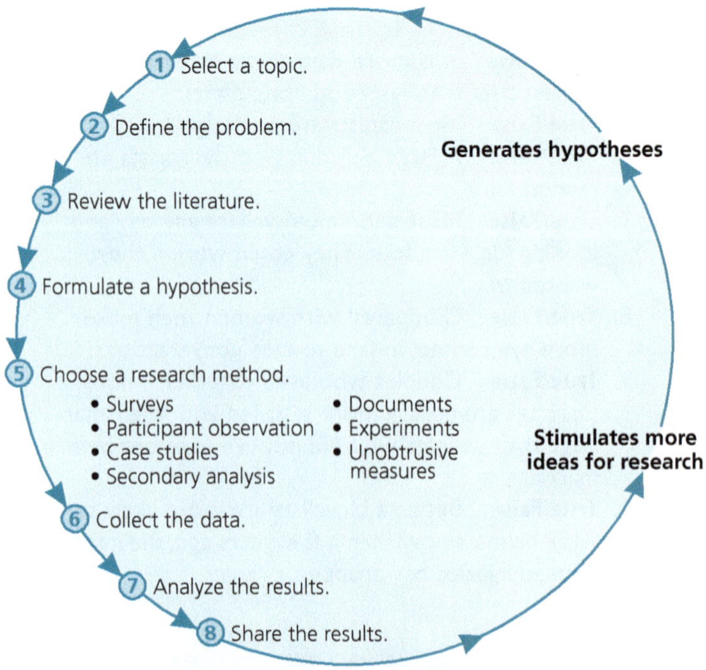

1. Select a topic.
2. Define the problem.
3. Review the literature.
4. Formulate a hypothesis.
5. Choose a research method.
   - Surveys
   - Participant observation
   - Case studies
   - Secondary analysis
   - Documents
   - Experiments
   - Unobtrusive measures
6. Collect the data.
7. Analyze the results.
8. Share the results.

Generates hypotheses

Stimulates more ideas for research

Source: Modification of Figure 2.2 of Schaeffer 1989.

To understand social life, we need to move beyond "common sense" and learn what is really going on. Let's look at how sociologists do their research.

A Research Model

As shown in Figure 4, scientific research follows eight basic steps. This is an ideal model, however, and in the real world of research some of these steps may run together. Some may even be omitted.

1. *Selecting a topic.* First, what do you want to know more about? Let's choose spouse abuse as our topic.
2. *Defining the problem.* The next step is to narrow the topic. Spouse abuse is too broad; we need to focus on a specific area. For example, you may want to know why men are more likely than women to be the abusers. Or perhaps you want to know what can be done to reduce domestic violence.
3. *Reviewing the literature.* You must review the literature to find out what has been published on the problem. You don't want to waste your time rediscovering what is already known.

4. *Formulating a hypothesis.* The fourth step is to formulate a **hypothesis,** a statement of what you expect to find according to predictions that are based on a theory. A hypothesis predicts a relationship between or among **variables,** factors that vary, or change, from one person or situation to another. For example, the statement "Men who are more socially isolated are more likely to abuse their wives than are men who are more socially integrated" is a hypothesis.

Your hypothesis will need **operational definitions,** that is, precise ways to measure the variables. In this example, you would need operational definitions for three variables: social isolation, social integration, and spouse abuse.

5. *Choosing a research method.* The means by which you collect your data is called a **research method** or *research design.* Sociologists use six basic research methods, which are outlined in the next section. You will want to choose the method that will best answer your particular questions.

6. *Collecting the data.* When you gather your data, you have to take care to assure their **validity;** that is, your operational definitions must measure what they are intended to measure. In this case, you must be certain that you really are measuring social isolation, social integration, and spouse abuse—and not something else. Spouse abuse, for example, seems to be obvious. Yet what some people consider to be abuse is not considered abuse by others. Which will you choose? In other words, your operational definitions must be so precise that no one has any question about what you are measuring.

You must also be sure that your data are reliable. **Reliability** means that if other researchers use your operational definitions, their findings will be consistent with yours. If your operational definitions are sloppy, husbands who have committed the same act of violence might be included in some research but excluded in other studies. You would end up with erratic results. You might show a 5 percent rate of spouse abuse, but another researcher may conclude that it is 30 percent. This would make your research unreliable.

7. *Analyzing the results.* You can choose from a variety of techniques to analyze the data you gather. If a hypothesis has been part of your research, you will test it during this step. (Some research, especially that done by participant observation, has no hypothesis. You may know so little about the setting you are going to research that you cannot even specify the variables in advance.)

8. *Sharing the results.* To wrap up your research, you will write a report to share your findings with the scientific community. You will review how you did your research, including your operational definitions. You will also show how your findings fit in with the published literature and how they support or refute the theories that apply to your topic. As Table 2 illustrates, sociologists often summarize their findings in tables.

Let's look in greater detail at the fifth step to see what research methods sociologists use.

Research Methods

As we review the seven research methods (or *research designs*) that sociologists use, we will continue our example of spouse abuse. As you will see, the method you choose will depend on the questions you want to answer. So that you can have a yardstick for comparison, you will want to know what "average" is in your study. Table 3 discusses ways to measure average.

Surveys

Let's suppose that you want to know how many wives are abused each year. Some husbands also are abused, of course, but let's assume that you are going to focus on wives.

Because sociologists find all human behavior to be valid research topics, their research runs from the unusual to the routines of everyday life. Their studies range from broad scale social change, such as the globalization of capitalism, to smaller scale social interaction, such as people having fun.

Barry Batchelor/PA Photos/Landov

hypothesis a statement of how variables are expected to be related to one another, often according to predictions from a theory

variables a factor thought to be significant for human behavior, which can vary (or change) from one case to another

operational definitions the way in which a researcher measures a variable

research method one of seven procedures that sociologists use to collect data: surveys, participant observation, case studies, secondary analysis, documents, experiments, and unobtrusive measures

validity the extent to which an operational definition measures what it is intended to measure

reliability the extent to which research produces consistent or dependable results

TABLE 2   How to Read a Table

Tables summarize information. Because sociological findings are often presented in tables, it is important to understand how to read them. Tables contain six elements: title, headnote, headings, columns, rows, and source. When you understand how these elements fit together, you know how to read a table.

1 The **title** states the topic. It is located at the top of the table. What is the title of this table? Please determine your answer before looking at the correct answer at the bottom of this page.

2 The **headnote** is not always included in a table. When it is, it is located just below the title. Its purpose is to give more detailed information about how the data were collected or how data are presented in the table. What are the first eight words of the headnote of this table?

3 The **headings** tell what kind of information is contained in the table. There are three headings in this table. What are they? In the second heading, what does n = 25 mean?

4 The **columns** present information arranged vertically. What is the fourth number in the second column and the second number in the third column?

5 The **rows** present information arranged horizontally. In the fourth row, which husbands are more likely to have less education than their wives?

6 The **source** of a table, usually listed at the bottom, provides information on where the data in the table originated. Often, as in this instance, the information is specific enough for you to consult the original source. What is the source for this table?

Comparing Violent and Nonviolent Husbands

Based on interviews with 150 husbands and wives in a Midwestern city who were getting a divorce.

Husband's Achievement and Job Satisfaction	Violent Husbands $n = 25$	Nonviolent Husbands $n = 125$
He started but failed to complete high school or college.	44%	27%
He is very dissatisfied with his job.	44%	18%
His income is a source of constant conflict.	84%	24%
He has less education than his wife.	56%	14%
His job has less prestige than his father-in-law's.	37%	28%

Source: Modification of Table 1 in O'Brien 1975.

Some tables are much more complicated than this one, but all follow the same basic pattern.

ANSWERS

1. Comparing Violent and Nonviolent Husbands
2. Based on interviews with 150 husbands and wives
3. Husband's Achievement and Job Satisfaction, Violent Husbands, Nonviolent Husbands. The *n* is an abbreviation for number, and *n* = 25 means that 25 violent husbands were in the sample.
4. 56%, 18%
5. Violent Husbands
6. A 1975 article by O'Brien

---

survey the collection of data by having people answer a series of questions

population a target group to be studied

An appropriate method for this purpose would be the **survey,** in which you would ask individuals a series of questions. Before you begin your research, however, you must deal with practical matters that face all researchers. Let's look at these issues.

Selecting a Sample. Ideally, you might want to learn about all wives in the world. Obviously, your resources will not permit such research, and you will have to narrow your **population,** the target group that you are going to study.

TABLE 3 Three Ways to Measure "Average"

The Mean	The Median	The Mode
The term *average* seems clear enough. As you learned in grade school, to find the average you add a group of numbers and then divide the total by the number of cases that you added. Assume that the following numbers represent men convicted of battering their wives:	To compute the second average, the *median*, first arrange the cases in order—either from the highest to the lowest or the lowest to the highest. That arrangement will produce the following distribution.	The third measure of average, the *mode*, is simply the cases that occur the most often. In this instance the mode is 57, which is way off the mark.

EXAMPLE	EXAMPLE		EXAMPLE
321	57	1,795	57
229	57	321	57
57	136	289	136
289	229 **or** 229		229
136	289	136	289
57	321	57	321
1,795	1,795	57	1,795

The Mean	The Median	The Mode
The total is 2,884. Divided by 7 (the number of cases), the average is 412. Sociologists call this form of average the *mean*. The mean can be deceptive because it is strongly influenced by extreme scores, either low or high. Note that six of the seven cases are less than the mean. Two other ways to compute averages are the median and the mode.	Then look for the middle case, the one that falls halfway between the top and the bottom. That number is 229, for three numbers are lower and three numbers are higher. When there is an even number of cases, the median is the halfway mark between the two middle cases.	Because the mode is often deceptive, and only by chance comes close to either of the other two averages, sociologists seldom use it. In addition, not every distribution of cases has a mode. And if two or more numbers appear with the same frequency, you can have more than one mode.

Let's assume that your resources (money, assistants, time) allow you to investigate spouse abuse only on your campus. Let's also assume that your college enrollment is large, so you won't be able to survey all the married women who are enrolled. Now you must select a **sample,** individuals from among your target population. How you choose a sample is crucial, for your choice will affect the results of your research. For example, married women enrolled in introductory sociology and engineering courses might have quite different experiences. If so, surveying just one or the other would produce skewed results.

Because you want to generalize your findings to your entire campus, you need a sample that accurately represents the campus. How can you get a representative sample?

The best way is to use a **random sample.** This does *not* mean that you would stand on some campus corner and ask questions of any woman who happens to walk by. *In a random sample, everyone in your population (the target group) has the same chance of being included in the study.* In this case, because your population is every married woman enrolled in your college, all married women—whether first-year or graduate students, full- or part-time—must have the same chance of being included in your sample.

How can you get a random sample? First, you need a list of all the married women enrolled in your college. Then you assign a number to each name on the list. Using a table of random numbers, you then determine which of these women will become part of your sample. (Tables of random numbers are available in statistics books and online, or they can be generated by a computer.)

A random sample will represent your study's population fairly—in this case, married women enrolled at your college. This means that you can generalize your findings to *all* the married women students on your campus, even if they were not included in your sample.

sample the individuals intended to represent the population to be studied

random sample a sample in which everyone in the target population has the same chance of being included in the study

stratified random sample a sample from selected subgroups of the target population in which everyone in those subgroups has an equal chance of being included in the research

respondents people who respond to a survey, either in interviews or by self-administered questionnaires

Sociologists usually cannot interview or observe every member of a group or participant in an event that they want to study. To be able to generalize their findings, they select samples. Sociologists would have several ways to study this protest in San Francisco against U.S. foreign policy.

closed-ended questions
questions that are followed by a list of possible answers to be selected by the respondent

open-ended questions
questions that respondents answer in their own words

rapport (ruh-POUR) a feeling of trust between researchers and the people they are studying

What if you want to know only about certain subgroups, such as freshmen and seniors? You could use a **stratified random sample.** You would need a list of the freshmen and senior married women. Then, using random numbers, you would select a sample from each group. This would allow you to generalize to all the freshmen and senior married women at your college, but you would not be able to draw any conclusions about the sophomores or juniors.

Asking Neutral Questions. After you have decided on your population and sample, your next task is to make certain that your questions are neutral. Your questions must allow **respondents,** the people who answer your questions, to express their own opinions. Otherwise, you will end up with biased answers—which are worthless. For example, if you were to ask, "Don't you think that men who beat their wives should go to prison?" you would be tilting the answer toward agreement with a prison sentence. The *Doonesbury* cartoon below illustrates a blatant example of biased questions. For examples of flawed research, see the Down-to-Earth Sociology box.

Types of Questions. You must also decide whether to use closed- or open-ended questions. **Closed-ended questions** are followed by a list of possible answers. This format would work for questions about someone's age (possible ages would be listed), but not for many other items. For example, how could you list all the opinions that people hold about what should be done to spouse abusers? The answers provided for closed-ended questions can miss the respondent's opinions.

As Table 4 illustrates, the alternative is **open-ended questions,** which allow people to answer in their own words. Although open-ended questions allow you to tap the full range of people's opinions, they make it difficult to compare answers. For example, how would you compare these answers to the question "Why do you think men abuse their wives?"

"They're sick."

"I think they must have had problems with their mother."

"We ought to string them up!"

Establishing Rapport. Will women who have been abused really give honest answers to strangers? If you were to walk up to women on the street and ask if their husbands have ever beaten them, there would be little reason to take your findings seriously. If, however, researchers establish **rapport** ("ruh-POUR"), a feeling of trust, with their respondents, victims will talk about sensitive matters. A good example is rape. Each year, researchers interview a random sample of 100,000 Americans. They ask them whether they have been victims of burglary, robbery, and other crimes. After establishing rapport, the researchers ask about rape. They find that rape victims will talk about their experiences. The national crime victimization survey shows that the actual incidence of rape is about 40 percent higher than the number reported to the police—and that attempted rapes are *nine* times higher than the official statistics (*Statistical Abstract* 2011:Table 311).

A new technique to gather data on sensitive areas, Computer-Assisted Self-Interviewing, overcomes lingering problems of distrust. In this technique, the interviewer gives a

Improperly worded questions can steer respondents toward answers that are not their own, which produces invalid results.

Doonesbury © G. B. Trudeau. Reprinted with permission of Universal Press Syndicate. All rights reserved.

Down-to-Earth Sociology
Loading the Dice: How *Not* to Do Research

fotoshoot/Alamy Royalty Free

The methods of science lend themselves to distortion, misrepresentation, and downright fraud. Consider these findings from surveys:

Americans overwhelmingly prefer Toyotas to Chryslers.
Americans overwhelmingly prefer Chryslers to Toyotas.

Obviously, these opposite conclusions cannot both be true. In fact, both sets of findings are misrepresentations, even though the responses came from surveys conducted by so-called independent researchers. These researchers, however, are biased, not independent and objective.

It turns out that some consumer researchers load the dice. Hired by firms that have a vested interest in the outcome of the research, they deliver the results their clients are looking for (Armstrong 2007). Here are six ways to load the dice.

1. **Choose a biased sample.** If you want to "prove" that Americans prefer Chryslers over Toyotas, interview unemployed union workers who trace their job loss to Japanese imports. You'll get what you're looking for.

2. **Ask biased questions.** Even if you choose an unbiased sample, you can phrase questions in such a way that you direct people to the answer you're looking for. Suppose that you ask this question:

   We are losing millions of jobs to workers overseas who work for just a few dollars a day. After losing their jobs, some Americans are even homeless and hungry. Do you prefer a car that gives jobs to Americans, or one that forces our workers to lose their homes?

   This question is obviously designed to channel people's thinking toward a predetermined answer—quite contrary to the standards of scientific research. Look again at the Doonesbury cartoon.

3. **List biased choices.** Another way to load the dice is to use closed-ended questions that push people into the answers you want. Consider this finding:

   U.S. college students overwhelmingly prefer Levis 501 to the jeans of any competitor.

Sound good? Before you rush out to buy Levis, note what these researchers did: In asking students which jeans would be the most popular in the coming year, their list of choices included no other jeans but Levis 501!

4. **Discard undesirable results.** Researchers can keep silent about results they find embarrassing, or they can continue to survey samples until they find one that matches what they are looking for. As has been stressed in this chapter, research must be objective if it is to be scientific. Obviously, none of the preceding results qualifies. The underlying problem with the research cited here—and with so many surveys bandied about in the media as fact—is that survey research has become big business. Simply put, the money offered by corporations has corrupted some researchers.

   The beginning of the corruption is subtle. Paul Light, dean at the University of Minnesota, put it this way: "A funder will never come to an academic and say, 'I want you to produce finding X, and here's a million dollars to do it.' Rather, the subtext is that if the researchers produce the right finding, more work—and funding—will come their way."

The first four sources of bias are inexcusable, intentional fraud. The next two sources of bias reflect sloppiness, which is also inexcusable in science.

5. **Misunderstand the subjects' world.** This route can lead to errors every bit as great as those just cited. Even researchers who use an adequate sample and word their questions properly can end up with skewed results. They may, for example, fail to anticipate that people may be embarrassed to express an opinion that isn't "politically correct." For example, surveys show that 80 percent of Americans are environmentalists. Most Americans, however, are probably embarrassed to tell a stranger otherwise. Today, that would be like going against the flag, motherhood, and apple pie.

6. **Analyze the data incorrectly.** Even when researchers strive for objectivity, the sample is good, the wording is neutral, and the respondents answer the questions honestly, the results can still be skewed. The researchers may make a mistake in their calculations, such as entering incorrect data into computers. This, too, of course, is inexcusable in science.

Sources: Based on Crossen 1991; Goleman 1993; Barnes 1995; Resnik 2000; Hotz 2007.

TABLE 4 Closed- and Open-Ended Questions	
A. Closed-Ended Question	**B. Open-Ended Question**
Which of the following best fits your idea of what should be done to someone who has been convicted of spouse abuse? 1. probation 2. jail time 3. community service 4. counseling 5. divorce 6. nothing—it's a family matter	What do you think should be done to someone who has been convicted of spouse abuse?

participant observation research in which the researcher participates in a research setting while observing what is happening in that setting

case study an analysis of a single event, situation, or individual

secondary analysis the analysis of data that have been collected by other researchers

Participant observation, participating and observing in a research setting, is usually supplemented by interviewing, asking questions to better understand why people do what they do. In this instance, the sociologist would want to know what this hair removal ceremony in Gujarat, India, means to the child's family and to the community.

laptop computer to the respondent, then moves aside, while the individual enters his or her own answers into the computer. In some versions of this method, the respondent listens to the questions on a headphone and answers them on the computer screen. When the respondent clicks the "Submit" button, the interviewer has no idea how the respondent answered any question (Mosher et al. 2005).

Participant Observation (Fieldwork)

In **participant observation,** or **fieldwork,** the researcher *participates* in a research setting while *observing* what is happening in that setting. Obviously, this method does not mean that you would sit around and watch someone being abused. But if you wanted to learn how abuse has affected the victims' hopes and goals, their dating patterns, or their marriages, you could use participant observation.

For example, if your campus has a crisis intervention center, you might be able to observe victims of spouse abuse from the time they report the attack through their participation in counseling. With good rapport, you might even be able to spend time with them at their home or with friends. What they say and how they interact with others might help you to understand how the abuse has affected them. This, in turn, could give you insight into how to improve college counseling services.

If you were doing participant observation, you would face this dilemma: How involved should you get in the lives of the people you are observing? Consider this as you read the Down-to-Earth Sociology box.

Case Studies

To do a **case study,** the researcher focuses on a single event, situation, or even individual. The purpose is to understand the dynamics of relationships, power, or even the thought processes that motivate people. Sociologist Ken Levi (2009), for example, wanted to study hit men. He would love to have had a large number of hit men to interview, but he had access to only one. He interviewed this man over and over, giving us an understanding of how someone can kill others for money. A case study of spouse abuse would focus on a single wife and husband, exploring the couple's history and relationship.

As you can see, case studies reveal a lot of detail about some particular situation, but the question always remains: How much of this detail applies to other situations? This problem of *generalizability*, which plagues case studies, is the primary reason that few sociologists use this method.

Secondary Analysis

If you were to analyze data that someone else has already collected, you would be doing **secondary analysis.** For example, if you were to examine the original data from a study of women who had been abused by their husbands, you would be doing secondary analysis.

Documents

Documents, or written sources, include books, newspapers, bank records, immigration records, and so on. To study spouse abuse, you might examine police reports to find out how many men in your community have been arrested for abuse. You might also use court records to find out what proportion of those men were charged, convicted, or put on probation. If you wanted to learn about the social and emotional adjustment of the

Down-to-Earth Sociology

Gang Leader for a Day: Adventures of a Rogue Sociologist

Next to the University of Chicago is an area of poverty so dangerous that the professors warn students to avoid it. One of the graduate students in sociology, Sudhir Venkatesh, the son of immigrants from India, who was working on a research project with William Julius Wilson, decided to ignore the warning.

With clipboard in hand, Sudhir entered "the projects." Ignoring the glares of the young men standing around, he went into the lobby of a high-rise. Seeing a gaping hole where the elevator was supposed to be, he decided to climb the stairs, where he was almost overpowered by the smell of urine. After climbing five flights, Sudhir came upon some young men shooting craps in a dark hallway. One of them jumped up, grabbed Sudhir's clipboard, and demanded to know what he was doing there.

Sudhir blurted, "I'm a student at the university, doing a survey, and I'm looking for some families to interview."

One man took out a knife and began to twirl it. Another pulled out a gun, pointed it at Sudhir's head, and said, "I'll take him."

Then came a series of rapid-fire questions that Sudhir couldn't answer. He had no idea what they meant: "You flip right or left? Five or six? You run with the Kings, right?"

Grabbing Sudhir's bag, two of the men searched it. They could find only questionnaires, pen and paper, and a few sociology books. The man with the gun then told Sudhir to go ahead and ask him a question.

Sweating despite the cold, Sudhir read the first question on his survey, "How does it feel to be black and poor?" Then he read the multiple-choice answers: "Very bad, somewhat bad, neither bad nor good, somewhat good, very good."

As you might surmise, the man's answer was too obscenity laden to be printed here.

As the men deliberated Sudhir's fate ("If he's here and he don't get back, you know they're going to come looking for him"), a powerfully built man with a few glittery gold teeth and a sizable diamond earring appeared. The man, known as J.T., who, it turned out, directed the drug trade in the building, asked what was going on. When the younger men mentioned the questionnaire, J.T. said to ask *him* a question.

Amidst an eerie silence, Sudhir asked, "How does it feel to be black and poor?"

"I'm not black," came the reply.

"Well, then, how does it feel to be African American and poor?"

"I'm not African American either. I'm a nigger."

Sudhir was left speechless. Despite his naïveté, he knew better than to ask, "How does it feel to be a nigger and poor?"

As Sudhir stood with his mouth agape, J.T. added, "Niggers are the ones who live in this building. African Americans live in the suburbs. African Americans wear ties to work. Niggers can't find no work."

Not exactly the best start to a research project.

But this weird and frightening beginning turned into several years of fascinating research. Over time, J.T. guided Sudhir into a world that few outsiders ever see. Not only did Sudhir get to know drug dealers, crackheads, squatters, prostitutes, and pimps, but he also was present at beatings by drug crews, drive-by shootings done by rival gangs, and armed robberies by the police.

How Sudhir got out of his predicament in the stairwell, his immersion into a threatening underworld—the daily life for many people in "the projects"—and his moral dilemma at witnessing so many crimes are part of his fascinating experience in doing participant observation of the Black Kings.

Sudhir, who was reared in a middle-class suburb in California, even took over this Chicago gang for a day. This is one reason that he calls himself a rogue sociologist—the decisions he made that day were serious violations of law, felonies that could bring years in prison. There are other reasons, too: During the research, he kicked a man in the stomach, and he was present as the gang planned drive-by shootings.

Sudhir eventually completed his Ph.D., and he now teaches at Columbia University.

Based on Venkatesh 2008.

Professor Sudhir Venkatesh, who now teaches at Columbia University, New York.

Paresh Gandhi Courtesy of Sudhir Venkatesh, Columbia University

---

victims, however, these documents would tell you nothing. Other documents, though, might provide those answers. For example, a crisis intervention center might have records that contain key information—but gaining access to them is almost impossible. Perhaps an unusually cooperative center might ask victims to keep diaries that you can study later.

Documents in its narrow sense, written sources that provide data; in its extended sense, archival material of any sort, including photographs, movies, CDs, DVDs, and so on.

FIGURE 5 The Experiment

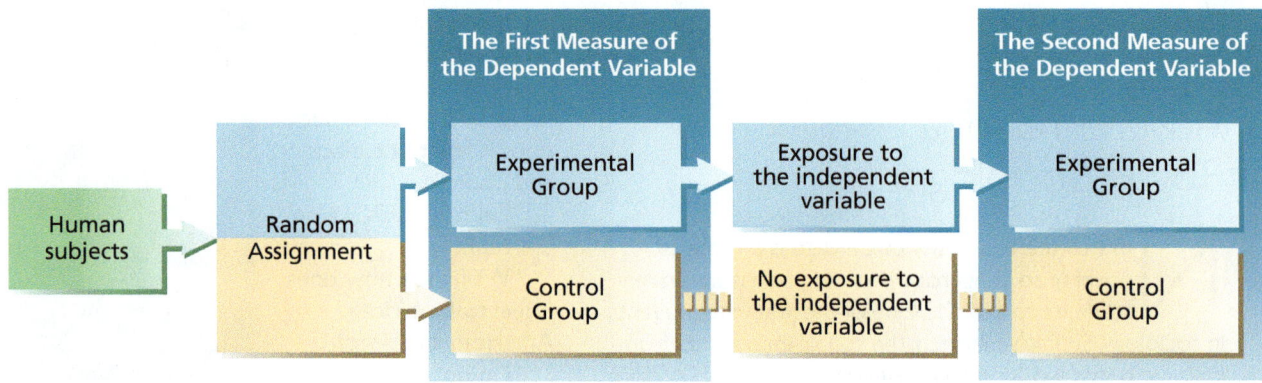

Source: By the author.

Experiments

A lot of people say that abusers need therapy. Yet no one knows whether therapy really works. **Experiments** are useful for determining cause and effect, whose basic requirements are outlined on Table 5. Let's suppose that you propose an experiment to a judge and she gives you access to men who have been arrested for spouse abuse. As in Figure 5, you would divide the men randomly into two groups. This helps to ensure that their individual characteristics (attitudes, number of arrests, severity of crimes, education, race-ethnicity, age, and so on) are distributed between the groups. You then would arrange for the men in the **experimental group** to receive some form of therapy. The men in the **control group** would not get therapy.

Your **independent variable,** something that causes a change in another variable, would be therapy. Your **dependent variable,** the variable that might change, would be the men's behavior: whether they abuse women after they get out of jail. Unfortunately, your operational definition of the men's behavior will be sloppy: either reports from the wives or records indicating which men were rearrested for abuse. This is sloppy because some of the women will not report the abuse, and some of the men who abuse their wives will not be arrested. Yet it might be the best you can do.

Let's assume that you choose rearrest as your operational definition. If you find that the men who received therapy are *less* likely to be rearrested for abuse, you can attribute the difference to the therapy. If you find *no difference* in rearrest rates, you can conclude that the therapy was ineffective. If you find that the men who received the therapy have a *higher* rearrest rate, you can conclude that the therapy backfired.

Unobtrusive Measures

Researchers sometimes use **unobtrusive measures,** observing the behavior of people who are not aware that they are being studied. For example, social researchers studied the level of whiskey consumption in a town that was legally "dry" by counting empty bottles in trashcans. (Lee 2000). Casino operators use chips that transmit radio frequencies, allowing them to track how much their high rollers are betting at every hand of poker or blackjack (Sanders 2005; Grossman 2007). Billboards read information embedded on a chip in your car key. As you drive by, the billboard displays *your* name with a personal message (Feder 2007). The same device can *collect* information as you drive by.

It would be considered unethical to use most unobtrusive measures to research spouse abuse. You could, however, analyze 911 calls. Also, if there were a public forum held by abused or abusing spouses on the Internet, you could record and analyze the online conversations. Ethics in unobtrusive research are still a matter of dispute: To secretly record the behavior of people in public settings, such as a crowd, is generally considered acceptable, but to do so in private settings is not.

experiments the use of *control* and *experimental groups* and *dependent* and *independent variables* to test causation

experimental group the subjects in an experiment who are exposed to the independent variable

control group the subjects in an experiment who are not exposed to the independent variable

independent variable a factor that causes a change in another variable, called the dependent variable

dependent variable a factor in an experiment that is changed by an independent variable

unobtrusive measures ways of observing people so they do not know they are being studied

TABLE 5   Cause, Effect, and Spurious Correlations

Causation means that a change in one variable is caused by another variable. Three conditions are necessary for causation: correlation, temporal priority, and no spurious correlation. Let's apply each of these conditions to spouse abuse and alcohol abuse.

1 The first necessary condition is *correlation*.

If two variables exist together, they are said to be correlated. If batterers get drunk, battering and alcohol abuse are correlated.

Spouse Abuse + Alcohol Abuse

People sometimes assume that correlation is causation. In this instance, they conclude that alcohol abuse causes spouse abuse.

Alcohol Abuse ⟶ **Spouse Abuse**

But *correlation never proves causation. Either* variable could be the cause of the other. Perhaps battering upsets men and they then get drunk.

Spouse Abuse ⟶ **Alcohol Abuse**

2 The second necessary condition is *temporal priority*.

Temporal priority means that one thing happens before something else does. For a variable to be a cause (*the independent variable*), it must *precede* that which is changed (*the dependent variable*).

precedes
Alcohol Abuse ⟶ **Spouse Abuse**
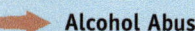

If the men had not drunk alcohol until after they beat their wives, obviously alcohol abuse could not be the cause of the spouse abuse. Although the necessity of temporal priority is obvious, in many studies this is not easy to determine.

3 The third necessary condition is *no spurious correlation*.

This is the necessary condition that really makes things difficult. Even if we identify the correlation of getting drunk and spouse abuse and can determine temporal priority, we still don't know that alcohol abuse is the cause. We could have a *spurious correlation;* that is, the cause may be some underlying third variable. These are usually not easy to identify. Some sociologists think that male culture is that underlying third variable.

Male Culture ⟶ **Spouse Abuse**
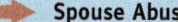

Socialized into dominance, some men learn to view women as objects on which to take out their frustration. In fact, this underlying third variable could be a cause of both spouse abuse and alcohol abuse.

Male Culture   →   **Spouse Abuse**
    →   **Alcohol Abuse**

But since only some men beat their wives, while all males are exposed to male culture, other variables must also be involved. Perhaps specific subcultures that promote violence and denigrate women lead to both spouse abuse and alcohol abuse.

Male Subculture   →   **Spouse Abuse**
    →   **Alcohol Abuse**

If so, this does *not* mean that it is the only causal variable, for spouse abuse probably has many causes. Unlike the movement of amoebas or the action of heat on some object, human behavior is infinitely complicated. Especially important are people's *definitions of the situation*, including their views of right and wrong. To explain spouse abuse, then, we need to add such variables as the ways that men view violence and their ideas about the relative rights of women and men. It is precisely to help unravel such complicating factors in human behavior that we need the experimental method.

MORE ON CORRELATIONS

Correlation simply means that two or more variables are present together. The more often that these variables are found together, the stronger their relationship. To indicate their strength, sociologists use a number called a *correlation coefficient*. If two variables are always related, that is, they are always present together, they have what is called a *perfect positive correlation*. The number 1.0 represents this correlation coefficient. Nature has some 1.0's, such as the lack of water and the death of trees. 1.0's also apply to the human physical state, such as the absence of nutrients and the absence of life. But social life is much more complicated than physical conditions, and there are no 1.0's in human behavior.

Two variables can also have a *perfect negative correlation*. This means that when one variable is present, the other is always absent. The number –1.0 represents this correlation coefficient.

Positive correlations of 0.1, 0.2, and 0.3 mean that one variable is associated with another only 1 time out of 10, 2 times out of 10, and 3 times out of 10. In other words, in most instances the first variable is *not* associated with the second, indicating a weak relationship. A strong relationship may indicate causation, but not necessarily. Testing the relationship between variables is the goal of some sociological research.

Gender in Sociological Research

You know how significant gender is in your own life, how it affects your orientations and your attitudes. You also may be aware that gender opens and closes doors to you. Because gender is also a factor in social research, researchers must take steps to prevent it from biasing their findings. For example, sociologists Diana Scully and Joseph Marolla (1984, 2007) interviewed convicted rapists in prison. They were concerned that their gender might lead to *interviewer bias*—that the prisoners might shift their answers, sharing certain experiences or opinions with Marolla, but saying something else to Scully. To prevent gender bias, each researcher interviewed half the sample.

Gender certainly can be an impediment in research. In our imagined research on spouse abuse, for example, could a man even do participant observation of women who have been beaten by their husbands? Technically, the answer is yes. But because the women have been victimized by men, they might be less likely to share their experiences and feelings with men. If so, women would be better suited to conduct this research, more likely to achieve valid results. The supposition that these victims will be more open with women than with men, however, is just that—a supposition. Research alone will verify or refute this assumption.

Gender issues can pop up in unexpected ways in sociological research. I vividly recall an incident in San Francisco.

The streets were getting dark, and I was still looking for homeless people. When I saw someone lying down, curled up in a doorway, I approached the individual. As I got close, I began my opening research line, "Hi, I'm Dr. Henslin from. . . . ?" The individual began to scream and started to thrash wildly. Startled by this sudden, high-pitched scream and by the rapid movements, I quickly backed away. When I later analyzed what had happened, I concluded that I had intruded into a woman's bedroom.

This incident also holds another lesson. Researchers do their best, but they make mistakes. Sometimes these mistakes are minor, and even humorous. The woman sleeping in the doorway wasn't frightened. It was only just getting dark, and there were many people on the street. She was just assertively marking her territory and letting me know in no uncertain terms that I was an intruder. If we make a mistake in research, we pick up and go on. As we do so, we take ethical considerations into account, which is the topic of our next section.

Ethics and Values in Sociological Research

In addition to choosing an appropriate research method, we must also follow the ethics of sociology (American Sociological Association 1999). Research ethics require honesty, truth, and openness (sharing findings with the scientific community). Ethics clearly forbid the falsification of results. They also condemn plagiarism—that is, stealing someone else's work. Another ethical guideline states that research subjects should generally be informed that they are being studied and never be harmed by the research. Sometimes people reveal things that are intimate, potentially embarrassing, or otherwise harmful to themselves—and their anonymity must be protected. Finally, although not all sociologists agree, it generally is considered unethical for researchers to misrepresent themselves. Sociologists take their ethical standards seriously. To illustrate the extent to which they will go to protect their respondents, consider the research conducted by Mario Brajuha.

Protecting the Subjects: The Brajuha Research

Mario Brajuha, a graduate student at the State University of New York at Stony Brook, was doing participant observation of restaurant workers. He lost his job as a waiter when the restaurant where he was working burned down—a fire of "suspicious origin," as the police said. When detectives learned that Brajuha had taken field notes (Brajuha and Hallowell 1986), they asked to see them. Because he had promised to keep the information confidential, Brajuha refused to hand them over. When the district attorney subpoenaed the notes, Brajuha still refused. The district attorney then threatened to put Brajuha in jail. By this time, Brajuha's notes had become rather famous, and unsavory characters—perhaps those who had set the fire—also wanted to know what was in them. They, too, demanded to see them, accompanying their demands with threats of a different nature. Brajuha found himself between a rock and a hard place.

For two years, Brajuha refused to hand over his notes, even though he grew anxious and had to appear at several court hearings. Finally, the district attorney dropped the subpoena. When the two men under investigation for setting the fire died, the threats to Brajuha, his wife, and their children ended.

Ethics in social research are of vital concern to sociologists. As discussed in the text, sociologists may disagree on some of the issue's finer points, but none would approve of slipping LSD to unsuspecting subjects like these Marine recruits in basic training at Parris Island, South Carolina. Researchers did this to U.S. soldiers in the 1960s just "to see what would happen."
©Drew Crawford/The Image Works

Misleading the Subjects: The Humphreys Research

Sociologists agree on the necessity to protect respondents, and they applaud the professional manner in which Brajuha handled himself. Although it is considered acceptable for sociologists to do covert participant observation (studying some situation without announcing that they are doing research), to deliberately misrepresent oneself is considered unethical. Let's look at the case of Laud Humphreys, whose research forced sociologists to rethink and refine their ethical stance.

Laud Humphreys, a classmate of mine at Washington University in St. Louis, was an Episcopal priest who decided to become a sociologist. For his Ph.D. dissertation, Humphreys (1970, 1971, 1975) studied social interaction in "tearooms," public restrooms where some men go for quick, anonymous oral sex with other men.

Humphreys found that some restrooms in Forest Park, just across from our campus, were tearooms. He began a participant observation study by hanging around these restrooms. He found that in addition to the two men having sex, a third man—called a "watch queen"—served as a lookout for police and other unwelcome strangers. Humphreys took on the role of watch queen, not only watching for strangers but also observing what the men did. He wrote field notes after the encounters.

Humphreys decided that he wanted to learn about the regular lives of these men. For example, what about the wedding rings that many of the men wore? He came up with an ingenious technique: Many of the men parked their cars near the tearooms, and Humphreys recorded their license plate numbers. A friend in the St. Louis police department gave Humphreys each man's address. About a year later, Humphreys arranged for these men to be included in a medical survey conducted by some of the sociologists on our faculty.

Disguising himself with a different hairstyle and clothing, Humphreys visited the men's homes. As he interviewed the men, supposedly for the medical study, he found that they led conventional lives. They voted, mowed their lawns, and took their kids to Little League games. Many reported that their wives were not aroused sexually or were afraid of getting pregnant because their religion did not allow them to use birth control. Humphreys concluded that many heterosexual men were using the tearooms for a form of quick sex.

value free the view that a sociologist's personal values or biases should not influence social research

values the standards by which people define what is desirable or undesirable, good or bad, beautiful or ugly

objectivity value neutrality in research

replication the repetition of a study in order to test its findings

This study stirred controversy among sociologists and nonsociologists alike. Many sociologists criticized Humphreys, and a national columnist wrote a scathing denunciation of "sociological snoopers" (Von Hoffman 1970). One of our professors even tried to get Humphreys' Ph.D. revoked. As the controversy heated up and a court case loomed, Humphreys feared that his list of respondents might be subpoenaed. He gave me the list to take from Missouri to Illinois, where I had begun teaching. When he called and asked me to destroy it, I burned the list in my backyard.

Was this research ethical? This question is not decided easily. Although many sociologists sided with Humphreys—and his book reporting the research won a highly acclaimed award—the criticisms continued. At first, Humphreys defended his position vigorously, but five years later, in a second edition of his book (1975), he stated that he should have identified himself as a researcher.

Values in Research

Max Weber said that sociology should be **value free.** By this, he meant that a sociologist's **values**—beliefs about what is good or desirable in life and the way the world ought to be—should not affect social research. Weber wanted **objectivity,** value neutrality, to be the hallmark of social research. If values influence research, he said, sociological findings will be biased.

That bias has no place in research is not a matter of debate. All sociologists agree that no one should distort data to make them fit their values. It is equally clear that sociologists are infused with arbitrary values of all sorts, for like everyone else we are members of a particular society at a given point in history. Because values can lead to unintended distortions in how we interpret our research, sociologists stress the need of **replication,** repeating a study in order to compare the new results with the original findings. If an individual's values have distorted the research, replication by others should uncover the bias and correct it.

Despite this consensus, however, values remain a hotly debated topic in sociology (Buroway 2007; Piven 2007). As summarized in Figure 6, the disagreement centers on the proper purposes and uses of sociology. Some sociologists take the position that their goal should be to advance the understanding of social life—to gather data on any topic that interests them and to use the most appropriate theory to interpret their findings. Others are convinced that this is not enough. Sociologists, they say, should research the social arrangements that harm people—poverty, crime, racism, war, and other forms of human exploitation—with the goal of improving social life.

In the midst of this controversy, sociologists do their research: From racism and sexism to the globalization of capitalism on the macro level to the micro level of face-to-face interaction—talking, touching, and gestures. These are all topics that sociologists study and that we will explore in this text. This beautiful variety in sociology—and the contrast of going from the larger picture to the smaller picture and back again—is part of the reason that sociology holds such fascination for me. I hope that you also find this variety appealing.

Before we close this chapter, though, I would like you to consider two trends that are shaping sociology.

FIGURE 6   The Debate over Values in Sociological Research

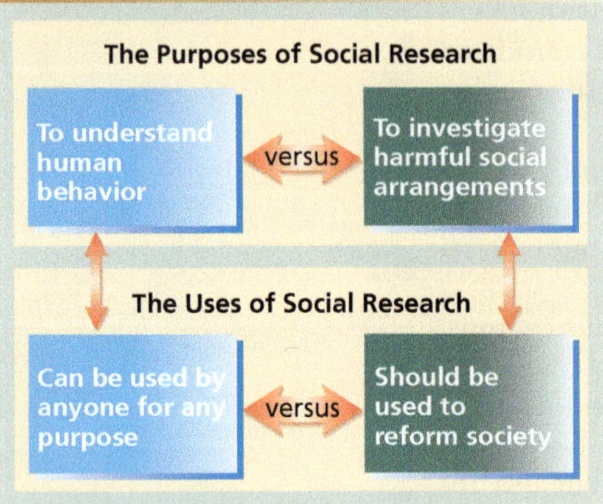

The Purposes of Social Research

To understand human behavior — versus — To investigate harmful social arrangements

The Uses of Social Research

Can be used by anyone for any purpose — versus — Should be used to reform society

Source: By the author.

Trends Shaping the Future of Sociology

Two major trends indicate changing directions in sociology. Let's look again at the relationship of sociology to social reform and then at globalization.

Sociology's Tension: Research Versus Reform

Public Sociology.   As we have discussed, a tension between social research and social reform runs through the history of sociology. Today, the American Sociological Association (ASA)

is promoting **public sociology,** a middle ground between research and reform. By this term, the ASA refers to the public becoming more aware of the sociological perspective, especially to politicians and policy makers using sociological data and applying the sociological understanding of how society works as they develop social policy (American Sociological Association 2004).

Public sociology is a safe way to make strides toward social reform. Few people get upset if sociologists publicize the sociological perspective by giving testimonies at hearings, serving on government committees, and submitting papers to policy makers. If those in power find the sociologists' recommendations to their liking, they can adopt them. If they don't, they can disregard them and go on their merry way. This is certainly safer than working directly with oppressed people to demand social change. The risk of government agents using what they learn from the sociological perspective to strengthen the elites in their positions of privilege, however, seems to have gone unnoticed. This is not to say that this middle ground does not hold the potential for social reform, for it does. As you can see from the Cultural Diversity box, data from basic sociological research can become a stimulus for social policy.

With the backing of the ASA, then, the pendulum is swinging toward applying sociological knowledge. At the same time, another trend is also beginning to have a profound effect on sociology. Let's look at the implications of globalization for the future of sociology.

public sociology sociology being used for the public good; especially the sociological perspective (of how things are related to one another) guiding politicians and policy makers

Cultural Diversity in the United States

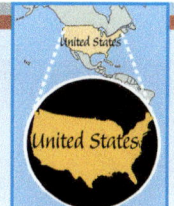

Unanticipated Public Sociology: Studying Job Discrimination

Basic sociology—research aimed at learning more about some behavior—can turn into public sociology. Here is what happened to Devah Pager, a graduate student at the University of Wisconsin in Madison, who was doing volunteer work in a homeless shelter. Some of the men told her how hard it was to find work if they had had been in prison. Were the men exaggerating she wondered? To find out what difference a prison record makes in getting a job, she sent pairs of college men to apply for 350 entry-level jobs in Milwaukee. One team was African American, and one was white. Pager prepared identical résumés for the teams, but with one difference: On each team, one of the men said he had served 18 months in prison for possession of cocaine.

Figure 7 shows the difference that the prison record made. Men without a prison record were two or three times as likely to be called back.

But Pager came up with another significant finding. Look at the difference that race–ethnicity made. White men with a prison record were more likely to be offered a job than African American men who had a clean record!

Sociological research often remains in obscure journals, read by only a few specialists. But Pager's findings got around, turning into public sociology. Someone told President George W. Bush about the research, and he announced in his State of the Union speech that he

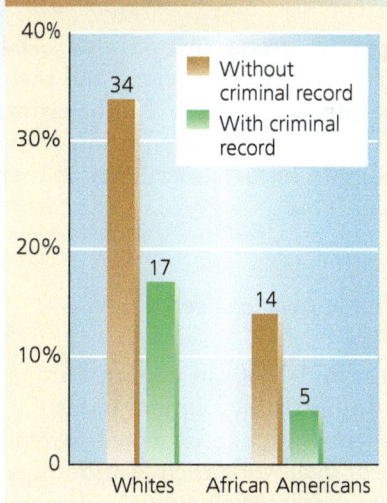

FIGURE 7 Call-Back Rates by Race–Ethnicity and Criminal Record

Source: Courtesy of Devah Pager.

wanted Congress to fund a $300 million program to provide mentoring and other support to help former prisoners get jobs (Kroeger 2004).

As you can see, sometimes only a thin line separates basic and public sociology.

For Your Consideration

What findings would you expect if women had been included in this study?

Globalization

Globalization is the breaking down of national borders because of advances in communications, trade, and travel, and a resulting dispersal of products and ideas around the world. Because the United States dominates sociology and we U.S. sociologists tend to concentrate on events and relationships that occur in our own country, most of our findings are based on U.S. samples. Globalization is destined to broaden our horizons, directing us to a greater consideration of global issues. This, in turn, is likely to motivate us to try more vigorously to identify universal principles.

Application of Globalization to This Text.   With each passing year, the world grows smaller as we become more connected to the global village. Increasingly, our welfare is tied to that of people in other nations. To help broaden your horizons, we will visit many cultures around the world, examining what life is like for the people who live in those cultures. Seeing how *their* society affects their behavior and orientations to life helps us to understand how *our* society influences what we do and how we feel about life.

You and I are living at a great historical moment, personally experiencing one of the most significant events in all of world history. Think about the impact of globalization on your life, especially how it is likely to shape your future. The developing new world order, if it can shave off its rough edges, appears destined to play a significant role in your future.

SUMMARY *and* REVIEW

The Sociological Perspective

What is the sociological perspective?

The **sociological perspective** stresses that people's social experiences—the groups to which they belong and their experiences within these groups—underlie their behavior. C. Wright Mills referred to this as the intersection of biography (the individual) and history (social factors that influence the individual).

Origins of Sociology

When did sociology first appear as a separate discipline?

Sociology emerged in the mid-1800s in western Europe, during the onset of the Industrial Revolution. Industrialization affected all aspects of human existence—where people lived, the nature of their work, their relationships, and how they viewed life. Early sociologists who focused on these social changes include Auguste Comte, Herbert Spencer, Karl Marx, Emile Durkheim, Max Weber, Harriet Martineau, and W. E. B. Du Bois.

Sociology in North America

What was the position of women and minorities in early sociology?

The few women who received the education required to become sociologists tended to focus on social reform. The debate between social reform and social analysis was won by male university professors who ignored the contributions of the women. W. E. B. Du Bois faced deep racism in his sociological career.

Why are the positions of Parsons and Mills important?

C. Wright Mills took the position that sociology like Talcott Parsons' dispassionate analysis of the components of society does nothing for social reform, which should be the goal of sociologists. The significance of this position is that the debate about the purpose and use of sociology continues today.

Theoretical Perspectives in Sociology

What is a theory?

A **theory** is a statement about how facts are related to one another. A theory provides a conceptual framework for interpreting facts.

What are sociology's major theoretical perspectives?

Sociologists use three primary theoretical frameworks to interpret social life. **Symbolic interactionists** examine how people use symbols (meanings) to develop and share their views of the world. Symbolic interactionists usually focus on the **micro level**—on small-scale, face-to-face interaction. **Functional analysts,** in contrast, focus on the **macro level**—on large-scale patterns of society. Functional theorists stress that a social system is made up of interrelated parts. When working properly, each part contributes to the stability of the whole, fulfilling a function that contributes to the system's equilibrium. **Conflict theorists** also focus on large-scale patterns of society. They stress that society is composed of competing groups that struggle for scarce resources.

With each perspective focusing on select features of social life, and each providing a unique interpretation, no single perspective is adequate. The combined insights of all three yield a more comprehensive picture of social life.

What is the relationship between theory and research?

Theory and research depend on one another. Sociologists use theory to interpret the data they gather. Theory also generates questions that need to be answered by research, while research, in turn, helps to generate theory. Theory without research is not likely to represent real life, while research without theory is merely a collection of empty facts.

Doing Sociological Research

Why do we need sociological research when we have common sense?

Common sense is unreliable. Research often shows that commonsense ideas are limited or false.

What are the eight basic steps in sociological research?

1. Selecting a topic 2. Defining the problem 3. Reviewing the literature 4. Formulating a **hypothesis** 5. Choosing a **research method** 6. Collecting the data 7. Analyzing the results 8. Sharing the results

Research Methods

How do sociologists gather data?

To gather data, sociologists use seven **research methods** (or **research designs**): **surveys, participant observation,** **case studies, secondary analysis, documents, experiments,** and **unobtrusive measures.**

Ethics and Values in Sociological Research

How important are ethics in sociological research?

Ethics are of fundamental concern to sociologists, who are committed to openness, honesty, truth, and protecting their subjects from harm. The Brajuha research on restaurant workers and the Humphreys research on "tearooms" illustrate ethical issues of concern to sociologists.

What value dilemmas do sociologists face?

The first dilemma is how to make certain that research is objective, not unintentionally distorted by the researchers' values. To overcome this possible source of bias, sociologists stress **replication.** The second dilemma is whether to do research solely to analyze human behavior or with the goal of reforming harmful social arrangements.

Trends Shaping the Future of Sociology

What trends are likely to have an impact on sociology?

The first is **public sociology,** an attempt to apply sociology by publicizing sociological data and the sociological perspective. This renewed emphasis on applying sociology could take sociology closer to its roots. The second is **globalization,** which is likely to broaden sociological horizons, refocusing research and theory away from its concentration on U.S. society.

THINKING CRITICALLY

1. Do you think that sociologists should try to reform society or study it dispassionately?
2. Of the three theoretical perspectives, which one would you prefer to use if you were a sociologist? Why?
3. Considering the macro- and micro-level approaches in sociology, which one do you think better explains social life? Why?
4. In your opinion, is it right (or ethical) for sociologists to not identity themselves when they do research? To misrepresent themselves? What if identifying themselves as researchers will destroy their access to a research setting or to informants?

ADDITIONAL RESOURCES

What can you find in MySocLab? mysoclab www.mysoclab.com

- Complete Ebook
- Practice Tests and Video and Audio activities
- Mapping and Data Analysis exercises

- Sociology in the News
- Classic Readings in Sociology
- Research and Writing advice

Where Can I Read More on This Topic?

Suggested readings follow this chapter.

SUGGESTED READINGS

Allan, Kenneth D. *Explorations in Classical Sociological Theory: Seeing the Social World.* Thousand Oaks, Calif.: Pine Forge Press, 2006. The author's emphasis is that sociological theory can be a guide for selecting research projects and for interpreting the results.

Berger, Peter L. *Invitation to Sociology: A Humanistic Perspective.* New York: Doubleday, 1972. This analysis of how sociology applies to everyday life has become a classic in the field.

Brooks, Arthur C. *Gross National Happiness: Why Happiness Matters for America and How We Can Get More of It.* New York: Basic Books, 2008. To see how happiness, ordinarily considered to be an intensely personal matter, can be explained by the sociological perspective, read this book.

Charon, Joel M. *Symbolic Interactionism: An Introduction, an Interpretation, an Integration,* 9th ed. Upper Saddle River, N.J.: Prentice Hall, 2008. The author lays out the main points of symbolic interactionism, providing an understanding of why this perspective is important in sociology.

Henslin, James M., ed. *Down to Earth Sociology: Introductory Readings,* 15th ed. New York: Free Press, 2010. This collection of readings about everyday life and social structure is designed to broaden the reader's understanding of society, and of the individual's place within it.

Jeffries, Vincent, ed. *Handbook of Public Sociology.* Lanham, MD: Rowman & Littlefield, 2009. The authors examine how sociology can be taken out of its academic isolation to engage wider audiences. Somewhat advanced reading.

Lengermann, Patricia Madoo, and Gillian Niebrugge. *The Women Founders: Sociology and Social Theory, 1830–1930.* Long Grove, Ill.: Waveland Press, 1998. Through their analyses and the writings they reprint, the authors/editors illuminate the struggles of female sociologists during the early period of sociology.

Mills, C. Wright. *The Sociological Imagination.* New York: Oxford University Press, 2000. First published in 1960, this classic analysis provides an overview of sociology from the framework of the conflict perspective.

Ritzer, George. *Classic Sociological Theory,* 5th ed. New York: McGraw-Hill, 2008. To help understand the personal and historical context of how theory develops, the author includes biographical sketches of the theorists.

How Sociologists Do Research

Bryman, Alan. *Social Research Methods,* 3rd ed. Oxford: Oxford University Press, 2008. An overview of the research methods used by sociologists, with an emphasis on the logic that underlies these methods.

Creswell, John W. *Research Design: Qualitative, Quantitative, and Mixed Methods Approaches,* 3rd ed. Beverly Hills, Calif.: Sage, 2008. This introduction to research methods walks you through the research experience and helps you to understand when to use a particular method.

Drew, Paul, Geoffrey Raymond, and Darin Weinberg. *Talk and Interaction in Social Research Methods.* Thousand Oaks, Calif.: Sage Publications, 2006. The authors stress the importance of talk in a variety of social research methods.

Lee, Raymond M. *Unobtrusive Methods in Social Research.* Philadelphia: Open University Press, 2000. This overview of unobtrusive ways of doing social research summarizes many interesting studies.

Neuman, W. Lawrence. *Social Research Methods: Qualitative and Quantitative Approaches,* 6th ed. Boston: Allyn and Bacon, 2006. This "how-to" book of sociological research describes how sociologists gather data and the logic that underlies each method.

Schuman, Howard. *Method and Meaning in Polls and Surveys.* Cambridge, Mass.: Harvard University Press, 2008. Examines how the wording of questions can change findings and how to understand the results of surveys.

Whyte, William Foote. *Creative Problem Solving in the Field: Reflections on a Career.* Lanham, Md.: AltaMira Press, 1997. Focusing on his extensive field experiences, the author provides insight into the researcher's role in participant observation.

Wysocki, Diane Kholos, ed. *Readings in Social Research Methods,* 3rd ed. Belmont, Calif.: Wadsworth, 2008. The authors of these articles provide an overview of research methods.

Journals

Applied Behavioral Science Review, Clinical Sociology Review, International Clinical Sociology, Journal of Applied Sociology, The Practicing Sociologist, Sociological Practice: A Journal of Clinical and Applied Sociology, and *Sociological Practice Review* report the experiences of sociologists who work in applied settings, from peer group counseling and suicide prevention to recommending changes to school boards.

Contexts: Understanding People in Their Social Worlds, published by the American Sociological Association, uses a magazine format to present sociological research in a down-to-earth fashion.

Humanity & Society, the official journal of the Association for Humanist Sociology, publishes articles intended "to advance the quality of life of the world's people."

Journal of Contemporary Ethnography, Qualitative Sociology, and *Symbolic Interaction* feature articles on symbolic interactionism and analyses of everyday life.

Electronic Journals

Electronic Journal of Sociology (http://www.sociology.org) and *Sociological Research Online* (http://www.socresonline.org.uk) publish articles on various sociological topics. Access is free.

Writing Papers for Sociology

Booth, Wayne C., Gregory G. Colomb, and Joseph M. Williams. *The Craft of Research,* 3rd ed. Chicago: University of Chicago, 2008. How to plan a paper, build an argument, anticipate and respond to the reservations of readers, and create introductions and conclusions that answer the demanding question, "So what?"

Richlin-Klonsky, Judith, William G. Roy, Ellen Strenski, and Roseann Giarusso, eds. *The Sociology Writing Group. A Guide to Writing Sociology Papers,* 6th ed. New York: Worth Publishers, 2007. The guide walks students through the steps in writing a sociology paper, from choosing the initial assignment to doing the research and turning in a finished paper. Also explains how to manage time and correctly cite sources.

About Majoring in Sociology

You like sociology and perhaps are thinking about majoring in it, but what can you do with a sociology major? Be sure to check the epilogue of this book (pages 336–337). Also check out the resources that are available from the American Sociological Association. Go to www.asanet. org. This will bring you to the ASA's home page. Here, you can click around and get familiar with what this professional association offers students.

On the menu at the top of ASA's home page, click Students. This will bring you to a page that has links to resources for students. You may be interested in The Student Sociologist, a newsletter for students. The link, Careers, will take you to several free online publications, including those that feature information on careers in both basic and applied sociology. You will also see such links as the student forum, student involvement, and funding.

If you want to contact the ASA by snail mail or by telephone or fax, here is that information: American Sociological Association, 1430 K Street NW, Suite 600, Washington, D.C. 20005. Tel. (202) 383-9005. Fax (202) 638-0882. E-mail: Executive.Office@asanet.org

You might also be interested in *Careers in Sociology Module.* New York: Wadsworth, 2009, and Lambert, Stephen. *Great Jobs for Sociology Majors,* New York: McGraw-Hill, 2009. How can you make a living with a major in sociology? These two publications explore careers in sociology, from business and government to health care and the law.

Socialization

From Chapter 3 of *Sociology: A Down-to-Earth Approach Core Concepts, Census Update,* Fourth Edition. James M. Henslin. Copyright © 2012 by Pearson Education, Inc. Published by Allyn & Bacon.

©Jeff Greenberg/The Image Works

Socialization

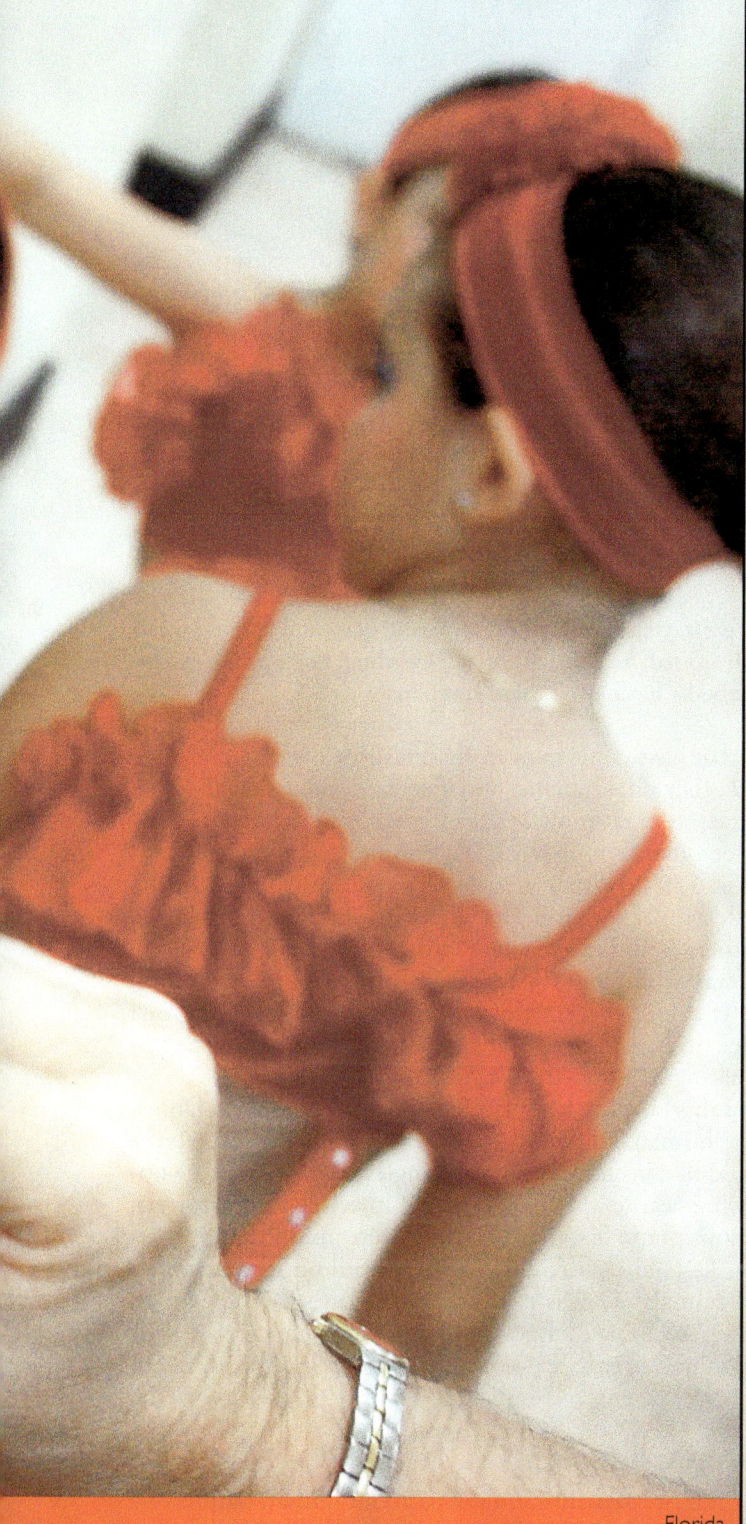

Florida

The old man was horrified when he found out. Life never had been good since his daughter lost her hearing when she was just 2 years old. She couldn't even talk—just fluttered her hands around trying to tell him things.

Over the years, he had gotten used to that. But now . . . he shuddered at the thought of her being pregnant. No one would be willing to marry her; he knew that. And the neighbors, their tongues would never stop wagging. Everywhere he went, he could hear people talking behind his back.

> Her behavior toward strangers, especially men, was almost that of a wild animal, manifesting much fear and hostility.

If only his wife were still alive, maybe she could come up with something. What should he do? He couldn't just kick his daughter out into the street.

After the baby was born, the old man tried to shake his feelings, but they wouldn't let loose. Isabelle was a pretty name, but every time he looked at the baby he felt sick to his stomach.

He hated doing it, but there was no way out. His daughter and her baby would have to live in the attic.

Unfortunately, this is a true story. Isabelle was discovered in Ohio in 1938 when she was about 6½ years old, living in a dark room with her deaf-mute mother. Isabelle couldn't talk, but she did use gestures to communicate with her mother. An inadequate diet and lack of sunshine had given Isabelle a disease called rickets.

> [Her legs] were so bowed that as she stood erect the soles of her shoes came nearly flat together, and she got about with a skittering gait. Her behavior toward strangers, especially men, was almost that of a wild animal, manifesting much fear and hostility. In lieu of speech she made only a strange croaking sound. (Davis 1940/2007:156–157)

When the newspapers reported this case, sociologist Kingsley Davis decided to find out what had happened to Isabelle after her discovery. We'll come back to that later, but first let's use the case of Isabelle to gain insight into human nature.

social environment the entire human environment, including direct contact with others

feral children children assumed to have been raised by animals, in the wilderness, isolated from humans

Society Makes Us Human

"What do you mean, society makes us human?" is probably what you are asking. "That sounds ridiculous. I was born a human." The meaning of this statement will become more apparent as we get into the chapter. Let's start by considering what is human about human nature. How much of a person's characteristics comes from "nature" (heredity) and how much from "nurture" (the **social environment,** contact with others)? Experts are trying to answer the nature–nurture question by studying identical twins who were separated at birth and reared in different environments, such as those discussed in the Down-to-Earth Sociology box. Another way is to examine children who have had little human contact. Let's consider such children.

Feral Children

The naked child was found in the forest, walking on all fours, eating grass and lapping water from the river. When he saw a small animal, he pounced on it. Growling, he ripped at it with his teeth. Tearing chunks from the body, he chewed them ravenously.

This is an apt description of reports that have come in over the centuries. Supposedly, these **feral** (wild) **children** could not speak; they bit, scratched, growled, and walked on all fours. They drank by lapping water, ate grass, tore ravenously at raw meat, and showed insensitivity to pain and cold. Why am I even mentioning stories that sound so exaggerated?

It is because of what happened in 1798. In that year, such a child was found in the forests of Aveyron, France. "The wild boy of Aveyron," as he became known, would have been written off as another folk myth, except that French scientists took the child to a laboratory and studied him. Like the feral children in the earlier informal reports, this child, too, gave no indication of feeling the cold. Most startling, though, the boy would growl when he saw a small animal, pounce on it, and devour it uncooked. Even today, the scientists' detailed reports make fascinating reading (Itard 1962).

Ever since I read Itard's account of this boy, I've been fascinated by the seemingly fantastic possibility that animals could rear human children. In 2002, I received a report from a contact in Cambodia that a feral child had been found in the jungles. When I had the opportunity the following year to visit the child and interview his caregivers, I grabbed it. The boy's photo is to the left. If we were untouched by society, would we be like feral children? By nature, would our behavior be like that of wild animals? That is the sociological question. Unable to study feral children, sociologists have studied isolated children, like Isabelle in our opening vignette. Let's see what we can learn from them.

One of the reasons I went to Cambodia was to interview a feral child—the boy shown here—who supposedly had been raised by monkeys. When I arrived at the remote location where the boy was living, I was disappointed to find that the story was only partially true. During its reign of terror, the Khmer Rouge had shot and killed the boy's parents, leaving him, at about the age of two, abandoned on an island. Some months later, villagers found him in the care of monkeys. They shot the female monkey who was carrying the boy. Not quite a feral child—but the closest I'll ever come to one.

James M. Henslin

Isolated Children

What can isolated children tell us about human nature? We can first conclude that humans have no natural language, for Isabelle and others like her are unable to speak.

But maybe Isabelle was mentally impaired. Perhaps she simply was unable to progress through the usual stages of development. It certainly looked that way—she scored practically zero on her first intelligence test. But after a few months of language training, Isabelle was able to speak in short sentences. In just a year, she could write a few words, do simple addition, and retell stories after hearing them. Seven months later, she had a vocabulary of almost 2,000 words. In just two years, Isabelle reached the intellectual level that is normal for her age. She then went on to school, where she was "bright, cheerful, energetic . . . and participated in all school activities as normally as other children" (Davis 1940/2007:157–158).

Down-to-Earth Sociology

Heredity or Environment? The Case of Jack and Oskar, Identical Twins

Identical twins are identical in their genetic heritage. They are born when one fertilized egg divides to produce two embryos. If heredity determines personality—or attitudes, temperament, skills, and intelligence—then identical twins should be identical not only in their looks but also in these characteristics.

The fascinating case of Jack and Oskar helps us unravel this mystery. From their experience, we can see the far-reaching effects of the environment—how social experiences override biology.

Jack Yufe and Oskar Stohr are identical twins. Born in 1932 to a Roman Catholic mother and a Jewish father, they were separated as babies after their parents divorced. Jack was reared in Trinidad by his father. There, he learned loyalty to Jews and hatred of Hitler and the Nazis. After the war, Jack and his father moved to Israel. When he was 17, Jack joined a kibbutz and later served in the Israeli army.

Oskar's upbringing was a mirror image of Jack's. Oskar was reared in Czechoslovakia by his mother's mother, who was a strict Catholic. When Oskar was a toddler, Hitler annexed this area of Czechoslovakia, and Oskar learned to love Hitler and to hate Jews. He joined the Hitler Youth (a sort of Boy Scout organization, except that this one was designed to instill the "virtues" of patriotism, loyalty, obedience—and hatred).

In 1954, the two brothers met. It was a short meeting, and Jack had been warned not to tell Oskar that they were Jews. Twenty-five years later, in 1979, when they were 47 years old, social scientists at the University of Minnesota brought them together again. These researchers figured that because Jack and Oskar had the same genes, any differences they showed would have to be the result of their environment—their different social experiences.

Not only did Jack and Oskar hold different attitudes toward the war, Hitler, and Jews, but their basic orientations to life were also different. In their politics, Jack was liberal, while Oskar was more conservative. Jack was a workaholic, while Oskar enjoyed leisure. And, as you can predict, Jack was proud of being a Jew. Oskar, who by this time knew that he was a Jew, wouldn't even mention it.

The question of the relative influence of heredity and the environment in human behavior has fascinated and plagued researchers. To try to answer this question, researchers have studied identical twins. In this photo, what behaviors can you see that are clearly due to the environment? Any that are due to biology?

Frank Siteman Photography

That would seem to settle the matter. But there were other things. As children, Jack and Oskar had both excelled at sports but had difficulty with math. They also had the same rate of speech, and both liked sweet liqueur and spicy foods. Strangely, both flushed the toilet both before and after using it, and they both enjoyed startling people by sneezing in crowded elevators.

For Your Consideration

Heredity or environment? How much influence does each have? The question is not yet settled, but at this point it seems fair to conclude that the *limits* of certain physical and mental abilities are established by heredity (such as ability at sports and aptitude for mathematics), while attitudes are the result of the environment. Basic temperament, though, seems to be inherited. Although the answer is still fuzzy, we can put it this way: For some parts of life, the blueprint is drawn by heredity; but even here the environment can redraw those lines. For other parts, the individual is a blank slate, and it is up to the environment to determine what is written on that slate.

Sources: Based on Begley 1979; Chen 1979; Wright 1995; Segal and Hershberger 2005; De Moor et al. 2007.

Language is the key to human development. Without language, people have no mechanism for developing thought and communicating their experiences. Unlike animals, humans have no instincts that take the place of language. If an individual lacks language, he or she lives in a world of internal silence, without shared ideas, lacking connections to others.

Without language, there can be no culture—no shared way of life—and culture is the key to what people become. Each of us possesses a biological heritage, but this heritage does not determine specific behaviors, attitudes, or values. It is our culture that superimposes the specifics of what we become onto our biological heritage.

Institutionalized Children

Other than language, what else is required for a child to develop into what we consider a healthy, balanced, intelligent human being? We find part of the answer in an intriguing experiment from the 1930s. Back then, orphanages were common because parents were more likely than now to die before their children were grown. Children reared in orphanages tended to have low IQs. "Common sense" (which is unreliable) made it obvious that their low intelligence was because of poor brains ("They're just born that way"). But two psychologists, H. M. Skeels and H. B. Dye (1939), began to suspect a social cause.

Skeels (1966) provides this account of a "good" orphanage in Iowa, one where he and Dye were consultants:

Until about six months, they were cared for in the infant nursery. The babies were kept in standard hospital cribs that often had protective sheeting on the sides, thus effectively limiting visual stimulation; no toys or other objects were hung in the infants' line of vision. Human interactions were limited to busy nurses who, with the speed born of practice and necessity, changed diapers or bedding, bathed and medicated the infants, and fed them efficiently with propped bottles.

Perhaps, thought Skeels and Dye, the problem was the absence of stimulating social interaction, not the children's brains. To test their controversial idea, they selected thirteen infants who were so mentally slow that no one wanted to adopt them. They placed them in an institution for mentally retarded women. They assigned each infant, then about 19 months old, to a separate ward of women ranging in mental age from 5 to 12 and in chronological age from 18 to 50. The women were pleased with this. They enjoyed taking care of the infants' physical needs—diapering, feeding, and so on. And they also loved to play with the children. They cuddled them and showered them with attention. They even competed to see which ward would have "its baby" walking or talking first. In each ward, one woman became particularly attached to the child and figuratively adopted him or her:

As a consequence, an intense one-to-one adult–child relationship developed, which was supplemented by the less intense but frequent interactions with the other adults in the environment. Each child had some one person with whom he [or she] was identified and who was particularly interested in him [or her] and his [or her] achievements. (Skeels 1966)

The researchers left a control group of twelve infants at the orphanage. These infants received the usual care. They also had low IQs, but they were considered somewhat higher in

Infants in this orphanage in Siem Reap, Cambodia, are drugged and hung in these mesh baskets for up to ten hours a day. The staff of the orphanage pockets most of the money contributed by Westerners for the children's care. The treatment of these children is likely to affect their ability to reason and to function as adults.

intelligence than the thirteen in the experimental group. Two and a half years later, Skeels and Dye tested all the children's intelligence. Their findings are startling: Those cared for by the women in the institution gained an average of 28 IQ points while those who remained in the orphanage lost 30 points.

What happened after these children were grown? Did these initial differences matter? Twenty-one years later, Skeels and Dye did a follow-up study. The twelve in the control group, those who had remained in the orphanage, averaged less than a third-grade education. Four still lived in state institutions, and the others held low-level jobs. Only two had married. The thirteen in the experimental group, those cared for by the institutionalized women, had an average education of twelve grades (about normal for that period). Five had completed one or more years of college. One had even gone to graduate school. Eleven had married. All thirteen were self-supporting or were homemakers (Skeels 1966). Apparently, "high intelligence" depends on early, close relations with other humans.

A recent experiment in India confirms this early research. Many of India's orphanages are like those that Skeels and Dye studied—dismal places where unattended children lie in bed all day. When experimenters added stimulating play and interaction to the children's activities, the children's motor skills improved and their IQs increased (Taneja et al. 2002). The longer that children lack stimulating interaction, though, the more difficulty they have intellectually (Meese 2005).

Let's consider Genie, a 13-year-old girl who had been locked in a small room and tied to a chair since she was 20 months old:

Apparently Genie's father (70 years old when Genie was discovered in 1970) hated children. He probably had caused the death of two of Genie's siblings. Her 50-year-old mother was partially blind and frightened of her husband. Genie could not speak, did not know how to chew, was unable to stand upright, and could not straighten her hands and legs. On intelligence tests, she scored at the level of a 1-year-old. After intensive training, Genie learned to walk and to say simple sentences (although they were garbled). Genie's language remained primitive as she grew up. She would take anyone's property if it appealed to her, and she went to the bathroom wherever she wanted. At the age of 21, she was sent to a home for adults who cannot live alone. (Pines 1981)

In Sum: From Genie's pathetic story and from the research on institutionalized children, we can conclude that the basic human traits of intelligence and the ability to establish close bonds with others depend on early interaction with other humans. In addition, there seems to be a period prior to age 13 in which children must learn language and experience human bonding if they are to develop normal intelligence and the ability to be sociable and follow social norms.

Deprived Animals

Finally, let's consider animals that have been deprived of normal interaction. In a series of experiments with rhesus monkeys, psychologists Harry and Margaret Harlow demonstrated the importance of early learning. The Harlows (1962) raised baby monkeys in isolation. They gave each monkey two artificial mothers. One "mother" was only a wire frame with a wooden head, but it did have a nipple from which the baby could nurse. The frame of the other "mother," which had no bottle, was covered with soft terrycloth. To obtain food, the baby monkeys nursed at the wire frame.

Like humans, monkeys need interaction to thrive. Those raised in isolation are unable to interact with others. In this photograph, we see one of the monkeys described in the text. Purposefully frightened by the experimenter, the monkey has taken refuge in the soft terrycloth draped over an artificial "mother."

Nina Leen/Time Life Pictures/Getty Images

When the Harlows (1965) frightened the baby monkeys with a mechanical bear or dog, the babies did not run to the wire frame "mother." Instead, as shown in the photo on the previous page, they would cling pathetically to their terrycloth "mother." The Harlows concluded that infant–mother bonding is not the result of feeding but, rather, of what they termed "intimate physical contact." To most of us, this phrase means cuddling.

The monkeys raised in isolation could not adjust to monkey life. Placed with other monkeys when they were grown, they didn't know how to participate in "monkey interaction"—to play and to engage in pretend fights—and the other monkeys rejected them. They didn't even know how to have sexual intercourse, despite futile attempts to do so. The experimenters designed a special device, which allowed some females to become pregnant. Their isolation, however, made them "ineffective, inadequate, and brutal mothers." They "struck their babies, kicked them, or crushed the babies against the cage floor."

In one of their many experiments, the Harlows isolated baby monkeys for different lengths of time and then put them in with the other monkeys. Monkeys that had been isolated for shorter periods (about three months) were able to adjust to normal monkey life. They learned to play and engage in pretend fights. Those isolated for six months or more, however, couldn't make the adjustment, and the other monkeys rejected them. In other words, the longer the period of isolation, the more difficult its effects are to overcome. In addition, there seems to be a critical learning stage: If that stage is missed, it may be impossible to compensate for what has been lost. This may have been the case with Genie.

Because humans are not monkeys, we must be careful about extrapolating from animal studies to human behavior. The Harlow experiments, however, support what we know about children who are reared in isolation.

In Sum: Babies do not develop "naturally" into social adults. If children are reared in isolation, their bodies grow, but they become little more than big animals. Without the concepts that language provides, they can't grasp relationships between people (the "connections" we call brother, sister, parent, friend, teacher, and so on). And without warm, friendly interactions, they can't bond with others. They don't become "friendly" or cooperate with others. In short, it is through human contact that people learn to be members of the human community. This process by which we learn the ways of society (or of particular groups), called **socialization,** is what sociologists have in mind when they say "Society makes us human."

Further keys to understanding how society makes us human are our self-concept, ability to "take the role of others," reasoning, morality, and emotions. Let's look at how we develop these capacities.

Socialization into the Self and Mind

When you were born, you had no ideas. You didn't know that you were a son or daughter. You didn't even know that you were a he or she. How did you develop a **self,** your image of who you are? How did you develop your ability to reason? Let's find out.

Cooley and the Looking-Glass Self

About a hundred years ago, Charles Horton Cooley (1864–1929), a symbolic interactionist who taught at the University of Michigan, concluded that the self is part of how *society* makes us human. He said that *our sense of self develops from interaction with others.* To describe the process by which this unique aspect of "humanness" develops, Cooley (1902) coined the term **looking-glass self.** He summarized this idea in the following couplet:

> **Each to each a looking-glass**
> **Reflects the other that doth pass.**

The looking-glass self contains three elements:

1. *We imagine how we appear to those around us.* For example, we may think that others perceive us as witty or dull.

---

socialization the process by which people learn the characteristics of their group—the knowledge, skills, attitudes, values, norms, and actions thought appropriate for them

self the unique human capacity of being able to see ourselves "from the outside"; the views we internalize of how others see us

looking-glass self a term coined by Charles Horton Cooley to refer to the process by which our self develops through internalizing others' reactions to us

taking the role of the other putting oneself in someone else's shoes; understanding how someone else feels and thinks and thus anticipating how that person will act

significant other an individual who significantly influences someone else's life

generalized other the norms, values, attitudes, and expectations of people "in general"; the child's ability to take the role of the generalized other is a significant step in the development of a self

2. *We interpret others' reactions.* We come to conclusions about how others evaluate us. Do they like us for being witty? Do they dislike us for being dull?

3. *We develop a self-concept.* How we interpret others' reactions to us frames our feelings and ideas about ourselves. A favorable reflection in this *social mirror* leads to a positive self-concept; a negative reflection leads to a negative self-concept.

Note that the development of the self does *not* depend on accurate evaluations. Even if we grossly misinterpret how others think about us, those misjudgments become part of our self-concept. Note also that *although the self-concept begins in childhood, its development is an ongoing, lifelong process.* During our everyday lives, we monitor how others react to us. As we do so, we continually modify the self. The self, then, is never a finished product—it is always in process, even into our old age.

Mead and Role Taking

Another symbolic interactionist, George Herbert Mead (1863–1931), who taught at the University of Chicago, pointed out how important play is as we develop a self. As we play with others, we learn to **take the role of the other.** That is, we learn to put ourselves in someone else's shoes—to understand how someone else feels and thinks and to anticipate how that person will act.

This doesn't happen overnight. We develop this ability over a period of years (Mead 1934; Denzin 2007). Psychologist John Flavel (1968) asked 8- and 14-year-olds to explain a board game to children who were blindfolded and to others who were not. The 14-year-olds gave more detailed instructions to those who were blindfolded, but the 8-year-olds gave the same instructions to everyone. The younger children could not yet take the role of the other, while the older children could.

As we develop this ability, at first we can take only the role of **significant others,** individuals who significantly influence our lives, such as parents or siblings. By assuming their roles during play, such as dressing up in our parents' clothing, we cultivate the ability to put ourselves in the place of significant others.

As our self gradually develops, we internalize the expectations of more and more people. Our ability to take the role of others eventually extends to being able to take the role of "the group as a whole." Mead used the term **generalized other** to refer to our perception of how people in general think of us.

Taking the role of others is essential if we are to become cooperative members of human groups—whether they be our family, friends, or co-workers. This ability allows us to modify our behavior by anticipating how others will react—something Genie never learned.

As Figure 1 illustrates, we go through three stages as we learn to take the role of the other:

1. *Imitation.* Under the age of 3, we can only mimic others. We do not yet have a sense of self separate from others, and we can only imitate people's gestures and words. (This stage is actually not role taking, but it prepares us for it.)

2. *Play.* During the second stage, from the ages of about 3 to 6, we pretend to take the roles of specific people. We might pretend that we are a firefighter, a wrestler, a nurse, Supergirl, Spiderman, a princess, and so on. We also like costumes at this stage and enjoy dressing up in our parents' clothing, or tying a towel around our neck to "become" Superman or Wonder Woman.

3. *Team Games.* This third stage, organized play, or team games, begins roughly when we enter school. The

Ariel Skelley/Corbis

FIGURE 1 How We Learn to Take the Role of the Other: Mead's Three Stages

Stage 1: Imitation
Children under age 3
No sense of self
Imitate others

Stage 2: Play
Ages 3 to 6
Play "pretend" others
(princess, Spiderman, etc.)

Stage 3: Team Games
After about age 6 or 7
Team games
("organized play")
Learn to take multiple roles

To help his students understand the term *generalized other,* Mead used baseball as an illustration. Why are team sports and organized games excellent examples to use in explaining this concept?

Mead analyzed *taking the role of the other* as an essential part of learning to be a full-fledged member of society. At first, we are able to take the role only of *significant others*, as this child is doing. Later we develop the capacity to take the role of the *generalized other*, which is essential not only for cooperation but also for the control of antisocial desires.

significance for the self is that to play these games we must be able to take multiple roles. One of Mead's favorite examples was that of a baseball game, in which each player must be able to take the role of all the other players. To play baseball, it isn't enough that we know our own role; we also must be able to anticipate what everyone else on the field will do when the ball is hit or thrown.

Mead also said there were two parts of the self, the "I" and the "me." The "*I*" is *the self as subject,* the active, spontaneous, creative part of the self. In contrast, the "*me*" is *the self as object.* It is made up of attitudes we internalize from our interactions with others. Mead chose these pronouns because in English "I" is the active agent, as in "I shoved him," while "me" is the object of action, as in "He shoved me." Mead stressed that we are not passive in the socialization process. We are not like robots, with programmed software shoved into us. Rather, our "I" is active. It evaluates the reactions of others and organizes them into a unified whole. Mead added that the "I" even monitors the "me," fine-tuning our ideas and attitudes to help us better meet what others expect of us.

In Sum: In studying the details, you don't want to miss the main point, which some find startling: *Both our self and our mind are social products.* Mead stressed that we cannot think without symbols. But where do these symbols come from? Only from society, which gives us our symbols by giving us language. If society did not provide the symbols, we would not be able to think and so would not possess a self-concept or that entity we call the mind. The self and mind, then, like language, are products of society.

Piaget and the Development of Reasoning

Shown here is Jean Piaget with one of the children he studied in his analysis of the development of human reasoning.

The development of the mind—specifically, how we learn to reason—was studied in detail by Jean Piaget (1896–1980). This Swiss psychologist noticed that when young children take intelligence tests, they often give similar wrong answers. This set him to thinking that the children might be using some consistent, but incorrect, reasoning. It might even indicate that children go through some natural process as they learn how to reason.

Stimulated by such an intriguing possibility, Piaget set up a laboratory where he could give children of different ages problems to solve (Piaget 1950, 1954; Flavel et al. 2002). After years of testing, Piaget concluded that children do go through a natural process as they develop their ability to reason. This process has four stages. (If you mentally substitute "reasoning skills" for the term *operational* as we review these stages, Piaget's findings will be easier to understand.)

1. **The sensorimotor stage** (from birth to about age 2) During this stage, our understanding is limited to direct contact—sucking, touching, listening, looking. We aren't able to "think." During the first part of this stage, we do not even know that our bodies are separate from the environment. Indeed, we have yet to discover that we have toes. Neither can we recognize cause and effect. That is, we do not know that our actions cause something to happen.

2. **The preoperational stage** (from about age 2 to age 7) During this stage, we *develop the ability to use symbols.* However, we do not yet understand common concepts such as size, speed, or causation. Although we are learning to count, we do not really understand what

Syracuse Newspapers/H. Bragman/The Image Works

Bill Anderson/Photo Researchers, Inc.

numbers mean. Nor do we yet have the ability to take the role of the other. Piaget asked preoperational children to describe a clay model of a mountain range. They did just fine. But when he asked them to describe how the mountain range looked from where another child was sitting, they couldn't do it. They could only repeat what they saw from their view.

3. **The concrete operational stage** (from the age of about 7 to 12) Our reasoning abilities are more developed, but they remain *concrete.* We can now understand numbers, size, causation, and speed, and we are able to take the role of the other. We can even play team games. Unless we have concrete examples, however, we are unable to talk about concepts such as truth, honesty, or justice. We can explain why Jane's answer was a lie, but we cannot describe what truth itself is.

4. **The formal operational stage** (after the age of about 12) We now are capable of abstract thinking. We can talk about concepts, come to conclusions based on general principles, and use rules to solve abstract problems. During this stage, we are likely to become young philosophers (Kagan 1984). If we were shown a photo of a slave during our concrete operational stage, we might have said, "That's wrong!" Now at the formal operational stage we are likely to add, "If our county was founded on equality, how could anyone own slaves?"

Global Aspects of the Self and Reasoning

Cooley's conclusions about the looking-glass self appear to be true for everyone around the world. So do Mead's conclusions about role taking and the mind and self as social products, although researchers are finding that the self may develop earlier than Mead indicated. The stages of reasoning that Piaget identified probably also occur worldwide, although researchers have found that the stages are not as distinct as Piaget concluded and the ages at which individuals enter the stages differ from one person to another (Flavel et al. 2002). Even during the sensorimotor stage, for example, children show early signs of reasoning, which may indicate an innate ability that is wired into the brain. Although Piaget's theory is being refined, his contribution remains: *A basic structure underlies the way we develop reasoning, and children all over the world begin with the concrete and move to the abstract.* Interestingly, some people seem to get stuck in the concreteness of the third stage and never reach the fourth stage of abstract thinking (Kohlberg and Gilligan 1971; Suizzo 2000). College, for example, nurtures the fourth stage, and people with this experience apparently have more ability for abstract thought. Social experiences, then, can modify these stages.

Learning Personality, Morality, and Emotions

Our personality, morality, and emotions are vital aspects of who we are. Let's look at how we learn these essential aspects of our being.

Freud and the Development of Personality

Along with the development of the mind and the self comes the development of the personality. Sigmund Freud (1856–1939) developed a theory of the origin of personality that has had a major impact on Western thought. Freud, a physician in Vienna in the early 1900s, founded *psychoanalysis,* a technique for treating emotional problems through long-term exploration of the subconscious mind. Let's look at his theory.

Freud believed that personality consists of three elements. Each child is born with the first element, an **id,** Freud's term for inborn drives that cause us to seek self-gratification. The id of the newborn is evident in its cries of hunger or pain. The pleasure-seeking id operates throughout life. It demands the immediate fulfillment of basic needs: food, safety, attention, sex, and so on.

id Freud's term for our inborn basic drives

Sigmund Freud in 1932 in Hochroterd, Austria. Although Freud was one of the most influential theorists of the 20th century, most of his ideas have been discarded.

The id's drive for immediate gratification, however, runs into a roadblock: primarily the needs of other people, especially those of the parents. To adapt to these constraints, a second component of the personality emerges, which Freud called the ego. The **ego** is the balancing force between the id and the demands of society that suppress it. The ego also serves to balance the id and the **superego,** the third component of the personality, more commonly called the *conscience.*

The superego represents *culture within us,* the norms and values we have internalized from our social groups. As the *moral* component of the personality, the superego provokes feelings of guilt or shame when we break social rules, or pride and self-satisfaction when we follow them.

According to Freud, when the id gets out of hand, we follow our desires for pleasure and break society's norms. When the superego gets out of hand, we become overly rigid in following those norms and end up wearing a straitjacket of rules that inhibit our lives. The ego, the balancing force, tries to prevent either the superego or the id from dominating. In the emotionally healthy individual, the ego succeeds in balancing these conflicting demands of the id and the superego. In the maladjusted individual, the ego fails to control the conflict between the id and the superego. Either the id or the superego dominates this person, leading to internal confusion and problem behaviors.

Sociological Evaluation.   Sociologists appreciate Freud's emphasis on socialization—his assertion that the social group into which we are born transmits norms and values that restrain our biological drives. Sociologists, however, object to the view that inborn and subconscious motivations are the primary reasons for human behavior. *This denies the central principle of sociology:* that factors such as social class (income, education, and occupation) and people's roles in groups underlie their behavior (Epstein 1988; Bush and Simmons 1990).

Feminist sociologists have been especially critical of Freud. Although what I just summarized applies to both females and males, Freud assumed that what is "male" is "normal." He even referred to females as inferior, castrated males (Chodorow 1990; Gerhard 2000). It is obvious that sociologists need to continue to research how we develop personality.

Kohlberg, Gilligan, and the Development of Morality

If you have observed young children, you know that they want immediate gratification and show little or no concern for others. ("Mine!" a 2-year-old will shout, as she grabs a toy from another child.) Yet, at a later age this same child will become considerate of others and try to be fair in her play. How does this change happen?

Kohlberg's Theory.   Psychologist Lawrence Kohlberg (1975, 1984, 1986; Reed 2008) concluded that we go through a sequence of stages as we develop morality. Building on Piaget's work, he found that children start in the *amoral stage* I just described. For them, there is no right or wrong, just personal needs to be satisfied. From about ages 7 to 10, children are in what Kohlberg called a *preconventional stage.* They have learned rules, and they follow them to stay out of trouble. They view right and wrong as what pleases or displeases their parents, friends, and teachers. Their concern is to avoid punishment. At

ego Freud's term for a balancing force between the id and the demands of society

superego Freud's term for the conscience; the internalized norms and values of our social groups

about age 10, they enter the *conventional stage.* During this period, morality means following the norms and values they have learned. In the *postconventional stage,* which Kohlberg says most people don't reach, individuals reflect on abstract principles of right and wrong and judge people's behavior according to these principles.

Gilligan and Gender Differences in Morality. Carol Gilligan, another psychologist, grew uncomfortable with Kohlberg's conclusions. They just didn't match her own experience. Then she noticed that Kohlberg had studied only boys. By this point, more women had become social scientists, and they had begun to question a common assumption of male researchers, that research on boys would apply to girls as well.

Gilligan (1982, 1990) decided to find out if there were differences in how men and women looked at morality. After interviewing about 200 men and women, she concluded that women are more likely to evaluate morality in terms of *personal relationships.* Women want to know how an action affects others. They are more concerned with personal loyalties and with the harm that might come to loved ones. Men, in contrast, tend to think more along the lines of *abstract principles* that define right and wrong. As they see things, an act either matches or violates a code of ethics, and personal relationships have little to do with the matter.

Researchers tested Gilligan's conclusions. They found that *both* men and women use personal relationships and abstract principles when they make moral judgments (Wark and Krebs 1996). Although Gilligan no longer supports her original position (Brannon 1999), the matter is not yet settled. Some researchers have found differences in how men and women make moral judgments (White 1999; Jaffee and Hyde 2000). Others stress that both men and women learn cultural forms of moral reasoning (Tappan 2006).

As with personality, in this vital area of human development, sociological research is also notably absent.

Socialization into Emotions

Emotions, too, are an essential aspect of who we become. Sociologists who research this area of our "humanness" find that emotions are not simply the results of biology. Like the mind, emotions depend on socialization (Hochschild 2008). This may sound strange. Don't all people get angry? Doesn't everyone cry? Don't we all feel guilt, shame, sadness, happiness, fear? What has socialization to do with emotions?

Global Emotions. At first, it may look as though socialization is not relevant, that we simply express universal feelings. Paul Ekman (1980), a psychologist who studied emotions in several countries, concluded that everyone experiences six basic emotions: anger, disgust, fear, happiness, sadness, and surprise. He also observed that we all show the same facial expressions when we feel these emotions. A person from Peru, for example, could tell from just the look on an American's face that she is angry, disgusted, or fearful, and we could tell from the Peruvian's face that he is happy, sad, or surprised. Because we all show the same facial expressions when we experience these six emotions, Ekman concluded that they are wired into our biology.

Expressing Emotions. If we have universal facial expressions to express basic emotions, then this is biology, something that Darwin noted back in the 1800s (Horwitz and Wakefield 2007:41). What, then, does sociology have to do with them? Facial expressions are only one way by which we show emotions. We also use our bodies, voices, and gestures.

> **Jane and Sushana have been best friends since high school. They were hardly ever apart until Sushana married and moved to another state a year ago. Jane has been waiting eagerly at the arrival gate for Sushana's flight, which has been delayed. When Sushana exits, she and Jane hug one another, making "squeals of glee" and even jumping a bit.**

If you couldn't tell from their names that these were women, you could tell from their behavior. To express delighted surprise, U.S. women are allowed to make "squeals of glee" in public places and to jump as they hug. In contrast, in the exact circumstances, U.S. men

   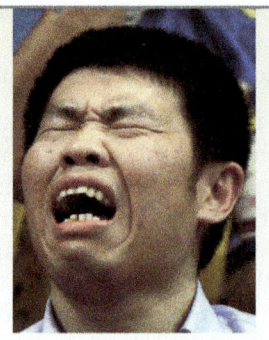 

What emotions are these people expressing? Are these emotions global? Is their way of expressing them universal?

are expected to shake hands, and they might even give a brief hug. If they gave out "squeals of glee," they would be violating a fundamental "gender rule."

In addition to "gender rules" for expressing emotions, there also are "rules" of culture, social class, relationships, and settings. Consider *culture*. Two close Japanese friends who meet after a long separation don't shake hands or hug—they bow. Two Arab men will kiss. *Social class* is so significant that it, too, cuts across other lines, even gender. Upon seeing a friend after a long absence, upper-class women and men are likely to be more reserved in expressing their delight than are lower-class women and men. *Relationships* also make a big difference. We express our feelings more openly if we are with close friends, more guardedly if we are at a staff meeting with the corporate CEO. The *setting*, then, is also important, with each setting having its own "rules" about emotions. As you know, the emotions we can express at a rock concert differ considerably from those we can express in a classroom. A good part of our socialization during childhood centers on learning our culture's *feeling rules*.

What We Feel.

Joan, a U.S. woman who had been married for seven years, had no children. When she finally gave birth and the doctor handed her a healthy girl, she was almost overcome with happiness. Tafadzwa, in Zimbabwe, had been married for seven years and had no children. When the doctor handed her a healthy girl, she was almost overcome with sadness.

The effects of socialization on our emotions go much deeper than guiding how, where, and when we express our feelings. From this example, you can see that socialization also affects *what* we feel (Clark 1997; Shields 2002). To understand why the woman in Zimbabwe felt sadness, you need to know that in her culture to not give birth to a male child is serious. It lowers her social status and is a good reason for her husband to divorce her (Horwitz and Wakefield 2007:43).

People in one culture may even learn to experience feelings that are unknown in another culture. For example, the Ifaluk, who live on the western Caroline Islands of Micronesia, use the word *fago* to refer to the feelings they have when they see someone suffer. This comes close to what we call sympathy or compassion. But the Ifaluk also use this term to refer to what they feel when they are with someone who has high status, someone they highly respect or admire (Kagan 1984). To us, these are two distinct emotions, and they require separate words to express them.

Research Needed.

Although Ekman identified six emotions as universal in feeling and facial expression, I suspect that there are more. It is likely that all people around the world have similar feelings and facial expressions when they experience helplessness, despair, confusion, and shock. We need cross-cultural research to find out whether these are universal emotions. We also need research into how culture guides us in feeling and expressing emotions.

Society Within Us: The Self and Emotions as Social Control

Much of our socialization is intended to turn us into conforming members of society. Socialization into the self and emotions is essential to this process, for both the self and our emotions mold our behavior. Although we like to think that we are "free," consider for a moment just some of the factors that influence how you act: the expectations of friends and parents, of neighbors and teachers; classroom norms and college rules; city, state, and federal laws. For example, if in a moment of intense frustration, or out of a devilish desire to shock people, you wanted to tear off your clothes and run naked down the street, what would stop you?

The answer is your socialization—*society within you.* Your experiences in society have resulted in a self that thinks along certain lines and feels particular emotions. This helps to keep you in line. Thoughts such as "Would I get kicked out of school?" and "What would my friends (parents) think if they found out?" represent an awareness of the self in relationship to others. So does the desire to avoid feelings of shame and embarrassment. Your *social mirror,* then—the result of your being socialized into a self and emotions—sets up effective controls over your behavior. In fact, socialization into self and emotions is so effective that some people feel embarrassed just thinking about running naked in public!

In Sum: Socialization is essential for our development as human beings. From interaction with others, we learn how to think, reason, and feel. The net result is the shaping of our behavior—including our thinking and emotions—according to cultural standards. This is what sociologists mean when they refer to "*society within us.*"

Socialization into Gender

Learning the Gender Map

For a child, society is uncharted territory. A major signpost on society's map is **gender,** the attitudes and behaviors that are expected of us because we are a male or a female. In learning the gender map (called **gender socialization**)**,** we are nudged into different lanes in life—into contrasting attitudes and behaviors. We take direction so well that, as adults, most of us act, think, and even feel according to this gender map, our culture's guidelines to what is appropriate for our sex.

Let's briefly consider some of the "gender messages" that we get from our family and the mass media.

Gender Messages in the Family

Our parents are the first significant others who show us how to follow the gender map. Sometimes they do so consciously, perhaps by bringing into play pink and blue, colors that have no meaning in themselves but that are now associated with gender. Our parents' own gender orientations have become embedded so firmly that they do most of this teaching without being aware of what they are doing.

This is illustrated in a classic study by psychologists Susan Goldberg and Michael Lewis (1969), whose results have been confirmed by other researchers (Fagot et al. 1985; Connors 1996; Clearfield and Nelson 2006).

> Goldberg and Lewis asked mothers to bring their 6-month-old infants into their laboratory, supposedly to observe the infants' development. Covertly, however, they also observed the mothers. They found that the mothers kept their daughters closer to them. They also touched their daughters more and spoke to them more frequently than they did to their sons.
>
> By the time the children were 13 months old, the girls stayed closer to their mothers during play, and they returned to their mothers sooner and more often than the boys did. When Goldberg and Lewis set up a barrier to separate the children from their mothers, who were holding toys, the girls were more likely to cry and motion for help; the boys, to try to climb over the barrier.

Goldberg and Lewis concluded that mothers subconsciously reward daughters for being passive and dependent, and sons for being active and independent.

gender the behaviors and attitudes that a society considers proper for its males and females; masculinity or femininity

gender socialization the ways in which society sets children on different paths in life *because* they are male or female

The *gender roles* that we learn during childhood become part of our basic orientations to life. Although we refine these roles as we grow older, they remain built around the framework established during childhood.

Frank and Ernest

SOON WE'LL GIVE UP DOLLS AND HOPSCOTCH---BUT THEY'LL BE INTO FOOTBALL FOREVER.

THAVES 12-10

www.cartoonistgroup.com

Our gender lessons continue throughout childhood. On the basis of our sex, we are given different kinds of toys. Boys are more likely to get guns and "action figures" that destroy enemies. Girls are more likely to get dolls and jewelry. Some parents try to choose "gender neutral" toys, but kids know what is popular, and they feel left out if they don't have what the other kids have. The significance of toys in gender socialization can be summarized this way: Almost all parents would be upset if someone gave their son Barbie dolls.

Parents also subtly encourage boys to participate in more rough-and-tumble play. They expect their sons to get dirtier and to be more defiant, their daughters to be daintier and more compliant (Gilman 1911/1971; Henslin 2007). In large part, they get what they expect. Such experiences in socialization lie at the heart of the sociological explanation of male–female differences. For a fascinating account of how socialization trumps biology, read the Cultural Diversity box on the next page.

Gender Messages from Peers

peer group a group of individuals of roughly the same age who are linked by common interests

Sociologists stress how this sorting process that begins in the family is reinforced as the child is exposed to other aspects of society. Of those other influences, one of the most powerful is the **peer group,** individuals of roughly the same age who are linked by common interests. Examples of peer groups are friends, classmates, and "the kids in the neighborhood."

The family is one of the primary ways that we learn gender. Shown here is a woman in South Africa. What gender messages do you think her daughter is learning?

Gavriel Jecan/www.DanitaDelimont.com

Cultural Diversity around the World

Women Becoming Men: The Sworn Virgins

"I will become a man," said Pashe. "I will do it."

The decision was final. Taking a pair of scissors, she soon had her long, black curls lying at her feet. She took off her dress—never to wear one again in her life—and put on her father's baggy trousers. She armed herself with her father's rifle. She would need it.

Going before the village elders, she swore to never marry, to never have children, and to never have sex.

Pashe had become a sworn virgin—and a man.

There was no turning back. The penalty for violating the oath was death.

In Albania, where Pashe Keqi lives, and in parts of Bosnia and Serbia, it is the custom for some women to become men. They are neither transsexuals nor lesbians. Nor do they have a sex-change operation, something unknown in those parts.

The custom is a practical matter, a way to support the family. In these traditional societies, women must stay home and take care of the children and household. They can go hardly anywhere except to the market and mosque. Women depend on men for survival.

And when there is no man? That is the problem.

Pashe's father was killed in a blood feud. In these traditional groups, when the family patriarch (male head) dies and there are no male heirs, how are the women to survive? In the fifteenth century, people in this area hit upon a solution: One of the women takes an oath of lifelong virginity and takes over the man's role. She then becomes a social he, wears male clothing, carries a gun, owns property, and moves freely throughout the society.

She drinks in the tavern with the men. She sits with the men at weddings. She prays with the men at the mosque.

When a man wants to marry a girl of the family, she is the one who approves or disapproves of the suitor.

In short, the woman really becomes a man. Actually, a social man, sociologists would add. Her biology does not change, but her gender does. Pashe had become the man of the house, a status she occupied her entire life.

Taking this position at the age of 11—she is in her 70s now—also made Pashe responsible for avenging her father's murder. But when his killer was released from prison, her 15-year-old nephew (she is his uncle) rushed in and did the deed instead.

Sworn virgins walk like men, they talk like men, they hunt with the men, and they take up manly occupations. They become shepherds, security guards, truck drivers, and political leaders. Those around them know that they are women, but in all ways they treat them as men. When they talk to women, the women recoil in shyness.

The sworn virgins of Albania are a fascinating cultural contradiction: In the midst of a highly traditional group, one built around male superiority that severely limits women, we find both the belief and practice that a biological woman can do the work of a man and function in all of a man's social roles. The sole exception is marriage.

Under a communist dictator until 1985, with travel restricted by law and custom, mountainous northern Albania had been cut off from the rest of the world. Now there is a democratic government, and the region is connected to the rest of the world by better roads, telephones, and even television. As modern life trickles into these villages, few women want to become men. "Why should we?" they ask. "Now we have freedom. We can go to the city and work and support our families."

Stuart Freedman/Corbis

Pashke Ndocaj, shown here in Thethi, Albania, became a sworn virgin after the death of her father and brothers.

For Your Consideration

How do the sworn virgins of Albania help to explain what gender is? Apply functionalism: How was the custom and practice of sworn virgins functional for this society? Apply symbolic interactionism: How do symbols underlie and maintain women becoming men in this society? Apply conflict theory: How do power relations between men and women underlie this practice?

Based on Zumbrun 2007; Bilefsky 2008; Smith 2008.

As you grew up, you saw girls and boys teach one another what it means to be a female or a male. You might not have recognized what was happening, however, so let's eavesdrop on a conversation between two eighth-grade girls studied by sociologist Donna Eder (2007).

CINDY: The only thing that makes her look anything is all the makeup . . .
PENNY: She had a picture, and she's standing like this. (Poses with one hand on her hip and one by her head)
CINDY: Her face is probably this skinny, but it looks that big 'cause of all the makeup she has on it.
PENNY: She's ugly, ugly, ugly.

Do you see how these girls were giving gender lessons? They were reinforcing images of appearance and behavior that they thought were appropriate for females. Boys, too, reinforce cultural expectations of gender. Sociologist Melissa Milkie (1994), who studied junior high school boys, found that much of their talk centered on movies and TV programs. Of the many images they saw, the boys would single out those associated with sex and violence. They would amuse one another by repeating lines, acting out parts, and joking and laughing at what they had seen.

If you know boys in their early teens, you've probably seen a lot of behavior like this. You may have been amused, or even have shaken your head in disapproval. But did you peer beneath the surface? Milkie did. What is really going on? The boys, she concluded, were using media images to develop their identity as males. They had gotten the message: "Real" males are obsessed with sex and violence. Not to joke and laugh about murder and promiscuous sex would have marked a boy as a "weenie," a label to be avoided at all costs.

Gender Messages in the Mass Media

As you can see with the boys Milkie studied, a major guide to the gender map is the **mass media,** forms of communication that are directed to large audiences. Let's look further at how media images reinforce **gender roles,** the behaviors and attitudes considered appropriate for our sex.

Advertising. The advertising assault of stereotypical images begins early. The average U.S. child watches about 25,000 commercials a year (Gantz et al. 2007). In these commercials, girls are more likely to be shown as cooperative and boys as aggressive (Larson 2001). Girls are also more likely to be portrayed as giggly and less capable at tasks (Browne 1998).

The gender messages continue in advertising directed at adults. I'm sure you have you noticed the many ads that portray men as dominant and rugged and women as sexy and submissive. *Your mind and internal images* are the target of this assault of stereotypical, culturally molded images—from cowboys who roam the wide-open spaces to scantily clad women, whose physical assets couldn't possibly be real. Although the purpose is to sell products—from booze and bras to cigarettes and cell phones—the ads also give lessons in gender. Through images both overt and exaggerated and subtle and below our awareness, they help teach what is expected of us as men and women in our culture.

Television. Television reinforces stereotypes of the sexes. On prime-time television, male characters outnumber female characters. Male characters are also more likely to be portrayed in higher-status positions (Glascock 2001). Sports news also maintains traditional stereotypes. Sociologists who studied the content of televised sports news in Los Angeles found that female athletes receive less coverage and are sometimes trivialized (Messner et al. 2003). Male newscasters often focus on humorous events in women's sports or turn the female athlete into a sexual object. Newscasters even manage to emphasize breasts and bras and to engage in locker-room humor.

Stereotype-breaking characters, in contrast, are a sign of changing times. In comedies, women are more verbally aggressive than men (Glascock 2001). The powers of the teenager *Buffy, The Vampire Slayer,* were remarkable. On *Alias,* Sydney Bristow exhibited extraordinary strength. In cartoons, Kim Possible divides her time between cheerleading practice and saving the world from evil, while, also with tongue in cheek, the Powerpuff

mass media forms of communication, such as radio, newspapers, television, and blogs that are directed to mass audiences

gender role the behaviors and attitudes expected of people because they are female or male

Girls are touted as "the most elite kindergarten crime-fighting force ever assembled." This new gender portrayal continues in a variety of programs, such as *Totally Spies*.

The gender messages on these programs are mixed. Girls are powerful, but they have to be skinny and gorgeous and wear the latest fashions. Such messages present a dilemma for girls, for this model continuously thrust before them is almost impossible to replicate in real life.

Video Games.   The movement, color, virtual dangers, unexpected dilemmas, and ability to control the action make video games highly appealing. High school and college students, especially men, find them a seductive way of escaping from the demands of life. The first members of the "Nintendo Generation," now in their thirties, are still playing video games—with babies on their laps.

Sociologists have begun to study how video games portray the sexes, but we still know little about their influence on the players' ideas of gender (Dietz 2000; Berger 2002). Women, often portrayed with exaggerated breasts and buttocks, are now more likely to be main characters than they were just a few years ago (Jansz and Martis 2007). Because these games are on the cutting edge of society, they sometimes also reflect cutting-edge changes in sex roles, the topic of the Mass Media in Social Life box on the next page.

Anime.   *Anime* is a Japanese cartoon form. Because anime crosses boundaries of video games, television, movies, and books (comic), we shall consider it as a separate category. As shown below, one of the most recognizable features of anime is the big-eyed little girls and the fighting little boys. Japanese parents are concerned about anime's antisocial heroes and its depiction of violence, but to keep peace they reluctantly buy anime for their children (Khattak 2007). In the United States, violence is often part of the mass media aimed at children—so with its cute characters, anime is unlikely to bother parents. Anime's depiction of active, dominant little boys and submissive little girls leads to the question, of course, of what gender lessons it is giving children.

In Sum: "Male" and "female" are such powerful symbols that learning them forces us to interpret the world in terms of gender. As children learn their society's symbols of gender, they learn that different behaviors and attitudes are expected of boys and girls. First transmitted by the family, these gender messages are reinforced by other social institutions. As they become integrated into our views of the world, gender messages form a picture of "how" males and females "are." Because gender serves as a primary basis for **social inequality**—giving privileges and obligations to one group of people while denying them to another—gender images are especially important in our socialization.

> **social inequality** a social condition in which privileges and obligations are given to some but denied to others

Anime is increasing in popularity—cartoons and comics aimed at children and pornography targeted to adults. Its gender messages, especially those directed to children, are yet to be explored.

Courtesy Everett Collection

173

MASS MEDIA In SOCIAL LIFE

Lara Croft, Tomb Raider: Changing Images of Women in the Mass Media

With digital advances, video games have crossed the line from what are usually thought of as games to something that more closely resembles interactive movies. Costing an average of $10 million to produce and another $10 million to market, some video games have intricate subplots and use celebrity voices for the characters (Nussenbaum 2004). Some introduce new songs by major rock groups (Levine 2008). Sociologically, what is significant is the *content* of video games. They expose gamers not only to action but also to ideas and images. Just as in other forms of the mass media, the gender images of video games communicate powerful messages.

Amidst the traditional portrayals of women as passive and subordinate, a new image has broken through. As exaggerated as it is, this new image reflects a fundamental change in gender relations. Lara Croft, an adventure-seeking archeologist and star of *Tomb Raider* and its many sequels, is the essence of the new gender image. Lara is smart, strong, and able to utterly vanquish foes. With both guns blazing, she is the cowboy of the twenty-first century, the term *cowboy* being purposefully chosen, as Lara breaks stereotypical gender roles and dominates what previously was the domain of men. She was the first female protagonist in a field of muscle-rippling, gun-toting macho caricatures (Taylor 1999).

Yet the old remains powerfully encapsulated in the new. As the photos on this page make evident, Lara is a fantasy girl for young men of the digital generation. No matter her foe, no matter her predicament, Lara oozes sex. Her form-fitting outfits, which flatter her voluptuous figure, reflect the mental images of the men who fashioned this digital character.

Vince Maher/WENN/Newscom

SHNS photo courtesy Eido via Newscom

The mass media not only reflect gender stereotypes but they also play a role in changing them. Sometimes they do both simultaneously. The images of Lara Croft not only reflect women's changing role in society, but also, by exaggerating the change, they mold new stereotypes.

Lara has caught young men's fancy to such an extent that they have bombarded corporate headquarters with questions about her personal life. Lara is the star of two movies and a comic book. There is also a Lara Croft action figure.

For Your Consideration

A sociologist who reviewed this text said, "It seems that for women to be defined as equal, we have to become symbolic males—warriors with breasts." Why is gender change mostly one-way—females adopting traditional male characteristics? To see why men get to keep their gender roles, these two questions should help: Who is moving into the traditional territory of the other? Do people prefer to imitate power or weakness?

Finally, consider just how far stereotypes have actually been left behind. One reward for beating time trials is to be able to see Lara wearing a bikini.

Agents of Socialization

agents of socialization individuals or groups that affect our self-concept, attitudes, behaviors, or other orientations toward life

Individuals and groups that influence our orientations to life—our self-concept, emotions, attitudes, and behavior—are called **agents of socialization.** We have already considered how three of these agents—the family, our peers, and the mass media—influence our ideas of gender. Now we'll look more closely at how agents of socialization prepare us in other ways to take our place in society. We shall first consider the family, then the neighborhood, religion, day care, school and peers, and the workplace.

This photo captures an extreme form of family socialization. The father seems to be more emotionally involved in the goal—and in more pain—than his daughter, as he pushes her toward the finish line in the Teen Tours of America Kid's Triathlon.

Lannis Waters/The Palm Beach Post

The Family

The first group to have a major impact on us is our family. Our experiences in the family are so intense that their influence is lifelong. These experiences establish our initial motivations, values, and beliefs. In the family, we receive our basic sense of self, ideas about who we are and what we deserve out of life. It is here that we begin to think of ourselves as strong or weak, smart or dumb, good-looking or ugly—or somewhere in between. And as already noted, the lifelong process of defining ourselves as female or male also begins in the family.

The Family and Social Class.   Social class makes a huge difference in how parents socialize their children. Sociologist Melvin Kohn (1959, 1963, 1976, 1977; Kohn et al. 1986) found that working-class parents are mainly concerned that their children stay out of trouble. For discipline, they tend to use physical punishment. Middle-class parents, in contrast, focus more on developing their children's curiosity, self-expression, and self-control. They are more likely to reason with their children than to use physical punishment.

But why such differences? As a sociologist, Kohn knew that the answer was life experiences of some sort. He found that answer in the world of work. Blue-collar workers are usually told exactly what to do. Since they expect their children's lives to be like theirs, they stress obedience. Middle-class parents, in contrast, have work that requires more initiative, and they socialize their children into the qualities they find valuable.

Kohn wanted to know why some working-class parents act more like middle-class parents, and vice versa. As he probed further, he found the key—the parents' type of job. Some middle-class workers, such as office workers, are supervised closely. It turned out that they follow the working-class pattern and emphasize conformity. And some blue-collar workers, such as those who do home repairs, have a good deal of freedom. These workers follow the middle-class model in rearing their children (Pearlin and Kohn 1966; Kohn and Schooler 1969).

Social class also makes a difference in the ideas that parents have of how children develop, ideas that have fascinating consequences for children's play (Lareau 2002).

Working-class parents think of children as similar to wild flowers—they develop naturally. Since the child's development will take care of itself, they see parenting primarily as providing food, shelter, and comfort. They set limits on their children's play ("Don't go near the railroad tracks") and let them play as they wish. Middle-class parents, in contrast, think of children as more like tender house plants—to develop correctly, they need a lot of guidance. With this orientation, they try to structure their children's play to help them develop knowledge and social skills. They may want them to play baseball, for example, not for the enjoyment of the sport, but to help them learn how to be team players.

The Neighborhood

As all parents know, some neighborhoods are better than others for their children. Parents try to move to those neighborhoods—if they can afford them. Their commonsense evaluations are borne out by sociological research. Children from poor neighborhoods are more likely to get in trouble with the law, to become pregnant, to drop out of school, and even to have worse mental health in later life (Brooks-Gunn et al. 1997; Sampson et al. 2001; Wheaton and Clarke 2003; Yonas et al. 2006).

Sociologists have also found that the residents of more affluent neighborhoods keep a closer eye on the children than do the residents of poor neighborhoods (Sampson et al. 1999). The basic reason is that the more affluent neighborhoods have fewer families in transition, so the adults are more likely to know the local children and their parents. This better equips them to help keep the children safe and out of trouble.

Religion

How important is religion in your life? You could be among the two-thirds of Americans who belong to a local congregation, but what if you are among the other third (Gallup Poll 2007b)? Why would religion be significant for you? To see the influence of religion, we can't look only at people who are religious. Even in the extreme—people who wouldn't be caught dead near a church, synagogue, or mosque—religion plays a powerful role. Perhaps this is the most significant aspect of religion: Religious ideas so pervade U.S. society that they provide the foundation of morality for both the religious and the nonreligious.

For many Americans, the influence of religion is more direct. This is especially true for the two of every five Americans who report that during a typical week they attend a religious service (Gallup Poll 2007). Through their participation in congregational life, they learn doctrine, values, and morality, but the effects on their lives are not limited to these obvious factors. For example, people who participate in religious services learn not only beliefs about the hereafter but also ideas about what kinds of clothing, speech, and manners are appropriate for formal occasions. Life in congregations also provides a sense of identity for its participants, giving them a feeling of belonging. It also helps to integrate immigrants into their new society, offers an avenue of social mobility for the poor, provides social contacts for jobs, and in the case of African American churches, has been a powerful influence in social change.

Day Care

It is rare for social science research to make national news, but occasionally it does. This is what happened when researchers published their findings on 1,200 kindergarten children they had studied since they were a month old. They observed the children multiple times both at home and at day care. They also videotaped and made detailed notes on the children's interaction with their mothers (National Institute of Child Health and Human Development 1999; Guensburg 2001). What caught the media's attention? Children who spend more time in day care have weaker bonds with their mothers and are less affectionate to them. They are also less cooperative with others and more likely to fight and to be "mean." By the time they get to kindergarten, they are more likely to talk back to teachers and to disrupt the classroom. This holds true regardless of the quality of the day care, the family's social class, or whether the child is a girl or a boy (Belsky 2006). On the positive side, the children also scored higher on language tests.

Are we producing a generation of "smart but mean" children? This is not an unreasonable question, since the study was designed well and an even larger study of children in England has come up with similar findings (Belsky 2006). Some point out that the differences between children who spend a lot of time in day care and those who spend less time are slight. Others stress that with 5 million children in day care (*Statistical Abstract* 2011:Table 576), slight differences can be significant for society. The researchers are following these children as they continue in school. The most recent report on the children, when they were in the 6th grade, indicates that these patterns are continuing (Belsky et al. 2007).

The School

Part of the **manifest function,** or *intended* purpose, of formal education is to teach knowledge and skills, such as reading, writing, and arithmetic. The teaching of such skills is certainly part of socialization, but so are the schools' **latent functions,** their *unintended* consequences that help the social system. Let's look at this less visible aspect of education.

At home, children learn attitudes and values that match their family's situation in life. At school, they learn a broader perspective that helps prepare them to take a role in the world beyond the family. At home, a child may have been the almost exclusive focus of doting parents, but in school, the child learns *universality*—that the same rules apply to everyone, regardless of who their parents are or how special they may be at home. The Cultural Diversity box on the next page explores how these new values and ways of looking at the world sometimes even replace those the child learns at home.

Sociologists have also identified a *hidden curriculum* in our schools. This term refers to values that, although not explicitly taught, are part of a school's "cultural message." For example, the stories and examples that are used to teach math and English may bring with them lessons in patriotism, democracy, justice, and honesty. There is also a *corridor curriculum,* what students teach one another outside the classroom. Unfortunately, the corridor curriculum seems to emphasize racism, sexism, illicit ways to make money, and coolness (Hemmings 1999). You can determine for yourself which of these is functional and which is dysfunctional.

Conflict theorists point out that social class separates children into different educational worlds. Children born to wealthy parents go to private schools, where they learn skills and values that match their higher position. Children born to middle- and lower-class parents go to public schools, which further refine the separate worlds of social class. Middle-class children learn that good jobs, even the professions, beckon, while children from blue-collar families learn that not many of "their kind" will become professionals or leaders. This is one of the many reasons that children from blue-collar families are less likely to take college prep courses or to go to college. In short, schools around the world reflect and reinforce their nation's social class, economic, and political systems.

Peer Groups

As a child's experiences with agents of socialization broaden, the influence of the family decreases. Entry into school marks only one of many steps in this transfer of allegiance.

Schools are one of the primary *agents of socialization.* One of their chief functions is to sort young people into the adult roles thought appropriate for them, and to teach them the attitudes and skills that match these roles. What sorts of attitudes, motivations, goals, and adult roles do you think this child is learning?

AsiaPix/Getty Images Royalty Free

manifest functions the intended beneficial consequences of people's actions

latent functions unintended beneficial consequences of people's actions

177

Cultural Diversity in the United States

Immigrants and Their Children: Caught Between Two Worlds

It is a struggle to adapt to a new culture, for its behaviors and ways of thinking may be at odds with the ones already learned. This can lead to inner turmoil. One way to handle the conflict is to cut ties with your first culture. Doing so, however, can create a sense of loss, one that is perhaps recognized only later in life.

Richard Rodriguez, a literature professor and essayist, was born to working-class Mexican immigrants. Wanting their son to be successful in their adopted land, his parents named him Richard instead of Ricardo. While his English–Spanish hybrid name indicates the parents' aspirations for their son, it was also an omen of the conflict that Richard would experience.

Like other children of Mexican immigrants, Richard first spoke Spanish—a rich mother tongue that introduced him to the world. Until the age of 5, when he began school, Richard knew only fifty words in English. He describes what happened when he began school:

Bob Daemmrich/The Image Works

> The change came gradually but early. When I was beginning grade school, I noted to myself the fact that the classroom environment was so different in its styles and assumptions from my own family environment that survival would essentially entail a choice between both worlds. When I became a student, I was literally "remade"; neither I nor my teachers considered anything I had known before as relevant. I had to forget most of what my culture had provided, because to remember it was a disadvantage. The past and its cultural values became detachable, like a piece of clothing grown heavy on a warm day and finally put away.

As happened to millions of immigrants before him, whose parents spoke German, Polish, Italian, and so on, learning English eroded family and class ties and ate away at his ethnic roots. For Rodriguez, language and education were not simply devices that eased the transition to the dominant culture. They also slashed at the roots that had given him life.

To face conflicting cultures is to confront a fork in the road. Some turn one way and withdraw from the new culture—a clue that helps to explain why so many Latinos drop out of U.S. schools. Others go in the opposite direction. Cutting ties with their family and cultural roots, they wholeheartedly adopt the new culture.

Rodriguez took the second road. He excelled in his new language—so much, in fact, that he graduated from Stanford University and then became a graduate student in English at the University of California at Berkeley. He was even awarded a Fulbright fellowship to study English Renaissance literature at the University of London.

But the past shadowed Rodriguez. Prospective employers were impressed with his knowledge of Renaissance literature. At job interviews, however, they would skip over the Renaissance training and ask him if he would teach the Mexican novel and be an adviser to Latino students. Rodriguez was also haunted by the image of his grandmother, the warmth of the culture he had left behind, and the language and thought to which he had become a stranger.

Richard Rodriguez represents millions of immigrants—not just those of Latino origin but those from other cultures, too—who want to be a part of life in the United States without betraying their past. They fear that to integrate into U.S. culture is to lose their roots. They are caught between two cultures, each beckoning, each offering rich rewards.

For Your Consideration

I saw this conflict firsthand with my father, who did not learn English until after the seventh grade (his last in school). German was left behind, but broken English and awkward expressions remained for a lifetime. Then, too, there were the lingering emotional connections to old ways, as well as the suspicions, haughtiness, and slights of more assimilated Americans. He longed for security by grasping the past, but at the same time, he wanted to succeed in the everyday reality of the new culture. Have you seen similar conflicts?

Sources: Based on Richard Rodriguez 1975, 1982, 1990, 1991, 1995.

Gradeschool boys and girls often separate themselves by gender, as in this playground in Schenectady, New York. The socialization that occurs during self-segregation by gender is a topic of study by sociologists.

One of the most significant aspects of education is that it exposes children to peer groups that help them resist the efforts of parents and schools to socialize them.

When sociologists Patricia and Peter Adler (1998) observed children at two elementary schools in Colorado, they saw how children separate themselves by sex and develop separate gender worlds. The norms that made boys popular were athletic ability, coolness, and toughness. For girls, popularity was based on family background, physical appearance (clothing and use of makeup), and the ability to attract popular boys. In this children's subculture, academic achievement pulled in opposite directions: For boys, high grades lowered their popularity, but for girls, good grades increased their standing among peers.

You know from your own experience how compelling peer groups are. It is almost impossible to go against a peer group, whose cardinal rule seems to be "conformity or rejection." Anyone who doesn't do what the others want becomes an "outsider," a "nonmember," an "outcast." For preteens and teens just learning their way around in the world, it is not surprising that the peer group rules.

As a result, the standards of our peer groups tend to dominate our lives. If your peers, for example, listen to rap, Nortec, death metal, rock and roll, country, or gospel, it is almost inevitable that you also prefer that kind of music. In high school, if your friends take math courses, you probably do, too (Crosnoe et al. 2008). It is the same for clothing styles and dating standards. Peer influences also extend to behaviors that violate social norms. If your peers are college-bound and upwardly striving, that is most likely what you will be; but if they use drugs, cheat, and steal, you are likely to do so, too.

The Workplace

Another agent of socialization that comes into play somewhat later in life is the workplace. Those initial jobs that we take in high school and college are much more than just a way to earn a few dollars. From the people we rub shoulders with at work, we learn not only a set of skills but also perspectives on the world.

Most of us eventually become committed to some particular line of work, often after trying out many jobs. This may involve **anticipatory socialization,** learning to play a role before entering it. Anticipatory socialization is a sort of mental rehearsal for some future activity. We may talk to people who work in a particular career, read novels about that type of work, or take a summer internship in that field. Such activities allow us to

anticipatory socialization the process of learning in advance an anticipated future role or status

179

gradually identify with the role, to become aware of what would be expected of us. Sometimes this helps people avoid committing themselves to an unrewarding career, as with some of my students who tried student teaching, found that they couldn't stand it, and then moved on to other fields more to their liking.

An intriguing aspect of work as a socializing agent is that the more you participate in a line of work, the more the work becomes a part of your self-concept. Eventually you come to think of yourself so much in terms of the job that if someone asks you to describe yourself, you are likely to include the job in your self-description. You might say, "I'm a teacher," "I'm a nurse," or "I'm a sociologist."

Resocialization

What does a woman who has just become a nun have in common with a man who has just divorced? The answer is that they both are undergoing **resocialization;** that is, they are learning new norms, values, attitudes, and behaviors to match their new situation in life. In its most common form, resocialization occurs each time we learn something contrary to our previous experiences. A new boss who insists on a different way of doing things is resocializing you. Most resocialization is mild—only a slight modification of things we have already learned.

Resocialization can also be intense. People who join Alcoholics Anonymous (AA), for example, are surrounded by reformed drinkers who affirm the destructive effects of excessive drinking. Some students experience an intense period of resocialization when they leave high school and start college—especially during those initially scary days before they find companions, start to fit in, and feel comfortable. The experiences of people who join a cult or begin psychotherapy are even more profound, for they learn views that conflict with their earlier socialization. If these ideas "take," not only does the individual's behavior change but he or she also learns a fundamentally different way of looking at life.

Total Institutions

Relatively few of us experience the powerful agent of socialization that sociologist Erving Goffman (1961) called the **total institution.** He coined this term to refer to a place in which people are cut off from the rest of society and where they come under almost total control of the officials who are in charge. Boot camp, prisons, concentration camps, convents, some religious cults, and some military schools, such as West Point, are total institutions.

A person entering a total institution is greeted with a **degradation ceremony** (Garfinkel 1956), an attempt to remake the self by stripping away the individual's current identity and stamping a new one in its place. This unwelcome greeting may involve fingerprinting, photographing, or shaving the head. Newcomers may be ordered to strip, undergo an examination (often in a humiliating, semipublic setting), and then put on a uniform that designates their new status. Officials also take away the individual's *personal identity kit,* items such as jewelry, hairstyles, clothing, and other body decorations used to express individuality.

Total institutions are isolated from the public. The bars, walls, gates, and guards not only keep the inmates in but also keep outsiders out. Staff members supervise the day-to-day lives of the residents. Eating, sleeping, showering, recreation—all are standardized. Inmates learn that their previous statuses—student, worker, spouse, parent—mean nothing. The only thing that counts is their current status.

No one leaves a total institution unscathed, for the experience brands an indelible mark on the individual's self and colors the way he or she sees the world. Boot camp, as described in the Down-to-Earth Sociology box on the next page, is brutal but swift. Prison, in contrast, is brutal and prolonged. Neither recruit nor prisoner, however, has difficulty in knowing that the institution has had profound effects on attitudes and orientations to life.

resocialization the process of learning new norms, values, attitudes, and behaviors

total institution a place that is almost totally controlled by those who run it, in which people are cut off from the rest of society and the society is mostly cut off from them

degradation ceremony a term coined by Harold Garfinkel to refer to a ritual whose goal is to strip away someone's position (social status); in doing so, a new social and self-identity is stamped on the individual

Down-to-Earth Sociology
Boot Camp as a Total Institution

The bus arrives at Parris Island, South Carolina, at 3 A.M. The early hour is no accident. The recruits are groggy, confused. Up to a few hours ago, the young men were ordinary civilians. Now, as a sergeant sneeringly calls them "maggots," their heads are buzzed (25 seconds per recruit), and they are quickly thrust into the harsh world of Marine boot camp.

Buzzing the boys' hair is just the first step in stripping away their identity so that the Marines can stamp a new one in its place. The uniform serves the same purpose. There is a ban on using the first person "I." Even a simple request must be made in precise Marine style or it will not be acknowledged. ("Sir, Recruit Jones requests permission to make a head call, Sir.")

Every intense moment of the next eleven weeks reminds the recruits, men and women, that they are joining a subculture of self-discipline. Here pleasure is suspect and sacrifice is good. As they learn the Marine way of talking, walking, and thinking, they are denied the diversions they once took for granted: television, cigarettes, cars, candy, soft drinks, video games, music, alcohol, drugs, and sex.

Lessons are taught with fierce intensity. When Sgt. Carey checks brass belt buckles, Recruit Robert Shelton nervously blurts, "I don't have one." Sgt. Carey's face grows red as his neck cords bulge. "I?" he says, his face just inches from the recruit. With spittle flying from his mouth, he screams, " 'I' is gone!"

"Nobody's an individual" is the lesson that is driven home again and again. "You are a team, a Marine. Not a civilian. Not black or white, not Hispanic or Indian or some hyphenated American—but a Marine. You will live like a Marine, fight like a Marine, and, if necessary, die like a Marine."

Each day begins before dawn with close-order formations. The rest of the day is filled with training in hand-to-hand combat, marching, running, calisthenics, Marine history, and—always—following orders.

"An M-16 can blow someone's head off at 500 meters," Sgt. Norman says. "That's beautiful, isn't it?"

A recruit with drill sergeants

Norm Rowan/The Image Works

"Yes, sir!" shout the platoon's fifty-nine voices.

"Pick your nose!" Simultaneously fifty-nine index fingers shoot into nostrils.

The pressure to conform is intense. Those who are sent packing for insubordination or suicidal tendencies are mocked in cadence during drills. ("Hope you like the sights you see/Parris Island casualty.") As lights go out at 9 P.M., the exhausted recruits perform the day's last task: The entire platoon, in unison, chants the virtues of the Marines.

Recruits are constantly scrutinized. Subpar performance is not accepted, whether it be a dirty rifle or a loose thread on a uniform. The underperformer is shouted at, derided, humiliated. The group suffers for the individual. If one recruit is slow, the entire platoon is punished.

The system works.

One of the new Marines (until graduation, they are recruits, not Marines) says, "I feel like I've joined a new society or religion."

He has.

For Your Consideration
Of what significance is the recruits' degradation ceremony? Why are recruits not allowed video games, cigarettes, or calls home? Why are the Marines so unfair as to punish an entire platoon for the failure of an individual? Use concepts in this chapter to explain why the system works.

Sources: Based on Garfinkel 1956; Goffman 1961; Ricks 1995; Dyer 2007.

Socialization Through the Life Course

You are at a particular stage in your life now, and college is a good part of it. You know that you have more stages ahead of you as you go through life. These stages, from birth to death, are called the **life course** (Elder 1975; 1999). The sociological significance of the life course is twofold. First, as you pass through a stage, it affects your behavior and orientations. You simply don't think about life in the same way when you are 30, are

life course the stages of our life as we go from birth to death

In contemporary Western societies such as the United States, children are viewed as innocent and in need of protection from adult responsibilities such as work and self-support. Ideas of childhood vary historically and cross-culturally. From paintings, such as this 1559 Italian painting by Sofonisba Anguissola (1532–1625), "The Artist's Family," some historians conclude that Europeans once viewed children as miniature adults who assumed adult roles early in life.

married, and have a baby and a mortgage, as you do when you are 18 or 20, single, and in college. (Actually, you don't even see life the same way as a freshman and as a senior.) Second, your life course differs by social location. Your social class, race–ethnicity, and gender, for example, map out distinctive worlds of experience. This means that the typical life course differs for males and females, the rich and the poor, and so on. To emphasize this major sociological point, in the sketch that follows I will stress the *historical* setting of people's lives. Because of your particular social location, your own life course may differ from this sketch, which is a composite of stages that others have suggested (Levinson 1978; Carr et al. 1995; Quadagno 2007).

Childhood (from birth to about age 12)

Consider how different your childhood would have been if you had grown up in another historical era. Historian Philippe Ariès (1965) noticed that in European paintings from about A.D. 1000 to 1800 children were always dressed in adult clothing. If they were not depicted stiffly posed, as in a family portrait, they were shown doing adult activities.

From this, Ariès drew a conclusion that sparked a debate among historians: He said that during this era in Europe, childhood was not regarded as a special time of life. He said that adults viewed children as miniature adults and put them to work at an early age. At the age of 7, for example, a boy might leave home for good to learn to be a jeweler or a stonecutter. A girl, in contrast, stayed home until she married, but by the age of 7 she assumed her share of the household tasks. Historians do not deny that these were the customs of that time, but some say that Ariès' conclusion is ridiculous. They say that other evidence of that period indicates that childhood was viewed as a special time of life (Orme 2002).

Having children work like adults did not disappear with the Middle Ages. It is still common in the Least Industrialized Nations today, where children work in many occupations—from blacksmiths to waiters. They are most visible as street peddlers, hawking everything from shoelaces to chewing gum and candy.

Child rearing, too, was remarkably different. Three hundred years ago, parents and teachers considered it their moral duty to *terrorize* children to keep them in line. They would lock children in dark closets, frighten them with bedtime stories of death and hellfire, and force them to witness gruesome events. Consider this:

A common moral lesson involved taking children to visit the gibbet [an upraised post on which executed bodies were left hanging], where they were forced to inspect the rotting corpses as an example of what happens to bad children when they grow up. Whole classes were taken out of school to witness hangings, and parents would often whip their children afterwards to make them remember what they had seen. (DeMause 1975)

Industrialization transformed the way we perceive children. When children had the leisure to go to school and postponed taking on adult roles, parents and officials came to think of them as tender and innocent, as needing more care, comfort, and protection. Such attitudes of dependency grew, and today we view children as needing gentle guidance if they are to develop emotionally, intellectually, morally, even physically. We take our

transitional adulthood
a term that refers to a period following high school when young adults have not yet taken on the responsibilities ordinarily associated with adulthood; also called *adultolescence*

view for granted—after all, it is only "common sense." Yet, as you can see, our view is not "natural." It is, instead, rooted in geography, history, and economic development.

In Sum: Childhood is more than biology. Everyone's childhood occurs at some point in history and is embedded in particular social locations, especially social class and gender. *These social factors are as vital as our biology, for they determine what our childhood will be like.* Although a child's *biological* characteristics (such as being small and dependent) are universal, the child's *social* experiences (the kind of life the child lives) are not. Because of this, sociologists say that childhood varies from culture to culture.

Adolescence (ages 13–17)

It might seem strange to you, but adolescence is a *social invention,* not a "natural" age division. In earlier centuries, people simply moved from childhood to young adulthood, with no stopover in between. The Industrial Revolution allowed adolescence to be invented. It brought such an abundance of material surpluses that for the first time in history people in their teens were not needed in the labor force. At the same time, education became more important for achieving success. As these two forces in industrialized societies converged, they created a gap between childhood and adulthood. The term *adolescence* was coined to indicate this new stage in life (Hall 1904), one that has become renowned for inner turmoil.

To mark the passage of children into adulthood, tribal societies hold *initiation rites.* This grounds their self-identity. They know how they fit in the society. In the industrialized world, however, adolescents must "find" themselves, grappling with the dilemma of "I am neither a child nor an adult. Who am I?" As they attempt to carve out an identity that is distinct from both the "younger" world being left behind and the "older" world that is still out of reach, adolescents develop their own subcultures, with distinctive clothing, hairstyles, language, gestures, and music. We usually fail to realize that contemporary society, not biology, created this period of inner turmoil that we call *adolescence.*

Transitional Adulthood (ages 18–29)

If society invented adolescence, can it also invent other periods of life? As Figure 2 illustrates, this is actually happening now. Postindustrial societies are adding another period of extended youth to the life course, which sociologists call **transitional adulthood** (also known as *adultolescence*). After high school, millions of young adults postpone adult responsibilities by going to college. They are mostly freed from the control of their parents, yet they don't have to support themselves. After college, many live at home, so they can live cheaply while they establish themselves in a career—and, of course, continue to "find themselves." During this time, people are "neither psychological adolescents nor sociological adults" (Keniston 1971). At some point during this period of extended youth, young adults ease into adult responsibilities. They take a full-time job, become serious about a career, engage in courtship rituals, get married—and go into debt.

In many societies, manhood is not bestowed upon males simply because they reach a certain age. Manhood, rather, signifies a standing in the community that must be achieved. Shown here is an initiation ceremony in Indonesia, where boys, to lay claim to the status of manhood, must jump over this barrier.

Michael MacIntyre/The Hutchison Library

FIGURE 2 Transitional Adulthood: A New Stage in the Life Course

Who has completed the transition?

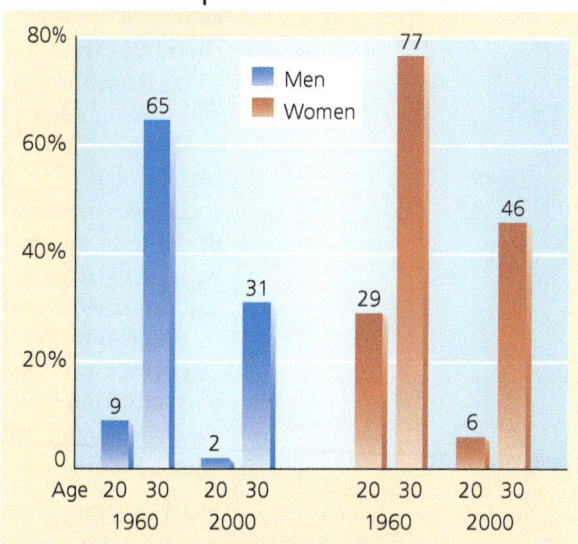

The data show the percentage who have completed the transition to adulthood, as measured by leaving home, finishing school, getting married, having a child, and being financially independent.

Source: Furstenberg, et al. 2004.

The Middle Years (ages 30–65)

The Early Middle Years (ages 30–49).   During their early middle years, most people are more sure of themselves and of their goals in life. As with any point in the life course, however, the self can receive severe jolts. Common in this period are divorce and losing jobs. It may take years for the self to stabilize after such ruptures.

The early middle years pose a special challenge for many U.S. women, who have been given the message, especially by the media, that they can "have it all." They can be super-workers, superwives, and supermoms—all rolled into one. Reality, however, hits them in the face: too little time, too many demands, even too little sleep. Something has to give, and attempts to resolve this dilemma are anything but easy.

The Later Middle Years (ages 50–65).   During the later middle years, health issues and mortality begin to loom large as people feel their bodies change, especially if they watch their parents become frail, fall ill, and die. The consequence is a fundamental reorientation in thinking—*from time since birth to time left to live* (Neugarten 1976). With this changed orientation, people attempt to evaluate the past and come to terms with what lies ahead. They compare what they have accomplished with what they had hoped to achieve. Many people also find themselves caring not only for their own children but also for their aging parents. Because of this double burden, which is often crushing, people in the later middle years sometimes are called the "sandwich generation."

Life during this stage isn't stressful for everyone. Many find late middle age to be the most comfortable period of their lives. They enjoy job security and a standard of living higher than ever before; they have a bigger house (one that may even be paid for), drive newer cars, and take longer and more exotic vacations. The children are grown, the self is firmly planted, and fewer upheavals are likely to occur.

As they anticipate the next stage of life, however, most people do not like what they see.

The Older Years (about age 65 on)

The Transitional Older Years.   In agricultural societies, when most people died early, old age was thought to begin at around age 40. As industrialization brought improved nutrition, medicine, and public health, allowing more people to live longer, the beginning of "old age" gradually stretched out. People who are in good health today are coming to experience their 60s not as old age, but as an extension of their middle years. This change is so recent that a *new stage of life* seems to be evolving, the period between retirement (averaging about 63) and old age—which people are increasingly coming to see as beginning around age 75 ("Schwab Study . . . " 2008). We can call this stage the *transitional older years.*

Researchers are focusing more on this transitional stage of life. They have found that social isolation harms both the body and brain, that people who are more integrated into social networks stay mentally sharper (Ertel et al. 2008). With improved heath, two-thirds of the men and two-fifths of the women between their late 60s and age 75 continue to be sexually active (Lindau et al. 2007). Not only are people in this stage of life having more sex, but they also are enjoying it more (Beckman et al. 2008).

Because we have a self and can reason abstractly, we can contemplate death. In our early years, we regard death as a vague notion, a remote possibility. As people see their parents and friends die and observe their own bodies no longer functioning as before, however, the thought of death becomes less abstract. Increasingly during this stage in the life course, people feel that "time is closing in" on them.

The Later Older Years.   As with the preceding periods of life, except the first one, there is no precise beginning point to this last stage. For some, the 75th birthday may mark entry into this period of life. For others, that marker may be the 80th or even the 85th birthday. For most, this stage is marked by growing frailty and illness; for all who reach this stage, it is ended by death. For some, the physical decline is slow, and a rare few manage to see their 100th birthday mentally alert and in good physical health.

The Sociological Significance of the Life Course

The sociological significance of the life course is that it does not merely represent biology, things that naturally occur to all of us as we add years to our lives. Rather, *social* factors influence our life course. As you just saw, *when* you live makes a huge difference in the course that your life takes. And with today's rapid social change, the difference in historical time does not have to be vast. Being born just ten years earlier or later may mean that you experience war or peace, an expanding economy or a depression—factors that vitally affect what happens to you not just during childhood but throughout your life.

Your *social location,* such as social class, gender, and race–ethnicity, is also highly significant. Your experience of society's events will be similar to that of people who share your social location, but different from that of people who do not. If you are poor, for example, you likely will feel older sooner than most wealthy people for whom life is less demanding. Individual factors—such as your health or marrying early or entering college late—may throw your life course "out of sequence."

For all these reasons, this sketch of the life course may not adequately reflect your own past, present, and future. As sociologist C. Wright Mills (1959) would say, because employers are beating a path to your door, or failing to do so, you are more inclined to marry, to buy a house, and to start a family—or to postpone these life course events. In short, changing times change lives, steering the life course into different directions.

This January 1937 photo from Sneedville, Tennessee, shows Eunice Johns, age 9, and her husband, Charlie Johns, age 22. The groom gave his wife a doll as a wedding gift. The new husband and wife planned to build a cabin, and, as Charlie Johns phrased it, "go to housekeepin'." This couple illustrates the cultural relativity of life stages, which we sometimes mistake as fixed. It also is interesting from a symbolic interactionist perspective—that of changing definitions.

The marriage lasted. The couple had 7 children, 5 boys and 2 girls. Charlie died in 1997 at age 83, and Eunice in 2006 at age 78. The two were buried in the Johns Family Cemetery.

Are We Prisoners of Socialization?

From our discussion of socialization, you might conclude that sociologists think of people as robots: The socialization goes in, and the behavior comes out. People cannot help what they do, think, or feel, for everything is simply a result of their exposure to socializing agents.

Sociologists do *not* think of people in this way. Although socialization is powerful, and affects all of us profoundly, we have a self. Established in childhood and continually modified by later experience, our self is dynamic. Our self is not a sponge that passively absorbs influences from the environment but, rather, a vigorous, essential part of our being that allows us to act on our environment.

It is precisely because people are not robots that their behavior is so hard to predict. The countless reactions of others merge in each of us. As the self develops, we each internalize or "put together" these innumerable reactions, producing a unique whole called the *individual.* Each of us uses our mind to reason and to make choices in life.

In this way, *each of us is actively involved in the construction of the self.* Although our experiences in the family lay down our fundamental orientations to life, we are not doomed to keep those orientations if we do not like them. We can purposely expose ourselves to other groups and ideas. Those experiences, in turn, will have their own effects on our self. In short, although socialization is powerful, we can change even the self within the limitations of the framework laid down by our social locations. And that self—along with the options available within society—is the key to our behavior.

By the Numbers: *Then and Now*

Percentage of men who complete the transition to adulthood by age 30

1960	NOW
65%	**31**%

Percentage of women who complete the transition to adulthood by age 30

1960	NOW
77%	**46**%

About when does old age begin?

40 PREINDUSTRIAL TIMES	**75** NOW (IN TRANSITION)

SUMMARY *and* REVIEW

Society Makes Us Human

How much of our human characteristics come from "nature" (heredity) and how much from "nurture" (the social environment)?

Observations of isolated, institutionalized, and **feral children** help to answer the nature–nurture question, as do experiments with monkeys that were raised in isolation. Language and intimate social interaction—aspects of "nurture"—are essential to the development of what we consider to be human characteristics.

Socialization into the Self and Mind

How do we acquire a self?

Humans are born with the *capacity* to develop a **self,** but the self must be socially constructed; that is, its contents depend on social interaction. According to Charles Horton Cooley's concept of the **looking-glass self,** our self develops as we internalize others' reactions to us. George Herbert Mead identified the ability to **take the role of the other** as essential to the development of the self. Mead concluded that even the mind is a social product.

How do children develop reasoning skills?

Jean Piaget identified four stages that children go through as they develop the ability to reason: (1) *sensorimotor,* in which understanding is limited to sensory stimuli such as touch and sight; (2) *preoperational,* the ability to use symbols; (3) *concrete operational,* in which reasoning ability is more complex but not yet capable of complex abstractions; and (4) *formal operational,* or abstract thinking.

Learning Personality, Morality, and Emotions

How do sociologists evaluate Freud's psychoanalytic theory of personality development?

Sigmund Freud viewed personality development as the result of our **id** (inborn, self-centered desires) clashing with the demands of society. The **ego** develops to balance the id and the **superego,** the conscience. Sociologists, in contrast, do not examine inborn or subconscious motivations, but, instead, consider how *social* factors—social class, gender, religion, education, and so forth—underlie personality.

How do people develop morality?

Children are born without morality. Lawrence Kohlberg identified four stages children go through as they learn morality: amoral, preconventional, conventional, and postconventional. As they make moral decisions, both men and women use personal relationships and abstract principles.

How does socialization influence emotions?

Socialization influences not only *how we express our emotions* but also *what emotions we feel.* Socialization into emotions is one of the means by which society produces conformity.

Socialization into Gender

How does gender socialization affect our sense of self?

Gender socialization—sorting males and females into different roles—is a primary means of controlling human behavior. Children receive messages about gender even in infancy. A society's ideals of sex-linked behaviors are reinforced by its social institutions.

Agents of Socialization

What are the main agents of socialization?

The **agents of socialization** include the family, neighborhood, religion, day care, school, **peer groups,** the **mass media,** and the workplace. Each has its particular influences in socializing us into becoming full-fledged members of society.

Resocialization

What is resocialization?

Resocialization is the process of learning new norms, values, attitudes, and behavior. Most resocialization is voluntary, but some, as with residents of **total institutions,** is involuntary.

Socialization Through the Life Course

Does socialization end when we enter adulthood?

Socialization occurs throughout the life course. In industrialized societies, the **life course** can be divided into childhood, adolescence, young adulthood, the middle years, and the older years. The West is adding a new stage, **transitional adulthood.** Life course patterns vary by geography, history, gender, race–ethnicity, and social class, as well as by individual experiences such as health and age at marriage.

Are We Prisoners of Socialization?

Although socialization is powerful, we are not merely the sum of our socialization experiences. Just as socialization influences human behavior, so humans act on their environment and influence even their self-concept.

THINKING CRITICALLY

1. What two agents of socialization have influenced you the most? Can you pinpoint their influence on your attitudes, beliefs, values, or other orientations to life?

2. Summarize your views of the "proper" relationships of women and men. What in your socialization has led you to have these views?

3. What is your location in the life course? How does the text's summary of that location match your experiences? Explain the similarities and differences.

ADDITIONAL RESOURCES

What can you find in MySocLab? mysoclab www.mysoclab.com

- Complete Ebook
- Practice Tests and Video and Audio activities
- Mapping and Data Analysis exercises

- Sociology in the News
- Classic Readings in Sociology
- Research and Writing advice

Where Can I Read More on This Topic?

Suggested readings follow this chapter.

SUGGESTED READINGS

Ariès, Philippe. *Centuries of Childhood: A Social History of Family Life.* New York: Vintage Books, 1972. The author analyzes how childhood in Europe during the Middle Ages differs from childhood today.

Greco, Monica, and Paul Stenner, eds. *Emotions: A Social Science Reader.* New York: Routledge, 2008. The authors examine the increasing significance of the study of emotions in the social sciences.

Grusec, Joan E., and Paul D. Hastings, eds. *Handbook of Socialization: Theory and Research.* New York: Guilford Press, 2007. Extensive overview of socialization from earliest childhood into adulthood.

Handel, Gerald, Spencer Cahill, and Frederick Elkin. *Children and Society: The Sociology of Children and Childhood Socialization.* New York: Oxford University Press, 2007. A symbolic interactionist perspective of childhood from birth to adolescence with an emphasis on the development of the self.

Hunt, Stephen J. *The Life Course: A Sociological Introduction.* New York: Palgrave McMillan, 2006. Gives an overview of the life course while considering what is distinct about a sociological approach to this topic.

Lareau, Annette. *Unequal Childhoods: Class, Race, and Family Life.* Berkeley: University of California Press, 2003. The author documents differences in child rearing in poor, working-class, and middle-class U.S. families.

Pugh, Allison J. *Longing and Belonging: Parents, Children, and Consumer Culture.* Berkeley: University of California Press, 2009. Through participant observation and interviewing, the author analyzes why parents, even though they are financially strapped, give in to their children's material wants.

Settersten, Richard A., Jr., and Timothy J. Owens, eds. *New Frontiers in Socialization.* Greenwich, Conn.: JAI Press, 2003. The authors of these articles focus on the adult years in the life course, examining the influence of families, neighborhoods, communities, friendship, education, work, volunteer associations, medical institutions, and the media.

Sociological Studies of Child Development: A Research Annual. Greenwich, Conn.: JAI Press, published annually. Along with theoretical articles, this publication reports on sociological research on the socialization of children.

Turmel, André. *A Historical Sociology of Childhood: Developmental Thinking, Categorization and Graphic Visualization.* New York: Cambridge University Press, 2008. The author examines how the idea of what a "normal" child is has changed over time.

Gerontology

AGING TODAY

Jessie Taylor called for a cab and headed downtown for her last appointment of the day. She works for the state office on aging. She monitors nursing-home standards and teaches staff ways to improve patient care. Jessie is 63 years old. She has a pear-shaped figure, a pixie grin, and a mop of gray hair. As she got out of the cab, the driver got out too. He grabbed her elbow, ushered her across the street, and deposited her on the sidewalk. "You can't be too careful crossing the street these days," he said, then smiled and waved good-bye. Jessie says that when she goes to her local supermarket, the checkout clerk often asks other customers to wait a moment while she checks Jessie's things through. Then, one of the workers helps her to her car with her groceries.

All of this used to surprise Jessie. After all, she works at a job like everyone else, drives her own car when she travels out of town, and serves as a leader in her profession. Yet sometimes people treat her like a frail old woman. People see her kind face, gray hair, and wrinkles and they want to help her. They imagine that she needs help doing simple things because of her age. I asked Jessie whether she ever tells people that she doesn't need their help. She said that sometimes she does, but she doesn't want to discourage these people from helping someone in the future, so often she goes along and grins to herself.

Jessie knows that stereotypes can be useful. They help us get along in a complex world where we know only a fraction of the people we see and meet every day. But stereotypes can lead to problems. Jessie sees **stereotyping** every day in her work. She listens as nursing-home aides call patients "dearie" and "sweetie." She watches as workers use baby talk with their adult patients.

Stereotypes can lead us to misjudge people, to treat them inappropriately, and in the case of older people to assume that they need help.[1] Stereotyping can also lead to **prejudice**, a negative attitude toward a person, and to **discrimination**, unfair treatment based on prejudice rather than merit. **Gerontology**, the systematic study of aging, attempts to counteract stereotyping and prejudice. It presents a more balanced view of later life. This chapter looks at (1) the benefits of studying aging, (2) the social basis of age stereotyping, and (3) changes in society that will lead to new images of later life.

WHY STUDY AGING?

Everyone can benefit from the study of aging. First, gerontology can help you understand current social issues. A society with an increasingly older population, for example, will experience changes in **social institutions**. Consider the following changes that will occur in three institutions: the family, the health care system, and recreation programs.

- More people than ever before will live in what some gerontologists call *beanpole families*. These families have three, four, or more generations alive at the same time. Each generation has relatively few members due to smaller numbers of children being born. Older people in these families will live into late old age. Some of them will need caregiving help from their younger family members. Others will live independently or with some formal help in late old age.
- Older people will get more of their health care services in the community. Programs such as visiting nurse services, Meals on Wheels, and foot clinics at senior centers will help keep seniors in their homes longer.

---

[1]The terms *old, elderly,* and *aged* in this text refer to people 65 and over unless another age is given. This fits the definition of the elderly used by the U.S. Census Bureau, the Social Security Administration, and many pension plans. Be aware, however, that many differences exist among people in this age group. Older people differ by race, gender, and region of the country. Older people also differ by age. Some older people today were 40 years old when other older people were children. The term *old people* and other related terms refer at best to a typical older person, not all older people.

- Older people will take part in more active recreation programs, including fitness programs, adventure travel, and university courses.

These changes will lead to different social service needs, and this will require a shift in economic resources. Should the government give more money to older people? Will this mean less money for other age groups? Will it lead to tensions between the generations? Answers to these questions will shape public policy in the future. The study of aging allows you to understand and respond sensibly to such issues.

The second reason for studying aging is that you might plan to work in a field that serves older people. Students in nursing, social work, or physiotherapy will almost certainly work with older people. Students in recreation studies, architecture, or family studies will also benefit from understanding aging. Even students in business programs need to know about aging. Companies, from banks to restaurants to travel agencies, now see older customers as an important part of their clientele. You will work with older people in almost any field you choose. Knowledge of aging will give you a better understanding of your clients and their needs.

Third, most of us live in families with older members. Your parents and grandparents will soon face many of the issues discussed here. You can help them deal with the issues of later life by studying aging.

Jeanne, a student in one of my classes, used her knowledge of aging to help her grandmother stay involved in family life. She noticed that her grandmother had begun to avoid Sunday family dinners. Jeanne discovered that her mother had told her grandmother not to bother making the potato salad for dinners anymore. Jeanne's mother wanted to make life easier for her grandmother, whose arthritis had gotten worse.

The grandmother felt that she had lost an important role in the family. If she couldn't help cook the family dinner, she decided she wouldn't come at all. Jeanne explained the situation to her mother, and they arranged for Jeanne to work with her grandmother in preparing the potato salad. The grandmother enjoyed teaching Jeanne her recipe, Jeanne got to know her grandmother in a new way, and her grandmother started coming to Sunday dinners again. Greater awareness of aging issues can make you a resource to your community, your family, and yourself.

Most people know something about aging before they study the subject. They know about aging from their personal experiences, from their contact with older people in their families and neighborhoods, and from the media. Still, this gives a limited view of aging, one that sometimes mixes truth with bias and myth. A person who has watched a relative or friend die of Alzheimer's disease, for example, may fear aging. But relatively few people contract this disease. Most older people are healthy into late old age.

Likewise, the media present many negative images of older people. But older people form a diverse group. Some people have problems, while others report high life satisfaction. "Apart from dementia," Zarit says, "... older people have lower rates of mental disorders than other adult age groups and generally report higher emotional well-being. ... This is a finding supported by virtually every epidemiological survey" (2009, pp. 675–676). Zarit concludes that "older people may, in fact, be somewhat better off—happier, less depressed, and even less lonely than the other adult age-groups" (p. 678).

Gerontologists work to replace myths and stereotypes with facts and knowledge. They have conducted many studies that look at current images of aging and attitudes toward old age.

AGEISM

Some years ago Robert Butler (1969) coined the term **ageism** to describe these negative attitudes toward aging. The International Longevity Center (2006, p. 21) defines ageism as "Ideas, attitudes, beliefs, and practices on the part of individuals that are biased against persons or groups based on their older age." Ageism "reflects a deep seated uneasiness on the part of the young and middle-aged—a personal revulsion to and distaste for growing old, disease, disability; and fear of powerlessness, 'uselessness,' and death" (Butler, 1969, p. 243). Palmore (2001) reports that, in one sample of older people, 77% said they had experienced more than one incident of ageism. They most often reported disrespect or the assumption that they had an illness.

Hess (2006, p. 384) reviewed the psychological literature on aging stereotypes. He found that overall "the literature suggests an underlying negative component to most categories of older adults." Laboratory studies of attitudes about aging show a consistent bias against older people (Hummert, Garstka, & O'Brien, 2002). Nosek, Banaji, and Greenwald (2002) compared subjects' attitudes toward race, gender, and age. They found stronger negative associa-

tions with age than with race or gender. They also found that older adults showed just as strong an age bias as did younger adults.

Older people may even try to distance themselves from being old. Cohen (2001) says that some older adults buy into the negative stereotypes, reject aging, and try to stay middle-aged forever. Nancy Perry Graham (2010, p. 4), editor of *AARP—The Magazine*, tells the following story. She and fellow editors attended a Bruce Springsteen concert in New Jersey in October 2009. A woman approached them and asked, "Why would you wear an AARP [American Association of Retired Persons] T-shirt to a Springsteen concert?" Graham explained that she worked for AARP and that, by the way, Springsteen himself was 60 years old. The woman took this in, then asked, "But why would you want people to know you're *old?*" Graham says this response would make sense from a teenaged Springsteen fan. But this woman was in her 60s. Graham says a friend of hers calls this attitude "chronological racism."

A national study of perceptions of aging in the United States found that fewer than half of older people reported "very serious" or "somewhat serious" problems with health, crime, income, and loneliness. But this same group of older people thought that nearly all older people had "very serious" or "somewhat serious" health, safety, income, or relationship problems (Cutler, Whitelaw, & Beattie, 2002) (see Table 1).

Some older people, for example, refuse to use bus passes that give discounts to seniors. They would rather pay the higher fares than admit their age. A 72-year-old man I met on a bus told me he was going to visit the "old folks" at a local nursing home. He does not see himself as an old person. Most people, it seems, feel that "old" is 5 years older than they are.

Some years ago, Kalish (1979) and Estes (1979) described a **new ageism**. This refers to the desire to help older people who need special treatment due to poor health, poverty, or lack of social supports. Although this positive form of ageism tries to do good, it supports the stereotype of old age as a time of decline and loss. Binstock (1983, 2005a) calls this a **compassionate stereotype** or compassionate ageism. This stereotype attempts to create sympathy for older people, but it doesn't give a true picture of later life.

Estes found that a federal bureaucracy to care for older people, what she calls the **aging enterprise**, grew out of compassionate stereotyping. Supporters

TABLE 1 "Very Serious" or "Somewhat Serious" Problems Facing Older People, 2000: A Survey of American Older People

	A Problem for Me (%)		A Problem for Other Older People (%)	
	1974	**2000**	**1974**	**2000**
Health	54	42	96	92
Fear of crime	50	36	84	82
Not having enough money to live on	46	36	92	88
Loneliness	36	21	94	84

This nationwide study found that, compared with 1974, in 2000, a smaller proportion of older people reported very or somewhat serious problems. Older people's subjective sense of well-being improved over the 25 years. But older people's view of other older people stayed roughly the same. Older people continue to think that nearly all other people their age suffer from health, crime, money, and personal relationship problems. Older people have a stereotyped view of other older people. Further analysis of the data in this study showed that middle-aged people (ages 35 to 53) had an even more negative view of older people. More than 90% of the Baby Boom group thought that older people today had serious problems with the items on this list.

How do your friends feel about aging? How do you think they would answer if asked about the "very serious" or "somewhat serious" problems that older people face?

Source: Adapted from N. E. Cutler, N. A. Whitelaw, & B. L. Beattie, *American Perceptions of Aging in the 21st Century: A Myths and Realities of Aging Chartbook* (Washington, DC: National Council on the Aging, 2002), Figure 1, p. 2, and Figure 2, p. 4. Used with permission of the National Council on the Aging.

of older people created the stereotype of older people as poor, frail, and dependent. This image created sympathy for older people and led to programs such as **Medicare,** the **Older Americans Act,** and improved **Social Security.** These programs did improve older people's lives, but they also set the stage for the current round of **scapegoating**.

People now question whether the old deserve such apparently lavish treatment. Some policy analysts and the press declare that older people have plenty of money and political power and they cost too much to care for. Stereotyping, whether negative or compassionate, in the end decreases public support for the older person who really needs help.

CULTURE AS A SOURCE OF AGEISM

At a conference a few years ago, a sales representative gave me a page of comments about getting older. The page had his name and phone number in the outside margins. I suppose he thought that people would pass this page along to colleagues. They would share this bit of humor and his name as well. The page said:

You know you're getting old when . . .

- Everything hurts and what doesn't hurt doesn't work.
- Your pacemaker makes the garage door go up every time a pretty girl walks by.
- Your back goes out more often than you do.
- The last time you helped a little old lady across the street it was your wife.

I've read these lines to many audiences and classes of students, and people find them funny. But at the risk of ruining the fun, I suggest that all of these jokes foster ageism. For one thing, they all make older people seem physically and psychologically weak. They also make older people seem less able to do things or imply that they cannot control their bodily functions.

The man who gave me this list saw no harm in the humor, and since then I have received copies of this list from other sources. One copy of this list appeared in *Reader's Digest.* Imagine that a similar list had a racial or ethnic bias. Would you pass it along to your customers or show it to your professor? Would it be published in a national magazine? Few people see these jokes as ageist at first. All of us have grown up with the stereotype of older people as run-down and decrepit. Jokes like these and many other sources in our culture support ageist beliefs.

Great writings from the past, for example, present ageist images of older people. Aristotle's (1941, Bk. II: Ch. 13, pp. 1405–1406) image of aging shows many of the biases people express today. Old men, he says,

are sure about nothing and under-do everything. . . . They are small-minded, because they have been humbled by life: their desires are set upon nothing more exalted or unusual than what will help them to keep alive. . . . They live by memory rather than by hope. . . . This, again, is the cause of their loquacity; they are continually talking of the past, because they enjoy remembering it. . . . Their sensual passions have either altogether gone or have lost their vigour.

Machiavelli presents the old man in his play *La Clizia* as a lecher. Shakespeare, at the start of *King Lear,* presents the king as a fool. Children's stories throughout history feature rag men, bogeymen, and wicked witches, all caricatures of old people. Montepare and Zebrowitc (2002) report that children get exposure to attitudes and views of aging and older people in preschool. Psychologist Becca Levy (2003, cited in Dittmann, 2003; also Calasanti, 2006) reports, "Age stereotypes are often internalized at a young age—long before they are even relevant to people," and early attitudes tend to be reinforced over their lifetimes.

BOX 1
WHAT'S IN A NAME?

Every group has its preferred name for itself. Do we call someone an American Indian, an Aboriginal Person, a Native American? Groups generally adopt and promote a term that presents them in a positive way. However, no acceptable term has evolved to refer to the older population, and anyone who writes about older people or speaks to groups about aging faces a dilemma. What should we call people age 65 and over?

I have not found a term that all the older people I meet will accept. This poses a dilemma for someone who needs to write about older people as a group.

Canadians, for example, feel comfortable with the term *seniors*, as in "senior centre." But in the United States, senior center directors want to find a new term for their organizations. They feel that the word *senior* turns off new generations of older people. Likewise, terms such as *Gruppies* (Graying Urban Professionals) seem silly. Beck (1990b) reports on several other options: "Whoopies (Well-Heeled Older People), OPALS (Older Persons with Active Lifestyles) and Grumpies (Grown-up Mature People)." None of these has caught on.

"The real problem," Beck (1990b) says, "is that any term associated with *old* is still considered derogatory." And until we tackle and overcome our societal rejection of aging, someone will be offended no matter what term we choose.

If you know some older people, ask them what term they use to describe their age group.

The Media as a Source of Ageism

The media provide more up-to-date examples of ageist treatment. The cartoon show *The Simpsons* depicts Grandpa Simpson as ignorant, forgetful, and timid. In one episode he and his nursing-home friends break out of the home to freedom. They make it to the sidewalk, look around, get scared, and shuffle back inside.

Studies of prime-time television shows, television commercials, and children's shows have generally found that television underrepresents older people (Signorielli, 2001). Donlon, Ashman, and Levy (2005) found that fewer than 2% of prime time TV characters were age 65 years or older (though the older population makes up nearly 13% of American society). Studies of television commercials also find an underrepresentation of older people in advertisements (Miller, Levell, & Mazachek, 2004). When television does portray older people, as in commercials, it often puts them in stereotyped roles.

In 2003, the Screen Actors Guild (SAG) reported that only 27% of all women's roles on prime-time television went to women over age 40, and they were typically cast as victims: betrayed, abandoned, and abused. The SAG also reported that more than twice as many roles are available for actors under the age of 40 as for actors older than 40 (International Longevity Center, 2006). Older people express concern about these negative stereotypes (Robinson, Popovich, Gustafson, & Fraser, 2003).

Levitt and Dubner (2005, p. 79), in their book *Freakonomics,* describe a TV show called *The Weakest Link.*

On this show, contestants vote to eliminate other players. In the early rounds, weak players are eliminated because they lack the information needed to help the others succeed. In the later rounds, players are eliminated if they know too much because they increase the competition. Levitt and Dubner found that "elderly players [on the show] . . . are victims of taste-based discrimination: in the early rounds *and* late rounds, they are eliminated far out of proportion to their skills. It seems as if the other contestants—this is a show on which the average age is thirty-four—simply don't want the older players around."

Most studies show that the print media also underrepresent older people. A study of pictures in magazines and newspapers in the United Kingdom (Whitfield, 2001), for example, found that they included relatively few pictures of older people. Older people make up 16% of that society. But pictures of older people made up 3% or fewer of pictures in newspapers and magazines. The study found that even magazines for seniors showed relatively few pictures of older people.

De Luce (2001, p. 40) reviewed advertising and articles in 31 American popular magazines, including *Time* and *Newsweek*. She found that a number of magazines (e.g., *The New Yorker* and *The New York Times Magazine*) had no ads targeted at people age 50 and over. Nineteen publications in her study had only one to five ads targeted to older people. De Luce says that these findings reveal the "invisibility" of older consumers. Ads that did have older people in them included ads for cancer survivors, for sufferers of memory loss and for loss of sexual vigor.

A study titled *Ageism in America* (International Longevity Center, 2006, p. 55) reports that the TV show *Murder She Wrote* "starred the legendary stage and film actress Angela Lansbury. Having run successfully for ten years, the show was canceled at the height of its popularity because the audience was deemed too old and therefore the time sold not sufficiently profitable."

Krueger (2001) says that only about 50 newspapers in the United States have a reporter dedicated to reporting on aging issues. He says that the lack of stories on older adults supports stereotyping. It also limits the amount of useful information that the public needs to understand aging. Kleyman (2002) says that, even though few newspapers put resources into reporting on aging, the topic will grow in interest. The aging of the Baby Boom generation, the aging of senior news managers, and a growing interest in topics related to aging will lead to more stories on older people.

Studies have found signs of ageism in magazine articles (Whitfield, 2001), country music (Aday & Austin, 2000), and jokes. Bowd (2003) reviewed 4,200 jokes and found eight categories of negative stereotypes, including the impotent male, the unattractive female, the sick older person, and the forgetful older person.

Thornton and Light (2006, p. 276) describe the use of **elderspeak** and its effect on older people. Elderspeak refers to "a specialized speech register resembling baby talk in addressing older adults." This form of speech uses fewer clauses, shorter phrases, more filler phrases (e.g., *like* or *you know*), words with fewer syllables, slower speech, and longer pauses. In other words, elderspeak sounds like baby talk. It also includes the use of words such as *dearie, cutie,* and *sweetie*. Institutional workers may use words like these to address residents (for example, "Good morning, dearie, it's time for breakfast") (Hess, 2006). Thornton and Light say that stereotyping drives elderspeak. The speaker assumes that the older person has low mental ability or some other impairment.

Elderspeak has a negative effect on the older person. It creates low self-esteem, it reduces a person's ability to communicate effectively, it decreases the quality of interaction, and it reduces the older person's sense of control (Thornton & Light, 2006).

Ageism even influences retail sales. One student, as part of an assignment to study ageism, entered a women's clothing store with her mother and grandmother.

The store sold moderately priced clothes for women of all ages. The three women walked around the store separately to see whom the sales staff would approach first. The staff approached the student first to offer help and the grandmother last.

Ruth Reichl, former *New York Times* food critic, conducted a similar experiment. She went to lunch at Tavern on the Green in New York with two older women. One was an acting coach, the other a wealthy older woman dressed in cashmere and fur. Reichl dressed in disguise for the lunch in order to remain anonymous to the restaurant staff. She wore the clothes and took on the personality of a poor old woman.

She reports that the waiters either ignored their table or appeared impatient when serving them. Their table seemed to get slower service than others. Reichl writes,

> The service was so slow that after a great deal of small talk and five pots of tea, I felt compelled to apologize. "I always seem to get bad service," I told Helen [the wealthy woman]. "I don't know why." "Well, I do," she [Helen] snapped. "You look like an old lady. And waiters consider old ladies their natural enemies. They think that they will complain constantly, order the cheapest dishes on the menu, and leave a six percent tip. I have found that it is essential to appear prosperous when going out to eat." (Reichl, 2005, pp. 211–212, 215)

Obvious poverty or low income compounds the ageism that an older person faces. In her disguise as an old and poor woman, Reichl became invisible. "As I walked up Riverside Drive," she says, "not one of the many people walking dogs, wheeling strollers, or carrying briefcases glanced my way. No doorman tipped his hat as I went by. By the time I got to the corner, I felt as insubstantial as the wind; when people looked my way they saw only the buildings at my back. When I waved my hand the taxis hurtled past as if I were not there. I finally resorted to stepping into the middle of the street."

When she finally got a cab, the driver hit the gas so hard it threw her against the back of the seat. When she protested and asked him to slow down, he ignored her. "Perhaps it was how he always drove," she says, "but it made me feel like an old boot, a piece of junk that he was desperate to deposit at its destination."

Reichl experienced a sudden entry into the world of an older person. But many older people experience ageism daily.

One woman, in a study of attitudes toward older people, said, "Salespersons can be impatient if you are choosing something and are not swift enough." Another woman said, "Salespeople will talk to me rather than to my mother who is 85" (National Advisory

BOX 2
DISGUISED
The Story of Patricia Moore: A Woman Who Disguised Herself as Old

How does it feel to be an older person? Most of us will have to wait many years to find out, but knowing what it feels like might give us each new insights into aging. Patricia Moore, a 26-year-old industrial designer at the time, decided to turn herself into an 85-year-old woman.

Her journey into old age began with a custom-made latex mask and a white wig. She dressed the part with her mother's purse, canvas shoes, and a cane. She wore bandages on her legs, support stockings, and a cinch to flatten her chest. Old glasses and a pillbox hat completed the disguise.

Pat put her disguise on almost every week for 3 years. She played the role of an old woman in 116 cities in 14 states and 2 provinces in Canada. She says that geography made little difference in how people treated her as an older person. Some people offered her help and treated her kindly. Other people ignored her. Sometimes she faced overt ageism.

Pat gave up her disguise after 3 years, but not before she got mugged, met poor and abused older people, and also met kind strangers who helped her on her way. She counts older people among the kindest strangers she met during her time as an old woman.

Does Pat Moore, the young one with the smooth skin and the pretty eyes, ever miss the "old lady"?

"Oh, I miss her," Pat answers without hesitation. "She was a good friend. We meant a great deal to each other, but for now we've said good-bye.

"It's not a sad parting, though," she adds with a mischievous smile, "I expect to see her again—in the mirror—in about 50 years!"

Below, you can see how Pat looked in and out of her disguise at the time.

Pat Moore in her disguise as an old woman and as she looks today.

Source: Patricia Moore, *DISGUISED—The Story of Patricia Moore: A Woman Who Disguised Herself as Old.* Used with permission.

Council on Aging, 1993, p. 20). Ageism negatively affects older people's self-images and lowers their status in society. It makes everyday life less pleasant and in some cases more difficult.

Writer Malcolm Cowley (1980) describes the effects of ageism on his self-image. "We start by growing old in other people's eyes," he says, "then slowly we come to share their judgment." He recalls the time he backed out of a parking lot and nearly collided with another car. The driver got out, ready to fight. "Why, you're an old man," he said after seeing Cowley. Then he got back in his car and drove away. Cowley bristles when he remembers the event.

Some years later, he says, "a young woman rose and offered me her seat in a Madison Avenue bus. That message was kind and also devastating. 'Can't I even stand up?' I thought as I thanked her and declined the seat. But the same thing happened twice the following year, and the second time I gratefully accepted the offer, though with a sense of having diminished myself. 'People are right about me,' I thought. . . . All the same it was a relief to sit down and relax" (Cowley, 1980, pp. 5–6).

Gladwell (2005) shows that exposure to negative views of aging can have a subtler—but no less damaging—effect on the person. One psychology experiment gave subjects five scrambled words and asked them to make a four-word sentence—for example, "shoes give replace old the." (Replace the old shoes.) The study asked subjects to complete 10 of these sentences. Most people found the job easy and completed all 10 sentences. But, Gladwell says, "After you finished that test—believe it or not—you would have walked out of my office and back down the hall more slowly than you walked in" (p. 53). Why? Because the researchers included in the sentences words that referred to aging—*old, lonely, wrinkle*, etc.

Gladwell says that in this study, subjects' unconscious minds began to think about old age. As a result, their bodies responded as if they had aged. Their minds, he says, "took all this talk of old age so seriously that by the time [they] finished and walked down the corridor, [they] acted old. [They] walked slowly" (p. 53). In other words, in this study mere exposure to words related to aging had a subliminal effect. It led to stereotypical negative behavior.

Lack of Knowledge as a Source of Ageism

Some of what looks like ageism comes from ignorance. Few people know much about aging today except what they see and hear in the media and popular culture. Gerontologist Erdman Palmore (1977) created a Facts on Aging Quiz (FAQ) to explore people's knowledge about aging. Palmore designed the quiz to test physical, mental, and social knowledge as well as common misconceptions about old age. The FAQ has led to a small explosion of studies as researchers from around the world criticized, validated, and modified the original quiz (Palmore, 1998; Pennington,

Pachana, & Cole, 2001; Seufert & Carrozza, 2002).

Palmore himself published Part Two of the quiz in 1981. He later developed a multiple-choice quiz (Harris, Changas, & Palmore, 1996). Here is a brief FAQ that draws on Palmore's quizzes.[2] Read the questions and answer them either true or false.

1. All five senses tend to decline in old age.
2. Over 20% of the U.S. population is now age 65 or over.
3. The life expectancy of African Americans at age 75 is about the same as that of whites.
4. The majority of older people have incomes below the poverty level (as defined by the federal government).
5. Older workers have fewer accidents than younger workers.
6. People tend to become more religious as they age.
7. Lung capacity tends to decline in old age.
8. At least 10% of the aged are living in long-stay institutions (i.e., nursing homes, mental hospitals, homes for the aged).
9. Over three fourths of older people can carry out their daily activities without help.
10. The aged have higher rates of criminal victimization than persons under age 65.

How did you score? (The answers appear on the next page.)

Palmore (1998, p. 43) reports a "most disturbing general finding" from the use of the FAQs. "Most people know little about aging and have many misconceptions . . . the average person appears to have almost as many misconceptions about aging as correct conceptions." He found that people scored better on some questions than on others. The questions most often missed included the proportion of older people in long-term stay institutions, the older person's inability to change, and the proportion of older people below the poverty line.

A study by the AARP (formerly the American Association of Retired Persons) and the University of Southern California (2004) found similar results. This national study of almost 1,500 Americans found that people answered about half the items on a 25-point quiz correctly. Sixty-four percent of respondents mistakenly thought that a majority of older people lived in poverty, 73% percent mistakenly thought older people were lonely, and 85% mistakenly thought that 10% of older people live in nursing homes.

[2]*Source:* Adapted from Palmore, E. B. 1977. Facts on Aging: A short quiz. *The Gerontologist, 17*, 315–320; and Palmore, E. B. 1981. The Facts on Aging Quiz: Part two. *The Gerontologist, 21*, 431–437.

Palmore (1998) found that test takers tended to assume a negative view of older people. He also found that even people with expertise in aging missed many of the FAQ questions. Graduate students and professionals who worked with older people missed about one third of the true/false questions. Gerontology students and faculty members missed from 10% to 30% of the items. These findings suggest that most people have an uneven knowledge about aging. In general, people seemed to have more knowledge of physical changes that come with age and less knowledge of social facts about aging.

Both the Palmore research and the study by the AARP and University of Southern California show that the most frequent misconceptions about aging come from negative views of old age. Palmore found that people with more education scored better on the FAQ. People with a high school education averaged between 52% and 60% correct, undergraduates averaged between 55% and 69%, graduate students scored 65% to 76% correct, and gerontology students and faculty scored 66% to 92% correct. Finally, specialists in the field of aging scored 90% or better (Palmore, 1998).

Hess (2006) reviewed the research on attitudes toward older people. He found that people with more knowledge about aging had a more positive view of later life. They could see things from the perspective of the older person. Also, people who had personal contact with older adults tend to stereotype less. Negative stereotypes come into play most often when we know little about a person or group (Funderburk, Damron-Rodriguez, Storms, & Solomon, 2006).

BOX 3
TO DYE OR NOT TO DYE: THAT IS THE QUESTION

"I had light streaks put in my dark hair when I was younger," Genie says. "Now I do the opposite. I have dark streaks put in my gray hair.

"As I got older," she says, "I had my hair colored its original black. I had it done every 3 or 4 weeks. It cost a fortune. But I made it part of my budget. Had to have it done. I couldn't stop. If I stopped, I'd have a line across my head where the gray would grow in and where the black color stopped."

"Then I got sick and they shaved my head. That was my opportunity. I stopped coloring my hair. I let it go silver. But one day I looked in the mirror and I thought, 'Gosh, she looks old.' So I started again, but this time with dark highlights in the gray."

Genie faced the dilemma that many women (and men) face as they age—to dye or not to dye. In a society that idolizes youth, gray hair marks a person as old and less desirable. Hair dye covers one sign of aging and allows a person to appear more youthful.

Anne Kreamer (2007) reports that a Procter & Gamble survey found that 65% of women dyed their hair in 2004—many times the proportion in the 1950s. This, Kreamer (p. 72) says, "is why going gray has become a difficult . . . choice for modern women to make." A gray-haired older woman now stands out from her age group.

A 2007 *Time* magazine poll asked people whether they thought gray hair is an advantage or disadvantage today. Nearly four fifths of respondents (79%) thought gray hair disadvantaged a person in personal or social life, and 67% thought it disadvantaged a person in the workplace.

Nora Ephron (2006), in her book *I Feel Bad About My Neck*, says, "There's a reason why forty, fifty, and sixty don't look the way they used to, and it's not because of feminism or better living through exercise. It's because of hair dye. . . . Hair dye has changed everything, but it almost never gets the credit. It's the most powerful weapon older women have against the youth culture" (p. 36).

The new role of women in the workplace plays some role in women's decisions to dye their hair. The workplace values a youthful look, and women may feel pressured by social attitudes to use hair color. But this poses a dilemma. The independent working woman represents a liberation from the past definitions of femininity.

The women's liberation movement promised freedom from narrow (male-dominated) views of female beauty. A woman who dyes her hair to appear younger seems to give in to the stereotypical images of youth and beauty that women wanted to escape.

Will new generations of women, the Baby Boomers, continue to dye their hair? Boomers created the "do your own thing" ethic of the 1960s. Will they reject social convention and stop coloring their hair as they enter the third age? Will Boomers let their inner gray show?

===

What do you think about the tendency of women (and some men) to color their hair? Should people dye their hair as they age in order to look younger? Or should they allow their gray hair to show? Does hair coloring give in to societal ageism? Does it encourage the continuation of negative attitudes toward getting older?

Note: Answers to the FAQ on p.8: Odd numbered items are true. Even numbered items are false.

SOME FACTS ON AGING TODAY

Consider some of the correct answers to questions on the FAQ. For now, consider the facts presented here and think about why people might have missed these items.

True or False: Over 20% of the U.S. population is now age 65 or over.

False. The proportion of older people in the United States has grown over the past 100 years. In 1900, about 4% of the population was age 65 or over. By 2010, the proportion of older people had more than tripled to 12.97% (U.S. Census Bureau, 2008b). The proportion of older people in the population will continue to grow. By the year 2050, when the last Baby Boomers reach late old age, the U.S. Census Bureau projects that older people will make up 20.17% of the population. This aging of the population will transform U.S. society. It will transform policies and programs for older people, open new opportunities for people of all ages, and change our views of later life.

True or False: The majority of older people have incomes below the poverty level (as defined by the federal government).

False. In 2007, 9.7% of people age 65 and over had incomes below the government's poverty line (U.S. Census Bureau, 2010a). This proportion has dropped from the early 1960s, when more than 30% of older people had incomes below the poverty line. Older people today get more of their income from work or pensions than in the past.

In addition, a number of government programs provide a stronger economic safety net than ever before. This net consists of improved Social Security benefits, yearly cost-of-living increases in Social Security, and a Supplemental Security Income program. Some groups of older people still suffer from high rates of poverty, as we will see. But Schulz (2001, p. 2) concludes that overall, "older people today are *economically much better off than they were a little more than two decades ago*" [emphasis in the original].

True or False: At least 10% of the aged are living in long-stay institutions (i.e., nursing homes, mental hospitals, or homes for the aged).

False. On any given day, about 5% of people age 65 and over live in an institution. Some will stay for a short time and return to their homes. Most older people today and in the future will live on their own or with family members in the community. Most have reasonably good health and manage to care for themselves.

Those older people who have physical problems and need help often use community care programs that range from Meals on Wheels to visiting nurse services. Older people who need help rely mostly on family and friends. People who live in institutions, in most cases, are very old, have poor health, and have few informal supports to help them stay in the community.

True or False: The life expectancy of African Americans at age 75 is significantly less than that of whites.

False. African Americans, compared to whites, have a lower **life expectancy** at birth. An African American child born in 2005 could expect to live to age 73.2. A white child born in that year could expect to live to age 78.3. These figures mean a difference of 5.3 fewer years of life expectancy for the African American child.

But this question asks about life expectancy at age 75. In 2002, the life expectancy for African American men and women at age 75 was 86.4 years. The life expectancy for white men and women age 75 in that year was 86.9 years, a difference of only half a year or about the same (National Center for Health Statistics, 2009). These figures show the effects of high African American **mortality** in childhood and young adulthood. Poverty, poor health care, and unhealthy living conditions put many African American infants and children at greater risk than whites. Once African Americans reach age 75, they have survived most of these harsh conditions.

True or False: Compared to people under age 65, the aged have higher rates of criminal victimization.

False. Older people have the lowest rates of criminal victimization across all crime categories. (See Table 2.) Older people, compared with younger people, have a much lower risk of violent crime or property crime. In addition, rates have fallen by one third since the 1970s (Federal Interagency, 2004). However, older people do have a high risk for certain types of crimes—for example, larceny with personal contact, such as purse snatching and pocket picking. Older people show some of the highest rates for these types of crimes in urban settings.

Doyle (1990) used an opportunity framework to explain patterns of crime against older people. *Opportunity* refers to the attractiveness of a target, the exposure of the target, and the guardianship or protection of the target. Older people have less exposure to criminals. They tend to stay at home at night and to live in relatively safe neighborhoods. Retired people spend

TABLE 2 Estimated Personal Violent Victimization Rates by Type of Victimization at Selected Ages, per 1,000 persons, United States, 2009

Age	Total	Rape/Sexual Assault	Robbery	Aggravated Assault	Simple Assault
12–15	36.8	0.9*	3.1	6.9	25.9
16–19	30.3	0.6*	5.2	5.3	19.3
20–24	28.1	0.8*	3.5	7.5	16.3
25–34	21.5	0.8*	2.8	4.5	13.4
35–49	16.1	0.4*	2.0	2.6	11.1
50–64	10.7	0.3*	1.1	1.9	7.5
65+	3.2	0.2*	0.4*	0.3*	2.2

*Based on 10 or fewer cases.

This table shows the decrease in violent criminal victimization that takes place from middle-age onward. Older people show extremely low rates of violent victimization. Except in the case of simple assault (e.g. purse snatching) data show less than 10 cases per 1,000 older people.

Source: Adapted from Truman, J. L., and Rand, M. R. (2010). *Criminal victimization, 2009. National Crime Victimization Survey.* Washington, DC: U.S. Department of Justice. Office of Justice Programs. Bureau of Justice Statistics. Table 5. Retrieved October 19, 2010, from http://bjs.ojp.usdoj.gov/content/pub/pdf/cv09.pdf

more time at home and so protect their property more. At the same time, they do offer an attractive target for purse snatchers and pickpockets on the street.

Other studies support this framework. Many minority older people live in high-crime neighborhoods and have more exposure to criminals. African American men, for example, show high rates of assault and intimidation against them. Older men in these neighborhoods may look like easy targets to criminals.

Victimization by Fraud

Older people seem more susceptible to certain types of crime than others. Con artists and swindlers, for example, tend to target this population. Older people have savings that make them attractive targets. They also may have fewer social supports to help them steer clear of bogus deals such as home repair and medical and insurance scams.

Cons and swindles take many forms. Con artists often use the "bank examiner" swindle on older people. In that case, a con artist calls an older person, often a woman who lives alone, and says that someone is embezzling money from her bank. The caller asks if she will help catch the thief. The caller tells her to withdraw money from her account and give the money to a bank messenger who will arrive at her door. The caller explains that the messenger will take the money back to the bank. The bank will then check the serial numbers and catch the crooked teller. The messenger, of course, works for the con artist and gets away with the money.

"'Once you hand over your money, there is no recovery,' says Melvin L. Jeter, southern regional security director for NationsBank. 'There's no way any money's going to get back'" (McLeod, 1995, p. 14).

Home repair con artists also target older people. They look for homes that need repairs—loose shingles or a broken eaves trough. The swindler then knocks on the older person's door and offers to estimate the cost of repairs. He or she gives a low estimate and says that the older person will have to pay for the work right away to get this deal. The con artist usually asks for cash payment before any work gets done.

Some crooks even drive the older person to the bank to withdraw the money. Once the swindler has the money, the work may never get done, or it is done poorly with cheap materials. Con artists of this type may come back again and again to do more repairs. They may even try to borrow money from the older person once they have a relationship.

No exact figures exist on the cost of fraud to older people. But a report from the City and County of Denver, Colorado, gives some idea of the losses older people face. One criminal case filed with the Denver District Attorney's Economic Crime Unit found that older victims lost $20 million to fraud. In another case, an investment advisor swindled older clients out of $17 million. In still another case, a probate attorney stole more than $3.5 million from older people or their estates (Curtis, 2006).

Swindlers have increased their use of technology to bilk older people. *Slamming*, for example, switches a person's phone to another provider without the owner's permission. *Cramming* occurs when a person gets charged for phone services that he or she never ordered. Money offers from Nigerian sources often come as email messages. They promise to transfer funds to a person's bank account. The victim will supposedly receive part of these funds as a reward for helping with the transfer. But after the person has agreed to help, further letters demand money for transfer fees and other expenses. The victim never receives the promised funds or any reward.

These and other electronic schemes use technology to play on a person's ignorance or greed. Older people who have little experience with electronic media serve as easy targets for thieves. Greisman (2005), in a presentation on behalf of the Federal Trade Commission, estimated that Internet auction scams, identity theft, and lottery, prize, and sweepstakes scams cost older Americans $152 million in 2004. The FTC estimates that Internet scams account for about two fifths of fraud complaints. The Federal Trade Commission (2010) and the FBI (2010) provide fraud prevention information on their websites.

Effects of Victimization

Barbara Barer, an anthropologist at the University of California, San Francisco, found that fraud can lower an older person's self-image. She reports the case of a 96-year-old woman cheated out of money for an emergency alert system. The woman felt so embarrassed about losing the money that she never reported the crime. She felt that if her friends or family knew, they might question her competence.

Barer says that older people also feel that if they report crimes, they may face further victimization. One man arranged for car repairs with a neighbor. The neighbor never did the repairs. The man feared that the neighbor's children would smash his car windows and slash his tires if he reported the crime.

Barer says that crimes like these against older people can lead to feelings of inferiority and loss of self-esteem. Crimes against very old people can lead to a loss of independence and possibly institutionalization. Barer says that with most crimes, society sees the criminal at fault, but "when a crime is committed against an elderly individual, the victim is implicated for being at fault for allowing it to happen. The mistake is unforgivable. Thus it is preferable to conceal the shame" (Unreported Crime, 1994, p. 4).

The AARP (1999) conducted a study of consumers age 18 and over. The study found that compared with younger people, older people were more vulnerable to unfair or deceptive business practices. The oldest age group, age 75 and over, had the highest proportion of vulnerable people. Older people with low education

levels and low incomes had the highest rates of vulnerability. These people also can least afford the cost of unfair business practices.

Older people, compared with younger people, had less knowledge of consumer rights. Younger people, compared with older people, tended to take a less trusting attitude toward businesses. These differences between older and younger consumers make older people more susceptible to con artists. Police often have special pamphlets prepared to alert older people to schemes directed at them. Twenty states share information to foil fraud schemes. Other states sponsor consumer hotlines for older people, train police, and scan junk mail for current scams.

Fear of Crime

A national study in 2000 by the National Council on Aging (Cutler et al., 2002) found that 36% of older people felt that fear of crime was a "very" or "somewhat" serious problem for them. This figure dropped from 50% in 1974. But it still means that more than one older person in three considers crime a serious problem. Also, specific groups may fear crime more than others. Acierno and Kilpatrick (2004) asked 106 adults age 55 and over about their fear of crime. The researchers found that women, visible minority group members, people who felt depressed, and socially isolated people reported the most fear of crime.

Some fear of crime may have a sound basis. Older people who live in urban areas with high crime rates, for example, report a greater fear of crime than those in rural areas. They do in fact face a greater risk of victimization than suburban older people. Likewise, older people may fear crime because a purse snatching can lead to personal injury. Older people who live on fixed incomes may fear the effects of petty theft on their ability to pay their bills. The topics of fear of crime and ways to reduce this fear need more careful study.

Ageism and the Workplace

The U.S. Age Discrimination in Employment Act (ADEA) prohibits mandatory retirement at any age (except in cases where age influences ability). Congress (29 U.S.C. 621(b)—1967, cited in McCann & Ventrell-Monses, 2010) enacted the ADEA "to promote the employment of older persons based on their ability rather than age; [and] to prohibit arbitrary age discrimination in employment." The act attempts to reduce discrimination against older workers.

But researchers have a hard time judging the success of this legislation or the extent of discrimination. Employers who discriminate on the basis of age cannot admit it for fear of legal action. Schulz and Binstock (2006, p. 158) say that the law has driven most discrimination "underground." McCann and Ventrell-Monses (2010, p. 356) say that "more than 40 years after the ADEA's enactment, age discrimination continues to impede the achievement of equal treatment for older persons in the workplace."

The number of formal complaints lodged by workers gives a glimpse of the problem. Older workers filed 19,103 discrimination complaints with the Equal Employment Opportunity Commission (EEOC) in 2007. This figure increased by 29% to 24,582 in 2008—the highest figure in 15 years. The economic recession and layoffs in 2008 in part accounts for this spike in complaints (Levitz & Shishkin, 2009).

An AARP study (Groeneman, 2006) found that 60% of workers age 45 and over believe that age discrimination exists in the workplace. Among this group, 95% think it is "very common" or "somewhat common." A majority of this group felt that age discrimination began after age 50. One worker told the Conference Board (Parkinson, 2002, pp. 17, 33), "After about (age) 45, the company does not continue to recognize one's contribution, and further advancement is denied if one is not already at the VP level." Another worker said, "All meaningful assignments or other opportunities are given to employees who are the same age as, or younger than, the boss—who is most often in his or her 40s."

"I do not expect to retire for approximately 6 years," one worker said. But his supervisor denied him opportunities for advancement due to his age. Haralson and Parker (2003) found that 63% of job seekers said they would leave dates off their resumes to hide their age.

Even before the recent recession, middle-aged workers worried about age discrimination at work. In an AARP (2008a) study 60% of workers age 45–74 said they believe age discrimination exists in the workplace. Of those who believed age discrimination exists at work, nearly all (90%) consider it very common or somewhat common. Most of them felt that age discrimination begins at age 50. Thirteen percent of workers in this study said they experienced some form of age discrimination during the past 5 years. This included not getting hired, being passed over for promotion, being denied access to training, or being passed up for a raise.

Another survey by the AARP (2007b, p. 59) found that, compared to younger workers, workers age 50 and over had much less confidence in their ability to find a job. "Age discrimination," the report says, "is viewed as the single largest barrier to finding jobs for workers over age 50."

A Merrill Lynch (2006) survey supports these findings. The study found that only 25% of people age 60 and over who wanted to work said they had a problem finding a job. But of those who could not find work, 80% said that they faced age discrimination.

A number of experimental studies document age discrimination in the workplace. The studies found that "younger job applicants were favored over older applicants who were identical in all respects save age" (Rix, 2004, p. 15). Lahey (2006, cited in Herd, 2009), for example, sent out resumes for equally experienced older and younger workers. The resumes went to 4,000 companies in Florida and Massachusetts. She found that the people presented as younger applicants in their resumes had a 40% greater chance of getting called for an interview.

What sorts of things do employers believe about older workers? And what are the facts about older workers?

Cooke (2006) says that employers view older workers as more expensive and less effective than younger workers. They believe this "despite anti-discrimination laws and evidence that older workers are indeed capable of learning new tasks and tend to have higher loyalty and less absenteeism" (p. 396). Firms that want to retire older workers will do so through "voluntary buy-outs" even where states make mandatory retirement illegal.

The AARP (2007a, p. 59) sponsored a study of seven developed nations. The study found that "age discrimination in hiring practices continues to be a serious concern around the world." People age 50 and over, compared to younger workers, said they felt less confident about their ability to find a new job. They also felt that age discrimination posed the single greatest barrier to finding a job. In this AARP study, 28% of people age 50 and over said that they had experienced age discrimination. Sixty percent of these people said that they experienced age discrimination when looking for a job. More than 35% reported age discrimination in promotion decisions.

McMullin and Berger (2006, pp. 211–218) conducted in-depth interviews with 30 unemployed women and men ages 45–65. All of these people actively tried to find work—and they all reported overt and covert ageism in their job search. "No one will tell you; no one will admit it," one 60-year-old woman told the researchers. "But I have a friend who owns his own company and he said, 'If I interview three people, even though you have the experience, if I think I can get more years out of another one, I would hire another person.' And you know, they don't have to say that, that's just the way it's done."

In answer to a question about age discrimination, one 45-year-old woman made reference to the role that gender plays in age discrimination. "Well definitely because I am a woman and because of my age. They want young, attractive women, not women who are forty-five, fifty or older." Men in this study also experienced rejection based on their age. One 62-year-old man said, "I went to two interviews there. They finally rejected me. . . . I, as they put it, was 'over-qualified.' . . . But I couldn't get anyone to hire me."

McMullin and Berger found throughout their research that employers often used euphemisms in order to reject older workers. Some companies say that they feel the work is too fast-paced for an older worker, instead of saying the person is too old for the job. The authors say that these phrases and excuses try "to avoid charges of ageism and age-based discrimination." Employers "seem to disguise their ageist hiring practices by rejecting older applicants with the use of more age neutral terms."

Employers use years of experience to identify a person's age. Workers find that their strong resumes may work against them. They signify the age of the worker and that alone may eliminate them from consideration. One worker, a woman of 60, said: "They don't say anything, but you know when there is absolutely no reason why you shouldn't be considered—to just look at my resume, they know how many years I've been in the business and they can sort of deduct that I'm not thirty-five or forty."

These workers report the effects of ageism and (in the case of the women) sexism in later life. Ageism in these cases affects more than a person's self-image. It can lead to low wages when a person does find a job (Rix, 2006). This can keep a person from living a decent life.

McCann and Ventrell-Monses (2010) trace the presence of discrimination to weak legislation. These authors say that, compared to legislation that prohibits racial or gender-based discrimination, the law takes a weak stand against age discrimination. For example, a person discriminated against based on race or gender can sue for compensatory or punitive damages due to discrimination. The law does not give the older worker this same right. "Congress's failure to provide for such damages in an age case implies that the older victim does not deserve a remedy" (McCann & Ventrell-Monses, 2010, p. 360).

The courts have taken a similar stand and "have been consistently unsympathetic to constitutionally based claims of age discrimination." For example, the courts do not support claims based on ageist comments. A U.S. Court of Appeals for the Fifth Circuit considered ageist statements irrelevant when presented as evidence of discrimination. One court ruling said, "Ageism is not a vice, or at least not enough of an evil to warrant judicial intervention" (Eglit, 1986, cited in McCann & Ventrell-Monses, 2010, p. 362).

The legal system views age discrimination as less harmful than other forms of discrimination. But the effects of ageism equal those of racial or gender discrimination. Discrimination against an older worker leads to loss of a job, loss of income, and personal humiliation. It has the same damaging effects as other forms of discrimination. But for the older worker fair treatment often depends on corporate policy and practice rather than legal support.

Some companies do a better job than others at reducing age discrimination. Deutsche Bank, for example, developed a task force on age diversity led by senior managers. The National Health Service in the United Kingdom conducts training on the value of older workers and promotes intergenerational mentoring. Danny Green, Human Resources Director of Merck Frost in Quebec, says, "Frankly, it's good business for government and employers to make it easier for over-50 employees to continue working. It's a win-win all around—it adds to the GDP of the country" (AARP, 2007a). These companies and others recognize the experience and dedication that many older workers bring to their jobs. They also recognize that a company must take a proactive stance to overcome age discrimination in the workplace.

The Ageless Self: Another Form of Ageism

Aging celebrities such as George Clooney or Cher serve as role models for Baby Boomers. They make aging look glamorous, and they challenge negative stereotypes. But they may create a new stereotype of the sophisticated, successful, beautiful senior. These new images of aging may lead to a new form of ageism: the ageless self.

Katz and Marshall (2003), for example, note that our consumer society pressures older people to use drugs and products to remain sexually and physically youthful. The authors say that this promotes an impossible ideal, one that ignores other ways to age. Many of the new images of aging, they say, marginalize the very old, older people with disabilities, and older people with a different view of aging.

Some authors see the current interest in longevity, the increases in surgery to alter the effects of aging, and the desire to act young into old age as a rejection of aging. Calasanti and Slevin (2006, p. 3) say that successful aging, when it promotes the image of eternal youth "means not aging not being 'old,' or, at the very least, not looking old."

Women may feel especially vulnerable as they age. Holstein (2001–2002) says that throughout life women get social approval for their looks. The ideal older woman according to the ageist stereotype, Calasanti and Slevin (2006) say, is "healthy, slim, discreetly sexy and independent."

Clarke, Griffin, and Maliha (2009) interviewed 36 women ages 71–93 about their clothing choices. These women used clothing to mask changes in their bodies that signaled aging. They opted for traditional styles and clothing that masked flabby underarm skin (referred to as bat wings), wrinkles, pear-shaped bodies, and loose skin at their necks. One woman said she wears turtlenecks because, "Most women as they get older, they get the turkey wattle here you know . . . the fat sinks from here, goes to under your chin and you'll find that older women have a bunch of fat hanging down here. . . . I like things with a turtleneck because they hide that ugly part" (p. 718). Their comments hint at the underlying anxiety that affects most older people as they age in American society.

BOX 4
THE BOOMING BOOMER MARKET

Boomers take a unique view of later life. Market researchers have begun to track the habits and preference of this big generation. Here are some of their findings:

- Boomers look forward to the future. They plan to begin some big new experiences. Many Boomers plan to start new businesses after they retire. Others want to give back to their communities through volunteer work. They want to find meaning in their post-retirement years.

- Boomers feel concerned with their physical well-being, and they plan to do something about it. Rich Kelleher, age 60, jogs daily. He had an operation on his knee recently that sidelined him for a while. But now he plays tennis daily with the retirees in his condo complex. He and his wife bicycle along the boardwalk near their home in Florida. Rich also owns a kayak that he uses for trips into the mangrove swamps near his home. He's training to run a half-marathon. Rich lives a more active lifestyle now than when he was in college. Like many Boomers, Rich wants to stay in good health as long as he can. He's begun to take care of his body through diet, weight control, and exercise.

- Boomers represent a relatively young and wealthy market. They go out for dinner to fast-food and to fine restaurants, they enjoy luxury cars, and they spend money on grandchildren. Some even buy new homes that reflect their new lifestyle in retirement. Studies show that Boomers also like to travel. They take vacations, and they include vacation expenses in their financial plans. Willens (2003, p. 45) says that "60 percent [of Boomers] have taken at least one vacation trip in past 12 months and plan for another next year." Novelli and Workman (2006) report that the 50 and over age group accounts for 70% of cruise passengers and accounts for 72% of all trips in a recreational vehicle.

- Myers and Nielson (2003, pp. 55, 57) say that "Boomers want unique life experiences." They report that 40% of travelers age 50 and over hold passports (compared to only 17% for all Americans). Also, "Among all travelers, people aged 50 and over use 80 percent of all luxury travel—e.g., vacations that cost at least $350 per day, they average 3 trips per year (more than the young), they stay places almost 1.5 times longer when they go somewhere, [and] they spend 75 percent more money at a vacation site than people aged 18–48."

- Boomers have embraced computer technology. They used technology at work, and they continue to use it in their private lives. Boomers use computers for email, trip planning, medical advice, shopping, and financial management.

Can you detect any other trends in the media that show the influence of the Baby Boom generation? Consider advertising, consumer products, and changes in attitudes toward aging.

Baker and Gringart (2009, p. 989) found that older men also expressed dissatisfaction with their physical appearance as they aged. The researchers found that men tended to engage in physical fitness activity to stay in shape. The researchers propose that men (particularly those under age 70) "engage in physical activity . . . to maintain a certain body-shape ideal." Men at older ages lose their interest in fitness as they age, possibly because they can no longer maintain the ideal of a youthful body. This study found that men become "progressively dissatisfied with their physical appearance" as they age. The researchers conclude that "cultural pressures to conform to youthful ideals are experienced by both genders" (p. 990).

Catherine Mayer (2009) coined the term *amortality* to describe the ageless self. Amortals, she says, obey no age norms. "The defining characteristic of amortality," she writes, "is to live the same way, at the same pitch, doing and consuming much the same things, from late teens right up until death." Amortals deny aging. In their most extreme pronouncements they deny death itself—hoping for a scientific breakthrough before they meet the reaper. A National Consumers League (2004) survey, for example, estimates that about 90 million Americans each year buy products or undergo procedures to hide physical signs of aging. In 2004 alone, the antiaging industry reported more than a $45.5 billion gross in products and services (Business Communications, 2005).

Katz (2001–2002) found that advertisements for retirement communities focus on active lifestyles and make life seem problem free. Older people in these ads appear to live in a paradise of mature adulthood. These ads promote a lifestyle for healthy, ageless older people. Katz says that these images can make the problems of aging—such as poverty, poor health, or the frailty of late old age—seem deviant. Stoller and Gibson (2000, p. 76) say that "recommendations to join an exercise class, learn ballroom dancing, or take up lap swimming imply sufficient discretionary income to purchase lessons or gain access to appropriate facilities."

Likewise, the move to a retirement paradise implies that the person has enough money to live in one of these communities. These models of aging create new problems for older people. "We find ourselves yearning to be like people in these pictures," one older woman writes, "and belabor ourselves for failing these role models" (Preston, cited in Stoller & Gibson, 2000).

This image of the ageless self ignores the diversity among older people and the fact that the body declines with age. Holstein (2005, p. 28) cautions that the ideal of "successful aging" "can also serve to threaten the self-esteem of people who cannot or choose not to live up to those new norms." Cruikshank (2003, p. 168) proposes that older people and American society show "frankness about decline and loss of capacity." She argues against the "false cheerfulness" of the ageless self.

This critique of popular images of aging points to the diverse experiences of aging in the twenty-first century. It also shows the need for older people to confront ageist stereotypes. Clarke (2002), for example, studied the attitudes of older women toward beauty in later life. The women in this study felt pressure from the fashion industry to stay thin. But they rejected the current ideal of extreme thinness. They preferred a more rounded body shape for themselves.

These women emphasized the importance of inner beauty. They found beauty in a person's personality, a person's relationships with others, and a person's inner happiness. Clarke (2002, p. 440; also Clarke et al., 2009) concludes that social ideals shape an older woman's view of herself and that "ageist norms . . . denigrate older women and older women's bodies." But, she says, older women can and do challenge these norms. "Many of the women in my study," she says, "provide an important example of how oppressive social values can be resisted and how individuals may . . . offer alternatives to ageist interpretations of later life" (Clarke, 2002, p. 440).

We need to allow for many ways to grow old. Some people want to engage in energetic activities that we associate with youth. Other older people define later life as a time to use their wisdom, share their memories, and offer community leadership. Some people live vibrant, healthy lives into late old age. Others live with chronic illnesses. Some seem youthful to us; others look old. No single right way to grow old exists. And none of these ways should meet with social rejection.

RESPONSES TO AGEISM

A study by Cutler, Whitelaw, and Beattie (2002) found that 45% of older people believed that their later years were "the best years of my life." Sixty-one percent of the people in this survey said they would feel "very happy" if they knew they could live another 10 years. People in this survey said that the key to a meaningful old age lies in having close family and friendships, good health, and a rich spiritual life. Middle-aged people in this sample agreed that these three items held the keys to a good old age. In this same survey, 68% of the older people said that as they grew older, "things seem better than I thought they would be." And 89% of the older people said that as they looked back on their lives they felt "fairly well satisfied."

People with good incomes, married couples, people with a secure pension, and healthy people report some of the greatest life satisfaction in later life (Holden & Hatcher, 2006). But as this survey shows, nearly all older people feel satisfied with life in general and they look forward to the years ahead. George (2006) reviewed the literature on life satisfaction.

She says that in both short-term and long-term studies, life satisfaction in old age remains high. This view from old age contradicts many of the stereotypes of aging.

Research shows that stereotypes exist because of ignorance about later life and the fear of aging. Even positive stereotypes can lead to prejudice and discrimination against older people. Authors suggest a number of ways to produce a more balanced view of aging. These include the use of the media, education programs, intergenerational programs, and legislation that prohibits discrimination based on age.

BOX 5
THE LIFE EXPERIENCES OF TODAY'S CENTENARIANS VIEWED THROUGH HISTORICAL EVENTS

Year	Age in That Year	Event
1914	1	World War I begins
1918	5	World War I ends
1929	16	Stock market crashes; Great Depression begins
1931	18	Penicillin discovered
1935	22	Social Security Act passed
1937	24	U.S. Housing Act passed; establishes public housing
1941	28	Pearl Harbor; United States enters World War II
1945	32	Yalta conference; Cold War begins
1946	33	Baby Boom begins
1950	37	United States enters Korean War
1955	42	Nationwide polio vaccination program begins
1964	51	United States enters Vietnam War; Baby Boom ends
1969	56	First man on the moon
1980	67	First AIDS case is reported to the Centers for disease control and prevention
1980	67	Era of the personal computer begins
1989	76	Berlin wall falls
1990	77	United States enters Persian Gulf War
2000	87	Dot-com stock market bubble bursts
2001	88	September 11 attack on the World Trade Center; terrorist threat worldwide increases
2003	90	United States enters Iraq war
2006	93	Broadband Internet, the World Wide Web, and mobile communications create a global community; concern about global warming takes hold
2008	95	First baby boomers turn 62, eligible for Social Security retired worker benefits
2008	95	Housing market bubble bursts; economy declines

One stereotype of older people says that they are rigid and inflexible. But older people have adapted to a wide range of challenges and opportunities throughout their lives. And most older people continue to successfully adapt today. This chart shows some of the social, political, and technological changes a typical older person has experienced in his or her lifetime. What changes have

occurred in your grandparents' lifetime? Your parents' lifetime? In your own? Create a chart that lists the changes you have witnessed in history, technology, and society. How have you responded to these changes? Can you guess what changes you will witness in the future? How do you think you'll respond?

Source: Adapted from the Federal Interagency Forum on Aging-Related Statistics. *Older Americans 2008: Key Indicators of Well-Being.* (Washington, DC: U.S. Government Printing Office, 2008). Retrieved December 21, 2009, from http://www.agingstats.gov/agingstatsdotnet/Main_Site/Data/2008_Documents/OA_2008.pdf

CHANGE ON THE HORIZON

The Media

Some improvement in attitudes toward older people may be taking place. Janelli and Sorge (2001) reviewed 61 children's storybooks published between 1991 and 1999. They found that most authors presented realistic stories. These stories showed both grandmothers and grandfathers as affectionate toward their grandchildren.

Magazines and television ads now feature famous seniors. Hall of Fame football player and coach Mike Ditka and former U.S. Senator Bob Dole promote drugs to correct erectile dysfunction. Jack Nicklaus promotes a ceramic and titanium hip replacement. Fashion model Lauren Hutton, now over 60 years old, wears a low-cut gown to promote a soy-based cereal that "may reduce the risk of heart disease." They send the message that they have control of their lives. They actively respond to the physical challenges that come with aging.

Luttropp (1995) reports that Oil of Olay skin lotion launched an ad campaign that presented healthy, happy women in their 40s. The campaign also responded to the diversity of the older population. It depicted African American as well as white women who feel content with their age. An African American woman in the ads says she is "looking forward to being the best-looking grandmother on the block" (Luttropp, 1995, p. 5). Other cosmetics companies, such as Clinique, have removed ageist language from their ads, and companies such as Nike target some of their ads to a middle-aged audience.

Unilever, the maker of Dove beauty products, has taken a bold step to attract older consumers. It created a new line of products called "Pro Age" that help people look good without denying their age. The advertising for the Dove products feature full-figured women, nonmodels, over age 50. Unilever takes a risk in promoting a product that helps people look their age (rather than deny it). After all, millions of Americans get Botox treatments each year, use antiaging makeup, and buy toothpaste to whiten aging teeth.

The Unilever (2010) company conducted a global study of women ages 50–64 and found that 91% of these women "believe it is time for society to change its views about women and ageing." Nancy Etcoff, a psychologist at the Harvard Medical School, consulted on a study that led to the new Dove products. She may be optimistic when she says, "We're seeing a real shift in how people are approaching beauty. Up to now, it's been about fighting aging with everything you have. Now you have a chance not to" (cited in Tsiantar, 2007).

Today the mass media also present an image of healthier, more active older people than in the past. *Time* magazine ran a story (complete with an ad for Levitra, an erectile dysfunction drug) titled "Still Sexy After Sixty" (Golden, 2004). The article presented vignettes that described the happy sex lives of seniors. Some years ago the TV comedy series *The Golden Girls* broke ground when it featured four older women who lived together. The series portrayed the women as active, engaged, and involved in complex relationships with men. It gained a wide audience and ran for several seasons.

Betty White, age 88 in 2010 and one of the Golden Girls, continues to entertain Americans. She starred in a 2010 Super Bowl commercial for Snickers candy where she played a football player. She also hosted *Saturday Night Live* on May 8 that year. Her show received the highest ratings of the past 18 months.

Architect Frank Gehry, when he was in his 70s, designed and oversaw construction of the Disney Concert Hall in Los Angeles. The concert hall has gotten critical raves. Gehry's Guggenheim Museum in Bilbao, Spain, and now the Disney Concert Hall mark him as one of the most creative men of our time. Pulitzer Prize–winning author Toni Morrison, now past 80, continues to write, teach, and influence our culture.

Astronaut John Glenn returned to space flight at age 77. David Bowie, at age 57, performed through a 112-date tour in 2004. Bob Dylan, now past 70, spends as much as 20 weeks touring on the road and continues to produce new music, as do the Rolling Stones. Frere-Jones (2005, p. 94) says, "In 2004, many of the best shows came from older groups who—perhaps owing to experience, new sobriety, humility, or all three—improved their repertory through performance, in ways that their juniors can't."

The Senior Market: A New Image of Aging

A few years ago a young market researcher sat down with three senior executives: one from a cosmetics firm, one from an egg-producing plant, and one from a pantyhose company. She explained that she wanted to study the spending patterns of older people. The executives laughed at her idea. None of them could understand why she wanted to do this. They each explained that they couldn't see this as relevant to their companies' future.

Some marketing directors still hold these views (Lippert & Scott, 2003). But the growing aging market has changed many advertisers' minds and will soon change many more. **Demographers** trumpet the aging of society, and economists tell us that older people today make up the richest generation of older people in history. As a group, they sit on a pile of wealth that includes their homes, pensions, savings, investments, and in some cases income from work.

Novelli and Workman (2006, p. 145) report that Baby Boomer households "pull in more than $2 trillion in annual income, account for 50% of all discretionary income, and are house-rich." Boomers hold 40 million credit cards, nearly half of all the credit cards in the United States. This group controls a large majority of the country's financial assets (Lippert & Scott, 2003).

The older market will grow in the future, but few companies have an idea of how to attract this older consumer. So far, attempts to target this market have had mixed results. Beck (1990a) notes that Kellogg's, for example, changed the name of "Bran Flakes" to "40+Bran Flakes" to capture the older market. She says that Kellogg's dropped the "40+" six months later when the name change failed to help sales.

Marketing experts say that people do not want a cereal that reminds them of their age. Other products, such as a line of gourmet foods called "Singles" (for people who live alone), have also failed to attract older consumers. In this case, experts say that people don't want to be reminded that they eat alone. Bradley and Longino (2001) report that pureed food for seniors and shampoo for people with gray hair both failed to sell.

Products that play on disabilities or problems turn people off. George Moschis, a researcher at the Center for Mature Consumer Studies at Georgia State University, found that older people will avoid a product if they think the company negatively stereotypes their age group (cited in Beck, 1990a; also Bradley & Longino, 2001). Success in attracting older consumers demands knowledge of what motivates them.

Ambrosius (1994, p. 11), for example, says that younger and older consumers want different things. Younger people focus on building families, careers, and success in their social roles. Older people want psychological fulfillment (rather than social-role fulfillment) and want to achieve life satisfaction. Ambrosius says, "We need to be more concerned with personal development . . . and deeper values. . . . Remember, no one buys anything merely because of age."

Baby Boomers will pay for quality and service when they buy a product. But they want products that fit their lifestyles and needs. Novelli & Workman (2006, p. 143) says that "Good Grips," a line of kitchen tools, "ease household tasks and boast a smart,

---

BOX 6
SOME MODELS OF GOOD AGING

Do people lose their abilities with age? Is aging a constant downhill course? Some well-known people should cause us to question our beliefs about old age. They show that people can continue to excel long past the normal retirement age. The following cases show the potential of later life.

- As of April 2009, the average age of the Supreme Court justices was 69 years.
- As of October 20, 2010, 4 senators are in their 80s, 23 are in their 70s, 34 are in their 60s (61% are age 60 or over).
- Former Senator John Glenn, the first American to orbit Earth in 1962, returned to space at age 77. He served as a payload specialist.
- Former Federal Reserve chairman Alan Greenspan oversaw the U.S. economy from age 61 to age 80.

- Actress Betty White starred on *Saturday Night Live* at age 87 and has had a career revival in her late 80s.
- Hugh Hefner, age 83, continues to oversee the Playboy empire.
- Pete Seeger, renowned folk-singer, released a new CD at age 90.
- Leroy "Satchel" Paige was the oldest baseball player, age 59. He pitched three scoreless innings in 1965 for the Kansas City Athletics. When asked about the secret of a good age, Paige said:
  - Don't look back. Something might be gaining on you.
  - Avoid fried meats which angry up the blood.
  - Age is a question of mind over matter. If you don't mind, it doesn't matter.

ageless design." All of these products support a new model of later life. They meet the needs of older people who see themselves as active, energetic, and engaged. This view of later life rejects the image of aging as a decline.

Advertisements have also begun to take a more positive view of older people. Investment companies, such as Smith Barney Transamerica and E*Trade, use full-page magazine ads to target Baby Boomers. An E*Trade ad plays on Boomers' concerns for their income in retirement. The ad says, "You're still working. Is your retirement account?" These companies want to offer investment advice to this rich and expanding market. Retail companies have also begun to target the older consumer. Ikea, the assemble-it-yourself furniture company, now offers delivery and assembly to attract older customers.

The September 2010 issue of the AARP *Bulletin* contained articles on Alzheimer's disease, health insurance for people with a preexisting condition, and retirement. You might expect to see these articles in a magazine for seniors. But it also contained articles on travel, smartphone use, and Harry Potter. These articles reflect the diverse interests and lifestyles of older people today.

Harris (2003b, pp. 2, 5) says, "In the same way that not every automobile is a Ford, not every member of the Boomer generation is the same. It is a diverse group, consisting of multiple sub-groups, with each sub-group having its own wants and needs." The Boomer generation, for example, stretches over 20 years. Boomers in

their early 50s still hold their mid-career jobs and have children in college. Many older Boomers have retired from their first careers and may have begun second careers. People in each of these life stages have different interests and will respond to different products and services.

According to the International Longevity Center (2006, p. 57, citing Dobrow, 2005), "Products targeting baby boomers are set to become the next big ad category in the coming years." Each year new people enter the ranks of the old. These people have better education, better financial resources, and better health than past generations of older people. They lead active, engaged lives until late old age, and they will reshape our ideas about aging.

Education Programs

Gerontology and geriatric education courses exist for professionals who work with older people. But some professions provide more education than others. And education programs need to improve enrollment rates.

Lee (2002) studied graduate schools of social work in the United States. The study found that 81.6% of schools offered courses on aging (an increase from 74% in 1992). About one quarter of the schools offered a concentration in aging. The field of social work recognizes the need to train more geriatric social workers. A grant from the John A. Hartford Foundation has funded a major effort to strengthen social workers' competencies in gerontology. Projects

---

BOX 7
TOWARD AN AGE-IRRELEVANT SOCIETY

Historian Andrew Achenbaum (1983) says that we may go too far in giving preferred treatment to older people. This amounts to a reverse form of discrimination. It gives one group access to special programs and services based on their age. In an age-irrelevant society, should older people get special benefits?

Achenbaum says we need to look at whether age should serve as the basis for a policy or practice. Mandatory retirement, for example, discriminates against older people because age alone cannot predict ability on the job. On the other hand, he says, shelter allowances should be based not on age, but on need. Many age groups need help with housing costs.

This logic could apply to seniors' discounts as well. A young family of four may have as much need for a

discount at a restaurant as a senior couple. A review of age-based policies would sometimes benefit older people and other times not. "Programs that unduly favor or disfavor people because they happen to be 'old,'" Achenbaum says, "should be reconsidered, and then either scrapped or reformulated" (p. 171).

The cry of ageism can play on our guilt about our negative feelings toward aging. Achenbaum asks us to use a rational basis for deciding how we treat all people.

Do you agree with Achenbaum's view? Do older people deserve discounts? Or should people get discounts only if they can show they are needy?

funded under this grant developed competencies and guidelines for generalist social workers and specialists in geriatrics. Schools of social work will have the option of adopting and implementing these guidelines (Greene & Galambos, 2002).

The Alliance for Aging Research (2010) reports that fewer than 10% of medical schools require unique course work or a rotation in geriatrics. Fewer than 3% of medical school graduates have taken elective courses in geriatrics. Only 9,000 geriatric specialists practice in the United States, and this number could fall to 6,000 as a result of retirements and declines in recertification. This will take place as the older population doubles in the next 20 years.

The International Longevity Center (2006, p. 70) sums up the problem that older people face: "Physicians and other health care providers, including nurses and social workers, are not adequately trained to understand the specific conditions of old age, so that high-quality affordable care has not been available by well-trained health care providers in the field of geriatrics."

Those who work directly with frail older people (e.g., nurses' aides) may have less factual knowledge about aging than supervisors and administrators (e.g., registered nurses). Direct-care workers often get the least gerontology education. Their heavy workloads and low pay make continuing education more difficult. They rarely have professional development funds they can use for courses or conferences. In-service gerontology programs for these workers can increase their knowledge and give them a more balanced view of their patients.

The Alliance for Aging Research (2010) calls for the "restoration and expansion of federal funding for Title VII programs including Geriatric Education Centers, Geriatric Health Professions Training and Geriatric Career Awards." The Alliance predicts that the lack of training "will have a tremendous impact on the quality of care older adults receive."

Studies show that fact-based programs alone will not change ageist stereotypes (Stuart-Hamilton & Mahoney, 2003). A study of medical school students (MacKnight & Powell, 2001), for example, found that home visits had little positive effect on attitudes toward older people. And on some measures the students showed a less positive attitude toward aging. Students in the health sciences who see only ill and institutionalized older people may have a negative attitude toward aging at the end of their studies.

A study of college students (Ragan & Bowen, 2001) found that only groups that got reinforcement for their knowledge showed a change in attitude after 1 month. Gerontology curricula for health professionals need to balance a problems focus with information about successful aging. Health care workers such as doctors, nurses, and physiotherapists especially need to learn about successful aging. They need to understand the possibilities for wellness and growth in their patients.

Intergenerational Programs

Research by Becca Levy and her colleagues at the Yale School of Public Health (Levy, Slade, Kunkel, & Kasl, 2002; also Hess, Auman, Colcombe, & Rahhal, 2003) report that Americans develop stereotypes of aging in childhood. Society reinforces these stereotypes throughout life. People then enter later life with the same prejudices toward older people as others in the population. These stereotypes can lead to decreased mental ability and poor cardiovascular responses to stress, and they can even shorten life. On the other hand, one study showed that people who hold positive views of aging lived an average of 7.5 years longer than people who held negative views.

Studies show that social contact between older and younger people can reduce stereotyping. My first contact with older people outside my family, for example, led to my career in gerontology. In 1973, a colleague asked me to speak to a group of older people in a university-sponsored discussion group. I decided to speak on school reform (my main interest at that time).

Thinking I would shock the group with a criticism of traditional schooling, I told them about open

zumawireworldphotosthree033315/Newscom

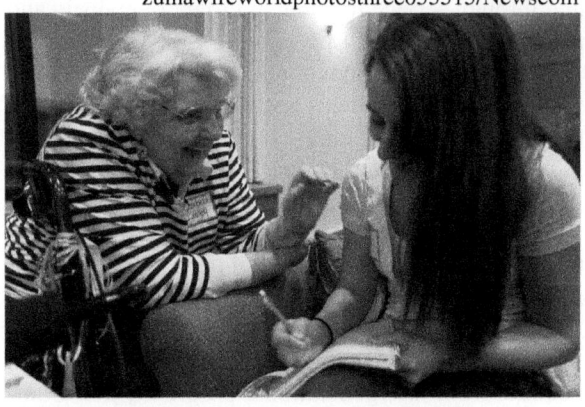

"Elizabeth Lasley, 85, tells a story to Sherri Dahl, 21. Sherri's creative writing class finds their inspiration from a group of seniors who live down the street."

classroom structures, new concepts of learning, and the new role of the teacher as facilitator. After I finished, the group looked at me in silence. Then one woman said, "You know, I was the principal at Pine Ridge Elementary School until two years ago when I retired. I brought in most of the changes you've just told us about." She then told me how she put these innovative programs in place. Other group members also had taught in the public schools until they retired. They spoke about the administrative and day-to-day problems that new programs posed for teachers.

I left the room stunned. These people had calmly shattered my stereotype of old age. They knew as much as I did about my topic. They were articulate and had a great sense of humor. They had just taken me through one of the most enjoyable seminars I had ever led. I resolved to learn more about older people and spend more time with them. This seminar launched me into the next 30 years of my career.

My own experience convinces me that contact between older and younger people can remove ageist stereotypes. But contact alone does not guarantee more knowledge about older people or less bias against them. Studies of education programs show that positive attitudes arise from balanced contact and guided reflection.

Knapp and Stubblefield (2000) asked students in a psychology of aging course to work with older people in the community. The students also interacted with fellow classmates age 55 and over. Students kept a journal and discussed their experiences in class. The researchers compared these students with a control group in a criminal justice course. The researchers concluded that interaction with older people in class and through service learning led to more realistic and positive views of older people.

Roth (2005) describes a volunteer program for university students. Students spent time interacting with residents of a nearby long-term care facility. The program asked students to learn about the residents' views of life. Students wrote weekly reports that reflected on their experience. The researchers conclude that the students developed a more positive view of frailty and later life.

A study of Experience Corps volunteers, who work with children in schools, found that older people gain benefits from intergenerational programs, too. Compared to nonvolunteers, volunteers took part in more social interaction, read more books, and watched less television. Other studies show that older people who volunteer with children burn more calories and do better on memory tests (Rebok et al., 2004).

A program in Salem, Oregon, paired chronically truant teenagers with homebound seniors in a friendly visiting program. The students visited the seniors 1 day a week. Butts and Lent (2009, p. 154) say that many of the seniors would get dressed up and open their curtains only on the day that their visitors arrived. Likewise, the teachers could count on these students to attend school on their visiting day. "They both had to be there for each other. They knew they were needed."

These programs show the value of interaction between the generations. "One antidote to ageism," Butler (1993, p. 77) says, "is knowledge, the primary intervention." He reports that knowledge and satisfying contact with older people lead to a more positive view of aging. Butts and Lent (2009, p. 153) say that "thoughtfully planned intergenerational programs that engage the generations in a purposeful way with clear goals have positive outcomes."

Legislation and Social Action

Education can help reduce ageism. But discrimination can also be fought directly through legislation. Past success includes passage of the Age Discrimination in Employment Act of 1967 and the Age Discrimination Act of 1975. Under the 1967 Employment Act (amended in 1974 and 1978), an employer cannot fire someone because of age, cannot refuse to hire someone because of age, and cannot discriminate in pay because of age.

This kind of legislation, like other kinds of antidiscriminatory legislation, will not end discriminatory acts. Nevertheless, antidiscrimination laws clearly state society's values and the intent to allow workers to stay at work if they choose.

An end to ageism, prejudice, and discrimination will require all of the strategies proposed here: education, balanced contact, and social action. It will require that we develop a society that judges people by who they are and what they can do, rather than by their ages. The seeds of this kind of society may already exist. Some years ago, Sharon Curtin (1972, p. 50) said, "Almost everyone has someone they know, they love, who is also old. But they regard these loved ones as rather special cases. They may be the rule rather than the exception."

CONCLUSION

Ageism can lead to stereotyping, prejudice, and discrimination against older people. It can lead us to misjudge them, to treat them inappropriately, and to assume that they have less ability than they do. Alex Comfort writes:

> We can't take the pain out of the facts that humans aren't immortal or indefinitely disease-proof, or that illnesses accumulate as we age. We can, however, wholly abolish the mischievous idea that after a fixed age we become different, impaired or nonpeople. The start of this demystification has to be in our own rejection of it for ourselves, and then in our refusal to impose it on others. (1976, pp. 32–33)

Novelist and travel writer Paul Theroux (2003) says this about aging and old age:

> What all older people know, what had taken me almost sixty years to learn, is that an aged face is misleading. . . . I now knew: the old are not as frail as you think, and they are insulted to be regarded as feeble. They are full of ideas, hidden powers, even sexual energy. Don't be fooled by the thin hair and battered features and skepticism. The older traveler knows it best: in our hearts we are youthful, and we are insulted to be treated as old men and burdens, for we have come to know that the years have made us more powerful and streetwise. Years are not an affliction. Old age is strength enough.

These writers point the way to the future, toward a fuller understanding of age and aging—one that includes the reality of physical change. But one that also includes the potential for wisdom and continued engagement with the world.

George Burns (1896–1996) worked as a comedian into his late 90s. He smoked, drank, and stayed out late. Someone once asked him, "What do your doctors say about all this?" Burns answered, "They don't say anything; they're all dead." George Burns presented a new model of old age: active, purposeful, joyful, and enviable.

Gerontology focuses on older people, but it also asks us to look at ourselves. It asks us to look at our beliefs, values, and actions. Some people want to study aging for the joy of learning something new, but many people have a practical or professional interest in aging. We are all aging, and we have friends, relatives, and neighbors who are now in or will soon enter old age. Alex Comfort gave one of the best reasons for studying aging: self-interest. After all, he said, old age is a minority group nearly all of us will join one day. The more we know about aging, the better our ability to create a good old age for ourselves and the people we love.

SUMMARY

- Gerontology is the systematic study of aging. This chapter explains the benefits of studying aging, the social basis of age stereotyping, and the changes that will lead to new images of aging.
- Robert Butler used the term *ageism* to describe negative attitudes toward aging. New ageism tries to do good by advocating for policies and programs to help older people. But it also supports the stereotype of old age as a time of decline and loss.
- Ageism leads to stereotyping, prejudice, and discrimination against older people.
- The media, advertising, literature, and popular culture are common sources of ageism in our society.
- Ageism results from ignorance about aging and misconceptions about old age. The Facts on Aging Quiz (FAQ) suggests that people with more education have fewer misconceptions about aging.
- Gerontologists gather and teach facts about aging. This creates a better understanding of later life and a better quality of life for people of all ages.
- Ageism in the workplace leads to discrimination against older workers. Legislation attempts to prevent this. But

it still takes place. Older workers often find it hard to reenter the workplace, or they have to take jobs at low pay.
- The promotion of the ageless self rejects the reality of aging. This creates another form of ageism. It promotes ideal of a youthful appearance and an active lifestyle. People who don't fit this ideal can appear as failures.
- Gerontologists suggest that the media, education, intergenerational programs, and legislation can produce a more positive and balanced view of aging.
- The Baby Boom generation will change our image of later life. This group will challenge the stereotype of aging as a time of decline. At the same time, an increase in older people of all ages will lead to acceptance of diversity in later life. This will include acceptance of physical changes that come with age.
- An acceptance of aging as a normal part of life will help end ageism in the future. It may lead to an **age-irrelevant society**. This type of society judges people by who they are and what they contribute, rather than their age.

DISCUSSION QUESTIONS

1. Define *ageism* according to Robert Butler. Explain how it can lead to social and personal problems.
2. Discuss the effects of ageism on older people and propose several strategies to discourage (or end) ageism in our society. How does compassionate stereotyping lead to scapegoating older people?
3. What are some common sources of ageism? Can you list several examples of ageism in your environment?
4. List some common misconceptions about old age today. Did you believe some of these misconceptions yourself, or did you have a more accurate view of aging?
5. How does the "ageless self" lead to ageism? How can we promote a good image of aging without rejecting people who do not conform to a youthful ideal of old age?
6. What industries, besides those listed in this chapter, could target the older market?
7. How can younger people and university or college students increase their social interactions with older people? How would this benefit society?
8. How will the Baby Boomers change our view of aging? Will society and individuals stop denying aging and accept normal changes that come with age?
9. Do you think American society in the future will provide a better opportunity for successful aging?

SUGGESTED READING

Cohen, Gene D. (2000). *Creative Age: Awakening Human Potential in the Second Half of Life*. New York: Avon Books.

This book counteracts the myth of decline in later life. The author refers to historical examples, scientific research, and case studies to support the idea that older people can live creative lives. The book shows that age, experience, and creativity can lead to inner growth and new potential in later life. The book also suggests ways that older people can enhance their creativity in everyday life.

Martz, S. H. (1994). *If I Had My Life to Live Over I Would Pick More Daisies*. Watsonville, CA: Papier Mache.

This is a classic collection of fiction, poetry, and photos on what it means to age as an older woman. It provides insight into the experience of older women from their own perspectives. The book offers a dose of reality to combat the myths that lead to ageism.

Morrow-Howell, N., Hinterlong, J., & Sherraden, M. (Eds.). (2001). *Productive Aging: Concepts and Challenges*. Baltimore, MD: Johns Hopkins University Press.

This collection of essays by well-known gerontologists advances the concept of productive aging. The essays explore the personal, psychological, social, and economic meaning of productive aging in America today. Race, gender, age, and education all influence productive aging. Several of the essays describe programs that provide opportunities for productive aging.

Palmore, E. B., Branch, L. G., & Harris, D. K. (Eds.). (2005). *Encyclopedia of Ageism*. Binghamton, NY: Haworth.

This book takes a comprehensive look at negative attitudes and behaviors toward aging and older people. Topics include elder abuse, inequality, the cost of ageism, and human rights of older people. An understanding and awareness of ageism can lead to better treatment of older people.

Websites to Consult

The Third Age—The Age of Change
www.thirdage.com

A website that focuses on Baby Boomer health, retirement, and lifestyle topics. Think of yourself as an anthropologist studying a newly discovered tribe. This site offers a look at topics of interest to the tribe we call Baby Boomers. This site has a magazine-style format. It tells us about the culture of this new generation of older people—what issues they face (e.g., caregiving to parents) and what keeps them going (e.g., sex in long-term relationships).

National Academy on an Aging Society—Selected Resources
www.agingsociety.org/agingsociety/links/links_ageism.html

This provides a short reference list of articles on aging in the media, age discrimination, and ways to fight ageism.

AARP Magazine
www.aarpmagazine.org

The AARP Magazine is the premier magazine from America's largest association of older people. This website contains human-interest stories, case studies, and information about aging in U.S. society. Articles on technology, relationships, and cooking show the range of interests of older people today. Check back frequently for updates.

THEORIES AND METHODS

I visited Frances Kennedy, 68 years old, in her apartment on a cool autumn afternoon. I had just begun a study of how people make **transitions** in later life. Frances agreed to take part in the study, and I arranged to visit her home. She had lived alone since her youngest son moved out several years ago. I wanted to understand how she had adapted to living by herself.

"Oh, I love it," she said. "At first I had to adjust. For instance, I couldn't understand how the toothpaste spray got on the bathroom mirror now that I lived alone. I had always blamed that on Jimmy, my son. Finally, I had to admit that it must have been at least partly me all along.

"I love the idea that I can leave a chicken leg or a half container of milk in the refrigerator and find it still

there the next day. I can sleep late on Saturdays if I want to, and I can have quiet suppers alone after work.

"I've also developed some tricks to make life interesting. You know, it's not much fun every night coming home and making your own supper. There's no surprise in it. So I found a way to surprise myself. One Sunday a month I prepare a batch of dinners—things like eggplant parmigiana, beef stew, lasagna. Then I put them in containers, seal the lids, and put them in the freezer. I don't label them.

"In the morning, before I go out, I take out two containers and put them on the counter to defrost. When I come home at night I open the containers, pop them in the microwave, and surprise myself with whatever's for dinner.

"I have other ways to make living alone more fun. For instance, I hate to clean house. But there's no one to share the work with now. So I put on a 20- or 25-minute piece of fast music. I have to clean the whole house before the music ends. I've got a whole lot of these games (like putting a label on the window cleaner bottle with the date when I think it will be used up) to make life interesting."

Frances has a creative streak that makes play out of the simplest jobs. Living alone allows her to express this creativity. My afternoon with her showed me why she enjoys living alone. It also gave me insight into why many older women prefer to live on their own.

Research on aging can take many forms. My meeting with Frances took the form of an in-depth interview. I used a few leading questions to guide our discussion, but mostly I wanted her to talk about her life in her own words. The open-ended interview method allowed Frances to reveal her private world to me.

Other research methods help to answer different research questions. And they produce different results. Research methods provide guides on how to collect information, ways to analyze research findings, and ways to report findings so other researchers can verify the results.

Some researchers, for example, use survey methods. They mail questionnaires to hundreds or even thousands of people, then they analyze the results on a computer. Other researchers conduct controlled studies in laboratories. They ask people to take a paper-and-pencil test or they test a person's reaction time. Historical researchers study diaries and letters. Researchers who want to understand a group's culture or everyday life spend many hours doing field research.

No single method can answer all research questions. Gerontologists choose the methods and theories that best suit their research questions. Sociologists define a *theory* as a "conceptual model of some aspect of life" (Online Dictionary, 2004). Theories try to make sense out of a complex reality. They link concepts and ideas into a single pattern. Scientists use theories to develop hypotheses about the way the world works. They then test these hypotheses through their research.

Gerontologists use many theories to guide their research. Some theories apply to individuals and their personal relationships. A gerontologist, for example, might want to understand whom older people turn to for help. The researcher might theorize that older people turn to family members for help before they turn to government services. This theory of social support says that people use informal supports before they turn to formal helpers.

Each theory and method has its limits and its strengths. This chapter looks at (1) theories that guide gerontologists in their research; (2) methods that gerontologists use to gather their data; and (3) future trends in aging research in the United States.

THE STUDY OF AGING IN THE PAST

Historians trace the study of aging to the ancient scriptures of the Far East, the Bible, and the work of Greek philosophers such as Plato and Aristotle. Before the 17th century, authors based their writings on their own experiences. The writings reflected writers' fears and the biases of the time.

In the 17th century, writers began to base their studies on scientific methods and systematic observations. Most of the early researchers who studied aging were trained in the natural sciences and medicine. By the 18th century, scientists began to use mathematical techniques to study aging. Sir Edmund Halley, the discoverer of the comet named after him, created the first table of life expectancy. Benjamin Rush, in 1793, published the first American geriatrics work, *Account of the State of the Body and Mind in Old Age*. This started a modern period in which researchers saw aging as something other than disease. It also marked the start of the medical study of aging.

Quetelet in the mid-19th century proposed a "social physics"—a science that would study human facts and events, express them in numbers, and locate cause-and-effect relationships. Quetelet, for example, collected physical and social data on people of different ages. He studied birth and death rates and looked at how crime and suicide varied by age. His study, *On the Nature of Man and the Development of His Faculties* (1835), described how human strength and weight varied by age. By the late 19th century, the social sciences—sociology and psychology—had also begun to study aging.

Historians credit Elie Metchnikoff of the Pasteur Institute in Paris with the first use of the term *gerontology* in 1905 (Freeman, 1979). Metchnikoff wrote the first gerontology text, *The Problem of Age, Growth, and Death*, in 1908. A short time later, in 1912, the Society of Geriatry—one of the first groups to study aging in North America—was formed in New York. G. Stanley Hall wrote *Senescence, the Last Half of Life* in 1922, one of the first scientific studies of aging in the United States. Hall used survey data to understand religious beliefs and attitudes toward death among older people. He and other writers at this time focused on the problems of old age (Achenbaum, 1987).

GERONTOLOGY RESEARCH TODAY

Research output on aging grew rapidly after World War II. Research on aging in the 1960s moved beyond a study of problems to include studies of normal aging. This included studies of positive developments in later life. Major journals in the United States began to be published after 1946.

Today, dozens of academic journals around the world publish research on aging, and new ones start all the time. Journals such as *The Journals of Gerontology*, *The Gerontologist*, and *The International Journal of Human Development* serve a wide audience. Other journals target specific groups such as nurses, social workers, or recreation professionals. A series of handbooks in biology, psychology, and the social sciences synthesize knowledge on key topics.

A bibliography of sources on aging for the years 1954 to 1974 listed 50,000 entries (Woodruff & Birren, 1975). This list contained more sources than all the writings on aging in the previous 100 years. Today, a complete bibliography would contain many times this number of sources. Computerized bibliographies such as *AGELINE* (a general database) or CINAHL (focused mostly on health-related sources) attempt to keep track of the thousands of sources published on aging each year. A search for even one keyword in a database can turn up hundreds of sources published in the past 20 years.

IS GERONTOLOGY A DISCIPLINE?

The varied approaches that researchers take to aging (biological, psychological, social) raise some questions: Is gerontology a discipline, or is it a subfield within existing disciplines (such as sociology or biology)?

Some years ago the Gerontological Society of America (GSA) sponsored the Foundations Project (Foundations Project, 1980). This project asked experts to reflect on the status of gerontology as a discipline. A *discipline,* the project said, has "a distinct body of knowledge, requiring the establishment of a separate academic unit" (p. 6). A number of leaders in the field of aging at that time thought that gerontology met this criterion. They proposed that universities and colleges develop gerontology departments with their own faculty members and with administrative status.

Few schools, however, have taken this route. Gerontologists almost always belong to traditional disciplines such as sociology, psychology, or biology. In most cases gerontology programs exist within a social science department, although some schools offer an interdisciplinary option that spans more than one field.

The status of gerontology as a discipline rests on whether gerontology has claim to a "distinct body of knowledge." The GSA put this to a test. The GSA asked 111 experts on aging from fields as varied as biomedicine and economics whether gerontology has a distinct body of knowledge (Foundations Project, 1980). The study asked them to define the core and scope of the field. Although the experts differed on the exact content and boundaries of the field, they did agree that three areas made up the core of aging studies: biomedicine, psychosocial studies, and socioeconomic-environmental studies.

Biomedicine studies look at the changes in the body that come with age, including studies of DNA, the cells, the body's systems, stress, and dementia. The experts showed the most agreement on the content of this subfield. This may be due to the long history of biomedical research on aging. Geriatrics, the medical specialty that deals with older people, draws heavily on biomedical knowledge of aging. Geriatricians, physicians who treat older people, also contribute to this body of knowledge through clinical research.

Psychosocial studies look at the changes that take place inside the individual and between individuals and groups. Researchers study memory, creativity, and learning. They also study personality, relationships, and death and dying.

Socioeconomic-environmental studies look at the effects of aging on social institutions. Sociologists define a *social institution* as a pattern of social interaction that has a relatively stable structure and persists over time (Online Dictionary, 2004). Institutions include the economy, the family, and the health care system. Socioeconomic-environmental studies ask, for example, how an aging society will affect the health care system or the economy. These studies also look at the effect of social institutions on aging individuals. For example, how does the U.S. retirement income system (pension plans and retirement policies) affect the experience of aging?

Social gerontology makes up a part of the total body of gerontological knowledge. It includes the psychosocial, socioeconomic-environmental, and practice-related studies of aging. Clark Tibbitts first introduced the idea of social gerontology in 1954.

Social gerontology views aging from the perspective of the individual and the social system. When social gerontologists look at biomedical issues, they focus on the social effects of physical aging. For example, they ask how changes in a person's ability to walk affect that person's needs for social services. Or they ask how physical aging differs by race and ethnicity. Do older African Americans and whites have the same diseases at the same rates and from the same causes? Social gerontologists also look at changes throughout the life course. They study changes in family life, relationships, and activities. Social gerontology has grown in importance in the past 20 years.

THEORIES OF AGING

My grandmother used to keep her eyeglasses pushed up onto her head. I remember one day watching her walk around the house with a puzzled look on her face.

"Grandma," I asked, "what are you looking for?"

"My glasses. I can't find them anywhere."

"They're on your head," I said with a laugh.

"Oh," she said, as she patted her head. "I must be getting old."

In that moment my grandmother expressed a theory of aging: When you get old, you forget things, like where you put your eyeglasses. She didn't think of this as a theory; she didn't know anything about theories. But she had one. When she forgot where she put her glasses, it confirmed her belief that you forget things when you age.

Many psychologists use this same theory in their research. They suspect that memory declines with age, and they have produced volumes of literature to test this theory. In this way researchers differ from my grandmother. They suspect that memory decreases with age, but they try to prove or disprove this idea.

Theories often start with beliefs, commonsense ideas, or hunches. But scientific theories differ from everyday theories in that scientists try to state a theory clearly. A theory may contain formal propositions linked to one another. The theory will also produce testable hypotheses that can guide research. Social scientists then study their research findings to see whether they support, reject, or modify the theory.

Bengtson, Gans, Putney, and Silverstein (2009, p. 5) say, "Theories are like lenses. Look at an object through one kind of lens, and the viewer will see one thing; look at it through another lens, and the viewer will be able to see something different." Theories help

researchers to organize and give focus to their work. For example, you can think of a family in terms of power, authority, and kinship relations. Or you can think of the family as an economic unit related to the larger economy. In each case theory leads to a different description and explanation of family life.

Gerontologists have developed many theories to explain aging. These range from biological theories of why the skin wrinkles to theories of why some societies revere their elders. Some gerontologists borrow theories from sociology and psychology and apply them to the study of aging. For example, psychologists have applied theories of mental function to the study of memory (Dixon, Backman, & Nilsson, 2004). Social psychologists use theories of stress to study the buffering effects of social relations (Antonucci, Birditt, & Akiyama, 2009). Sociologists have applied political economy theory to the study of pensions (Quadagno, 2005).

Gerontologists create theories to help them explain a set of facts. For example, research shows that older people may need housing with more physical and social supports as they age. The theory of person–environment fit, first advanced by Lawton and Nahemow (1973), explains this trend. This theory says that the supports a person needs depend on two things: a person's ability and the demands of the environment. As ability decreases, demand increases, and a person needs more support. This theory interprets the facts and puts them in a framework. It allows researchers to test the relationship between different forces that shape housing needs. It also allows service providers to offer supports that improve an older person's quality of life.

Each theory contains a set of assumptions about people and the world. For example, exchange theory focuses on what people give and get from one another. It helps explain caregivers' service to their spouses or parents. But it has its limits. For example, it says nothing about the impact of modern industrial society on the family, or about state policies that limit home care benefits to older people. Gerontologists use other theories, such as modernization theory or political economy theory, to understand social change and social policy.

Gerontologists differ in the kinds of theories they favor. The choice of a theory depends on a researcher's training, the subject under study, and even personal preference. The study of gerontological theories shows the scope of gerontological research and the ways that gerontologists think about aging.

TWO LEVELS OF THEORIES

Social gerontologists use theories to explain everything from child–parent relations to the treatment of older people by the government. The following discussion arranges some of the major theories in a framework and gives examples of how gerontologists have applied them in their work. Gerontologists use at least two types of theory: micro-level theories and macro-level theories.

Micro-level theories describe people and their relationships. They focus on small-scale events such as interactions between staff and patients in a nursing home, changes in personality with age, and choice of leisure activities. These theories encompass studies of how individuals change as they age. They include the study of memory and intelligence, as well as the study of adjustments to retirement or widowhood.

Macro-level theories look at social institutions (such as the family), social systems (such as health care or housing), and whole societies. These theories examine the way that social institutions shape experiences and behavior. These theories focus on large-scale events such as historical changes in family size and structure, health care policies, and how industrial or agricultural societies treat their older people.

Modernization theory serves as an example of a macro-level theory.

THREE THEORETICAL PERSPECTIVES

Micro-level and macro-level theories look at different phenomena. Taken together, they show the scope of gerontological study. Researchers can choose from three major theoretical perspectives within these two levels of study: the interpretive perspective, the functionalist perspective, and the conflict perspective.

Interpretive Perspective

The interpretive perspective most often focuses on the micro-level of social life. It looks at how people relate to one another, how they define situations, and how they create social order. Theories within this perspective include social constructionism, social exchange theory (Homans, 1961), the symbolic-interactionist perspective, social phenomenology, and ethnomethodology (Garfinkel, 1967), as well as an even earlier tradition pioneered by Max Weber (1905/1955). A relatively small number of gerontologists have used this perspective.

BOX 1
THEORIES OF AGING

Levels of Theory

Micro	*Macro*	
(individual social interaction)	(social structures, social processes)	

Theoretical Perspectives

Interpretive	*Functionalist*	*Conflict*
(how individuals define and create social world)	(social order based on cooperation and consensus)	(society based on conflict between social groups)

Theories

Social constructionism	Structural functionalism	Political economy
Symbolic interactionism	Modernization	Moral economy
Social phenomenology	Disengagement	Feminist theories
Ethnomethodology	Continuity	
Social exchange	Activity	
	Age stratification	
	Life course	

This chart presents the most influential theories in the study of aging. It summarizes the discussion in the text.

Source: Aging and Society, A Canadian Perspective, Fifth Edition by NOVAK/CAMPBELL. © 2006. Reprinted with permission of Nelson, a division of Thomson Learning: www.thomsonrights.com. Fax 800-730-2215.

Symbolic interaction, based on the work of George Herbert Mead (1934), and social phenomenology, based on the work of Alfred Schutz (1967), fit this perspective. Symbolic interactionists study how symbols such as clothing, body language, and written words shape social relations. For example, an older man in a derby hat with a pipe and an umbrella gives one impression. A young woman in jeans and a bustier and with platinum-colored hair gives another. We would address each of these people differently and make different assumptions about their backgrounds and interests. People learn to read and respond to the symbols around them.

Social phenomenologists take a more extreme view. They speak of "the social construction of reality" (Berger & Luckmann, 1967). They view social order as a creation of everyday interaction (Longino & Powell, 2009). Social phenomenologists often look at conversation to find the methods people use to maintain social relations. For example, if I ask, "How are you?" you understand that I don't want to hear about your athlete's foot. You answer, "Fine." We smile and move on.

A doctor who asks this same question wants to know about your health. You give a different answer to this question in a doctor's office. If you answer, "Fine," the doctor may probe and ask some very personal questions. You will play along and assume that this is part of the doctor's job. A social phenomenologist studies the way that a doctor's conversation builds and creates a social reality that we call "the medical exam."

The interactionist perspective sees the person as an actor and a creator of social life. People do more than live in social groups and organizations. They play a part in creating and maintaining them. They do this every day and in every interaction. People negotiate who goes through a door first, who sits where at the dinner table, and what kind of clothes to wear to a job interview. All of these actions have meaning, and people learn to read and interpret these meanings. People also take these actions for granted and rarely notice their impact.

Symbols come loaded with meaning. I once asked a graphic designer to create a brochure for a gerontology program that I planned to offer. I explained that I would send the brochure to health care professionals. The designer came back with a brochure that had an abstract image on it. The image looked like a bent and crooked figure leaning on a cane. This image reflected the designer's idea of aging. It presented an image that he felt the public shared. I could have used this brochure cover in the program, but only as a case study in ageism.

Gray hair, wrinkles, a walker—all symbolize aging. Symbols or images can have a strong influence on us. The wheelchair symbolizes sickness, weakness, and dependence. Wheelchair designers have worked to change this image. Some wheelchairs now have angled wheels, high-performance tires, and special seats for athletic use. Some physically challenged older people prefer indoor scooters to wheelchairs.

One older woman I know, who owned a wheelchair, says that her scooter changed her self-image. She felt helpless and stigmatized in her wheelchair. She now rides around her local shopping mall with confidence and self-esteem. Why does the image of a scooter differ from that of a wheelchair? The wheelchair symbolizes illness. The scooter symbolizes freedom and an active lifestyle. People attach different meanings to each. Sociologist W. I. Thomas summed this up in what sociologists call the **Thomas theorem**: "If people define situations as real, they are real in their consequences" (Thomas & Thomas, 1928, p. 572).

The interpretive perspective can give a good understanding of how people interpret their social world, how they interact with one another, and why they do what they do. Studies that focus on language, for example, "can 'give voice' to people as individual informants" (Coupland, 2009, p. 851). For example, a report on conversations with people who live in retirement communities shows how these people understand their own condition (Norrick, 2009). Interviews with older Japanese women (Matsumoto, 2009) and a study of the self-expression of poor older women in Detroit (Onolemhemhen, 2009) give insight into these people's social world. Gerontologists have used this approach to study how people adapt to retirement, loss of a spouse, and changes in health (Koch, 2000).

Schaefer (2010) studied the experience of older adult students who attended college classes. The students' children had grown up and they no longer needed to spend time on childrearing. This allowed them to return to school. Schaefer conducted in-depth interviews and used reflective questionnaires with nine of these students ages 50 to 62. She felt that higher education institutions do not necessarily meet the needs of older learners, so she set out to understand these students' experiences in college. She wanted to understand what was "personally meaningful" to them.

This study explored students' past education experiences and their future goals, what brought them to higher education, and what supports they found useful in their program. Schaefer locates her study within the tradition of social phenomenology. This allows her to understand what is "real and meaningful" in the minds of these students.

Schaefer found that the Baby Boomers in her study attended school to develop their careers (rather than for personal enrichment); they were first-generation students who needed a better understanding of the higher education process; and they had complex support needs. Schaefer reports the students' experiences in their own words.

One student said, in explaining her return to school, "I think I went through a big, serious empty nest problem there. It was just this loss—what do I do now? The being isolated, children were gone, and what am I here on earth [for]—what is my purpose anymore?" (p. 77).

Another student expressed emotions related to her role as homemaker. "I felt so isolated," she said. "I think that's primarily what it was. I felt so isolated at home day in, day out taking care of children, taking care of the home, and not getting out in the real world because, you know he wouldn't let me work either outside the home."

These students discovered a new role for themselves through a return to school. School helped them deal with existential crises. It helped them develop a new sense of self. Schaefer also discovered that the students faced unique challenges. One student said, "This was walking through a whole new door I hadn't been to in years, and things had changed considerably. There was a lot of confusion of what I needed to do to start, the fear of getting started."

These expressions of doubt and uncertainty give a rich understanding of these students' lives as they enter the institution. The interpretive perspective allows us to see and understand the world from the student's point of view. This type of study provides rich information for students of life transitions. Administrators of higher education can use these insights to create more responsive programs for older learners.

Kaufman (1993) used an interactionist theory to guide her study of stroke patients because she thought "the voices of individual old people were deemphasized or lost in the conduct of . . . [scientific] research" (p. 13). She wanted to explore the meaning older people gave to their lives. She found that stroke patients experience a sharp break with past life patterns. She also found that people try to maintain continuity in their lives. They interpret the past and link it to the present. Kaufman determined that stroke patients worked hard to build links from their past to their fu-

ture. People who completed this task recovered, even if they still had physical disability. Stroke patients needed to show that they were the same people after their illness as before.

Kaufman (1993) places her work within a phenomenological framework. "Phenomenology," she says, "attends to the reality of experience" (p. 15). It studies a phenomenon—sickness, rehabilitation, health—from the subject's point of view. This type of research requires a close collaboration between the researcher and the subject. The subject's story and the way the subject comes to create that story become the research finding. This approach to research opens the researcher to the world of the subject. The researcher in a well-crafted study learns to see the world through the eyes of the subject and to understand the meaning the subject gives to the world.

Gubrium points to a growing interest in the interpretive perspective. He reports a "decided surge of interest in the place of personal meaning, the unstandardized, and the emergent in everyday life" (Gubrium, 1993, p. 60; Gubrium & Holstein, 1999). But Gubrium cautions against romanticizing this experience. The interactionist perspective, he says, must include an awareness of culture and history. This allows the researcher to see how people create and maintain the meaning of old age in a specific social setting.

Critique of the Interpretive Perspective

Like every perspective, the interactionist perspective gives only one view of social life. Critics of this perspective say, first, that it overlooks the links between the individual and larger social institutions. For example, an interactionist view of older students' self-understanding misses the impact of the school bureaucracy—paperwork, deadlines, fees—on students' lives. It also misses the effects of hospital bureaucracy on stroke patients.

Second, the interactionist perspective does not look at the impact of social policies on people or groups. For example, policies may restrict the number of courses students can take. This can affect the older student's ability to move through the curriculum. Policies can also affect the kinds of rehabilitation services that a stroke patient receives.

Third, the interactionist perspective does not discuss power and conflict between social groups. The interactionist perspective would not, for example, study the effects of race on educational opportunity for older students in America. Likewise, stroke patient

---

BOX 2
A QUESTION OF METHOD
Self-Portrait of Rembrandt van Rijn

Rembrandt van Rijn (1606–1669) began painting self-portraits in the 1620s. He completed his last self-portrait the year of his death, 1669. Here we see him in late middle age. In all, he painted more than 90 self-portraits. Experts have called his self-portraits a "visual diary." They stand as one of the great achievements in the history of Western art.

Does Rembrandt's self-portrait count as a "research study" of aging? If not, why not? If so, why do you consider it a research study? How does it differ from studies done by social scientists? What do artists discover through their "research"? What can an artist's work teach us about aging?

Peter Horree/Alamy

---

ethnicity and social class influences the treatment they receive. The functionalist and conflict perspectives focus on these issues.

Functionalist Perspective

The functionalist perspective includes structural-functionalist theory (or *functionalism*) in sociology. Emile Durkheim promoted this theory in the 19th century in *The Division of Labor in Society* (1893). Talcott Parsons developed this theory further in *The Social System* (1951). Functionalism views society as a system made up of many parts. These include religion, the family, education, and politics. Changes to one part of the system lead to changes in the whole system.

Functionalism sees society as an organism that tries to stay in equilibrium. Biologists refer to this as *homeostasis*. Society regulates itself in the same way your body keeps a steady temperature. When you exercise, you overheat your body. Sweat cools you down. A change in one part of the system brings into play mechanisms that reestablish order.

An increase in the number of older people in society, for example, leads to more government money directed to programs for the elderly. More support to

older people can create a dysfunction (e.g., a fear that too little money exists for other age groups). This may lead to political backlash and reduced support. The system tries to stay in balance through changes in policies and programs.

Functionalism can explain large-scale political change as well as the way small groups maintain their structure. Functionalism says that norms (shared rules of behavior) and roles (expectations for behavior in a certain social status) shape behavior. People learn these norms and learn to play social roles as they grow older. People conform to these norms through social pressure, but also through belief in society's underlying value system. The values expressed in the commandment "Honor thy father and mother" show up in everyday behavior and in social policies. Failure to honor a parent may lead to informal sanctions, such as criticism from a sister or brother. Extreme neglect may lead to the charge of abuse and legal sanctions.

Informal and formal sanctions create a smooth-running society. People know what to do and what others expect of them. Functionalism focuses on consensus and social order. It assumes that society changes or evolves in a positive direction. It explains social problems as dysfunctions, and it proposes to correct these dysfunctions through the use of experts in planning and the helping professions.

Historically, gerontologists used the functionalist perspective more than any other perspective in their study of aging. Gerontology's most influential early theories are disengagement theory (Cumming & Henry, 1961), activity theory (Neugarten, Havighurst, & Tobin, 1968), and modernization theory (Cowgill & Holmes, 1972). All three rely on structural-functionalist assumptions. Riley and colleagues (Riley, 1987; Riley, Foner, & Waring, 1988) also produced a dominant theory based on structural-functionalist principles: age stratification theory.

Age Stratification Theory: An Example of the Functionalist Perspective

Age stratification theory, or its more recent identification as the "aging and society paradigm" (Riley, Foner, & Riley, 1999), links individual aging to social institutions. The theory discusses individual aging, societal aging, and **cohort flow** (Riley et al., 1988). Age stratification theory describes a "dynamic interplay between two interdependent processes: individual aging and social change" (Riley, 1985, p. 371).

Individual Aging

Age stratification theory views aging as a lifelong process. People experience biological changes with age. They also experience changes in roles and social positions. Each society sets out a series of roles that people enter and leave as they age. These include the role of child, student, spouse, parent, worker, retiree, and grandparent. These roles and the norms that go with them change over time. Many older people, for example, learned that a person should not have sex outside of marriage. Some of these people now find themselves widowed. If they want to have an active sex life without marrying again, they will have to rethink their childhood beliefs about marriage, sex, and old age. This can lead to a broader change in social values and behavior. In this way individuals and cohorts can create social change.

Societal Change

Every society has a set of age grades that stratifies its members. Societies attach certain rights and responsibilities to each age grade. Age grades in the United States include childhood, adolescence, young adulthood, middle age, and old age. These age grades may change over time. Today, for example, gerontologists speak of the Third Age (young retirees) and the Fourth Age (the very old). More people now live in the Third and Fourth age grades than ever before.

The U.S. Census Bureau often divides statistics on older people into two or more groups (e.g., ages 65 to 74, 75 to 84, and 85 and over). This division recognizes that people move through different stages in later life (e.g., many people have to cope with increased frailty after age 85). Gerontologists can learn about a society by studying its age stratification system.

Cohort flow describes the dynamics of the age stratification system. People belong to an **age cohort**, a group of people born at about the same time. People born between 1950 and 1959, for example, form an age cohort. Age cohorts move through society's age grade system together. They go through the same age grades and transitions at about the same time.

People in their 80s today experienced the end of World War II in their early adult years. Many of them married just after the war, and they produced the Baby Boom generation. These people share memories of the postwar years as young parents. They also share the memory of the Big Band era, the first television shows, and early commercial air travel.

The Baby Boom generation will remember some of these events, but they may recall more about the first cartoon shows than anything else on television. The Baby Boomers will recall little of the McCarthy hearings or Dwight Eisenhower's presidency in the 1950s. Historical events affect each cohort, but each cohort experiences these events differently because they go through the event at a different time in the life cycle.

Each age cohort moves through life as if on an escalator. One group leaves an age grade, and the next group enters it. Each age grade places expectations on its members and offers members new roles to play. At the same time, each cohort brings into an age grade a new set of norms and values that lead to changes in social life.

New cohorts and historical events can lead to changes in the age grade system itself. For example, each generation brings into later life unique shared experiences. World War II shaped the worldview of my father's generation. The Viet Nam war and Woodstock shape Baby Boomers' thinking, philosophy, and worldview today. Elder (1999, p. 15) says that "individuals are thought to acquire a distinct outlook and philosophy from the historical world, defined by their birth date, an outlook that reflects lives lived interdependently in a particular historical context."

Older people today as a group enter old age with more income than older people in the past. The Social Security system, corporate pension plans, and good nutrition allow them to live more active lifestyles and to engage in new activities. The current generation of older people has begun to change our notion of old age. They travel, take courses, and exercise. These new seniors have given rise to new education programs, new travel options, and new products that cater to their needs. Gerontologists now speak of the young-old (age 65 to 74), the old-old (age 75 to 84), and the oldest-old (age 85 and over) because the single age grade "old age" has lost its meaning.

Age stratification theory relies on many of the assumptions of the structural-functionalist approach to aging. First, it assumes that norms and values influence individual aging. Second, it describes the relationship between the individual and society as a feedback loop. Change begins with the individual cohort or with large-scale historical or social change. These changes then lead to change in other parts of the social system. Third, the theory tends to see society as a homogeneous set of structures and functions that all people in a cohort experience in the same way.

Age stratification theory has a number of strengths. First, it has helped to separate age differences (between cohorts) from age changes over the life course (aging). Second, it highlights the impact of historical and social changes on individuals and cohorts. Third, it highlights the relationship between aging and social structures. Bengtson, Burgess, and Parott (1997, p. S82) say that age stratification theory "provides new ways to explore differences related to time, period, and cohort."

Critique of the Functionalist Perspective

Criticisms of age stratification theory show the limits of the functionalist perspective. First, age stratification theory tends to see society as a homogeneous set of structures and functions that all people in an age cohort experience the same way. This approach focuses on the differences between cohorts, but misses the diversity within them. For example, people in the same cohort differ by gender, race, and ethnicity.

Age stratification theory puts little focus on how gender, social class, race, and ethnicity create inequalities within age cohorts. For example, it says little about the differences between growing old as a lower-class woman and growing old as a middle-class man. Income differences within a cohort may have a greater influence on a person's life than the norms and values related to his or her age grade.

A person's race or gender leads to different behaviors and to different responses to sociohistorical events. A person's race or gender also determines the choices available as the person ages. For example, compared to a poor older woman, a wealthy older man will have more opportunity to invest in an Individual Retirement Account (IRA). This will increase the gap in income between these two people.

A second criticism is that the age stratification theory overlooks the person's interpretation of the social world. It emphasizes the impact of society and history on the individual but says little about how the individual makes sense of these conditions and responds to them. People in the same age cohort interpret the world and respond to events in unique ways. A war may turn one person into a patriot and another into a pacifist. An elderly Chinese woman who has just arrived in California from Hong Kong will see the world differently from a retired New England farmer. Age stratification theory overlooks how each of these people interpret the world. It makes little reference to individual control or action.

Third, functionalist theories have a conservative bias. Functionalism sees equilibrium and social order as preferred social conditions. Age stratification theory, for example, focuses on cohorts, norms, and social order, but it fails to account for conflicts and tensions between social groups in society or for issues of power. These conflicts often shape a person's life. Race, gender, social class, and ethnicity create unequal access to a good life in society. Older African Americans today, for example, have poorer health than whites. Racial inequality may explain more about African Americans' life changes than do the norms and values of their age cohort.

Functionalist theories, like the age stratification theory, have their shortcomings. Still, they order the complex changes that take place over the life course.

The *life course approach*, also a functionalist approach, bridges both the micro-level and macro-levels of analysis. It incorporates social interaction and social structure within its framework (Settersten, 2006). Idler (2006, p. 283) says the life course perspective "focuses on timing, sequencing, and duration of roles or periods" of life.

Elder and Johnson (2003) describe five principles of the life course perspective:

1. Human development and aging take place throughout life.
2. History and location shape an individual's life.
3. Life transitions and events vary depending on when they take place in a person's life.

4. Individuals are linked to others and live interdependently.
5. Individuals give shape to their lives by taking action and making choices.

Researchers use the life course approach to explain (1) the changes that take place in an individual over time, (2) age-related and socially recognized life transitions, and (3) the interaction of social life, history, culture, and personal biography (Moen & Spencer, 2006; Settersten, 2006). At the micro-level or individual level, the life course approach looks at how events and conditions early in life affect later life.

Zarit (2009) gives the example of how earlier experiences affect mental disorder in later life. Major depressive disorder (MDD) shows up in about 1% to 5% of older people. But research shows that usually this problem started earlier in a person's life. Rarely does MDD show up for the first time in old age. New cases, Zarit says, steadily decline after age 30 (with a slight increase after age 75). Anxiety disorders show the same pattern. Most people face this disorder first in adolescence or young adulthood. These mental disorders form a lifelong pattern of disturbance.

At the macro-level or societal level, the life course approach shows how social change and historical events can create differences between cohorts (Elder, 2000). For example, teenagers and adults in New Orleans will feel different effects from the damage caused by hurricane Katrina. The hurricane caused some university students to drop out of school. This may influence their earning power for many years to come. Older adults experienced a different kind of loss. They lost homes and businesses that they may never have time or resources to replace. The life course approach studies the impact of macro-level events on individual lives.

The life course approach overcomes some of the limitations of age stratification theory. It recognizes variety in life course patterns and differences between age cohorts. It also recognizes differences within age cohorts due to differences in race, ethnicity, social class, and gender. This approach takes into account the diversity of roles and role changes across the life course. It recognizes aging as a lifelong, dynamic, interactive, and multidirectional process. For example, an older woman may maintain good relations with her children, she may have trouble walking up stairs, but she may take up a new hobby such as painting. Aging involves stability in some areas of life, decline in others, and improvement in others.

The life course approach looks at transitions and trajectories. Transitions refer to changes in social status or social roles (in particular, when transitions occur, how long they last, how people get through the transitions). Transitions include marriage, divorce, remarriage, widowhood, and parenthood. Work-related transitions also occur—for example, getting a first job or retiring.

Trajectories refer to long-term patterns of stability and change. They may include many transitions. One marital status trajectory may involve the transition to marriage, a subsequent divorce, then a remarriage, and finally a transition to widowhood. Another marital status trajectory may involve only one marriage for life. This involves only the transition to a first marriage and, for one of the couple, the transition to widowhood. The life course approach has made a number of contributions to the study of aging.

First, it bridges the macro-level and the micro-level of analysis by recognizing the importance of social structures and historical context, as well as individual experiences and meanings. It helps us understand the diversity within and between cohorts.

Second, the approach brings together sociological, psychological, anthropological, and historical approaches to the study of aging.

Third, the life course approach understands aging as a dynamic process that takes place throughout life.

The life course approach in particular appreciates the link between earlier stages of adulthood and later life. Research on topics such as diet, health and illness, family life, and work all show the impact of earlier life conditions on later life. For example, women more often than men show a broken work history. This leads to lower incomes for women in midlife, but also poorer pensions and lower incomes in old age. Likewise, a divorce or the decision to stay single may lead to fewer family supports in later life. Even conditions such as poor nutrition in childhood have an impact on old age.

This approach has some limitations. It puts the greatest emphasis on social structures and on individual responses to those structures. It focuses less on how individuals or cohorts create social change. Like most functionalist theories, it puts the greatest emphasis on social stability. Also, its broad focus on society, history, culture, and the individual makes it hard to define as a single theory.

Some researchers say that no unified, systematic approach to the life course exists. Rather, the life course approach merges theoretical approaches from many disciplines, including sociology and psychology (Settersten, 2006). Bengtson and colleagues (1997, p. S80) say, "It is very difficult to incorporate into a single analysis the many contextual variables . . . that this approach identifies." Still, the life course approach encourages us to think about the many individual and social forces that affect aging.

Conflict Perspective

Conflict theory looks at the tensions that exist between groups in society. It grows out of the work of Karl Marx (1867–1895/1967), who viewed society as a struggle between social classes. Conflict theorists look at the ways socially powerful groups or the government (as a tool of these groups) shapes the lives of others. Few gerontologists have used the conflict perspective in their work. Those who do often look at how the economy or state policies influence old age.

In the early 20th century, for example, new machines demanded faster work. Older workers faced greater stresses than ever before. They often found it hard to keep up with the pace of the new machines. Many companies at this time replaced slower older workers with younger workers. The conflict perspective views these social tensions as part of a class struggle. The owners of factories exploited workers to increase their profits. Older people became victims of the system.

Gerontologists also make use of *political economy theory*, a type of conflict theory that looks at the state, the economy, social class, and their impact on people. The political economy approach traces the origins of older people's problems to the political and economic structure of capitalist society (Kail, Quadagno, & Keene, 2009). It looks at how the market economy and public policies produce inequality. The economic order and social programs and policies for older people can reinforce class, gender, and racial inequalities in later life. The political economy of aging framework sees old age as a social construction that mirrors the unequal distribution of resources in youth and middle age.

Cumulative disadvantage theory (a type of conflict theory) focuses on the lifelong effects of inequality. This theory says that disadvantages earlier in life accumulate and are magnified over the life course. "Thus, the more disadvantages individuals experience, the more likely they are to accrue subsequent and greater disadvantages" (Kail et al., 2009, p. 557)

For example, compared with men, women in their younger years are more likely to earn less income, work part time, or have disrupted work histories due to child care or care for other family members. Public and private pension programs tend to reward those with higher incomes and stable work histories. This means that, compared with older men, older women find themselves with fewer pension benefits and less savings.

Researchers have begun to study the causes of poverty in later life, women and gender discrimination, the ideology of aging as a social problem, and pensions and policies. Gerontologists have looked at the impact of retirement and pensions on the quality of life in old age (Moen & Spencer, 2006), the social structures that influence retirement for women (Zimmerman, Mitchell, Wister, & Gutman, 2000), and social policy in an aging society (Hudson, 2004).

Early work by Estes (1979) took a political economy approach to the study of welfare programs in the United States. She found that these programs tended to stigmatize older people. They defined the needs of older people as a need for services. This justified the expansion of the social service bureaucracy. Within the social welfare system, older people have little control over the services they can get or the ones they receive. Control lies in the hands of middle-class service workers. These workers define the older person's needs (e.g., for homemaker services or Meals on Wheels) and dole out services based on their assessment. Estes concluded that those who run the welfare state gain more than those served by it.

Estes's work shows the strength of the political economy approach. First, it places the study of aging in the context of large political, historical, economic, and social forces. Second, it views public pensions and income in later life as the outcome of a struggle between competing groups. Third, it predicts that economic and political forces will shape future changes in public pensions.

The political economy approach emphasizes the impact of history and economics on individuals. It shows how the state and social policies can increase or decrease social inequalities. But the political economy approach tends to overemphasize the poverty and problems older people face. It also tends to view the individual as the product of political and economic forces. It pays little attention to individuals' interpretations of social life. It says little about the ways that individuals shape their world through interactions with others. As Bengtson and colleagues (1997, p. S83) say, this perspective too often "paints a picture of all elders as powerless, forced to exist under oppressive structural arrangements with no control over their own lives."

Within the conflict perspective, *feminist theories* bridge both the micro-level and macro-level of analysis. They recognize the importance of social interaction and social structure in the study of aging. Feminist theories hold that society is gendered by nature. Feminist social gerontologists believe that gender defines social interaction and life experiences, including the experience of aging.

A feminist approach recognizes gender as a social organizing principle, not just a category on a census form (Calasanti & Slevin, 2006). Furthermore, within a patriarchal system (such as North American society), gender-based inequalities are created and perpetuated (for example, through pay inequality in the workplace). This results in social advantages for men (for instance, higher wages and better pensions) and disadvantages for women (higher rates of poverty in old age).

Feminist gerontologists criticize other theories of aging and other gerontologists for not focusing enough on gender relations or on older women's experiences (Calasanti, 2009; Allen & Walker, 2009). Feminist scholars also criticize the positivist assumption that social scientists stand outside the social world they study. Feminist theory and research includes a commitment to social change. Quadagno and Reid (1999, p. 344) say that "the challenge for social gerontology is not simply to understand how people interpret their private troubles but rather to consider also how these private troubles become public issues, thereby generating a societal response."

Feminist research in aging has focused on many unique issues: sexual relations in later life (Connidis, 2006), "double-duty care" by female health professionals who care for older parents (Ward-Griffin et al., 2005), the health of older men (Calasanti, 2004a), and identity and the aging body (Slevin, 2006).

Feminist theories make an important contribution to the study of aging. First, feminist theories, like the life course approach, recognize the importance of social structure, social interaction, and individual characteristics (primarily gender, but also race, ethnicity, and social class). Second, feminist theories present a more inclusive picture of aging and older adults, by focusing on the majority of the older population—women—and on issues that are relevant to women's lives. Third, feminist theories of aging challenge the traditional focus on men in research and the ageist biases in mainstream feminist theories that ignore

issues of age (Calasanti, 2004b; Calasanti & Slevin, 2006). Fourth, feminist theories challenge political economy studies that focus on the labor market and inequality related to work. These studies continue to devalue caregiving for children, spouses, and parents.

There are some limitations to feminist theories. For example, some gerontologists see gender as too narrow a focus for the study of aging. They say that feminist theories attempt to feminize the study of aging and that they ignore the experiences important to older men (Calasanti, 2004a). Critics also say that feminist theories dwell too much on social problems. They overlook the positive experience many women have in later life and women's contributions to society. Still, feminist theories of aging contribute to our understanding of aging. They have made gender an explicit theme in the study of aging and later life.[1]

Critique of the Conflict Perspective

Conflict theories ask questions neither of the other perspectives can. Conflict theories link individual problems to larger social issues of the economy and the state. Still, conflict theories have their limits. First, they overemphasize the poverty and problems that older people face. Second, they overemphasize the effect of social structures on individual aging. Third, they tend to see the person as the product of social and political forces. Conflict theories pay little attention to the responses older people make to social pressures.

Gerontologists need theories to make sense of the mass of detailed information that researchers gather. A statement made more than a decade ago by Bengtson and his colleagues (1997, S84) remains true today. They say that "theory is not a marginal, meaningless 'tacked-on' exercise to presenting results in an empirical paper. Rather, cumulative theory-building represents the core of the foundation of scientific inquiry and knowledge" (see also Biggs, Hendricks, & Lowenstein, 2003).

Gerontological theories offer many explanations of aging. Their variety reflects the many dimensions of gerontological research. Gerontologists have borrowed theoretical perspectives from most of the social sciences. They have modified these theories to fit the study of aging. In some cases, they have developed new theories (such as age stratification theory and the life course approach) to fit the issues that gerontologists study. Gerontologists can select from the theories presented here and from many more specific

---

[1] I thank my colleague, Professor Lori Campbell, McMaster University, for developing this review of feminist gerontology.

theories in their attempts to understand aging. Each of these theories and perspectives gives us a different insight into what it means to age.

New Developments in Theory

What theoretical ideas have emerged in social gerontology in recent years? What approaches will emerge or grow in the years ahead? Some researchers and theorists support the wider use of interpretive frameworks for studying aging. Narrative gerontology offers one new framework (Randall & Kenyon, 2004). This approach seeks to understand the "inside" of aging. It studies the stories that people tell in order to organize and make sense of their lives. These stories create meaning around their experience of aging. Becker (2001) used the narrative approach to study older people who live with chronic pain. Other writers have studied the life stories of people with dementia and terminal illness (Basting, 2003; Kuhl & Westwood, 2001). Narrative gerontology shows that people "compose" their lives through their life stories. These stories are retold, revisited, and reinterpreted as people age.

Moral economy theory, a complement to political economy theory, grew out of the work of E. P. Thompson in England. Political economy theorists and researchers have begun to use this perspective to explore issues such as retirement, long-term care (Minkler & Estes, 1999), and community volunteerism (Narushima, 2005). This approach to the study of aging looks at the shared moral assumptions held by members of a society. Studies that use this approach look at values such as justice and fairness in society and how they affect social policies. The moral economy theory is concerned with the social consensus that underlies issues such as justice between the generations, pension entitlements, and access to health care.

Critical gerontology emerged to address limitations in mainstream gerontological theory. Ray (2003, 2008) makes the distinction between "theory" and "critical theory." Theory helps to guide research and interpret research findings. Critical theory questions these findings. It reminds "us that all theories are partial, that other meanings are always possible, that meaning-making itself is an exercise in power and authority, and that we promote some meanings at the expense of others" (Ray, 2003, p. 34).

Estes (2003; also Katz, 2003), for example, criticizes mainstream theory for not "looking within" to examine and question its underlying and "taken-for-granted" assumptions about aging. This view asks gerontologists to look at "what is missing, ignored, or denied" within aging theories and research. This approach has produced some fresh insights from gerontologists who reflect on their own lives.

Stephen Katz (2008, p. 141), for example, traces his thoughts and feelings about old age to his youth in Toronto's Jewish quarter in Kensington Market. There he identified "old" with "the majority adults; Yiddish; rye bread; barrels of pickled and salted foods. . . ." His warm reflections on his youth show the roots of his interest in aging today. "Indeed," he says, "if one probes the career of any author or thinker or critic, one will find a narrative of life whose experiences, revelations, and suffering are the voice and soul of their work" (p. 145).

Bengtson and colleagues (2009) see a trend toward novelty as they look across the field of theory in gerontology. They note that theories today differ in their origins, their scope, and their focus of interest. But these writers also recognize "an integration of theoretical perspectives both within and across disciplines." For example, they see a growing awareness in all disciplines of aging as a lifelong process. In psychology and biology this takes the form of life-span development. It takes the form of the life course approach in sociology. It takes the form of a life-cycle model in the economy of aging.

They see similarities across disciplines in an interest in: (1) the study of cumulative advantages and disadvantages of aging; (2) the interrelationship of the environment and the person; (3) the variability that comes with aging; and (4) the need for cross-disciplinary thinking.

New theoretical approaches will include biological and genetic approaches to aging as well as an interest in the effects of globalization on aging.

Theory will remain central to studying aging. Bengtson, Rice, and Johnson (1999) say that "theory is the compass with which to navigate through vast seas of data. It is the means by which data are transformed into meaningful explanations, or stories, about the processes and consequences of aging." Gerontological theories offer many explanations of aging. Their variety reflects the many dimensions of gerontological research. Each of these perspectives gives us a different insight into what it means to age.

RESEARCH ISSUES AND METHODS

Gerontologists use many different methods to study aging. Methods vary by discipline, by subfields within a discipline, and by the question under study. Methods range from the laboratory work of biomedical scientists to the intelligence tests of psychologists, from studies of diaries and literature, to surveys such as the U.S. Census. Some studies use more than one method. The U.S. Health and Retirement Study (U.S. Department of Health and Human Services, 2007), for example, used face-to-face interviews in people's homes, telephone interviews, and physiological measurements to study the retirement process. The proper use of research methods ensures that gerontologists end up with reliable and valid results. The following discussion looks at some of the methodological issues that gerontologists face.

Experimental Designs

Social gerontologists want to understand the changes that take place in individuals over time. For example, a gerontologist might want to know how drinking milk in childhood affects bone density in old age. An experiment could answer this question. A researcher could divide a group of children into two groups in childhood. One group would drink milk. The other would not. After 60 years, the researchers would measure the effects of milk drinking on bone density. Of course, gerontologists cannot conduct this kind of experiment. They could not risk the health of a group of children. Even if they could do the experiment, they would have to wait nearly a lifetime to get the results.

Instead, social gerontologists more often work with groups that already exist. For example, a gerontologist might study bone density in two groups of women born at different times. These groups might differ naturally in the diet they ate. Women who grew up during the Great Depression, for example, may have had a poorer diet than women born 10 years later. A gerontologist could compare the bone density in these two groups of women in old age.

Gerontologists often conduct this kind of study. These studies take the place of formal experiments and often serve as the quickest, least expensive way to gather information. But this type of study presents problems for the researcher. For instance, imagine a researcher who conducts a study of diet and bone density in older women in 2010. She looks at bone density in two groups of women—one group born in 1940 (70 years old) and the other born in 1930 (80 years old and born during the Great Depression). The researcher finds that women born during the Depression (who had poor diets) have less bone density than women born after the Depression.

Does this mean that poor diet in childhood leads to less bone density in old age? Not necessarily. The researchers want to know whether one variable (diet) causes a change in another variable (bone density). They have found a **correlation** or regular relationship between these two variables, but a high correlation between two variables (such as childhood diet and bone

---

BOX 3
TIMING AND THE LIMITATIONS OF SURVEY DATA

The AARP conducted a survey titled "Staying Ahead of the Curve: The AARP Work and Career Study." The AARP conducted the study in the spring of 2007. The survey sample included 1,500 workers between the ages of 45 and 74. All had jobs at the time or were looking for work. The researchers included the following note at the start of their report.

A NOTE ON THE TIMING: When respondents were interviewed for this survey in the spring of 2007, the economy was relatively strong and unemployment was lower than at the time that the writing of this report was being completed in the spring of 2008. If the survey were taken during the current economic slowdown, it is possible that responses to questions would be different—especially those concerning job security, age discrimination, and motivations to work.

This comment shows the sensitivity of data to changing social conditions. Think about a survey that asks 65- to 69-year-olds about their attitudes toward retirement and their financial resources. Five years later a survey asks these same people the same questions. Will they give the same answers that they gave the first time?

A change in Social Security policies, a downturn in the housing market, or an economic boom could change their answers. Likewise, a new cohort of 65- to 69-year-olds at the time of the second survey might give answers very different from those of the first cohort five years ago. Readers of survey reports need to keep in mind that surveys provide a snapshot of a population at one point in time.

density in old age) does not prove that one caused the other. Consider some other possibilities.

First, the 1930 group is 10 years older than the 1940 group at the time of the study. Bone density may decrease with age. The two groups may differ because bone density decreases between ages 70 and 80. Diet in childhood may have little or nothing to do with this.

Second, the two groups may have begun life with different bone densities due to differences in their mothers' diets. Children born during the Depression may suffer throughout their lives from the effects of their mothers' poor nutrition.

Third, historical events may have influenced these two groups differently. For example, older women from both the 1930 and 1940 groups have begun to exercise in the past few years. This increase in activity will increase bone density, but it may have less effect on older women. This effect makes it unclear whether childhood diet led to the differences in bone density that the researcher found.

These examples show the kinds of problems gerontologists face when they search for the causes of change in later life. Gerontologists generally place changes in old age into one of three categories: age effects, cohort effects, or period effects.

Age effects, due to physical decline, appear with the passage of time. They include an increase in the body's fat-to-muscle ratio, a decrease in lung elasticity, and decreases in bone density. They also include environmentally caused changes such as wrinkled skin and cataracts caused by the sun.

Cohort effects are related to the time of a person's birth. A *cohort* refers to a group of people born around the same time (usually within a 5-year period). People born in a certain cohort often share a common background and view of the world. People born just after World War II, for example, were the first cohorts exposed to large doses of television. This shaped their entertainment habits, values, and lifestyles.

Period effects are due to the time of measurement. This would include historical effects on measurement, such as an ongoing war, or changes in health habits, such as increased exercise. These effects have different influences on different age cohorts.

Gerontologists try to disentangle these effects to understand the causes of aging. Maddox and Campbell (1985, p. 20) called this the "age/period/cohort (APC) problem." Gerontologists use a number of research designs to look at these three effects and understand change in later life.

Cross-Sectional Designs

A cross-sectional study takes place when a researcher studies several age groups at one point in time. Many studies use this approach (Neuman & Robson, 2009). Brach and colleagues (Brach, Simonsick, Kritchevsky, Yaffe, & Neuman, 2004), for example, used data from a questionnaire study to compare the physical functioning of older people who exercised or stayed active with those who were inactive. The researchers found that people in the exercise group had significantly better physical functioning than the active group and the inactive group. They conclude that twenty to thirty minutes of exercise most days leads to better physical functioning.

Bond and colleagues (2003) studied the relationship between alcohol consumption and depression among Japanese Americans and white Americans between the ages of 65 and 101. The study analyzed data from more than 4,000 people. The study found that the younger people in the study consumed more alcohol and had lower depression scores.

Researchers use cross-sectional designs for a number of reasons. First, cross-sectional data sets may already exist. This saves time and money. The cross-sectional exercise and activity data used by Brach and colleagues (2004), for example, came from a larger longitudinal study, the Aging and Body Composition (Health ABC) study. This information cost thousands of dollars and many weeks to collect. The researchers wanted to compare the responses of several age groups at one point in time, and the data from this already completed study could answer this question.

Second, cross-sectional designs control for environmental events that might affect the study. For example, if the season of the year affects answers on a housing study, then a one-time study can get responses from everyone in the same season. Third, cross-sectional designs allow the researcher to gather data about many age groups in one study.

Cross-sectional studies show differences between age groups. However, they may confuse differences between age groups (differences due to when a person was born) with changes due to aging. For example, many cross-sectional studies done in psychology until the 1960s found that older age groups had lower intelligence scores than younger age groups. This led to the conclusion that intelligence decreases with age.

But other things could explain this apparent decline in intelligence with age. For example, educational differences between the older and younger groups account, at least in part, for the cross-sectional findings. Older cohorts with less education tended to do less well on paper-and-pencil tests and felt more test anxiety. This led to lower intelligence scores.

Most researchers who study aging still use cross-sectional designs. They often do this for practical reasons. Cross-sectional studies cost less to conduct, and researchers can analyze the data immediately. But cross-sectional studies can lead to errors in interpretation. They confound aging and cohort effects. They rely on the untested assumption that between-person differences reflect within-person changes over time. Researchers try to overcome this problem. They can combine results from a number of cross-sectional studies. This gives a picture of change over time. It allows gerontologists to study social trends and to assess the impact of social policies. The use of more than one cross-sectional study creates a longitudinal design. Longitudinal studies correct for some of the problems that cross-sectional studies face.

Longitudinal Designs

Longitudinal studies look at age cohorts or individuals over time. Longitudinal studies of intelligence, for example, help untangle the effects of background and environment (cohort effects) from changes due to age. A longitudinal study, for example, can compare a person's test scores at age 45, 50, and 55. This provides a record of how a person's mental ability changes over the years. Hofer and Sliwinski (2006) report the existence of more than 40 large-scale longitudinal studies of people aged 50 and over. These studies took place in the United States and in other countries. They offer information about changes within individuals over time.

The Health and Retirement Study (National Institute on Aging and National Institutes of Health, 2007) conducted in the United States offers a good example of a longitudinal study. Researchers collected a first round of data from 12,600 people aged 51 to 61 in 1992. Researchers also drew an oversample of people from Florida, people of African American descent, and people with Hispanic heritage. Follow-up waves of this study take place every 2 years. A second study, the Study of Assets and Health Dynamics Among the Oldest Old, began in 1993, and the data from the two studies were merged into a single study. The study also added two new groups in 1998. It included age groups not in the two original studies, and it included a group in their 50s to replace people in the original group who had aged.

This study looks at the retirement experience, savings, health insurance coverage, and economic condition of older Americans. The study focuses on health and economic transitions in later life. It also looks at the role that families play in the economic support of older people. The longitudinal design follows the same people over many years (at 2-year intervals). Researchers can use these findings to see what events influence retirement decisions and how people manage the challenges of later life.

One study based on these findings, for example, found that, over time, education level best predicted a person's retirement decision. People with high levels of education and good emotional health tended to stay on the job. The researchers say that the current trend toward early retirement could end as more educated cohorts enter the retirement years (Boeri & Baunach, 2002). These and other findings will help policy makers plan for an aging society.

Longitudinal studies pose practical problems. First, they take many years to complete. The researcher, the funding agency, or the public may want faster results. Second, they cost more money than cross-sectional studies. A longitudinal study requires a number of tests or surveys. Third, fewer grants exist for longitudinal studies than for cross-sectional studies. Longitudinal studies depend on a stream of funding over many years that granting bodies and the government find hard to promise.

Fourth, longitudinal studies lose members over time (through dropouts or death) (Alwin, Hofer, & McCammon, 2006). This may lead to confusing findings. For example, if lower intelligence leads to shorter life, then, over time, as less intelligent people die off, the average intelligence score for a group may improve. This confounds the study results (Hofer & Sliwinski, 2006). The same holds true for studies of disease (Vogler, 2006). Those who die during a study leave a healthier, less diseased group behind. This group no longer represents the original sample's characteristics. Some longitudinal studies try to overcome this problem. They bring new people into the study as people die off or drop out.

Longitudinal studies also have other drawbacks. They confound age effects (due to aging) with period effects (due to the time of testing). For example, intelligence test results reflect economic, social, and political conditions at the time of the test. A war or other stressful social event may affect results. Also, people may improve their test scores with practice as they get tested many times. This reflects a change unrelated to aging.

BOX 4
THE BALTIMORE LONGITUDINAL STUDY OF AGING

Longitudinal studies take time, money, and management skill. A lack of any of these will cause a study to fizzle and die. Studies that have lasted many years stand as a tribute to the planning and dedication of their creators and current researchers.

The Baltimore Longitudinal Study of Aging (BLSA) (National Institute on Aging, 2010a), begun in 1958, celebrated its 50th anniversary in 2008. It is the longest-running scientific study of human aging in the United States. The study aims to (1) measure biological and behavioral changes as people age, (2) relate these measures to one another, and (3) separate universal aging processes from disease and the effects of the environment. Researchers have produced more than 800 articles and reports using the data from this study. These findings have shaped scientists' and practitioners' thinking about the aging process.

People in the study come to Baltimore every 2 years for a battery of tests and measurements. In 2010, the BLSA included 1,400 men and women (women first entered the study in 1978). People range in age from their 20s to their early 100s. The oldest person is 102. Many people have taken part in the study for most of their adult lives. The study has included more than 2,500 people in its history, and it adds new people every year. Some people are fourth-generation BLSA volunteers.

All longitudinal studies face the problem of dropouts. How does the BLSA manage to keep so many of its volunteers in the study over so many years? The BLSA, from the start, treated the people in the study as coworkers. One volunteer said the study "made me feel not like a guinea pig, but like a human being who is part of a great scientific enterprise."

Louise Capone, a 47-year-old woman in the study, who has been tested seven times so far, says:

This is really what keeps me coming back. . . . We get the results of our own tests, which are nice to have, but also we learn what the study is learning, overall. There is a real sense of being a partner in the study, of working with the researchers toward a goal. (U.S. Department of Health and Human Services, BLSA, 1993)

The BLSA has produced many breakthroughs and supports for our understanding of aging. Consider the following findings:

- Differences between individuals increase with age.
- People can reduce the decline in oxygen use that comes with age, if they stay active.
- Disease-free older people at rest have cardiac output similar to that of younger people.
- Until at least age 70, problem-solving ability shows little or no decline.
- Personality remains stable through most of life. A cheerful person in youth will stay that way in old age.

These longitudinal findings present a clearer picture of the changes that come with time, and they suggest how people can improve functions that decline through neglect or misuse.

Paul Costa, a personality psychologist, says that the BLSA gives us a new view of aging. "We need not worry that we will become crotchety with age or that only firm resignation can save us from despair and fear of death. . . . We need not dread our future" (U.S. Department of Health and Human Services, 1993).

Source: National Institute on Aging. (2010a). *Baltimore Longitudinal Study of Aging*. National Institutes of Health. Retrieved October 25, 2010, from www.grc.nia.nih.gov/branches/blsa/blsanew.htm

---

A third method, time-lag comparison design, tries to overcome the problems raised by simple cross-sectional and simple longitudinal designs. Time-lag studies look at groups of people of the same age at different points in time (e.g., 65-year-olds in 1990, 2000, and 2010; 60-year-olds over this same time period). This type of study tries to measure differences between cohorts.

Like cross-sectional and longitudinal methods, the time-lag method also presents problems. It confounds cohort effects with environmental effects. If a research study finds that 70-year-olds in 2005 visited doctors less often than 70-year-olds did in 1985, this difference may be due to the better health of 70-year-olds in 2005 (a cohort effect). Or it may be due to a change in the health care system, perhaps higher costs to users that discourage visits to doctors (an environmental effect).

Each of these designs attempts to understand the effects of aging on individuals, and each design has its place in the researcher's tool kit. (See Figure 1.) Gerontologists must use these methods to get a clearer picture of how people change over time. Longitudinal studies prove especially useful in studies of health over time. This approach can track the influence of behaviors (such as smoking or exercise) on health.

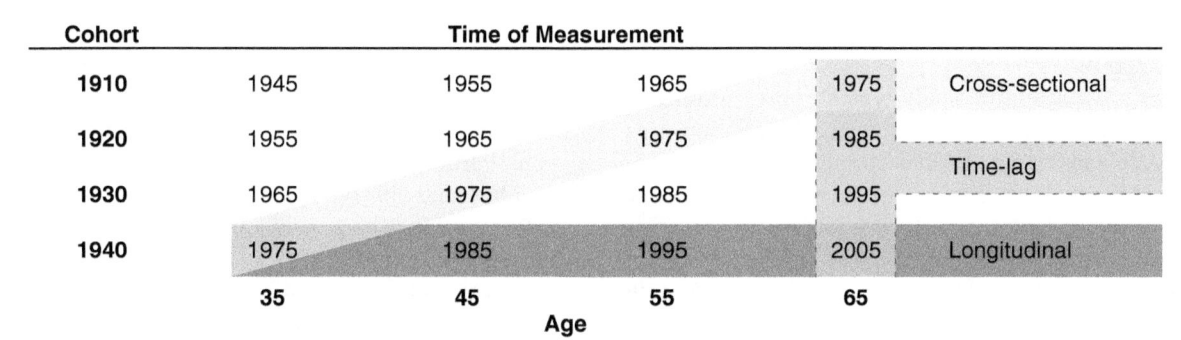

This chart shows the different approaches used in three types of study design.

The hypothetical cross-sectional study took place in 1975 and studied four age groups (35, 45, 55, and 65) in that year. It compared findings across age groups. This study took a snapshot of age differences at one point in time.

The longitudinal study also began in 1975, but it went on for 30 years. It measured the 1940 cohort four times (in 1975, 1985, 1995, and 2005) at four different ages (35, 45, 55, and 65). The study had fewer people in it at each time of measurement due to dropouts and deaths. (Some research studies of this type replace people who die or leave the study.) This study could follow age changes in the 1940 cohort.

The time-lag study measured 65-year-olds at four times (1965, 1975, 1985, and 1995). This study had different people in the sample at each time of measurement. It could show how 65-year-olds differed at each time of measurement.

FIGURE 1 Cross-Sectional, Longitudinal, and Time-Lag Designs

Source: Adapted from P. B. Baltes, H. W. Reese, and J. R. Nesselroade, *Life-Span Developmental Psychology: Introduction to Research Methods*, 1977, Monterey, CA: Brooks/Cole.

Longitudinal studies can also assess the influence of early life experiences on health in later life.

Salthouse (2006) says that only longitudinal studies allow researchers to assess the long-term effects of interventions. For example, it may take years for an exercise program to affect health in later life. An immediate effect of the exercise program (e.g., an improved self-image) might lessen and disappear over time. Salthouse admits that long-term studies cost a lot and consume time and energy. But they provide the only accurate assessment of an intervention's effect on the process of aging.

Complex methods such as time-lag designs help sort out the effects of age, cohort, and period. But these results still leave unanswered questions (Alwin et al., 2006). For example, a longitudinal design may clearly show that lung elasticity decreases with age. And it may show that this holds true for all age cohorts and at different points in time. But this study says nothing about why the lung changes. After studies sort out these effects, the gerontologist's work has only begun. "Separating the confounds," Botwinick says, "is not the end of the line, it is but the beginning" (1984, p. 400). Whatever method the researcher chooses, researchers must look closely to find the causes of the change.

Quantitative and Qualitative Methods

Paradigms are frameworks used to think about and organize an understanding of natural or social phenomena (Online Dictionary, 2004). They define what questions scientists ask and how scientists conduct their studies.

Gerontology has a long history of using a natural science paradigm. This began with studies of physiology and disease. Later, social scientists followed biomedical science in using mathematical measurement. Today, gerontologists often apply the methods of natural science—mathematical measurement, statistical methods, cause-and-effect models—to the study of aging.

Philosophers refer to this type of science as **positivism**. Positivism seeks to control natural events like aging. It underlies the work in the biology and physiology of aging. Positivist science has led to many of the breakthroughs in medicine in the past century. It has also led to a more detailed understanding of the aging process.

Positivism assumes a nonreflexive object of study. Hormones, muscles, and vitamins fit this picture. The successes of positivist study in biology and physiology have led to its application to other fields—recreation, family life, and creativity. Positivism has become the main approach to scientific study in gerontology and other social sciences (Achenbaum, 2000a; Cole & Ray, 2000).

Positivist scientific study typically uses **quantitative methods**. These methods emphasize relationships between and among variables through numerical measurement (quantity, amount, frequency) (Del Balso & Lewis, 2008; Neuman & Robson, 2009). Quantitative methods range from pharmaceutical research on the effects of drugs on older people to census reports on income or marital status.

Quantitative studies often take the form of surveys or questionnaires. Researchers then summarize responses into numerical values for statistical analysis.

This model of scientific rationality serves certain ends. It discovers the facts about income, health care services, recreation, and other subjects of interest to gerontologists. It also suggests ways to improve later life (e.g., by showing the need for more health care services). But this approach may apply less well to understanding why people do what they do. A study might show that a high percent of people quit exercise programs after they sign up for a gym. But this finding doesn't say why people quit. Census data may provide information on mortality rates for men and women. But they can't tell us why, compared to women, men tend to marry again shortly after widowhood. Positivism limits the study of aging to certain topics and approaches. It rules out other questions and methods.

Critical gerontology questions the ideals of positivist science. Critical gerontologists say the positivist approach creates a system that dominates older people (Moody, 1993). For example, medical science turns the older person into a patient. It prescribes drugs, plans treatment, and controls access to health services. It does all this in the name of health care. But to provide this care, medical science turns the older person into a passive object. Critical gerontology exposes the effects of positivism on older people. Critical research seeks to empower people by giving them an understanding of the forces that shape their lives.

Critical gerontologists often use **qualitative methods** such as in-depth interviews, life histories, case studies, analysis of the content of documents or artifacts, and observation. Qualitative methods use an interpretive theoretical approach to understand these data. "Qualitative research is characterized by a verbal or literary presentation of data" (Del Balso & Lewis, 2008, p. 40).

The use of qualitative methods in research on aging has grown significantly in recent years. Qualitative researchers "look at social life from multiple points of view and explain how people construct identities" (Neuman, 2003, p. 146). They seek to understand the social world and social experience of individuals from the subjects' own perspectives.

Qualitative methods include participant observation. Participant observers spend time with group members and observe what they do. Researchers want to learn as much as possible about social life from the participants' points of view. Participant observation studies include studies of national identity formation among minority older people (Tammeveski, 2003), studies of how spouses respond to caregiving (Calasanti, 2006), and studies of older people in assisted-living facilities (Ball et al., 2004). Neuman (2003, p. 146) says that "instead of trying to convert social life into variables or numbers, qualitative researchers borrow ideas from the people they study." Researchers try to understand the meanings people bring to social interactions. Qualitative research wants to give voice to the study participants. Studies often report results in the subjects' own words.

Beard (2004) conducted a participant observation study of people diagnosed with Alzheimer's disease. She also used in-depth interviews and focus group discussions to study the experience of memory loss. The study took place over 6 months. Like many researchers who use this method, Beard used unstructured interviews and accounts of the participants' experiences. She found that, in spite of memory loss, participants found ways to manage the effects of the illness and preserve their sense of self.

Saarnio and Isola (2009) conducted an observational study of elderly people in institutions in Finland. The researchers wanted to study the use of physical restraints in these settings. The researchers collected data on restraints for 4 months. They spent between 6 and 16 hours each week in the institutions. They observed staff and patients on all shifts. The researchers took notes during their time in the institutions and kept a journal of their emotions during the research.

The study found that the staff frequently used restraints to control patients. Staff used belts to keep people in their chairs, they tied patients to beds with linens, they used physical force, and they issued sharp verbal commands.

Sometimes staff reduced patients' mobility through passive restraint. For example, they restrained patients by removing a person's walker or wheelchair. They sometimes intentionally removed alarm bells so patients could not call for help. Nurses even kept patients underdressed so they would be less likely to appear in public.

A field note from this study gives an example of what one researcher observed: "The elderly patient is sitting in a wheelchair in his underpants and tells me right away that he hasn't been given any trousers by the nurses although he has asked for them. He says that he's too embarrassed to walk around in the corridor without his trousers on" (p. 283).

The researchers conclude that this environment does not serve older patients' needs. Staff systematically ignored patients and kept them immobile to decrease their workload. This frustrated patients and created a dangerous and unpleasant environment. These conditions raise ethical questions about the treatment of patients and the quality of care they receive.

Participant observation allowed the researchers to observe the actual conditions in the nursing home. It's doubtful that the researchers could have gotten this information any other way.

This study also shows the amount of time and effort it takes to do participant observation research. Participant observation researchers need to get the permission to enter the organization they plan to study. They must carefully observe and document what they see and hear.

Because entering and working in the field takes a lot of time, relatively few researchers use this method. But this study shows that participant observation produces unique and insightful results.

Critical gerontology looks for those places and moments where alternative models of aging would improve the lives of older people. The interests of critical gerontology and positivist gerontology differ. Positivist gerontology wants prediction and control over aging. Positivist studies produce knowledge that the state or experts in the field of aging can use to cure disease, improve housing, or develop effective fitness programs. This takes the form of control by professionals, government agencies, and policies. Critical gerontology, on the other hand, has a different agenda. It works to "open up possibilities of communication, mutual understanding, and coordinated social action" (Moody, 1993, p. xxiii). It aims to empower older people and enhance their freedom.

Quantitative and qualitative methods each have their strengths and limitations. Quantitative methods allow researchers to gather a great deal of information on a wide range of issues. Moreover, they can analyze a large sample and generalize their results to a larger population. But quantitative researchers structure their research questions and give respondents limited choices. This kind of research offers little opportunity to capture the rich description of individuals' subjective experiences or their perceptions of their social world (Lincoln & Guba, 2000; Neuman, 2003).

Qualitative methods allow researchers to appreciate the complexity of social interactions and behaviors. These methods study how individuals understand and give meaning to their lives (Del Balso & Lewis, 2008; Neuman & Robson, 2009). They allow the words and subjective experiences of participants to be heard.

Qualitative research also has its limits. Researchers often use small sample sizes. This limits generalization to a larger population. Some researchers combine both quantitative and qualitative methods in one study (Neuman & Robson, 2009).

BOX 5
STRENGTHS AND WEAKNESSES OF QUALITATIVE AND QUANTITATIVE METHODS

	Quantitative Methods	*Qualitative Methods*
Strengths	• Data can be quantified, standardized, and measured	• Hear voice of participants
	• Generalizable to larger population	• Captures subjective experiences
	• Can study wide range of topics	• Data detailed, rich, in depth
	• Study can be replicated	• Suitable for "sensitive" topics
Weaknesses	• Data general and lacks depth	• Not generalizable
	• Cannot capture subjective experience or meanings	• Interviewer effect
	• Responses forced into "tick boxes"	• Unintentional subjectivity or bias of researcher
	• Not suitable for "sensitive" topics	• Time and labor intensive

This table summarizes some general advantages and disadvantages of qualitative and quantitative methods, based on Neuman and Robson (2009).

Source: From *Basics of Social Research: Qualitative and Quantitative Approaches, Canadian Edition,* by W. L. Neuman and K. Robson, 2009, Toronto, ON: Pearson Education Canada. Reprinted with permission.

The Humanities

The study of aging has grown to include the humanities (e.g., literature, philosophy, fine arts) as well as biomedicine and social science (Cole & Ray, 2000). Frankel says, "The humanities are that form of knowledge in which the knower is revealed . . . when we are asked to contemplate not only the proposition but the proposer, when we hear the human voice behind what is said" (cited in Moody, 1988b).

Scholars in the humanities use many methods to study aging. Vesperi (2002) shows how literary interpretation opens up new ways of thinking about aging. Yahnke (2000), for example, studied the portrayal of aging in films and videos. He looked at how these media presented the themes of intergenerational relations and regeneration in later life. He found that most films give a positive view of aging by showing satisfying relationships and fulfillment in old age.

Shenk and Schmid (2002) list the use of photo archives, self-portraits, photocollage, and photography as resources and methods for studying aging. Winkler (1992) studied pictures of aging by great artists, selecting examples from Ghirlandaio (15th century) to Käthe Kollwitz (20th century). These pictures guide us, she says, to reflect on the end of life. Historians have studied population trends, church records, and diaries (Haber, 2000). These studies allow us to compare aging today with old age at other times and in other places.

Some gerontologists have written autobiographical sketches (Katz, 2008; Calasanti, 2008) to expand their own understanding of aging. This goes against the positivist bias of gerontology research, but it fits well within a humanistic approach, and it reveals the human face of aging.

Aging studies in the humanities stand on the margins of gerontology today, but interest in this approach continues to grow (Achenbaum, 2000a). The Gerontological Society of America, for example, at its annual meetings sponsors an interest group in the humanities, and the second edition of *Handbook of the Humanities and Aging* appeared in 2000 (Cole & Ray, 2000). Studies in the humanities reflect on the universal experience of aging. They show us the value that great writers, artists, and scholars place on old age. They expose us to new ways of thinking about aging and offer us new ways to explore our own lives.

Information Literacy: The Challenge of the Internet

Anyone with a computer can now read and download volumes of information about aging. Web sites offer everything from complex government documents (e.g., census data) to infomercials (e.g., investment advice). How can a person assess the quality of information available today?

The American Library Association's (ALA) *Presidential Committee on Information Literacy: Final Report* (1989) states, "To be information literate, a person must be able to recognize when information is needed and have the ability to locate, evaluate, and use effectively the needed information." Information literacy is a vital skill for anyone who wants to understand aging today.

Consider a request for health information. I just typed the word "arthritis" into the Google search engine (December 18, 2010). The first page of Web sites retrieved included the Arthritis Foundation, Wikipedia (the free encyclopedia), WebMD, a Mayo Clinic site on rheumatoid arthritis, the U.S. Centers for Disease Control and Prevention (CDC), and a site related to the U.S. National Institutes of Health (NIH). These sources provide a range of information on arthritis. But the quality of information on these sites varies.

The government sources, the CDC (2010) site, for example, links to information about research grants, scientific findings on this topic, and practical information on personal care. It also links to research reports and information on government agencies. This site provides a high standard of information quality. For example, the scientific reports have passed inspection by top scientists.

But all information has a bias. The government site takes Western scientific method and knowledge as a cornerstone of truth. Someone questioning the government's goals, someone skeptical of scientific methods and findings, someone who wants a more personal view of aging will question the value of this site.

Wikipedia (2011) on the other hand, provides this disclaimer: "Older articles tend to grow more comprehensive and balanced; newer articles may contain misinformation, unencyclopedic content, or vandalism. Awareness of this aids obtaining valid information and avoiding recently added misinformation."

Wikipedia, an encyclopedia created by a community of users and changed constantly by those users, does not claim to offer true or valid knowledge. The managers of the Wikipedia site admit bias in the listings. They warn readers about potentially misleading information.

Wikipedia shows sensitivity to the quality of the information it provides. This is good. But it leaves the reader to sort out the truth from the misinformation. For example, a section on the cognitive effects of aging takes up only one paragraph, though it links to many other submissions. A link to memory provides only four paragraphs, but again provides many links to other articles. And these entries have many further links.

Wikipedia shows the strengths and the weaknesses of Web-based information. It allows a reader to surf from one topic to another according to his or her needs, and it offers a lot of information from a wide range of authors. But it offers no expert review or screening of the information. The Wikipedia community members can change information they consider inaccurate. But Wikipedia leaves it to the reader to decide on the validity and reliability of the information. Wikipedia might serve as a starting point for research, but it can mislead a naïve reader who has little experience in a field.

A site called WebMD (2010) provides a third example of information available on the Web. It sits somewhere between the government sources and Wikipedia on the reliability scale. The site provides up-to-date information on arthritis and health tips designed to inform the general public. But a close look at the site shows that it accepts advertising. And this could bias the information presented. For example, the editor of this site chooses what information to present. Does the editor subtly or overtly choose news items to attract or keep advertisers? Would the editor leave out an item that reflected badly on an advertiser? The reader needs to keep these questions in mind. A serious student of this subject would not use this source alone for information on arthritis.

Today you have more information available to you than ever before. And you can get that information at the touch of a button. Blogs, wikis, YouTube, and Twitter all offer opportunities for people to express and publish their views. Web sites that can seem informational (sites put up by financial advisors, insurance agents, etc.) may actually be infomercials for a product. These sites exist side by side on the Web with U.S. government studies and scholarly reports. This places a greater burden than ever before on your ability to assess the quality of the information you receive.

To understand this issue firsthand, try a Google search on some aging-related topics (e.g., retirement, pensions, or arthritis). Look carefully at the types of sites retrieved (government, for-profit, nonprofit, individual, etc.). Go to a few of these sites and consider the variations in the quality of information provided.

Also, go to Wikipedia and enter the same keywords as you did in the Google search. Explore the topic by reading a section and then going to related links in the article. Note how easily you can gather information as you go from topic to topic. But think about the sources of the information. Critically evaluate the information you gather. Look at the variation in the completeness of entries, in the types of references given, and in the content of the entries. These exercises will sharpen your thinking and build your information literacy skills.

ETHICAL ISSUES IN RESEARCH

Research studies on human subjects face ethical challenges. And studies of certain frail or vulnerable groups pose unique problems. Researchers need to consider the ethical implications of studying institutionalized older people, those living in poverty, the socially isolated (Russell, 1999), and people with Alzheimer's disease or other cognitive impairments (Karlawish, 2004; Sevick et al., 2003). They also need to consider the ethics of doing field research where the researcher observes people (e.g., in a nursing home) without their permission.

Saarnio and Isola (2009) in their study of physical restraints, for example, had to get permission to conduct their research. They report the following method for getting permission: "After obtaining the permits to conduct the study, an information session was organized for the staff working on the units; after the session they could decide whether to take part in the study. The decision about taking part in the study was collective, and the head nurse of each unit passed on the information about the unit's participation to the researcher (R.S.)."

Note that first the researchers needed to get "permits" to conduct the study (it's unclear from their report who issued these permits). They then took care to inform participants (nurses) about the research and its purposes. Participants could opt out of the research if they chose. Note also that they got group consent. It appears that a nurse who did not want to participate had no choice once the group made its decision. Also, note that the patients had no say in this decision. Should the patients have been consulted? Did the researcher need their permission to proceed? An ethics committee would have to consider these issues before granting permission for the research to go ahead.

Most professional associations have a code of ethics that they require members to follow. (See Box 6.) Universities also have ethical guidelines and standards for research. They often have a research ethics committee that reviews proposed projects. The ethics review board must approve each study, weigh the potential risks and benefits, and then give permission for re-search to proceed. Research committees today demand informed consent from the people under study. They also require full disclosure to the subjects of the researcher's intent.

Universities do this for several reasons: to protect themselves from lawsuits, to ensure that subjects understand the studies they take part in, and to protect subjects from harm. My own university requires ethical review for all faculty and student projects that involve an older person. This includes class projects such as interviewing an older person or observing activities at a senior center.

BOX 6
ETHICAL PRINCIPLES OF PSYCHOLOGISTS AND CODE OF CONDUCT

Most professional associations have a code of ethics that guides members' conduct. The American Psychological Association, for example, has an ethics code titled *Ethical Principles of Psychologists and Code of Conduct*. This ethics code sets standards of practice for members and states penalties for violating the code.

Standard 8, entitled "Research and Publication," discusses the need for institutional approval, informed consent from participants, and the use of deception in research.

8.01 Institutional Approval

When institutional approval is required, psychologists provide accurate information about their research proposals and obtain approval prior to conducting the research. They conduct the research in accordance with the approved research protocol.

8.02 Informed Consent to Research

(a) When obtaining informed consent as required in Standard 3.10, Informed Consent, psychologists inform participants about (1) the purpose of the research, expected duration, and procedures; (2) their right to decline to participate and to withdraw from the research once participation has begun; (3) the foreseeable consequences of declining or withdrawing; (4) reasonably foreseeable factors that may be expected to influence their willingness to participate such as potential risks, discomfort, or adverse effects; (5) any prospective research benefits; (6) limits of confidentiality; (7) incentives for participation; and (8) whom to contact for questions about the research and research participants' rights. They provide opportunity for the prospective participants to ask questions and receive answers. (See also Standards 8.03, Informed Consent for Recording Voices and Images in Research; 8.05, Dispensing With Informed Consent for Research; and 8.07, Deception in Research.)

(b) Psychologists conducting intervention research involving the use of experimental treatments clarify to participants at the outset of the research (1) the experimental nature of the treatment; (2) the services that will or will not be available to the control group(s) if appropriate; (3) the means by which assignment to treatment and control groups will be made; (4) available treatment alternatives if an individual does not wish to participate in the research or wishes to withdraw once a study has begun; and (5) compensation for or monetary costs of participating including, if appropriate, whether reimbursement from the participant or a third-party payer will be sought. (See also Standard 8.02a, Informed Consent to Research.)

Other subsections of the ethics code include guidelines on deception in research, debriefing subjects, offering inducements to take part in studies, and maintaining confidentiality. The ethics code requires psychologists to pay special attention to the rights of their subjects.

Ethical issues arise, in particular, when researchers study cognitively impaired older people. These people cannot understand the meaning of the research or their role in the studies. Researchers need to take special care to protect the rights of these participants. They need to get consent from family members, institution officials, or other responsible parties before proceeding with their research.

Researchers want to safeguard their subjects, but they also have a selfish reason for keeping high ethical standards. Unethical studies sour the public on research. A few years ago, I visited some senior centers to speak about a study I had begun. A woman raised her hand at the end of my talk.

"You're not the fellow that went around a little while ago asking people about sex, are you?" she asked.

"No, I'm not," I said.

"Well," she said, "that guy asked a lot of questions he had no business asking."

A number of other people in the audience nodded agreement. I met the same question in two or three other groups I visited. I learned that someone had done a questionnaire study on sexuality several years before. This person had not explained the study to the subjects and had left questions unanswered in their minds. I never found out who did this research, but I know that the study upset older people in the community and made it harder for me to gain their trust and support.

Researchers need to consider at least three ethical issues: (1) the need for informed consent, (2) the need to guard subjects against harm or injury, and (3) the need to protect individuals' privacy (Neuman, 2003).

Informed consent means that the researcher tells the subjects the facts about the research and gets written permission from them before they take part in a study. Older people who live in long-term care facilities and socially isolated people may feel some pressure to take part in a study. Individuals must freely give their consent, without any coercion. They need to understand that they can decide not to answer any questions without explanation. And they need to know that they can withdraw from the study at any time.

Researchers must also guard against doing harm or injury to study participants. This includes physical harm and psychological harm. Some people might feel embarrassed or upset at some questions they feel they have to answer. Researchers need to minimize risk to participants throughout the research process. Researchers also seek to protect participants from potential harm by keeping the participants' identities private. Researchers can do this by making sure that data analysis cannot reveal an individual's identity. The researcher should also promise to keep personal information private.

Older people with Alzheimer's disease or other types of dementia present special challenges in research. For example, they may not be able to give true voluntary informed consent (Bravo et al., 2005;

Neuman & Robson, 2009). If the mental competency of an individual is in question, the researcher must get written permission from someone who has the legal authority to make such decisions. A family member or staff member in a nursing home may have this authority. Permission from a substitute decision maker allows for research at all stages of the disease (Karlawish, 2004).

THE FUTURE OF GERONTOLOGICAL THEORY AND METHODS

What theories and methods will gerontologists use in the future? Some or all of the following trends will create new theories and methods in the years to come.

- Gerontologists will create new and more sophisticated quantitative methods. These include structural equation models, longitudinal factor analysis, and multivariate effects models. These methods will emerge as computer power increases and as gerontologists apply methods used in other social sciences. They will allow gerontologists to test new and more complex theories.
- Gavrilov and Gavrilova (2001) propose the use of recent models from natural science—chaos theory and catastrophe theory—to explain aging. These theories and models question the assumptions of linear, probabilistic analyses that gerontologists use today. Hendricks (1997, p. 205) challenges gerontology "to develop mind-sets and measures that address the possibility of non-linear processes." This approach would include the study of unpredictable and dramatic changes in individuals' lives and in their families, work, and neighborhoods. It would also include a study of how people modify their life courses through their own interpretations of their lives.
- Gerontologists would like to link the micro-levels and macro-levels of theory. The age stratification theory, the life course approach, and feminist theories come closest to doing this now, though each has its limits. These approaches and theories look at the intersection of individual biography and history. They also look at the influence of earlier life experiences on old age. These approaches point to the need for multidisciplinary and interdisciplinary studies.
- Researchers will further develop political economy and phenomenological theories, as well as feminist theories, and life course approaches. These approaches

reveal hidden sides of aging. They challenge the myths of aging and explore ways to create a good old age.

- Qualitative methods will continue to play a role in gerontological research. Qualitative methods can explore the experience of aging at a time when more and more people want to know about that experience. Qualitative methods can also reveal the diversity of later life.

- Studies in the humanities will add new methods to gerontological research, such as linguistic analysis, the study of paintings and photos, and autobiographical analysis. New topics of interest in the future will lead to new approaches to the study of aging. Achenbaum (2000a) says that cross-disciplinary studies show promise. These studies blend social science with the studies of art or history.

- Technology will expand research opportunities. Laptop computers, for example, allow researchers to enter interview data in the field. Researchers can use video technology to study behavior problems in long-term care settings. Video recording technology permits researchers to observe behavior without a researcher present. This method allows researchers to gather data throughout the day, and a number of researchers can observe and analyze the same data. Researchers have used this technology to study wandering behavior and the causes of falls in nursing homes.

Researchers will use all of these approaches and more as they explore new topics in the study of aging.

CONCLUSION

Gerontologists use a variety of theories and methods to study aging. Theories range from micro-level studies of individuals and interaction to macro-level studies of whole societies. Researchers use interactionist, functionalist, and conflict theories. Methods range from laboratory studies in the biological sciences to surveys and observation studies in the social sciences. Researchers choose the theories and methods that best help them answer their questions.

The range of theories and methods reflects the varied interests of gerontologists. Gerontologists traditionally came from the biological and social sciences. In the past few years, scholars from the humanities have turned to the study of aging. These scholars have added the study of art, literature, and history to the traditional methods of gerontological research.

The increase in the older population will lead to greater interest in aging and more research in the future. Researchers will come from ever more varied disciplines. They will create new methods and develop new theories as they explore new questions in the field of aging.

SUMMARY

- Gerontology has three subfields: biomedicine, psychosocial studies, and socioeconomic-environmental studies.
- Gerontologists create theories to help explain sets of facts. They use micro-level theories to describe people and their relationships, and they use macro-level theories to describe social institutions.
- The micro-level and macro-level of theory can each take an interactionist, functionalist, or conflict perspective.
- New developments in theory include narrative gerontology, moral economy theory, and critical gerontology. Also, different disciplines have begun to use similar theoretical models—for example, variability among aging populations and the link between the person and the environment.
- Gerontologists use a variety of research methods to study aging. These include experiments, mailed surveys, face-to-face interviews, participant observation, and studies of historical documents. The proper use of these methods ensures reliable and valid results.

- Age, period, and cohort effects influence people as they age. Researchers use a variety of methods to disentangle these effects.
- Cross-sectional, longitudinal, and time-lag designs each have strengths and weaknesses. Researchers try to use the approach that best answers their questions, given the resources they have available.
- Quantitative methods allow researchers to test theories and hypotheses. They look at relationships between variables and typically use numerical measures. They use a positivist approach to social phenomena, an approach similar to the study of natural science.
- Critical gerontology tries to understand the forces that shape people's lives. Researchers in this tradition often use qualitative methods, such as in-depth interviews and participant observation, in their studies.
- Historians and researchers in the humanities, such as classicists and English scholars, bring new theories and

methods to the study of aging. The multidisciplinary study of aging brings richness to gerontology and to our understanding of later life.

- The tremendous amount of information available on the Internet places new demands on students of aging. Information available online varies in quality and reliability. Everyone needs to improve their information literacy to make the best use of information available today.

- Researchers need to consider ethical issues related to their research. Professional associations and universities provide ethical standards, guidelines, and review committees to ensure ethical treatment of subjects in research.

- New theories developed in the natural sciences, interdisciplinary studies, and new technologies will all influence gerontological theories and methods in the future.

DISCUSSION QUESTIONS

1. List the three areas that make up the field of gerontology. Describe the kinds of questions each area asks and the kinds of things each area studies.
2. Explain the difference between micro-level and macro-level theories. Give examples of each. State the benefits and limits of each type of theory.
3. What are the three theoretical perspectives that gerontologists use in their studies? Explain the advantages and disadvantages of each perspective. Give at least one example of a study that uses each perspective.
4. What is the age/period/cohort problem? How can it influence research results? How do gerontologists try to overcome this problem?
5. Why do gerontologists use cross-sectional, longitudinal, and time-lag designs? Explain the advantages and disadvantages of each type of design.
6. Define the term *critical gerontology*. What methods do critical gerontologists use in their studies? Give an example of a study done using this approach.
7. What is information literacy? How has the use of the Internet made information literacy more important than ever before?
8. What safeguards exist to ensure ethical treatment of older subjects in research?
9. What are some of the future directions that gerontology theories and methods may take?

SUGGESTED READING

Biggs, S., Lowenstain, A., & Hendricks, J. (Eds.). (2003). *The need for theory: Critical approaches to a social gerontology*. Amityville, NY: Baywood.

The editors have collected a series of essays on the applications of critical theory to the study of aging. Studies look at personal meaning in gerontology theory, the ways that people negotiate identity in later life, and the family in the context of modernization. A student new to the field may find these essays difficult, but they show how some gerontologists think.

Bengtson, V. L., Gans, D., Putney, N., & Silverstein, M. (2008). *Handbook of theories of aging*, 2nd ed. New York: Springer.

This book contains chapters written by 67 prominent gerontologists. It reviews developments in gerontological theories over the decade prior to its publication. The chapters cover biological, social, and psychological theories. The book also includes a section on theory and social policy. It offers an excellent summary of major theories and provides references that you can follow up for in-depth study.

Gubrium, J. F., & Holstein, J. A. (Eds.). (2000). *Aging and everyday life*. Malden, MA: Blackwell.

This book contains essays by 30 gerontologists on the subject of the aging experience. The essays span a range of topics, including the cultural construction of aging, changing age consciousness as a person ages, and grief among daughters
who have lost a parent. Other essays present examples of aging experiences, including the management of aging among exotic dancers, life in a single-room occupancy hotel, and the experience of the body through autobiography. The essays show the variety of studies that qualitative researchers have conducted.

Websites to Consult

The Gerontological Society of America—Journals
www.geron.org/Publications

This Gerontological Society of America website presents a list of the peer-reviewed journals and other publications sponsored by the GSA. These are among the premier academic publications in the field of aging. The journals cover a broad range of topics. They include articles on biological, psychological, and social facets of aging. The site offers free abstracts of articles from the association's journals. Check with your school's library to see if it provides access to physical or electronic copies of these journals.

AgeLine
www.ebscohost.com/thisTopic.php?marketID=1&topicID=23

This site contains a database of academic and high-quality popular writings on aging. The database includes journal articles, books, chapters, research reports, dissertations, and educational videos from more than 200 sources. You can search AgeLine by topic, author, keyword, date, or a combination of these methods. AgeLine provides detailed bibliographical information for each source it retrieves. It also provides abstracts of each of its entries. Some entries offer the full text of the item online. AgeLine is an invaluable research tool. You may need to access this site through your university library in order to make full use of its resources. If your library does not have access to AgeLine, request that it subscribe.

AARP's Database on Internet Resources

www.aarp.org/research/internet_resources/

This site links to more than 1,200 of the best sites for people age 50+. You can browse this site or search for resources using the URL given here.

National Institute on Aging

www.nia.nih.gov

This site offers a brief description of 250 health care and aging organizations. The site gives contact information for these organizations. Some of these sources will overlap with sources found in the AARP Web site database, but it offers another way to search for information you need.

Federal Interagency Forum on Aging-Related Statistics

www.agingstats.gov

This portal contains links to census data, current government studies, and discussions of aging-related topics. It is a great resource for data and research topics.

DEMOGRAPHY

Flirt/SuperStock

Astrid Thoenig, 100 years old, lives in Parsippany, NJ. She says she's lived so long because she comes from "good stock." She spent her life as an office worker in a variety of businesses. Now she works 40 hours a week in her son's insurance agency. She reads, she knits. She says that having a purpose in life keeps her happy.

Like Ms. Thoenig, more Americans than ever before live past the age of 100. Long life has become the norm as average life expectancy has increased. And not just in the United States. We may be blessed to have more 90- and 100-year-olds than ever before. But in countries throughout the world, populations have aged. The average life expectancy has increased worldwide. In particular, more people live to old age and late old age than ever before (Hobson, 2010, p. 36).

In 2000, for example, the world had 421 million people age 65 years and over. The United Nations projects that by 2050 this figure will more than triple and the world will have almost one and a half billion people age 65 and over (United Nations, 2002b; Davidson, 2009). In 2050, the population of older persons will be larger than the population of children (0–14 years) for the first time in human history.

Population aging will affect different societies in different ways. The United Nations divides the world's nations into two groups—the more developed and the less developed—based on their demographic and socioeconomic characteristics. "The less developed regions include all regions of Africa, Asia (excluding Japan), Latin America and the Caribbean, and Oceania (excluding Australia and New Zealand). The more developed regions include all other regions plus the three countries excluded from the less developed regions" (United Nations, 2002a, p. iv).

The **developed nations**, such as France, Sweden, and the United States, will have large proportions of older people in their populations. The proportion of older people in most of these countries has increased gradually over many decades. Their populations will get older in the future. Some developed countries, such as Japan, had relatively young populations until recently. They have seen rapid population aging in recent years.

The **less developed nations**, such as China and Viet Nam, already have large numbers of older people. In 2000, for example, the majority of the world's older persons (54%) lived in Asia (Kinsella & Velkoff, 2001). These countries also have large numbers of young people (due to high **birth rates**). For this reason, compared with the developed nations, they will have lower *proportions* of older people in their populations. Still, the *large numbers* of older people will put new demands on these societies.

The less developed nations also include very undeveloped nations, such as the countries of Africa, Oceania, parts of the Caribbean, and parts of Latin America. These **least developed nations** will have large numbers of older people in their populations. They will have the least resources to cope with the demands of population aging.

Each type of society will face population aging in the years ahead. Each will face different challenges as their older populations grow. And each will need to make different responses to the challenge of population aging.

This chapter (1) looks at population aging in three types of societies, (2) describes some of the challenges created by population aging, and (3) considers population aging in the United States and its impact on American society.

THE CHALLENGE OF POPULATION AGING

What Is Population Aging?

When we talk about aging we generally refer to a person or even an animal or a thing. But what do we mean when we say that populations age?

Demographers, experts in the study of population change, use at least three measures to describe population aging: (1) the **absolute number of older people** in a population, (2) the **median age** of the population, and (3) the increased proportion of older people. These measures allow comparisons between societies and between a single society at two points in time. A population ages when any of these measures increase. Populations with large numbers of older people or with high proportions of older people are said to be old or aging societies.

The following discussions of societies will often make reference to the number or proportion of older people in the society. Be aware that a society can have a large number of older people, but still have a relatively small proportion of its population in old age. The less developed nations show this pattern. This kind of society will have a high birth rate and a large number of young people. More developed nations will have a low birth rate and a high proportion of older people. Each of these types of societies faces different challenges as they respond to population aging.

THE DEMOGRAPHIC TRANSITION

The **demographic transition** describes a pattern of population change that took place in Western nations over the past 250 years. The **developing nations** will probably go through this transition, and some of these nations have already started the process. Figure 1 shows the population trends over time that created the transition.

The developed nations that have gone through the demographic transition—from high to low birth and **death rates**—face new issues related to a large older population. For one thing, the demographic transition leads to a new perspective on the life cycle. Nearly all children can now expect to live to old age. Most middle-aged people can expect to live a decade or more in retirement, and many older people will live to late old age. A larger population than ever before will live more than 100 years.

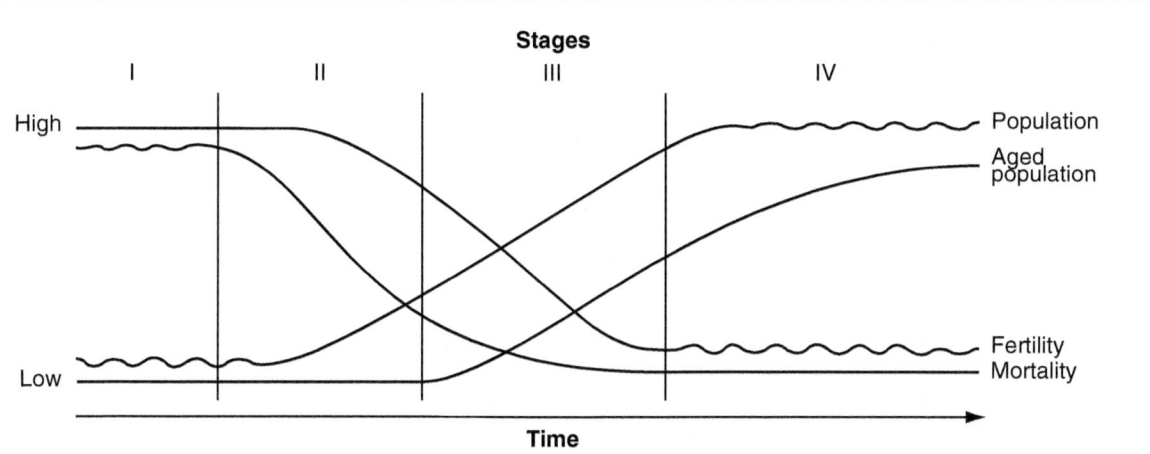

Stage I: High fertility and high mortality. Small population. Slow and varied population growth. High proportion of young people, small proportion of older people.

Stage II: High fertility; mortality begins to decline. Population begins to grow as more children survive. Population explosion may occur and society may get younger. Small proportion of elderly people.

Stage III: Fertility declines and mortality declines further. Population growth begins to level off at larger size. *This is the stage of the transition from a young high-growth to an older low-growth population.* Older population begins to grow as a proportion of the population.

Stage IV: Low fertility, low mortality. Low population growth and large proportion of older people in the population.

FIGURE 1 Stages of the Demographic Transition

Source: Reprinted from "Demography of Aging" by G. C. Myers, in R. H. Binstock & L. K. George, Eds., *Handbook of Aging and the Social Sciences,* 3rd ed. (p. 25). Copyright 1990, with permission from Elsevier.

The developing nations that go through this transition will experience similar benefits and challenges as their populations age (see Figure 2).

THREE TYPES OF SOCIETIES AND POPULATION AGING

The Less Developed Nations

The less developed nations of Africa, Asia, Oceania, the Caribbean, and Latin America make up three quarters of the world's population. Most of these nations have young populations with a small proportion of older people. In some cases they have as few as 2% of their populations age 65 and over. These countries will age in the years ahead, though they will still have relatively small proportions of older people.

African nations (some of the least developed nations) will average only a little over 4% age 65 and over in the year 2025. Overall the developing nations will average only about 8% in that year (United Nations, 2002a). High birth rates will keep the *proportion* of older people relatively low in these countries, but these nations will see explosive growth in the *number* of older people.

"By the year 2025," Myers (1990, p. 27) says, "over two-thirds of the world's older population will be found in the developing countries." Asia will gain over a quarter of a billion older people. China alone will have 194 million people age 65 and over by 2025. (By comparison, the entire U.S. population will be about 346 million people in that year [United Nations, 2002b].) High **fertility** in the past and greater survival of older people in the present will produce this explosive growth.

An increase in older people in developing nations will strain current social, health, and economic programs. Sennott-Miller (1994) says that developing nations need more information about their older populations, and they need to plan for an aging society. Countries with

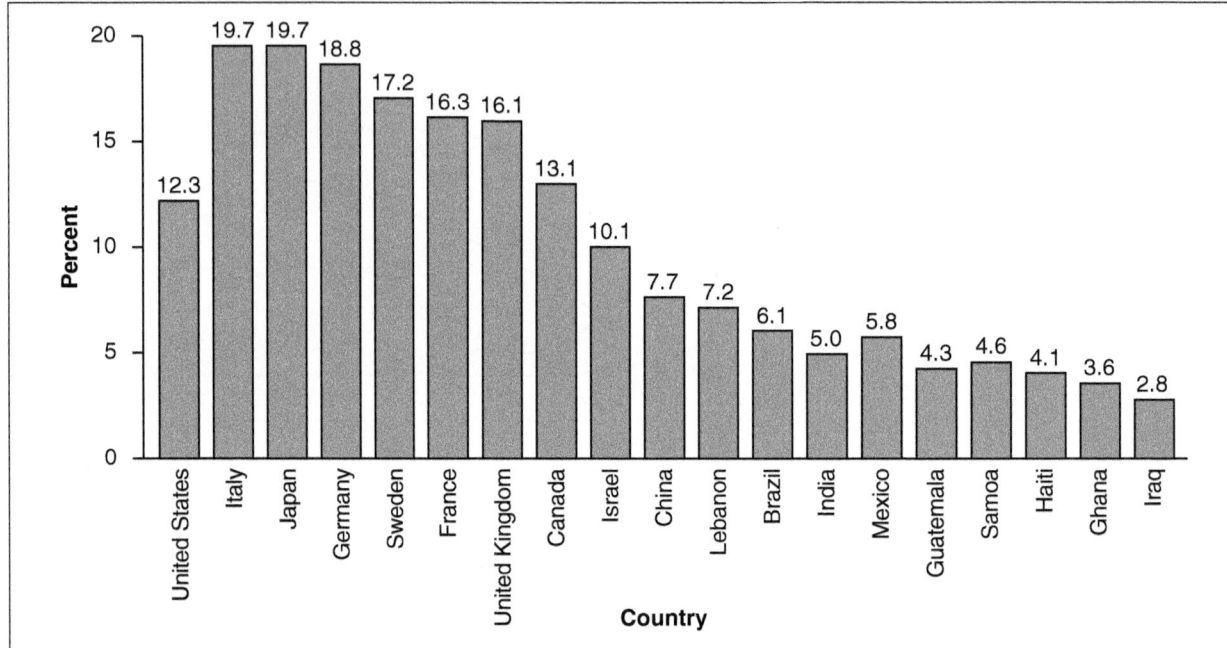

This chart reveals that the developed countries of Europe and North America have the largest proportions of older people. The developing nations (e.g., Brazil and China) have smaller proportions of older people. These proportions will increase if their birth rates decline and life expectancy increases. The least developed nations have the smallest proportions of older people, the highest birth rates, and the highest death rates.

FIGURE 2   Elder Populations in Selected Countries, 2005, Age 65 and Over

Source: Population Division of the Department of Economic and Social Affairs of the United Nations Secretariat, *World Population Prospects: The 2006 Revision* and *World Urbanization Prospects: The 2005 Revision,* http://esa.un.org/unpp. Retrieved November 15, 2007, from http://esa.un.org/unpp/p2k0data.asp.

TABLE 1   Elder Population Increases, Age 65 and Over from World and Major Regions, 2000 to 2050

	Population (in millions)			*Increase (2000 as base = 100)*	
	2000	*2025*	*2050*	*2025*	*2050*
World	421.4	832.2	1,464.9	197	348
More developed*	171.0	260.3	320.7	152	188
Less developed**	250.3	571.8	1,144.2	228	457
Africa	26.6	56.9	128.8	214	484
Latin America	29.1	70.1	143.7	241	494
North America	39.0	70.0	92.6	179	237
Asia	216.2	480.6	910.5	222	421
Europe	107.4	148.5	180.1	138	168
Oceania	3.0	6.1	9.2	203	307

*More developed: Europe, Japan, North America, Australia, and New Zealand.

**Less developed: Africa, Asia (excluding Japan), Latin America/Caribbean, Melanesia, Micronesia, and Polynesia.

The absolute number of older people given in this chart: (1) shows the distribution of older people worldwide; (2) allows for a comparison of the size of older populations that each country and region will have to deal with; and (3) shows the growth rate of the older population in each region. This growth rate gives an idea of how much demographic change each society will undergo.

This table shows that, worldwide, the less-developed countries have a larger number of older people than the more developed countries (although they have smaller percentages of older people). It also shows that the older population will increase in the less developed countries at a faster rate than in the more developed countries.

In 2000, for example, Asia had five and a half times more older people than North America. This reflects the larger size of the total Asian population. Projections show that the Asian older population will increase at a faster rate than the North American older population. This reflects increased life expectancies in Asian countries. By the year 2050, compared to North America, Asia will have more than nine and a half times more older people.

Source: Medium variant data in Population Division of the Department of Economic and Social Affairs of the United Nations Secretariat, *World Population Prospects: The 2004 Revision* and *World Urbanization Prospects: The 2003 Revision.* Retrieved April 14, 2005, from http://esa.un.org/unpp

social programs and pension plans in place will need to adapt these programs to serve more older people. China provides a good example of a developing nation that faces the challenge of population aging.

China: A Case Study of Population Aging in a Developing Nation

China had a total population of 1.3 billion people in 2000. Demographers expect the population to grow to almost 1.5 billion people by 2050. Over these same 30 years, the population age 65 will grow from 88 million in 2000 to 341 million in 2050 (United Nations, 2002b). Retirees at midcentury (people between the ages of 50 and 60, depending on their jobs) will make up about one third of China's population or 430 million people (*New York Times,* 2007).

Researchers trace this rapid increase in population aging to a decrease in China's **fertility rate.** The one-child policy begun in 1979 accounts for much of this decline in fertility. Due to this fertility decline (a rate of 1.8 in 2000) China will age sooner and more rapidly than other developing nations (Kinsella & Velkoff, 2001). Zhang (2001, p. 12) says that "China has a population that is aging . . . so fast that it has outpaced **industrialization** and **modernization**." Experts call this "one of the greatest **demographic changes** in history" (French, 2006).

At current rates of population change, China will get old before it gets rich. It will have to deal with the issues of a developing nation, such as feeding its people. And it will have to deal with issues of a developed society, such as caring for the elderly. It will also have to develop the pension and health care systems to care for its older population at the same time that it privatizes industry and grows its economy.

China today has the largest population of older people in the world. It also has the largest share of the world's oldest old (age 80+). These figures raise questions about China's ability to respond to its rapidly aging population. For example, the **elderly support ratio** (the number of people age 65 and over per 100 people ages 20 to 64 years old) between 2000 and 2030 will double from 12 to 26. And its parent support ratio (the number of people age 80 and over per 100 people ages 50 to 64) during those same years will more than quadruple from 3 to 14. These crude figures suggest that Chinese society and its members will need to provide more support for its older population in the years ahead. Most of these older people (about 76% of all older Chinese) live in rural areas.

In the cities many older people get a pension. But in rural areas older people depend mostly on family financial, social, and health care support (Peng & Hui, 2009). This can cause stress, and sometimes it leads to family breakdown. Also, younger people often move away from their families to find work in the cities. This further reduces the support for rural older people.

Older people in cities face a different set of challenges. More older people than ever before in China live on their own, especially in cities. The Chinese Association of Senior Citizens reports that more than 25% of older people in China live alone or with only their spouse (Zhang, 2001). These people face poverty, and they may lack a family support network. Osnos (2007, p. 7A) interviewed Zhang Junrui, a 79-year-old who retired from a state-owned factory in Beijing. Zhang says that "for elderly people, the biggest issue is to avoid getting sick. . . . Because savings might not be enough."

Chinese tradition puts the responsibility for elder care on the family. But in urban centers, this can also lead to burden and burnout. A study in Beijing found that 50% of families report financial, emotional, or other hardship in caring for their older relatives. This pressure will grow in the future as small young families with one child care for four or more older relatives.

An increase in the very old population (80+) will put a further burden on the young. The very old population will increase almost sixfold from 16 million in 2006 to 94 million people in 2050 (Johnson, 2006). Li Bengong, the executive deputy director of the China National Committee on Aging, says, "The situation is very serious. . . . We have weak economic capability to cope with the aging of the population" (Johnson, 2006, p. 20A).

China, like other developing nations, will find it hard to meet the needs of its growing older population. The high cost of building and running long-term care institutions will limit the growth of nursing homes. Also, older people in China prefer to stay at home and get support from their families. China has begun to develop home care options that fit its culture and that meet the needs of its aging population.

The increased number and proportion of older people in China and their need for support will lead to social change. Kinsella and Velkoff (2001, p. 79) say that in the near future China "may anticipate a social and economic fabric radically different from that of today."

The Least Developed Nations

The least developed nations face unique challenges due to population aging. Older people in parts of Africa, for example, face hardships because urban life, wage labor, and national political movements have lowered their status. Some countries in Africa will experience sudden demographic aging due to the HIV/AIDS epidemic. Botswana, for example, has seen a decrease in life expectancy from around 60 years in the 1950s "to a low of 42 years for females and 45 years for males" in the 1990s. The deaths of middle-aged and younger people will lead to rapid societal aging (Oduaran & Molosi, 2009, p. 123; also Wolff, Kabunga, Tumwekwase, & Grosskurth, 2009).

Cattell (1994), in a study of older people in Kenya, says that "delocalization," the shift of power outside the community and family, has occurred. This leads to loose family bonds and loss of authority for older people. A study of groups near Lake Victoria found that, in the past, grandmothers played a vital role in raising granddaughters. Today, granddaughters spend most of their day at school, and some live away during the school term. Schoolteachers and more worldly ideas now replace grandmothers and their teachings.

Older people in African countries often lack basic services. A study of South Africa, for example, found that only 47% of urban black older people and 15% of rural black older people had access to conveniences such as running water, sanitation, and electricity. A study of southern Africa found that in Botswana, Lesotho, Namibia, Swaziland, and Zimbabwe, few older people get a pension. For this reason most work into their 70s and 80s (Gist, 1994; Martin & Kinsella, 1994).

Many of these older people still give support to their families. Some give direct financial support to younger people. Kinsella calls pension sharing "the norm." Others provide services (such as babysitting) that allow younger people to work outside the home.

Very old people in these countries rely on family support for their well-being, but lower fertility, the movement of young people to find jobs, and deaths due to AIDS among the young will reduce the amount of family support older people can count on. This occurs at a time when the older population in southern Africa will nearly triple between 2000 and 2025 from 1.2 million to 3.5 million people (United Nations, 2002a). The country of Ghana provides a good example of the challenges facing the least developed nations.

Ghana: A Case Study of Population Aging in a Least Developed Nation

The number of older people (60+) in Ghana will increase from 1.3 million in 2005 to almost 5.6 million people in 2050. During this same time people age 80+ will increase six times from 100,000 to almost 600,000 in 2050. Once people in Africa enter old age, their life expectancy mirrors that of people throughout the world. This means that this large older population will live longer than ever before.

These demographic facts challenge Ghanaian society to provide support for older people. African nations in general have few social security programs for older people. These societies face "economic stagnation, heavy indebtedness, severely constrained public resources and sustained pervasive poverty of populations" (Aboderin, 2006, p. 19). The United Nations (UNDP, 2003, cited in Aboderin, 2006) reports that in Ghana 45% of the people live below $1 per day. And 79% live below $2 per day. Under these conditions welfare programs for the young and middle aged compete with the needs of the elderly for scarce resources.

People in Ghana cannot depend on social security in later life. Nor can they save enough during their working years to provide for themselves in old age. This leaves the responsibility for their care on the family.

Aboderin (2006, p. 108) found that current economic and social conditions undermine traditional models of family support. Today, for example, support for an older person falls mainly on adult children. In the past, the entire community shared in the care for older members. One respondent told Aboderin, "In the olden days older people were cared for not just by the children but also the relatives. Everybody was sharing food and so on but now . . . only the children look after the old person."

Adult children find it difficult to support their parents and pay their own family expenses. For this reason support for older parents has declined and in some cases has ceased. Older people who lack support from their children sink deep into poverty. One respondent says, "If I usually chop [eat] three times a day, [some] days I will chop only once. . . . So I will force to tighten my belt because *there is nowhere for me to go*" (Aboderin, 2006, p. 110, emphasis added by author).

Aboderin (2006, p. 111) found that "the middle aged child often has to choose between support for their own children or support for their parents." And people tend to choose support for the young. Aboderin summarizes the comments of the people she interviewed. "*The . . . older generation has no right to stand in the way of—or absorb resources that are needed for—the future life and well-being of the younger generations.*" One person told Aboderin, "Right now I can't help my mother how I want because I don't have" (p. 113, emphasis in the original).

Some people propose that governments find ways to support the family in its traditional role. Other planners argue for laws that would force middle-aged children to care for their aging parents. The lack of funds makes either of these options unlikely in the near future.

This case study shows the challenges that face the least developed nations as they try to plan for an aging population. Older people can no longer rely on support from their children. And the wider community no longer provides support to older members. Poverty among young adults undermines their ability provide support for their parents.

Older people in a least developed nation have little or no social security. They have no savings. And they have only tenuous support from their adult children. As more people enter old age in Ghana and as they live longer in old age, this lack of support could turn into a crisis. "The major single cause of the decline [in support for elders]," Aboderin (2006, p. 146) says, "without doubt . . . has been a reduced resource capacity of the middle generation." And unless the economic conditions in the country improve, older people cannot count on support from any source. This makes old age an uncertain and painful time for many people in Ghana.

Summary of Aging in Developing and Least Developed Nations

The ability of a country to help its older people largely depends on its economy. A country with a strong economy can make more resources available to its older people. But few developing nations have strong economies. Responses that fit Western industrialized societies will not fit developing nations.

The developing nations need solutions that fit their cultures and current economic conditions. Developing nations such as India, cannot afford expensive pension programs. India's large population (1.3 billion people, about 3.6 times that of the United States) and its developing economy challenge its ability to care for people of all ages. More than one quarter of the population lives below the poverty line.

India uses most of its public resources for poverty alleviation, job creation, and food subsidies to the poor. India provides pension relief only to its poorest elders (about 5.3 million people), and then only 75 rupees per month (about $1.50 U.S. in 2010) (Rao, 2001).

Sokolovsky (2000) concludes that the family remains the primary source of support for older people throughout the world. Where public supports exist, especially in developing nations, they can, at their best, support traditional family commitments to the old. He cites Nana Apt, an African sociologist, to support this point. "It is not enough," she says, "to talk about the bind of tradition, and it's not enough to talk about its

---

BOX 1
REFLECTIONS ON AGING IN AFRICA

Novelist and travel writer Paul Theroux traveled by land from Cairo to Cape Town. He detailed his journey in his book *Dark Star Safari: Overland from Cairo to Cape Town* (2003). During his travels he passed his 60th birthday. This caused him to examine the meaning of age and aging—for him and for the people he met. In the excerpt below, Theroux reflects on what aging means in the African context.

> I decided to avoid any birthday celebration. I was so self-conscious of my age that I often asked Africans to guess how old I was, hoping—perhaps knowing in advance—they would give me a low figure. They always did. Few people see elderly in Africa. Forty was considered old, a man of fifty was at death's door, sixty year olds were just crocks or crones. Despite my years I was healthy, and being agile and resilient I

found traveling in Africa a pleasure. I did not seem old here, did not feel it, did not look it to Africans, and so it was a great place to be, another African fantasy, an adventure in rejuvenation.

> "You are forty-something," Kamal had guessed in Addis. The highest number I got was fifty-two. Little did they know how much they flattered my vanity. But no one was vain about longevity in Africa, because the notion of longevity hardly existed. No one lived long and so age didn't matter, and perhaps that accounted for the casual way Africans regarded time. In Africa no one's lifetime was long enough to accomplish anything substantial, or to see any task of value completed. Two generations in the West equaled three generations in African time, telescoped by early marriage, early child-bearing, and early death. (pp. 197–198)

disintegration. We must find ways and means of transforming it into a modern form that will make multigenerational relationships much more viable" (Apt, 1998, p. 14, cited in Sokolovsky, 2000).

Sokolovsky (2000, p. 44) goes on to say that traditional systems work best when they fit into local economic and cultural systems. "These systems need to give both youth and elders reason to support each other."

THE DEVELOPED NATIONS

The United Nations (2002a) reports that the developed nations of the world will see increases in their proportions of older people. The U.N. projects that these countries on average will have more than one quarter of their populations age 65 and over by 2025. And they will have one third of their populations over age 60 in that year. Population aging will extend a trend that, for some of these countries, began in the 19th century.

Increased population aging will create challenges for the developed nations. For example, all of these countries will face the issue of rising health care and pension costs. These societies may need to shift funds from other types of programs to serve older people. Or they may develop new programs that better fit an older population.

Societies like those of Western Europe, Canada, Japan, and the United States today have relatively few people who work in manufacturing and food production. Instead, most people work in the service sector. This includes nurses, teachers, and investment counselors. These people sell their technical expertise. People in a **postindustrial society** generally have a high standard of living. These societies have high social mobility, a concern for equality and individual rights, and long life expectancies.

Christensen and colleagues (Christensen, Doblhammer, Rau, & Vaupel, 2009) say that if the increase in life expectancy in developed nations continues, "most babies born since 2000 . . . will celebrate their 100th birthdays."

The high proportion of older people in developed nations and the large number of very old people will pose challenges to their pension and health care systems. Japan shows the challenges that face developed nations today.

Japan: A Case Study of Population Aging in a Developed Nation

Japan had a population of 84 million people in 1950. By 2000, the population had increased to 127 million

Jean Schweitzer/Alamy

Korea has modernized rapidly. This Korean woman sells vegetables at the indoor market in Gyeongjus, South Korea. Many older people in Korea keep shops. Others sew and sell their goods. They help their extended families with the income and they stay active in the community.

(United Nations, 2002b). Over these same 50 years the population age 65 and over increased more than five times. The Japanese today have one of the longest average life expectancies in the world. According to the United Nations (2002b), at birth a Japanese female can expect to live 85 years, a Japanese male, 77.8 years.

In the year 2006, Japan had 21% of its population age 65 and over (the highest percentage in the world) (Chandler, 2006). Low fertility rates and low death rates will lead to continued population aging in the future. Projections to the year 2050 show that in that year nearly two of every five people in Japan will be age 65 or older (Maeda, 2009). Myers (1990, p. 26) calls this "a spectacular growth" in the proportion of older people. And Chandler (2006) calls the pace of population aging in Japan "without precedent in the industrial world."

The large increase in the oldest old (age 80+) poses unique problems for Japan. This population will grow to over 17 million people by 2050, a 2.7-fold increase from 2005. Nearly one person in five in Japan will be age 80 and over in 2055. This large increase in the very old will place heavier demands on government, community, and family support systems.

The Japanese call this *koreika,* societal aging. A 1995 survey conducted by the Ministry of Health and Welfare in Japan (National Institute of Population, 2004) found that 57.3% of the respondents considered population aging "a trouble" or "a serious trouble." And 68% of the respondents said that Japan should increase its birth rate to slow population aging. Knight and Traphagan (2003, p. 13) say people in rural communities use low birth rates and population aging to explain all kinds of problems. They use this "depopulation consciousness" to explain poor treatment of older people, problems at work, and the inability to find a bride.

Japan has a history of providing social security and health care to its older people. The government has provided a national pension plan and a universal health insurance program since the 1960s. A report by the National Institute of Population and Social Security Research (2002–2003) says that these two programs "have become the two main pillars of Japanese social security system." Population aging will strain the capacity of these systems in the years ahead. This will require new responses from individuals and the government.

Japan faces challenges similar to those of other developed nations. These challenges include higher costs for pensions, more chronic disease, and the need to rethink health care services for an older population. Japan differs from other developed nations in the speed of its transition to an aging society. In only 26 years (1970 to 1996), the Japanese older population grew from 7% to 14% of the population. By contrast, some European societies took as long as 115 years to see this kind of change (Kinsella & Velkoff, 2001). Japan will have to make changes quickly to meet the needs of its aging population and to maintain its standard of living.

Mass retirement in the next few years also poses a threat to Japan's prosperity. More than 2 million people age 60 retired in 2007. These experienced workers will leave the labor force, but fewer young people will be there to take their place. And this will mean fewer people to pay into the national pension system. Ibe (2000, p. 8) concludes that a "revision of pension benefits and payments is therefore inevitable."

Proposed changes that might solve this problem include increasing the birth rate, raising the retirement age (now age 60), encouraging women to enter the labor force to increase productivity, and allowing more immigrant labor in order to boost the national economy (Chandler, 2006; Doi, 2007). Some combination of these options will be needed to manage societal aging in Japan.

Population aging affects nations and people throughout the world. The developed nations will have greater proportions of older people in their populations in the future. The developing nations will have larger numbers of older people than ever before. These changes will take place in the context of rapid **urbanization**, industrialization, globalization, and changes to the environment. We cannot look back. New conditions call for new responses. The large number of older people in the world today "remains irreducibly novel," Laslett (1976, p. 96) says, and "it calls for invention rather than imitation."

POPULATION AGING IN THE UNITED STATES

Increased Numbers of Older People

In 2006, 37 million people age 65 and over lived in the United States. Older people accounted for just over 12% of the total population. Over the 20th century, the older population grew more than 10-fold from 3 million to 37 million. Projections show that it will more than double again from the year 2006 to 2050, from 37 million to 86.7 million people.

The oldest-old population (those age 85 and over) grew from just over 100,000 in 1900 to 5.3 million in 2006. The U.S. Census Bureau projects that this group could grow to nearly 21 million people by 2050. Some experts predict an even faster growth of this older population due to lower death rates at later ages (Federal Interagency Forum, 2008). (Figure 3 shows the actual and projected increase in the number of older people in the United States from 1900 to 2050.)

This growth in the older population will take place unevenly over the forty-year period from 1990 to 2030. From 1990 to 2010, the older population grew relatively slowly by about 1.3% per year. This reflects the relatively small number of births during the 1930s. But from 2010 to 2030, when the large Baby Boom cohorts enter old age, the older population will grow by as much as 2.8% per year.

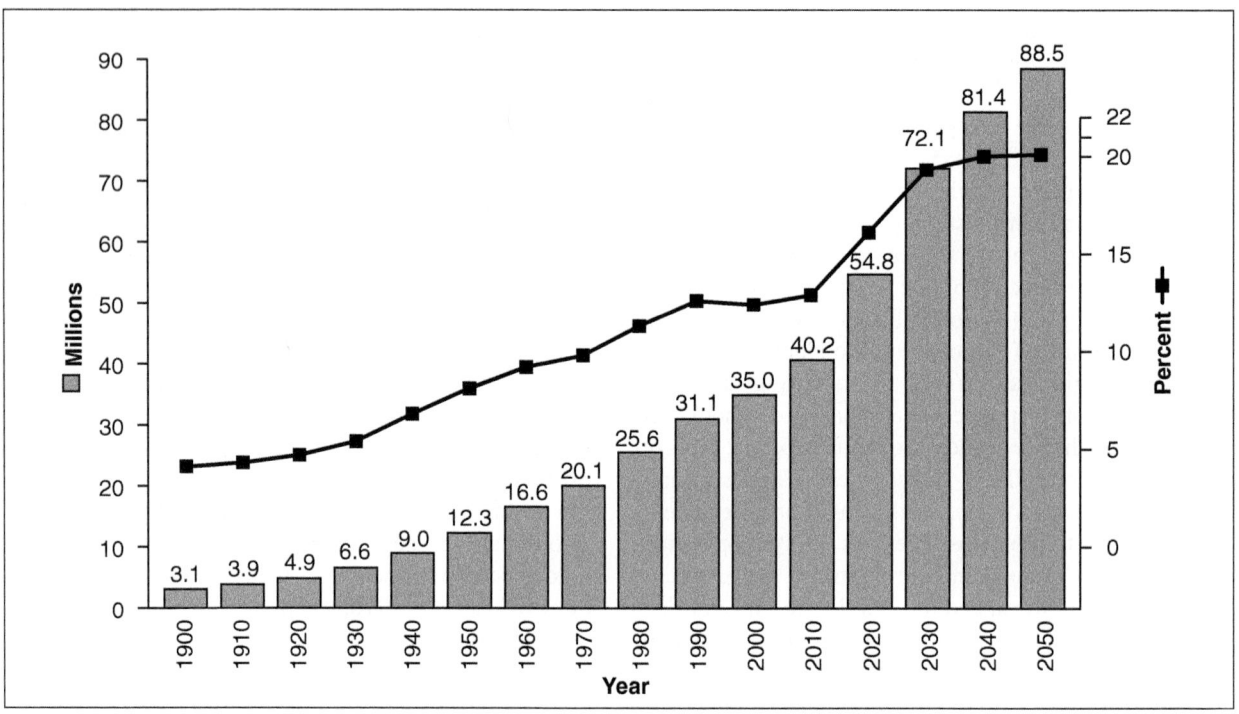

FIGURE 3 U.S. Elder Population, Age 65 and Over, 1900–2050*

*The projections presented here reflect the U.S. Census Bureau's "middle series" projections. The U.S. Census Bureau makes a number of projections based on a number of fertility, mortality, and migration assumptions. The middle series assumes a fertility rate in 2050 of 2,150 births per 1,000 women, life expectancy at birth in 2050 of 79.7 years for men and 85.6 years for women, and an ultimate net migration of 880,000 per year.

The 1900 to 1980 data are tabulated from the Decennial Censuses of the Population and exclude Armed Forces overseas. Projections (1990 onward) are middle series projections and include Armed Forces overseas.

Sources: Adapted from L. Hetzel & A. Smith, *The 65 Years and Over Population: 2000–Census 2000 Brief,* 2001. Retrieved on March 21, 2004, from www.census.gov/prod/2001pubs/c2kbr01-lo.pdf. F. Hobbs & N. Stoops, *Demographic Trends in the 20th Century,* U.S. Census Bureau, Census 2000 Special Reports, Series CENSR-4 (Washington DC: U.S. Government Printing Office, 2002). Retrieved on January 19, 2004, from www.census.gov/prod/2002pubs/censr-4.pdf. National Center for Health Statistics. (2010a). Health, United States, 2009: With Special Feature on Medical Technology. Hyattsville, MD. 2010. Figure 1, p. 15. Projected 2010–2050 figures.

Demographers rarely use the absolute number of older people in a society alone to analyze population aging. They rarely use it to compare aging in different societies. This figure, if used alone, can mislead a researcher. For example, a doubling or tripling of the older population can seem like an overwhelming change to a society, but its effect will depend on many things, including the society's economy, its policies, and its total rate of population growth.

Increased Median Age of the Population

Half the population is older and half younger than the median age. Median age gives a rough estimate of a population's age structure. It offers a sensitive measure of increases or decreases in population aging.

An increase in the median age means that the population has gotten older. Note in Figure 4 that the median age has more than doubled over the years, from seventeen years in 1820 to a projected thirty-nine years in 2050. Note also that the increase halted during the 1960s and 1970s. This signals a reversal in the process of population aging for those years.

Why did this occur? These declines in median age mark the effects of the Baby Boom that took place after World War II. The median age increased again between 1970 and 2000 from twenty-eight to thirty-five years. The U.S. Census projects a further increase in median age to 39 years by 2030 (He, Sangupta, Velkoff, & De Barros, 2005). Demographers rarely use the median age alone as a measure of population aging. The median age says little about the relative size of age groups within the population, or about changes in the size of age groups relative to one another.

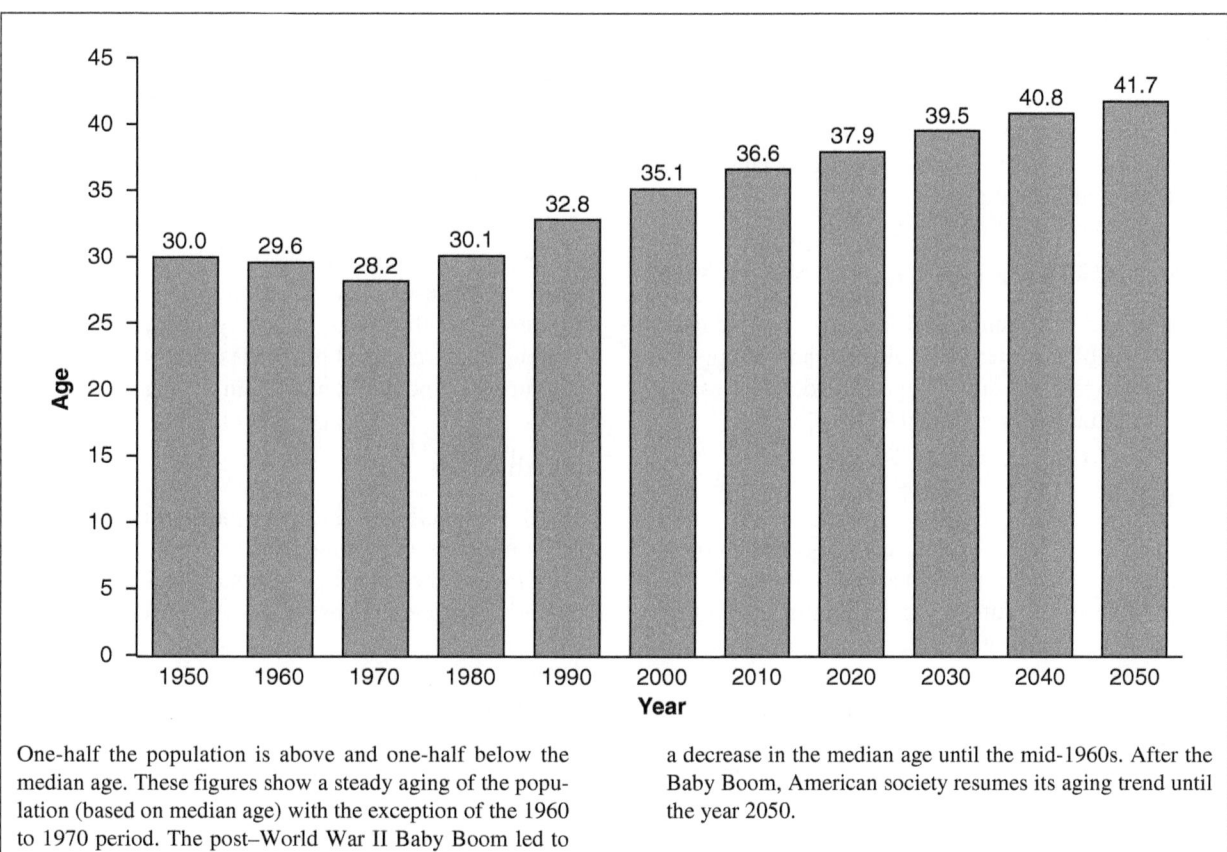

One-half the population is above and one-half below the median age. These figures show a steady aging of the population (based on median age) with the exception of the 1960 to 1970 period. The post–World War II Baby Boom led to a decrease in the median age until the mid-1960s. After the Baby Boom, American society resumes its aging trend until the year 2050.

FIGURE 4   Median Age of U.S. Population, 1950–2050

Source: Population Division of the Department of Economic and Social Affairs of the United Nations Secretariat. (2009). *World Population Prospects: The 2008 Revision,* http://esa.un.org/unpp. Retrieved: November 05, 2010—http://esa.un.org/unpp/p2k0data.asp

Increased Proportion of Older People

Gerontologists most often use the proportion of people age 65 and over in the population as a measure of population aging. This measure shows the relationship between the older group and the rest of society. An increase in the proportion of older people, for example, means a decrease in the proportion of other age groups. It gives an indication of how much influence the older group will have on social life. Figure 3 shows the proportion of people age 65 and over in the United States for the years 1900 to 2050. Note that the proportion increases from 4% in 1900 to 20% in 2050 when the last of the Baby Boom generation reaches late old age.

Measuring Trends

Each of these measures of population aging shows the same trend: *the aging of the U.S. population.* Each measure gives a unique perspective on this phenomenon. For example, the absolute number of older people gives an idea of how many people will enter retirement at a certain time. It also gives some idea of the number of customers who might want to invest in condominiums or buy cars. The median age points to shifts in the political interests of the population. A higher median age means more people interested in programs and policies for later middle-aged and older adults.

The proportion of older people shows the relationship between older and younger age groups. For example, in 1900, older people made up 4% of the population, but people under age 18 made up 40% of the population. In 1980, older people made up 11% and young people made up 28% of the population. By the year 2050, older people (age 65 and over) will make up 20.6% and younger people (ages 0 to 14) will make up only 18.5% of the population (Hetzel &

Smith, 2001; United Nations, 2002b). These figures suggest that societal resources will need to shift to serve older people in the future. Gerontologists use these measures to assess various impacts of population aging on social life and to project social changes due to population aging.

THE CAUSES OF POPULATION CHANGE

A population can change in three ways: people move into or out of a society, people die, and people are born. Demographers study migration, death rates, and birth rates to understand population aging.

Migration

Migration has played a relatively small role in population aging in the United States and will likely play a smaller role in the future. Because immigrants typically arrive in the United States as young adults, their presence tends to lower the country's median age. They also tend to have children, which further lowers the median age.

Migrants who come of age in the United States have an impact on population aging 45 or 50 years later. This delayed effect accounts for some of the increase in the older population until 1960. Many of the people who came of age before 1960 immigrated to the United States between 1905 and 1914. Between 1901 and 1910, for example, nearly 9 million immigrants arrived in the United States, by far the highest rate of immigration in the past 100 years (U.S. Census Bureau, 2002).

Immigrants have less impact on population aging today than at certain times in the past. First, the immigrants from earlier in the last century have died off. Second, more restrictive immigration laws have kept the group of foreign-born older people relatively small. (Immigration averaged around 700,000 people per year of all ages in the 1980s.) This has relaxed somewhat. In 1990, the government lifted quotas on family reunification, which led to larger numbers of immigrants than in the 1980s (some of them older people).

Still, the numbers remain relatively small. For the years 2007–2009, for example, about 1.1 million people became legal permanent residents of the United States each year. New arrivals totaled less than half a million people each year (Monger, 2010).

Third, projected low immigration levels in the future will mean small proportions of foreign-born older people. The U.S. Census Bureau middle series projections put immigration in the year 2050 at about 880,000,

a number similar to the recent past, but a relatively small proportion of the total U.S. population.

Changes in immigration laws, the quality of border control, and the flow of immigrants make future migration figures uncertain. Illegal immigration, mostly by young people, would slow population aging in the short run, but demographers find it hard to assess the impact of this group. Zopf (1986, p. 5) concludes that "the largest impact of immigration on the aging of the population has probably passed." For this reason, death rates and birth rates will have the greatest impact on population aging in the years ahead.

Death Rates

Death rates fell throughout the past century for whites and nonwhites and for men and women. (See Table 2.) This means that more people survived into old age than ever before. Life expectancy at birth in 1900 was 47.3 years. It reached a record high of 77.7 years in 2006 (Heron et al., 2009; Arias, 2010). These gains in life expectancy largely reflect decreases in infant mortality. The National Center for Health Statistics (2003; Xu, Kochanek, & Tejada-Vera, 2009) reports that from 1960 to 2001, infant mortality fell

TABLE 2 U.S. Life Expectancy at Birth (in Years)

	White		African American	
	Male	*Female*	*Male*	*Female*
1970	68.0	75.6	60.0	68.3
1980	70.7	78.1	63.8	72.5
1990	72.7	79.4	64.5	73.6
2000	74.7	79.9	68.2	75.1
2010	76.5	81.3	70.2	77.2
2020	77.7	82.4	72.6	79.2

This table shows the increase in life expectancy at birth for whites and African Americans in the United States for selected years from 1970 to 2010. All four groups show an increase in life expectancy. African American men and women, from 1970 to 2000, have narrowed the gap in life expectancy with their white counterparts. Whites of either sex continue to have longer life expectancies than African Americans. But the projection to 2020 shows an increase for all groups and a narrower gap between whites and African Americans.

Source: Adapted from U.S. National Center for Health Statistics, National Vital Statistics Reports (NVSR). (2009). *Deaths: Final Data for 2006,* Vol. 57, No. 14, April 17, 2009. Retrieved: October 19, 2010, from http://www.census.gov/compendia/statab/2010/tables/10s0102.pdf

U.S. Census Bureau, Statistical Abstract of the *United States* (Washington, DC: U.S. Government Printing Office, 2002b). Retrieved March 21, 2004, from www.census.gov/prod/www/statistical-abstract-02.html; Arias, E. (2004). United States life tables, 2001, *National Vital Statistics Reports, Vol. 52*(14) (Hyattsville, MD: National Center for Health Statistics, 2004). Retrieved March 21, 2004, from www.cdc.gov/nchs/data/nvsr/nvsr52/nvsr52_14.pdf.

steadily. The rate decreased from 26.0 (per 1,000 live births) in 1960 to 6.77 in 2007.

This is the lowest rate ever recorded in the United States. Both African Americans and whites showed a decline in infant mortality from 1960 to 2007. African Americans showed a decline from 44.3 in 1960 to 12.92 in 2007 for both sexes. Whites showed a decline from 22.9 in 1960 to 5.72 in 2007 (National Center for Health Statistics, 2003; Xu et al., 2007).

Both races show improvements in infant survival, but the 2007 figures show that African Americans have an infant mortality rate 2.3 times the rate of whites. This reflects lower incomes, poverty, and less access to high-quality medical care for African Americans.

The United States could see further decreases in infant mortality. Countries such as Hong Kong, Japan, and Singapore have rates below 4 per 100,000. But these countries have small, homogeneous populations.

Demographers also project increases in life expectancy for people over age 65. They project these gains for whites and nonwhites, men and women. The trend that supports these future gains already exists. For example, between 1980 and 2006, life expectancy at age 65 increased from 14.2 years to 17.1 years for white males, from 18.4 to 19.8 years for white females, from 13.0 to 15.1 years for black males, and from 16.8 to 18.6 years for black females (National Center for Health Statistics, 2009; Arias, 2010).

Changes in life expectancy will affect the size and structure of the older population in the years ahead. By the years 2045–2050, men at age 65 can expect on average to live another 18.8 years, and women at age 65 can expect to live another 23 years (United Nations, 2002b).

The conquest of cancer or further declines in stroke and heart disease death rates could lead to further increases in life expectancy in old age. This will mean, among other things, continued increases in the number and proportion of the oldest old people in the population, and a greater proportion of women in the old and very old population.

In the past, population aging took place because of decreased infant mortality. Today and in the future, population aging will occur mostly because of increased longevity.

Birth Rates

The decline in the **fertility rate** and the **birth rate**, more than any other cause, explains population aging during the past century. This may surprise you. Why should the rate of children born influence aging?

Demographers define the fertility rate as the number of live births per 1,000 women ages 15 to 44; they define the birth rate as the number of live births per 1,000 population. A high fertility rate (many births) will increase the proportion of younger people in society. This will keep the population relatively young. A low fertility rate will mean a proportionately greater number of older people. Couple a low fertility rate (fewer children) with a low death rate (people living longer), and you get population aging in the United States today.

At least three specific changes in birth rate influenced population aging in the United States. First, an increase in births took place before 1920 (Easterlin, 1987). The end of World War I in part accounts for this increase. The same may be said for the large number of young immigrants in the early 1900s, who began having children at this time. These people (the children born around 1920) entered old age in the mid-1980s. They will make up the very old population in the United States in the early years of this century.

Second, an explosion in births, the Baby Boom, took place after World War II, between 1946 and 1964. The first Baby Boomer, Kathleen Casey-Kirschling, was born 1 second after midnight on January 1, 1946. Between her birth and the end of 1964, America added one new baby to its population every 8 seconds. This meant a total of 78.2 million people added to the population during these years. Boomers formed the largest generation in U.S. history. In 2006, Baby Boomers totaled 78 million people or 26.1% of the population (U.S. Census Bureau, 2006e).

Nearly all of this group will have entered old age by the year 2030. In that year the United States will have an estimated 72 million older people (around 20% of the population at that time). This will come to more than twice the number of older people alive in 2000 (He et al., 2005). The oldest-old population will grow rapidly after 2030, when the Baby Boomers move into this age group.

The Baby Boom generation has shaped U.S. society and culture since the 1950s. The education system built schools for them in their childhood; the housing industry built homes for them as young adults; and the travel, leisure, and health care industries await their arrival into old age. This group, compared with past generations, has greater expectations for its living standards in later life. The size of the older Baby Boom generation will reshape the marketplace, social services, and politics in the next century. (See Box 2.)

BOX 2
THE BABY BOOM

One of my earliest memories is from 1951. I'm sitting in a car on a hot summer day with my uncle and grandmother. We're waiting outside a gray brick building. I can see the steps that lead to the front door far away. My uncle sits in the driver's seat. I see my mother coming down the step. She's carrying a blanket in her arms. A woman dressed in white walks beside her. The car door opens. My mother gets in and everyone in the car cranes their necks to look at the blanket.

The bundle was my sister Lynne. I was 3 years old at the time. I wasn't the only child with a new sister. Throughout my neighborhood and across the country boys and girls welcomed newborn sisters and brothers into their homes. The Baby Boom was in full swing.

During World War II my father and my uncles left their fiancées and girlfriends at home and went off to war. When the men came home they picked up where their lives had left off. They got jobs, got married, and moved to the suburbs. They also started families. And they did this with vigor.

The returning soldiers and their new brides made up for time lost during the war. They began to produce children at a furious rate.

The United States had a fairly steady number of births each year before the Baby Boom—hovering around 8 to 10 million children born per year. The Baby Boom years saw roughly double these numbers of births for two decades (between 1946 and 1964). This burst of children affected every American institution.

I was born in 1948, at the "leading edge" of the Baby Boom, so I know. Builders created suburbs to house us. Communities built schools to educate us. And industries (such as the food industry) created new products—first, prepared baby foods, then shelves of sugared cereals—to feed us. The streets in my neighborhood teemed with kids on Saturdays and during summer vacations. Every family it seemed had at least two children, some more. On my father's side of the family, for example, my sister and I have eight cousins. On my mother's side we have thirteen cousins—most of them born during the Baby Boom years.

The Baby Boom continued to shape American culture as we grew up. Boomers brought a new mindset to the country. If society didn't meet our needs, we changed society. Elvis. The Beatles. Bob Dylan. The Civil Rights Movement. Marijuana. LSD. Free love. The antiwar protests of the 1960s and early 1970s. All of this social unrest said "We'll have it our way."

Boomer influence continues today. As the first Boomers reached age 60, some radio stations dedicated themselves to "classic rock." Translation: rock music from the 60s and 70s that Boomers like. These stations play to the largest and one of the wealthiest groups in America.

The Baby Boom will continue to shape American culture, economics, and politics in the years ahead. The population pyramids show that by the middle of this century, Boomers will make up the largest older population ever. For example, between 2000 and 2030, the older population will more than double, from 35 million to 72 million, and almost one in five people will be age 65 or older (He et al., 2005).

"Every day," Myers and Nielson (2003, p. 56) say, "more than 10,000 Leading Edge Baby Boomers in the U.S. reach 55 years of age." Between 2011 and 2030, the years when the Baby Boom cohorts enter old age, the older population will grow by as much as 2.8% per year. The U.S. Census Bureau projects a population of 69 million people ages 50 to 59 in the year 2010 (cited in Harris, 2003). The Census Bureau (1996, pp. 2–5) calls this a "massive increase" in the number of older people.

The sheer number of older people in the future will influence economic and social life. As they enter later life, Baby Boomers will place demands on the retirement income system, the health care system, and every other system in U.S. society. They will also serve as a market for new goods and services—travel tours, education, electronic gear, housing, and more.

Health clubs, once the home of yogurt-loving, wheat germ-eating eccentrics, now exist in most hotels and shopping malls. An entire genre of books focuses on later-life issues and lifestyles—retirement, relationships, parent care, and personal growth. This interest in health and well-being in later life will accelerate in the years ahead. The cosmetics industry, the pharmaceutical industry, and business in general will shift attention to this growing market of affluent Boomers.

Russell (2001, p. 3) sums up the influence of the Boomer generation: "Boomers continue to be the most powerful generation the nation has ever experienced. Not only is . . . [this] group large, but its influence extends into the younger and older generations as it guides its children and aids its parents."

Third, fertility has declined from the mid-1960s to the early years of this century. The U.S. birth and fertility rates began to fall after 1960 (with a birth rate of 118 per 1,000 births to women ages 15 to 44) and hit an all-time low of 61 in 2002 (Downs, 2003). This has led to a sharp increase in the median age and an increase in the proportion of older people. Zopf (1986, p. 24) says, "The birth rate has fallen so significantly in virtually all parts of the nation that the aging of the population is one of [America's] universal demographic phenomena."

Will birth rates stay low in the future? Will the population keep getting older? No one can say for sure. For example, a surprising increase in births in 2007 led to the highest number of births ever registered in the United States in 1 year (more than 4.3 million). The general fertility rate in that year increased by 1% to 69.5—the highest level since 1990 (Hamilton, Martin, & Ventura, 2009).

This increase in fertility rates reverses a U.S. decline in fertility rates and bucks a worldwide trend among developed nations. Other developed nations have seen sharp decreases in fertility rates. Sweden, Japan, and Italy have birth rates far below the rate needed to replace their populations. Some countries, such as Sweden and Japan, have tried to reverse this trend, but they have had little success.

Birth rates reflect changing social and demographic conditions. Consider the following social forces that lead to a decreased birth rate:

1. New methods of birth control allow couples to choose how many children they will have. Gee (1982, p. 61) called population aging an "unplanned by-product of planned parenthood."
2. Young people in developed nations spend more years in school and in starting their careers than ever before.
3. Most young women today, compared with the past, work outside the home. They start families later and want fewer children.

These trends point to lower birth rates in the future. But no one can predict the direction of future rates. For example, the recent increase in birth rate took place even though more American women work outside the home than ever before.

Also, birth rates differ for various ethnic and racial groups. The Hispanic population has historically had a birth rate higher than the white population and other ethnic/racial groups. This young population will play a future role in the politics of population aging, especially in states with large Hispanic populations (e.g., California and other southwestern states).

Gerontologists point to the potential for conflict between the relatively large older white population and the large younger Hispanic population. For example, this young group may resist paying for benefits to the older white population through taxes and other state subsidies.

If birth rates stay high, this will moderate the aging of the population. An increased birth rate will decrease the proportion of older people in the population and will lower the median age. Still, it won't reduce the large effect of the aging Baby Boomer population on American society.

THE CHALLENGES OF AN AGING POPULATION

The older group will grow over the next 50 years or so, but it will not grow steadily. For example, population aging will slow and in some years will reverse itself. Myers (1990, p. 32) calls this the "metabolism of the population."

Between 1990 and 2000, for instance, the proportion of older people in the population decreased. The slow growth in the 65- to 74-year-old group accounts for this trend. But this will change in the early to middle years of the 21st century when the Baby Boom cohorts enter old age. These new cohorts will bring with them better health, better incomes, and a new view of later life.

At the same time, a larger number of people than ever before will live into late old age. These people, some of them over 100 years old, will have unique health and social service needs. The composition of the older population (the number of younger and the number of older seniors) can tell us about the challenges the United States will face as the population ages.

The Aging of the Older Population

Settersten and Trauten (2010, p. 143) call old age "life's longest period, extending three or more decades." Demographers divide the older group into subgroups. In the past, gerontologists defined the group ages 55 to 74 as the young-old and those age 75 and over as the old-old. But population aging has led to a refinement of this scheme. Research reports now often divide the older population into three groups: 65 to 74, 75 to 84, and 85 and over. All of these groups have grown in size.

He and colleagues (2005) report that the 65- to 74-year-old age group in 2000 was 8 times larger than in 1900, the 75- to 84-year-old age group was 16 times larger, and the 85 and over age group was 35 times larger. These groups will all grow in size in this century. But the oldest age group will be among the fastest-growing groups in the population. For example, between 1990 and 2000 the oldest age group increased by more than one third (from 3.1 million to 4.2 million) (He et al., 2005). (See Box 3 and Figure 5.)

People age 85 and over form a unique group within the older population. This group will grow about five times in size between 2000 and 2050 (Gonyea, 2010, citing Federal Interagency Forum on Aging-Related Statistics, 2006). By 2050, nearly a fifth of the older population (age 65 and over) will be 85 years old or over. This makes the oldest old population one of the fastest growing age groups in the country. Better health care and disease prevention have led to longer life in old age, and they will extend the lives of more people in the future. (See Figure 6.)

The oldest old population (age 85 and over) looks very different demographically from the young-old population (ages 65 to 74). Dunkle, Roberts, and Haug (2001) analyzed data from a longitudinal study of people in their 80s and 90s who lived in the Midwestern United States. They found that many of these people had small social networks. Although more than half the men in their study (52.2%) had spouses, only 11% of women were married. One third of the people in this study had no living children. The researchers found that the social networks of these people declined over time. (See Box 4.)

BOX 3
CENTENARIANS

Peter Keating (2010), writing for *Smart Money Magazine*, reports the following cases of centenarian achievement:

> Last year Emma Hendrickson, 101, became the oldest person ever to compete in the U.S. Bowling Congress Women's Championships, when she rolled a 318 series in Reno, Nev.

> Harriet Ames, 100, of Concord, N.H., earned her bachelor's degree in January, then died the next day.

> Frank DiPaolo Jr., 103, Providence political operative, still holds down his job as a doorman at the Rhode Island State House.

These people represent the leading edge of a population explosion of centenarians. The U.S. Administration on Aging reports that in 2008 the United States had 92,127 people age 100 and over (one quarter of one percent of the total 65+ population). This is a 147% increase from the 1990 figure of 37,306.

The Census Bureau predicts that by the year 2080, the United States will have over 1 million people age 100 or over. This will be a 10-fold increase over current figures. Vierck (2002, p. 2) calls this a "centenarian boom." Never in history have so many people reached their hundredth birthday.

What is it like to live to 100 years old? Will more centenarians mean more chronic health problems such as Alzheimer's disease? Will it mean more years of suffering for more people? Thomas Perls (1995), associate professor of geriatrics at Boston University School of Medicine, directed the New England Centenarian Study.

He thinks that people who live to age 100, as a group, will have better health than people 20 years younger. His pilot work found low proportions of centenarians with Alzheimer's disease. These people had better cognitive ability and health than expected. Perls says, "Centenarians disprove the perception that 'the older you get, the sicker you get. . . . They teach us that the older you get, the healthier you've been" (Keating, 2010).

Perls (1995) found that men in their 90s have better mental functioning than men in their 80s. Also, he has found what he calls a "gender crossover." Women tend to outlive men, but men who live beyond age 80 live healthier, more independent lives than women. Men who survive to late old age have greater physical and mental resources than expected.

Alfred Benedetti, age 101, serves as a model for the old age Perls describes. Benedetti performed in the Senior Olympics for the past 11 years, entering the javelin, shot put, and basketball free throw events. He bowls twice a week. He said that his health and long life came from avoiding tobacco and alcohol—except for the shot of port wine he drank every day. He stayed busy reading, writing, and working with his hands.

Genetics may explain part of the reason for long life and well-being in late old age. Those who live long may have genes that protect them from routine physical decline. They may also have genes that increase their ability to overcome disease and keep organs functioning well. Good health and a strong physical system lead to survival into late old age.

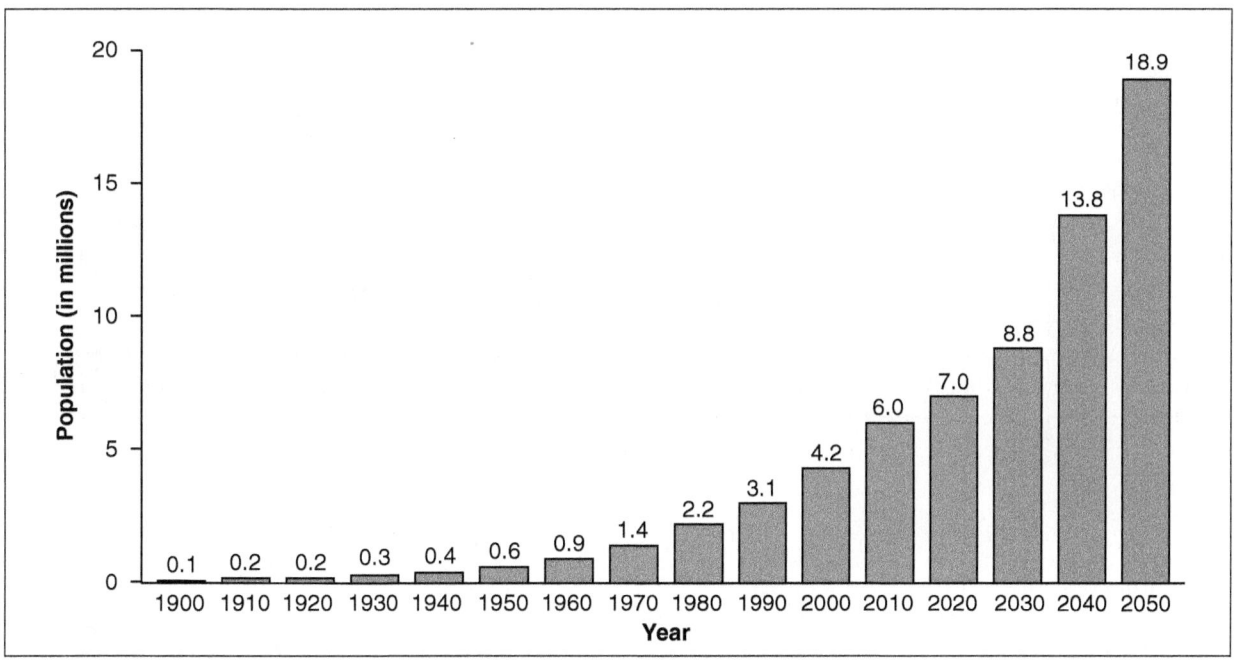

FIGURE 5 Population 85 Years and Over, 1900 to 2050

Source: U.S. Census Bureau. (1993). *Decennial censuses for specified years* and *population projections of the United States by age, sex, race, and Hispanic origin, 1993 to 2050,* Current Population Reports, P25-1104. Washington, DC: U.S. Government Printing Office. The data for 1990 are from He, W., Sangupta, M., Velkoff, V. A., & De Barros, K. A. (2005). *1990 census of population and housing,* CPH-L-74, *Modified and actual age, sex, race, and Hispanic origin data, 65+ in the United States: 2005,* U.S. Census Bureau, Current Population Reports, P23-209. Washington, DC: U.S. Government Printing Office.

BOX 4
A GERONTOLOGIST REFLECTS ON LATE OLD AGE

Elaine Brody, at age 88, provided a 50th anniversary feature article for *The Gerontologist* in 2010. Brody is one of the best-known gerontologists of her generation. Among other achievements, she coined the term "women in the middle" to capture the caregiving demands on middle-aged women.

In this article she provides a personal view of late old age. Below you will find some excerpts that focus on her experience.

My present perspective, then, is that of an 86-year-old woman who, I suppose, was prepared for old age intellectually but not emotionally. Even my children are growing into the stages of life I studied. Common experiences of old age, such as illness and losses, were unexpected, even though expectable. . . .

I do not remember becoming old. All of a sudden, I was there. Others perceive me as old. Cars stop to let me cross. People offer to help carry my packages. My grandchildren "check up" on me when my children are out of town and hold my arm when we cross a street. People my age walk more slowly and fatigue more quickly. Our waistlines thicken and our hair thins. Our balance is not great. We develop lots of wrinkles. One of my granddaughters is observant in detecting which of my friends have had what she calls "a little work done" on their faces (though having such "work" is by no means limited to the old). Some have had to give up driving—with the accompanying loss of independence and feelings of competence that entails. . . .

Our perspective on age has changed. One day, three people in succession said to me, "Did you hear about poor Harold? He was too young to die. He was only 83." A 92-year-old man died suddenly. Until that moment, he had been a regular member of his Neighborhood Security Patrol. As Jerry Seinfeld said, "Who dies at 70 anymore? It's old-fashioned.". . .

Source: Adapted from Brody, E. M. (2009). On being very, very old: an insider's perspective. *The Gerontologist, 50*(1), pp. 2–10.

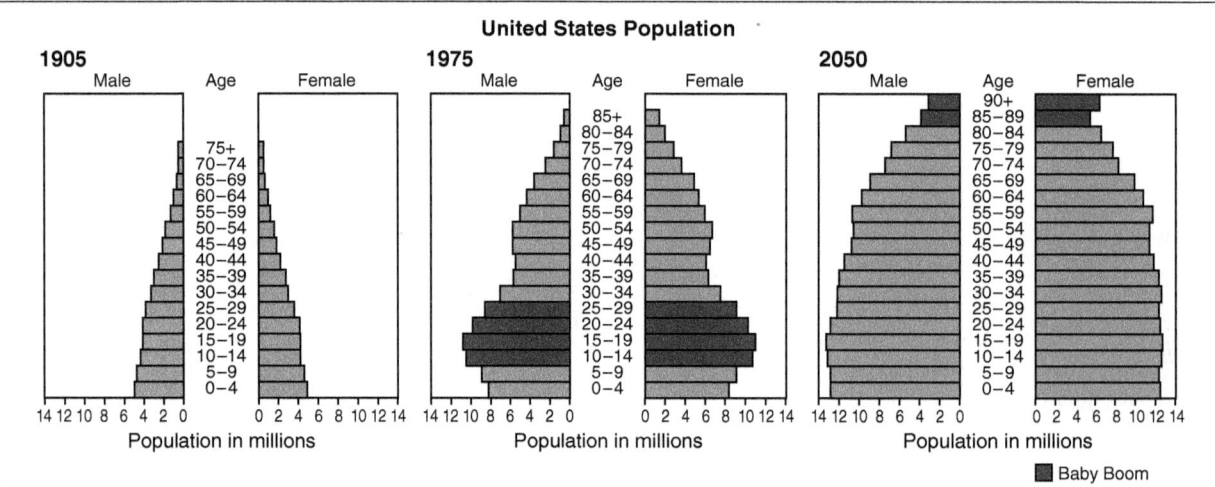

United States Population

Population pyramids consist of stacked bars that represent 5-year age cohorts. The bottom bar shows the youngest age group (0 to 4 years), the top bar the oldest group (90 and over). The left side of the bar contains the data for men, the right side for women.

A population pyramid gives a graphic profile of a society's age structure. Pyramids allow demographers to compare the age structures of two countries. They allow a viewer to compare male and female age structures in one society. And they allow a viewer to compare segments of the population (e.g., the size of the 5- to 9-year-old age group with the 0- to 4-year-old age group).

The three pyramids presented here show the impact of the Baby Boom, the Baby Bust, and longer life at the oldest ages. These three influences lead to the square-shaped pyramid of 2050. The movement of the Baby Boom generation can be seen through the life cycle by comparing the pyramids from 1975 and 2050. The Baby Boom appears as the 10- to 29-year-old age groups in 1975. It shows up as the 85 and over age group in 2050. At this point, many members of the Baby Boom generation have died. Note the large size of the 85 and over age groups in 2050 compared with 1975. Longer life expectancies and the continued large size of the Baby Boom generation lead to this large group of very old people.

FIGURE 6 Images of Aging: Population Pyramids for the United States, 1905, 1975, 2050

Sources: U.S. Census Bureau. (1965). *Estimates of the population of the United States, by single years of age, color, and sex: 1900 to 1959,* Current Population Reports, Series P-25, No. 311. Washington, DC: U.S. Government Printing Office. U.S. Census Bureau. (1982). *Preliminary estimates of the population of the United States, age, sex, and race: 1970 to 1981,* Current Population Reports, Series P-25, No. 917. Washington, DC: U.S. Government Printing Office. Day, J. C., & U.S. Census Bureau (1993). *Population projections of the United States, age, sex, race, and Hispanic origin: 1993 to 2050,* Current Population Reports, Series P2-1104. Washington, DC: U.S. Government Printing Office, middle series projections.

Gonyea (2010) says that people age 80 and over have the lowest average income of all age groups over age 65. Median income in 2006 for people age 80 and over came to $15,462 compared to $20,518 for people ages 64 to 69. More than 1 person in 10 among the oldest old lives in poverty (11.4%) and 3 in 10 live near poverty. Women and minority members of the oldest group report the lowest incomes.

African American women age 75 and over and Hispanic women age 85 and over have the lowest incomes of all. For example, older white men age 75 and over have a poverty rate of 4.4%. African American women in this age group have a poverty rate of 30.2%—more than seven times the rate of older white men. These figures reflect a lifetime of low income for minority women, lack of pensions and savings, and time out of the workforce taken to raise a family. These low-income groups rely most heavily on Social Security for their income.

The oldest old people have multiple chronic conditions and high rates of disability. They also consume large amounts of services, considering their numbers. Freedman, Aykan, Wolf, and Marcotte (2004) studied the amount of care services people age 75 and over used each month during a 3-year period. The researchers found that over the 3 years this group increased its care hours by 38%.

Wang (2004) reports that the 85 and over population accounts for 1.5% of the population, but uses 16.1% of Medicare fee-for-service payments. This group also uses the most nursing home services. He and colleagues (2005) report that in 2000, 18.2% of people age 85 and over lived in institutions compared with only 1.1% of people ages 65 to 74 and 4.5% of those ages 75 to 84. This represents a decrease in nursing home use from 1990. But it shows the continued need for heavy health care services for the very old.

The increase in the very old population in the years ahead will lead to an increase in the use of long-term care services. Some of that care will take place in institutions. But where possible, long-term care will take place in the community. In either case, increases in the oldest old population will have a large impact on national health care costs and policies.

Ethnic and Racial Variations

The racial and ethnic composition of the older population changes as new people enter old age. Today, for example, the nonwhite population of the United States is younger than the white population. Older people make up only 8% of the African American and 5% of the Hispanic American populations compared with 13.4% of the white population (National Center for Health Statistics, 2003). This difference reflects higher fertility rates (more young people in minority populations) and higher mortality among nonwhites. However, these rates may change in the years ahead, and this would lead to changes in the older population.

He and colleagues (2005) say that the proportion of non-Hispanic Whites in the older population will decrease from 83% in 2003 to 72% by 2030. During this same period the population of older African Americans will increase from 8% to 10% of the older population. Hispanics will increase from about 6% to 11% of the older population. And the proportion of Asians in the older population will increase from 3 to 5% of the older population. These changes will lead to greater ethnic and racial diversity in the older population.

Regional Distribution

Internal migration (**in-migration**) in the United States in the past several decades has led to decreases in the proportion of older people in the Northeast, increases in the proportion of older people in the Midwest, and increases in the proportions of older people in the South and the West. These findings reflect three trends that lead to an older population: accumulation, recomposition, and congregation (Longino, 2001).

Accumulation

Accumulation takes place when older people stay behind and young people move out of an area. Midwestern states (Iowa, Missouri, Nebraska, North Dakota, and South Dakota) made up 5 of the 15 states with the highest concentrations of older people in 2000 (He et al., 2005). The **out-migration** of younger people accounts for this. Young people leave this region to find work, often in the Sunbelt states. Projections show that northeastern states like Maine, Pennsylvania, and Rhode Island will age in the future in part because of out-migration. If present trends continue, they will rank among the 10 oldest states in the year 2020 (U.S. Census Bureau, 1996).

Recomposition

Recomposition takes place when older people move into an area that younger people leave. For example, some older people move to rural areas to retire. These areas may offer little opportunity for young workers. But they offer a low cost of living and beautiful scenery that suits older people (Hunt, Marshall, & Merrill, 2002). Arkansas and Missouri fit this pattern. They had large numbers of older people in 2000. Projections show that they will have some of the highest proportions of older people in the country in 2020 (19.3% and 17.5% of the population, respectively).

Congregation

Congregation takes place when people of all ages move to an area, but older people arrive at the fastest pace. Florida, Arizona, and North Carolina fit this pattern. The large number of older people who have moved to Florida made this the oldest state in the country in 2000 (with 17.6% of its population age 65 or over). Only Arkansas and Arizona will reach this level by the year 2020. By that time, Florida is projected to have over one quarter of its population age 65 and over.

Other Sunbelt and Western states (e.g., California and Texas) with a large number of older people also attract a large number of young people. This keeps the proportion of older people relatively low. Both California and Nevada rank in the bottom 10 states by proportion of older people, with 10.6% and 9.9% age 65 or older, respectively (He et al., 2005).

The movement of many Baby Boomers to the Sunbelt has delayed population aging in that region until later in this century. But Longino (2001, citing Frey,

"The kids are grown before you know it, aren't they?"

Published in The New Yorker 5/16/1988 by W.B. Park/Cartoonbank.com

1999) says, "This pattern should continue to fuel the aging of the Sunbelt in the early decades of the 21st century." Only Florida has both a large number and a large proportion of older people. Florida in 2000 had 6 of the 10 cities in the United States with the highest proportions of older people. Clearwater, Florida, in that year had 21.5% of its population age 65 and over (Hetzel & Smith, 2001).

Interstate Migration

Willa Reich lived in Manhattan all of her adult life. When she was in her 60s, her son and his family moved to Florida, but her daughter and her daughter's family remained in the city, a few minutes away by car. Willa's apartment was a short subway ride from her job, and with her daughter nearby, she felt content where she was.

Nevertheless, when Willa retired at age 65, she began to consider a move. She had a good pension from the city, Social Security, and some savings. The neighborhood had gotten worse, the winters felt more severe, and her son in Florida kept asking her to move south. She went to look at a condominium apartment north of Miami during one visit to her son. The complex had a clubhouse, swimming pools, a lake, a transportation system, and recreation activities. Her son lived only an hour away by car. She decided to move. Two years later her daughter and family moved to a town a few miles away. Willa now has her children and grandchildren nearby, and she enjoys the lifestyle she wants. Willa will probably live in her new community for the rest of her life.

Willa's decision to move to a southern small town fits a pattern similar to that of many older people today. Demographers find that migration patterns follow the life course. Studies done in the 1980s found a stable pattern that has lasted for decades. The tendency to move peaks at around age 20 to 24. This coincides with students leaving school and with marriage. Younger people move to find jobs and set up their own families.

From age 35 on, the tendency to move declines slowly until retirement. Children, a job, and community ties all limit the tendency to move during the middle years. Migration picks up again for some people between ages 60 and 70 after people retire. An increase in migration occurs again at the end of life due to declines in health (Longino, 2004).

Amenity Migration

The first type of move, at retirement, Longino (1992) calls **amenity migration**. People move to enjoy a new lifestyle, to be with friends who have moved, or to establish a new identity as a retiree. He also describes another kind of amenity move: a move back to a person's childhood home state. People who do this often moved in their youth to find work. They then return to their roots in retirement.

Kadlec (2007) cites the U.S. Census when he reports that "nearly 18% of people over 60 who moved across state lines say they are returning to their home town." African Americans have a relatively high rate of this type of migration. Migration researchers say that retirees often have "'remote thoughts' or daydreams about moving before they make a move. They also gather information about new locations that shape their decision to move" (Longino & Bradley, 2006, p. 77).

Longino (2001) says that people tend to move for three reasons in old age: retirement, moderate disability, and major chronic disability.

Retirement

Longino (1990, p. 52) says that people who make their first move after retirement look for "places of natural beauty and more pleasant climates." Studies in Canada, Great Britain, and the United States show that

BOX 5
LIFE IN A RETIREMENT COMMUNITY
Pro and Con

I recently visited a friend who lives in a retirement community near Fort Lauderdale, Florida. At the main entrance, a line of cars waited to get in. A security guard walked up to my car with a clipboard and asked whom I was visiting. I told him and said that my host had called ahead to clear my arrival. He went into a guardhouse to check the guest list. When he returned, he asked to see my driver's license, then walked around the car to check the license plate and jot down the number. Finally, he waved me through. By this time I felt hot, bothered, and ready to turn around.

I have had an easier time crossing national borders than getting into this community. The delay may have annoyed me as a visitor, but the person I visited loves living here. She has made new friends and keeps busy with exercise classes, mah jong, and movies. She also likes the sense of security she gets from the high fence and the guardhouse at the entrance.

Many other older people feel the same way about their retirement communities. These enclaves attract more people every year. They offer a lifestyle that many older people want in retirement. Sun City in Arizona, one of the largest retirement communities in the United States, has 50,000 residents and its own banks, shopping plazas, golf courses, and restaurants. Retirement communities offer a self-contained world. They offer convenience, social activity, and security.

Critics see a downside to retirement communities. Kastenbaum (1993b) says these communities can create a "fortress mentality." They often cut themselves off from the local community and from local social issues. Some communities refuse to pay taxes for the local school system. People in these settings may even cut themselves off from their families. "An old man and woman move down here and build a mansion," Jim Martin, retiree and social activist says. "Then he dies and she's left living in his mausoleum. Then what? They cut all their lifelines to everybody!" (cited in Crispell & Frey, 1994).

Some communities limit the length of stay of anyone under age 18. Some communities discourage visits by families with young children. Gerber and colleagues (1989) quote one of the rules at a retirement community in Florida: "Children require the constant supervision of those responsible for them. They must be kept from interfering in any way with the quiet and comfort of residents."

What are the pros and cons of retirement community living? Would you want to live in a community like this? Would you want your parents or grandparents to move to one? Would you like to visit them there?

retirees tend to migrate to specific areas. Mobile older people tend to move to places with a mild climate, often by the coast. They also look for places with a reasonable cost of living (Walters, 2002).

An active senior couple at the Snowbird Ski Resort, Utah. People will often visit a place for a vacation before they decide to move there full or part-time.

James Kay/Stock Connection/Alamy

"The pattern is never random," Longino (1990, p. 52) says, "nor are migrants randomly selected from among all older people." Hazelrigg and Hardy (1995) found that most migrants are retired, married, and generally have higher incomes than peers in their new location. They also have more education and better health than older people who stay put. Migrants are also "overwhelmingly Anglo" (Longino, 1990, p. 53).

Research shows that destination characteristics tend to determine the place people choose, more than nearness or distance from the preretirement home. Some states in the United States have a great attraction for retirees (e.g., Florida and Arizona) (Longino & Bradley, 2006). Ten states received 54.3% of out-of-state migrants age 60 and over in 2000.

The recession following 2008 may have had a moderating effect on interstate migration. Longino and Bradley (2006) note that the top receiving states lost some share of interstate migrants between 1990 and 2000. Also, California slid from 13.6% of all older migrants in 1960 to 6.1% in 2000. The high cost of living, the loss of jobs, and relatively high taxes in California help explain this decrease in migration.

Still, the Sunbelt and Western states get the largest share of migrating retirees. Mild winter temperatures and scenic beauty lead people to the South and West (Stafford, 2009). Florida, California, Arizona, Texas, and North Carolina get the largest streams of older migrants from states outside their regions. Longino (2001, p. 111) calls these "national destination states." Florida, the lead destination state, adds more older migrants each year than Arizona, California, and Texas combined (Longino & Bradley, 2006).

Longino (2001, 2004) notes some counterintuitive trends. For example, many retirees migrate to attractive places in neighboring states. New Yorkers and people from Pennsylvania often migrate to the New Jersey shore. Cape Cod, the Wisconsin Dells, and the Pocono Mountains of Pennsylvania also attract retirees. Some older people move out of Sunbelt states. Florida, for example, contains the 100 top counties that send migrants out of state. Disability and the need to live near their children motivate these moves. Los Angeles County seniors often move to Arizona, Nevada, or Oregon. Relief from the high cost of living and a more relaxed lifestyle draw them to these locations.

Often, migrants have visited a place before. Some have even lived in the place for part of the year in the years before they move. Some never move permanently. They live in a Sunbelt location until the weather turns hot. Then they head back to their northern homes.

A case will illustrate this pattern. Jack Exeter owns a computer services business in Connecticut. His company creates websites for local businesses. He and his wife wanted an escape from the cold northern winters. They enjoyed vacationing in Florida, so they began exploring housing options there. They visited a number of condominium complexes, compared prices, and looked for a community that felt comfortable. They finally found a setting that offered the amenities they liked. Jack, an outdoors type, could play tennis, kayak, and hike on nearby trails. His wife Josie wanted warm weather and a chance to relax with a good book in quiet surroundings.

They bought a condo, but they didn't move there all at once. For one thing, their children and grandchildren still lived in Connecticut. And they enjoy summers at nearby beaches. They use the condo only during the winter. Josie spends most of the cold months there—from Thanksgiving to Easter. Jack commutes there for 2-week stints throughout the winter. He works hard with his staff when he's in Connecticut. He runs his business by phone and via email while he's away.

Jack's not ready to retire yet. He needs to keep working. But when he does retire, he'll spend all winter in Florida with Josie. They'll come back for the summer and for holidays and special events with their kids. Their winter home also offers a place for their family and friends to gather during winter vacations.

Longino (2001) refers to people like Jack as "seasonal" or "cyclical" migrants. As many as 80% of these migrants never settle permanently in their seasonal homes. These people live a lifestyle different from that of permanent migrants. When their health declines they make fewer and shorter visits to their seasonal location. Eventually they give up their seasonal visits.

Some permanent migrants take part in community life. Others remain aloof and bond with other migrants, never becoming part of the community. A person who plans to migrate should think about social needs as well as the climate before they make a move. The charm of golf or fishing, Longino says, will wear off in a year. People need to think about the community life, the culture, and the kinds of services they use (e.g., a library or a theater). "Long-term satisfaction," he says, "is more strongly determined by whether or not they can do the things they want to do and be the person they want to be in retirement" (Longino, 1992, p. 30).

The migration of older people to Sunbelt states after retirement sometimes creates tension between the migrants and the long-time residents. Some Sunbelt communities fear that older migrants will increase health and social service costs. But when Longino (1990) reviewed the data on health, transportation, and service use in host communities, he found no evidence for the supposed high costs of older people.

In the South, for example, except for Florida, most older migrants came from the region or were returning to their native states. Local residents saw them as natives. Longino (2001) reports that Florida's income from older migrants came to $8.3 billion between 1985 and 1990 (up from $4 billion in 1975 to 1980). Sastry (1992) found that retiree migrants had large positive economic effects on the Florida economy. Retirees contribute by spending their pension funds and paying taxes. This benefits older and younger people. The migration of older people also creates jobs in host communities.

Experts still disagree on the benefits of older people's migration to an area. Research shows that older people create economic growth in smaller towns and retirement settings. But as these older people age, they may place new demands on their communities. The long-term cost to a community may outweigh the short-term benefit of older migrants. Continued migration by younger retirees will offset this cost in some cases, as will out-migration that often takes place late in life. The complexity of migration decisions and trends makes it difficult to predict future costs or benefits.

Moderate Disability

The second type of move is what Wiseman and Roseman (1979) call "kinship migration," or what Walters (2002) calls "assistance-seek migration." This takes place when the older retiree moves back near his or, more often, her children. Illness, disability, or widowhood lead to this move (Stoller & Longino, 2001). People who live in rural areas will move to more urban centers at this time so they can get the health care and support they need from their children and from social services.

Roberts (2007, no page) gives some examples of this trend. Ida Kotowitz, age 88, says, "I was failing in health, most of my friends have passed away and I was alone." She moved to a retirement home in the Bronx, New York, after 22 years in Florida. "Friends are all right when you're well," she says, "but when you're not, you need family." Al Petzke, age 82, tells a similar story. After his wife died he continued to live in their home in Houston. But "it didn't make one bit of sense," the retired steelworker says, "[for his son] to be spending all that money every month flying down to see me." Al left Houston and moved back to Ohio in order to live near his son. Kadlec (2007) says that "even if you have plenty of money, eventually you are going to want the support of the people you know best."

Major Chronic Disability

The third move comes near the end of life. Meyer and Speare (1985) call this a move in "preparation for aging." Older people move from a community setting (their own home, an apartment, or living with their children) to an institution. This move often takes place within the person's local community. Generally, it coincides with increased disability and the need for institutional health care. A person who needs nursing home care may migrate to a nursing home from a location

with few nursing home beds. This applies especially to people with severe disability (Walters, 2002).

Urban–Rural Distribution

In the United States, about three-quarters of older people live in metropolitan counties (with a city of 50,000 or more people) (He et al., 2005). Longino (2001) says that from the 1950s onward, older people have tended to live in suburbs of these cities. Central cities have attracted more young people. Older populations in suburbs have increased proportionately as children move out and older people age in place.

Two trends explain the presence of older people in cities. First, many older people in the city centers have always lived there and will age in place. They have close friends in the neighborhood. They see neighbors and friends when they shop or go to church. Those who live in cities tend to be nonwhite, have the least money, have low mobility, and live alone.

In 2000, for example, elderly Hispanic Americans had a nine times greater likelihood of living inside than outside a metropolitan area. Elderly African Americans had a five times greater likelihood of living in a city than outside one. Whites had only a three times greater likelihood of living in a city than outside one. Older minority group members in cities sometimes have problems getting to and using social and health care services. Barriers such as language, poverty, poor transportation, and lack of knowledge about services may keep people from using programs.

These problems and the desire to live a simpler life help explain why some African Americans over age 60 return to southern states in retirement (Longino & Bradley, 2006). These moves fit into a historical cycle. African American workers move North in their younger years and return to their roots in later life. Hispanic Americans today who move to northern cities for jobs may show this pattern in the future.

The second trend, described by Smith (2004a, b), is the tendency for educated former suburbanites to move back to the city in later life. She reports that this group of older people enjoys the culture and services that big cities offer. One couple who moved from the Washington suburbs to a downtown neighborhood said that the museums and cultural events only partly explain their move. "It's the restaurants, it's the stores, it's the sense of vitality on the streets, the diversity of age and ethnic groups. It's a lively atmosphere to live in."

This trend may grow as the Baby Boom ages and some of its members choose the excitement of city living. Smith reports that Del Webb, the company that pioneered the Sun City lifestyle in the Southwest, has begun to develop city-oriented properties. They have considered developing an urban high-rise retirement community for active people who want to live downtown.

Suburban communities also show an increase in older people and in the proportion of older people. At least three trends account for this increase. First, suburbs attracted young couples after World War II. As these people age in place, they increase the number and proportion of older people in the suburbs. This trend accounts for most of the increase in older people in suburbs today.

Second, the children of these older people grow up and move away. This leads to a greater proportion of older people in certain suburbs. Third, some older people move to the suburbs when they retire (Longino, 2001). These people tend to be married, have more money, and live in their own homes. They may move into suburban or small-town retirement communities. Preston (1993) projects an increase in the size of smaller centers when Baby Boomers retire.

Changes in the Sex Ratio

The **sex ratio** shows the proportion of men to women in the population. The formula for the sex ratio looks like this:

$$\text{Sex ratio} = \frac{\text{Number of men} \times 100}{\text{Number of women}}$$

A ratio of 100 for people age 65 and over would mean an older population with one man for every woman. The lower the ratio, the smaller the proportion of men in the older population.

In 1900, men age 60 and over in the United States outnumbered women in that age group 105 to 100 (Hobbs & Stoops, 2002). These figures reflect the high rates of female deaths due to childbirth at the turn of the century. This ratio declined throughout most of the 20th century. In 2000, the older population (65 and over) had a ratio of 70 men for every 100 women. The ratio ranged from 86 for those ages 65 to 69 to 41 for those age 85 and over (He et al., 2005).

At least two trends account for the increase of women over men in later life: (1) better health care for women during their childbearing and middle years and (2) increases in cigarette smoking and work-related diseases among men in the 20th century. But recently, this trend has begun to reverse itself. Between 1980 and 2002, the gap in life expectancy

between men and women narrowed. A girl born in 1980 could expect to live 7.4 years longer than a boy born in that year. But a girl born in 2002 could expect to live only 5.2 years longer than her male counterpart (National Center for Health Statistics, 2004b).

These figures show a convergence of life expectancies for men and women. This may be due to increased cigarette use by women. Pampel (2002) reports that cigarette smoking among women from the 1960s to the 1980s accounts for *all* of the narrowing in mortality figures for men and women. Also, large numbers of women have entered the workforce, and they now face the same working conditions as men.

Table 3 shows the sex ratio at various ages. Notice that the ratio declines with each older age group. In 2001, the group ages 95 to 99 has a ratio about one third that of the 65- to 69-age group. This reflects the greater life expectancy of older women compared with older men.

This low sex ratio points to another characteristic of the older population today. Compared to men, women face a greater chance of being single in later life. Several factors account for this. First, women tend to marry older men. Second, men have a shorter life expectancy than women in later life. Third, whereas men

TABLE 3   U.S. Sex Ratios by Age for Selected Years

	Year			
Age	*2001*	*2030*	*2050*	*2070*
65–69	85.2	89.1	90.2	91.7
70–74	80.1	85.9	87.5	89.9
75–79	72.1	80.6	83.4	87.7
80–84	62.2	72.9	77.9	82.9
85–89	49.5	63.2	70.2	75.9
90–94	37.5	52.8	60.6	67.5
95–99	28.9	43.0	51.0	58.7
100+	22.0	33.1	40.9	49.4

The sex ratio is the proportion of men to women in the population. The figures in the table represent the number of men for every 100 women. In any given year, compared with younger age groups, older age groups show lower sex ratios. This occurs because the proportion of men in an age cohort decreases over time. Note that demographers expect more men to survive in each age group in the future. This leads to higher sex ratios. Demographers predict that the life expectancies of men and women will come closer together in the future. This will mean a decrease in the rates of widowhood and more married couples in the older population.

Source: U.S. Census Bureau. (2000). *Projections of the total resident population by 5-year age groups,* and *Sex with special age categories: Middle series, 2001 to 2005, 2025 to 2045, 2050 to 2070,* Population Projections Program, Population Division. Washington, DC: U.S. Government Printing Office. Retrieved April 26, 2004, from www.census.gov/population/projections/nation/summary/np-t3-b.pdf and np-t3-f.pdf, and np-t3-g.pdf.

tend to remarry, women tend to stay single. In 2002, for example, only 13.9% of men age 65 and over were widowed; in that same year and age group, 45.5% of women were widowed (U.S. Census Bureau, 2004).

The higher proportion of women in later life and their greater chance of widowhood makes old age a different experience for women and men today. Women, more than men, have to adapt to a singles lifestyle. They need to create social supports outside of marriage. And they have a greater stake in the quality and availability of services and supports in later life.

The future of aging for men and women may look different due to the increases in the life expectancy of men. Married couples in happy marriages will live more years together. And women who experience widowhood will typically do so at a later age. This will provide women as well as men with more in-home (spousal) support in later life.

THE IMPACT OF POPULATION AGING

Support (or Dependency) Ratios

The aging of the older population will lead to change in what demographers call the **total dependency ratio**. This is the ratio of the 0 to 14 and 65 and older age groups to the rest of the population (ages 15 to 64). This ratio gives a crude measure of how many middle-aged (working) people exist to support younger and older people in the population.

Demographers express the total dependency ratio in the following formula:

$$\text{Total dependency ratio} = \frac{\text{Population 0 to 19 plus Population 65+}}{\text{Population 20 to 64}} \times 100$$

Table 4 introduces the concept of the elderly and youth dependency ratios. The **elderly dependency ratio** refers to the number of people age 65 and over divided by the population ages 20 to 64, multiplied by 100. The **youth dependency ratio** refers to the number of people ages 0 to 19 divided by the population ages 20 to 64, multiplied by 100. These ratios show how these two subgroups contribute to the total dependency ratio.

Table 4 gives a good summary of recent demographic change in the United States. The total dependency ratio decreases from 1990 to 2000 and picks up again into the middle of this century. In 2030, it reaches a level similar to that of 1930.

TABLE 4 Dependency Ratios: 1980 to 2050

Year	Total	Youth	Older
1980	76.2	56.4	19.9
1990	70.2	48.8	21.4
2000	69.6	48.5	21.1
2010	66.5	44.8	21.7
2020	74	46	28
2030	83	48	35
2040	85	48	37
2050	85	48	37

The old age dependency ratio measures the relationship between the population age 65 and over and the general population (ages 20 to 64). The youth dependency ratio measures the relationship between the population under age 20 and the general population (ages 20 to 64). Addition of these two ratios gives the total dependency ratio. These figures provide an indication of how many people in the general population exist to support younger and older people in the population.

Note that the composition of the total ratio changes over time. In 1980, young people made up about three quarters of the total ratio. This means that in 1980, compared to older people, younger people (by this measure) required more support from the middle-aged population. At the middle of this century (2050), older people will make up almost half (44%) of the total dependency ratio. Older people will have almost doubled in their need for support by the middle-aged population between 1980 and 2050. The traditional view of the old age dependency ratio holds that older people make large demands on society's resources. But as healthier, better educated, and active older people enter old age, they may not follow this traditional pattern.

Note: The reference population for these data is the resident population.

Sources: U.S. Bureau of the Census. (1983). *1980 census of population, vol. 1, Characteristics of the population, Chapter B, General population characteristics, Part 1, United States summary,* PC80-1-B1. Washington, DC: Government Printing Office, Table 42. U.S. Bureau of the Census. (1991). *1990 census of population and housing summary tape file 1* (STF1). Washington, DC: Government Printing Office. U.S. Census Bureau. (2001). *Census 2000 summary file 1* (SF1). Washington, DC: Government Printing Office, Table QT-P1; Table PCT12; 2010 to 2030. U.S. Census Bureau, International Programs Center, International Data Base. (2004). U.S. Department of Commerce Economics and Statistics Administration. www.census.gov/ipc/www/idbnew.html. Vincent, G. K., & Velkoff, V. A.. (2010, May). *The next four decades: The older population in the United States: 2010 to 2050. Population estimates and projections.* Current Population Reports. P25-1138. U.S. National Center for Health Statistics. (2009, April 17). National Vital Statistics Reports (NVSR), *Deaths: Final data for 2006,* Vol. 57, No. 14. Retrieved October 19, 2010, from www.census.gov/compendia/statab/2010/tables/10s0102.pdf

Several considerations are worth noting.

- First, the elderly and youth dependency ratios make up different proportions of the total dependency ratio at different points in time. Until 1950, for example, the youth dependency ratio made up almost the entire total dependency ratio. In 2030, older people account for almost half the total dependency ratio.

- Second, the elderly dependency ratio generally increases throughout this period. But it makes a sudden jump after the year 2010.

- Third, the youth dependency ratio stays roughly the same from 1990 to 2030.
- Fourth, the ratio of working people ages 20 to 64 to those age 65 and over decreases dramatically in this century. By 2030, the United States will have only 2.5 younger adults for each older person.

This table shows that the increase in total dependency ratio is due to an increase in older people in the population. Some see this as a sign of trouble in the future. They see this as a shift from lower-cost programs for younger people to high-cost programs for older people. Kotlikoff (1993), for example, warns about increased costs for health care and potentially less investment in long-term programs such as care for the environment, infrastructure improvements (roads and bridges), and education.

A smaller number of children may reduce the costs for schooling. This could allow local and state governments to meet the higher costs of an aging population. But, not counting the costs for public schools, children rely mostly on private support from their parents. An older population depends more on public sources of support. This means that the same total dependency ratio, but with a higher elderly dependency ratio, may mean greater public cost in the future.

Programs such as Medicare and Social Security depend on intergenerational support. They assume that society will transfer some funds from the younger generation to the older generation. This works well today with a large working-age population and a relatively small older population. But the future will see a large group of older people depend on a smaller group of younger people. Peterson (1999, cited in Korczyk & Public Policy Institute, AARP, 2002) takes a gloomy view of the future. He calls the increase in older people a "global hazard" that "may actually do more to shape our collective future than deadly super-viruses, extreme climate change or the proliferation of nuclear, biological and chemical weapons."

Not everyone agrees with this conclusion. A look at other countries with populations older than the United States suggests how the United States can adapt to an aging population. Many societies have greater elderly dependency ratios than the United States. Sweden and Austria, for example, already have dependency ratios similar to those projected for the United States later this century. These countries have not faced a crisis due to their aging populations. They have well-developed social support systems and some of the highest standards of living in the world. This suggests that the

United States can adapt to an older population in the future without crisis or social upheaval (Schulz & Binstock, 2006).

Jackson and colleagues (2003) studied old age dependency ratios in twelve countries. The study assessed, among other things, the public burden of an aging population. The study placed the United States (along with Australia and the United Kingdom) in a low-vulnerability category. The authors say that the modest dependency ratio in the future and a pension system balanced between public and private sources will allow the United States to adapt to its aging population. These authors and others (Korczyk & Public Policy Institute, AARP, 2002) take a close look at dependency ratios and fail to see an economic crisis due to population aging.

Critique of Dependency Ratios

The conclusions drawn from dependency ratios seem self-evident. The word *dependency* itself leads to the conclusion that an increase in older people will place a greater burden on society. Some reports use the less loaded term *support* ratio, although this refers to the same measure (He et al., 2005). A closer look at this measure raises questions about its ability to predict the future.

For example, this formula assumes that all people in an age group behave the same and have the same needs. Dependency ratios assume that all people ages 20 to 64 work, support themselves, and support the older and younger populations. But many people ages 20 to 64 (college students, for example, or people who are disabled or unemployed) depend on others or public funds for their income.

Dependency ratios also assume that all people age 65 and over depend primarily on younger people (or public support). But this doesn't fit the facts today and will be less true in the future.

First, studies show that Baby Boomers plan to stay active in their retirement. A Harvard University–MetLife (2004) study reports a trend toward later retirement ages. The report predicts that Baby Boomers will likely increase this trend. An end to mandatory retirement for most workers, an increase in the age for receiving full Social Security benefits, and the need for more labor all point toward later retirement ages in the future.

Attitudes toward retirement have also changed. Many Boomers now plan to work part-time for interest, enjoyment, or extra income. In addition, the recent economic downturn has led workers to rethink early retirement plans.

Many Baby Boomers also plan for second careers as entrepreneurs, teachers, or workers in nonprofit agencies. These people prefer new career opportunities and income to government pensions (Reynolds, 2004). If this trend continues, these people will stay at work long past the current retirement age of 65. This group will continue to add to the economy as they age.

Second, health care experts expect that, compared to past generations of older people, Baby Boomers will enter later life in better health. Willens (2003) reviewed the research on Baby Boom health practices. He summarizes three national random samples of Boomers done in 2001–2002. He reports that they are "highly concerned with their physical well-being and doing something about it" (p. 43).

Fifty-five percent of Boomers in these studies say they try to cut back on unhealthy foods and on the quantity they eat. Fifty-two percent take vitamin and mineral supplements, 49% walk for exercise three to five times per week, 32% have exercise equipment at home and use it, 13% belong to a health club, and 10% belong to a commercial weight reduction program. Willens (2003, p. 44) concludes, "Boomers . . . have decided to begin taking care of their bodies—bodies that in many instances have been neglected over the years."

Third, Boomers plan to stay engaged in social life as they age. They look forward to retirement, actively plan for it, and want to do more than recreation. Willens (2003, p. 40) says that "this group is ready to begin some big new experience." The dependency ratio may serve as an easy way to look at the cost of an aging society, but it fails to predict the impact of the older population today. And it will do an even worse job of predicting the impact of the Baby Boom generation.

The use of this ratio does damage when it creates a sense of crisis or panic about societal aging. The dependency ratio creates a fiction based on weak assumptions. It assumes that an older population will only increase societal costs. But more older people in society may lead to a better use of resources. An older society, for example, may have a lower crime rate, a lower auto accident rate, and an increased concern for fitness and disease prevention.

Older people, many with good incomes, will spend their pensions and savings on travel, restaurants, and professional services. Many older people will help support their younger family members and will give to their communities as volunteers. These trends will make better use of social resources and create a better quality of life for all age groups.

Korczyk and Public Policy Institute, AARP (2002) says that the characteristics of older people (e.g., their health) and social policies have the greatest effect on the cost of an older population. Many retirement policies today, for example, encourage retirement at age 65. Ironically, countries with the highest elderly dependency ratios encourage older people to leave the workforce early. They appear to demand economic dependency by the older population.

In the future, these countries may rethink these policies. The United States has already taken action. Over the next few years, it will gradually raise the age of eligibility for full Social Security payments. The government must also control Medicare and other health care costs. Marmor (2001) shows that practices like the use of Diagnosis Related Groups, begun in the 1980s, helped control and reduce hospital fees. Projections of current health care costs, based on an aging population, create the demand for change.

A stronger economy and improved private pension plans would reduce the impact of an older population on public funds. Korczyk and Public Policy Institute, AARP (2002) says that society's economic stability and growth would expand the job market. It would allow people to save for retirement, and it would provide young people with good salaries. This will help them pay for services that will support an older population. Better private pension plans would help people stay financially independent in later life.

Friedland and Summer (1999, p. 5) say that "society can and will adjust [to an aging population] as it has done before. But adjustment will be easier if the challenges are addressed in a rational manner today." How well the United States manages this shift will depend on how well people understand population aging and how well our society prepares for change. Much of this planning has begun, but more will have to take place in the years ahead. Preparation for the future will take planning, thought, and creative social action, and all of us will play a part in this societal transformation.

CONCLUSION

I worked for some years at a university campus in a northern city. I headed home one day in January and noticed my wife about a block ahead of me, pushing one of our children in a baby carriage. She reached the corner of the busiest intersection in town and began to cross when the light changed. The slush from the cars slowed the wheels of the carriage in the street and she only made it to the center island. There she climbed the snow bank and hauled the carriage (and our child) up to safety.

As she caught her breath, she noticed that an elderly woman had just reached the bottom of the snow bank and was trying to climb up. The traffic had started and the woman looked scared. My wife reached down and helped the woman to safety. They stood breathing hard in the cold air with a look of weary triumph. They had both braved the city streets and won a small victory.

People imagine that more social services, longer traffic lights, or new architectural designs to serve an older population will inhibit social life. The demographic doomsayers imagine that an older population will bring only higher costs. But an older society can benefit all of us. In this story, the older woman needed a longer red light to cross the street, but so did my wife and our baby. And I wouldn't mind if I didn't have to climb over snow mountains to get on the bus or risk a concussion when the bus whips into traffic just as I move

toward my seat. An older society might be a more humane society. And a more enjoyable place for all of us.

The world will face population aging in the years ahead. The developing and the developed nations will face challenges due to the costs associated with an aging population. In every case societies will need to review past practices and think of new ways to support their aging populations.

The United States cannot copy any other society as it moves into the future. It cannot look back to recover a golden age of the past. But it can learn from other societies about a good old age. Throughout the world, older people do best when they can give to their society. They get the highest esteem when they contribute to society and express themselves.

Some societies make this possible. Older people served as matchmakers in China and Japan; they served as spiritual and community leaders in early America. They still serve as ritual leaders among the Coast Salish Indians in the Pacific Northwest. When older people play useful roles, they contribute to society and receive respect. The United States can create policies and social opportunities for older people with this in mind.

SUMMARY

- The developing nations still have relatively young populations. They will have increased numbers of older people in the years ahead due to decreased death rates. An increase in the number of older people in these societies will strain current social, health, and economic programs for older people.
- The developed nations of the world have increasing proportions of older people in their populations. They also have growing proportions of very old people (age 85 and over). Societal population aging, and the aging of the older population, will create new economic and social challenges for these nations.
- The U.S. population aged steadily during the last century and will continue to age in the future. Social scientists believe that population aging will lead to social change, but they do not think that it will lead to conflict, crisis, and more social problems.
- Demographers study the aging of society and the impact of societal aging on social institutions. Demographers use three measures of population aging: the absolute number of older people in a society, the median age of the population, and the increased proportion of older people.
- Population change occurs due to migration, deaths, and births. The decline in the fertility rate is the major cause of population aging in the United States today.

- Demographers divide the older population into subgroups. They refer to young-, middle-, and old-old. Each of these groups has unique needs.
- Internal migration has led to a shift in the proportions of the older population in different parts of the United States. We see decreases in the proportion of older people in the Northeast and increases in the proportion of older people in the South, Midwest, and West.
- People tend to move for three reasons in old age. Gerontologists call the first type of move a retirement move, the second type a moderate disability move, and the third type a major chronic disability move.
- Two things account for the greater number of women to men at every age in later life. First is better health care for women during their childbearing and middle years. Second are the increases in cigarette smoking and work-related diseases for men. Current trends show an improvement in life expectancy for men. This may lead to similar numbers of men and women in old age in the future.
- Demographic studies show an increase in the elderly dependency ratio. Some researchers believe that this increase will lead to a future crisis in the cost of services for older people. Other researchers believe that the older population will lead society to a better use of resources. Most gerontologists agree that U.S. society needs to pre-

pare for an aging population. New policies and new approaches to services can meet the challenges of population aging.

- The oldest members of the Baby Boom generation turned 60 in 2005. This generation will enter old age in large numbers in the next 30 years. They will change the meaning of later life during their Third Age (between ages 60 and 85).

- U.S. society will need to change to meet the needs of older people. Many of these changes will lead to a better quality of life for all age groups.

- The past cannot give answers to the new challenges that aging societies will face. But history can teach us one thing. When older people have a useful role to play in society, they live a good old age. And society benefits from their contributions and their wisdom.

DISCUSSION QUESTIONS

1. Compare and contrast the challenges facing the developed and developing nations as a result of the increase in the proportion and number of older people in their societies. Discuss some responses each type of society can make to these challenges.

2. What are the stages of the demographic transition? Describe the changes in birth and death rates at each stage. What impact do birth and death rates at each stage have on social institutions? What impact do they have on everyday life?

3. List the measures that demographers use to describe population aging. Give the strengths and weaknesses of each measure.

4. State three changes in social institutions that will come about due to population aging.

5. What are the three causes of population change in the United States today? What effect does a declining birth rate have on population aging? Why does it have this effect?

6. List some of the pros and cons of having children today. Do you think that young people in the United States today want to have many or few children? Think for a moment about how many children you would like to have. What about your friends and other people your age? What effect will today's decisions about having children have on the future age structure of the U.S. population?

7. How long do you expect to live? How does that influence your decisions with respect to diet, exercise, relationships, career, and any other important component

of your life? What if life expectancy was 120 years or 150 years? How would you think differently about your life? What differences would it make in planning your future?

8. Describe the migration patterns of older people in the past 20 years or so. Do you know anyone who has migrated within the United States after retirement? Where did they move from? Where did they move to? Why did they move? Were they satisfied with their move?

9. Look at the three population pyramids presented in this chapter (Figure 6). Compare the size of the older population (age 65 and older) with the younger population (age 14 and under). What do you see? Compare the ratio of men and women in the three oldest age groups. Now compare one pyramid with another and look at the total size of the three oldest age groups. What accounts for the different shapes of these pyramids?

10. Give three reasons why an older woman stands a greater chance than an older man of living without a spouse. What social changes may make widowhood for women less common in the future?

11. Present the pros and cons of using dependency ratios to project future social conditions. What can the United States do now to prepare for an aging society in the years ahead?

12. Give three reasons why the "Merchants of Doom" are likely to be wrong in their predictions of a social crisis due to population aging.

SUGGESTED READING

Carmel, S., Morse, C., & Torres-Gil, F. (Eds.). (2007). *Lessons on aging from three nations*, Vol. I and Vol. II. New York: Baywood Press.

The editors look at aging in three multicultural modern societies: the United States, Israel, and Australia. Each of these countries faces issues related to immigration, social diversity, and population aging. The articles in these volumes show how each of these societies develop unique policies and programs for older people. The authors draw on their own experiences in

each society to suggest improvements in programs and practices. A rare study that allows cross-cultural and cross-national comparisons.

Palmore, E., Whittington, F., & Kunkel, S. (eds.). (2009). *The international handbook on aging* (3rd ed.). Santa Barbara, CA: ABC-CLIO.

A collection of articles by social scientists in 47 countries. Each author provides the social, political, and economic backdrop to population aging. The articles describe the challenges that each country will face as its population ages. The handbook also contains overview essays on world regions (e.g., Asian-Pacific Region) and a directory of gerontological and geriatric associations worldwide. A good reference volume.

Korczyk, S. M., & Public Policy Institute, AARP. (2002). *Back to which future: The U.S. aging crisis revisited.* Washington, DC: Public Policy Institute, AARP. Available online at http://research.aarp.org/econ/2002_18_aging.pdf.

This paper looks at many of the issues presented in this chapter. It also assesses the impact of population aging on health and income in later life as well as the cost of health care. The paper concludes that **demography** is not destiny. The effect of population aging on society will depend on the health and abilities of the older population as well as on public policy.

Websites to Consult

HelpAge International
www.helpage.org/Home

This site contains information about aging in an international context. If you need information about how other countries and cultures confront the physical, social, and economic challenges associated with aging, HelpAge can provide it.

AARP AgeSource/AgeStats Worldwide
http://www.aarpinternational.org/database/

These two databases support the exchange of policy and program information around the world. AgeSource Worldwide offers several hundred information sources in 25 countries. Sources include libraries, databases, major reports, and other Web metasites. AgeStats Worldwide provides access to comparative statistical data on older adults across countries or regions. You can browse by country, topic, and type of information (e.g., report, text, reading list). The database provides some projections as far ahead as 2050.

International Association of Gerontology and Geriatrics
www.iagg.info

This site contains links to international collections of information as well as a photo bank that depicts active, healthy seniors from around the world. It is an excellent resource for presentations and access to international news on aging.

The U.S. Census Bureau
www.census.gov

Reliable and updated regularly, the U.S. Census Bureau produces the most reliable demographic data and information on population changes. It also releases periodic aging-related studies.

The U.S. Census Bureau's DataFerrett
http://dataferrett.census.gov

DataFerrett is an advanced search program that downloads, organizes, and stores datasets from a number of government programs. If you need to cross-reference data from a number of government programs, DataFerrett can help you find and organize the information. Topics include race and ethnicity, social security data, and economic data.

National Institute on Aging Demography Centers
http://agingcenters.org/

The NIA's Demography Centers provide links to a wide variety of aging-related databases and publications. On this site, you can find demographic data from a number of organizations and archives. You can also find information about the latest demographic studies being conducted at each of the Institute's centers.

Psychology

Psychology

Psychology
Yesterday and Today

66 *If you could discern and explain the factors that led to Tiger Woods's meteoric rise to fame, you would be a very insightful psychologist.* 99

CHAPTER OUTLINE

O N A BALMY APRIL DAY IN 2002, A YOUNG MAN WAS PLAYING GOLF. NOTHING unusual about that. But when this young man sank his final putt, the watching crowd let out a roar, and he looked for his parents and embraced them, fighting back tears. The occasion was the PGA Masters Tournament, and the young man was Tiger Woods.

Think of the magnitude of his victory: At 26, Woods was the youngest three-time winner of the Masters. And golf's reigning champion, in a sport that had long been effectively closed to all but Whites, was of Asian, Black, White, and Native American ancestry. Tiger Woods dominated the sport of golf like no one before him or perhaps to come—all at a very young age. Before he came on the scene, golf was truly "the White man's sport," and the only place for a minority was as a caddy. After he burst into our collective awareness, he not only opened the sport to minorities, but also brought it into the mainstream—golf courses nationwide have become more crowded since Woods's rise to prominence.

If you could discern and explain the factors that led to Tiger Woods's meteoric rise to fame, you would be a very insightful psychologist.

But where would you begin? You could look at Woods's hand-eye coordination, his concentration and focus, and his ability to judge distances and calculate factors of wind, temperature, and humidity.

You could look at his personality—his reaction to racist hate mail (as a college student at

Psychology

Stanford University, he even kept one particularly vile letter taped to his wall), his religious beliefs (he was raised in his mother's faith, Buddhism), his demeanor during play, and his discipline in training.

You could look at his relationships with the social world around him—his family, his competitors, his fans.

Is this psychology? Indeed it is. Psychologists ask and, in scientific ways, attempt to answer questions about why and how people think, feel, and behave as they do. Because we are all human and so have much in common, sometimes the answers are universal. But we are also, like snowflakes, all different, and psychology helps to explain our uniqueness. Psychology is about mental processes and behavior, both exceptional and ordinary. In this chapter, we show you how to look at and answer such questions by methods used in current research and (because the inquiry into what makes us tick has a history) how psychologists over the past century have approached these questions.

The Science of Psychology: Getting to Know You

Virtually everything any of us does, thinks, or feels falls within the sphere of psychology. You are dealing with the subject matter of psychology when you watch people interacting in a classroom or at a party, or notice that a friend is in a really terrible mood. The field of psychology aims to understand what is at work when you daydream as you watch the clouds drift by, when you have trouble recalling someone's name, even when you're asleep.

LOOKING AHEAD: Learning Objectives

1. *Psychology can illuminate all aspects of your life, but what is psychology?*
2. *What is the concept of levels of analysis, and how can you use it to understand psychology?*

What Is Psychology?

Although it may seem complex and wide-ranging, the field you are studying in this textbook can be defined in one simple sentence: **Psychology** *is the science of mental processes and behavior*. Let's look at the key words in this definition.

First, *science*: From the Latin *scire*, "to know," science avoids mere opinions, intuitions, and guesses and instead strives to nail down facts—to *know* them—by using objective evidence to answer questions like these: What makes the sun shine? Why does garlic make your breath smell strong? How is Tiger Woods able to execute his swings so superbly? A scientist uses logic to reason about the possible causes of a phenomenon and then tests the resulting ideas by collecting additional facts, which will either support the ideas or refute them, and thus nudge the scientist further along the road to the answer.

Psychology: The science of mental processes and behavior.

What Is Psychology?

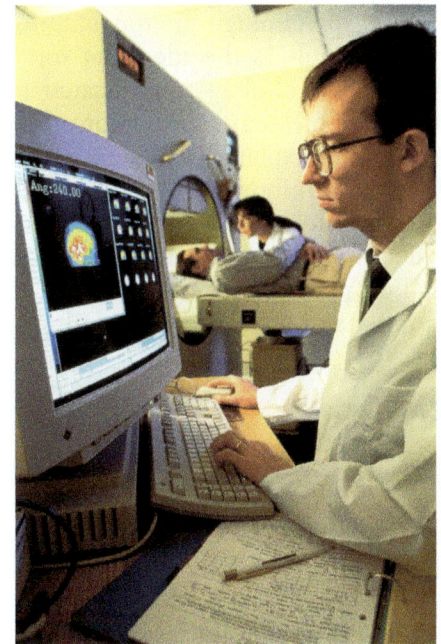

Science

Mental Processes

Behavior

Second, *mental processes*: **Mental processes** are what your brain is doing not only when you engage in "thinking" activities such as storing memories, recognizing objects, and using language, but also when you feel depressed, jump for joy, or savor the experience of being in love. How can we find objective facts about mental processes, which are hidden and internal? One way, which has a long history in psychology, is to work backward, observing what people do and inferring from outward signs what is going on "inside." Another, as new as the latest technological advances in neuroscience, is to use brain-scanning techniques to take pictures of the living brain that show its physical changes as it works.

Third, *behavior*: By **behavior**, we mean the outwardly observable acts of a person, either alone or in a group. Behavior consists of physical movements, voluntary or involuntary, of the limbs, facial muscles, or other parts of the body. A particular behavior is often preceded by mental processes, such as a perception of the current situation (how far the golf ball must travel) and a decision about what to do next (how forcefully to swing the club). A behavior may also be governed by the relationship between the individual and a group. Tiger Woods might not have performed the way he did in 2002 had he been playing in 1920, when many in the crowd would not have wanted a non-White person to win. So there are layers upon layers: An individual's mental processes affect his or her behavior, and these processes are affected by the surrounding group (the members of which, in turn, have their own individual mental processes and behaviors).

When you think about a friend's "psychology," you might wonder about his or her motivations ("Why would she say such a thing?"), knowledge ("What does she know that led her to make that decision?"), or goals ("What is she trying to accomplish by acting like that?"). In all cases, you are trying to *describe* (such as by

Mental processes: What the brain does when a person stores, recalls, or uses information or has specific feelings.

Behavior: The outwardly observable acts of an individual, alone or in a group.

Psychology

inferring what your friend knows or believes) and *explain* (such as by inferring your friend's motivations) your friend's mental processes and behavior. Most people try to describe and explain other people's psychology on the basis of "common sense" or generalizations they've heard (such as the idea that some people are grouchy in the morning). The field of psychology is dedicated to helping us understand each other by using the tools of science. But more than that, psychology's goals are not simply to describe and explain mental processes and behavior, but also to *predict* and *control* them. As an individual, you'd probably like to be able to predict what kind of person would make a good spouse for you or which politician would make sound decisions in crisis situations. As a society, we all would greatly benefit by knowing how people learn most effectively, how to control addictive and destructive behaviors, and how to cure mental illness.

Levels of Analysis: The Complete Psychology

The areas you might explore to answer questions about Tiger Woods's success—his coordination and focus, his beliefs and attitudes, his relationships with his parents and his audience—can be understood in terms of three types of events, each of which provides a field for analysis. Think for a moment about a computer. How can we understand what it does?

1. First, we can ponder the machine itself. The computer is a *mechanism*. One event causes another. You enter a Save command, it saves a file to a disk; you enter a Print command, it sends the file to the printer, and so forth. Each input triggers a specific event—cause and effect. The computer program is like a mental process; it specifies the steps the mechanism takes in particular circumstances.

2. Second, we can ask about the *content* of the computer—the specific information it contains and what's being done to it. The mechanism behaves exactly the same way if you type a research paper, a love letter, or directions to a barbecue. Nevertheless, the differences in content obviously matter a great deal. The content relies on the mechanism (for instance, if the computer is not turned on, you cannot type in any content), but the mechanism and content are not the same.

3. Third, we can hook the computer into a network. We now focus on how different computers *affect each other and the network itself*. What happens when you type in a query to Google? Your computer (both the mechanism and the particular content you type) interacts with others that relay the query and finally send back information in response.

These three *levels of analysis* (to use the most widely accepted terminology) build on one another, with each level adding something new to our understanding of computing. Specifically, the content relies on the mechanism (as anyone knows who has tried to use a computer with a broken hard drive or malfunctioning power supply), and the network depends on both the content (such as the particular commands or requests you enter) and the mechanism (a functioning computer).

Do we really need to consider these three levels of analysis? To see why we do, suppose you log onto the Internet and your computer suddenly freezes. Why? It could be that your hard drive has crashed (mechanism); or perhaps you entered an invalid command (content); or perhaps the network itself is down (network). To consider all of the possible reasons for your computer's malfunction, you need to contemplate disruptions at each level of analysis.

Now let's see how this analogy applies to humans.

Three Levels of Analysis in Psychology

At any moment in Tiger Woods's day, or yours, events are happening at the same three levels we just considered in our computer analogy. Considering psychological phenomena from these three levels reveals much that would be hidden were we to look at only one level.

In humans, the *mechanism* is the brain and all of the biological factors that affect it. At this **level of the brain**, psychologists consider not only the activity of the brain but also the structure and properties of the organ itself—brain cells and their connections, the chemical soup in which they exist (including the hormones that alter the way the brain operates), and the genes that give rise to them. At the level of the brain, a psychologist might want to design an experiment to study how Tiger Woods can adjust the force of his swing so exquisitely well for driving, chipping, and putting and might speculate that the parts of his brain that control hand-eye coordination are especially well developed.

At the next level, consider how we use the information that our brains store and process. At this **level of the person**, psychologists focus on the *content* of mental processes, not just the internal mechanics that are the focus at the level of the brain. Unlike the level of the brain, we no longer talk about the characteristics of brain areas or how they operate to process information; rather, we talk about mental contents such as beliefs (including ideas, explanations, expectations), desires (such as hopes, goals, needs), and feelings (fears, guilts, attractions, and the like). Although the brain is the locus and vehicle for content, the two are not the same—any more than a computer and a love letter written on it are the same. Rather, the brain is in many ways a canvas on which life's experiences are painted. Just as we can discuss how aspects of a canvas (such as its texture) allow us to paint, we can discuss how the brain supports mental contents. But just as we can talk about the picture itself (a portrait, a landscape, and so on), we can talk about mental contents. To do so, we must shift to another level of analysis. At the level of the person, a psychologist who is studying Tiger Woods might want to investigate the factors—among them, possibly, his Buddhist faith—behind the inner calm he displays under pressure.

And third, just as computers in a network affect each other, people affect one another. "No man is an island," the poet John Donne wrote. We all live in *social environments* that vary over time and space and that are populated by our friends and professors, our parents, the other viewers in a movie theater, the other drivers on a busy highway. Our lives are intertwined with other people's lives, and from birth to old age, we take our cues from other people around us. The relationships that arise within groups make them more than simply collections of individuals. Psychologists not only study isolated individuals, but also investigate the mental processes and behavior of members of groups. Members of street gangs and political parties both have distinct identities based on shared beliefs and practices that are passed on to new members as *culture*, which has been defined as the "language, beliefs, values, norms, behaviors, and even material objects that are passed from one generation to the next" (Henslin, 1999). Thus, at the **level of the group**,

Level of the brain: Events that involve the structure and properties of the organ itself—brain cells and their connections, the chemical soup in which they exist, and the genes.

Level of the person: Events that involve the nature of beliefs, desires, and feelings—the *content* of the mind, not just its internal mechanics.

Level of the group: Events that involve relationships between people (such as love, competition, and cooperation), relationships among groups, and culture. Events at the level of the group are one aspect of the environment; the other aspect is the physical environment itself (the time, temperature, and other physical stimuli).

Psychology

psychologists consider the ways that collections of people (as few as two, as many as a society) shape individual mental processes and behavior. At the level of the group, a psychologist might want to examine the role of a supportive and enthusiastic audience in helping Tiger Woods birdie instead of bogey.

Events that occur at every level of analysis—brain, person, and group—are intimately tied to conditions in the physical world. All our mental processes and behaviors take place within and are influenced by a specific *physical environment*. A windy day at the golf course changes the way Tiger Woods plays a shot. The group is only part of the world; to understand the events at each level of analysis, we must always relate them to the physical world that surrounds all of us.

All Together Now

Many people seem delighted to discover that their brains are not, in fact, computers. We noted above that the computer acts the same way when it is used to write a love letter or directions to someone's house. The human brain does not. When you feel an emotion (at the level of the person), that experience is accompanied by changes in how your brain operates (Davidson, 2004; Sheehan et al., 2004). In humans, unlike computers, events at the different levels are constantly interacting. For example, as you sit in a lecture hall, the signals among your brain cells that enable you to understand the lecture, and the new connections among your brain cells that enable you to remember it, are happening because you decided to take the course (perhaps because you need it to graduate): That is, events at the level of the person (your interests or perhaps knowledge of your school's requirements) are affecting events at the level of the brain. But, as you listen to the lecture, your neighbor's knuckle cracking is really getting to you, and you're finding it hard to concentrate: Events at the level of the group are affecting events at the level of the brain. Because you really want to hear this stuff, you're wondering how to get your neighbor to cut it out, and you decide to shoot a few dirty looks his way: Events at the level of the person are affecting events at the level of the group (which, as we've seen, affect events at the level of the brain). And all of this is going on within the physical environment of the room, where the sunlight that had seemed warm and welcoming is now pretty hot, and you're getting drowsy, and you're *really* irritated, and you finally change your seat. . . . And round and round. Events at the three levels of analysis, in a specific physical context, are constantly changing and influencing one another. To understand fully what's going on in any life situation, you need to look at all three.

The concept of levels of analysis has long held a central role in science in general (Anderson, 1998; Nagel, 1979; Schaffner, 1967) and in the field of psychology in particular (Fodor, 1968, 1983; Kosslyn & Koenig, 1995; Looren de Jong, 1996; Marr, 1982; Putnam, 1973; Saha, 2004), and for good reason: This view of psychology not only allows you to see how different types of theories and discoveries illuminate the same phenomena, but it also lets you see how these theories and discoveries are interconnected—and thus how the field of psychology as a whole emerges from them.

In each of the rest of the chapters of this book, in a feature called Looking at Levels, we will consider one aspect of psychology in detail, showing how it is illuminated when we investigate events at the three levels of analysis and their interactions. Moreover, we shall draw on the different levels continually as we encounter different aspects of the field throughout the book. The fact that interactions of events at the different levels of analysis are always present is one thread that holds the different areas of psychology together, that makes the field more than a collection of separate topics.

Psychology

1. *Psychology can illuminate all aspects of your life, but what is psychology?* Psychology is the science of mental processes and behavior. Science is a way of answering questions that relies on, first, using logic to reason about the possible causes of a phenomenon and, then, collecting new facts to test the resulting ideas. Psychology focuses on both the internal events that underlie our thoughts, feelings, and behavior and the behavior itself.

2. *What is the concept of* levels of analysis, *and how can you use it to understand psychology?* Any psychological phenomenon can best be understood by considering events at three levels of analysis: the brain (its functioning and its structure), the person (his or her beliefs, desires, and feelings), and the group (social interactions and cultural influences). All these events occur in the context of the physical world. Events at the different levels are constantly interacting, and thus it is impossible to explain mental processes or behavior adequately in terms of only a single level of analysis.

LOOKING BEYOND: *Critical Thinking*

In your own life, can you identify instances where events at the different levels of analysis were clearly at work?

How would you react if it could be shown conclusively that all criminals have an abnormal structure in a certain part of their brains? If this were true, what should we do with this knowledge? Or, what if it could be shown that criminals have perfectly normal brains, but they all had weak parents who didn't give them enough discipline when they were children? Neither of these single-perspective views is likely to be correct, but what if one level of analysis turns out to be more important than the others?

Psychology Then and Now

How do you think psychologists 50 or 100 years ago might have interpreted Tiger Woods's performance? Would they have focused on the same things that psychologists do today? One hallmark of the sciences is that rather than casting aside earlier findings, researchers use them as stepping stones to the next set of discoveries. Reviewing how psychology has developed over time helps us understand where we are today. In the century or so during which psychology has taken shape as a formal discipline, the issues under investigation have changed, the emphasis has shifted from one level of analysis to another, and events at each level have often been viewed as operating separately or occurring in isolation.

LOOKING AHEAD: *Learning Objectives*

1. *How did psychology develop over time?*
2. *What do today's psychologists actually do?*

The Evolution of a Science

In one form or another, psychology has probably always been with us. People have apparently always been curious about why they and others think, feel, and behave the ways they do. In contrast, the history of psychology as a scientific field is relatively brief, spanning little more than a century. The roots of psychology lie in *philosophy* (the use of logic and speculation to understand the nature of reality, experience, and values) on the one hand and *physiology* (the study of the biological workings of the body, including the brain) on the other. From philosophy, psychology borrowed theories of the nature of mental processes and behavior. For example, the 17th-century French philosopher René Descartes focused attention on the distinction between mind and body and the relation between the two (still a focus of considerable debate). John Locke, a 17th-century English philosopher (and friend of Sir Isaac Newton), stressed that all human knowledge arises from experience of the world and from reflection about it. Locke argued that we only know about the world via how it is represented in the mind. From physiology, psychologists learned to recognize the role of the brain in giving rise to mental processes and behavior and acquired tools to investigate these processes. These twin influences of philosophy and physiology remain in force today, shaped and sharpened by developments over time.

Early Days: Beginning to Map Mental Processes and Behavior

The earliest scientific psychologists were not much interested in why we behave as we do. Instead, these pioneers typically focused their efforts on understanding the operation of perception (the ways in which we sense the world), memory, and problem solving—events at what we now think of as the level of the brain. But even at the beginning, psychologists focused on events at several levels of analysis.

Structuralism. Wilhelm Wundt (1832–1920), usually considered the founder of scientific psychology, set up the first psychology laboratory in 1879 in Leipzig, Germany. The work of Wundt and his colleagues led to ==structuralism==, the first formal movement in psychology. The structuralists sought to identify the "building blocks" of consciousness (*consciousness* is the state of being aware). Part of Wundt's research led him to characterize two types of elements of consciousness. The first comprised sensations, which arise from the eyes, ears, and other sense organs; the second consisted of feelings, such as fear, anger, and love. The goal of structuralism was to describe the rules that determine how particular sensations or feelings may occur at the same time or in sequence, combining in various ways into mental *structures*. Edward Titchener (1867–1927), an American student of Wundt, broadened the structuralist approach to apply it to the nature of concepts and thinking in general.

The structuralists developed and tested their theories partly with objective techniques, such as measures of the time it takes to respond to different sensations. Their primary research tool, however, was ==introspection==, which means literally "looking within." Here is an example of introspection: Try to recall how many windows and doors are in your parents' living room. Are you aware of "seeing" the room in a mental image, of scanning along the walls and counting the windows and doors? Introspection is the technique of noticing your mental processes as, or immediately after, they occur. Insofar as the structuralists' theories were about the structure of consciousness, they addressed the mechanisms of mental processes—and hence considered events at the level of the brain. But they also considered the contents of consciousness itself, at the level of the person.

Had the structuralists been asked to analyze Tiger Woods's golf success—how, for example, he perceives distances, fairway terrain, and wind direction—they

Margaret Floy Washburn was not only Edward Titchener's first graduate student to receive a Ph.D., but was also the first woman to earn a Ph.D. in psychology (at Cornell in 1894).

Structuralism: The school of psychology that sought to identify the basic elements of experience and to describe the rules and circumstances under which these elements combine to form mental *structures*.

Introspection: The process of "looking within."

probably would have trained him to use introspection to describe his mental processes. However, there was a major problem with such uses of introspection. Let's say that although you are able to use mental imagery as a tool to recall the numbers of windows and doors in your parents' living room, your best friend doesn't seem to be able to do the same. How could you prove that mental images actually exist and objects can indeed be visualized? For the early psychologists, this was the core of the problem. Barring the ability to read minds, there was no way to resolve disagreements about the mental processes that introspection revealed.

Functionalism.   Rather than trying to chart the elements of mental processes, the adherents of **functionalism** sought to understand how our minds help us to adapt to the world around us—in short, to *function* in it (Boring, 1950). Whereas the structuralists asked *what* mental processes are and *how* they operate, the functionalists wanted to know *why* humans think, feel, and behave as we do. The functionalists had less interest in events at the level of the brain than did the structuralists and greater interest in events at the level of the group. The functionalists, many of whom were Americans, shared the urge to gather knowledge that could be put to immediate use. Sitting in a room introspecting simply didn't seem worthwhile to them. The functionalists' interest lay in the methods by which people learn and in how goals and beliefs are shaped by environments. As such, their interests spanned the levels of the person and the group.

The functionalists were strongly influenced by Charles Darwin (1809–1882), whose theory of evolution by natural selection stressed that some individual organisms in every species, from ants to oaks, possess characteristics that enable them to survive and reproduce more fruitfully than others. The phrase "survival of the fittest," often quoted in relation to natural selection, doesn't quite capture the key idea. (For one thing, these days "the fittest" implies the muscle-bound star of the health club, whereas in Darwin's time it meant something "fit for" or "suited to" its situation.) The idea of natural selection is that certain inborn characteristics make particular individuals more fit for their environments, enabling them to have more offspring that survive, and those in turn have more offspring, and so on, until the characteristics that led the original individuals to flourish are spread through the whole population. Darwin called the inborn characteristics that help an organism survive and produce many offspring *adaptations*.

Wilhelm Wundt (the man with the long gray beard standing behind one table) in his laboratory.

The functionalists sought to apply knowledge of psychology and helped to improve education in the United States.

Functionalism: The school of psychology that sought to understand how the mind helps individuals *function*, or adapt to the world.

The functionalists applied Darwin's theory to mental characteristics. For example, William James (1842–1910), who set up the first psychology laboratory in the United States at Harvard University, studied the ways in which consciousness helps an individual survive and adapt to an environment. The functionalists likely would have tried to discover how Tiger Woods's goals and beliefs enable him to press on in the face of adversity, such as losing an important match or receiving hate mail.

The functionalists made several enduring contributions to psychology. Their emphasis on Darwin's theory of natural selection and its link between humans and nonhuman animals led them to theorize that human psychology is related to the psychology of animals. This insight meant that the observation of animals could provide clues to human behavior. The functionalists' focus on social issues, such as improving methods of education, also spawned research that continues today.

Gestalt Psychology.   Although their work began in earnest nearly 50 years later, the Gestalt psychologists, like the structuralists, were interested in consciousness, particularly as it arises during perception (and thus, they too focused on events at the levels of the brain and the person). But instead of trying to dissect the elements of experience, Gestalt psychology—taking its name from the German word *Gestalt*, which means "whole"—emphasized the overall patterns of thoughts or experience. Based in Germany, Max Wertheimer (1880–1943) and other scientists noted that much of the content of our thoughts comes from what we perceive and, further, from inborn tendencies to structure what we see in certain ways.

Have you ever glanced up to see a flock of birds heading south for the winter? If so, you probably didn't pay attention to each individual bird but instead focused on the flock. In Gestalt terms, the flock was a *perceptual unit*, a whole formed from individual parts. The Gestalt psychologists developed over 100 perceptual laws, or principles, that describe how our eyes and brains organize the world. Most of the Gestalt principles illustrate the dictum that "the whole is more than the sum of its parts." When you see the birds in flight, the flock has a size and shape that cannot be predicted from the size and shape of the birds viewed one at a time. To Gestalt psychologists, just as the flock is an entity that is more than a collection of individual birds, our patterns of thought are more than the simple sum of individual images or ideas. Gestaltists would want to know how Tiger Woods can take in the overall layout of each hole, or even an 18-hole course, and plan his strategy accordingly.

We do not see isolated individual musicians, but a marching band. In the words of the Gestalt psychologists, "the whole is more than the sum of its parts."

Today, the study of perception is no longer the province of Gestalt psychology alone but rather a central focus of psychology, as well it should be. Perception is, after all, our gateway to the world; if our perceptions are not accurate, our corresponding thoughts and feelings will be based on a distorted view of reality. The research of the Gestaltists addressed how the brain works, and today Gestaltism has become integrated into studies of the brain itself.

Gestalt psychology: An approach to understanding mental processes that focuses on the idea that the whole is more than the sum of its parts.

Psychology

Psychodynamic Theory: More Than Meets the Eye

Sigmund Freud (1856–1939), a Viennese physician specializing in neurology (the study and treatment of diseases of the brain and nervous system), developed a detailed and subtle theory of how thoughts and feelings affect our actions.

Freud stressed the notion that the mind is not a single thing, but in fact has separate components. Moreover, some of these mental processes are **unconscious**; that is, they are outside our awareness and beyond our ability to bring to awareness at will. Freud believed that we have many unconscious sexual, and sometimes aggressive, urges. Moreover, Freud also believed that a child absorbs his or her parents' and culture's moral standards, which then censor the child's (and, later, the adult's) goals and motivations. Thus, he argued, we often find our urges unacceptable and so keep them in check, hidden in the unconscious. According to Freud, these unconscious urges build up until, eventually and inevitably, they demand release as thoughts, feelings, or action.

Freud developed what has since been called a **psychodynamic theory**. From the Greek words *psyche*, or "mind," and *dynamo*, meaning "power," the term refers to the continual push-and-pull interaction among conscious and unconscious forces. Freud believed that it was these interactions that produced abnormal behaviors, such as obsessively washing one's hands until they crack and bleed. According to Freud, such hand washing might be traced to unacceptable unconscious sexual or aggressive impulses bubbling up to consciousness (the "dirt" perceived on the hands) and that washing symbolically serves to remove the "dirt." What would followers of psychodynamic theory say about Tiger Woods? A Freudian would probably ask Woods about his earliest memories and experiences and try with him to analyze the unconscious urges that led to his intense interest in golf. This theory focuses on the level of the person but addresses mental processes and behavior at all three levels of analysis: The theory of mental mechanisms is at the level of the brain, but an individual's experience affects events at the level of the person, and the nature of one's upbringing is to be understood at the level of the group. Freud developed an extraordinarily ambitious theory, which attempted to reach into all corners of human thought, feeling, and behavior.

Rather than deriving from objective scientific studies, however, the guiding principles of psychodynamic theory rest primarily on subjective interpretations of what people say and do. Moreover, psychodynamic theory became so intricate and complicated that it could usually explain any given observation or research result as easily as the opposite result, and thus became impossible to test—obviously a serious drawback.

Nevertheless, the key idea of psychodynamic theory—that behavior is driven by a collection of mental processes—had a crucial influence on later theories. In addition, the idea that some mental processes are hidden from conscious awareness has proven invaluable. Furthermore, psychodynamic theory focused attention on novel kinds of observations, such as the interpretation of slips-of-the-tongue and the analysis of dreams. These observations sparked much subsequent research. Psychodynamic theory led to entirely new approaches to treating psychological problems, which have since been modified and refined.

Behaviorism: The Power of the Environment

By the early part of the 20th century, a new generation of psychologists calling themselves behaviorists began to question a key assumption shared by their

Sigmund Freud, the father of psychodynamic theory.

Unconscious: Outside conscious awareness and not able to be brought to consciousness at will.

Psychodynamic theory: A theory of how thoughts and feelings affect behavior; refers to the continual push-and-pull interaction among conscious and unconscious forces.

"Stimulus, response! Stimulus, response! Don't you ever *think*?"

predecessors, that psychologists should study hidden mental processes. Because they found the theories of mental processes so difficult to pin down, American psychologists such as Edward Lee Thorndike (1874–1949), John B. Watson (1878–1958), and Clark L. Hull (1884–1952) rejected the idea that psychology should focus on these unseen phenomena. Instead, these followers of **behaviorism** concluded that psychology should concentrate on understanding directly observable behavior.

Later behaviorists, especially B. F. Skinner (1904–1990) and his followers, acknowledged that mental processes probably exist, but argued that it was not useful for psychology to focus on them. Instead, Skinner and his followers held that to understand behavior, we should study behavior. For instance, rather than trying to study the nature of "affection" so as to understand why someone treats dogs well ("affection" being an unobservable mental process), these behaviorists would look at when and how a person approaches dogs, protects them from harm, pets them, and otherwise treats them well. Such a scientific investigation would be aimed at discovering how particular responses came to be associated with the stimulus of perceiving a dog. Because of their concern with the content of the stimulus–stimulus and stimulus–response associations, the behaviorists focus on events at the level of the person.

The behaviorists have had many important insights, among them the fact that responses usually produce consequences, either negative or positive, which in turn affect how the organism responds the next time it encounters the same stimulus. Say you put money in a vending machine (a response to the stimulus of seeing the machine) and the machine dispenses a tasty candy bar; chances are good that you will repeat the behavior in the future. If, on the other hand, the machine serves up a stale candy bar with a torn wrapper, you will be less inclined to use this or another machine like it again.

How might the behaviorists explain Tiger Woods's success? A key idea in behaviorism is *reinforcement,* any consequence that results from a given behavior and strengthens or supports the behavior. A reward, such as payment for a job, is a common type of reinforcement. If the consequence of a behavior is reinforcing, we are likely to repeat the behavior. Conversely, if a behavior produces an undesirable outcome ("punishment"), we are less likely to do it again. From his earliest days, Tiger Woods received an extraordinary amount of reinforcement for playing well, at first from his father and then from an increasingly larger affirming public. It was this reinforcement, the behaviorists would argue, that spurred him to repeat those acts that brought desirable consequences, while shunning behaviors (including ineffective golfing techniques) that did not help him play well.

The behaviorists have developed many principles that describe the conditions in which specific stimuli lead to specific responses, many of which have stood up well in later investigations. Moreover, the behaviorists' emphasis on controlled, objective observation has had a deep and lasting impact on psychology. Today, even studies of mental processes must conform to the level of rigor established by the behaviorists. Behaviorist insights also have improved

Behaviorism: The school of psychology that focuses on how a specific stimulus (object, person, or event) evokes a specific response (behavior in reaction to the stimulus).

psychotherapy and education. On the other hand, as we will see, many of the behaviorists' objections to the study of mental processes have been refuted by subsequent research.

Humanistic Psychology

Partly as a reaction to the theories of the Freudians and behaviorists, which viewed people as driven either by the content of their mental processes or by external stimuli, a new school of psychological thought emerged in the late 1950s and early 1960s. According to **humanistic psychology**, people have positive values, free will, and deep inner creativity, which in combination allow them to choose life-fulfilling paths to personal growth. The humanistic approach (focused on the level of the person) rests on the ideas that the "client" (no longer the "patient" as in psychodynamic approaches) must be respected as equal to the therapist and that each person has dignity and self-worth.

Psychologists such as Carl Rogers (1902–1987) and Abraham Maslow (1908–1970) developed therapies based on the humanistic approach. Rogers's *client-centered therapy* incorporated Maslow's theory that people have an urge to *self-actualize*—that is, to develop to their fullest potentials—and that, given the right environment, this development will, in time, occur. Rather than serving as an expert in a position of authority, the client-centered therapist provides a "mirror" in the form of an unconditionally supportive and positive environment. How might humanistic psychologists explain Tiger Woods's success? No doubt they would point to him as someone who is striving to reach his full potential. They might question, however, whether in the long run his intense focus on golf will prove entirely satisfying, especially if he ignores other aspects of life.

Although humanistic psychology never had the impact that the other schools had, it is important in part because it represented a renewed interest in mental processes. This school continues to attract followers today, but it is not a major force in the field. Nevertheless, many of the therapies now in use reflect the influence of humanistic thinking.

The Cognitive Revolution

The tension between approaches—on the one hand, structuralism, functionalism, and psychodynamic psychology, which studied unobservable mental processes, and on the other hand, behaviorism, which considered only directly observable behavior—was resolved by a new arrival on the scene, the computer. The computer led to the *cognitive revolution* of the late 1950s and early 1960s; its proponents looked to the computer as a model for the way human mental processes work. This movement came into full flower in the mid-1970s, led by, among others, psychologists/computer scientists Herbert A. Simon and Alan Newell (Simon went on to win a Nobel Prize, in part for this work) and linguist Noam Chomsky. (Gardner [1985] provides a detailed history of the cognitive revolution.)

We saw earlier in the chapter how useful computer metaphors can be, but the cognitive revolution focused not on the levels of analysis we have discussed, but rather solely on a new way to conceive of mental processes. This perspective gave birth to **cognitive psychology**, which attempts to characterize the nature of human *information processing*, that is, the way information is stored and operated on internally (Neisser, 1967). In this view, mental processes are like computer software (programs), and the brain is like the hardware (the machine itself).

Humanistic psychology: The school of psychology that assumes people have positive values, free will, and deep inner creativity, the combination of which leads them to choose life-fulfilling paths to personal growth.

Cognitive psychology: The approach in psychology that attempts to characterize how information is stored and operated on internally.

Computers provided a new way to conceptualize mental processes and to develop detailed theories about them.

Computers showed, once and for all, why it is important that there be a science of the unobservable events that take place in the head, not just a science of directly observable behavior. Consider, for example, how you might react if your word-processing program produced *italics* whenever you entered the command for **boldface**. Noticing the software's "behavior" would be only the first step in fixing this error: You would need to dig deeper in order to find out where the program had gone wrong. This would involve seeing what internal events are triggered by the command and how those events affect what the machine does. So, too, for people. If somebody is acting odd, we must go beyond the essential step of noticing the unusual behavior; we also need to think about what is happening inside and consider what is causing the problem. Indeed, the cognitive revolution led to new ways of conceptualizing and treating mental disorders, such as depression.

The theories and research methods developed by cognitive psychologists have also proven crucial in the development of <mark>cognitive neuroscience</mark>, which blends cognitive psychology and neuroscience (the study of the brain). Cognitive neuroscientists argue that "the mind is what the brain does" (Gazzaniga, 2004; Kosslyn & Koenig, 1995) and hope to discover the nature, organization, and operation of mental processes by studying the brain. One of the goals of cognitive neuroscience is to distinguish among different sorts of mental processes. For example, after Tiger Woods began to lose consistently, he was asked how he felt—and was upbeat in his response. It seems unlikely that this is how he actually felt, but he may have believed he had to "put on a happy face" and try to deceive the reporters. Researchers have found that the particular mental processes used in deception depend on whether a person draws on previously rehearsed and memorized stories or on new stories made up on the spot; brain scanning has revealed that there is more than one way to tell a lie, with separate neural systems being used in the different sorts of lying—which in turn differ from the neural systems used when one tells the truth (Ganis et al., 2003). This is one of the most exciting areas of psychology today, in part because brain-scanning technologies have allowed us, for the first time in history, to observe human brains at work.

The cognitive neuroscience approach considers events at the three levels of analysis, but with a primary focus on the brain. Cognitive neuroscientists seeking to explain Tiger Woods's golfing achievements would likely investigate how different parts of his brain function while he plays golf, looking to discover the way his brain processes information. For example, how does the visual input he receives standing at the tee allow him to judge distance to the pin? They would also compare Woods's brain function with that of less accomplished golfers and would even program computers to mimic the way his brain works during play.

Evolutionary Psychology

One of the most recent developments in the field, evolutionary psychology, first made its appearance in the late 1980s. This school of thought has a heritage—with a twist—in the work of the functionalists and their emphasis on Darwin's

Cognitive neuroscience: A blending of cognitive psychology and neuroscience (the study of the brain) that aims to specify how the brain stores and processes information.

theory of natural selection. Central to <mark>evolutionary psychology</mark> is the idea that certain cognitive strategies and goals are so important that natural selection has built them into our brains. But instead of proposing that evolution has selected any specific behaviors as such (as earlier evolutionary theorists, including Charles Darwin himself, believed), these theorists believe that general cognitive strategies (such as using deception to achieve one's goals) and certain goals (such as finding attractive mates) are inborn. This approach addresses events at all three levels of analysis and is being developed by researchers such as Lida Cosmides and John Tooby (1996), David Buss (1994, 1999), and Steven Pinker (1994, 1997) and reviewed by others (Barkow et al., 1992; Plotkin, 1994, 1997; Schmitt, 2002). For example, these theorists claim that we have the ability to lie because our ancestors who could lie had an advantage: They could trick their naïve companions into giving up resources. These more devious ancestors had more children who survived than did their nonlying contemporaries, and their lying children had more children, and so on, until the ability to lie was inborn in all members of our species. Notice that lying is not a specific behavior; it is a strategy that can be expressed by many behaviors, all of them deceitful.

Evolutionary psychologists also compare human abilities with those of animals, particularly nonhuman primates (Hauser, 1996). For example, by studying the way animals communicate, researchers try to infer which abilities formed the basis of human language. By studying animals, researchers hope to discover the abilities of our common ancestors and, from those data, develop theories about the way those abilities may have been refined over the course of evolution. When asked about what might underlie Tiger Woods's achievements, an evolutionary psychologist might note that although our species did not evolve to play golf, the abilities that arose via natural selection for hunting game and avoiding predators can also be used in other ways—in playing sports, for example.

But evidence of the universality of certain behaviors among humans or of shared abilities in nonhuman animals and humans does not tell us *why* those characteristics are present. Are they really adaptations? Evolutionary theories are notoriously difficult to test because we don't know what our ancestors were like and how they evolved. Just because we are born with certain tendencies and characteristics does not mean that these are evolutionarily selected adaptations. As Stephen Jay Gould and Richard Lewontin (1979) pointed out, at least some of our modern characteristics are simply by-products of other characteristics that

Evolutionary psychology: The approach in psychology that assumes that certain cognitive strategies and goals are so important that natural selection has built them into our brains.

Probably the best source of evidence for theories in evolutionary psychology is *cultural universals*, behaviors or practices that occur across all cultures, including playing music, dancing, lying, telling stories, gossiping, expressing emotions with facial expressions, fearing snakes, giving gifts, and making medicines (Brown, 1991).

Psychology

Table 1　Schools of Psychological Thought

Name	Landmark Events	Key Ideas
Structuralism	Wundt founds first psychology laboratory, 1879.	Use introspection to discover the elements of mental processes and rules for combining them.
Functionalism	James's *Principles of Psychology*, published 1890.	Study why thoughts, feelings, and behavior occur, how they are adaptive.
Gestalt psychology	Wertheimer's paper on perceived movement, 1912.	Focus on overall patterns of thoughts or experience; "the whole is more than the sum of its parts."
Psychodynamic theory	Freud publishes *The Ego and the Id*, 1927.	Conflicts among conscious and unconscious forces underlie many thoughts, feelings, and behaviors.
Behaviorism	Watson's paper *Psychology as the Behaviorist Views It*, 1913; Skinner's *The Behavior of Organisms*, 1938.	Behavior is the appropriate focus of psychology, and it can be understood by studying stimuli, responses, and the consequences of responses.
Humanistic psychology	Maslow publishes *Motivation and Personality*, 1954.	Nonscientific approach; belief that people have positive values, free will, and deep inner creativity.
Cognitive psychology	Neisser's book *Cognitive Psychology* gives the "school" its name, 1967.	Mental processes are like information processing in a computer.
Cognitive neuroscience	First issue of the *Journal of Cognitive Neuroscience* appears, 1989.	"The mind is what the brain does."
Evolutionary psychology	Barkow, Cosmides, and Tooby edit *The Adapted Mind*, 1992.	Mental strategies and goals are often inborn, the result of natural selection.

Note: Dates prior to Maslow based on Boring (1950).

were in fact selected. Your nose evolved to warm air and detect odors; and once you have a nose, you can use it to hold up your eyeglasses. But just as nobody would claim that the nose evolved to hold up glasses, nobody should claim that all the current functions of the brain resulted from natural selection.

The various schools of psychological thought are summarized in Table 1.

The State of the Union: Psychology Today

Although schools of psychology gave rise to other schools over time, the original schools did not simply fade away. Rather than being replaced by their descendents, the parent schools often continued to develop and produce new and important discoveries. Moreover, the different schools began to influence each other. Today, we have a rich mix of different sorts of psychology, which are cross-fertilizing and interacting with one another in fascinating ways. For example, techniques in cognitive neuroscience (most notably brain scanning) are being used to test hypotheses about the effects of social context on reasoning and to test behaviorist principles about stimulus–response relations (Blakemore et al., 2004), and research in cognitive psychology is having an impact on many questions that motivated the functionalists, particularly in the area of improving methods of education (Kozhevnikov et al., 2005). In addition, behaviorist techniques have been used to train animals to respond only to certain visual patterns, which then has allowed scientists to discover how interactions among individual brain cells give rise to some of the Gestalt laws of organization (Merchant et al., 2003). Moreover, psychodynamic theory has influenced questions being asked in cognitive psychology and cognitive neuroscience, such as those concerning the nature of forgetting (Anderson et al., 2004). Similarly, evolutionary psychology is making intriguing points of contact with modern behaviorist theories, most notably regarding the idea that behaviors may obey economic laws (for example, by maximizing gain while minimizing expended effort).

All of these varied approaches to psychology not only co-exist but feed off one another. The result is that we are learning about mental processes and behavior at an ever-increasing clip. If you are interested in psychology, these are truly exciting times in which to live!

The Psychological Way: What Today's Psychologists Do

If you read that Tiger Woods had seen a psychologist, would you think that he had a personal problem, or that he was suffering from too much stress? Neither guess is necessarily true; psychologists do much more than help people cope with their problems. As the field of psychology developed, different schools of thought focused on different aspects of mental processes and behavior; their varying influences are felt in what today's psychologists do. And just what is that?

Here we consider three major types of psychologists: those who help people deal with personal problems or stress, those who teach and usually also study the science of mental processes and behavior, and those who seek to solve specific practical problems, such as helping athletes perform better.

Clinical and Counseling Psychology: A Healing Profession

Andrea is a **clinical psychologist** who specializes in treating people with eating disorders. Many of Andrea's clients have a disorder called *anorexia nervosa*, characterized by refusal to maintain a healthy weight. Others, who have a disorder called *bulimia nervosa*, eat and then force themselves to vomit or take laxatives immediately afterward. Andrea sees such patients once or twice a week, for 50 minutes per session. During these sessions, Andrea's job is usually to discover why behaviors that are so destructive in the long run seem so desirable to the patient in the short run. She then helps her patients phase out the destructive behaviors and replace them with more adaptive behaviors—for instance, responding to anxiety after eating by taking a quick walk around the block instead of vomiting. Depending on the setting in which Andrea works (probably a private office, clinic, or hospital), she will spend varying portions of her day with patients; meeting with other psychologists to discuss how to be more helpful to patients; supervising psychotherapists in training; going out into the community, perhaps lecturing about eating disorders at high school assemblies; and doing paperwork, including writing notes on each patient, submitting forms to insurance companies for payment, and reading professional publications to keep up with new findings and techniques.

Andrea has been trained to provide **psychotherapy**, which involves helping clients learn to change so that they can cope with troublesome thoughts, feelings, and behaviors. She also administers and interprets psychological tests, which can help in diagnosis and in planning the appropriate treatment. *Clinical*

Clinical psychologist: The type of psychologist who provides psychotherapy and is trained to administer and interpret psychological tests.

Psychotherapy: The process of helping clients learn to change so they can cope with troublesome thoughts, feelings, and behaviors.

There are many kinds of psychotherapy, and different training prepares therapists in different ways. Psychiatrists, for example, typically would not treat families, but clinical psychologists and social workers—as well as other mental health professionals—might.

neuropsychologists are clinical psychologists who work specifically with tests designed to diagnose the effects of brain damage on thoughts, feelings, and behavior and to indicate which parts of the brain are impaired following trauma. Other clinical psychologists work with organizations, such as corporations, to help groups function more effectively; for example, a psychologist might advise a company about reducing stress among workers in a particular unit or might teach relaxation techniques to all employees. Some clinical psychologists have a Ph.D. (doctor of philosophy) degree, awarded by a university psychology department; these graduate programs teach students not only how to do psychotherapy and psychological testing, but also how to conduct and interpret psychological research. Other clinical psychologists have a Psy.D. (doctor of psychology), a graduate degree from a program with less emphasis on research. In some states, clinical psychologists can obtain additional training and be granted the right to prescribe drugs (the first state to grant this privilege was New Mexico, in 2002).

If Andrea had been trained as a **counseling psychologist**, she would have learned to help people deal with issues we all face, such as choosing a career, marrying, raising a family, and performing at work. Counseling psychologists often provide career counseling and vocational testing to help people decide which occupations best suit their interests and abilities. These professionals sometimes provide psychotherapy, but they may have a more limited knowledge of therapeutic techniques than do clinical psychologists. They may have a Ph.D. (often from a program that specifically trains people in this area) or often an Ed.D. (doctor of education) degree from a school of education.

Andrea could also have become a **psychiatrist**. If she had gone this route, her training and area of competence would have differed from those of the other mental health professionals. First, as a physician with an M.D. (doctor of medicine) degree, a psychiatrist has extensive medical training and can prescribe drugs, whereas, in general, psychologists cannot. Second, as a medical doctor, a psychiatrist (unlike a clinical psychologist) has typically not been trained to interpret and understand psychological research or psychological research or psychological testing.

There are two other types of clinical mental health practitioners who are not psychologists. Her interest in clinical work might have led Andrea to choose either of those professions: social work or psychiatric nursing. If she had earned an M.S.W. (master of social work) degree, as a **social worker**, she would typically focus on using psychotherapy to help families and individuals, and she also would teach clients how to use the social service systems in their communities. A **psychiatric nurse** holds a master's degree (M.S.N., master of science in nursing) as well as a certificate of clinical specialization (C.S.) in psychiatric nursing. A psychiatric nurse provides psychotherapy, usually in a hospital or clinic or in private practice, and works closely with medical doctors to monitor and administer medications; in some cases, a psychiatric nurse can prescribe medications.

Counseling psychologist: The type of psychologist who is trained to help people with issues that naturally arise during the course of life.

Psychiatrist: A physician who focuses on mental disorders; unlike psychologists, psychiatrists can prescribe drugs, but they are not trained to administer and interpret psychological tests, nor are they trained to interpret and understand psychological research.

Social worker: A mental health professional who uses psychotherapy to help families (and individuals) and teaches clients to use the social service systems in their communities.

Psychiatric nurse: A nurse with a master's degree and a clinical specialization in psychiatric nursing who provides psychotherapy and works with medical doctors to monitor and administer medications.

Academic Psychology: Teaching and Research

James is a professor of psychology at a large state university. Most mornings he prepares lectures, which he delivers three times a week. He also has morning office hours, when students can come by to ask questions about their program of courses in the department or their progress in one of James's classes. Once a week he has a noontime committee meeting; for example, the committee on computer technology may discuss how best to structure the department computer network. His afternoons are taken up mostly with research. If he worked at a smaller college, he might spend more time teaching and less time on research; alternatively, if he worked at a hospital, he might spend the lion's share of his time doing research and very little time teaching. In fact, if John worked in a research institute (perhaps affiliated with a medical school), he might not teach at all, but instead would make discoveries that others could teach; if he worked in a small college, he might not do research, but instead would dedicate himself to teaching the accumulated knowledge of the science of psychology. James's specialty is *developmental psychology*, the study of how thinking, feeling, and behaving develop with age and experience. His research work takes place at a laboratory preschool at the university, where he and his assistants are testing the ways children become attached to objects such as dolls and blankets. James also must find time to write papers for publication in professional journals, and he regularly writes grant proposals requesting funding for his research, so that he can pay students to help him test the children in his studies. He also writes letters of recommendation, grades papers and tests, and reads journal articles to keep up with current research in his and related fields. James tries to eat lunch with colleagues at least twice a week to keep up-to-date on departmental events and the work going on at the university in other areas of psychology.

Developmental psychologists often take special care to prevent their presence from affecting the child's behavior in any way.

Although the activities of most ==academic psychologists== are similar in that most teach and many also conduct research, the kinds of teaching and research vary widely. Different types of academic psychologists focus on different types of questions. For example, if James had become a *cognitive psychologist* (one who studies thinking, memory, and related topics), he might ask, "How is Tiger Woods able to hit the ball with the appropriate force in the correct direction?" but not, "What is the role of the audience at a major golf tournament, and would it have been different 50 years ago?" If he had become a *social psychologist* (one who studies how people think and feel about themselves and other people and how groups function), he might ask the second question, but not the first. And in neither case would he ask, "What aspects of Tiger Woods's character help him deal with the extreme stress he faces?" That question would interest a *personality psychologist* (one who studies individual differences in preferences and inclinations).

Because psychology is a science, it rests on objective tests of its theories and ideas. It is through research that psychologists learn how to diagnose people's problems and how to cure them; it is through research that they determine what kind of career will make good use of a particular person's talents; it is through research that they discover how to present material so that students can understand

Academic psychologist: The type of psychologist who focuses on teaching and conducting research.

Applied psychologist: The type of psychologist who studies how to improve products and procedures and conducts research to help solve specific practical problems.

and remember it most effectively. Theories about such issues can come from anywhere, but there is no way to know whether an idea is right or wrong except by testing it scientifically, through research.

There are at least as many different types of academic psychologists as there are separate sections in this book. In fact, this book represents a harvest of their research. Thousands of researchers are working on the topics covered in each chapter, and it is their efforts that allow a book like this one to be written.

Applied Psychology: Better Living Through Psychology

Maria is an applied psychologist; more specifically, she is a *human factors psychologist*, a professional who works to improve products so that people can use them more intuitively and effectively. In general, **applied psychologists** use the principles and theories of psychology in practical areas such as education, industry, and marketing. An applied psychologist may have a Ph.D. or, sometimes, only a master's degree in an area of psychology (in North America, a master's degree typically requires two years of postgraduate study instead of the four to six for a Ph.D.). Applied psychologists not only work on improving products and procedures but also conduct research aimed at solving specific practical problems.

Applied psychologists have many roles, one of which is to help attorneys decide which potential jurors are likely to be sympathetic or hostile to the defendant.

Working in applied psychology, a *developmental psychologist* may be employed by or consult with the product development department of a toy company. Using her knowledge of children, she can help design toys that will be appropriate for particular age levels; she then brings children to a playroom at the company to see how they play with the new toys. A *physiological psychologist* studies the brain and brain–body interactions and may work at a company that makes drugs or brain-scanning machines. A *social psychologist* may help lawyers decide which potential jurors should be rejected. A *personality psychologist* may design a new test to help select suitable personnel for a job. An *industrial/organizational (I/O) psychologist* focuses on using psychology in the workplace; he or she might help an employer create a more comfortable and effective work environment so as to increase worker productivity or might redesign work spaces to promote more effective employee communication. A *sport psychologist* works with athletes to help them improve their performances, by helping them learn to concentrate better, deal with stress, and practice more efficiently (Tiger Woods has consulted a sport psychologist). An *educational* or *school psychologist* works with educators (and sometimes families), devising ways to improve the cognitive, emotional, and social development of children at school.

The occupations of the various types of psychologists are summarized in Table 2.

The Changing Face of Psychology

You may have noticed a lack of female names when we reviewed the history of psychology, and for good reason. In earlier times, few opportunities were available for women to make major contributions to this field; however, in spite of the barriers of those days, a few women did make their mark on psychology, such as Margaret Floy Washburn, who was Edward Titchener's first student to earn a Ph.D. (in 1894), and Mary Whiton Calkins, the first woman to become president of the American Psychological Association (in 1905).

Mary Whiton Calkins, the first woman president of the American Psychological Association (1905).

Table 2 What Psychologists Do

Clinical psychologist	Administers and interprets psychological tests; provides psychotherapy.
Clinical neuropsychologist	Diagnoses effects of brain damage on thoughts, feelings, and behavior, and diagnoses the locus of damage.
Counseling psychologist	Helps people with issues that arise during everyday life (career, marriage, family, work).
Developmental psychologist	Researches and teaches the development of mental processes and behavior with age and experience.
Cognitive psychologist	Researches and teaches the nature of thinking, memory, and related aspects of mental processes.
Social psychologist	Researches and teaches how people think and feel about themselves and other people, and how groups function.
Personality psychologist	Researches and teaches individual differences in preferences and inclinations.
Physiological psychologist	Researches and teaches the nature of the brain and brain/body interactions.
Human factors psychologist	Applies psychology to improve products.
Industrial/organizational psychologist	Applies psychology in the workplace.
Sport psychologist	Applies psychology to improve athletic performance.
Educational or school psychologist	Applies psychology to improve cognitive, emotional, and social development of schoolchildren.

As shown in Figure 1, the situation is changing—increasing numbers of women, such as Anne Treisman, Ursula Bellugi, Susan Carey, and Elizabeth Spelke, are making major contributions in all areas of psychology (we will review fruits of their labors in the pages to come). In fact, in the last major survey (National Science Foundation, 2001), fully 77% of college graduates with psychology majors were women. Thus, we can expect to see increasing representation of women in the field at large.

LOOKING BACK: *Review*

1. *How did psychology develop over time?* Wundt, Titchener, and the other structuralists aimed to understand the elements of mental processes and how they are organized; this approach relied largely on introspection ("looking within"), which turned out to be not very reliable and not always valid—people often have no idea how their mental processes work, at least not in ways they can easily report. The functionalists rejected this approach as disconnected from real-world concerns and focused instead on how mental processes adapt to help us survive in the natural world; their pragmatic concerns led them to apply psychology to education and other social activities. In contrast, the Gestalt psychologists, who reacted to the attempt to dissect mental processes into isolated elements, studied the way the brain organizes material into overarching patterns. Freud shifted attention primarily to the level of the person; his psychodynamic theory was concerned largely with the operation of unconscious mental processes and primitive impulses (often related to sex)

Figure 1 **Women Winning the APA Award for Distinguished Scientific Contributions**

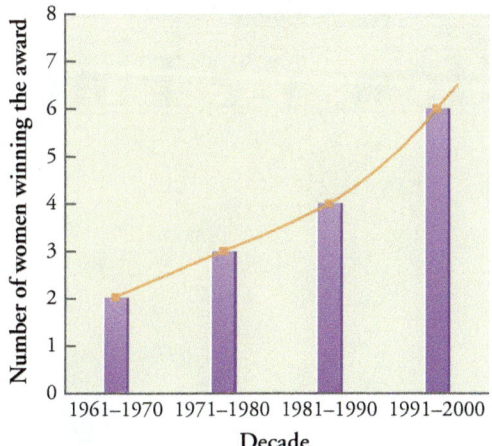

Women are playing an increasingly prominent role in scientific psychology. In 1997, two-thirds of all Ph.D. degrees in psychology were earned by women (American Psychological Association, www.apa.org/pi/wpo/wapa/final.html).

in dictating what people think, feel, and do. The behaviorists denounced the assumption, shared by all their predecessors, that mental processes should be the focus of psychology; they urged us to stick with what we could see—stimuli, responses, and the consequences of responses. But this view turned out to be too limiting. The humanists, in part reacting against the scientific approach, developed psychotherapies that relied on respect for individuals and their potentials. Elements of the various strands came together in the cognitive revolution, and many researchers who study cognition today conceive of mental processes as "what the brain does." Evolutionary psychology treats many cognitive strategies and goals as adaptive results of natural selection.

2. *What do today's psychologists actually do?* Clinical and counseling psychologists administer diagnostic tests and help people with their problems; academic psychologists teach and do research; and applied psychologists trained in various areas of psychology seek to solve specific practical problems, such as making better products and improving procedures in the workplace.

LOOKING BEYOND: *Critical Thinking*

If Tiger Woods were to be studied by adherents of a single school of psychological thought, which one would be least likely to produce useful insights? Most likely? When asked to account for his remarkable skill, Woods professes to have no conscious knowledge about how he plays so well. How would this report affect the approaches taken by the different schools?

Would the President be more effective if he had a chief psychologist? If so, which sort of psychologist would be most helpful? (Don't assume it would necessarily be a clinical psychologist.) Why?

The Research Process: How We Find Things Out

You could probably speculate for hours about how Tiger Woods came to be such a superb golfer. Let's say, however, that you want to *know* why some people like him are able to perform at high levels in spite of extraordinary pressure. How could you find out for sure? You would need to investigate in a careful and systematic way to reach a conclusion.

LOOKING AHEAD: *Learning Objectives*

1. *What is the scientific method, and how is it used to study psychology?*
2. *What scientific research techniques are commonly used in psychology?*
3. *What are key characteristics of good scientific studies in psychology?*
4. *How are ethical principles applied to scientific studies in psychology?*

Psychology

The Scientific Method

Psychology is a science because it relies on a specific type of method of inquiry, and this method, in principle, allows psychologists to discover characteristics that predict human behavior. The <mark>scientific method</mark> is a way to gather facts that will lead to the formulation and validation of a theory. It involves *specifying a problem, systematically observing events, forming a hypothesis of the relation between variables, collecting new observations to test the hypothesis, using such evidence to formulate and support a theory, and finally, testing the theory*. Let's take a closer look at the scientific method, one step at a time.

Step 1: Specifying a Problem

What do we mean by "specifying a problem"? Science tries to answer questions, any one of which may be rephrased as a "problem." Despite the way the word is often used in ordinary conversation, a problem is not necessarily bad: It is simply a question you want to answer or a puzzle you want to solve. For example, a scientist might note that even as a child, Tiger Woods's abilities and discipline made him stand out from his peers. Why? Was there something different about his brain or the way he was being raised?

Step 2: Observing Events

After the problem is specified, it is investigated by "systematically observing events." Scientists are not content to rely on impressions or interpretations. They want to know the facts, as free from any particular notions of their significance as possible. Facts are established by collecting <mark>data</mark>, which are numerical measurements or careful observations of a phenomenon. Properly collected data can be obtained again in a <mark>replication</mark> of a study; that is, they can be collected again by the original investigator or someone else. Scientists often prefer quantitative data (numerical measurements), such as how many words on a list a person can learn in a given time. In addition to collecting numerical data, scientists rely on systematic observations, which simply document that a certain event occurs. But unless the data include numbers, it is often difficult to sort the observation from the interpretation. The data are just the facts, ma'am, nothing but the facts—when data are collected, the interpretation must be set aside, saved for later.

What do we mean by "events"? An event in the scientific sense is the occurrence of a particular phenomenon. Scientists study two kinds of events: those that are themselves directly observable (such as how many times in an hour a mother speaks to her infant) and those that, like thoughts, motivations, or emotions, can only be inferred. For example, when people smile without really meaning it (as they often do when posing for photographs), the muscles they use are not the same ones used to produce a sincere smile (Ekman, 1985). It is possible to observe directly which set of muscles is in use. But a researcher's interest goes beyond the directly observable muscle contractions to the link with inner (and invisible) thoughts and feelings. By studying what's observable (the muscles), researchers can learn about the unobservable (the mental state of the smiler).

But observations are just the beginning; they typically can be interpreted in more than one way. For example, a smile could mean happiness, agreement, politeness, or amusement.

Scientific method: The scientific method involves specifying a problem, systematically observing events, forming a hypothesis of the relation between variables, collecting new observations to test the hypothesis, using such evidence to formulate and support a theory, and finally testing the theory.

Data: Objective observations.

Replication: Collecting the same observations or measurements and finding the same results as were found previously.

Step 3: Forming a Hypothesis

What about "forming a hypothesis of the relation between variables"? First, by the term **variable**, researchers mean an aspect of a situation that is liable to change (or, in other words, that can vary); more precisely, a variable is a characteristic of a substance, quantity, or entity that is measurable. A **hypothesis** is a tentative idea that might explain a set of observations. Say you are inspired by Tiger Woods and decide to take golf lessons. On the course, you notice a particularly good player and ask her for tips. She says that when she's off the course, she often practices her swings mentally, imagining herself whacking the ball straight down the fairway or out of a sand trap; she assures you that the mental practice has improved her game. Well, maybe there's a connection here between two variables: between time spent visualizing swings and golf score. The idea appeals to you, in part because it means that you can practice at night, or whenever you are bored, or when the course is covered with snow. But it's a hypothesis only. Before you go to the trouble of imagining yourself swinging a club, over and over and over, you ought to test the hypothesis to find out whether it's correct.

Step 4: Testing the Hypothesis

Thus, you must go about "collecting new observations to test the hypothesis." The first thing you need to do is create operational definitions of the key concepts, which make them concrete enough to test. An **operational definition** specifies a variable by indicating how it is measured or manipulated. For example, "improvement" could be defined in terms of the number of putts sunk or the distance the ball is driven. In fact, much research has been conducted on mental practice, and many studies have documented that it actually does improve performance, measured in various ways. In a typical study, people are divided into two groups, and the performance of both groups is assessed. One group then uses mental practice for a specified period, while the other makes no preparation. Then the performance of both groups is assessed again. Usually, the people who engage in mental practice show greater improvement (Doheny, 1993; Driskell et al., 1994; Druckman & Swets, 1988; White & Hardy, 1995; Yagueez et al., 1998).

Step 5: Formulating a Theory

Now consider "using such evidence to formulate and support a theory." A **theory** consists of an interlocking set of concepts or principles that explains a set of observations. A theory does not appear out of thin air; rather, a theory is formulated on the basis of empirical findings that were obtained before the theory existed. Unlike a hypothesis, a theory is not a tentative idea and doesn't focus on possible relationships among variables. Instead, theories are rooted in an established web of facts and concepts and focus on the *reasons* for established relationships among variables. In our example, the idea that mental practice leads to better performance is a hypothesis, not a theory. A theory might explain that mental practice works because the brain activity that allows you to perform an action is also induced when you practice mentally; thus, when you engage in the actual behavior later, after practicing it mentally, the appropriate processes are more efficient.

Hypotheses and theories both produce **predictions**, which are new hypotheses. These hypotheses are expectations about specific events that should occur in particular circumstances if the original theory is correct. The new hypotheses can then be put to the test.

Variable: An aspect of a situation that can vary, or change; specifically, a characteristic of a substance, quantity, or entity that is measurable.

Hypothesis: A tentative idea that might explain a set of observations.

Operational definition: A definition of a variable that specifies how it is measured or manipulated.

Theory: An interlocking set of concepts or principles that explain a set of observations.

Prediction: An expectation about specific events that should occur in particular circumstances if the theory or hypothesis is correct.

Figure 2 The Scientific Method

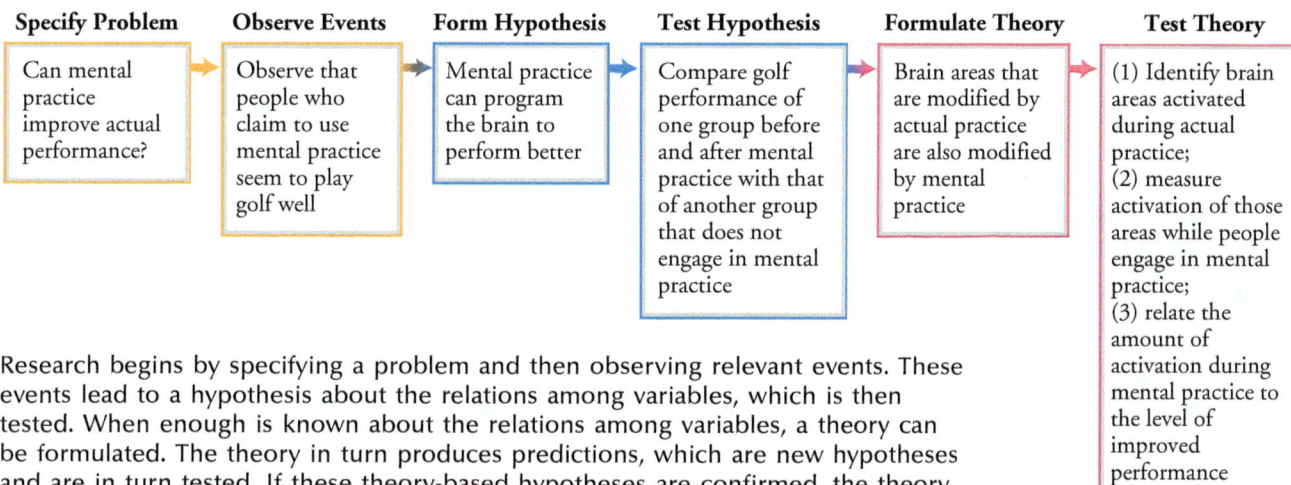

Specify Problem	Observe Events	Form Hypothesis	Test Hypothesis	Formulate Theory	Test Theory
Can mental practice improve actual performance?	Observe that people who claim to use mental practice seem to play golf well	Mental practice can program the brain to perform better	Compare golf performance of one group before and after mental practice with that of another group that does not engage in mental practice	Brain areas that are modified by actual practice are also modified by mental practice	(1) Identify brain areas activated during actual practice; (2) measure activation of those areas while people engage in mental practice; (3) relate the amount of activation during mental practice to the level of improved performance

Research begins by specifying a problem and then observing relevant events. These events lead to a hypothesis about the relations among variables, which is then tested. When enough is known about the relations among variables, a theory can be formulated. The theory in turn produces predictions, which are new hypotheses and are in turn tested. If these theory-based hypotheses are confirmed, the theory is supported; if they fail to bear fruit, then the theory must be altered and the whole process repeated.

Step 6: Testing the Theory

Finally, what do we mean by "testing the theory"? The history of science is littered with theories that turned out to be wrong. Researchers evaluate a theory by testing its predictions. As illustrated in Figure 2, once a theory has been formulated, it plays a key role in the process of formulating hypotheses. Each prediction of the theory is, in fact, a new hypothesis to be tested. The theory of mental practice predicts that the parts of the brain used to produce a behavior—in our example, swinging a golf club—are activated by merely imagining the behavior. This prediction has also been tested by using brain-scanning techniques to observe what happens in the brain when an individual imagines making certain movements. And, in fact, parts of the brain used in controlling actual movements have been found to be activated when the movements are only imagined (Jeannerod, 1994, 1995; Kosslyn et al., 1998; Parsons, 1987, 1994; Parsons & Fox, 1998).

Each time a theory makes a correct prediction, the theory is supported, and each time it fails to make a correct prediction, the theory is weakened. If enough of its predictions are unsupported, the theory must be rejected and the data explained in some other way. A good theory is *falsifiable*; that is, it makes predictions it cannot "squirm out of." A falsifiable theory can be rejected if the predictions are not confirmed. Part of the problem with astrology, for example, is that its predictions are so vague and general that they are difficult to disprove.

Putting the Steps Together

Now that you understand all the steps of the scientific method, you could use it to investigate other questions. Say you've heard that putting a crystal under your bed will focus cosmic energies and improve your athletic ability. Should you believe this? First, you specify the problem, phrasing it as a question: Can crystals under your bed improve performance? Second, you systematically observe events: Perhaps you notice that on days after the members of a golf team place crystals under their beds, they do perform better. Third, from those data, you form a

Would putting a crystal under his bed make him play better?

hypothesis: Something about the crystals themselves—not the beliefs of the players who use them or any other factors—is responsible for the improvement. Fourth, you test the hypothesis: Before some of Tiger Woods's games, you sneak a crystal under his bed, making sure he never knows when it is there and when it isn't; then you observe whether he plays better on days after the crystal was present. Fifth, if the hypothesis is supported and Woods does play better on those days, you need a theory to explain how the crystal works (for example, you might hypothesize that it somehow alters the magnetic field of the earth). Finally, you test the theory: You might put the crystal in a magnetically shielded box and see whether its being under Woods's bed still raises his level of play.

The Psychologist's Toolbox: Techniques of Scientific Research

Although all sound psychological investigations rely on the scientific method, researchers working in the different areas of psychology often pose and answer questions differently. Psychologists use a variety of research tools, each with its own advantages and disadvantages.

Descriptive Research: Just the Facts, Ma'am

Although the scientific method is always described in terms of testing hypotheses, this isn't quite the whole story. Not all research is sparked by specific hypotheses. Some research is devoted simply to describing "things as they are." It's no accident that "observing events" is a key part of the scientific method: Theorizing without facts is a little like cooking without ingredients.

Naturalistic Observation. For the scientist, facts are *not* intuitions, impressions, or anecdotes. Essential to the scientific method is careful, systematic, and unbiased observation that can be repeated by others, and some researchers specialize in collecting such data from real-world settings. For example, researchers observed caregivers interacting with young children, and noted that the caregivers changed their language and speech patterns, using short sentences and speaking in a high pitch. This modified way of speaking is known as *child-directed speech* (Morgan & Demuth, 1996; Snow, 1991, 1999).

Although naturalistic observation is an essential part of science, it is only a first step. The discovery of child-directed speech does not tell us whether caregivers use it in order to help children understand them, or to entertain the children, or simply to imitate other caregivers they have heard. It is difficult to test specific interpretations of a finding using only naturalistic observation (although not impossible, as any astronomer will tell you). The problem is that to test your hypothesis, you must seek out a specific situation where nature has set the relevant variables in just the right way. In science, observing an event is typically only the first step.

Some scientists observe animals in the wilds of Africa; others observe sea life in the depths of the ocean; and others observe humans in their natural habitats.

Case study: A scientific study that focuses on a single instance of a situation, examining it in detail.

Case Studies. Sometimes nature or human affairs produce unique situations, which change an independent variable in a novel way. A **case study** focuses on a single instance of a situation, examining it in detail. For example, a researcher might study a single professional athlete, looking closely at her life and circumstances in an effort to formulate hypotheses about the psychological underpinnings that allow someone to succeed at that level. Many neuropsychologists study individual brain-damaged patients in depth to discover which abilities are "knocked out" following certain types of damage. A psychologist who studies abnormal behavior might study a reported case of multiple personalities to discover whether there's anything to the idea (books such as *Sybil* and *The Three Faces of Eve* describe such cases in great detail); a cognitive psychologist may investigate how an unusually gifted memory expert is able to retain huge amounts of information almost perfectly; a personality psychologist might study in detail how aspiring professional athletes remain motivated through years and years of hard work with no guarantee that they will ever enjoy major success.

However, we must always be cautious about generalizing from a single case; that is, we must be careful in assuming that the findings in the case study extend to all other similar cases. Any particular person may be unusual for many reasons and so may not be at all representative of people in general.

Brain damage following an accident can cause someone to fail to name fruits and vegetables while still able to name other objects (Hart et al., 1985). A case study would examine such a person in detail, documenting precisely what sorts of things could and could not be named.

Surveys. A **survey** is a set of questions put to a number of participants about their beliefs, attitudes, preferences, or activities. Surveys are a relatively inexpensive way to collect a lot of data fairly quickly, and they are popular among psychologists who study personality and social interactions. Surveys provide data that can be used to formulate or test a hypothesis. However, the value of surveys is limited by what people are capable of reporting accurately. You could use a survey to ask people how much they like golf, but not to ask people how their brains work or to ask them to report subtle behaviors, such as body language, that they may engage in unconsciously. Moreover, even if they are capable of answering, people may not always respond honestly; this is especially a problem when the survey touches on sensitive personal issues, such as sex. And even if people do respond honestly, what they say does not always reflect what they do. Finally, not everyone who is asked to respond does, in fact, fill in the survey. Because a particular factor (such as income or age) may incline some people, but not others, to respond, it is difficult to know whether the responses obtained are actually representative of the whole group that the survey was designed to assess.

Survey questions have to be carefully worded so that they don't lead the respondents to answer in a certain way and yet still get at the data of interest. Similarly, the nature of the response scale (for example, the range of values presented) affects what people say, as does the order in which questions are asked (Schwarz, 1999).

Correlational Research: Do Birds of a Feather Flock Together?

Researchers use another method to study the relations among variables, a method that relies on the idea of correlation. A correlation is a relationship in which changes in the measurements of one variable are accompanied by changes in the measurements of another variable. For example, height is correlated with weight: Taller people tend to be heavier than smaller people. A **correlation coefficient** (often simply called a *correlation*) is an index of how closely related two measured variables are. Figure 3 illustrates three predicted correlations between variables.

Survey: A set of questions, typically about beliefs, attitudes, preferences, or activities.

Correlation coefficient (or correlation): An index of how closely interrelated two sets of measured variables are, which ranges from −1.0 to +1.0. The higher the correlation (in either direction), the better we can predict the value of one type of measurement when given the value of the other.

Researchers have found that the lower the level of a chemical called monoamine oxidase (MAO) in the blood, the more the person will tend to seek out thrilling activities (such as sky diving and bungee jumping; Zuckerman, 1995). Thus, there is a negative correlation between the two measures: As MAO levels go down, thrill seeking goes up. But we don't know whether MAO level causes the behavior or vice versa—or whether some other chemical, personality trait, or social factor causes the levels of both MAO and thrill seeking to vary together.

In Figure 3a, we see a positive correlation, a relationship in which increases in one variable (height) are accompanied by increases in another (weight); a positive correlation is indicated by a correlation value that falls between 0 and 1.0. In Figure 3b, we see a negative correlation, a relationship in which increases in one variable (age) are accompanied by decreases in another (health); a negative correlation is indicated by a correlation value that is between 0 and −1.0. Finally, in Figure 3c, we see a zero correlation, which indicates no relationship between the two variables (height and aggressiveness); they do not vary together. The closer the correlation is to 1.0 or −1.0, the stronger the relationship; visually, the more tightly the data points cluster around the line, the higher the correlation.

Correlational research involves measuring at least two things about each of a number of individuals or groups (or measuring the same individuals or groups at a number of different times), and looking at the way one set of measurements goes up or down in tandem with another set of measurements; correlations always compare one pair of measurements at a time. The main advantage of correlational research is that it allows researchers to compare variables that cannot be manipulated directly. The main disadvantage is that correlations indicate only that two variables tend to vary together, not that one *causes* the other. For

Figure 3 Strength of Correlation

POSITIVE CORRELATION
BETWEEN 0 AND 1.0

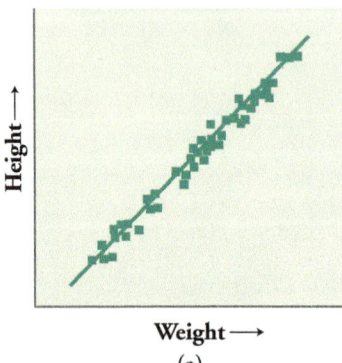

Weight →
(a)

Here, increases in one variable (height) are accompanied by increases in another (weight); this is a positive correlation, indicated by a correlation value that falls between 0 and 1.0.

NEGATIVE CORRELATION
BETWEEN 0 AND −1.0

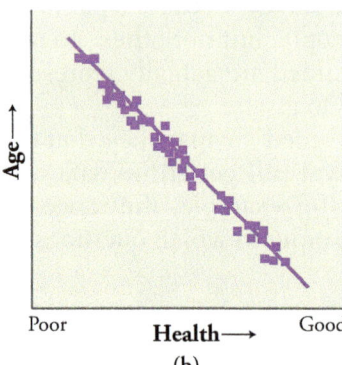

Poor   Health →   Good
(b)

Here, increases in one variable (age) are accompanied by decreases in another (health); this is a negative correlation, indicated by a correlation value that is between 0 and −1.0.

ZERO CORRELATION

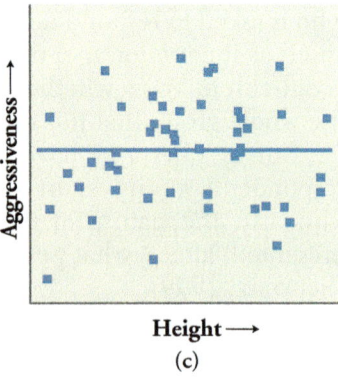

Height →
(c)

A zero correlation indicates no relationship between the two variables, height and aggressiveness here; they do not vary together. The closer the correlation is to 1.0 or −1.0, the stronger the relationship; visually, the more tightly the data points cluster around the line, the higher the correlation.

example, evidence suggests a small correlation between poor eyesight and intelligence (Belkin & Rosner, 1987; Miller, 1992; Williams et al., 1988), but poor eyesight doesn't cause someone to be smarter! Remember: *Correlation does not imply causation*.

Experimental Research: Manipulating and Measuring

Much psychological research relies on conducting *experiments*, controlled situations in which variables are manipulated. Experiments provide the strongest way to test a hypothesis, in that they can provide evidence that one event causes another.

Independent and Dependent Variables. The variables in a situation—for example, "time spent mentally practicing" and "golf score"—are the aspects of the situation that can vary. In an experiment, the investigator deliberately alters one aspect of a situation, which is called the ==independent variable==, and measures another, called the ==dependent variable==. In other words, in an experiment, the value of the dependent variable depends on the value of the independent variable. For our mental practice of golf example, the amount of time participants in the experiment spend mentally practicing is the independent variable (it is deliberately varied), and their golf score is the dependent variable (it is measured); see Figure 4. By examining the link between independent and dependent variables, a researcher hopes to discover exactly which factor is causing an ==effect==, which is the difference in the dependent variable that results from a change in the independent variable. In our mental practice example, the effect is the degree of improvement in participants' golf score from the first assessment of their performance (before mental practice) to the second assessment (after mental practice).

Once researchers have found a relation between two variables, they need to test that relation to rule out other possible explanations for it; only by eliminating other possibilities can they know whether a hypothesized relation is correct. In our example, say we had tested only one group, the one that used mental practice. The fact that these players improved would not necessarily show that mental practice can improve actual golf performance. Perhaps simply practicing during the first assessment (before mental practice) is enough to cause an improvement at the second assessment. Or perhaps people are simply more relaxed at the time of the second assessment, and that is why they perform better.

A ==confound==, or *confounding variable*, is any other aspect of the situation (such as the anxiety that accompanies a test) that has become entangled with the aspects that the researcher has chosen to vary. Confounds thus lead to results that are ambiguous, that do not have a clear-cut interpretation (see Figure 5).

Experimental and Control Groups and Conditions. One way to disentangle confounds is to use a control group. The ==experimental group== receives the complete *treatment*, that is, the complete procedure that defines the experiment.

Figure 4 Relationship Between Independent and Dependent Variables

INDEPENDENT VARIABLE: Amount of time the person practices mentally	DEPENDENT VARIABLE: Subsequent performance on the golf course

 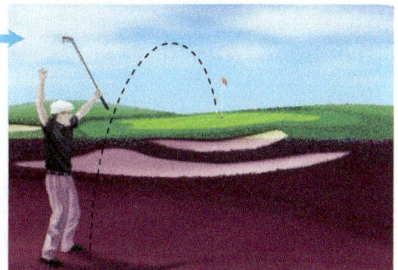

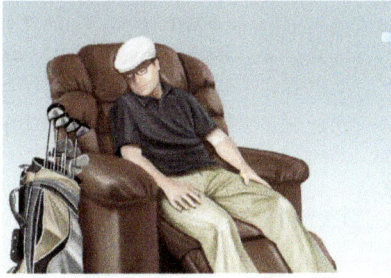 

The independent variable is what is manipulated—in this example, the amount of time participants spend mentally practicing. The dependent variable, what is measured, is in this case their golf score.

Independent variable: The aspect of the situation that is intentionally varied while another aspect is measured.

Dependent variable: The aspect of the situation that is measured as an independent variable is changed; the value of the dependent variable depends on the independent variable.

Effect: The difference in the dependent variable that is due to the changes in the independent variable.

Confound (or confounding variable): An independent variable that varies along with the ones of interest, and could be the actual basis for what you are measuring.

Experimental group: A group that receives the complete procedure that defines the experiment.

Figure 5 Confounding Variables in Everyday Life

Professor Jones has made a startling observation: Students with poor posture are more intelligent than those who stand up straight. He plans to alert the college admissions office to this finding, and urge them to require applicants to supply full-body photos. But is it intelligence that accompanies poor posture? Perhaps a strong motivation to do well leads to more intense poring over books, with hunched posture. Or is it that shy people both tend to hunch and to be more comfortable spending time alone studying? Can you think of other possible confounding variables that should make Professor Jones take pause?

Control group: A group that is treated exactly the same way as the experimental group, except that the one aspect of the situation being studied is not manipulated for this group. The control group holds constant—"controls"—all of the variables in the experimental group except the one of interest.

Random assignment: The technique of assigning participants randomly, that is, by chance, to the experimental and the control groups, so that no biases can sneak into the composition of the groups.

A **control group** is treated identically to the experimental group except with regard to the one variable that is the focus of study; a good control group holds constant—or controls—all of the variables in the experimental group except the one of interest. In the mental practice experiment, the experimental group does mental practice, the control group does not. If the kinds of people assigned to the two groups differ markedly, say, in age, gender, or learning ability (or any combination of the three), those factors could be confounds that would mask a clear reading of the experiment's results; any difference in the groups' golf scores could have been caused by any of those elements. In a properly conducted experiment, therefore, the researchers rely on **random assignment**: Participants are assigned randomly, that is, by chance, to the experimental and the control groups, so that no confounds can sneak into the composition of the groups.

Similarly, you can use an **experimental condition** and a **control condition**, either for a group of people or a single person. Instead of testing a separate control group, you test the same group another time, keeping everything the same as in the experimental condition except for the single independent variable of interest. To avoid confounding the order of testing with the condition (experimental versus control), you would test half the participants in the control condition before testing them in the experimental condition and would test the other half of the participants in the experimental condition before testing them in the control condition.

Quasi-Experimental Design

One element of a true experiment is that the participants are assigned randomly to the different groups. But in the real world, it is not always possible or desirable to achieve randomness, and so sometimes research designs must be quasi-experimental (*quasi* means "as if" in Latin). A *quasi-experimental design* includes independent and dependent variables and assesses the effects of different values of the independent variable on what is measured. However, participants are not randomly assigned to conditions, and the conditions typically are selected from naturally occurring variations in situations (not created by the investigator's manipulating the independent variable).

For instance, let's say that you want to discover whether the effects of mental practice are different for people of different ages, and so you decide to test four groups of people: teenagers, college students, middle-aged people, and elderly people. Obviously, you cannot assign people to the different age groups randomly. Rather, you select groups from what nature has provided. When composing the groups, you should control for as many variables—such as health and education level—as you can in order to make the groups as similar as possible. Similarly, if you want to track changes over time, it is not possible to assign people randomly to the groups as time goes by because you are taking measurements only from people you have measured before. In quasi-experiments, participants are not assigned randomly to groups; instead, such studies rely on comparing multiple groups or multiple sets of measurements, attempting to eliminate potential confounds as much as possible. Unfortunately, because the groups can never be perfectly equated on all characteristics, you can never be certain exactly what differences among groups are responsible for the observed results. The conclusions you draw from quasi-experiments cannot be as strong as those from genuine experiments.

Psychology

Table 3   Summary of Research Methods

Method	Key Characteristic(s)	Advantage(s)	Disadvantage(s)
Naturalistic observation	Observed events are carefully documented.	Forms the foundation for additional research by documenting the existence of an event or situation	Cannot control for confounding variables or change the variables to discover the critical factor in a particular mental process or behavior
Case study	A single instance of a situation is analyzed in depth.	Can provide in-depth understanding of the particular situation	Cannot assume that the findings extend to all other similar cases
Survey	A number of participants answer specific questions.	Relatively inexpensive way to collect a lot of data fairly quickly	Limited by how the questions are stated and by what people can and are willing to report
Correlational research	Relations among different variables are documented.	Allows comparison of variables that cannot be manipulated directly	Cannot infer causation
Experimental design	Participants are assigned randomly to groups, and the effects of manipulating one or more independent variables on a dependent variable are studied.	Allows rigorous control of variables; is able to establish causal relations between independent and dependent variables	Not all phenomena can be studied in controlled laboratory experiments (in part, because not all characteristics can be manipulated).
Quasi-experimental design	Similar to an experiment but participants are not assigned to groups randomly and conditions are often selected, not created.	Allows the study of real-world phenomena that cannot be studied in experiments	Cannot control relevant aspects of the independent variables

Table 3 summarizes the basic research methods used in psychology, along with their relative strengths and weaknesses. When thinking about the various methods, keep in mind that even though experiments are the most rigorous, they cannot always be performed—particularly if you are interested in studying large groups or if it is difficult (or unethical) to manipulate the variables. In addition, keep in mind that different combinations of the methods are often used. For example, observational methods are used as part of correlational research, and observational, correlational, or experimental research can be conducted with single individuals (case studies).

Meta-Analysis

Science is a communal effort. Usually many people are studying the same phenomenon, each one painting additional strokes onto an emerging picture. Meta-analysis is a technique that allows researchers to combine results from different studies. This is particularly useful when results have been mixed, with some studies showing an effect and some not. Meta-analysis can determine whether there is a relationship among variables that transcends any one study, a strand that cuts across the entire range of findings.

Sometimes results that are not evident in any individual study become obvious in a meta-analysis. Why? Studies almost always involve observing or testing a

Experimental condition: A part of a study in which the participant receives the complete procedure that defines the experiment. Usually this is accompanied by a control condition, with the same participants receiving both experimental and control conditions.

Control condition: A condition administered to the same participants who receive the experimental condition; this effectively makes the participants both the experimental and the control group.

Meta-analysis: A statistical technique that allows researchers to combine results from different studies, which can determine whether there is a relationship among variables that transcends any one study.

sample from a population; the **sample** is the group that is measured or observed, and the **population** is the entire set of relevant people or animals (perhaps defined in terms of age or gender). The crucial fact is that there is always variation in the population. Just as people vary in height and weight, they also vary in their behavioral tendencies, cognitive abilities, and personality characteristics. Thus, samples taken from the population will vary, and if a sample is relatively small, the luck of the draw could obscure an overall difference that actually exists in the population. For example, if you stopped the first two males and first two females you saw on the street and measured their heights, the females might actually be taller than the males. The problem of variation in samples is particularly severe when the difference of interest—the effect—is not great. If men averaged 8 feet tall and women 4 feet tall, small samples would not be a problem; you would quickly figure out the usual height difference between men and women. But if men averaged 5 feet 10 inches and women averaged 5 feet 9 inches (and the heights of those in both samples differed by up to 6 inches), you would need to measure many men and women before you were assured of finding the difference. Meta-analysis is a way of combining the samples from many studies, which allows you to detect even subtle differences or relations among variables (Rosenthal, 1991).

Be a Critical Consumer of Psychology

No research technique is always used perfectly, so you must be a critical consumer of all science, including the science of psychology. Metaphorically speaking, there are no good psychologists on salt-free diets—we take everything with at least a grain of salt! But this doesn't mean that you should be cynical, doubting everything you hear or read. Rather, whenever you read a report of a psychological finding in a newspaper, a journal article, or a book (including this one), look for aspects of the study that could lead to alternative explanations. You already know about the possibility of confounds; here are a few other issues that can cloud the interpretation of studies.

Reliability: Count on It!

Not all data are created equal; some are better than others. One way to evaluate data is in terms of reliability. **Reliability** means consistency. A reliable car is one you can count on to behave consistently, starting even on cold mornings and not dropping random parts on the highway. A reliable set of measurements is one that can be replicated, that is, obtained again if the study is repeated. When you read about the results of a study, find out whether they have been replicated; if so, then you can have greater confidence that the measurements were reliable.

Validity: What Does It Really Mean?

Something is said to be valid if it is what it claims to be; a valid driver's license, for example, is one that was, in fact, issued by the state and has not expired (and thus does confer the right to drive). In science, **validity** means that a method provides a true measure of what it is supposed to measure. A study may be reliable but not valid, or vice versa. Table 4 lists four of the major types of validity (Carmines & Zeller, 1979).

To understand the concept of validity, let's see what it's like to be a participant in a study. So, before reading further, try this exercise. Table 5 contains a list of words. Decide whether the first word names a living object or a nonliving one

Sample: A group that is drawn from a larger population and measured or observed.

Population: The entire set of relevant people or animals.

Reliability: Data are reliable if the same results are obtained when the measurements are repeated.

Validity: A measure is valid if it does in fact measure what it is supposed to measure.

Table 4 Four Major Types of Validity

Type	Description	Example
Face validity	Design and procedure appear to assess the variables of interest.	Sample essay as part of an entrance exam for journalism school.
Content validity	Measures assess all aspects of phenomenon of interest.	Test of knowledge of research methods that covers all methods.
Criterion validity	A measure or procedure is comparable to a different, valid measure or procedure.	A paper-and-pencil test of leadership ability correlates highly with poll results of leadership of actual leaders.
Construct validity	Measures assess variables specified by a theory.	A theory defines "fatigue" in terms of lack of alertness, and the measure assesses this lack.

(circle the word "living" at the right if it is living; otherwise move to the next word); then decide whether the second word begins with the letter t (circle the words "begins with t" if it does; otherwise move to the next word); then decide whether the third word names a living or a nonliving object, whether the fourth word begins with the letter t, and so on, alternating judgments as you go down the list. Please do this now.

Table 5 What's in a Word?

Circle the word or phrase on the right if the word on the left has the named property; otherwise, move on to the next word. After you finish the list, read on.

salmon	living	trout	living
tortoise	begins with *t*	donkey	begins with *t*
airplane	living	teapot	living
toad	begins with *t*	house	begins with *t*
guitar	living	table	living
goat	begins with *t*	terrain	begins with *t*
truck	living	tiger	living
automobile	begins with *t*	rosebush	begins with *t*
snake	living	bacteria	living
tent	begins with *t*	carpet	begins with *t*
toast	living	staple	living
television	begins with *t*	tricycle	begins with *t*
wagon	living	lawn	living
tarantula	begins with *t*	ocean	begins with *t*
toadstool	living	tuna	living
elephant	begins with *t*	terrier	begins with *t*

Psychology

When you have finished marking the list, take out a piece of paper and (without looking!) write down as many of the words as you can. How many words from the list were you able to remember?

The standard result from this kind of study is that people will remember more words after making a living/nonliving judgment than after making a t/non-t judgment (for example, see Craik & Tulving, 1975). This result is usually interpreted to mean that the more we think about (or "process") the material, as we must in order to make the living/nonliving decision, the better we remember it; for the t words, we only need to look at the first letter, not think about the named object at all. In fact, if we are forced to think about something in detail but don't consciously try to learn it, we end up remembering it about as well as if we did try to learn it.

Does this demonstration of differences in memory following differences in judgment really support this interpretation? What if you remembered the words you judged as living/nonliving better because you had to read the whole word to make the required judgment, but you only looked at the first letter of the other words to decide whether they began with t? If this were the case, your better memory of words in the living/nonliving category would have nothing to do with "thinking about it more." Therefore, the experiment would not be valid—it would not be measuring what the investigator designed it to measure.

When you read a result, always try to think of as many interpretations for it as you can; you may be surprised at how easy this can be. And, if you can think of an alternative interpretation, see whether you can think of a control group or condition that would allow you to tell who was right, you or the authors of the study.

Bias: Playing With Loaded Dice

Sometimes beliefs, expectations, or habits alter how participants in a study respond or affect how a researcher sets up or conducts a study, thereby influencing its outcome. This leaning toward a particular result, whether conscious or unconscious, is called **bias**, and it can take many forms. One form of bias is **response bias**, in which people have a tendency to respond in a particular way regardless of their actual knowledge or beliefs. For example, many people tend to say "yes" more than "no," particularly in some Asian cultures (such as that of Japan). This sort of bias toward responding in "acceptable" ways is a devilish problem for survey research. For example, consider the difference between these two versions of a question: "Do you support using public funds to build golf courses, which will increase recreational options?" versus "Do you support using public funds to build golf courses, which will encourage people to exercise and be healthier?" Given the way the second question is phrased, you would be hard-pressed to say "no."

Another form of bias is **sampling bias**, which occurs when the participants or items are not chosen at random but instead are selected so that an attribute is over- or underrepresented—which leads to a confound. For example, say you wanted to know the average heights of male and females, and you went to shopping malls to measure people. What if you measured males outside a toy store (and so were likely to be measuring little boys), but measured females outside a fashion outlet for tall people (and so were likely to find especially tall women)? Or, what if the words in the living/nonliving category in Table 5 were interesting words such as "centipede" and "boomerang," and the words in the t/non-t category were bland words such as "toe" and "broom"? Or, perhaps the living/

Bias: When beliefs, expectations, or habits alter how participants in a study respond or affect how a researcher sets up or conducts a study, thereby influencing its outcome.

Response bias: A tendency to respond in a particular way regardless of respondents' actual knowledge or beliefs.

Sampling bias: A bias that occurs when the participants or items are not chosen at random, but instead are chosen so that one attribute is over- or underrepresented.

nonliving words were more emotionally charged than the t/non-t words, or were more familiar. What if only language majors were tested, or only people who read a lot and have terrific vocabularies? Could we assume that all people would respond the same way? Take another look at Table 5; can you spot any potential sampling bias?

Sampling bias isn't just something that sometimes spoils otherwise good studies. Do you remember the U.S. Presidential election of 2000? Albert Gore and George W. Bush were in a dead heat, and the election came down to the tally in a few counties in Florida. Based on surveys of voters exiting their polling places, the TV commentators predicted that Gore would be the winner. What led them astray? Sampling bias. The news organizations that conducted the surveys did not ask absentee voters how they cast their ballots. In such a close election, this was an important factor because the absentee voters included many members of the armed services, who tend to be Republicans. Thus, sampling only from those who voted on election day produced a biased view of how the entire population voted—and the TV commentators had to eat their words.

Experimenter Expectancy Effects: Making It Happen

Clever Hans, a horse that lived in Germany in the early 1890s, apparently could add (Rosenthal, 1976). When a questioner (one of several) called out two numbers to add, for example, "6 plus 4," Hans would tap out the correct answer with his hoof. Was Hans a genius horse? Was he psychic? No. Despite appearances, Hans wasn't really adding. He seemed to be able to add, and even to spell out words (with one tap for the letter a, and an additional tap for each letter in the alphabet), but he responded only if his questioner stood in his line of sight and knew the answer. The questioner, who expected Hans to begin tapping, always looked at Hans's feet right after asking the question—thereby cuing Hans to start tapping. When Hans had tapped out the right number, the questioner always looked up—cuing Hans to stop tapping. Although, in fact, Hans could neither add nor spell, he was a pretty bright horse: He was not trained to do this; he "figured it out" on his own.

The cues offered by Hans's questioners were completely unintentional; they had no wish to mislead (and, in fact, some of them were probably doubters). But unintentional cues such as these lead to <mark>experimenter expectancy effects</mark>, which occur when an investigator's expectations lead him or her (consciously or unconsciously) to treat participants in a way that encourages them to produce the expected results. Such effects can occur in all types of research, from experiments to surveys—in all cases, the investigator can provide cues that influence how participants behave. For instance, if you were polling voters about their choice for President, your own views could color what they say; if you smile whenever they mention your candidate and frown when they mention the other candidate, they may try to please you by saying what they think (perhaps unconsciously) you want to hear.

At least for experiments, it's clear how to guarantee that experimenter expectancy effects won't occur: In a <mark>double-blind design</mark>, not only is the participant "blind" to (unaware of) the predictions of the study and hence unable consciously or unconsciously to serve up the expected results, but the experimenter is also "blind" to the condition assigned to the participant and thus is unable to induce the expected results. What would have happened if a questioner of Clever Hans had not known the answer to the question?

Experimenter expectancy effects: Effects that occur when an investigator's expectations lead him or her (consciously or unconsciously) to treat participants in a way that encourages them to produce the expected results.

Double-blind design: The participant is "blind" to (unaware of) the predictions of the study (and so cannot consciously or unconsciously produce the predicted results), and the experimenter is "blind" to the condition assigned to the participant (and so experimenter expectancy effects cannot produce the predicted results).

Dogbert (Dilbert's dog) is thinking scientifically about astrology. He proposes a relationship among seasonal differences in diet, sunlight, and other factors and personality characteristics. These variables can be quantified, and their relationships tested. If these hypotheses are not supported by the data but Dogbert believes in astrology nevertheless, he's crossed the line into pseudopsychology.

Psychology and Pseudopsychology: What's Flaky and What Isn't?

Are you a fire sign? Do you believe that your Zodiac sign matters? So many people apparently do that the home page for *Yahoo!* will automatically provide your daily horoscope. But astrology—along with palm reading and tea-leaf reading, and all their relatives—is not a branch of psychology; it is pseudopsychology. **Pseudopsychology** is superstition or unsupported opinion pretending to be science. Pseudopsychology is not just "bad psychology," which rests on poorly documented observations or badly designed studies and, therefore, has questionable foundations. Pseudopsychology is not psychology at all. It may look and sound like psychology, but it is not science. Unfortunately, advice to be found in some self-help books falls into this category. For instance, at one point we were told that screaming would "let it all out," and so was good for us—but there was absolutely no evidence that such screams did any more than annoy the neighbors. (This is why it is a good idea to check whether the advice dispensed in a self-help book you are contemplating buying is supported by research.)

Appearances can be misleading. Consider extrasensory perception (ESP). Is this pseudopsychology? ESP refers to a collection of mental abilities that do not rely on the ordinary senses or abilities. Telepathy, for instance, is the ability to read minds. This sounds not only wonderful but magical. No wonder people are fascinated by the possibility that they, too, may have latent, untapped, extraordinary abilities. The evidence that such abilities really exist is shaky. But the mere fact that many experiments on ESP have come up empty does not mean that the experiments themselves are bad or "unscientific." One can conduct a perfectly good experiment, guarding against confounds, bias, and expectancy effects, even on ESP. Such research is not necessarily pseudopsychology.

Let's say you want to study telepathy. You might arrange to test pairs of participants, with one member of each pair acting as "sender" and the other as "receiver." Both the sender and receiver would look at hands of playing cards that contained the same four cards. The sender would focus on one card (say, an ace) and would "send" the receiver a mental image of the chosen card. The receiver's job would be to guess which card the sender is focusing on. By chance alone, with only four cards to choose from, the receiver would guess right about 25% of the time. So the question is, can the receiver do better than mere guesswork? In

Pseudopsychology: Theories or statements that at first glance look like psychology, but are in fact superstition or unsupported opinion pretending to be science.

Psychology

this study, you would measure the percentage of times the receiver picks the right card, and compare this to what you would expect from guessing alone.

But wait! What if the sender, like the questioners of Clever Hans, provided visible cues (accidentally or on purpose) that have nothing to do with ESP, perhaps smiling when "sending" an ace, grimacing when "sending" a two. A better experiment would have sender and receiver in different rooms, thus controlling for such possible confounds. Furthermore, what if people have an unconscious bias to prefer red over black cards, which leads both sender and receiver to select them more often than would be dictated by chance? This difficulty can be countered by including a control condition, in which a receiver guesses cards when the sender is not actually sending. Such guesses will reveal response biases (such as a preference for red cards), which exist independently of messages sent via ESP.

Whether ESP can be considered a valid, reliable phenomenon will depend on the results of such studies. If they conclusively show that there is nothing to it, then people who claim to have ESP or to understand it will be trying to sell a bill of goods—and will be engaging in pseudopsychology. But as long as proper studies are under way, we cannot dismiss them as pseudopsychology.

Ethics: Doing It Right

Let's say that Tiger Woods wants to learn how to overcome pain so that he can practice hard even when he is hurt, but that practicing when injured might cause long-term damage to his body. Would it be ethical for a sport psychologist to teach Woods—or anyone else—techniques for continuing to work out even in the presence of damaging pain? Or, what if Woods developed a "block" that impaired his playing? Would it be ethical for a therapist to treat him with new, unproven techniques?

Ethics in Research

Following World War II, people were horrified to learn that the Nazis had performed ghastly experiments on human beings. The war trials in Nuremberg led directly to the first set of rules, subscribed to by many nations, outlawing those sorts of experiments. Sometimes the actions of psychologists also call for a set of rules, especially when participants' rights conflict with a research method or clinical treatment. Certain methods are obviously unethical: No psychologist would cause people who participate in experiments to become addicted to drugs to see how easily they can overcome the addiction or beat people to help them overcome a psychological problem. But many research situations are not so clear-cut.

Research With People: Human Guinea Pigs? In 1996, some New York psychiatrists were tapping the spines of severely depressed teenagers at regular intervals in order to see whether the presence of certain chemicals in the spinal fluid could predict which particular teens would attempt suicide. As required by law, the youths' parents had given permission for the researchers to draw the fluids. However, this study was one of at least ten that a court ruling brought to a screeching halt on December 5, 1996 (*New York Times*, page A1). The New York State Appeals Court found that the existing rules for the treatment of children and mentally ill people in experimental settings were unconstitutional because they did not properly protect these participants from abuse by researchers. However, the researchers claimed that without these studies they would never be able to develop the most effective drugs for treating serious impairments, some of which

Informed consent: The requirement that a potential participant in a study be told what he or she will be asked to do and be advised of possible risks and benefits of the study before agreeing to take part.

Debriefing: An interview after a study to ensure that the participant has no negative reactions as a result of participation and understands why the study was conducted.

might lead to suicide. Do the potential benefits of such studies outweigh the pain they cause?

New York was more lax in its policies than many other states. California, Connecticut, Massachusetts, and Illinois allow researchers to conduct experiments in which the pain outweighs the gain or experiments that have risks but do not benefit participants directly *only* when the participants themselves (not someone else for them) provide **informed consent**. Informed consent means that before agreeing to take part, potential participants in a study must be told what they will be asked to do and must be advised of the possible risks and benefits of the procedure. They are also told that they can withdraw from the study at any time without being penalized. Only after an individual clearly understands this information and gives consent by signature can he or she take part in a study. But not all states have such rules, and there are no general federal laws that regulate all research with human participants.

Nevertheless, a study that uses funds from the U.S. government or from most private funding sources must be approved by an institutional review board (IRB) at the university, hospital, or other institution that sponsors or hosts the study. The IRB monitors all research projects at that institution, not just those of psychologists. An IRB usually includes not only scientists but also physicians, clergy, and representatives from the local community. The IRB considers the potential risks and benefits of each research study and decides whether the study can be performed. These risks and benefits are considered from all three levels of analysis: Effects on the brain (for example, of drugs), the person (for example, through imparting false beliefs), and the group (for example, from embarrassment or humiliation). In many universities and hospitals, researchers are asked to discuss their proposed studies with the board, to explain in more detail what they are doing and why.

Concerns about the ethical treatment of human participants lead most IRBs to insist that participants be **debriefed**, that is, interviewed after the study about their experience. The purpose of debriefing is to ensure that participants are having no negative reactions as a result of their participation and that they have understood the purposes of the study. Deceiving participants with false or misleading information is allowable only when the participants will not be harmed and the knowledge gained clearly outweighs the use of dishonesty.

Research With Animals. Animals are studied in some types of psychological research, particularly studies that focus on understanding the brain. Animals, of course, can't give informed consent, don't volunteer, and can't decide to withdraw from the study if they get nervous or uncomfortable. But this doesn't mean that animals lack protection. Animal studies, like human ones, must have the stamp of approval of an IRB. The IRB makes sure the animals are housed properly (in cages that are large enough and cleaned often enough) and that they are not mistreated. Researchers are not allowed to cause animals pain unless that is explicitly what is being studied—and even then, they must justify in detail the potential benefits to humans (and possibly to animals, by advancing veterinary medicine) of inflicting the pain.

Is it ethical to test animals at all? This is not an easy question to answer. Researchers who study animals argue that their research is ethical. They point out that although there are substitutes for eating meat and wearing leather, there is no substitute for the use of animals in certain kinds of research. So, if the culture allows the use of animals

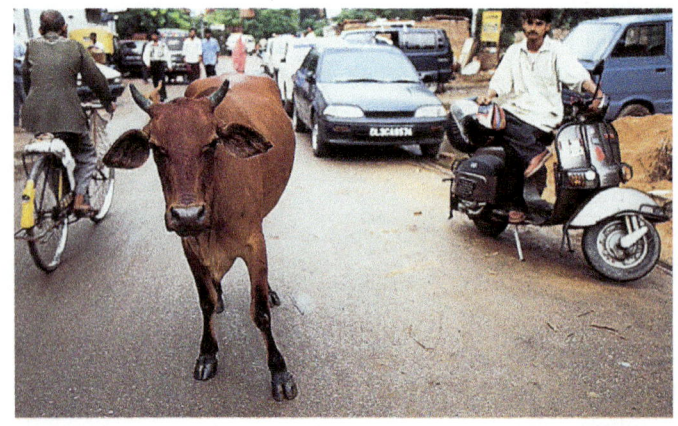

In large parts of India, animals are not eaten (some are even considered sacred). Many in that culture may believe that animal research is not appropriate.

for food and clothing, it is not clear why animals should not be studied in laboratories if the animals do not suffer and the findings produce important knowledge. This is not a cut-and-dried issue, however, and thoughtful people disagree. As brain-scanning technologies improve, the need for some types of animal studies of the brain may diminish.

Ethics in Clinical Practice

Imagine a Dr. Smith who has developed a new type of therapy that she claims is particularly effective for patients who are afraid of some social situations, such as public speaking or meeting strangers. You are a therapist who has a patient struggling with such difficulties and not responding to conventional therapy. You haven't been trained in Smith therapy, but you want to help your patient. Should you try this therapy? According to the American Psychological Association guidelines (see Table 6), the answer is clear: No. If you have not been trained appropriately or are not learning the therapy under supervision, you have no business delivering it.

This sort of ethical decision is relatively straightforward. But the process of psychotherapy sometimes requires careful stepping through emotional and ethical minefields. Psychologists are bound by their states' laws of confidentiality and may not communicate about a patient without specific permission from the patient, except in certain extreme cases, as when a life or (in some states) property is at

Table 6   General Ethical Principles and Code of Conduct for Psychologists

Principle A: Beneficence and Nonmaleficence	"Psychologists strive to benefit those with whom they work and take care to do no harm. . . . Because psychologists' scientific and professional judgments and actions may affect the lives of others, they are alert to and guard against personal, financial, social, organizational, or political factors that might lead to misuse of their influence."
Principle B: Fidelity and Responsibility	"Psychologists uphold professional standards of conduct, clarify their professional roles and obligations, accept appropriate responsibility for their behavior, and seek to manage conflicts of interest that could lead to exploitation or harm."
Principle C: Integrity	"Psychologists seek to promote accuracy, honesty, and truthfulness in the science, teaching, and practice of psychology. In these activities psychologists do not steal, cheat, or engage in fraud, subterfuge, or intentional misrepresentation of fact. Psychologists strive to keep their promises and to avoid unwise or unclear commitments."
Principle D: Justice	"Psychologists recognize that fairness and justice entitle all persons to access to and benefit from the contributions of psychology and to equal quality in the processes, procedures, and services being conducted by psychologists."
Principle E: Respect for People's Rights and Dignity	"Psychologists respect the dignity and worth of all people, and the rights of individuals to privacy, confidentiality, and self-determination. . . . Psychologists are aware of and respect cultural, individual, and role differences, including those based on age, gender, gender identity, race, ethnicity, culture, national origin, religion, sexual orientation, disability, language, and socioeconomic status and consider these factors when working with members of such groups."

Note: This is a direct quote with portions abridged; a complete description can be found at http://www.apa.org/ethics/code2002.html.

stake. Therapists have gone to jail rather than reveal personal information about their patients. Indeed, difficult cases sometimes cause new laws to be written. A patient at the University of California told a psychologist at the student health center that he wanted to kill someone and named the person. The campus police were told; they interviewed the patient and let him go. The patient then killed his targeted victim. The dead woman's parents sued the university for "failure to warn." The case eventually wound its way to California's highest court. One issue was whether the therapist had the right to divulge confidential information from therapy sessions. The court ruled that a therapist is obligated to use reasonable care to protect a potential victim. More specifically, in California (and in most other states now), if a patient has told his or her psychologist that he or she plans to harm a specific other person, and the psychologist has reason to believe the patient can and will follow through with that plan, the psychologist must take steps to protect the targeted person from harm, even though doing so may violate the patient's confidentiality. Similar guidelines apply to cases of potential suicide.

Further, a therapist cannot engage in sexual relations with a patient or mistreat a patient physically or emotionally. The American Psychological Association has developed many detailed ethical guidelines based on the principles listed in Table 6.

New Frontiers: Neuroethics

As research in psychology continues to progress at an increasing pace, new issues have emerged that would have been in the realm of science fiction a few years ago. To address one set of these issues, a new branch of ethics, called *neuroethics*, is focusing on the possible dangers and benefits of research on the brain. Still in its infancy, this field is already a hotbed of debate (a recent Google search on

The Center for Cognitive Liberty and Ethics (www.cognitiveliberty.org) asserts that two fundamental principles should form the core of neuroethics: First, individuals should never be forced to use technologies or drugs that interact with their brains. Second, individuals should not be prohibited from using such technologies or drugs if they so desire, provided that such use would not lead them to harm others.

"neuroethics" turned up more than 140,000 hits). So far, however, neuroethicists have more questions than answers. For example, Is it ethical to use brain-altering drugs to force prisoners to be docile? To scan people's brains to discover whether they are telling the truth? To require young children to take medication that makes them pay attention better in school?

Some scholars have been particularly concerned about the use of neuroscience to predict and control individual behavior (see Markus, 2002). For example, suppose that the brains of murderers could be shown conclusively to have a distinctive characteristic (perhaps one region that is much smaller than normal). Should we then scan people's brains and watch them carefully if they have this characteristic? Should this characteristic be used as a criterion for parole for prisoners?

Looking at Levels

Graph Design for the Human Mind

Scientists, such as those who study the effects of mental practice, often need to consider (and show others) complex findings. Graphs are a way to convey a lot of information without overwhelming the user. But what kind of graph should be used? It depends on what message needs to be conveyed. For example, Jeffrey Zacks and Barbara Tversky (1999) found that bar graphs are better than line graphs when you need to make or illustrate comparisons between discrete data points (such as specific numbers of Democratic versus Republican voters in various regions), whereas line graphs are better when you need to understand or illustrate trends (such as changes in the numbers of Democratic and Republican supporters in different parts of the United States over time). Bars end at discrete locations, and thus it's easy to compare data points simply by comparing the heights of the bars. In contrast, bars are not as useful for conveying trends because the reader needs mentally to connect the tops of bars, creating a line in order to determine visually whether there is a trend. Hence, if that's what you want to convey, it's better to give the reader the line in the first place. But if the reader needs to compare discrete data points, a line isn't so good: Now the reader must "mentally break down" the line into specific points, which requires effort (Kosslyn, 1994a; 2006).

Think about this finding from the levels-of-analysis perspective: When designing a graph, you need to respect the way the human perceptual and conceptual systems work (level of the brain). If you choose an inappropriate graph, you will force the reader to work hard to understand your message—which he or she may not be willing to do. But that's not all there is to it. Researchers who focus on the level of the group argue that people use graphs not only to communicate, but also to impress others. "For example, the use of gratuitous graphics [for example, adding the third dimension] may allow presenters to demonstrate their mastery of state-of-the-art technology, or their 'professionalism'; they may demonstrate the extra effort they have put into setting up the presentation or show their care about the contentment of their audience. Thus, social considerations in organizations are likely to promote self-presentation behavior in the context of information presentation" (Tractinsky & Meyer, 1999; p. 401; material in square brackets added for clarification).

In addition, researchers have studied events at the level of the person, such as the qualities of graphs that presenters prefer. One finding is that a presenter's preferences depend in part on the quality of the data. Tractinsky and Meyer (1999) asked participants to choose a display to present data; they found that participants preferred visually elaborate three-dimensional graphs when the graphs were presenting bad results. Why might this be? Perhaps because the graph obscures the data? Or perhaps because a fancy graph might partly compensate for poor results?

As usual, events at the three levels interact: Depending on the graph you choose for a specific purpose, you will affect the readers (level of the group) more effectively if the readers do not have to work hard to understand the display (level of the brain), and the particular message (level of the person) may not only influence the type of graph you choose but also how motivated the readers are to understand it. Not only do events at the different levels interact, but also these events *themselves* often must be understood at the different levels. For example, what occurs in the brain when someone is "impressed"? Trying to impress someone is clearly a social event, but it relies on events at the other levels of analysis. Similarly, "communication" is more than a social event—it also involves conveying content to readers (level of the person) and, ultimately, engaging their brains. Any psychological event can be understood fully only by considering it from all three levels.

LOOKING BACK: *Review*

1. *What is the scientific method, and how is it used to study psychology?* The scientific method is a way to gain objective knowledge that involves specifying a problem, systematically observing events, forming a hypothesis of the relation between variables, collecting new observations to test the hypothesis, using such evidence to formulate and support a theory, and, finally, testing the theory.

2. *What scientific research techniques are commonly used in psychology?* Psychologists use naturalistic observation, involving careful documentation of events; case studies, which are detailed analyses of a single instance of a situation; surveys, in which participants are asked sets of specific questions; correlational research, in which the relations among variables are documented but causation cannot be inferred; experimental designs, assigning participants randomly to groups and studying the effects of one or more independent variables on a dependent variable; and quasi-experimental designs, which are similar to experimental designs except that participants are not randomly assigned to groups. Finally, psychologists also use meta-analysis, in which the results of many studies are considered in a single overall analysis.

3. *What are key characteristics of good scientific studies in psychology?* The measures taken must be reliable (repeatable), valid (assess what they are supposed to assess), unbiased, and free of experimenter expectancy effects (leading participants to respond in specific ways). The studies must be well designed (eliminating confounds and having appropriate controls), and results properly interpreted (alternative accounts are ruled out).

4. *How are ethical principles applied to scientific studies in psychology?* For humans, informed consent is necessary before a person can participate in a study (informed consent requires that the person appreciate the potential risks and benefits); in the vast majority of cases, studies must be approved in advance by an Institutional Review Board (IRB); and participants must be debriefed after the study, to ensure that they have no negative reactions and to confirm their understanding of the purpose of the study. Animals must be treated humanely; animal studies must be approved in advance by an IRB; and animals cannot be caused pain or

discomfort unless that is what is being studied (even then, researchers must justify the potential benefits to humans or animals). Although guidelines vary across states, in general, strict confidentiality is observed unless a specific person may be harmed, suicide appears to be a real possibility, or (in some states) another's property may be damaged. Therapists must not take advantage of their special relationships with patients in any way. A new branch of ethics, called neuroethics, is focusing on the potential benefits and dangers of research on the brain.

LOOKING BEYOND: *Critical Thinking*

If you wanted to know whether Tiger Woods's upbringing played a crucial role in leading him to become a professional golfer, how would you go about studying this? Don't assume that it has to be a case study. Which specific questions would you ask? What are the best methods for answering them?

What characteristics and qualities do you think a pro golfer should have? Do you think psychology should prevent anyone from trying to enter this profession who does not have these characteristics and qualities? Why and why not?

LET'S SUM IT UP

I. The Science of Psychology: Getting to Know You

A. Psychology is the science of mental processes and behavior.

B. The goals of psychology are to describe, explain, predict, and control mental processes and behavior.

C. Psychology can best be understood by studying events at different levels of analysis: the levels of the brain, the person, and the group.

D. The level of the brain is where we examine the activity of certain brain systems, structural differences in people's brains, and effects of genes and chemicals (such as hormones) on mental processes and behavior.

E. The level of the person is where we study the content of mental processes, not just the mechanisms that give rise to them. Our beliefs, goals, and feelings are part and parcel of who we are.

F. The level of the group includes all our social interactions, past and present.

G. Events at the different levels are interdependent and are always interacting. They are also influenced by the physical environment.

II. Psychology Then and Now

A. Psychology began as the study of mental processes, such as those that underlie perception, memory, and problem solving.

B. The structuralists tried to identify the elements of consciousness and the rules by which these elements are combined into mental structures. The primary method of the structuralists was introspection ("looking within").

C. The functionalists rejected the goal of identifying mental processes and how they operated in favor of seeking explanations for thoughts, feelings, and behavior. The functionalists were interested in how mental processes adapt to help people survive in the natural world.

D. The Gestalt psychologists reacted against the structuralists' emphasis on breaking mental processes into distinct elements. The Gestaltists studied the way the brain organizes material into overall perceptual patterns.

E. Freud shifted focus to events at the level of the person. His psychodynamic theory explains how thoughts and feelings affect a person's behavior.

F. The behaviorists rejected the assumption that psychology should focus on mental processes; they urged us to stick with what we could see—stimuli, responses, and the consequences of responses.

G. The humanists, in part reacting against Freud's theory, were interested in developing treatments of psychological problems that relied on respect for individuals and their potentials.

H. Elements of the various strands came together in the cognitive revolution, which began by thinking of the mind by analogy to a computer program; in this view, mental processing is information processing.

I. Cognitive neuroscientists study the relation between events at all three levels of analysis, with an emphasis on how the brain gives rise to thoughts, feelings, and behavior.

J. Evolutionary psychology treats many cognitive strategies and goals as adaptations that are the results of natural selection.

K. The three major types of psychologists are distinguished by their training, work settings, and types of work.

L. Clinical and counseling psychologists administer and interpret psychological tests, provide psychotherapy, offer career and vocational counseling, and help people with specific psychological problems.

M. Academic psychologists teach and do research, in addition to helping to run their universities, colleges, or institutions.

N. Applied psychologists use the findings and theories of psychology to solve practical problems.

III. The Research Process: How We Find Things Out

A. The science of psychology relies on the scientific method, which involves specifying a problem, systematically observing events, forming a hypothesis of the relation between variables, collecting new observations to test the hypothesis, using such data to formulate and support a theory, and testing the theory.

B. Psychologists test hypotheses and look for relations among variables using a variety of tools, including naturalistic observation, case studies, surveys, corre-

lational studies, experiments, quasi-experiments, and meta-analyses.

C. Naturalistic observation involves careful observation and documentation of events.

D. Case studies are detailed investigations of a single instance of a situation.

E. In surveys, participants are asked to answer sets of specific questions.

F. In correlational studies, the relationship between the values of pairs of variables is assessed, showing how the values of one go up or down as the values of the other increase (but not showing that changes in the values of one variable *cause* changes in the other).

G. In an experiment, the effect of manipulating one or more independent variables on the value of a dependent variable is measured, and participants are assigned randomly to groups.

H. Quasi-experiments are like experiments but participants are not assigned to groups randomly and conditions are selected from naturally occurring variations.

I. In a meta-analysis, researchers combine results from different studies in order to identify a relationship among variables that transcends any one study.

J. When reading reports of studies, you should be alert for the following: (1) evidence that the data are reliable, (2) evidence that the data are valid, (3) biases, including the tendency to respond in particular ways to everything (response bias) and the nonrandom selection of participants or experimental materials (sampling bias), and (4) experimenter expectancy effects.

K. Pseudopsychology differs from psychology not necessarily in its content, but in how it is supported by data.

L. Research with humans or nonhuman animals at universities, hospitals, and most industrial settings requires approval from an Institutional Review Board (IRB).

M. For research with humans, the IRB will insist that the participants provide informed consent, which means that they must be given information in advance about the possible risks and benefits of participation.

N. The IRB will also require debriefing, which is an interview after the study to ensure that the participant had no negative reactions and did, in fact, understand the purpose of the study.

O. The IRB will also rule out any deceiving of participants, unless the deception is harmless and absolutely necessary.

P. For research with animals, the IRB requires that the animals be treated well (for example, housed in clean cages) and that pain be inflicted only if that is what is being studied and it is justified by the benefits from the research.

Q. In clinical practice, psychotherapists have clear ethical guidelines to follow, which include maintaining confidentiality unless a specific other person (or, in some states, property) is clearly in danger, or suicide is an imminent genuine concern.

R. In addition, therapists cannot use techniques that they have not been trained to use or engage in inappropriate personal behavior with patients.

S. A new branch of ethics, called neuroethics, is focusing on the possible dangers and benefits of research on the brain.

Key Terms

academic psychologist
applied psychologist
behavior
behaviorism
bias
case study
clinical psychologist
cognitive neuroscience
cognitive psychology
confound
control condition
control group
correlation coefficient
counseling psychologist
data
debriefing
dependent variable
double-blind design
effect
evolutionary psychology

experimental condition
experimental group
experimenter expectancy effects
functionalism
Gestalt psychology
humanistic psychology
hypothesis
independent variable
informed consent
introspection
level of the brain
level of the group
level of the person
mental processes
meta-analysis
operational definition
population
prediction
pseudopsychology
psychiatric nurse

psychiatrist
psychodynamic theory
psychology
psychotherapy
random assignment
reliability
replication
response bias
sample
sampling bias
scientific method
social worker
structuralism
survey
theory
unconscious
validity
variable

LOOKING ONLINE: *Enhance Your Learning*

MyPsychLab is an interactive and instructive multimedia resource that can be used to supplement a traditional lecture course or as an online course. It is an all-inclusive tool with a text-specific e-book plus multimedia tutorials, videos, simulations, animations, and controlled assessment to completely engage students and reinforce learning. MyPsychLab meets the individual learning needs of every student. Visit *www.mypsychlab.com* for more information!

Practice Test

For each of the following items, choose the single best answer.

1. Why is psychology a science?
   a. It relies on popular opinion and intuition.
   b. It examines psychological questions.
   c. It uses logic to reason about phenomena and then tests the resulting ideas by collecting additional facts.
   d. It is not a science, although, when it becomes more mathematical, it may develop into one.

2. At the level of the person, the psychologist focuses on
   a. events that involve the nature of beliefs, desires, and feelings.
   b. events that involve the structure and properties of the brain—brain cells and their connections, the chemical soup in which they exist, and the genes.
   c. events that involve relationships between people, relationships among groups, and culture.
   d. physiological variables that differentiate among people (such as weight, height, shoe size, and eye color).

3. How are conditions in the physical environment related to events at the three levels of analysis?
   a. Conditions in the physical environment are not related to events at any of the levels of analysis.
   b. Conditions in the physical environment are intimately tied to events that occur at every level of analysis.
   c. Conditions in the physical environment relate to events occurring only at the level of the brain.
   d. Conditions in the physical environment influence only occasional events at the level of the person.

4. Who is usually considered the founder of scientific psychology?
   a. Max Wertheimer
   b. Sigmund Freud
   c. Edward Titchener
   d. Wilhelm Wundt

5. An approach to understanding mental processes that focuses on the idea that the whole is more than the sum of the parts is
   a. Gestalt psychology.
   b. psychodynamic theory.
   c. functionalism.
   d. structuralism.

6. Which school of psychology assumes that people have positive values, free will, and deep inner creativity?
   a. psychodynamic theory
   b. evolutionary psychology
   c. functionalism
   d. humanistic psychology

7. What type of psychologist provides psychotherapy and is trained to administer and interpret psychological tests?
   a. an applied psychologist
   b. a physiological psychologist
   c. a clinical psychologist
   d. a cognitive psychologist

8. Properly collected data can be replicated, meaning that
   a. objective observations were collected.
   b. an aspect of a situation that is liable to change was described.
   c. a control group was included.
   d. if the same observations or measurements are collected again, they will yield the same results as found previously.

9. A tentative idea that might explain a set of observations is called
   a. data.
   b. a hypothesis.
   c. replication.
   d. an operational definition.

10. An independent variable that varies along with the ones of interest and that could be the actual basis for what you are measuring is
    a. a dependent variable.
    b. a control group.
    c. a hypothesis.
    d. a confound.

11. Suppose Dr. Knight reported a correlation of 0.02 between height and income. This correlation indicates that
    a. taller people are very likely to have greater income, relative to shorter people.
    b. greater height causes greater income.
    c. height and income are not closely related.
    d. Dr. Knight used a quasi-experimental design.

12. Suppose Dr. Blaine has been told that he needs to improve the face validity of his study. To do so, he ought to make sure that his
    a. design and procedure appear to assess the variables of interest.
    b. measures assess all aspects of the phenomenon of interest.
    c. measure or procedure is comparable to a different, valid measure or procedure.
    d. measures assess variables specified by a theory.

13. What is a double-blind design?
    a. one in which both participants and experimenters wear blindfolds
    b. one in which experimenter expectancy effects will influence the results unless deception is used to obscure the actual purposes and predictions of the study
    c. one that is based on pseudopsychology
    d. one in which the participant is unaware of the predictions of the study and the experimenter is unaware of the condition assigned to the participant

14. An interview that takes place after a study to ensure that the participant has no negative reactions as a result of participation and understands why the study was conducted is called
    a. informed consent.
    b. debriefing.
    c. behaviorism.
    d. unconscious.

15. Suppose Dr. Smith has developed a new type of therapy that she claims is particularly effective for patients who are afraid of some social situations. You have a patient struggling with such difficulties and not responding to conventional therapy. You haven't been trained in Dr. Smith's therapy, but you want to help. Should you try Dr. Smith's therapy?
    a. yes
    b. only if your patient wants to
    c. no
    d. It depends on how long Dr. Smith's therapy takes to work

● ●

Answers: 1. c 2. a 3. b 4. d 5. a 6. d 7. c 8. d 9. b 10. d 11. c 12. a 13. d 14. b 15. c

References

Anderson, M. C., Ochsner, K. N., Kuhl, B., Cooper, J., Robertson, E., Gabrieli, S. W., Glover, G. H., and Gabrieli, J. D. E. (2004). Neural systems underlying the suppression of unwanted memories. *Science, 303,* 232–235.

Anderson, N. B. (1998). Levels of analysis in health science: A framework for integrating sociobehavioral and biomedical research. In S. M. McCann, J. M. Lipton, et al. (Eds.), *Annals of the New York Academy of Sciences: Vol. 840, Neuroimmunomodulation: Molecular aspects, integrative systems, and clinical advances* (pp. 563–576). New York: New York Academy of Sciences.

Barkow, J. H., Cosmides, L., & Tooby, J. (Eds.). (1992). *The adapted mind: Evolutionary psychology and the generation of culture.* New York: Oxford University Press.

Belkin, M. & Rosner, M. (1987). Intelligence, education, and myopia in males, *Archives of Opthamology, 105,* 1508–1511.

Blakemore, S., Winston, J., & Frith, U. (2004). Social cognitive neuroscience: Where are we heading? *Trends in Cognitive Sciences, 8,* 216–222.

Boring, E. G. (1950). *A history of experimental psychology* (2nd ed.). New York: Appleton-Century-Crofts.

Buss, D. M. (1994). *The evolution of desire: Strategies of human mating.* New York: Basic Books.

Buss, D. M. (1999). *Evolutionary psychology: The new science of the mind.* Boston: Allyn & Bacon.

Carmines, E. G., & Zeller, R. A. (1979). *Reliability and validity assessment.* Beverly Hills, CA: Sage.

Cosmides, L., & Tooby, J. (1996). Are humans good intuitive statisticians after all? Rethinking some conclusions from the literature on judgment under uncertainty. *Cognition, 58,* 1–73.

Craik, F. I. M., & Tulving, E. (1975). Depth of processing and the retention of words in episodic memory. *Journal of Experimental Psychology: General, 104,* 268–294.

Davidson, R. J. (2004). What does the prefrontal cortex "do" in affect: Perspectives on frontal EEG asymmetry research. *Biological Psychology, 67,* 219–233.

Doheny, M. (1993). Effects of mental practice on performance of a psychomotor skill. *Journal of Mental Imagery, 17* (3–4), 111–118.

Driskell, J., Copper, C., & Moran, A. (1994). Does mental practice enhance performance? *Journal of Applied Psychology, 79* (4), 481–492.

Druckman, D., & Swets, J. A. (Eds.). (1988). *Enhancing human performance: Issues, theories, and techniques.* Washington, DC: National Academy Press.

Ekman, P. (1985). *Telling lies: Clues to deceit in the marketplace, marriage, and politics.* New York: Norton.

Fodor, J. A. (1968). *Psychological explanation: An introduction to the philosophy of psychology.* New York: Random House.

Fodor, J. A. (1983). *The modularity of mind.* Cambridge, MA: MIT Press.

Ganis, G., Kosslyn, S. M., Stose, S., Thompson, W. L., & Yurgelun-Todd, D. (2003). Neural correlates of different types of deception: An fMRI investigation. *Cerebral Cortex, 13,* 830–836.

Gardner, H. (1985). *The mind's new science: A history of the cognitive revolution.* New York: Basic Books.

Gazzaniga, M. S., (Ed.). (2004). *The cognitive neurosciences III.* Cambridge, MA: MIT Press.

Gould, S. J., & Lewontin, R. C. (1979). The spandrels of San Marco and the Panglossian paradigm: A critique of the adaptationist programme. *Proceedings of the Royal Society of London, Series B, 205,* 581–598.

Hauser, M. (1996). *The evolution of communication.* Cambridge, MA: MIT Press.

Henslin, J. M. (1999). *Sociology: A down-to-earth approach* (4th ed.). Needham Heights, MA: Allyn & Bacon.

Jeannerod, M. (1994). The representing brain: Neural correlates of motor intention and imagery. *Behavioral & Brain Sciences, 17,* 187–245.

Jeannerod, M. (1995). Mental imagery in the motor context. *Neuropsychologia, 33,* 1419–1432.

Kosslyn, S. M. (1994a). *Elements of graph design.* New York: Freeman.

Kosslyn, S. M. (2006). *Graph design for the eye and mind.* New York: Oxford University Press.

Kosslyn, S. M., Digirolamo, G. J., Thompson, W. L., & Alpert, N. M. (1998). Mental rotation of objects versus hands: Neural mechanisms revealed by positron emission tomography. *Psychophysiology, 35,* 151–161.

Kosslyn, S. M., & Koenig, O. (1995). *Wet mind: The new cognitive neuroscience.* New York: Free Press.

Kozhevnikov, M., Kosslyn, S. M., & Shephard, J. M. (2005). Spatial versus object visualizers: A new characterization of visual cognitive style. *Memory and Cognition, 33* (4), 710–726.

Looren de Jong, H. (1996). Levels: Reduction and elimination in cognitive neuroscience. In C. W. Tolman, F. Cherry, et al. (Eds.), *Problems of theoretical psychology* (pp. 165–172). North York, ON, Canada: Captus Press.

Markus, S. J. (2002). *Neuroethics: Mapping the field.* New York: Dana Press.

Marr, D. (1982). *Vision: A computational investigation into the human representation and processing of visual information.* New York: Freeman.

Merchant, H., Battaglia-Mayer, A., & Georgopoulos, A. P. (2003). Functional organization of parietal neuronal responses to optic-flow stimuli. *Journal of Neurophysiology, 90,* 675–682.

Miller, E. M. (1992). On the correlation of myopia and intelligence. *Genetic, Social and General Psychology Monographs 118,* 361–383.

Morgan, J. L., & Demuth, K. D. (1996). *Signal to syntax: Bootstrapping from speech to grammar in early acquisition.* Hillsdale, NJ: Erlbaum.

Nagel, E. (1979). *The structure of science: Problems in the logic of scientific explanation* (2nd ed.). Indianapolis, IN: Hackett.

Neisser, U. (1967). *Cognitive psychology.* New York: Appleton-Century-Crofts.

Parsons, L. M. (1987). Imagined spatial transformation of one's body. *Journal of Experimental Psychology: General, 116,* 172–191.

Parsons, L. M. (1994). Temporal and kinematic properties of motor behavior reflected in mentally simulated action. *Journal of Experimental Psychology: Human Perception & Performance, 20,* 709–730.

Parsons, L. M., & Fox, P. T. (1998). The neural basis of implicit movements used in recognising hand shape. *Cognitive Neuropsychology, 15,* 583–615.

Pinker, S. (1994). *The language instinct: How the mind creates language.* New York: Morrow.

Pinker, S. (1997). *How the mind works.* New York: Norton.

Putnam, H. (1973). Reductionism and the nature of psychology. *Cognition, 2,* 131–146.

Rosenthal, R. (1976). *Experimenter effects in behavioral research.* New York: Irvington.

Rosenthal, R. (1991). *Meta-analytic procedures for social research.* Beverly Hills, CA: Sage.

Saha, L. J. (Ed.). (2004). Levels of analysis in the social psychology of education [Editorial]. *Social Psychology of Education, 7,* 253–255.

Schaffner, K. F. (1967). Approaches to reduction. *Philosophy of Science, 34,* 137–147.

Schmitt, D. P. (2002). How shall I compare thee? Evolutionary psychology viewed as a psychological science. *Psychology, Evolution & Gender, 4,* 219–230.

Schwarz, N. (1999). Self-reports: How the questions shape the answers. *American Psychologist, 54,* 93–105.

Sheehan, T. P., Chambers, R. A., & Russell, D. S. (2004). Regulation of affect by the lateral septum: Implications for neuropsychiatry. *Brain Research Reviews, 46,* 71–117.

Snow, C. E. (1991). The language of the mother–child relationship. In M. Woodhead & R. Carr (Eds.), *Becoming a person* (pp. 195–210). London: Routledge.

Snow, C. E. (1999). Social perspectives on the emergence of language. In B. MacWhinney (Ed.), *The emergence of language* (pp. 257–276). Mahwah, NJ: Erlbaum.

Tractinsky, N., & Meyer, J. (1999). Chartjunk or goldgraph? Effects of presentation objectives and content desirability on information presentation. *MIS Quarterly, 23,* 397–420.

White, A., & Hardy, L. (1995). Use of different imagery perspectives on the learning and performance of different motor skills. *British Journal of Psychology, 86* (2), 169–180.

Williams, S. M., Sanderson, G. F., Share, D. L., & Silva, P. A. (1988). Refractive error, IQ and reading ability: A longitudinal study from age seven to 11. *Developmental Medicine & Child Neurology, 30,* 735–742.

Yagueez, L., Nagel, D., Hoffman, H., Canavan, A., Wist, E., & Hoemberg, V. (1998). A mental route to motor learning: Improving trajectoral kinematics through imagery training. *Behavioral and Brain Research, 90,* 95–106.

Zacks, J., & Tversky, B. (1999). Bars and lines: A study of graphic communication. *Memory & Cognition, 27,* 1073–1079.

What is Social Psychology?

WHAT IS SOCIAL PSYCHOLOGY?

WHAT IS SOCIAL PSYCHOLOGY?
WHAT ARE THE ROOTS OF SOCIAL PSYCHOLOGY?
WHAT ARE THE DIFFERENT PERSPECTIVES OF SOCIAL PSYCHOLOGY?
IS SOCIAL PSYCHOLOGY JUST COMMON SENSE?

In 1968,

Jane Elliott, a teacher from Riceville, Iowa, demonstrated the arbitrary nature of prejudice by initiating a polarizing activity with her third-grade students. Elliott's activity was prompted by the assassination of Martin Luther King, Jr. Unsure of how to explain what King stood for and why he was killed to her young students, Elliott decided to teach her students, all of whom were white, what it is like to be discriminated against. Elliott divided her students into two groups, those with blue eyes and those with brown eyes. The blue-eyed group, or Blues, was designated the superior group, and the brown-eyed group, or Browns, was designated the inferior group. As the inferior group, the Browns were told that they were less intelligent and less important than their fellow students, and Elliott constantly belittled them. Eventually, the Blues joined in on the discriminatory behavior, making judgments against and showing hatred toward those in the inferior group. The next day, Elliott reversed the experiment, making the Browns the superior group, and the brown-eyed students expressed the same prejudicial behavior (Tozer, Violas, & Senese, 1993).

How much of a role do prejudice and bigotry play in your life? Have you ever been the victim of prejudice or bigotry, or have you ever been the perpetrator of this behavior? If you are a member of a minority group, you may have sometimes felt unjustly judged by other members of society. If you are a member of a majority group, you may have acted superior to a member of a minority group. As a society, we are programmed to assume that the divide that instigates bigotry between minority and majority groups is based on race, gender, or other socially significant factors (e.g., white versus black, men versus women, or gay versus straight). Our social norms support this idea, but social psychologists argue that discrimination is based on factors that are purely arbitrary and meaningless, such as height, hair color, or even shoe size. These kinds of seemingly insignificant factors can instigate discrimination just as easily as skin color or sex. Elliott's experiment highlights just how random and powerful prejudice can be. The Blues were quick to embody their initial superiority, while the Browns readily accepted their inferiority.

While Elliott's activity was simply a demonstration rather than an experiment in discrimination (and used methods that are ethically questionable—something that social psychologists have also had to deal with), it does expose the irrational nature of discrimination. Prejudice and bigotry can take their place in the long list of concepts that are widely misunderstood. Social psychologists seek to examine and analyze these types of concepts so that we can begin to understand the motivation and reasoning behind our behavior.

What Is Social Psychology?

What possessed explorers hundreds of years ago to leave their home countries to sail across virtually unknown seas? Why were members of the U.S. space program so eager to launch themselves into uncharted areas beyond the reach of Earth? If you were a psychologist, you might say that the possibility of locating new resources and the novelty of being the first to discover something was the motivation.

If you were a sociologist, you might say that humans are curious by nature, and that their interest in the unknown drove them to seek out uncharted territories. If you were a social psychologist, however, you might say that the motivation came from the individual cultures of the explorers. Christopher Columbus set out on his expedition because the people of Spain desired to gain political and economic power in Europe by discovering new trade routes. Neil Armstrong and the rest of the Apollo 11 crew were fulfilling the United States' desire to flaunt its capabilities in science and exploration and to secure its status as a superpower in the industrial world.

No explanation is right or wrong; they simply emerge from different schools of thought. Psychology, sociology, and social psychology can be viewed as existing on a continuum, with psychology at one end, sociology at the other, and social psychology somewhere in between. Sociologists focus on the entire group, or the societal level, while social psychologists are interested in the interaction of the individual person and the given situation. The focus of social psychology can be described as having three main facets: social perception, social influence, and social interaction. Additionally, social psychologists apply their research to help understand and address issues in other fields such as law, business, and health.

Social perception is the process through which individuals form impressions of others and interpret information about them. For example, when we see a person driving a flashy sports car, we may think that the driver has a lot of money and is successful in life. **Social influence** is the process through which other people affect an individual's thoughts or actions. A person may experience social influence when deciding what profession to pursue. For example, an individual may choose to become a doctor not just because she is interested in medicine, but also because her parent is a doctor. Or the choice could be influenced by the fact that in our society, medicine is viewed as a noble profession, and the individual wishes to be respected by others. Social influence results from social interaction. **Social interaction** refers to the relationship between two or more individuals. This is the basis of analysis for social psychologists, who strive to understand and explain how the thoughts, feelings, and behaviors of individuals are influenced by the actual, imagined, or implied presence of others (Allport, 1954).

Much like social psychology complements and interacts with the disciplines of sociology, it also intersects with a number of other subdivisions of the umbrella field of psychology. For instance, both social and personality psychologists study the behaviors, thoughts, and feelings of individuals. Personality psychologists seek to

NASA Langley Research Center

∧
∧ Social factors can influence many different
∧ types of behavior, **even a journey to the moon.**

understand what distinguishes one personality from another; social psychology complements that by taking into account situational factors.

Similarly, while cognitive psychologists examine mental processes, like thinking, reasoning, remembering, and learning, social psychologists can strengthen their findings by considering how the social world impacts thought processes. And clinical psychologists, who study mental disorders, can benefit from social psychological research that may help explain how situational and social factors can contribute to and affect mental health.

What Are the Roots of Social Psychology?

Social psychology is a fairly young discipline that did not distinguish itself within the field of psychology until the 20th century. In fact, in 1979, Dorwin Cartwright stated that approximately "90 percent of all social psychologists who have ever lived are alive at the present time" (Cartwright, 1979). While the activities that define concepts such as social interaction and social influence have been

Kate Kunath/Getty Images

<<< **Social perception causes us to think that people who** wear glasses are more intelligent than those who don't.

present for as long as there have been humans on Earth, a strong plat-form on which to study these concepts did not exist until the development of Western culture. Some might even pinpoint it to the development of modern American culture. When introducing social psychology to a new generation of American graduate students in 1954, psychologist Gordon Allport stated, "While the roots of social psychology lie in the intellectual soil of the whole Western tradition, its present flowering is recognized to be characteristically an American phenomenon" (Farr, 1996).

One of the earliest formal studies in social psychology occurred at the end of the 19th century. In 1898, Norman Triplett, a professor at Indiana University, conducted a study that asked the question, "What happens

> **SOCIAL PERCEPTION** the process through which individuals form impressions of others and interpret information about them
>
> **SOCIAL INFLUENCE** the process through which other people affect an individual's thoughts or actions

when individuals join together with other individuals?" As a fan of bicycling, Triplett noticed that competitive cyclists performed better during races than during solo rides. He timed their unpaced rides, only an effort to lower previously established times, and compared them to paced rides against other contestants (Triplett, 1898).

How does the individual view herself?:

A personality psychologist may develop a questionnaire to measure individual differences in body image. A clinical psychologist may test different approaches to treatment for individuals with anorexia. And a cognitive psychologist might measure response times when identifying how positive certain words are after viewing pictures of different body types.

How do an individual's friends affect the way the individual views herself?:

A social psychologist might manipulate the feedback from other individuals about our appearance and measure the effect it has on our self-esteem.

How does a culture judge the female body?:

A sociologist might compare how different cultures perceive what makes a body type optimal.

Psychology

Social Psychology

Sociology

Westend61/SuperStock   Mike Flippo/Shutterstock   Ariel Skelley/Getty Images

∧
∧
∧ **Teen Body Image Issues on the Method of Thinking Spectrum.** Psychology, sociology, and social psychology can be viewed as existing on a continuum, **with psychology at one end, sociology at the other, and social psychology somewhere in between.** But it doesn't have to be one or another; **an interdisciplinary approach merging two or all three can be taken as well.**

SOCIAL FACILITATION the enhancement of a well-learned performance when another person is present

SOCIAL LOAFING a phenomenon that occurs when individuals make less of an effort when attempting to achieve a particular goal as a group than they would if they were attempting to achieve the goal on their own

To understand how pace keeping and competition among others affect an individual's performance, Triplett arranged a study that measured the performance of 40 children while playing a simple game. The results of the study suggested that the children performed better when playing in pairs than when playing alone. This study, considered to be the first published study in social psychology, documented the concept of **social facilitation**, or the enhancement of performance when another person is present. You may feel the effects of social facilitation in your academic life. For example, your instructor asks you to complete a task that you are well skilled at, such as reading a paragraph in a foreign language, and you perform better in class than if you were alone.

While the concept of social facilitation has been supported in studies beyond Triplett's studies, at the time, it was at odds with an earlier study that involved performance evaluation. In 1883, French professor Max Ringelmann conducted a study (although it was not published until 1913) from which he concluded that an individual's performance actually gets worse in the presence of others. Ringelmann asked a group of individuals to tug on a rope both individually and as a team. He found that the

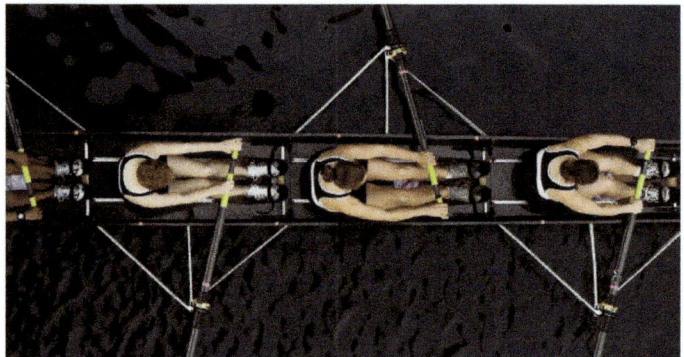

∧
∧ According to the concept of social loafing,
∧ the presence of others may cause these
rowers **to put forth less of an effort when working as a team than they would if they were working individually.**

The phenomenon of social facilitation would
∨ cause this athlete to lift more weight in
∨ front of a crowd than he would alone.

participants pulled harder when working as individuals than as a team. In fact, he found that the larger the group, the weaker the individual effort.

On the surface, Ringelmann's and Triplett's studies seem to be at odds, but when examined closely, one can see that the results actually highlight two different patterns of human behavior. In the bicycle study, the contribution of each individual member could not be identified, but in the rope study, each individual's contribution was not discernible, meaning that each individual's effort, or lack thereof, would not be noticed by the spectators.

Ringlemann's study illustrated the concept of **social loafing**, a phenomenon that occurs when individuals make less of an effort when attempting to achieve a goal as a group than they would if they were attempting to achieve the goal on their own. You may have had first-hand experience with social loafing if you have worked on a group project for class and one member of the group doesn't pull his or her weight. You might refer to this type of social loafer as a slacker. Social loafing can apply to more than just the individual. A subgroup that is part of a larger unit can participate in social loafing. This can occur in the corporate world when one department does not make an adequate contribution to the success of a company and leaves other departments to pick up the slack.

Other early social psychologists had profound impacts on the field. When people began to recognize social prejudice in the 1930s, researchers Katz and Braly gave shape to the idea of stereotypes as social psychologists study them now. After asking 100 Princeton University graduates to list five characteristics of 10 different racial and ethnic groups, Katz and Braly found that the subjects developed ideas about each group without having necessarily had any contact with members of these groups (Katz & Braly, 1933).

Another example of a landmark study is Richard LaPiere's empirical study of the discrepancies between individuals' attitudes and behaviors. LaPiere traveled around the country with a Chinese couple. Visiting over 350 restaurants and hotels, the couple was rejected entry just once. When surveyed after the trip, however, 92 percent of the businesses who answered the questions reported they would not accept Chinese individuals (LaPiere, 1934). The topic of the relationship between attitudes and behaviors became a mainstay among the topics social psychologists continue to study.

^ ^ ^ **Social Loafing vs. Social Facilitation.** Accountability is a major factor in determining **if a person will be a loafer or a facilitator, as illustrated here.** But if the task is important, loafing is diminished, and if we are good at it, we will likely perform well. **These factors can eclipse accountability.**

SOCIAL PSYCHOLOGY IN THE 20TH CENTURY

By the start of the 20th century, social psychology had begun to establish itself as an independent discipline through the development of a separate curriculum and the formation of a specialized organization. A major milestone in the development of social psychology curriculum was the publishing of textbooks. The first two textbooks on the subject of social psychology were published in 1908, one by sociologist Edward Ross and the other by psychologist William McDougall, titled *Social Psychology* and *Introduction to Social Psychology*,

>>> **Social psychologists address important social issues by working with refugees, or internally displaced persons (IDPs),** to help them deal with the stress of being forced to migrate from their homes and communities (Porter & Haslam, 2005).

respectively. Both works laid the groundwork for further study in the field. In 1924, psychologist Floyd Allport created a second version of *Social Psychology* that was heavily based on experimental research studies. Unlike McDougall's ideas, which focused on instinct as the main driver of behavior, many of the theories Allport established in his text focused on external influences (Katz, 1979). This contradiction helped bring a new depth and a new way of thinking to the field of social psychology. The *Handbook of Social Psychology*, now in its fifth edition, was first published in 1935 and is considered the quintessential reference guide for the field of social psychology.

In 1936, Gordon Allport, Floyd's younger brother, and other social psychologists formed the Society for the Psychological Study of Social Issues (SPSSI) in an effort to bring together a national group of socially minded psychologists to address social and economic issues, applying social psychological research to social issues and public policy. The organization established a mission to utilize theory and practice to focus on social problems of the group, the community, and the nation. Since its formation, the SPSSI has had a significant impact on the discipline of psychology and on society as a whole. Its publication, the *Journal of Social Issues*, has published research that has changed the way psychologists and other concerned members of society understand human behavior. The organization strives to inform public policy and encourages public education through its research and advocacy efforts. Today, SPSSI has grown into an international group of more than 3,000 psychologists, allied scientists, students, and other

Table 1: Topics in Social Psychology

Social Perception: Understanding How We View Ourselves and Others	• Why do we worry more about having safe flights than having safe car rides? • What impact does culture have on the way you see yourself? • How can you tell when someone is lying to you?
Social Influence: Understanding How We Influence One Another	• Why do your attitudes sometimes disagree with your actions? • Why are we more likely to say yes when we are already in a good mood? • How far would you go to obey someone? • How does competition affect performance?
Social Interaction: Understanding Why We Interact the Ways We Do With Others	• Is racial prejudice on the decline? • What impact does testosterone have on aggression? • Do opposites really attract? • Why does helping make you feel good?

academics who share a common interest in research on the psychological facets of important social issues (Society for the Psychological Study of Social Issues, 2010). Journals in social psychology include *Basic and Applied Social Psychology*, *Journal of Applied Social Psychology*, *Journal of Experimental Social Psychology*, *Journal of Personality*, *Journal of Personality and Social Psychology*, *Journal of Social Psychology*, *Personality and Social Psychology Bulletin*, *Social Cognition*, *Social Psychology Quarterly*, and many others in which social psychologists publish research on a vast area of topics such as those noted in Table 1.

The Impact of World War II

As social psychology moved into a more modern form during the mid-20th century, global events began to have a major influence on the development of the academic discipline. World War I had a significant impact on the social and political climate of the world, but it was World War II and the Nazis' occupation of Europe that completely changed the structure and direction of social psychology. In fact, Cartwright stated in his 1979 article for *Social Psychology Quarterly*, "If I were required to name the one person who has had the greatest impact upon the field, it would have to be Adolf Hitler" (Cartwright, 1979).

How could one person have such a significant impact on an entire academic field? The rise of fascism brought about by Hitler and the Nazi regime created a strong anti-Semitic and anti-intellectual environment in several of Europe's academic institutions. This forced several of the continent's leading social scientists, such as Kurt Lewin, Fritz Heider, and Solomon Asch, to migrate to the United States to escape persecution.

When the United States entered World War II, it took advantage of its wealth of native and immigrant social psychologists. As the United States watched countries and cultures willingly convert to a fascist form of thinking, government officials looked to social psychology to answer their questions about human behavior and the power of political propaganda. Social psychologists used their knowledge and results from government-funded research to develop several wartime programs, including the selection of officers for the Office of Strategic Services, precursor to the Central

Intelligence Agency (CIA), and the manipulation of enemy confidence and morale. The budding respect for the science behind social psychology and its useful application in solving real-world problems that occurred during World War II confirmed the beliefs of influential social psychologist Kurt Lewin, who is credited with the adage, "No research without action, and no action without research" (Ash, 1992). Lewin pioneered what is today called the *interactionist perspective*, combining internal factors (from personality psychology) and external factors (from social psychology). Lewin and his colleagues conducted research on leadership style (Lewin, Lippitt, & White, 1939). They found when groups of boys worked under three different types of leaders—autocratic, democratic, or laissez-faire—that they performed the best when they had a democratic leader .

> " *No* research without action, **and no action without research.**
> —Kurt Lewin "

Conformity had been a subject of research even before Hitler and World War II gave it a new relevance. In 1936, Turkish social psychologist Muzafer Sherif was the first researcher to take the complex idea of social

AP Images

∧ Adolf Hitler's ability to manipulate the
∧ values of thousands of Germans **generated many questions about human behavior and the power of propaganda.**

influence and apply a scientific method to it. Using the idea of *autokinetic effect*, the illusion that a stationary pinpoint of light in a dark room appears to move, Sherif asked subjects to estimate how far it moved. When accompanied by other participants in the room, the subjects altered their estimations, increasing or decreasing them to get them to most closely resemble the guesses of their counterparts (Sherif, 1936).

In the postwar era, social psychology research became an integral part of understanding how certain social changes could take place, specifically the widespread acceptance of Nazi ideology by Germans and other European citizens. Following World War II, there was an explosion of many of the theories that now make up the core of social psychology. For instance, Solomon Asch (1951) showed that people were readily willing to agree to a clearly wrong answer provided by the majority, and later, Stanley Milgram (1963) illustrated how people would compromise their personal values in the interest of obedience.

Leon Festinger further took these ideas about conformity and developed his theory of cognitive dissonance (1957), the idea that our attitudes are often at odds with our behaviors. He also developed social comparison theory (1954), a theory to explain how people perceive themselves in terms of others. Another building block of social psychology, attribution theory,

> **BASIC RESEARCH IN SOCIAL PSYCHOLOGY** the fundamental ideas behind behavior and cognitive processes
>
> **APPLIED RESEARCH IN SOCIAL PSYCHOLOGY** the use of the ideas of social psychology to address issues in other fields

developed by Fritz Heider (1958), examined how and why people explain their own behaviors and the behaviors of others. Using these basic theories of Sherif, Asch, Milgram, Festinger, and Heider, social psychologists today continue to expound upon these ideas and generate new questions and theories from them.

While social psychological research, both **basic** (the fundamental ideas behind behavior and cognitive processes) and **applied** (the use of the ideas of social psychology to address issues in other fields) flourished, so did debate. One debate centered on the use of laboratory research, which many argued was artificial and limited to applications outside the laboratory and outside the United States, where research primarily existed during this time. The second debate, over research ethics, became a hot topic during

ACTION LEARNING

Practicing What We Preach

Kurt Lewin, the father of modern social psychology, coined the term "action research" a half-century ago to describe research that is conducted with the goal of solving social problems. Lewin was interested in discovering how to get individuals to act in ways that are beneficial both to them and to society as a whole. Unlike the majority of his professional peers, Lewin was less interested in "pure research" that has no implication for practical application and more interested in research that encourages action learning, which he felt would lead to a better understanding of human behavior and a more considerate and peaceful world. He is credited with stating, "Research that produces nothing but books will not suffice" (Lewin, 1948).

Lewin found that the encouragement of actions is more effective when people make public commitments to them. For example, in one of his experiments on the power of public commitment, Lewin attempted to convince people to switch from eating white bread to eating wheat bread. When participants were asked to make a public commitment, such as raising their hands or verbally announcing that they intended to serve only wheat bread in their homes, they displayed a stronger commitment to the change.

Lewin's idea of action learning inspired a new generation of social psychologists who

aim to make the world a better place through research. Dacher Keltner, a psychologist from the University of California, Berkeley, used research to develop the GreaterGood Web site (www.greatergood.com), designed to promote the study and development of human happiness, compassion, and prosocial behavior through the delivery of scientific and educational resources. The GreaterGood Web site translates social psychology research on compassion and cooperation for a broad audience of educators, health care providers, government officials, and concerned citizens by offering resources that can help people learn how to forgive, apologize, and express gratitude, along with several other behaviors.

The GreaterGood Web site shows that experimental findings from social psychology are powerful tools for promoting a more compassionate and cooperative society because its resources, which are derived from research, can benefit the individual user as well as society as a whole. For example, a review of research on forgiveness encourages individuals to consider how the new field of remedial justice offers an alternative to the traditional legal justice system (Social Psychology Network, 2010). Lewin's concept of action learning has inspired other projects that use research to promote activities, such as reconciliation between conflicting nations and the reduction of youth violence.

Now that you know how social psychology can benefit the individual and society—take

action! Think about the issues that affect the students on your campus, for example, campus safety. Create a program that can decrease crime on your campus.

What will you learn from this action project?

1. Learn what makes students on your campus feel unsafe, and identify elements that can help deter crime on campus.
2. Understand the motivation behind the crimes that occur on campus.
3. Get firsthand knowledge of the benefits of applying the concepts of social psychology.

this time as well. Due to studies like Milgram's obedience study, in which individuals were ordered to administer what they believed were potentially lethal electric shocks to another individual, and which you will learn more about later, there are stringent ethical guidelines in place today to protect the rights of participants.

During the mid-1950s and 1960s, research turned to topics dealing with social relations and interactions like stereotyping and prejudice. The foundation of social psychology was further built upon by psychologists like Gordon Allport, who developed the Scale of Prejudice (1954); Latane and Darley, who researched altruism and prosocial behavior (1969); and Clark and Clark (1947), whose work later impacted the Supreme Court's 1954 decision to desegregate schools. Aggression and attraction also took a front seat during this period in social psychology.

During the 1970s and 1980s, a cognitive revolution impacted psychology as a whole, and this included social psychology. Festinger's theory of cognitive dissonance (1957) was central to this, and researchers Kahneman and Tversky (1973, 1974, 1982) developed the idea of different *heuristics*, or mental shortcuts, that people unintentionally take to make sense of the world around them. These ideas changed the approach researchers took to studying topics like stereotyping, personal relationships, and helping behaviors, among other ideas. Today, many researchers take a social-cognitive approach to understanding behavior.

It is important to remember that social psychology is primarily considered to be a Western-dominated discipline. In fact, 75–90 percent of social psychologists live in North America (Smith & Bond, 1993). However, during the 1990s, research by social psychologists in other cultures began to take on more prominence, and the impact of culture became a closely investigated subject (Triandis, 1994). For instance, social psychology is greatly impacted by the idea of *individualistic cultures*, or those that focus on independent individuals, like that of the United States; and the idea of *collectivist cultures*, or those that emphasize the individual in relation to his or her connectedness to those surrounding him or her.

wrangle/iStockphoto

∧∧∧ An evolutionary psychologist might say that we find a muscular build to be attractive because muscles are viewed as a sign of virility, **and humans have a natural desire to reproduce.**

What Are the Different Perspectives of Social Psychology?

All psychologists use the scientific method in their research, but since there is no one single perspective that can explain all human behavior or thinking, they may use several different theoretical approaches when testing hypotheses. Modern social psychological perspectives maintain that prior learning experiences and intrapsychic forces (e.g., the unconscious), as well as social and cultural context, shape human behavior and mental processes. The **sociocultural perspective** focuses on the relationship between social behavior and culture. This perspective is important because it highlights the fact that human behavior is not only influenced by an individual's close companions, but also by the culture in which the individual lives. For example, the children in the blue-eye/brown-eye experiment described in the chapter opener showed signs of prejudice as a result of the influence of their teacher and classmates, as well as the intolerant culture of their small town.

The **evolutionary perspective** takes a slightly different approach by focus-

>>> **Modern Social Perspectives on Why People Steal.** While each perspective takes a different approach, **they can work together to address the same issues.**

Sociocultural Perspective: People steal because our culture appreciates objects more than people.

Evolutionary Perspective: People steal because gaining certain objects, even if through stealing, improves a person's ability to survive.

Social Learning Perspective: A person steals because he learned through example that stealing is an acceptable behavior.

Social Cognitive Perspective: A person steals because he simply doesn't believe it is wrong.

Radius Images/Alamy

ing on the biological bases for universal mental characteristics that all humans share. Psychologists who follow the evolutionary perspective are interested in explaining general mental strategies and characteristics, such as how we attract members of the opposite sex, why we lie, why we like to play sports, and other similar concepts. The evolutionary perspective involves principles that are derived from evolutionary biology and Charles Darwin's principle of natural selection, and it focuses on the physical and biological predispositions that result in human survival (Boyd & Richerson, 1985). **Natural selection** is the process by which individuals with certain characteristics are more frequently represented in subsequent generations as a result of being better adapted to their environments. The evolutionary perspective would answer the question, "Why do we lie?" by claiming that lying somehow aided in our ancestors' survival, and over time, the characteristic of lying became so widely represented that it is now common in our society.

The **social cognitive perspective** and the **social learning perspective** accept and expand on conditioning principles, which assume direct correlations between learning and behavior. The social cognitive perspective builds on behavioral theories and demonstrates that an individual's cognitive process influences and is influenced by behavioral associations. The social learning perspective stresses the particular power of learning through social rewards and punishments.

A key theory to many of social psychology's core concepts, Albert Bandura's (1977) social learning theory argues that, in addition to learning through consequences in our environment, people also learn from each

> **NATURAL SELECTION** the process whereby individuals with certain characteristics are more frequently represented in subsequent generations as the result of being better adapted for their environment
>
> **SOCIAL COGNITIVE PERSPECTIVE** a perspective that builds on behavioral theories and demonstrates that an individual's cognitive process influences and is influenced by behavioral associations
>
> **SOCIAL LEARNING PERSPECTIVE** a perspective that stresses the particular power of learning through social reinforcements and punishments

other. This is called *observational learning*, when people are influenced by watching the modeled behaviors of others.

SOCIAL PSYCHOLOGY AND OTHER DISCIPLINES

Social psychologists do not work alone in their field. Economists, business leaders, and even neuroscientists help to guide and also benefit from the work of social psychologists. Because social psychologists are interested in what motivates particular behavior such as purchasing items, economists may team up with social psychologists to better understand the spending habits of certain populations. Similarly, business leaders may enlist the help of social psychologists to better understand and manage the behavior of their employees. Social loafing, for example, may be a problem that a company hopes to minimize. Social psychologists can help the

Health Care
Some people will conform to the popular opinion of what is healthy even if they feel otherwise.

Business
Some employees will conform to a company's standards even if they go against their personal standards.

Solomon Asch's Conformity Experiment

Consumer Science
Some consumers will purchase items that are popular even if they do not completely meet their needs.

Government
Some voters will agree with policies that are popular even if they go against their personal views.

LattaPictures/iStockphoto
Supri Suharjoto/Shuttertock
Jason Stitt/Shutterstock
Comstock/Thinkstock

Social Psychology and Other Fields. Social psychologists can work with individuals from other disciplines to perform research that is mutually beneficial.

> "Social psychologists do not work alone in their field. Economists, business leaders, and even neuroscientists help to guide and also benefit from the work of social psychologists."

company change how it assesses the accountability of employees. Conversely, individuals from these various disciplines can assist social psychologists by creating tools and platforms for research.

Neuroscientists have helped social psychologists literally look into the minds of humans through the development of magnetic resonance imaging (MRI) and positron emission tomography (PET) scans. These tools allow social psychologists, and neuroscientists, to observe brain activity when a study participant thinks about or engages in certain behavior, such as solving a problem or engaging in stereotyping. There is an emerging field called *social neuroscience*, which integrates the study of physiological mechanisms with social psychological perspectives (Cacioppo et al., 2007). The possibilities for social psychology to interact with other fields and industries are endless.

Is Social Psychology Just Common Sense?

As you were reading about Elliott's blue-eye/brown-eye experiment in the introduction to this chapter, you may not have been surprised that the children demonstrated prejudicial behavior. In fact, you may have even predicted the outcome. This reaction is not exclusive to Elliott's activity; it occurs in several major social psychology experiments.

For example, Asch's classic conformity experiment, mentioned earlier, also has seemingly predictable results. Asch administered a verbal vision test to a group of actual participants and several confederate participants. The **confederates**, or the individuals who are part of the research team and are placed in the experiment to play a particular role, were asked to answer select questions incorrectly, even when the correct answer was obvious, to see if the participants would conform to the majority opinion. The results of the study showed that 37 percent

>>> **In love, do "opposites attract"** or do "birds of a feather flock together"?

of the time, participants conformed to the wrong answer. Asch concluded that people conformed to what was obviously wrong because they were afraid of being ridiculed and wanted to fit in with the group (Asch, 1956). Does this conclusion seem obvious to you? Did you predict the results of this experiment before they were disclosed? You may answer yes to these questions because you already know that people want to fit in—it's common sense. But if common sense tells us all the answers to questions such as these, what need is there for social psychology?

Common sense is our natural understanding of things. We sometimes assume that social psychology is common sense because the subject matter is often personal and familiar. We believe that we are naturally knowledgeable about human behavior, but many of our common beliefs have been disproved by social psychologists. For example, the idea that "opposites attract" is believed by many, but a 2005 study published in the *Journal of Personality and Social Psychology* concluded that married couples were more likely to be similar in terms of religious beliefs, political attitudes, and values than randomly paired couples (de Vries, 2005). The study also found that married couples who showed similar personality traits in terms of anxiety and avoidance, agreeableness, and conscientiousness were more satisfied and happy in their marriages than the couples who did not show similar personality traits. The findings support the old adage that "birds of a feather flock together" rather than "opposites attract."

Psychologists cannot rely on common sense because they must base their conclusions on evidence that is acquired through careful and deliberate study. Through such studies, psychologists form theories that predict behavior before it occurs. When people use their common sense, they make "predictions" after the behavior occurs. This type of prediction occurs due to a phenomenon that psychologists call **hindsight bias**, or the tendency to think that you knew that something would occur all along. For instance, did you find yourself saying that you knew Barack Obama would win the 2008 presidential election especially if you had been planning all along to vote for him?

Although beliefs developed through common sense are often the result of good judgment, they can also generate ambiguous and conflicting explanations for behavior. Let's say you have a friend who is madly in love with her boyfriend. As she prepares to leave for a study-abroad program in Paris, she becomes worried about her ability to maintain her relationship with her boyfriend, who will be waiting for her at home. You reassure her that her relationship will overcome the distance because you believe that "absence makes the heart grow fonder." After two months abroad, however, your friend tells you that she's fallen in love with an artist named Pierre and wants to stay in France. You think, "I knew this was going to happen. After all, Paris is a romantic city, and when a person is out of sight, he is out of mind." If your friend's relationship survived the separation, then you probably would have said, "I told you so" and never doubted your original judgment.

DOESN'T EVERYONE AGREE WITH US?

Have you ever judged someone by claiming she has no common sense? As in, "Emma is book smart, but she has no common sense." As a child, your parents may have questioned your common sense after you did something foolish, such as crossing the street without looking. You didn't ignore your common sense when engaging in this behavior; at the

Image Source/Getty Images

time, you and your parents had different senses of danger. Common sense is a subjective concept, which makes it problematic to rely on common sense to explain behavior. What one person believes to be common sense might not fall in line with another person's belief. This is because common sense assumptions are usually based on personal observation and experience rather than solid evidence, and therefore bias becomes a factor.

> "Common sense is a subjective concept, which makes it problematic to rely on common sense to explain behavior."

For example, it's common knowledge that men are more authoritative than women, right? You might believe that if you grew up in a male-dominated household, but you might think quite differently if women were the authority figures in your upbringing. A person's values, principles, and tendencies can create bias in his or her perception of how broadly these beliefs are held (Ross, Greene, & House, 1977).

The False Consensus Effect

The assumption that everyone shares the same opinion as oneself occurs as the result of the **false consensus effect**. The false consensus effect increases when situations permit **differential construal**, or the act of judging circumstances differently (Gilovich, 1990). For example, you may think that everyone knows it is unprofessional to wear flip-flops in the workplace, but that is in reality a matter of opinion, not a matter of fact. Multiple parties can construe the idea of what is considered "professional" differently. False consensus can be problematic in activities such as creating public policy. If elected officials or committees assume that the majority of constituents are in favor of strong regulations on issues such as gun control, they could pass legislation that does not actually represent the desires of the public.

HOW DO YOU MINIMIZE BIAS?

Hindsight bias and the false consensus effect are two ways in which false conclusions can be derived through biased actions or thoughts. But sometimes, the conclusion itself can create biased actions or thoughts. Let's say you just moved to a new town and are looking to make new friends. You read a recent article in a major newspaper that cited a study that concluded that people who wear colorful clothing tend to be friendlier than people who wear neutral tones. As you mingle with people at a local event, you realize that the study was right—the people you met who were wearing colorful clothing were significantly friendlier than those in muted clothing. What you might not have realized is that by reading only the conclusion of the study, you created a bias that may have subconsciously caused you to demonstrate behavior that helped to confirm your thoughts. For example, you may have been more relaxed around the people who were wearing

>>> **If you are against the death penalty, then you may believe most people are as well.** But if you support it, you may overestimate how many people also support it.

CONFEDERATE an individual who is part of the research team and is placed in the experiment to play a particular role

HINDSIGHT BIAS the tendency to think that one knew that something would occur all along

FALSE CONSENSUS EFFECT a phenomenon that causes individuals to assume that everyone shares the same opinion they do

DIFFERENTIAL CONSTRUAL the act of judging circumstances differently

CONFIRMATION BIAS the tendency to notice information that confirms one's beliefs and to ignore information that disconfirms one's beliefs

SCIENTIFIC METHOD an approach to thinking that involves using systematic observations, measurements, and experiments to assess information

colorful clothing because you assumed that they were sociable, thereby making it easier to have a friendly conversation. This tendency to notice information that confirms one's beliefs and to ignore information that disconfirms one's beliefs is called **confirmation bias**.

How do social psychologists eliminate these biases when conducting their research? The answer to that question is complex because there is no way to completely remove bias from processes that humans administer. But social psychologists strive to minimize bias through the use of the scientific method. The **scientific method** is an approach to thinking that uses systematic observations, measurements, and experiments to assess information. It is used by other members of the scientific community such as chemists, physicists, biologists, and other psychologists to minimize bias and reduce errors. As you move forward in this course, you will need to apply the scientific method to your everyday thinking.

Social psychology is not just of interest to neuroscientists, other scientists, and people in the medical field. Understanding human behavior, and particularly how it relates to social and cultural aspects, can be beneficial to almost any field. So it is safe to say that the young field of social psychology will continue to grow and mature as it becomes increasingly useful and relevant to our modern world. As we continue our journey into learning about social psychology, we will explore many of these ideas in detail.

Tony Garcia/Getty Images

335

Review

Summary

WHAT IS SOCIAL PSYCHOLOGY?

• While psychology is the study of an individual's behavior, and sociology is the study of cultural behaviors, social psychology combines the two. Social psychology approaches discussing individual behaviors within the context of the individual's environment and culture, as well as many other factors. Concepts that are integral to the study of social psychology include social perception, social influence, and social interaction.

WHAT ARE THE ROOTS OF SOCIAL PSYCHOLOGY?

• Social psychology is a relatively new discipline within the larger field of general psychology. Two of the earliest formal studies in social psychology were Norman Triplett's social facilitation experiment and Max Ringelmann's social loafing study.

• Soon after, social psychology textbooks began to be published, and the Society for the Psychological Study of Social Issues (SPSSI) was established. Social psychology studies became particularly prominent in the wake of World War II, when people questioned how someone like Adolf Hitler was able to exert his influence over so many.

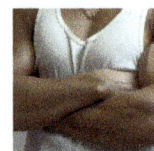

WHAT ARE THE DIFFERENT PERSPECTIVES OF SOCIAL PSYCHOLOGY?

• The four main perspectives that social psychologists may take are the sociocultural perspective, the evolutionary perspective, the social learning perspective, and the social cognitive perspective.

• The sociocultural perspective focuses on the relationship between social behavior and culture. The evolutionary perspective emphasizes the biological bases for universal mental characteristics that all humans share. The social cognitive perspective builds on behavioral theories and demonstrates how an individual's cognitive process influences and is influenced by behavioral associations. And the social learning perspective stresses that social rewards and punishments are responsible for the way people act.

IS SOCIAL PSYCHOLOGY JUST COMMON SENSE?

• Common sense is our natural understanding of things. We sometimes assume that social psychology is common sense because the subject matter is often personal and familiar. We believe that we are naturally knowledgeable about human behavior, but many of our common beliefs have been disproved by social psychologists.

• Social psychologists cannot rely on common sense because they must base their conclusions on evidence that is achieved through careful and deliberate study. In these studies, social psychologists form theories that predict behavior before it occurs. Avoiding relying on common sense helps researchers avoid bias.

Key Terms

applied research in social psychology the use of the ideas of social psychology to address issues in other fields

basic research in social psychology the fundamental ideas behind behavior and cognitive processes

confederate an individual who is part of the research team and is placed in the experiment to play a particular role

confirmation bias the tendency to notice information that confirms one's beliefs and to ignore information that disconfirms one's beliefs

differential construal the act of judging circumstances differently

evolutionary perspective a perspective that focuses on the physical and biological predispositions that result in human survival

false consensus effect a phenomenon that causes individuals to assume that everyone shares the same opinion they do

hindsight bias the tendency to think that one knew that something would occur all along

natural selection the process whereby individuals with certain characteristics are more frequently represented in subsequent generations as the result of being better adapted for their environment

scientific method an approach to thinking that involves using systematic observations, measurements, and experiments to assess information

social cognitive perspective a perspective that builds on behavioral theories and demonstrates that an individual's cognitive process influences and is influenced by behavioral associations

social facilitation the enhancement of a well-learned performance when another person is present

social influence the process through which other people affect an individual's thoughts or actions

social learning perspective a perspective that stresses the particular power of learning through social reinforcements and punishments

social loafing a phenomenon that occurs when individuals make less of an effort when attempting to achieve a particular goal as a group than they would if they were attempting to achieve the goal on their own

social perception the process through which individuals form impressions of others and interpret information about them

sociocultural perspective a perspective that focuses on the relationship between social behavior and culture

Test Your Understanding

MULTIPLE CHOICE

1. Which individuals are interested in the interaction of the person and situation?

   a. behavioral psychologists
   b. sociologists
   c. social psychologists
   d. social workers

2. Which is an example of social influence?

   a. seeing a person in a military uniform and assuming he is trustworthy
   b. eating only seafood that is sustainable to help the environment
   c. taking a fashion design class in an attempt to meet girls
   d. buying the same cell phone as your friend

3. What historic event was a precursor to the development of social psychology?

   a. the damage done by the Nazis during World War II
   b. the Industrial Revolution
   c. the Harlem Renaissance
   d. the start of the Golden Age in Europe

4. Which is an example of social loafing?

   a. finishing a race with a personal best time
   b. doing extra credit to raise your grade in class
   c. forgetting to turn in a research paper
   d. putting forth a minimal effort on a group project, in which every student will receive the same grade

5. What was a major milestone in the development of social psychology?

   a. the formation of organizations
   b. the development of field-specific textbooks
   c. the migration of psychologists to Europe
   d. the invention of the radio

6. Who do some think is the individual who had the greatest influence on social psychology?

   a. Theodore Roosevelt
   b. Martin Luther King, Jr.
   c. Adolf Hitler
   d. Sigmund Freud

7. Which social psychologist developed the theory of cognitive dissonance?

   a. Milgram
   b. Festinger
   c. Asch
   d. LaPiere

8. Which of the following is NOT a reason why common sense is unreliable?

   a. It is a subjective concept.
   b. It can be obstructed by hindsight bias.
   c. It is used to make predictions before events occur.
   d. It is not based on scientific research.

9. Which social psychology perspective focuses on the relationship between social behavior and culture?

   a. evolutionary perspective
   b. sociocultural perspective
   c. cognitive learning perspective
   d. social learning perspective

10. How might a member of congress use social psychology to improve his or her political campaign?

    a. impressing constituents with a large vocabulary
    b. using common sense to figure out what the people want
    c. making voting machines easier to use
    d. using research to find out what makes a candidate likable

ESSAY RESPONSE

1. Explain how a psychologist, a sociologist, and a social psychologist might approach an explanation of the mass shooting that occurred at Virginia Tech in 2007.

2. Have you ever been guilty of social loafing? Explain how you rationalized your lack of effort.

3. Explain why social psychology can apply to areas not involving science or psychology. Use an example from your own life where social psychology may apply.

4. Think about Jane Elliott's blue-eye/brown-eye experiment. What role might confirmation bias have had in this activity?

5. Examine the problem of student debt from a sociocultural perspective. How does the relationship between social behavior and culture affect students' finances?

APPLY IT!

Based on what you have learned about social psychology as a discipline, think about why it would be important to educate your campus or community about social psychological research. Prepare a two-page argument in which you try to convince students of the importance of taking a social psychology class and what they could learn from it that would impact their daily lives.

Remember to check www.thinkspot.com for additional information, downloadable flashcards, and other helpful resources.

Political Science

Politics and Political Science

From Chapter 1 of *Political Science: An Introduction*, 12/e. Michael G. Roskin. Robert L. Cord. James A. Medeiros. Walter S. Jones. Copyright © 2012 by Pearson Longman. All rights reserved.

Politics and Political Science

President Barack Obama speaks to a New Hampshire town hall meeting in 2010. (Rick Friedman/Corbis)

A major healthcare reform, bailouts of big corporations, and massive federal deficits have revived interest in politics in the United States. Students and attentive citizens who a few years ago turned away from politics are paying attention again. U.S. electoral turnout, with aroused voters, is up several percentage points from a low of 50 percent in presidential elections. For political scientists, the uptick in interest is welcome, but many still worry that Americans (and many other nationalities) are becoming depoliticized. Why did interest in politics decline for many years? Is it disgust at politicians and their constant, empty struggle for partisan advantage? Is it a feeling of helplessness, a sense that individual citizens do not matter? Is it the perception that the nation's capital is the playground of rich and powerful interest groups who simply buy whatever they want, including politicians? Or is it a healthy sign that, in relatively good times, people naturally turn to other concerns? If the economy is not bad and world problems seem distant, why follow politics? A bad economy and a long war renew interest in politics.

It is the thesis of this text that politics matters. If you do not take an interest and participate, others will, and they will influence the decisions that govern your life. Will they take us to war in a foreign land? Who might have to fight in that war? You. Will they alter the tax code to favor certain citizens and corporations? Who will have to pay in taxes what others avoid paying? You. Will they set up government programs whose costs escalate far beyond what anyone had foreseen? Who then will have to pay these costs? You. One of the tasks of this text is to make you aware of what politics is and how it works so that you can look after yourself and prevent others from using you. The ignorant are manipulated.

QUESTIONS TO CONSIDER

1. Why did politics fall out of favor? Is it now back?
2. What does it mean to "never get angry at a fact"?
3. Why did Aristotle call politics "the master science"?
4. What did Machiavelli bring to the study of politics?
5. How are legitimacy, sovereignty, and authority different but similar?
6. Is the Iraqi government now legitimate? How can you tell?
7. Is politics largely biological, psychological, cultural, rational, or irrational?
8. How can something as messy as politics be a science?

discipline A field of study, often represented by an academic department or major.

Many find politics distasteful, and perhaps they are right. Politics may be inherently immoral or, at any rate, amoral. Misuse of power, influence peddling, and outright corruption are prominent features of politics. But you need not like the thing you study. Biologists may behold a disease-causing bacterium under a microscope. They do not "like" the bacterium but are interested in how it grows, how it does its damage, and how it may be eradicated. Neither do they get angry at the bacterium and smash the glass slide with a hammer. Biologists first understand the forces of nature and then work with them to improve humankind's existence. Political scientists try to do the same with politics.

THE MASTER SCIENCE

Aristotle, the founder of the **discipline**, called politics "the master science." He meant that almost everything happens in a political context, that the decisions of the *polis* (the Greek city-state) governed most other things. Politics, in the words of Yale's Harold Lasswell (1902–1978), is the study of "who gets what." But, some object, the economic system determines who gets what in countries with free markets. True, but should we have a totally free-market system with no government involved? A decision to bail out shaky banks sparks angry controversy over this

Oil from the BP spill in the Gulf of Mexico in 2010 raised political questions about deep-sea drilling. Should U.S. need for oil override environmental concerns? (Julie Dermansky/Corbis)

point. Few love the bankers, but economists say it had to be done to save the economy from collapse. Politics is intimately connected to economics.

Suppose something utterly natural strikes, like a hurricane. It is the political system that decides whether and where to build dikes and whether and which of the victims to aid. The disaster is natural, but its impact on society is controlled in large part by politics. How about science, our bacteriologists squinting through microscopes? That is not political. But who funds the scientists' education and their research institutes? It could be private charity (the donors of which get tax breaks), but the government plays a major role. When the U.S. government decided that AIDS research deserved top priority, funding for other programs was cut. Bacteria and viruses may be natural, but studying them is often quite political. In this case, it pitted gays against women concerned with breast cancer. Who gets what: Funding to find a cure for AIDS or for breast cancer? The choice is political.

Because almost everything is political, studying politics means studying nearly everything. Some students select "interdisciplinary majors." Political science already is one, borrowing from and overlapping with all of the other social sciences. At times, it is hard to tell where history, human geography, economics, sociology, anthropology, and psychology leave off and political science begins. Here, briefly, is how political science relates to the other social sciences.

History

History is one of the chief sources of data for political scientists. When we discuss the politics of the Third French Republic (1871–1940), the growth of presidential power under Franklin Roosevelt (1933–1945), and even something as recent as the Cold War (1946–1989), we are studying history. But historians and political scientists

---

KEY CONCEPTS ■ "NEVER GET ANGRY AT A FACT"

This basic point of all serious study sounds commonsensical but is often ignored, even in college courses. It traces back to the extremely complex thought of the German philosopher Hegel, who argued that things happen not by caprice or accident but for good and sufficient reasons: "Whatever is real is rational." That means that nothing is completely accidental and that if we apply reason, we will understand why something happens. We study politics in a "naturalistic" mode, not getting angry at what we see but trying to understand how it came to be.

For example, we hear of a politician who took money from a businessperson. As political scientists, we push our anger to the side and ask questions like: Do most politicians in that country take money? Is it an old tradition, and does the culture of this country accept it? Do the people even expect politicians to take money? How big are campaign expenses? Can the politician possibly run for office without taking money? In short, we see if extralegal exchanges of cash are part of the political system. If they are, it makes no sense to get angry at an individual politician. If we dislike it, we may then consider how the system might be reformed to discourage the taking of money on the side. And reforms may not work. Japan reformed its electoral laws in an attempt to stamp out its traditional "money politics," but little changed. Like bacteria, some things in politics have lives of their own.

look for different things and handle data differently. Typically, historians study one episode in detail, digging up documents, archives, and memoirs on the topic. They have masses of data focused on one point but are reluctant to generalize. Political scientists, on the other hand, begin by looking for generalizations. They might take the findings of historians and compare and contrast them. A historian might do a detailed study of Weimar Germany (1919–1933); a political scientist might put that study alongside studies of France, Italy, and Russia of the same period to see what similarities and dissimilarities can be found. To be sure, some historians do comparative studies; they become de facto political scientists.

Human Geography

Human geography (as distinct from physical geography) has in recent decades been neglected by political scientists, although it influences politics more than many realize. The territorial components of human behavior—borders, regions, ethnic areas, trade flows, and centralization of power—have great political ramifications. Strife in Afghanistan, Iraq, India, and Turkey are heavily geographical problems, as is Canada's unsettled federalism, from which some Quebeckers wish to depart. French political scientist André Siegfried (1875–1959) pioneered the use of maps to explain regional political variations, a technique of today's electoral studies. The "red" and "blue" states in U.S. presidential elections show the relevance of political geography.

Economics

Economics, proclaim some economists, is the subject matter of politics. (Political scientists are apt to claim the opposite.) True, many political quarrels are economic: As Lasswell asked, "Who gets what?" Sufficient economic development may be the basis for democracy; few poor countries are democratic. A declining economy may doom democracy, as was the fate of Germany's Weimar Republic and recently of Russia. What policies promote economic development? How big a role should government have? Is the euro currency making Europe more united or ready to fall apart? When economists get into questions of policy, they become "political economists." A relatively new school of political science, "rational-choice theory," shares the economic perspective that humans pursue their self-interests.

Sociology

Sociology and political science overlap. Sociologist Seymour Martin Lipset (1922–2006) was equally renowned as a political scientist. He was among the first to demonstrate the close connection between democracy and level of wealth. Political science conventionally starts by looking at society to see "who thinks what" about politics. In demonstrating how political views vary among social classes, regions, religions, genders, and age groups, sociology gives an empirical basis to political-culture, public-opinion, and electoral studies.

Anthropology

Anthropology, which traditionally focused on preliterate societies, may seem of little relevance to political science. But the descriptive and interviewing techniques of anthropology have been heavily adopted by political scientists. The subfield of political culture can be viewed as a branch of anthropology. Japanese deference patterns, which we still see today, were laid down more than a millennium ago. Some current political systems are still run by traditionally influential families or clans. In Central Asia, the families of emirs who ruled under the Persians did so under the Russian tsars, the Communists, and now the newly independent states. In Africa, voting and violence follow tribal lines.

methodology The techniques for studying questions objectively.

political power Ability of one person to get another to do something.

Psychology

Psychology, particularly social psychology, contributes much to political science's understanding of which personalities are attracted to politics, why and under what circumstances people obey authority figures, and how people form national, group, and voting attachments. Studies of Hitler, Stalin, and Mao Zedong are often based on psychological theories. Psychologists are especially good with **methodology**; they devise ways to study things objectively and teach us to doubt claims that have holes in them. Asking questions in a "blind" manner and "controlling" for certain factors are techniques developed from psychology.

POLITICAL POWER

Political science often uses the findings of other social sciences, but one feature distinguishes it from the others—its focus on power: A gets B to do what A wants. Our second founding father (after Aristotle) is the Renaissance Florentine philosopher Niccolò Machiavelli, who emphasized the role of power in politics. You can take all the factors and approaches mentioned previously, but if you are not using them to study power—a very broad subject—you are probably not doing political science.

Some people dislike the concept of **political power**. It smacks of coercion, inequality, and occasionally of brutality. Some speakers denounce "power politics," suggesting governance without power, a happy band of brothers and sisters regulating themselves through love and sharing. Communities formed on such a basis do not last, or if they do last it is only by transforming themselves into conventional structures of leaders and followers, buttressed by obedience patterns that look suspiciously like power. Political power seems to be built into the human condition. But why do some people hold political power over others? There is no definitive explanation of political power. Biological, psychological, cultural, rational, and irrational explanations have been put forward.

legitimacy   Mass feeling that the government's rule is rightful and should be obeyed.

sovereignty   A national government's being boss on its own turf, the last word in law in that country.

Biological

Aristotle said it first and perhaps best: "Man is by nature a political animal." (Aristotle's words were *zoon politikon*, which can be translated as either "political animal" or "social animal." The Greeks lived in city-states in which the polis was the same as society.)

KEY CONCEPTS ■ LEGITIMACY, SOVEREIGNTY, AND AUTHORITY

These three related concepts—**legitimacy**, **sovereignty**, and **authority**—are basic to political science. Legitimacy originally meant that the rightful king or queen was on the throne by reason of "legitimate" birth. Since the Middle Ages, the term has broadened to mean not only the "legal right to govern" but also the "psychological right to govern." Legitimacy now refers to an attitude in people's minds—in some countries strong, in others weak—that the government's rule is rightful. Legitimacy in the United States is fairly high. Even Americans who do not particularly like the government generally obey it. We even pay taxes. One quick test of legitimacy: How many police are there? Few police, as in Sweden and Norway, indicates that little coercion is needed; legitimacy is high. Many police, as in North Korea or Iraq, indicates that much coercion is needed; legitimacy is low.

Where legitimacy is weak, few people feel obliged to pay their taxes and obey the law because the government itself is perceived as dirty and dishonest. Eventually, massive civil disobedience can break out, as it did in Serbia in 2000. Citizens rallied against the criminal misrule of President Slobodan Milošević; police batons and electoral rigging could not prevent him from being voted out of office. The Iraqi Governing Council of 2003–2004 was composed of highly educated Iraqis representative of all Iraqi groups, but it had little legitimacy because it had been installed by the U.S. occupiers. Arguably, the Council was the best government Iraq will ever have, but few valued it. Without legitimacy, governments are ineffective.

A government achieves legitimacy several ways. At the most elemental level, it must provide security, so that people feel reasonably safe. Many Iraqis complained that, bad as Saddam was, under him they could walk down the street. As Hobbes saw, no security means no legitimacy. Related to security is "rule of law." Regimes that provide it gain legitimacy. Just existing a long time fosters legitimacy. Citizens generally respect long-established governments. The fact that the U.S. Constitution is more than two centuries old confers great legitimacy on the U.S. government. New governments, on the other hand, have shaky legitimacy; their citizens have little or no respect for them.

A government gains legitimacy by governing well. Ensuring economic growth and jobs so that people can feed their families builds legitimacy. The government of West Germany, founded in 1949 after defeat in World War II, had little legitimacy at first, but level-headed political leadership with sound economic policies gradually earned the Bonn government legitimacy. On the other hand, the German Weimar Republic that followed World War I faced a series of economic and political catastrophes that undermined its legitimacy and let Hitler take power.

The structure of government contributes to its legitimacy. If people feel they are fairly represented and have a say in the selection of their officials, they are more likely to obey. Finally, governments shore up their legitimacy by national symbols. The flag, historic monuments, patriotic parades, and ringing speeches aim at convincing people that the government

Aristotle meant that humans live naturally in herds, like elephants or deer. Biologically, they need each other for sustenance and survival. It is also natural that they array themselves into ranks of leaders and followers, like all herd animals. Taking a cue from Aristotle, a modern biological explanation would say that forming a political system and obeying its leaders is innate human behavior, passed on to future generations with

authority   Political leaders' ability to command respect and exercise power.

is legitimate and should be obeyed. Although they ended centuries of monarchy in 1975, in 2002 the Laotian Communist regime kneeled before a new bronze statue of the king who founded Laos's monarchy 650 years earlier. The Communists were trying to prop up their fraying legitimacy by tying themselves to the old kings, a symbol of legitimacy most Laotians could understand. When legitimacy has collapsed, however, the manipulation of national symbols may appear to be a hollow joke. A gigantic statue of dictator Marcos of the Philippines became an object of ridicule and a symbol of what was wrong with his regime. Symbols by themselves do not create legitimacy.

Sovereignty (from the Old French "to rule over") originally meant the power of a monarch over his or her kingdom. Later, the term broadened to mean national control over the country's territory, boss of one's own turf. Nations safeguard their sovereignty. They maintain armies to deter foreign invasion; they control their borders with passports and visas; and they hunt down terrorists. Disputes over sovereignty are among the nastiest: Palestine, Chechnya, and Iraq are examples.

Sovereignty is sometimes a legal fiction. Iraq regained nominal sovereignty in 2004 but was still under U.S. influence. Sovereignty and legitimacy are connected. Lebanese Muslims, for example, saw the Christian-dominated government as illegitimate. In 1975, civil strife broke out among a dozen politico-religious militias. Syria occupied eastern Lebanon from 1976 to 2005, and Israel occupied southern Lebanon from 1982 to 2000. Lebanon in effect lost its

sovereignty, which it is now slowly regaining. For decades, it could neither control its own territory nor repel foreign invaders. A loss of legitimacy led to a loss of sovereignty.

Authority is the psychological ability of leaders to get others to obey them. It relies on a sense of obligation based on the legitimate power of office. A private obeys a captain; a motorist obeys a state trooper; a student obeys a professor. But not all people obey authority. Some privates are insubordinate, some motorists are speeders, and some students neglect the assigned reading. Still, most people obey what they perceive as legitimate authority most of the time.

Some authority comes with the office, but it must also be cultivated. An American president gets much authority just because he is president. Gerald Ford was respected and obeyed even though he was not elected president or vice president. As minority leader of the House of Representatives, Ford became vice president when Spiro T. Agnew resigned and president when Richard Nixon resigned. Nixon, implicated in the Watergate scandal of 1972, suffered an erosion of executive authority so acute that he could not govern effectively. A president cannot rule by decree but must obtain the willing consent of Congress, the courts, the civil service, and important interest groups. When Nixon lost this consent, his power as president declined.

In short, legitimacy means respect for a government; sovereignty, respect for a country; and authority, respect for a leader. None are automatic; all must be earned. Where you find one, you find the others. Where one erodes, so usually do the others.

one's genes. Some thinkers argue that human politics shows the same "dominance hierarchies" that other mammals set up. Politicians tend to be "alpha males"—or think they are.

The advantage of the biological approach is its simplicity, but it raises a number of questions. If we grant that humans are naturally political, how do we explain the instances when political groups fall apart and people disobey authority? Perhaps we should modify the theory: Humans are imperfectly political (or social) animals. Most of the time people form groups and obey authority, but sometimes, under certain circumstances, they do not. This begs the question of which circumstances promote or undermine the formation of political groups.

Psychological

Psychological explanations of politics and obedience are closely allied with biological theories. Both posit needs derived from centuries of evolution in the formation of political groups. The psychologists have refined their views with empirical research. One is the famous Milgram study, in which unwitting subjects were instructed by a professor to administer progressively larger electric shocks to a victim. The "victim," strapped in a chair, was actually an actor who only pretended to suffer. Most of the subjects were willing to administer potentially lethal doses of electricity simply because the "professor"—an authority figure in a white lab smock—told them to. Most of the subjects disliked hurting the victim, but they rationalized that they were just following orders and that any harm done to the victim was really the professor's responsibility. They surrendered their actions to an authority figure.

Psychological studies also show that most people are naturally conformist. Most members of a group see things the group's way. Psychologist Irving Janis found many foreign policy mistakes were made in a climate of "groupthink," in which a leadership team tells itself that all is well and that the present policy is working. Groups ignore doubters who tell them, for instance, that the Japanese will attack Pearl Harbor in 1941 or that the 1961 Bay of Pigs landing of Cuban exiles will fail. Obedience to authority and groupthink suggest that humans have deep-seated needs—possibly innate—to fit into groups and their norms. Perhaps this is what makes human society possible, but it also makes possible horrors such as the Nazi Holocaust and more recent massacres.

Cultural

How much of human behavior is learned as opposed to biologically inherited? This is the very old "nurture versus nature" debate. For much of the twentieth century, the cultural theorists—those who believe behavior is learned—dominated. Anthropologists concluded that all differences in behavior were cultural. Cooperative and peaceful societies raise their children that way, they argued. Political communities are formed and held together on the basis of cultural values transmitted by parents, schools, churches, and the mass media. Political science developed an interesting subfield, *political culture*, whose researchers found that a country's political culture was formed by many long-term factors: religion, child rearing, land tenure, and economic development.

Cultural theorists see trouble when the political system gets out of touch with the cultural system, as when the shah of Iran attempted to modernize an Islamic society that did not like Western values and lifestyles. The Iranians threw the shah out in 1979 and celebrated the return of a medieval-style religious leader who voiced the values favored by traditional Iranians. Cultural theories can also be applied to U.S. politics. Republicans often win elections by articulating the values of religion, family, and self-reliance, which are deeply ingrained into American culture. Many thinkers believe economic and political development depend heavily on **culture.**

> **culture** Human behavior that is learned as opposed to inherited.
>
> **rational** Based on the ability to reason.

The cultural approach to political life holds some optimism. If all human behavior is learned, bad behavior can be unlearned and society improved. Educating young people to be tolerant, cooperative, and just will gradually change a society's culture for the better, according to this view. Changing culture, however, is slow and difficult, as the American occupiers of Iraq discovered.

Culture contributes a lot to political behavior, but the theory has some difficulties. First, where does culture come from? History? Economics? Religion? Second, if all behavior is cultural, various political systems should be as different from each other as their cultures. But, especially in the realm of politics, we see similar political attitudes and patterns in lands with very different cultures. Politicians everywhere tend to become corrupt, regardless of culture.

Rational

Another school of thought approaches politics as a **rational** thing; that is, people know what they want most of the time, and they have good reasons for doing what they do. Classic political theorists, such as Hobbes and Locke, held that humans form "civil society" because their powers of reason tell them that it is much better than anarchy. To safeguard life and property, people form governments. If those governments become abusive, the people have the right to dissolve them and start anew. This Lockean notion greatly influenced the U.S. Founding Fathers.

The biological, psychological, and cultural schools downplay human reason, claiming that people are either born or conditioned to certain behavior, and individuals seldom think rationally. But how can we then explain cases in which people break away from group conformity and argue independently? How can we explain a change of mind? "I was for Jones until he came out with his terrible economic policy, so now I'm voting for Smith." People make rational judgments like that all the time. A political system based on the presumption of human reason stands a better chance of governing justly and humanely. If leaders believe that people obey out of biological inheritance or cultural conditioning, they will think they can get away with all manner of corruption and misrule. If, on the other hand, rulers fear that people are rational, they will respect the public's ability to discern wrongdoing. Accordingly, even if people are not completely rational, it is probably for the best if rulers think they are.

Irrational

Late in the nineteenth century, a group of thinkers expounded the view that people are basically **irrational**, especially when it comes to political power. They are

emotional, dominated by myths and stereotypes, and politics is really the manipulation of symbols. A crowd is like a wild beast that can be whipped up by charismatic leaders to do their bidding. What people regard as rational is really myth; just keep feeding the people myths to control them. The first practitioner of this school was Mussolini, founder of fascism in Italy, followed by Hitler in Germany. A soft-spoken Muslim fundamentalist, Osama bin Laden, got an irrational hold on thousands of fanatical followers. Believing the myth that America was the enemy of Islam, some willingly ended their lives in terrorist acts.

There may be a good deal of truth to the irrational view of human political behavior, but it has catastrophic consequences. Leaders who use irrationalist techniques start believing their own propaganda and lead their nations to war, economic ruin, or tyranny. Some detect irrationalism even in the most advanced societies, where much of politics consists of screaming crowds and leaders striking heroic poses.

Power As a Composite

There are elements of truth in all these explanations of political power. At different times in different situations, any one of them can explain power. Tom Paine's pamphlet *Common Sense* rationally explained why America should separate from Britain. The drafters of both the U.S. Declaration of Independence and the Constitution were imbued with the rationalism of their age. Following the philosophers then popular, they framed their arguments as if human political activity were as logical as Newtonian physics. Historian Henry Steele Commager referred to the Constitution as "the crown jewel of the enlightenment," the culmination of an age of reason.

But how truly rational were they? By the late eighteenth century, the 13 American colonies had grown culturally separate from Britain. People thought of themselves as Americans rather than as English colonists. They increasingly read American newspapers and communicated among themselves rather than with Britain. Perhaps the separation was more cultural than rational.

Nor can we forget the psychological and irrational factors. Samuel Adams was a gifted firebrand, Thomas Jefferson a powerful writer, and George Washington a charismatic general. The American break with Britain and the founding of a new order was a complex mixture of all these factors. The same complex mixture of factors goes into any political system you can mention. To be sure, at times one factor seems more important than others, but we cannot exactly determine the weight to give any one factor. And notice how the various factors blend into one another. The biological factors lead to the psychological, which in turn lead to the cultural, the rational, and the irrational, forming a seamless web.

One common mistake made about political power is viewing it as a finite, measurable quantity. Power is a connection among people, the ability of one person to get others to do his or her bidding. Political power does not come in jars or megawatts. Revolutionaries in some lands speak of "seizing power," as if power was kept in the national treasury and they could sneak in and grab it at night. The Afghan Taliban "seized power" in 1995–1996, but they were a minority of the Afghan population. Many Afghans hated and fought them. Revolutionaries think that they automatically get legitimacy and authority when they "seize power"— they do not. Power is earned, not seized.

Is power identical to politics? Some power-mad people (including more than a few politicians) see the two as the same, but this is an oversimplification. We might see politics as a combination of goals or policies plus the power necessary to achieve them. Power, in this view, is a prime *ingredient* of politics. It would be difficult to imagine a political system without political power. Even a religious figure who ruled on the basis of love would be exercising power over followers. It might be "nice power," but it would still be power. Power, then, is a sort of *enabling device* to carry out or implement policies and decisions. You can have praiseworthy goals, but unless you have the power to implement them, they remain wishful thoughts.

Others see the essence of politics as a *struggle for power*, a sort of gigantic game in which power is the goal. What, for example, are elections all about? The getting of power. There is a danger here, however. If power becomes the goal of politics, devoid of other purposes, it becomes cynical, brutal, and self-destructive. The Hitler regime destroyed itself in the worship of power. Obsessed with retaining presidential power, President Nixon ruined his own administration. As nineteenth-century British historian and philosopher Lord Acton put it, "Power tends to corrupt; absolute power corrupts absolutely."

KEY CONCEPTS ■ THE SUBFIELDS OF POLITICAL SCIENCE

Most political science departments divide the discipline into several subfields. The bigger the department, the more subfields it will likely have. We will get at least a brief introduction to all of them in this text.

U.S. Politics focuses on institutions and processes, mostly at the federal level but some at state and local levels. It includes parties, elections, public opinion, and executive and legislative behavior.

Comparative Politics examines politics within other nations, trying to establish generalizations and theories of democracy, stability, and policy. It may be focused on various regions, as in "Latin American politics" or "East Asian politics."

International Relations studies politics among nations, including conflict, diplomacy, international law and organizations, and international political economy. The study of U.S. foreign policy has one foot in U.S. politics and one in international relations.

Political Theory, both classic and modern, attempts to define the good polity, often focused on major thinkers.

Public Administration studies how bureaucracies work and how they can be improved.

Constitutional Law studies the applications and evolution of the Constitution within the legal system.

Public Policy studies the interface of politics and economics with an eye to developing effective programs.

quantify To measure with numbers.

hypothesis An initial theory a researcher starts with, to be proved by evidence.

IS POLITICS A SCIENCE?

If we cannot pinpoint which factors contribute what weight to politics, how can politics be a science? Part of the problem here is the definition of science. The original meaning of science, from the French, is simply "knowledge." Later, the natural sciences, which rely on measurement and calculation, took over the term. Now most people think of science as precise and factual, supported by experiments and data. Some political scientists (as we will consider later) have attempted to become like natural scientists; they **quantify** data and manipulate them statistically to validate **hypotheses**. The quantifiers make some good contributions, but usually they focus on small questions of detail rather than on large questions of meaning. This

---

HOW TO . . . ■ STUDY A CHAPTER

Read each chapter *before* class. And do not simply read the chapter; learn it by writing down the following:

A. Find what strikes you as the *three main points*. Do not outline; construct three complete sentences, each with a subject and predicate. They may be long and complex sentences, but they must be complete declarative sentences. You may find two, four, or six main points, but by the time you split, combine, and discard what may or may not be the main points, you will know the chapter. Look for abstract generalizations; the specifics come under point C, examples or case studies. Do not simply copy three sentences from the chapter. Synthesize several sentences, always asking yourself the following: What three sentences distilled from this chapter will most help me on the exam? These might be three main points from this Chapter:

1. Study politics as a scientist studies nature, trying to understand reality without getting angry at it.
2. Political science combines many disciplines but focuses on power: who holds it and how they use it.
3. Politics can be studied objectively, provided claims are supported by empirical evidence.

B. List a *dozen vocabulary words*, and be able to define them. These are words new to you or words used in a specialized way. This text makes it easier with the boldfaced terms defined in the margins; for terms not in boldface, read with a dictionary handy. These are the key terms from this Chapter:

authority	methodology
culture	political power
discipline	quantify
empirical	rational
hypothesis	scholarship
irrational	sovereignty
legitimacy	

C. Note specific *examples* or *case studies* that illustrate the main points or vocabulary words. Most will contain proper nouns (that is, capitalized). Examples are not main points or definitions; rather, they are empirical evidence that support a main point. The examples need not be complete sentences. These might be examples from this Chapter:

Aristotle's "master science"
AIDS versus breast-cancer research
West Germany's success story
Communist regimes in Eastern Europe
Iraq's chaos
Shah's regime in Iran erodes

is because they generally have to stick to areas that can be quantified: public opinion, election returns, and congressional voting.

empirical   Based on observable evidence.

But large areas of politics are not quantifiable. How and why do leaders make their decisions? Many decisions are made in secrecy, even in democracies. We do not know exactly how decisions are made in the White House in Washington, the Elysée in Paris, or the Zhongnanhai in Beijing. When members of Congress vote on an issue, can we be certain why they voted that way? Was it constituents' desires, the good of the nation, or the campaign contributions of interest groups? What did the Supreme Court have in mind when it ruled that laying off schoolteachers based on race is unconstitutional but hiring them based on race is not? Try quantifying that. Much of politics—especially dealing with how and why decisions are made—is just too complex and too secret to be quantified. Bismarck, who unified Germany in the nineteenth century, famously compared laws and sausages: It's better not to see them being made.

Does that mean that politics can never be like a natural science? Political science is an **empirical** discipline that accumulates both quantified and qualitative data. With such data, we can find persistent patterns, much like in biology. Gradually, we begin to generalize. When the generalizations become firmer, we call them theories. In a few cases, the theories become so firm that we may call them laws. In this way, the study of politics accumulates knowledge—the original meaning of science.

The Struggle to See Clearly

Political science also resembles a natural science when its researchers, if they are professional, study things as they are and not as they wish them to be. This is more difficult in the study of politics than in the study of stars and cells. Most political scientists have viewpoints on current issues, and it is easy to let these views contaminate their analyses of politics. Indeed, precisely because a given question interests us enough to study it indicates that we bring a certain passion with us. Can you imagine setting to work on a topic you cared nothing about? If you are interested enough to study a question, you probably start by being inclined

CLASSIC WORKS ■ CONCEPTS AND PRECEPTS

In the late eighteenth century, the great Prussian philosopher Immanuel Kant wrote, "Precepts without concepts are empty, and concepts without precepts are blind." This notion helped establish modern philosophy and social science. A precept is what you perceive through your sensory organs: facts, images, numbers, examples, and so on. A concept is an idea in your head: meanings, theories, hypotheses, beliefs, and so on. You can collect many precepts, but without a concept to structure them you have nothing; your precepts are empty of meaning. On the other hand, your concepts are "blind" if they cannot look at reality, which requires precepts. In other words, you need both theory and data.

scholarship Intellectual arguments supported by reason and evidence.

to one side. Too much of this, however, renders the study biased; it becomes a partisan outcry rather than a scholarly search for the truth. How can you guard against this? The traditional hallmarks of **scholarship** give some guidance. A scholarly work should be *reasoned*, *balanced*, supported with *evidence*, and a bit *theoretical*.

Reasoned   You must spell out your reasoning, and it should make sense. If your perspective is colored by an underlying assumption, you should say so. You might say, "For the purpose of this study, we assume that bureaucrats are rational," or "This is a study of the psychology of voters in a small town." Your basic assumptions influence what you study and how you study it, but you can minimize bias by honestly stating your assumptions. Early in the twentieth century, German sociologist Max Weber (1864–1920), who contributed vastly to all the social sciences, held that any findings that support the researcher's political views must be discarded as biased. Few attempt to be that pure, but Weber's point is well-taken: Beware of structuring the study so that it comes out to support a given view.

Balanced   You can also minimize bias by acknowledging that there are other ways of looking at your topic. You should mention the various approaches to your topic and what other researchers have found. Instructors are impressed that you know the literature in a given area. They are even more impressed when you can then criticize the previous studies and explain why you think they are incomplete or faulty: "The Jones study of voters found them largely apathetic, but this was an off-year election in which turnout is always lower." By comparing and criticizing several approaches and studies, you present a much more objective and convincing

---

KEY CONCEPTS ■ POLITICS VERSUS POLITICAL SCIENCE

Political science ain't politics. It is not necessarily training to become a practicing politician. Political science is training in the calm, objective analysis of politics, which may or may not aid working politicians. Side by side, the two professions compare like this:

Politicians	Political Scientists
love power	are skeptical of power
seek popularity	seek accuracy
think practically	think abstractly
hold firm views	reach tentative conclusions
offer single causes	offer many causes
see short-term payoffs	see long-term consequences
plan for next election	plan for next publication
respond to groups	seek the good of the whole
seek name recognition	seek professional prestige

The two professions of politician and political scientist bear approximately the same relation to each other as do bacteria and bacteriologists.

case. Do not commit yourself to a particular viewpoint or theory, but admit that your view is one among several.

Supported with Evidence   All scholarly studies require evidence, ranging from the quantified evidence of the natural sciences to the qualitative evidence of the humanities. Political science utilizes both. Ideally, any statement open to interpretation or controversy should be supported with evidence. Common knowledge does not have to be supported; you need not cite the U.S. Constitution to "prove" that presidents serve four-year terms.

But if you say presidents have gained more and more power over the decades, you need evidence. At a minimum, you would cite a scholar who has amassed evidence to demonstrate this point. That is called a "secondary source," evidence that has passed through the mind of someone else. Most student papers use only secondary sources, but instructors are impressed when you use a "primary source," the original gathering of data, as in your own tabulation of what counties in your state showed the strongest McCain vote. Anyone reading a study must be able to review its evidence and judge if it is valid. You cannot keep your evidence or sources secret.

Theoretical   Serious scholarship is always connected, at least a little, to a theoretical point. It need not be a sweeping new theory (that's for geniuses), but it should advance the discipline's knowledge a bit. At a minimum, it should confirm or refute an existing theory. Just describing something is not a theory, which is why Google or Wikipedia are seldom enough. You must relate the description to another factor, supported, of course, with empirical evidence. The general pattern of this is as follows: "Most of the time X accompanies Y." Theory-building also helps lift your study above polemics, an argument for or against something. Denouncing al Qaeda, which we all may do with gusto, is not scholarship. Determining why people join al Qaeda (currently studied by several scholars) would have important theoretical and practical impacts.

What Good is Political Science?

Some students come to political science supposing it is just opinions; they write exams or papers that ignore all or some of the preceding points. Yes, we all have political views, but if we let them dominate our study we get invalid results, junk political science. Professional political scientists push their personal views well to one side while engaged in study and research. First-rate thinkers are able to come up with results that actually refute their previously held opinion. When that happens, we have real intellectual growth—an exciting experience that should be your aim.

Something else comes with such an experience: You start to conclude that you should not have been so partisan in the first place. You may back away from the strong views you held earlier and take them with a grain of salt. Accordingly, political science is not necessarily training to become a practicing politician. Political science is training in objective and often complex analysis, whereas the practice of politics requires fixed, popular, and simplified opinions.

Political science can contribute to good government, often by warning those in office that all is not well, "speaking Truth to Power," as the Quakers say. Sometimes this advice is useful to working politicians. Public-opinion polls, for example, showed an erosion of trust in government in the United States starting in the mid-1960s. The causes were Vietnam, Watergate, and inflation. Candidates for political office, knowing public opinion, could tailor their campaigns and policies to try to counteract this decline. Ronald Reagan, with his sunny disposition and upbeat views, utilized the discontent to win two presidential terms.

As far back as 1950, the American Political Science Association warned about the weaknesses of U.S. political parties; they were decentralized and uncontrolled. Political parties in the United States cannot force views on members, nor do the parties control who call themselves members. In 1989, David Duke, a former leader of the Ku Klux Klan with ties to Nazis, won a seat as a Republican in the Louisiana state legislature. The Republican National Committee tried to distance itself from Duke, but he continued to call himself a Republican, and there was no legal way to stop him. Parties in the United States are too weak even to control who uses their names.

Some political scientists warned for years of the weak basis of the shah's regime in Iran. Unfortunately, such warnings were unheeded. Washington's policy was to support the shah, and only two months before the end of the shah's reign did the U.S. embassy in Tehran start reporting how unstable Iran had become. State Department officials had let politics contaminate their political analyses; they could not see clearly. Journalists were not much better; few covered Iran until violence broke out. Years in advance, American political scientists specializing in Iran saw trouble coming. More recently, political scientists warned that Iraq was unready for democracy and that a U.S. invasion would unleash chaos. Washington deciders paid no attention to the warnings. Political science can be useful.

mypoliscikit EXERCISES

Apply what you learned in this chapter on MyPoliSciKit (www.mypoliscikit.com).

Assessment   Review this chapter using learning objectives, chapter summaries, practice tests, and more.

Menu

Flashcards   Learn the key terms in this chapter; you can test yourself by term or definition.

Flashcards

Video   Analyze recent world affairs by watching streaming video from major news providers.

Videos

Comparative Exercises   Compare political ideas, behaviors, institutions, and policies worldwide.

Comparative Exercises

KEY TERMS

authority	irrational	rational
culture	legitimacy	scholarship
discipline	methodology	sovereignty
empirical	political power	
hypothesis	quantify	

FURTHER REFERENCE

Almond, Gabriel A. *Ventures in Political Science: Narratives and Reflections.* Boulder, CO: Lynne Rienner, 2002.

Boulding, Kenneth E. *Three Faces of Power.* Newbury Park, CA: Sage, 1989.

Elster, Jon. *Alexis de Tocqueville: The First Social Scientist.* New York: Cambridge University Press, 2009.

Friedrich, Carl J., ed. *Authority.* Cambridge, MA: Harvard University Press, 1958.

Huysmans, Jeff. *What Is Politics? A Short Introduction.* New York: Columbia University Press, 2004.

Janis, Irving L. *Victims of Groupthink: A Psychological Study of Foreign-Policy Decisions and Fiascoes.* Boston: Houghton Mifflin, 1972.

Kagan, Jerome. *Galen's Prophecy: Temperament and Human Nature.* New York: Basic Books, 1994.

Lasswell, Harold. *Politics: Who Gets What, When, How.* New York: McGraw-Hill, 1936.

Lewellen, Ted C. *Political Anthropology: An Introduction,* 3rd ed. Westport, CT: Greenwood, 2003.

Milgram, Stanley. *Obedience to Authority: An Experimental View.* New York: Harper & Row, 1974.

Minogue, Kenneth. *Politics: A Very Short Introduction.* New York: Oxford University Press, 1995.

Shively, W. Phillips. *The Craft of Political Research,* 8th ed. Upper Saddle River, NJ: Prentice Hall, 2010.

Theodoulou, Stella, and Rory O'Brien, eds. *Methods for Political Inquiry: The Discipline, Philosophy, and Analysis of Politics.* Upper Saddle River, NJ: Prentice Hall, 1999.

Wilson, Edward O. *Sociobiology: The New Synthesis.* Cambridge, MA: Harvard University Press, 1975.

Zimbardo, Philip. *The Lucifer Effect: Understanding How Good People Turn Evil.* New York: Random House, 2007.

Theories

From Chapter 2 of *Political Science: An Introduction*, 12/e. Michael G. Roskin. Robert L. Cord. James A. Medeiros. Walter S. Jones. Copyright © 2012 by Pearson Longman. All rights reserved.

Theories

Indonesia struggles to stabilize its democracy in its 2009 legislative elections. Many of the 38 competing parties used fruits as symbols to aid illiterate voters. (Himawan/epa/Corbis)

Why bother with theories at all, wonder many students new to political science. Why not just accumulate facts and let the facts structure themselves into a coherent whole? Because they won't. Gathering facts without an organizing principle leads only to large collections of meaningless facts, a point made by Kant. To be sure, theories can grow too complex and abstract and depart from the real world, but without at least some theoretical perspective, we do not even know what questions to ask. Even if you say you have no theories, you probably have some unspoken ones. The kind of questions you ask and which you ask first are the beginnings of theorizing.

QUESTIONS TO CONSIDER

1. Who founded political science?
2. What did Machiavelli, Confucius, Kautilya, and Ibn Khaldun have in common?
3. How did Hobbes, Locke, and Rousseau differ?
4. What is the crux of Marx's theory?
5. What is "positivism," and how does it underlie much of social science?
6. What is Easton's theory of the political system?
7. How does modernization theory borrow from Marx?
8. What is rational-choice theory?
9. Why must your paper have a "provable thesis"?

Take, for example, the structure of this text. We have adopted the view—widespread in political science for decades—that the proper starting point of political analysis is society. We assume that politics grows out of society. We start with people's values, attitudes, and opinions and see how they influence government. The subtitle of one influential book by a leading sociologist was *The Social Bases of Politics*. Its message: You start with society and see how it influences politics.

But that could stack the deck. If you assume that society is the basis of politics and that values and opinions are the important facts, you will gather much material on values and opinions and relatively little on the history, structure, and policies of government. Everything else will appear secondary to citizens' values and opinions. And indeed, political science went through a period in which it was essentially sociology, and many political scientists did survey research. This was part of the behavioral tide; survey research was seen as the only way to be "scientific" because it generated quantifiable data.

Most textbooks offered a "percolation up" model of politics. The first major bloc in most studies was concerned with the society and covered such things as how political views were distributed, how interest groups formed, who supported which political parties, and how people voted. That was the basis, the bottom part

Figure 1 ▶

Pyramid with social base and political superstructure. (Flow is from bottom to top.)

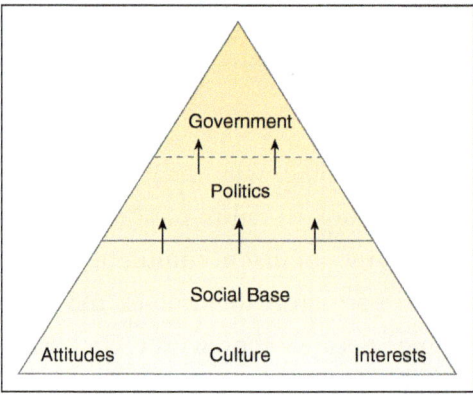

of the pyramid. The second major bloc was usually the institutions of government. They were assumed to be a reflection of the underlying social base. Legislatures and executives reacted to public opinion, interest groups, and political parties. The study of politics looked like Figure 1.

But just using the term social base assumes that society is the underlying element in the study of politics. Could it be the other way around? To use a coffee-making metaphor, instead of "percolating up," could politics "drip down"? Did healthcare reform percolate up from society or drip down from government officials? (Probably some of both.) One could imagine a book titled *The Political Bases of Society* that posits society as largely the result of political institutions and decisions made over the decades. Maybe politics leads society, in which case our model would look like Figure 2.

How can you prove which model is more nearly correct? It is possible (and very likely) that the flow is going both ways simultaneously and that both models are partly correct. Why, then, emphasize one model over the other? There is no good reason; it is simply the current fashion in political study, which began as a reaction against the emphasis on institutions that dominated political science before World War II. A seemingly simple matter of which topics to study first has theoretical implications. You cannot escape theory. We can only whet your appetite for political theories in our very brief discussion here. Consider further study of political theory; you will find that nothing is as practical as theory.

Figure 2 ▶

Pyramid with political institutions forming the social base. (Flow is from top to bottom.)

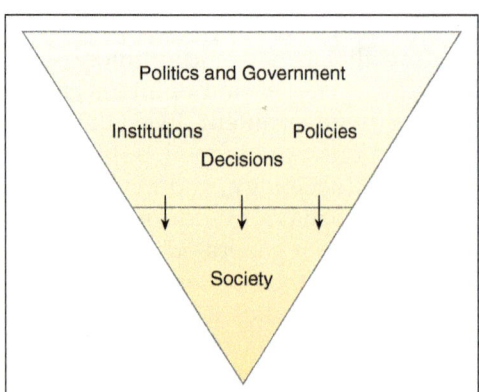

CLASSIC THEORIES

Some say Plato founded political science. His *Republic,* among other things, described an ideal polis, but his reasoning was largely speculative, and his ideal system ended up looking a bit like modern fascism or communism. Plato's student, Aristotle, on the other hand, was the first *empirical* political scientist. He regarded politics as the "master science" and sent out his students to gather data from the dozens of Greek city-states. With these data, he constructed his great work *Politics.* Both Plato and Aristotle saw Athens in decline; they attempted to understand why and to suggest how it could be avoided. They thus began a tradition that is still at the heart of political science: a search for the sources of the good, stable political system. Aristotle was not shy about defining what was politically "best," as in this passage from *Politics*:

descriptive Explaining what is.

normative Explaining what ought to be.

realism Working with the world as it is and not as we wish it to be; usually focused on power.

> [T]he best political community is formed by citizens of the middle class, and those states are likely to be well administered in which the middle class is large ... in which the citizens have moderate and sufficient property; for where some possess much and others nothing there may arise an extreme democracy or a pure oligarchy, or a tyranny may develop out of either extreme. ... [D]emocracies are safer and more permanent than oligarchies, because they have a middle class which is more numerous and has a greater share in government, for when there is no middle class, and the poor greatly exceed in number, troubles arise, and the state soon comes to an end.

Even though *Politics* was written in the fourth century B.C., Aristotle could be describing why democracy succeeds or fails today: Much depends on the size of the middle class, a point confirmed by modern research. Do China and Iraq have a middle class strong enough to sustain democracy? Ancient can still be relevant. Aristotle was both **descriptive** and **normative**: He used the facts he and his students had collected to prescribe the most desirable political institutions. Political scientists have been doing the same ever since, both describing and prescribing.

Most European medieval and Renaissance political thinkers took a religious approach to the study of government and politics. They were almost strictly normative, seeking to discover the "ought" or "should" and were often rather casual about the "is," the real-world situation. Informed by religious, legal, and philosophical values, they tried to ascertain which system of government would bring humankind closest to what God wished.

Niccolò Machiavelli in the early sixteenth century introduced what some believe to be the crux of modern political science: the focus on power. His great work *The Prince* was about the getting and using of political power. Many philosophers peg Machiavelli as the first modern philosopher because his motivations and explanations had nothing to do with religion. Machiavelli was not as wicked as some people say. He was a **realist** who argued that to accomplish anything good—such as the unification of Italy and expulsion of the foreigners who ruined it—the Prince had to be rational and tough in the exercise of power.

Although long depreciated by American political thinkers, who sometimes shied away from "power" as inherently dirty, the approach took root in Europe and contributed to the elite analyses of Mosca, Pareto, and Michels. Americans became acquainted with the power approach through the writings of the refugee German scholar of international relations Hans J. Morgenthau, who emphasized that "all politics is a struggle for power."

The Contractualists

Not long after Machiavelli, the "contractualists"—Hobbes, Locke, and Rousseau—analyzed why political systems should exist at all. They differed in many points

CLASSIC WORKS ■ NOT JUST EUROPEANS

China, India, and North Africa produced brilliant political thinkers long before their European counterparts. Unknown in the West until relatively recently, it is unlikely that their ideas influenced the development of Western political theory. The existence of these culturally varied thinkers suggests that the political nature of humans is basically the same no matter what the cultural differences and that great minds come to similar conclusions on how to deal with politics.

In China, Confucius—a sixth-century B.C. advisor to kings—propounded his vision of good, stable government based on two things: the family and correct, moral behavior instilled in rulers and ruled alike. At the apex, the emperor sets a moral example by purifying his spirit and perfecting his manners. He must think good thoughts in utter sincerity; if he does not, his empire crumbles. He is copied by his subjects, who are arrayed hierarchically below the emperor, down to the father of a family, who is like a miniature emperor to whom wives and children are subservient. The Confucian system bears some resemblance to Plato's ideal republic; the difference is that the Chinese actually practiced Confucianism, which lasted two and a half millennia and through a dozen dynasties. Some claim it formed the cultural basis for East Asia's recent remarkable economic growth.

Two millennia before Machiavelli and Hobbes, the Indian writer Kautilya in the fourth century B.C. arrived at the same conclusions. Kautilya, a prime minister and advisor to an Indian monarch, wrote in *Arthashastra* (translated as *The Principles of Material Well-Being*) that prosperity comes from living in a well-run kingdom. Like Hobbes, Kautilya posited a state of nature that meant anarchy. Monarchs arose to protect the land and people against anarchy and ensure their prosperity. Like Machiavelli, Kautilya advised his prince to operate on the basis of pure expediency, doing whatever it took to secure his kingdom domestically and against other kingdoms. Kautilya thus could be said to have founded both political economy and the realist school of statecraft.

In fourteenth century A.D. North Africa, Ibn Khaldun was a secretary, executive, and ambassador for several rulers. Sometimes out of favor and in jail, he reflected on what had gone wrong with the great Arab empires. He concluded, in his *Universal History*, that the character of the Arabs and their social cohesiveness was determined by climate and occupation. Ibn Khaldun was almost modern in his linking of underlying economic conditions to social and political change. Economic decline in North Africa, he found, had led to political instability and lawlessness. Anticipating Marx, Toynbee, and many other Western writers, Ibn Khaldun saw that civilizations pass through cycles of growth and decline.

Notice what all three of these thinkers had in common with Machiavelli: All were princely political advisors who turned their insights into general prescriptions for correct governance. Practice led to theory.

but agreed that humans, at least in principle, had joined in what Rousseau called a **social contract** that everyone now had to observe.

Thomas Hobbes lived through the upheavals of the English Civil War in the seventeenth century and opposed them for making individuals frightened and insecure. Hobbes imagined that life in "the **state of nature**," before **civil society** was founded, must have been terrible. Every man would have been the enemy of every other man, a "war of each against all." Humans would live in savage squalor with "no arts; no letters; no society; and which is worst of all, continual fear, and danger of violent death; and the life of man, solitary, poor, nasty, brutish, and short." To get out of this horror, people would—out of their profound self-interest—rationally join together to form civil society. Society thus arises naturally out of fear. People would also gladly submit to a king, even a bad one, for a monarch prevents anarchy. Notice how Hobbes's theory, that society is based on rational self-interest, is at odds with Aristotle's theory that humans are born "political animals." Which theory is right? (Hint: Have humans ever lived as solitary animals?) But also notice that Hobbesian situations appear from time to time, as in Iraq, where Sunni and Shia murdered each other as if there were no government.

Another Englishman, John Locke, also saw the seventeenth-century upheavals but came to less harsh conclusions. Locke theorized that the original state of nature was not so bad; people lived in equality and tolerance with one another. But they could not secure their property. There was no money, title deeds, or courts of law, so ownership was uncertain. To remedy this, they contractually formed civil society and thus secured "life, liberty, and property." Locke is to property rights as Hobbes is to fear of violent death. Some philosophers argue that Americans are the children of Locke. Notice the American emphasis on "the natural right to property."

Jean-Jacques Rousseau lived in eighteenth-century France and, some say, laid the philosophical groundwork for the French Revolution. He accepted the theories of Hobbes and Locke but gave them a twist. Life in the state of nature, Rousseau theorized, was downright good; people lived as "noble savages" without artifice or jealousy. (All the contractualists were influenced by not-very-accurate descriptions of American Indians.) What corrupted humans, said Rousseau, was society itself. The famous words at the beginning of his *Social Contract*: "Man is born free but everywhere is in chains."

But society can be drastically improved, argued Rousseau, leading to human freedom. A just society would be a voluntary community with a will of its own, the **general will**—what everyone wants over and above the "particular wills" of individuals and interest groups. In such communities, humans gain dignity and freedom. Societies make people, not the other way around. If people are bad, it is because society made them that way (a view held by many today). A good society, on the other hand, can "force men to be free" if they misbehave. Many see the roots of totalitarianism in Rousseau: the imagined perfect society; the general will, which the

social contract Theory that individuals join and stay in civil society as if they had signed a contract.

state of nature Humans before civilization.

civil society Humans after becoming civilized. Modern usage: associations between family and government.

general will Rousseau's theory of what the whole community wants.

Zeitgeist German for "spirit of the times"; Hegel's theory that each epoch has a distinctive spirit, which moves history along.

proletariat Marx's name for the industrial working class.

bourgeois Adjective, originally French for city dweller; later and current, middle class in general. Noun: *bourgeoisie*.

dictator claims to know; and the breaking of those who do not cooperate. Happily, the U.S. Founding Fathers were uninfluenced by Rousseau, but the architects of the French Revolution believed passionately in him, which perhaps explains why it ended badly.

Most of the U.S. Founding Fathers had studied Hobbes and Locke, whose influence is obvious. What is the Constitution but a social contract? Much of the Declaration of Independence reads as if it had been cribbed from Locke, which it had, by Jefferson. Please do not say political theories have no influence.

Marxist Theories

Another political theory that made a big difference was Marxism. A German living in London, Karl Marx, who was trained in Hegelian philosophy, produced an exceedingly complex theory consisting of at least three interrelated elements: a theory of economics, a theory of social class, and a theory of history. Like Hegel, Marx argued that things do not happen by accident; everything has a cause. Hegel posited the underlying cause that moves history forward as spiritual, specifically the **Zeitgeist**, the spirit of the times. Marx found the great underlying cause in economics.

Economics Marx concentrated on the "surplus value"—what we call profit. Workers produce things but get paid only a fraction of the value of what they produce. The capitalist owners skim off the rest, the surplus value. The working class—what Marx called the **proletariat**—is paid too little to buy all the products the workers have made, resulting in repeated overproduction, which leads to depressions. Eventually, argued Marx, there will be a depression so big the capitalist system will collapse.

Social Class Every society divides into two classes: a small class of those who own the means of production and a large class of those who work for the small class. Society is run according to the dictates of the upper class, which sets up the laws, arts, and styles needed to maintain itself in power. (Marx influenced the theory of elites. Most laws concern property rights, noted Marx, because the **bourgeoisie** (the capitalists) are obsessed with hanging on to their property, which, according to Marx, is nothing but skimmed-off surplus value anyway. If the country goes to war, said Marx, it is not because the common people wish it but because the ruling bourgeoisie needs a war for economic gain. The proletariat, in fact, has no country; proletarians are international, all suffering under the heel of the capitalists.

History Putting together his economic and social-class theories, Marx explained historical changes. When the underlying economic basis of society gets out of kilter with the structure that the dominant class has established (its laws, institutions, businesses, and so on), the system collapses, as in the French Revolution. Prior to 1789, France's ruling class was the feudal nobility. This system was from the Middle Ages, based on hereditary ownership of great estates worked by peasants, on laws stressing the inheritance of these estates and the titles that went with them, and on chivalry and honor. All were part and parcel of a feudal society. But the economic basis changed. Ownership of land and feudal values eroded with the rise of manufacturing, which brought a new class, the urban capitalists (or bourgeoisie), whose way of life and economy were quite different. By the late eighteenth century, France had an economy based on manufacturing but was still dominated by the feudal aristocrats of the past. The system was out of kilter: The economic basis had moved ahead, but the class **superstructure** had stayed behind. In 1789, the superstructure came down with a crash, and the bourgeoisie took over with its new capitalist and liberal values of a free market, individual gain, and legal (but not material) equality.

> **superstructure** Marx's term for everything that is built on top of the economy (laws, art, politics, etc.).
>
> **leftist** Favors social and economic change to uplift poor.

The capitalists did a good job, Marx had to admit. They industrialized and modernized much of the globe. They put out incredible new products and inventions. But they too are doomed, Marx wrote, because the faster they transform the economy, the more it gets out of kilter with the capitalist superstructure, just as the previous feudal society was left behind by a changing economy. This leads us back to Marx's theory of surplus value and recurring economic depressions. Eventually, reasoned Marx, the economy will be so far out of kilter from the bourgeois setup that it too will collapse. Socialism, predicted Marx, will come next, and we should aid in its coming. Marx was partly a theorist and partly an ideologist.

Marxism, as applied in the Soviet Union and other Communist countries, led to tyranny and failure, but, as a system of analysis, Marxism is still interesting and useful. Social class is important in structuring political views—but never uniformly. For example, many working-class people are conservative, and many middle-class intellectuals are liberals or **leftists**. Economic interest groups still ride high and—by means of freely spending on election campaigns—often get their way in laws, policies, and tax breaks. They seldom get all they want, however, as they are opposed by other interest groups. Marx's enduring contributions are (1) his understanding that societies are never fully unified and peaceful but always riven with conflict and (2) that we must ask "Who benefits?" in any political controversy.

One of the enduring problems and weaknesses of Marx is that capitalism, contrary to his prediction, has not collapsed. Marx thought the Paris Commune of 1870–1871 was the first proletarian uprising. (It was not.) True, capitalism has gone through some major depressions, in the 1890s and 1930s and a big scare in 2008–2009, but it has always bounced back.

Marx erred in at least a couple of ways. First, he failed to understand the flexible, adaptive nature of capitalism. Old industries fade, and new ones rise.

institutions   The formal structures of government, such as the U.S. Congress.

positivism   Theory that society can be studied scientifically and incrementally improved with the knowledge gained.

Imagine trying to explain Bill Gates and the computer software industry to people in the 1960s. They wouldn't believe you. Capitalism rarely gets stuck at one stage; it is the system of constant change. Second, Marx failed to understand that capitalism is not just one system; it is many. U.S., French, Singaporean, and Japanese capitalisms are distinct from each other. Marx's simplified notions of capitalism illustrate what happens when theory is placed in the service of ideology: Unquestioning followers believe it too literally.

Institutional Theories

From the nineteenth century through the middle of the twentieth century, American thinkers focused on **institutions**, the formal structures of government. This showed the influence of law on the development of political science in the United States. Woodrow Wilson, for example, was a lawyer (albeit unsuccessful) before he became a political scientist; he concentrated on perfecting the institutions of government. Constitutions were a favorite subject for political scientists of this period, for they assumed that what was on paper was how the institutions worked in practice. The rise of the Soviet, Italian, and German dictatorships shook this belief. The constitution of Germany's Weimar Republic (1919–1933) looked fine on paper; experts had drafted it. Under stress it collapsed, for Germans of that time did not have the necessary experience with or commitment to democracy. Likewise, the Stalin constitution of 1936 made the Soviet Union look like a perfect democracy, but it functioned as a dictatorship.

CONTEMPORARY THEORIES

Some thinkers of classic bent dismiss contemporary theories as trivial, obvious, superficial, or simply restatements of classic ideas. One such scholar sniffed that everything he learned from modern theories could be written on the inside of a matchbook cover. We need not be so harsh. Contemporary—meaning post–World War II—theories have made some contributions. Even when they ultimately fail and are abandoned, they leave a residue of interesting questions. True, compared to classic theories, most are pretty thin stuff.

Behavioralism

The Communist and Fascist dictatorships and World War II forced political scientists to reexamine their institutional focus, and many set to work to discover how politics really worked, not how it was supposed to work. Postwar American political scientists here followed in the tradition of the early nineteenth-century French philosopher Auguste Comte, who developed the doctrine of **positivism**, the application of natural science methods to the study of society. Comtean positivism was an optimistic philosophy, holding that as we accumulate valid data by means of scientific observation—without speculation or intuition—we will perfect a science of society and with it improve society. Psychologists are perhaps the most deeply imbued with this approach. **Behavioralists**, as they are called, claim to concentrate on actual behavior as opposed to thoughts or feelings.

Beginning in the 1950s, behaviorally inclined political scientists accumulated statistics from elections, public opinion surveys, votes in legislatures, and anything else they could hang a number on. Behavioralists made some remarkable contributions to political science, shooting down some long-held but unexamined assumptions and giving political theory an empirical basis. Behavioral studies were especially good in examining the "social bases" of politics, the attitudes and values of average citizens, which go a long way toward making the system function the way it does. Their best work has been on voting patterns, for it is here they can get lots of valid data.

During the 1960s, the behavioral school established itself and won over much of the field. In the late 1960s, however, behavioralism came under heavy attack, and not just by rear-guard traditionalists. Many younger political scientists, some of them influenced by the radicalism of the anti–Vietnam War movement, complained that the behavioral approach was static, conservative, loaded with its practitioners' values, and irrelevant to the urgent tasks at hand. Far from being "scientific" and "value-free," behavioralists often defined the current situation in the United States as the norm and anything different as deviant. Gabriel Almond (1911–2002) and Sidney Verba (1932–) found that Americans embody all the good, "participant" virtues of the "civic culture." By examining only what exists at a given moment, behavioralists neglected the possibility of change; their studies may be time-bound. Behavioralists have an unstated preference for the status quo; they like to examine established democratic systems, for that is where their methodological tools work best. People in police states or civil conflicts know that honestly stating their opinions could get them jailed or killed, so they voice the "correct" viewpoint.

Perhaps the most damaging criticism, though, was that the behavioralists focused on relatively minor topics and steered clear of the big questions of politics. Behavioralists can tell us, for example, what percentage of Detroit blue-collar Catholics vote Democratic, but they tell us nothing about what this means for the quality of Detroit's governance or the kinds of decisions elected officials will make. There is no necessary connection between how citizens vote and what comes out of government. Critics charged that behavioral studies were often irrelevant.

By 1969, many political scientists had to admit that there was something to the criticism of what had earlier been called the "behavioral revolution." Some called the newer movement **postbehavioral**, a synthesis of traditional and behavioral approaches. Postbehavioralists recognize that facts and values are tied together. They are willing to use both the qualitative data of the traditionalists and the quantitative data of the behavioralists. They look at history and institutions as well as public opinion and rational-choice theory. They are not afraid of numbers and happily use correlations, graphs, and percentages to make their cases. If you look around your political science department, you are apt to find traditional, behavioral, and postbehavioral viewpoints among the professors—or even within the same professor.

behavioralism The empirical study of actual human behavior rather than abstract or speculative theories.

postbehavioral Synthesis of traditional, behavioral, and other techniques in the study of politics.

Systems Theory

A major postwar invention was the "political systems" model devised by David Easton (1917–), which contributed to our understanding of politics by simplify-

thesis A main idea or claim, to be proved by evidence.

ing reality but in some cases departed from reality. The idea of looking at complex entities as systems originated in biology. Living entities are complex and highly integrated. The heart, lungs, blood, digestive tract, and brain perform their functions in such a way as to keep the animal alive. Take away one organ, and the animal dies. Damage one organ, and the other components of the system alter their function to compensate and keep the animal alive. The crux of systems thinking is this: You cannot change just one component, because that changes all the others.

Political systems thinkers argued that the politics of a given country work as a feedback loop, a bit like a biological system. According to the Easton model (Figure 3), citizens' demands, "inputs," are recognized by the government decision makers, who process them into authoritative decisions and actions, "outputs." These outputs have an impact on the social, economic, and political environment that

---

HOW TO . . . ■ MAKE THESIS STATEMENTS

You are assigned a paper in political science. Begin it with a clear, punchy **thesis**, a first sentence giving your main idea or claim, the thing you are going to prove. A thesis that cannot be proved with empirical evidence is just speculation, not solid research. An initial attempt at a thesis is a *hypothesis*. If your evidence does not support your thesis, discard or change it. Your thesis paragraph should be about as long as this one.

The simplest thesis is that something is (or is not) happening: "More and more interest groups set up shop in Washington." Avoid trivial theses, anything well-known or established: "The president is inaugurated on January 20 following the election." An interesting thesis explains how one thing relates to another: "White Protestant males vote strongly Republican." Gathering examples or case studies is often the initial step to developing a thesis. If you take the six counties in your state with the highest Obama vote, what generalizations can you make about them? Do not gently introduce your thesis (save that for your English class); move directly into it. A thesis is more definite than what the paper is "about." You left that behind in high school.

Indirect	**Direct**
Television has a big impact on politics, and many critics feel that it is not always a good impact.	U.S. television advertising makes viewers cynical and indifferent and leads to low voter turnout.
Unprovable	**Provable**
Democracy is government of the people, by people, and for the people.	Better-off countries tend to be democracies, poor countries not.
Trivial	**Nontrivial**
Tea Party supporters were unhappy with both of the main parties.	Tea Party supporters were mostly Republican voters angry over Obama's programs.
Vague	**Clear**
This paper is about U.S. policy toward Iran over three decades.	U.S. policy toward Iran failed to notice rising discontent against the shah.

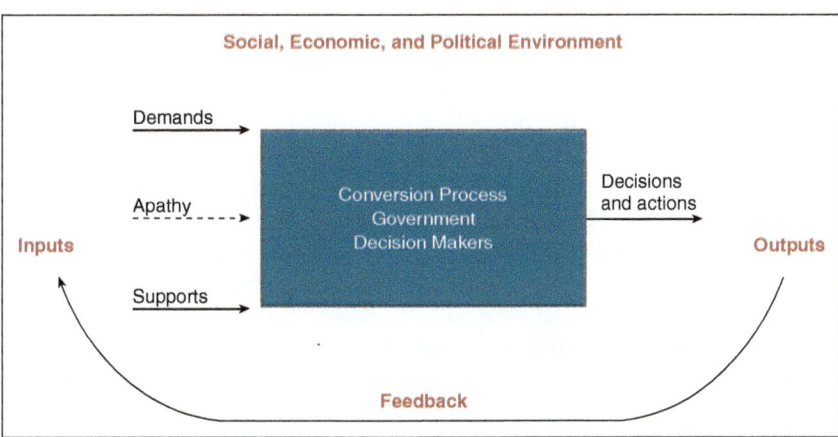

Figure 3
A model of the political system.

(*Adapted from David Easton*, A Systems Analysis of Political Life. *Chicago: University of Chicago Press, 1965,*.

the citizens may or may not like. The citizens express their demands anew—this is the crucial "feedback" link of the system—which may modify the earlier decision. Precisely what goes on in the "conversion process" was left opaque, a "black box."

In some cases, the political systems approach fits reality. During the Vietnam War, feedback on the military draft was very negative. The Nixon administration defused youthful anger by ending the draft in 1973 and changing to an all-volunteer army. Recent lavish bonuses for executives of failed big companies—at that time propped up with billions of federal dollars—brought rage from citizens and Congress. The Obama administration saw healthcare reform as important and necessary, but roughly half the U.S. population opposed it, a point the Republicans used in the 2010 elections. In the 1980s, the socialist economics of French President François Mitterrand produced inflation and unemployment. The French people, especially the business community, complained loudly, and Mitterrand altered his policy away from socialism and back to capitalism. In these cases, the feedback loop worked.

But in other cases, the systems model falls flat. Would Hitler's Germany or Stalin's Russia really fit the systems model? How much attention do dictatorships pay to citizens' demands? To be sure, there is always some input and feedback. Hitler's generals tried to assassinate him—a type of feedback. Workers in Communist systems had an impact on government policy by not working much. They demanded more consumer goods and, by not exerting themselves, communicated this desire to the regime. Sooner or later the regime had to reform. All over the Soviet bloc, workers used to chuckle: "They pretend to pay us, and we pretend to work." In the USSR, (botched) reform came with the Gorbachev regime—and it led to system collapse.

How could the systems model explain the Vietnam War? Did Americans demand that the administration send half-a-million troops to fight there? No, nearly the opposite: Lyndon Johnson won overwhelmingly in 1964 on an antiwar platform.

The systems model does show how discontent with the war ruined Johnson's popularity so that he did not seek reelection in 1968. The feedback loop did go into effect but only years after the decision for war had been made. Could the systems model explain the Watergate scandal? Did U.S. citizens demand that President Nixon have the Democratic headquarters bugged? No, but once details about the cover-up started leaking in 1973, the feedback loop went into effect, putting pressure on the House of Representatives to form an impeachment panel.

Plainly, there are some problems with the systems model, and they seem to be in the "black box" of the conversion process. Much happens in the mechanism of government that is not initiated by and has little to do with the wishes of citizens. The American people were little concerned about the health effects of smoking. Only the analyses of medical statisticians, which revealed a strong link between smoking and lung cancer, prodded Congress into requiring warning labels on cigarette packs and ending television advertising of cigarettes. It was a handful of specialists in the federal bureaucracy who got the anticigarette campaign going, not the masses of citizens.

The systems model is essentially static, biased toward the status quo, and unable to handle upheaval. This is one reason political scientists were surprised at the collapse of the Soviet Union. "Systems" are not supposed to collapse; they are supposed to continually self-correct.

We can modify the systems model to better reflect reality. By diagramming it as in Figure 4, we logically change little. We have the same feedback loop: outputs turning into inputs. But by putting the "conversion process" of government first, we suggested that it—rather than the citizenry—originates most decisions. The public reacts only later. That would be the case with the Iraq War: strong support in 2003 but disillusion and discontent by 2006.

Next, we add something that Easton himself later suggested. Inside the "black box," a lot more happens than simply the processing of outside demands. Pressures from the various parts of government—government talking mostly to itself and short-circuiting the feedback loop—are what Easton called "withinputs." These two alterations, of course, make our model more complicated, but this reflects the complicated nature of reality. The systems model, like all models in political science, must be taken with a grain of salt.

KEY CONCEPTS ■ MODELS: SIMPLIFYING REALITY

A model is a simplified picture of reality that social scientists develop to order data, to theorize, and to predict. A good model fits reality but simplifies it, because a model that is as complex as the real world would be of no help. In simplifying reality, however, models run the risk of oversimplifying. The real problem is the finite capacity of the human mind. We cannot factor in all the information available at once; we must select which points are important and ignore the rest. But when we do this, we may drain the blood out of the study of politics and overlook key points. Accordingly, as we encounter models of politics—and perhaps as we devise our own—pause a moment to ask if the model departs too much from reality. If it does, discard or alter the model. Do not disregard reality because it does not fit the model.

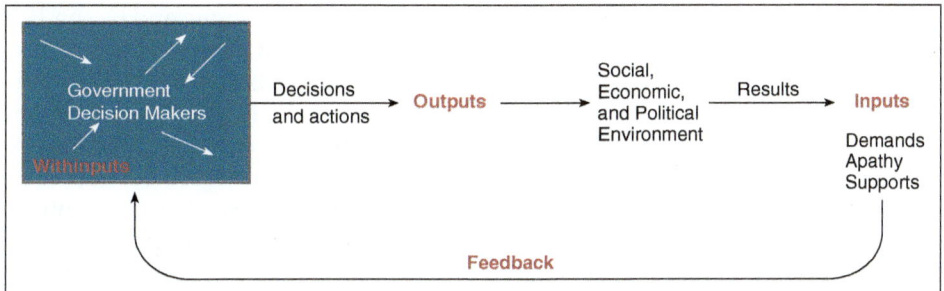

Figure 4
A modified model of the political system.

Modernization Theory

Modernization theory, a broad-brush term, is rooted in Hegel, who argued two centuries ago that all facets of society—the economic, cultural, and political—hang together as a package, which changes and moves all societies in the same direction. Hegel thought the underlying cause of this process was spiritual, but Marx argued that it was economic: "Steam engines and dynamos bring their own philosophy with them." You cannot have a feudal society with a modern economy, at least not for long. Max Weber argued that the cause was cultural, specifically, the rise of Protestantism. Others have emphasized the growth of education, communications, and the middle class, but all agree it happens as a package. Today's modernization theorists see the process as complex, multicausal, and little amenable to outside guidance. We do not develop countries; they develop themselves, a point neglected in Iraq.

gross domestic product (GDP) Sum total of goods and services produced in a given country in one year, often expressed per capita (GDPpc) by dividing population into GDP.

Most agree on the importance of industrialization. As a country industrializes, its economy, culture, communications, and politics also change. Giving new life to this theory was the remarkable of Seymour Martin Lipset's 1960 *Political Man*. Lipset classified countries as either "stable democracies" (such as Canada and Norway) or "unstable democracies and dictatorships" (such as Spain and Yugoslavia). With few exceptions, the stable democracies had more wealth, industry, radios, doctors, cars, education, and urban dwellers than the unstable democracies and dictatorships. In a word, they were more industrialized. And Lipset supplied an explanation: Industrialized countries have large middle classes, and they are the basis of democracy. Lipset combined Marx with Aristotle (see the quote from Aristotle earlier in this chapter).

More recent research tends to confirm a relationship between level of economic development and democracy. There is a dividing line between poor and middle-income countries, but it is not airtight. Lands with a per capita **gross domestic product (GDP)** of less than $5,000 are rarely democracies. If they attempt to found a democracy, it often fails, usually by military coup. Countries with a per capita GDP of more than $8,000, however, are mostly democracies. When they establish a democracy, it usually lasts. When South Korea and Taiwan were poor, they were dictatorships. As they industrialized, their middle classes and education levels grew, and by the 1990s both had turned into democracies. Much U.S. thinking on China is based on these hopeful examples. China's rapid economic growth suggests that it could soon become a middle-income country and hence be ripe for democracy. However, economic growth is rarely smooth, and China is a huge, complex nation ruled by a Communist Party that refuses to relinquish power. When Mexico topped $8,000 per cap, it was ready for its first democratic election, that of Vicente Fox in 2000. There is an interesting exception to this wealth-democracy connection: India, still with a per capita GDP of under $3,000, was founded and stayed democratic, likely the result of the age and authority of its founding Congress Party. For every theory, there are counterexamples.

Modernization theory also has some insights into the turmoil and instability that afflict many developing countries. It is because they modernize just one or two facets—often their economy and military—and leave the rest—such as religion and social structure—traditional. The two conflict; the traditional sectors resent and oppose the modern sectors. This helps explain the upsurge of Islamic fundamentalism in Iran, Egypt, Algeria, and Saudi Arabia. One must also note the high unemployment in these lands. If modernization theory is correct, if and when they reach middle-income levels, they should stabilize and democratize.

Rational-Choice Theory

In the 1970s, a new approach invented by mathematicians rapidly grew in political science—rational-choice theory. Rational-choice theorists argue that one

Shoppers in an upscale Beijing mall could watch 2010 World Cup soccer on a giant screen. Will China's rapid economic growth lead it to democracy? (AFP/Getty Images)

can generally predict political behavior by knowing the interests of the actors involved because they rationally choose to maximize their interests. As U.S. presidential candidates take positions on issues, they

> **paradigm** A model or way of doing research accepted by a discipline.

calculate what will give them the best payoff. They might think, "Many people oppose the war in Iraq, but many also demand strong leadership on defense. I'd better just criticize 'mistakes' in Iraq while at the same time demand strong 'national security.'" The waffle is not indecision but calculation, argue rational-choice theorists.

Rational-choice theorists enrage some other political scientists. One study of Japanese bureaucrats claimed you need not study Japan's language, culture, or history. All you needed to know was what their career advantages were to predict how they would decide issues. A noted U.S. specialist on Japan blew his stack at such glib, superficial shortcuts and denounced rational-choice theory. More modest rational-choice theorists immersed themselves in Hungary's language and culture but still concluded that Hungarian political parties, in cobbling together an extremely complex voting system, were making rational choices to give themselves a presumed edge in parliamentary seats.

Many rational-choice theorists backed down from some of their more know-it-all positions. Some now call themselves "neoinstitutionalists" (see following section) because all their rational choices are made within one or another institutional context—the U.S. Congress, for example. Rational-choice theory did not establish itself as the dominant **paradigm**—no theory has, and none is likely to—but it contributed a lot by reminding us that politicians are consummate opportunists, a point many other theories forget.

KEY CONCEPTS ■ POLITICS AS A GAME

Some rational-choice thinkers subscribed to a branch of mathematics called game theory, setting up political decisions as if they were table games. A Cuban missile crisis "game" might have several people play President Kennedy, who must weigh the probable payoffs of bombing or not bombing Cuba. Others might play Khrushchev, who has to weigh toughing it out or backing down. Seeing how the players interact gives us insights and warnings of what can go wrong in crisis decision making. If you "game out" the 1962 Cuban missile crisis and find that three games out of ten end in World War III, you have the makings of an article of great interest.

Game theorists argue that constructing the proper game explains why policy outcomes are often unforeseen but not accidental. Games can show how decision makers think. We learn how their choices are never easy or simple. Games can even be mathematized and fed into computers. The great weakness of game theory is that it depends on correctly estimating the "payoffs" decision makers can expect, and these are only approximations arrived at by examining the historical record. We know how the Cuban missile crisis came out; therefore, we adjust our game so it comes out the same way. In effect, game theory is only another way to systematize and clarify history (not a bad thing).

New Institutionalism

In the 1970s, political science began to rediscover institutions and, in the 1980s, proclaimed the "New Institutionalism." Its crux is that government structures—legislatures, parties, bureaucracies, and so on—take on lives of their own and shape the behavior and attitudes of the people who live within and benefit from them. Institutions are not simply the reflections of social forces. (Our discussion at the beginning of this chapter, on the importance of structures, is a neoinstitutionalist argument.) Legislators, for example, behave as they do largely because of rules laid down long ago and reinforced over the decades. Once you know these complex rules, some unwritten, you can see how politicians logically try to maximize their advantage under them, much as you can often predict when a baseball batter will bunt. It is not a mystery but the logic of the game they are playing. The preservation and enhancement of the institution becomes one of politicians' major goals. Thus, institutions, even if outmoded or ineffective, tend to rumble on. The Communist parties of the Soviet bloc were corrupt and ineffective, but they endured because they guaranteed the jobs and perquisites of their members.

The new institutionalism is a sound approach and popular in current research, and with it political science comes full circle, back to where it was before World War II, with some interesting new insights. It is, however, likely not the last model we shall see, for we will never have a paradigm that can consistently explain and predict political actions. Every couple of decades, political science comes up with a new paradigm—usually one borrowed from another discipline—that attracts much excitement and attention. Its proponents exaggerate its ability to explain or predict. Upon examination and criticism, the model usually fades and is replaced by another trend. Political science tends to get caught up in trends. After a few iterations of this cycle, we learn to expect no breakthrough theories. Politics is slippery and not easily confined to our mental constructs. By acknowledging this, we open our minds to the richness, complexity, and drama of political life.

mypoliscikit EXERCISES

Apply what you learned in this chapter on MyPoliSciKit (www.mypoliscikit.com).

 Assessment   Review this chapter using learning objectives, chapter summaries, practice tests, and more.

Flashcards   Learn the key terms in this chapter; you can test yourself by term or definition.

Video   Analyze recent world affairs by watching streaming video from major news providers.

Comparative Exercises   Compare political ideas, behaviors, institutions, and policies worldwide.

KEY TERMS

behavioralism	institutions	realism
bourgeois	leftist	social contract
civil society	normative	state of nature
descriptive	paradigm	superstructure
general will	positivism	thesis
gross domestic product (GDP)	postbehavioral	Zeitgeist
	proletariat	

FURTHER REFERENCE

Almond, Gabriel A., and James S. Coleman. *Politics of Developing Areas*. Princeton, NJ: Princeton University Press, 1960.

Boesche, Roger. *The First Great Political Realist: Kautilya and His Arthashastra*. Lanham, MD: Lexington, 2003.

Colomer, Josep M. *The Science of Politics: An Introduction*. New York: Oxford University Press, 2010.

Easton, David. *A Framework for Political Analysis*. Englewood Cliffs, NJ: Prentice Hall, 1965.

Hardt, Michael, and Antonio Negri. *Commonwealth*. Cambridge, MA: Harvard University Press, 2009.

Lane, Ruth. *Political Science in Theory and Practice: The "Politics" Model*. Armonk, NY: M. E. Sharpe, 1997.

Laver, Michael. *Private Desires, Political Action: An Invitation to the Politics of Rational Choice*. Thousand Oaks, CA: Sage, 1997.

Lipset, Seymour Martin. *Political Man: The Social Bases of Politics*, rev. ed. Baltimore, MD: Johns Hopkins University Press, 1981.

———, ed. *Political Philosophy: Theories, Thinkers, and Concepts*. Washington, DC: CQ Press, 2001.

Losco, Joseph, and Leonard Williams, eds. *Political Theory: Classic and Contemporary Readings*, 2nd ed., 2 vols. Los Angeles: Roxbury, 2002.

Morgenthau, Hans J., Kenneth W. Thompson, and David Clinton. *Politics Among Nations: The Struggle for Power and Peace*, 7th ed. Burr Ridge, IL: McGraw-Hill, 2005.

Sen, Amartya. *The Idea of Justice*. Cambridge, MA: Harvard University Press, 2009.

Tannenbaum, Donald, and David Schultz. *Inventors of Ideas: An Introduction to Western Political Philosophy*, 2nd ed. Belmont, CA: Wadsworth, 2003.

Tinder, Glenn. *Political Thinking: The Perennial Questions*, 6th ed. New York: Longman, 2003.

White, Stephen K., and J. Donald Moon, eds. *What Is Political Theory?* Thousand Oaks, CA: Sage, 2004.

Political Ideologies

From Chapter 3 of *Political Science: An Introduction*, 12/e. Michael G. Roskin. Robert L. Cord. James A. Medeiros. Walter S. Jones. Copyright © 2012 by Pearson Longman. All rights reserved.

Political Ideologies

The FDR memorial in Washington, DC, shows his emphasis on helping poorer citizens, an example of modern liberalism. (William Manning/Corbis)

The theories of politics lead to consideration of **ideologies**, which are often based on theories but simplified and popularized to sell to mass audiences, build political movements, and win elections. Ideologies might be called cheap theories. As is usual in U.S. politics, at least two of them contend.

Most Americans see themselves as **pragmatic**, but they can be quite ideological. Recently, for example, Republicans denounced the Democratic health-care and finance reforms as "liberal." Probably few Republicans knew it, but the basis of their opposition was actually *classic liberalism*, harkening back to Adam Smith's two-century-old admonition to get government out of the economy. Democrats, on the other hand, emphasized government solutions for financial crashes, poverty, health care, and home foreclosures. They were *modern liberals*, quite distinct from the classic variety. Ideology is alive and well in America.

QUESTIONS TO CONSIDER

1. Is it possible to be totally pragmatic, with no ideology?
2. How did classic liberalism turn into U.S. conservatism?
3. How close are modern liberalism and social democracy?
4. What changes did Lenin make to Marxism?
5. Why is nationalism the strongest ideology?
6. What are the main elements of fascism?
7. What is "Islamism," and why is it dangerous?
8. Do any ideologies attract today's students?
9. Could ideological politics die out?

WHAT IS IDEOLOGY?

An ideology begins with the belief that things can be better; it is a plan to improve society. As Anthony Downs put it, ideology is "a verbal image of the good society, and of the chief means of constructing such a society." Political ideologies are not political science; they are not calm, rational attempts to understand political systems. Rather, they are commitments to *change* political systems. (An exception is classic conservatism, which aimed to keep things from changing too much.) **Ideologues** make poor political scientists, for they confuse the "should" or "ought" of ideology with the "is" of political science.

In politics, ideology cements together movements, parties, and revolutionary groups. To fight and endure sacrifices, people need ideological motivation—something to believe in. Americans have sometimes not grasped this point. With their emphasis on moderation and pragmatism, they fail to understand the

ideology   Belief system that society can be improved by following certain doctrines; usually ends in -*ism.*

pragmatic   Using whatever works without theory or ideology.

ideologue   Someone who believes passionately in an ideology.

classic liberalism   Ideology founded by Adam Smith to keep government out of economy; became U.S. conservatism.

energizing effect of ideology in the world today. "Our" Vietnamese, the South Vietnamese, were physically no different from the Vietcong and North Vietnamese, and they were better armed. But in the crunch, the Vietnamese who had a doctrine to believe in—a mixture of Marx, Lenin, and Mao with heavy doses of nationalism and anticolonialism—won against the Vietnamese who didn't have much to believe in. We tend to forget that more than two centuries ago Americans were quite ideological, too, and—imbued with a passion for freedom and self-rule, via the pens of John Locke and Thomas Paine—beat a larger and better-equipped army of Englishmen and Hessians, who had no good reason to fight. Now we are aghast at the fanatics of a new ideology, Islamism.

Ideologies never work precisely the way their advocates claim. Some are hideous failures. All ideologies contain wishful thinking, which frequently collapses in the face of reality. Ideologues claim they can perfect the world; reality is highly imperfect. The **classic liberalism** of Adam Smith did contribute to the nineteenth century's economic growth, but it also led to great inequalities of wealth and recurring depressions. It was modified into modern liberalism. Communism led to brutal tyrannies, economic failures, and collapse. China quietly abandoned Maoism in favor of rapid economic growth. Ideologies, when measured against their actual performance, are more or less defective and should all be taken with a grain of salt.

THE MAJOR IDEOLOGIES

Classic Liberalism

Frederick Watkins of Yale called 1776 "the Year One of the Age of Ideology"— and not just for the American Revolution. That same year, Scottish economist Adam Smith published *The Wealth of Nations*, thereby founding classic laissez-faire economics. The true wealth of nations, Smith argued, is not in the amount of gold and silver they amass but in the amount of goods and services their people produce. Smith was refuting an earlier notion, called *mercantilism*, that the bullion in a nation's treasury determined its wealth. Spain had looted the New World of gold and silver but grew poorer. The French, too, since at least Louis XIV in the previous century, had followed mercantilist policies by means of government supervision of the economy with plans, grants of monopoly, subsidies, tariffs, and other restraints on trade.

Smith reasoned that this was not the path to prosperity. Government interference retards growth. If you give one firm a monopoly to manufacture something, you banish competition and, with it, efforts to produce new products and lower prices. The economy stagnates. If you protect domestic industry by tariffs, you take away incentives for better or cheaper products. By getting the government out of the economy, by leaving the economy alone (*laissez-faire*, in French), you promote prosperity.

Many ideologies stem from political theories. Classic liberalism traces back to the seventeenth-century English philosopher John Locke, who emphasized individual rights, property, and reason. Communism traces back to the early nineteenth-century German philosopher G. W. F. Hegel, who emphasized that all facets of a society—art, music, architecture, politics, law, and so on—hang together as a package, all the expression of an underlying *Zeitgeist*.

The philosophers' ideas, however, are simplified and popularized. Ideologists want plans for action, not abstract ideas. Marx, for example, "stood Hegel on his head" to make economics the great underlying cause. Most ideologies have a large economic component, for it is economics that will improve society. Lenin later stood Marx on his head to make his ideas apply to a backward country where Marx doubted they should. Mao Zedong then applied Lenin's ideas to an even more backward country, where they did not fit at all. Ideologies become warped.

One ideology gives rise to others (see figure below). Starting with the classic liberalism of Adam Smith, we see how liberalism branched leftward into radical, socialist, and communist directions. Meanwhile, on the conservative side, it branched rightward.

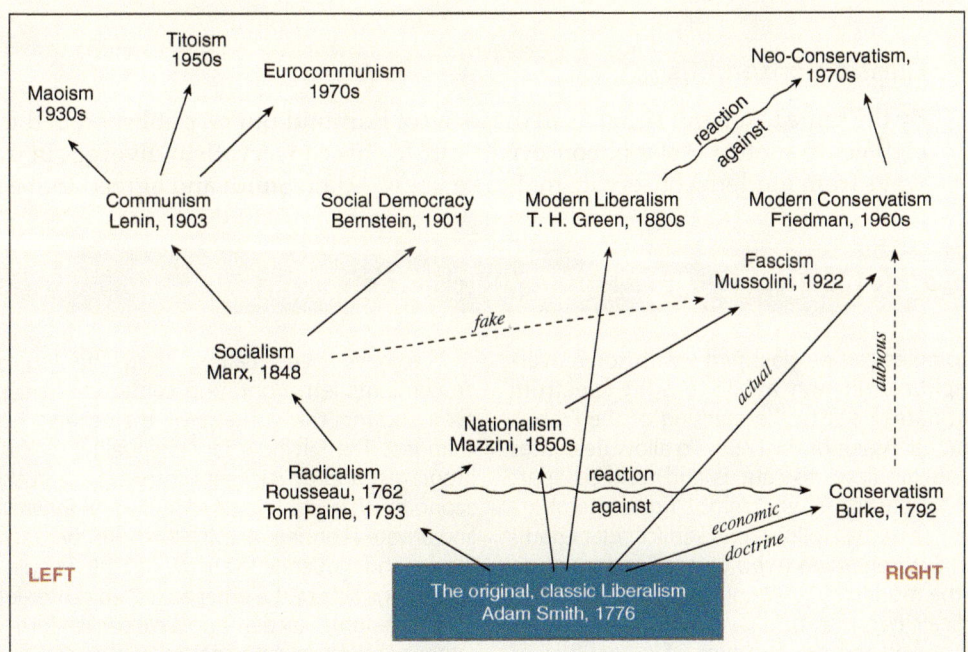

Figure 1
How political ideologies relate to one another: key thinkers and dates of emergence.

383

conservatism Ideology of keeping systems largely unchanged.

But won't free competition unsupervised by government lead to chaos? No, said Smith; the market itself will regulate the economy. Efficient producers will prosper and inefficient ones will go under. Supply and demand determine prices better than any government official. In the free marketplace, an "unseen hand" regulates and self-corrects the economy. If people want more of something, producers increase output, new producers enter the field, or foreign producers bring in their wares. The unseen hand—actually, the rational calculations of myriad individuals and firms all pursuing their self-interest—micro-adjusts the economy with no government help.

This ideology took the name liberalism from the Latin word for "free," *liber*: Society should be as free as possible from government interference. As aptly summarized by Thomas Jefferson, "That government is best that governs least." Americans took to classic liberalism like a duck takes to water. It fit the needs of a vigorous, freedom-loving population with plenty of room to expand. Noneconomic liberty also suited Americans. Government should also not supervise religion, the press, or free speech.

But, you say, what you're calling liberalism here is actually what Americans today call conservatism. True. In the late nineteenth century, liberalism changed and split into modern liberalism and what we now call conservatism, which we will discuss next. To keep our terminology straight, we call the original ideas of Adam Smith "classic liberalism" to distinguish it from the modern variety.

Classic Conservatism

By the same token, we should call the ideas of Edmund Burke, published in the late eighteenth century, "classic conservatism," for his **conservatism** diverges in many ways from modern conservatism. Burke knew Adam Smith and agreed that a free

KEY CONCEPTS ■ CLASSIFYING IDEOLOGIES

Ideologies can be classified—with some oversimplification—on a left-to-right spectrum that dates back to the meeting of the French National Assembly in 1789. To allow delegates of similar views to caucus and to keep apart strong partisans who might fight, members were seated as follows in a semicircular chamber: Conservatives (who favored continuation of the monarchy) were on the speaker's right, radicals (who favored sweeping away the old system altogether in favor of a republic of freedom and equality) were seated to his left, and moderates (who wanted some change) were seated in the center.

We have been calling their ideological descendants left, right, and center ever since, even though the content of their views has changed. The left now favors equality, welfare programs, and government intervention in the economy. The right stresses individual initiative and private economic activity. Centrists try to synthesize and moderate the views of both. People a little to one side or the other are called center-left or center-right. Sweden's political parties form a rather neat left-to-right spectrum: a small Communist party; a large Social Democratic party; and medium-sized Center (formerly Farmers'), Liberal, Christian, and Conservative parties.

market was the best economic system. Burke also opposed crushing the rebellious American colonists; after all, they were only trying to regain the ancient freedoms of Englishmen, said Burke. So far, Burke sounds like a liberal.

But Burke strongly objected to the way liberal ideas were applied in France by revolutionists. There, liberalism turned into *radicalism*, influenced by philosopher Jean-Jacques Rousseau and, fresh from the U.S. revolution, Thomas Paine. As is often the case, an ideology devised in one place becomes warped when applied to different circumstances. Liberalism in America was easy; once the English and their Tory sympathizers cleared out, it fell into place without resistance. But in France, a large aristocratic class and a state-supported Roman Catholic Church had a lot to lose. The revolutionaries tried to solve the problem with the guillotine and swept away all established institutions.

This, warned Burke, was a terrible mistake. Liberals place too much confidence in human reason. People are only partly rational; they also have irrational passions. To contain them, society over the years has evolved traditions, institutions, and standards of morality, such as the monarchy and an established church. Sweep these aside, said Burke, and man's irrational impulses lead to chaos, which in turn ends in tyranny far worse than the old system. Burke, in his 1792 *Reflexions on the Revolution in France*, predicted that France would fall into military dictatorship. In 1799, Napoleon took over.

Institutions and traditions that currently exist cannot be all bad, Burke reasoned, for they are the products of hundreds of years of trial and error. People have become used to them. The best should be preserved or "conserved" (hence the name conservatism). They are not perfect, but they work. This is not to say that things should never change. Of course they should change, said Burke, but only gradually, giving people time to adjust. "A state without the means of some change is without the means of its conservation," he wrote.

Burke was an important thinker for several reasons. He helped discover the *irrational* in human behavior. He saw that institutions are like living things; they grow and adapt over time. And, most important, he saw that revolutions end badly, for society cannot be instantly remade according to human reason. Although Burke's ideas have been called an *anti-ideology*—for they aimed to shoot down the radicalism then engulfing France—they have considerable staying power. Burke's emphasis on religion, traditions, and morality has been taken over by modern conservatives. His doubts about applying reason to solve social problems were echoed by political scientist Jeane Kirkpatrick, President Reagan's UN ambassador, who found that leftists always suppose that things can be much better when in fact violent upheaval always makes things worse. In these ways, classic conservatism is very much alive.

Modern Liberalism

What happened to the original, classic liberalism of Adam Smith? By the late nineteenth century, it was clear that the free market was not as self-regulating as Smith had thought. Competition was imperfect. Manufacturers rigged the market—a point Smith himself had warned about. There was a drift to bigness

modern liberalism Ideology favoring government intervention to correct economic and social ills; U.S. liberalism today.

and fewness: monopoly. The system produced a large underclass of the terribly poor (which Dickens depicted). Class positions were largely inherited; children of better-off families got the education and connections to stay on top. Bouts of speculative investing led to recurring economic depressions—2008–2009 is just the most recent example—which especially hurt the poor and the working class. In short, the laissez-faire economy created some problems.

The Englishman Thomas Hill Green rethought liberalism in the 1880s. The goal of liberalism, reasoned Green, was a free society. But what happens when economic developments take away freedom? The classic liberals placed great store in contracts (agreements between consenting parties with no government supervision): If you don't like the deal, don't take it. But what if the bargaining power of the two parties is greatly unequal, as between a rich employer and a poor person desperate for a job? Does the latter really have a free choice in accepting or rejecting a job with very low wages? Classic liberalism said let it be; wages will find their own level. But what if the wage is below starvation level? Here, Green said, it was time for government to step in. In such a case, it would not be a question of government infringing on freedoms but of government protecting them. Instead of the purely negative "freedom from," there had to be a certain amount of the positive "freedom to." Green called this *positive freedom*. Government was to step in to guarantee the freedom to live at an adequate level.

Classic liberalism expelled government from the marketplace; **modern liberalism** brought it back in, this time to protect people from a sometimes unfair economic system. Modern liberals championed wage and hour laws, the right to form unions, unemployment and health insurance, and improved educational opportunities. To do this, they placed heavier taxes on the rich than on the working class. They also regulated banking and finance to dampen the boom-and-bust cycle. This is the liberalism of the United States over the last century—the liberalism of Woodrow Wilson, Franklin D. Roosevelt, and Barack Obama. One strand of the old liberalism remains in the new, however: the emphasis on freedom of speech and press.

Modern Conservatism

What happened to the other branch of liberalism, the people who stayed true to Adam Smith's original doctrine of minimal government? They are still very important, only today we call them conservatives. (In Europe, they still call them liberals or *neoliberals*, much to the confusion of Americans.) American conservatives got a big boost from Milton Friedman (1912–2006), a Nobel Prize–winning economist. Friedman argued that the free market is still the best, that Adam Smith was right, and that wherever government intervenes, it messes things up. Margaret Thatcher in Britain and Ronald Reagan in the United States applied this revival of classic liberalism in the 1980s with mixed but generally positive results.

Modern conservatism also borrows from Edmund Burke a concern for tradition, especially in religion. American conservatives would put prayer into public schools, outlaw abortion and same-sex marriage, and support private and church-related schools. Modern conservatives also oppose special rights for women and minority groups, arguing that everyone should have the same rights. Modern conservatism is a blend of the economic ideas of Adam Smith and the traditionalist ideas of Edmund Burke.

Marxist Socialism

Liberalism (classic variety) dominated the nineteenth century, but critics deplored the growing gulf between rich and poor. Unlike T. H. Green, some did not believe that a few reforms would suffice; they wanted to overthrow the capitalist system. These were the socialists, and their leading thinker was Karl Marx. Marx wrote not as a scholar but to promote revolution. He hated the "bourgeoisie" long before he developed his elaborate theories that they were doomed. An outline of his ideas appeared in his 1848 pamphlet, *The Communist Manifesto*, which concluded with the ringing words: "The proletarians have nothing to lose but their chains. They have a world to win. Workers of all countries, unite!" Marx participated in organizing Europe's first socialist parties.

Marx's *Capital* was a gigantic analysis of why capitalism would be overthrown by the proletariat. Then would come socialism, a just, productive society without class distinctions. Later, at a certain stage when industrial production was very high, this socialist society will turn into *communism*, a perfect society without police, money, or even government. Goods will be in such plenty that people will just take what they need. There will be no private property, so there will be no need for police. Because government is simply an instrument of class domination, with the abolition of distinct classes there will be no need for the state. It will "wither away." Communism, then, was the predicted utopia beyond socialism.

Marx focused on the ills and malfunctions of capitalism and never specified what socialism would be like. He only said that socialism would be much better than capitalism; its precise workings he left vague. This has enabled a wide variety of socialist thinkers to put forward their own vision of socialism and say it is what Marx really meant. This has ranged from the mild "welfarism" of social-democratic parties, to *anarcho-syndicalism* (unions running everything), to Lenin's and Stalin's hypercentralized tyranny, to Trotsky's denunciation of same, to Mao's self-destructive permanent revolution, to Tito's experimental decentralized system. All, and a few more, claim to espouse "real" socialism. These different interpretations of socialism caused first the socialist and then the communist movement to splinter.

Social Democracy

By the beginning of the twentieth century, the German Social Democrats (SPD), espousing Marxism, had become Germany's biggest party. Marx had disparaged conventional parties and labor unions; bourgeois governments would simply crush them. At most, they could be training grounds for serious revolutionary action. But the German Social Democrats started succeeding. They got elected to the Reichstag

This statue of Karl Marx and Friedrich Engels, key figures in the Communist movement, presides over a park in Berlin named in their honor. (Dallas and John Heaton/Corbis)

and local offices; their unions won higher wages and better working conditions. Some began to think that the working class could accomplish its aims without revolution. Why use bullets when there are ballots?

Eduard Bernstein developed this view. In his *Evolutionary Socialism* (1901), he pointed out the real gains the working class was making and concluded that Marx had been wrong about the collapse of capitalism and revolution. Reforms that won concrete benefits for the working class could also lead to socialism, he argued. In revising Marxism, Bernstein earned the name **revisionist**, originally a pejorative hurled at him by orthodox Marxists. By the time of the ill-fated Weimar Republic in Germany (1919–1933), the Social Democrats had toned down their militancy and worked together with Liberals and Catholics to try to save democracy. Persecuted by the Nazis, the SPD revived after World War II and in 1959 dropped Marxism altogether, as did virtually all social democratic parties. As social democrats in many countries moderated their positions, they got elected more and more. They transformed themselves into center-left parties with no trace of revolution.

revisionist Changing an ideology or view of history.

social democracy Mildest form of socialism, stressing welfare measures but not state ownership of industry.

What, then, do **social democrats** stand for? They have abandoned the state ownership of industry. Only about 10 percent of Sweden's industry is state-owned, and much of that conservatives did long ago to keep firms from going under and creating unemployment. Said Olof Palme, Sweden's Social Democratic prime minister, "If industry's primary purpose is to expand its production, to succeed in new markets, to provide good jobs for their employees, they need have no fears. Swedish industry has never expanded so rapidly as during these years of Social Democratic rule." Instead of state ownership of industry, social democrats use *welfare* measures to improve living conditions: unemployment and medical insurance, generous pensions, and subsidized food and housing. Social democracies have become welfare states: *Welfarism* would be a more accurate term than *socialism*.

> **communism** Marxist theory merged with Leninist organization into a totalitarian party.
>
> **imperialism** Amassing of colonial empires, mostly by European powers; pejorative in Marxist terms.

There's one catch—there's always at least one catch—and that is that welfare states are terribly expensive. To pay for welfare measures, taxes climb. In Denmark and Sweden, taxes consume about half of the gross domestic product (GDP), exactly the kind of thing Milton Friedman warned about. With those kinds of taxes, soon you are not free to choose how you live. U.S. liberalism is tinged with social democratic ideas on welfare. The left wing of our Democratic Party resembles ideologically the moderate wings of European social democratic parties.

Communism

While the social democrats evolved into reformists and welfarists, a smaller wing of the original socialists stayed Marxist and became the Communists. The key figure in this transformation was a Russian intellectual, Vladimir I. Lenin. He made several changes in Marxism, producing *Marxism-Leninism*, another name for **communism**.

Imperialism Many Russian intellectuals of the late nineteenth century hated the tsarist system and embraced Marxism as a way to overthrow tsarism. But Marx meant his theory to apply in the most advanced capitalist countries, not in backward Russia, where capitalism was just beginning. Lenin, in his 17-year exile in Switzerland, remade Marxism to fit the Russian situation. He offered a theory of economic imperialism, one borrowed from German revolutionary Rosa Luxemburg and English economist J. A. Hobson, who wondered why the proletarian revolutions Marx had predicted had not broken out in the advanced industrialized lands. They concluded that the domestic market could not absorb all the goods the capitalist system produced, so it found overseas markets. Capitalism had transformed itself, expanding overseas into colonies to exploit their raw materials, cheap labor, and new markets. Capitalism thus won a temporary new lease on life by turning into **imperialism**. With profits from its colonies, the mother imperialist country could also pay off its working class a bit to render it reformist rather than revolutionary.

Imperialism had to expand, Lenin argued, but it was growing unevenly. Some countries, such as Britain and Germany, were highly developed, but where capitalism was just starting, as in Spain and Russia, it was weak. The newly industrializing countries were exploited as a whole by the international capitalist system. It was in them that revolutionary fever burned brightest; they were "imperialism's weakest link." Accordingly, a revolution could break out in a poor country, reasoned Lenin, and then spread into advanced countries. The imperialist countries were highly dependent on their empires. Once cut off from exploiting them, capitalism would fall. World War I, wrote Lenin, was the collision of imperialists trying to dominate the globe.

Lenin shifted the Marxian focus from the situation within capitalist countries to the global situation. The focus went from Marx's proletariat rising up against the bourgeoisie to exploited nations rising up against imperialist powers. Marx would probably not have endorsed such a redo of his theory.

Organization   Lenin's real contribution lay in his attention to organization. With the tsarist secret police always on their trail, Lenin argued, the Russian socialist party could not be like other parties—large, open, and trying to win votes. Instead, it had to be small, secretive, made up of professional revolutionaries, and tightly organized under central command. In 1903, the Russian Social Democratic Labor party split over this issue. Lenin had enough supporters at the party's Brussels meeting to win the votes of 33 of the 51 delegates present. Lenin called his faction *bolshevik* (Russian for "majority"). The losers, who advocated a more moderate line and a more open party, took the name *menshevik* ("minority"). In 1918, the Bolsheviks changed the party name to Communist.

Lenin's attention to organization paid off. Russia was in chaos from World War I. In March 1917, a group of moderates seized power from the tsar, but they were unable to govern the country. In November, the Bolsheviks shrewdly manipulated councils (*soviets* in Russian) that had sprung up in the leading cities and seized control from the moderates. After winning a desperate civil war, Lenin called on all true socialists around the world to join in a new international movement under Moscow's control. It was called the Communist International, or *Comintern*. Almost all socialist parties in the world split; their left wings went into the Comintern and became Communist parties in 1920–1921. The resultant social democratic and Communist parties have been hostile to each other ever since.

How much Marxism-Leninism did the rulers of the Soviet Union really believe? They constantly used Marxist rhetoric, but many observers argued they were cynical about ideology and just used it as window dressing. The Soviets never defined their society as Communist—that was yet to come; it was what they were working on. It is we in the West who called these countries "Communist." In 1961, party chief Nikita Khrushchev rashly predicted "communism in our generation," indicating that utopia would be reached by 1980. Instead, it declined, and at the end of 1991, the Soviet system collapsed.

Maoism and Titoism   In the 1930s, Mao Zedong concluded that the Chinese Communist Party (CCP) had to be based on poor peasants and guerrilla warfare. This was a break with Stalin's leadership, and after decades of fighting, the CCP took over mainland China in 1949. Mao pursued a radical course that included a failed attempt at overnight industrialization (the Great Leap Forward of 1958), the destruction of bureaucratic authority (the Proletarian Cultural Revolution in 1966–1976), and even border fighting with the Soviet Union in 1969. After Mao's death in 1976, pragmatic leaders moved China away from his extremism, which had ruined China's economic progress. A few revolutionary groups stayed Maoist: Cambodia's murderous Khmer Rouge and India's Naxalites. **Maoism** is an ultraradical form of communism.

Maoism Extreme form of communism, featuring guerrilla warfare and periodic upheavals.

Titoism Mild, decentralized form of communism.

nationalism A people's heightened sense of cultural, historical, and territorial identity, unity, and sometimes greatness.

Yugoslav party chief Josip Tito went the other way, developing a more moderate and liberal form of communism. Even though Tito's partisans fought the Germans in Stalin's name, Stalin did not fully control Tito, and in 1948 Stalin had Yugoslavia kicked out of the Communist camp. During the 1950s, the Yugoslav Communists reformed their system, basing it on decentralization, debureaucratization, and worker self-management. Trying to find a middle ground between a market and a controlled economy, Yugoslavia suffered economic problems in the 1980s. **Titoism** might have served as a warning to Communist rulers who wanted to experiment with "middle ways" between capitalism and socialism. The combination is unstable and worked only because Tito was undisputed ruler; when he died in 1980, Yugoslavia started coming apart until, by the early 1990s, it was a bloodbath.

Nationalism

The real winner among ideologies—one that still dominates today—is **nationalism**, the exaggerated belief in the greatness and unity of one's country. Nationalism is often born out of occupation and repression by foreigners. "We won't be pushed around by foreigners any more!" shout Cuban, Palestinian, Iraqi, Chinese, and many other nationalists. Nationalism has triumphed over and influenced all other ideologies, so that, in the United States, conservatism is combined with American nationalism, and, in China, nationalism was always more important than communism.

The first seeds of nationalism came with the Renaissance monarchs who proclaimed their absolute power and the unity and greatness of their kingdoms. Nationality was born out of sovereignty. *Nationalism*, however, appeared only with the French Revolution, which was based on "the people" and heightened French feelings about themselves as a special, leading people destined to free the rest of Europe. When a Prussian army invaded France in 1792, the "nation in arms" stopped them at Valmy; enthusiastic volunteers beat professional soldiers. The stirring "Marseillaise," France's national anthem, appeared that year.

Later, Napoleon's legions ostensibly spread the radical liberalism of the French Revolution but were really spreading nationalism. The conquered nations of Europe quickly grew to hate the arrogant French occupiers. Spaniards, Germans, and Russians soon became nationalistic themselves as they struggled to expel the French. Basic to nationalism is resentment of foreign domination, be it by British redcoats, Napoleon's legions, or European colonialists. Nationalism blanketed Europe in the nineteenth century and, in the twentieth century, spread to Europe's colonies throughout the world. It is in the developing countries that nationalism is now most intense.

By the mid–nineteenth century, thinkers all over Europe—especially in Germany and Italy—defined the nation as the ultimate human value, the source of all things good. Italian writer Giuseppe Mazzini espoused freedom not for individuals—that was mere liberalism—but for nations instead. One achieved true freedom by subordinating oneself to the nation. Education, for example, had to inculcate a sense of nationalism that blotted out individualism, argued Mazzini.

Nationalism arises when a population, invariably led by intellectuals, perceives an enemy or "other" to despise and struggle against. In the twentieth century, this has often been a colonial power such as Britain, France, or the Netherlands, against whom, respectively, Indians, Algerians, and Indonesians could rally in their fight for independence. Nationalism holds that it is terribly wrong to be ruled by others. Thus, Bosnian Serbs do not consent to be ruled by Bosnian Muslims, Palestinians by Israelis, and Lithuanians by Russians. Some Chinese and Iranians, feeling they have been repressed and controlled by outside powers, lash out with nationalistic military and diplomatic policies. Even some Canadians, fearful of U.S. economic and cultural dominance, turn nationalistic.

The big problem with nationalism is that it tends to lead to economic isolation. "We won't let foreigners take over our economy!" say nationalists, but rapid economic growth needs foreign investment and world trade. More than any of the previous ideologies, nationalism depends on emotional appeals. The feeling of belonging to a nation goes to our psychological center. What other human organization would we fight and kill for?

Regional Nationalism   In recent decades, the world has seen the rise of another kind of nationalism: regional nationalism, which aims at breaking up existing nations into what its proponents argue are the true nations. Militant Québécois want

---

HOW TO . . . ■ SUPPORT YOUR THESIS

"Well, that's what I think" isn't good enough. Writing a paper is like a lawyer making a case. Like a judge, your instructor decides if your evidence is valid and supports your point. In a short paper, you might back up your thesis with three to five supporting elements. You may wish to use subheads, little titles in the middle of your paper, to separate your supporting arguments. Subheads help you structure your ideas and make the paper easier to read and understand. If you cannot support your thesis with facts, numbers, quotes, or just plain reasoning, abandon or change it. As they say in the news business: "Back it up or back off."

Boldfaced and Centered

Boldface and center your subheads (like the above subhead) to make them stand out. A new subhead indicates you are moving on to another supporting element. A paragraph is one thought or point. Make about three of them per double-spaced page. A paragraph that rambles on for a whole page is hard to read. Have no more than one subhead per page. For example, if your thesis is that a sour economy hurts incumbent presidents in elections, you might make a subhead for each election: "The 2004 Elections," "The 2008 Elections," and so on. A five-page paper may have about three subheads, indicating you are supporting your thesis with three elements.

to separate from Canada, Basques from Spain, South Ossetians from Georgia, and Scots from Britain. It too is based on hatred of being ruled by unlike peoples.

fascism Extreme form of nationalism with elements of socialism and militarism.

Fascism

In Italy and Germany nationalism grew into **fascism**, one of the great catastrophes of the twentieth century. One sign of a fascist movement is members in uniforms; they like military structure and discipline. Before World War I, Italian journalist Benito Mussolini was a fire-breathing socialist; military service changed him into an ardent nationalist. Italy was full of discontented people after World War I. "Maximalist" socialists threatened revolution. In those chaotic times, Mussolini assembled a strange collection of people in black shirts who wanted to end democracy and political parties and impose stern central authority and discipline. These Fascists—a word taken from the ancient Roman symbol of authority, a bundle of sticks bound around an ax (the *fasces*)—hated disorder and wanted strong leadership to end it.

Amid growing disorder in 1922, the king of Italy handed power to Mussolini, and by 1924 he had turned Italy into a one-party state with himself as *Duce* (leader). The Fascists ran the economy by inserting their men into all key positions. Italy looked impressive: There was little crime, much monumental construction, stable prices, and, as they used to say, "The trains ran on time." Behind the scenes, however, fascism was a mess, with hidden unemployment, poor economic performance, and corruption.

With the collapse of the world economy in 1929, however, some thought fascism was the wave of the future. Adolf Hitler in Germany copied Mussolini's fascism but had his followers wear brown shirts and added *racism*. For Hitler, it was not just Germans as a nation who were fighting the punitive and unfair Versailles Treaty and chaos of the Weimar Republic; it was Germans as a distinct and superior race. Hitler did not invent German racism, which went back generations, but he hyped it. The racist line held that a special branch of the white race, the Aryans, were the bearers of all civilization. A subbranch, the Nordics, which included Germans, were even better. (Actually, Germans are of very mixed genealogy.) Nazis argued that the superior Nordics were being subjugated to the sinister forces of Judaism, communism, world capitalism, and even Roman Catholicism. This doctrine was the basis for the death camps.

Hitler was named chancellor (prime minister) in 1933 in a situation of turmoil and, like Mussolini, within two years had perfected a dictatorship. Probably a majority of Germans supported Hitler. With Nazis "coordinating" the economy, unemployment ended and many working people felt they were getting a good deal with the jobs, vacations, and welfare the regime provided. The Nazis' full name was the National Socialist German Workers Party, but the socialism was fake. Hitler's true aim was war, as war builds heroes. For a few years, Hitler dominated Europe and started turning the Slavic lands of Eastern Europe into colonies for Germans—*Lebensraum* (living space). Nazi death camps killed some 6 million Jews and a similar number of Christians who were in the way. Was Hitler mad? Many of his views

neoconservatism U.S. ideology of former liberals turning to conservative causes and methods.

were widely held among Germans, and he had millions of enthusiastic helpers. Rather than insanity, the Nazis demonstrated the danger of nationalism run amok.

The word *fascist* has been overused and misused. Some hurl it at everything they dislike. Spanish dictator Francisco Franco, for example, was long considered a fascist, but he was actually a "traditional authoritarian," for he tried to minimize mass political involvement rather than stir it up the way Mussolini and Hitler did. Brazilian President Getúlio Vargas decreed a fascist-sounding "New State" in 1937, but he was merely borrowing some fascist rhetoric at a time when the movement was having its heyday in Europe. Some right-wing American commentators denounce "Islamofascists."

The Ku Klux Klan in the United States is sometimes called fascist, and its members wear uniforms. The Klan's populist racism is similar to the Nazis', but the Klan strongly opposes the power of the national government, whereas the Nazis and Fascists worshipped it. Now some European anti-immigrant parties are tinged with fascism. Hungary's immigrant-hating Jobbik Party, for example, parades in uniform.

IDEOLOGY IN OUR DAY

The Collapse of Communism

By the 1980s, communism the world over was ideologically exhausted. Few people in China, Eastern Europe, and even the Soviet Union believed in it any longer. In the non-Communist world, leftists deserted Marxism in droves. Several West European Communist parties embraced "Eurocommunism," a greatly watered-down ideology that renounced dictatorship and state ownership of industry. Capitalism was supposed to have collapsed; instead, it was thriving in the United States, Western Europe, and East Asia. Many Communist leaders admitted that their economies were too rigid and centralized and that the cure lay in cutting back state controls in favor of free enterprise. Reform-minded Soviet President Mikhail Gorbachev (1985–1991) offered a three-pronged approach to revitalizing Soviet communism: *glasnost* (media openness), *perestroika* (economic restructuring), and *demokratizatzia* (democratization). Applied haltingly and half-heartedly, the reforms only heightened discontent, for now Soviets could voice their complaints. Starting in Eastern Europe in 1989, non-Communist parties took over. In the Soviet Union, a partially free parliament was elected and began debating change. Non-Communist parties and movements appeared. Gorbachev still could not make up his mind how far and fast reforms should go, and the economy, barely reformed, turned wildly inflationary. A 1991 coup failed, and, by the end of the year, the Soviet Union had ceased to exist.

Neoconservatism

In the 1970s, a new ideology emerged in the United States: **neoconservatism**, much of it from disillusioned liberals and leftists. As neoconservative writer Irving Kristol put it, "A neoconservative is a liberal who's been mugged by reality." Neoconservatives charged that the Democratic Party had moved too far left with unrealistic ideas on domestic reforms and a pacifist foreign policy. Neoconservatives reacted against the Great Society programs introduced by Lyndon Johnson in the mid-1960s that aimed to wipe out poverty and discrimination. Some liberals said the Great Society was never given a chance because funds for it were siphoned away by the Vietnam War. But neocons said it worked badly, that many of the programs achieved nothing. The cities grew worse; educational standards declined; medical aid became extremely costly; and a class of welfare-dependent poor emerged, people who had little incentive to work. Neocons spoke of negative "unforeseen consequences" of well-intentioned liberal programs. Especially bothersome to neocons: Affirmative action gave racial minorities preferential treatment in hiring, sometimes ahead of better-qualified whites.

Many neoconservatives were horrified at the extreme relativism that had grown in the 1960s. Simplistic ideas—such as "It's all right if it feels good" and "It just depends on your point of view" and "multiculturalism"—drove many liberals to neoconservatism. Ironically, some neocons were college professors who had earlier tried to broaden their students' views by stressing the relativity of all viewpoints and cultures. Instead, students became vacuous. In the Bush 43 administration, highly placed neocons promoted war with Iraq both to protect the United States and to pull the Muslim world into democracy. Many old-fashioned Republican conservatives, who dislike overseas crusades, despised the neocons, and they faded from power and prominence.

> **libertarianism** U.S. ideology in favor of shrinking all government power in favor of individual freedom.
>
> **feminism** Ideology of psychological, political, and economic equality for women.

Libertarianism

Slowly growing since the 1960s is an ideology so liberal that it became conservative, or vice versa. **Libertarians** would return to the original Adam Smith, with essentially no government interference in anything. They would deliver what Republicans only talk about. They note that modern liberals want a controlled economy but personal freedom while modern conservatives want a free economy but constraints on personal freedom. Why not freedom in both areas? Libertarians oppose subsidies, bureaucracies, taxes, intervention overseas, and big government itself. As such, they plugged into a very old American tradition and gained respectability. Although no Libertarian candidates won elections, their Cato Institute in Washington became a lively think tank whose ideas could not be ignored. (One Cato paper deplored cities building light rail systems when buses are better and cheaper. The paper's title: "A Desire Named Streetcar.") Some critics blame libertarian worship of unregulated markets for the reckless deals that produced the 2008–2009 financial meltdown.

Feminism

Springing to new life in the 1960s with a handful of female writers, by the 1970s the women's movement had become a political force in the United States and Western Europe. **Feminist** writers pointed out that women were paid less than men, were not

environmentalism Ideology that environment is endangered and must be preserved through regulation and lifestyle changes.

promoted, were psychologically and physically abused by men, were denied loans and insurance, and were in general second-class citizens.

The root problem was psychological, argued feminists. Women and men were forced into "gender roles" that had little to do with biology. Boys were conditioned to be tough, domineering, competitive, and "macho," and girls were taught to be meek, submissive, unsure of themselves, and "feminine." Gender differences are almost entirely learned behavior, taught by parents and schools of a "patriarchal" society, but this could be changed. With proper child rearing and education, males could become gentler and females more assertive and self-confident.

Feminists joined "consciousness-raising" groups and railed against "male chauvinist pigs." Feminism started having an impact. Many employers gave women a fairer chance, sometimes hiring them over men. Women moved up to higher management positions (although seldom to the corporate top). Working wives became the norm. Husbands shared in homemaking and child rearing. With more women going to college than men, many male-dominated professions—medicine, law, business—saw an influx of women.

Politically, however, feminists did not achieve all they wished. The Equal Rights Amendment (ERA) to the Constitution failed to win ratification by enough state legislatures. It would have guaranteed equality of treatment regardless of gender. Antifeminists, some of them conservative women, argued that the ERA would take away women's privileges and protections under the law, would make women eligible for the draft, and would even lead to unisex lavatories. Despite this setback, women learned that there was one way they could count for a lot politically—by voting. In the 1980 election, a significant "gender gap" appeared, and now women generally vote more Democratic than do men.

Environmentalism

Also during the 1960s, **environmentalism** began to ripple through the advanced industrialized countries. Economic development paid little heed to the damage it did to the environment. Any growth was good growth: "We'll never run out of nature." Mining, factories, and even farms poisoned streams; industries and automobiles polluted the air; chemical wastes made areas uninhabitable; and nuclear power leaked radioactivity. To the credo of "growth," environmentalists responded with "limits." They argued, "We can't go on like this without producing environmental catastrophe." Love Canal, Three Mile Island, and Chernobyl seemed to prove them right. The burning of fossil fuels and rain forests increases CO_2 that may trap heat inside the earth's atmosphere and change climates.

The ecologists' demands were only partly satisfied with the founding of the Environmental Protection Agency (EPA) in 1970. Industrial groups argued that EPA regulations restricted growth and ate into profits; under Republican presidents, the EPA was rendered ineffective. Energy production had to take first place over pristine environments, they argued.

Regulation was only part of the environmental credo. Many argued that consumption patterns and lifestyles in the advanced countries should change to conserve the earth's resources, natural beauty, and clean air and water. Americans, only about 4 percent of the world's population, consume a fourth of the world's manufactured goods and energy. In addition to being out of balance with the poor nations of the world, this profligate lifestyle is unnecessary and unhealthy, they argued. "Greens" urged public transportation and bicycles instead of cars, whole-grain foods and vegetables instead of meat, and decentralized, renewable energy sources, such as wind and solar energy, instead of fossil- or nuclear-fueled power plants.

Some environmentalists formed political parties, first the Citizens Party, then the Greens, but their main impact was within the two big parties, neither of which could ignore the environmental vote. In Western Europe in the 1980s, especially in Germany and Sweden, Green parties were elected to parliament, determined to end

Islamism Muslim religion turned into a political ideology.

COMPARING ■ ISLAMISM: A NEW IDEOLOGY WITH OLD ROOTS

Islamism illustrates how an ideology can suddenly arise by combining older elements. *Salafiyya*, or Islamic fundamentalism, started in the thirteenth century with a call to return to the pure ways of the Prophet and is the founding and current faith of Saudi Arabia. Al Qaeda is a *salafi* movement. Islamism exploded in 1979 with the Iranian revolution and the Soviet invasion of Afghanistan.

Islamism is an angry blend of religion, nationalism, socialism, and a "rage against modernity" that had long been brewing in the Muslim world. With America in the lead, Islamists argue, the West erodes Islamic morals and culture, subjugates the region economically (oil), and steals Islamic holy land (Israel). Some of this traces back to centuries of antipathy between Christendom and Islam, some to the frustrations of modernization. Islamism grows with rapid population increases and high unemployment and in reaction to corruption and misrule in Muslim countries.

Islamism resembles nationalism, but in Islam the political was always intertwined with the religious. Mosque and state are to be one. The Prophet Muhammad founded Islam as one giant community, the *umma*, that disdains nations as forms of idolatry. Accordingly, Osama bin Laden and his followers were uninterested in Palestinian or Iraqi nationalism except to use it on their march to a Muslim empire. Islamists seek to oust U.S. influence, destroy Israel, and take over all Muslim countries and eventually the world. Then a purified Islam will share the wealth now concentrated in the hands of a few corrupt rulers, a sort of socialism. Fanatic and uncompromising, Islamists jolted the world with terrorism. Some Muslim countries—Pakistan and Saudi Arabia among them—fearing Islamist overthrow, attempt to buy them off.

Islamism has several weaknesses. First, it is split between *Sunni* and *Shia* branches of Islam. Sunni is mainstream Islam, accounting for some 90 percent of the world's Muslims, but Shias dominate Iran and parts of Iraq, Saudi Arabia, Lebanon, and elsewhere. Sunnis despise and mistrust Shias. Second, Islamism, which has no economic plan, cannot put food on the table, something many Iranians now complain about. And most importantly, the Muslim extremists' indiscriminate murder of fellow Muslims has turned many Muslims against it, and Islamism has begun to fade.

nuclear power, toxic waste, and war. Many young Europeans found the Greens an attractive alternative to the old and stodgy conventional parties.

IS IDEOLOGY FINISHED?

In 1960, Harvard sociologist Daniel Bell argued that the century-long ideological debates were coming to a close. The failure of tyrannical communism and the rise of the welfare state were producing what Bell called the "end of ideology": There simply was not much to quarrel about. Henceforth, political debate would focus on almost technical questions of how to run the welfare state, said Bell, such as what to include under national health insurance. In 1989, political scientist Francis Fukuyama went even further: Not only had the great ideological debate ended with the victory of capitalist democracy, but also history itself could be ending. Widely misunderstood, Fukuyama did not mean that time would stand still but rather that the human endpoint propounded by Hegel—free people living in free societies—was now coming into view. Not only had we beaten communism, suggested Fukuyama, there were no longer any other ideologies to challenge ours. With the end of ideology would come the end of history in the sense of the struggle of great ideas. (Life could get boring, sighed the puckish Fukuyama.)

A glance at today's news makes one doubt the Bell and Fukuyama theses. First, the collapse of communism in Europe by itself did not disprove Marx's original ideas, although now Marxists carefully distance themselves from the Soviet type of socialism. (We use socialism here to mean state control of industry, not welfarism, which is just a variation on capitalist democracy.) Socialists still debate the possibility of a benign socialism. New and dangerous ideological challenges emerged just as communism collapsed: neofascism, breakaway nationalism, and Islamism. And within free democracy itself there are numerous ideological viewpoints: free market or government intervention, more welfare or less, a secular or religious state, and spreading democracy abroad or avoiding overseas involvement. Fukuyama need not worry about boredom.

mypoliscikit EXERCISES

Apply what you learned in this chapter on MyPoliSciKit (www.mypoliscikit.com).

 Assessment Review this chapter using learning objectives, chapter summaries, practice tests, and more.
Menu

Flashcards Learn the key terms in this chapter; you can test yourself by term or definition.
Flashcards

Video Analyze recent world affairs by watching streaming video from major news providers.
Videos

Comparative Exercises Compare political ideas, behaviors, institutions, and policies worldwide.
Comparative
Exercises

KEY TERMS

classic liberalism

communism

conservatism

environmentalism

fascism

feminism

ideologue

ideology

imperialism

Islamism

libertarianism

Maoism

modern liberalism

nationalism

neoconservatism

pragmatic

revisionist

social democracy

Titoism

FURTHER REFERENCE

Baradat, Leon P. *Political Ideologies: Their Origins and Impact*, 11th ed. New York: Longman, 2012.

Beer, Jeremy, Bruce Frohnen, and Jeffrey O. Nelson, eds. *American Conservatism: An Encyclopedia*. Wilmington, DE: ISI Books, 2006.

Bernstein, Andrew. *The Capitalist Manifesto: The Historic, Economic, and Philosophic Case for Laissez-Faire*. Lanham, MD: University Press of America, 2005.

Blumenthal, Max. *Republican Gomorrah: Inside the Movement That Shattered the Party*. New York: Basic Books, 2009.

Cohen, G. A. *Why Not Socialism?* Princeton, NJ: Princeton University Press, 2009.

Edwards, Mickey. *Reclaiming Conservatism: How a Great American Political Movement Got Lost—and How It Can Find Its Way Back*. New York: Oxford University Press, 2008.

Farber, David. *The Rise and Fall of Modern American Conservatism: A Short History*. Princeton, NJ: Princeton University Press, 2010.

Flynn, James R. *Where Have All the Liberals Gone? Race, Class, and Ideals in America*. New York: Cambridge University Press, 2008.

Frank, Thomas. *The Wrecking Crew: How Conservatives Rule*. New York: Metropolitan, 2008.

Frum, David. *Comeback: Conservatism That Can Win Again*. New York: Doubleday, 2009.

Goldwag, Arthur. *'Isms and 'Ologies: All the Movements, Ideologies, & Doctrines That Have Shaped Our World*. New York: Vintage, 2007.

Grosby, Steven. *Nationalism: A Very Short Introduction*. New York: Oxford University Press, 2005.

Heilbrunn, Jacob. *They Knew They Were Right: The Rise of the Neocons*. New York: Doubleday, 2008.

Krugman, Paul. *The Conscience of a Liberal*. New York: Norton, 2007.

Micklethwait, John, and Adrian Wooldridge. *The Right Nation: Conservative Power in America*. New York: Penguin, 2004.

Phares, Walid. *The War of Ideas: Jihadism against Democracy*. New York: Palgrave, 2007.

Sandle, Mark. *Communism*. New York: Longman, 2006.

Schmitt, Richard, ed. *Toward a New Socialism*. Lanham, MD: Lexington, 2007.

Schumpeter, Joseph A. *Can Capitalism Survive? Creative Destruction and the Future of the Global Economy*. New York: HarperCollins, 2009.

Snyder, Louis L. *The New Nationalism*. New Brunswick, NJ: Transaction, 2003.

Starr, Paul. *Freedom's Power: The True Force of Liberalism*. New York: Basic Books, 2008.

Sullivan, Andrew. *The Conservative Soul: How We Lost It, How to Get It Back*. New York: HarperCollins, 2007.

Tanenhaus, Sam. *The Death of Conservatism*. New York: Random House, 2009.

Walzer, Michael. *Politics and Passion: Toward a More Egalitarian Liberalism*. New Haven, CT: Yale University Press, 2004.

Wolfe, Alan. *The Future of Liberalism*. New York: Knopf Doubleday, 2010.

Economics

Economic Systems

LEARNING OBJECTIVES

1. Explain the concept of an economic system.
2. Describe how economic systems differ from one another.
3. Identify the elements of pure capitalism.
4. Draw and explain the circular-flow model of pure capitalism.
5. Explain how pure capitalism answers the three fundamental questions.
6. Discuss the strengths and weaknesses of pure capitalism.
7. Identify the elements of command socialism.
8. Draw and explain the pyramid model of command socialism.
9. Explain how command socialism answers the three fundamental questions.
10. Discuss the strengths and weaknesses of command socialism.
11. Explain why all real-world economies are mixed economies.

Every nation, from the richest to the poorest, faces the same economic dilemma: how to satisfy people's unlimited wants with its limited economic resources. Each society must decide which goods and services to produce, how to produce them, and for whom to produce them; in other words, it must establish an economic system. An **economic system** is a set of institutions and mechanisms for answering the three fundamental questions of economics—what, how, and for whom to produce.

In describing economic systems, it is helpful to ask two questions: (1) Who owns the means of production—the factories, farms, mines, and other resources used to produce goods and services? (2) Who makes the economic decisions; that is, who answers the three fundamental economic questions? The variety of real-world economic systems is probably as great as the number of world nations, but all economic systems combine elements of two divergent models. At one extreme, the means of production are privately owned, and individual buyers and sellers interacting in markets make the economic decisions. At the other extreme, the means of production are publicly owned, and a central authority makes the fundamental economic choices.

This chapter will begin by providing you with an overview of these two divergent models—the models of pure capitalism and pure command socialism. Models simplify reality, making it possible to see more clearly how the parts of a system function and interact. Once we have become familiar with how "pure" capitalism and "pure" command socialism would function, we can compare the U.S. economy and other selected economies against these theoretical models to discover how these real-world economic systems conform and how they deviate from the models.

THE MODEL OF PURE CAPITALISM

The *American Heritage Dictionary* defines something as *pure* if it is "free from impurities or contaminants." So pure capitalism is a hypothetical economic system that is totally or completely capitalist, one without traces of anything else. In this section we examine the elements of such a system, diagram its operation or functioning, see how it answers the three fundamental questions, and conclude by assessing its strengths and weaknesses.

Elements of Capitalism

We define **capitalism** as an economic system in which the means of production are privately owned and fundamental economic choices are made by individual buyers and sellers interacting in markets. The model of pure capitalism is entirely consistent with our definition and contains five basic elements, which we will describe briefly.

Private Property and Freedom of Choice
One of the principal features of capitalism is private property. In a capitalist economy, private individuals and groups are the owners of the **means of production**: the raw materials, factories, farms, and other economic resources used to produce goods and services. These resource owners may sell or use their resources, including their own labor, as they see fit. Businesses are free to decide what products they will produce and to purchase the necessary economic resources from whomever they choose. Consumers, in turn, are free to spend their incomes

any way they like. They can purchase whatever products they choose, and they can decide what fraction of their incomes to save and what fraction to spend.

Self-Interest

The driving force of capitalism is self-interest. In 1776 Adam Smith, the founder of economics, described a capitalist economy as one in which the primary concern of each player—of each producer, worker, and consumer—was to promote his or her own welfare.[1]

Smith introduced the **invisible hand** doctrine, which held that as individuals pursued their own interests, they would be led as if by an invisible hand to promote the good of the society as a whole. To earn the highest profits, predicted Smith, producers would generate the products consumers wanted most. Workers would offer their services where they were most needed because wages would be highest in those sectors. Consumers would favor producers who offered superior products and/or lower prices because they would seek the best value for their money. The result would be an economy that produced the goods and services desired by the society without the need for any central direction by government.

Markets and Prices

Capitalism is often described as a market system. This is because a capitalist economy contains numerous interdependent markets through which the functioning of the economy is coordinated and directed. A **market** consists of all actual or potential buyers and sellers of a particular item and can be local, regional, national, or international. For example, there are numerous local and regional markets for used automobiles, each consisting of all buyers and sellers of such vehicles in that particular area. Similar markets exist for all other goods and services and for all economic resources as well.

Market prices are determined by the interaction of buyers and sellers and serve two important functions. First, prices help to divide up, or ration, the society's limited output of goods and services among those who desire to receive it. Only those who are willing and able to pay the market price receive the product. Second, prices motivate businesses to produce more of some products and less of others. Businesses generally want to supply products that yield the highest profits, the ones with the highest prices in relation to their costs of production. These products tend to be those most desired by consumers. So, by motivating suppliers, price changes help to ensure that society's scarce resources are used to produce the goods and services most highly valued by consumers.

---

[1] Adam Smith's description of the functioning of a capitalist economy appeared in *An Inquiry into the Nature and Causes of the Wealth of Nations*, published in 1776.

Competition   Adam Smith recognized that for the invisible hand to work—for individuals seeking their own interests to promote the good of all—the pursuit of self-interest had to be guided and restrained by competition. Competition ensures that producers remain responsive to consumers and that prices remain reasonable.

Pure capitalism requires **pure competition**, a situation in which a large number of relatively small buyers and sellers interact to determine prices. Under conditions of pure competition, no individual buyer or seller can set—or even significantly influence—the prevailing price of a product or resource. Prices are thus determined by market forces, not by powerful buyers or sellers, and change only when market conditions change.

Limited Government Intervention   Pure capitalism is above all a **laissez-faire economy**. (*Laissez-faire* is a French phrase that in this context means "let the people do as they choose.") The model describes no role for government in making economic decisions. Through pricing, the market makes all production and distribution decisions—what, how, and for whom to produce—and competition ensures that consumers will be charged reasonable prices. The only role of government is to provide the kind of environment in which a market economy can function well. For example, government must define and enforce the private-property rights that enable individuals to own and use property.

The Circular-Flow Model

We can represent the operation of a capitalist economy in a diagram called the circular-flow model. Exhibit 1 models an economy composed of only two sectors: households and businesses. You can see that these two sectors are connected through transactions, or flows, that occur continuously between them. We'll examine how each sector processes the flow it receives and returns it to the other sector.

The Household and Business Sectors   The household sector is shown at the right in Exhibit 1. A **household** is defined as one or more people living in the same dwelling. Whether it consists of a single person or many people, each household will have a source of income and will spend that income. The household sector is composed of all the individual households in the economy. Because households own the land, labor, capital, and entrepreneurship that businesses need to produce goods and services, this sector is the source of all economic resources in the model of pure capitalism. It is also the source of consumer spending for the goods and services produced.

EXHIBIT 1

The Circular Flow of Pure Capitalism

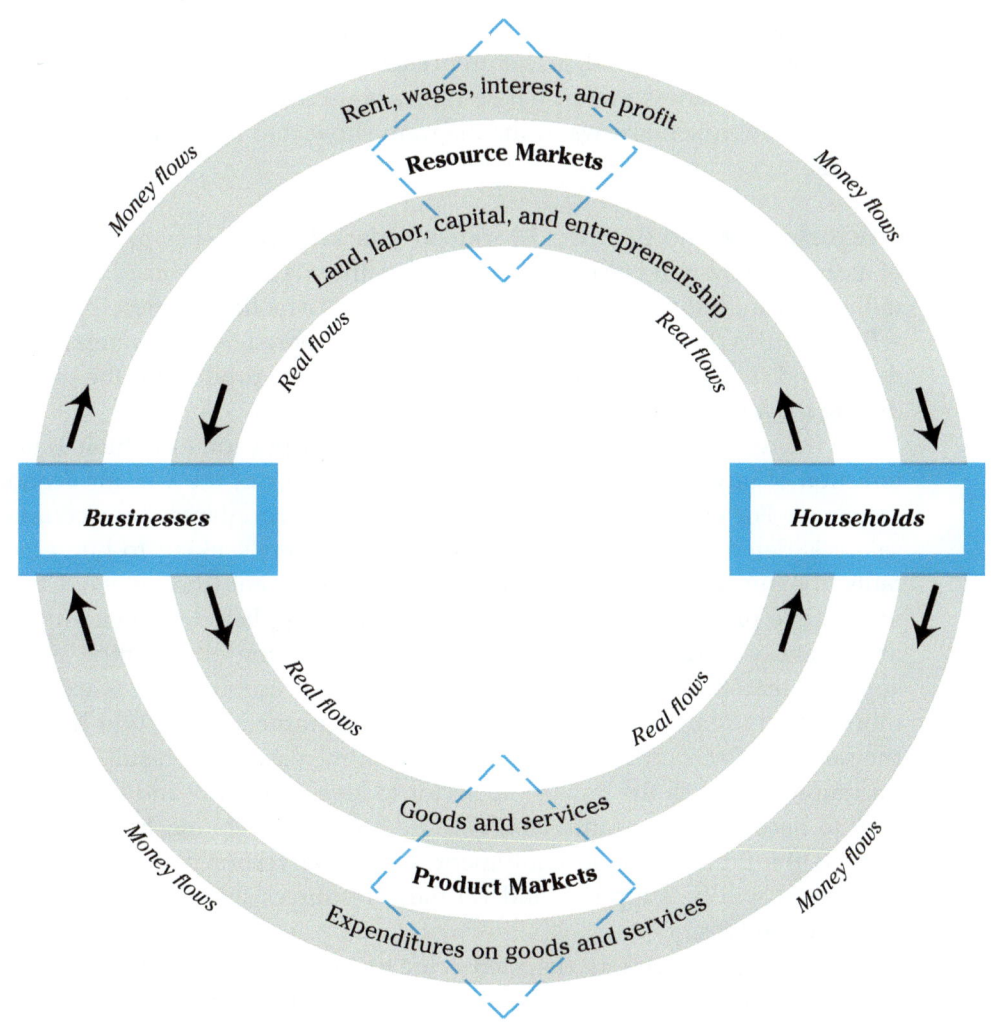

The business sector, on the left, is composed of all the businesses in the economy. The business sector purchases economic resources from households, converts those resources into products, and sells the products to the households.

Real Flows and Money Flows You can see in the diagram that two types of flows circle in opposite directions. In the outside circle *money flows*, in the form of rent, wages, interest, and profit, go from businesses to households to pay for economic resources. These flows return to businesses as households pay for products. *Real flows* involve the physical movement of the resources and products. The inner flow in the diagram shows economic resources in the form of land, labor, capital, and entrepreneurship flowing from the household sector to the business sector, where they are used to produce goods and services. The unbroken arrows in the diagram show that these circular flows are endless.

The Resource and Product Markets

Markets are the key to the operation of a capitalist system because they hold together its decentralized economy of millions of individual buyers and sellers. The interaction of these buyers and sellers ensures that the right products (the ones desired by consumers) are produced and that economic resources flow to the right producers (the ones producing the most-wanted products at the lowest prices).

In the resource markets, depicted in the upper portion of Exhibit 1, the interaction of buyers and sellers determines the prices of the various economic resources. For example, in the labor market for accountants, an accountant's salary is determined by the interaction of employers seeking to hire accountants (the buyers) and accountants seeking employment (the sellers). Changes in resource prices guide and motivate resource suppliers to provide the type and quantity of resources producers need most. Using our example of labor, suppose that the number of businesses desiring accountants is expanding more rapidly than new accountants are being trained. What will happen to the salaries of accountants? They will tend to increase. As a result, we can expect more people in the household sector to invest the time and money necessary to become accountants. You can see how the price mechanism ensures that (1) the types of labor, equipment, and other resources most needed by businesses will be supplied, and (2) these resources will be supplied in the proper quantities.

In the product markets, depicted in the lower portion of Exhibit 1, the prices of all products—from eggs and overcoats to haircuts and airline tickets—again are determined by the interaction of buyers and sellers. Prices serve the same function here as they do in the resource market: They make it possible to divide up, or ration, the limited amount of output among all those who wish to receive it. Only those consumers who are willing and able to pay the market price can obtain the product. When prices change, this informs producers about desired changes in the amount they are producing and motivates them to supply the new quantity. For example, when consumers want more of a product than is available, they tend to bid up its price. Producers, getting a clear signal that consumers like that item, thus have an incentive to supply more of it.

How Capitalism Answers the Three Fundamental Questions

Now that we have discussed the elements of pure capitalism and have a general idea of the role of markets in such an economy, we can determine more easily how this system answers the three fundamental questions.

What to Produce   One feature of pure capitalism is **consumer sovereignty**, an economic condition in which consumers dictate which goods and services businesses will produce. Because producers are motivated by profits and because the most profitable products tend to be the ones consumers desire most, producers must be responsive to consumer preferences. To illustrate consumer sovereignty in action, let's consider how automobile manufacturers in a pure capitalist economy would respond if consumer preferences suddenly took a dramatic turn away from sport-utility vehicles (SUVs) in favor of midsized cars. If people began to buy more midsized automobiles and fewer SUVs, the price of midsize cars would rise, and they would become more profitable, whereas SUVs would decline in price and become less profitable. Therefore, automobile manufacturers would produce more midsize vehicles and fewer SUVs—just what consumers want.

Because consumers are free to spend their incomes as they choose, producers who wish to earn profits must be responsive to consumers' desires. As a result, pure capitalism might be described as a system in which the consumer is the ruler and the producer an obedient servant.

How to Produce   Automobile producers have a number of options available for manufacturing midsized cars and other vehicles that consumers desire. They can produce these automobiles through highly mechanized techniques, or they can rely primarily on skilled labor and simpler tools. They can manufacture car bodies from steel, aluminum, fiberglass, or some combination of the three. In selecting which production technique and combination of resources to use, capitalist manufacturers will minimize the cost of production; they will adopt the *least-cost* approach because lower costs contribute to higher profits.

The search for the least-cost approach is guided by the market prices of the various economic resources. Because the scarcest resources cost the most, producers use them only when they cannot substitute less-expensive resources. For example, if steel is very expensive, automobile makers will tend to use it only where other materials would be inadequate, perhaps in the frame or in other parts of the car that require great strength. And if skilled labor is expensive, as it is in Japan and the United States, robots will be used to

In a capitalist economy, highly mechanized production methods—such as those utilizing robots—may be selected if labor is expensive.

perform as many jobs as possible. Thus, the prices of resources help to ensure that resources are used to their best advantage in a capitalist economy. Abundant, cheaper resources are used when they will suffice; scarcer, more costly resources are conserved.

For Whom to Produce   Finally, we consider the task of distributing our hypothetical economy's output of automobiles. We know that only those who can afford to buy automobiles will receive them. The ability to pay, however, is only half the picture; the other half is willingness to purchase, which takes into account consumer preferences. Some of those who can afford a new car will prefer to spend their money elsewhere: remodeling their homes perhaps or sending their children to college. Some who seemingly cannot afford a new car may be able to purchase one by doing without other things—new clothes or a larger apartment, for example. Of course, consumers with low incomes will face less-attractive choices than those earning high incomes. A low-income consumer may sacrifice basic necessities to afford an automobile, whereas a wealthy consumer need choose only between the new car and some luxury item, such as a sailboat or a winter vacation. In the final analysis, those with higher incomes will always have more choices than those with lower incomes and will receive a larger share of the economy's total output.

Capitalism: Strengths and Weaknesses

Before moving on from our discussion of pure capitalism, we will describe briefly some of the strengths and weaknesses inherent in such a system. One of the major strengths of pure capitalism is *economic efficiency*. In a market economy, businesses are encouraged to produce the products that consumers want most and to produce those products at the lowest cost in terms of scarce resources. A system that accomplishes those objectives goes a long way toward ensuring that a society achieves the maximum benefit possible from its limited resources.

A second positive feature of capitalism is *economic freedom*. Under pure capitalism, consumers, workers, and producers are free to make decisions based on self-interest. To many people, this economic freedom is the overwhelming virtue of the capitalist model.

Economist Milton Friedman, a vocal advocate of competitive capitalism, noted a third strength of the system: It promotes *political freedom* by separating economic and political power. The existence of private ownership of the means of production ensures that government officials are not in a position to deny jobs or goods and services to individuals whose political views conflict with their own.[2]

Pure capitalism also has some shortcomings. First, people are not uniformly equal in ability, and some will succeed to a greater extent than others. In a capitalist system the result is the unequal distribution of income and output. This inequality tends to be perpetuated because the children of the rich usually have access to better educational opportunities and often inherit the income-producing assets of their parents. Such inequality weakens capitalism's claim that it produces the goods and services that the *society* wants the most. It is more the case that capitalism produces the products that the *consumers who have the money* want most.

A second, closely related criticism was voiced by the late Arthur Okun, chairman of the Council of Economic Advisors during the Johnson administration. In a capitalist economy, observed Okun, money can buy a great many things that are not supposed to be for sale:

> Money buys legal services that can obtain preferred treatment before the law; it buys platforms that give extra weight to the owner's freedom of speech; it buys influence with elected officials and thus compromises the principle of one person,

---

[2]Milton Friedman, *Capitalism and Freedom* (Chicago: University of Chicago Press, 1962), p. 9.

one vote. . . . Even though money generally cannot buy extra helpings of rights directly, it can buy services that, in effect, produce more or better rights.[3]

Third, pure capitalism may be criticized for encouraging the destruction of the environment. Because air, rivers, lakes, and streams are **common-property resources** belonging to the society as a whole, they tend to be seen as free—available to be used or abused without charge or concern. The pursuit of self-interest would cause producers to dump their wastes into nearby rivers to avoid the cost of disposing of those wastes in an environmentally acceptable manner. Farmers would select pesticides according to their favorable impact on output and without regard to their undesirable effects on wildlife and water supplies. In this case, Adam Smith's invisible hand fails. The pursuit of self-interest by individuals may not promote the good of all but may instead lead to environmental destruction.[4]

THE MODEL OF PURE COMMAND SOCIALISM

The opposite of the model of pure capitalism is the model of pure command socialism. The socialist command economy described in this section represents no existing economic system. Like the model of pure capitalism, the model of pure command socialism is simply a tool to help us understand how command economies operate. Again, we will examine the basic elements of the model, diagram how the hypothetical economy operates, and see how the system decides what, how, and for whom to produce. Then we will examine the strengths and weaknesses of pure command socialism.

Elements of Command Socialism

We define **command socialism** as an economic system in which the means of production are publicly owned and the fundamental economic choices are made by a central authority. Four basic elements of command socialism support this definition.

Public Ownership   A socialist economy is characterized by state, or public, ownership of the means of production. In the model of pure command socialism,

---

[3] Arthur M. Okun, *Equality and Efficiency: The Big Tradeoff* (Washington: Brookings Institution, 1975), p. 22.

[4] It can be argued that the problem here is not capitalism, but too little capitalism. If someone were assigned the ownership of these common-property resources, that party would have both the ability and the incentive to protect those resources from abuse.

state ownership is complete. The factories, farms, mines, hospitals, and other forms of capital are all publicly owned. Even labor is publicly owned in the sense that workers and managers do not select their own employment but are assigned their jobs by the state.

Centralized Decision Making

One of the most distinctive features of command socialism is that economic choices are made by a central authority. This central authority may be either responsive to the feelings of the people (democratic socialism) or unresponsive to their wishes (authoritarian socialism or communism). In either case, this authority makes the fundamental production and distribution decisions and then takes the necessary actions to see that these decisions are carried out.

Economic Planning

In the model of command socialism, economic planning replaces the market as the method for coordinating economic decisions. The central authority, or central planning board, gathers information about existing production capacities, supplies of raw materials, and labor force capabilities. It then draws up a master plan specifying production objectives for each sector or industry in the economy. Industrywide objectives are translated into specific production targets for each factory, farm, mine, or other kind of producing unit. Central planning ensures that specific production objectives agree so that automobile manufacturers will not produce 1 million cars, for example, while tire manufacturers produce only 2 million tires.

Allocation by Command

In command socialism, resources and products are allocated by directive, or command, and the central authority uses its power to enforce these decisions. Once it determines production and distribution objectives, the central planning board dictates to each producing unit the quantity and assortment of goods the unit is to produce and the combination of resources it is to use. Commands are also issued to producers of raw materials and other production inputs to supply these inputs to the producing units that need them. Further commands direct individuals to places of employment—wherever the central planning board determines that their services are needed—and dictate distribution of the economy's output of goods and services. All the allocative functions that a capitalist economy leaves to the market and the pursuit of self-interest are accomplished in pure command socialism through planning and allocation by directive.

The Pyramid Model

Exhibit 2 represents a socialist command economy as a pyramid, with the central planning board at the top and the various producing and consuming

EXHIBIT 2

The Command Pyramid

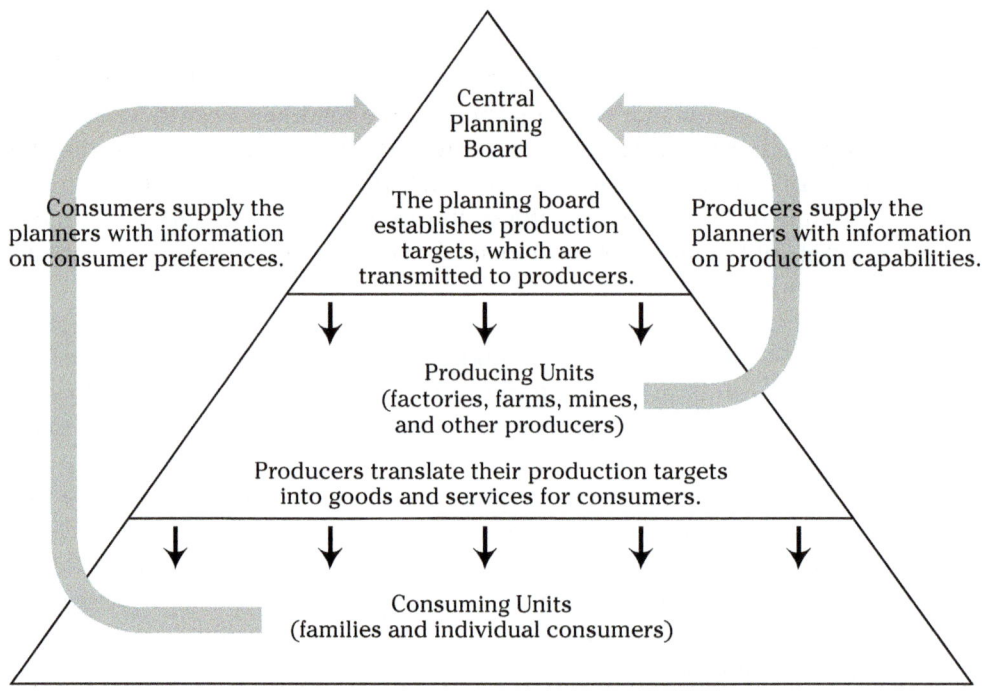

Central
Planning
Board

Consumers supply the
planners with information
on consumer preferences.

The planning board
establishes production
targets, which are
transmitted to producers.

Producers supply the
planners with information
on production capabilities.

Producing Units
(factories, farms, mines,
and other producers)

Producers translate their production targets
into goods and services for consumers.

Consuming Units
(families and individual consumers)

units below it. This diagram emphasizes the primary feature of a command economy: centralization of economic decision making.

The outer arrow at the right in Exhibit 2 shows how information about production capacities, raw material supplies, and labor capabilities flows up from the producing units in the middle of the pyramid to the central planning board at the top. Information, if requested, about which goods and services consumers desire also flows up from the consuming units at the base of the pyramid (outer left arrow). Production objectives, or targets, are transmitted back to the individual producing units, which then supply the targeted quantity and assortment of products and produce them as specified. Finally, the output is distributed to consumers in accordance with the plan.

How Command Socialism Answers the Three Fundamental Questions

In many respects the operation of a socialist command economy is easier to understand than the functioning of a capitalist economy. The answers to the three fundamental questions are decided by the central planning board, which then uses its authority to ensure that all directives are carried out.

The central planners can select any output targets, any mix of products within the limits set by the economy's production capacity. Of course, the planners will have to gather an abundance of information before they have a good picture of the economy's capabilities. They must determine the size of the labor force and the skills it possesses, for example, as well as how many factories exist and what they are capable of producing. Until the central planners have this kind of information, they cannot establish realistic output targets. And, even then, they will face some tough decisions because, as you already know, more of one thing means less of something else. So if they decide to produce more automobiles, they won't be able to manufacture as many refrigerators and military weapons and other products.

In deciding how to produce each product, central planners must try to stretch the economy's limited resources as far as possible. This requires that each resource be used efficiently—where it makes the greatest contribution to the economy's output. If some resource is particularly scarce, planners must be careful to use it only where no other input will suffice; otherwise they won't be able to maximize the economy's output.

Even with the best planning, an economy's resources will stretch only so far. The central planning board can allocate the economy's limited output in accordance with any objective it has set. If the planning board's primary objective is equality, it can develop a method of rationing, dividing up the society's output in equal shares to each member. If it wants to promote loyalty to the government, the central authority can give supporters extra shares while penalizing dissenters. Whatever its objectives, the central planning board can use distribution as a method to further them.

Command Socialism: Strengths and Weaknesses

Like pure capitalism, the economy of pure command socialism has certain strengths and certain weaknesses. Some people argue that a major strength of command socialism is its ability to promote a high degree of equality in the distribution of income and output. Because the central planners control the distribution of goods and services, they can elect to distribute output in ways that achieve whatever degree of equality in living standard they consider appropriate. Thus, it is theoretically possible for command socialism to avoid the extremely unequal income and output distribution that characterizes pure capitalism.

Another major strength of command socialism is its potential for achieving economic objectives in a relatively short period of time. As an example, consider the power of the planners to foster more rapid economic growth. If a society wants to increase its capacity for producing goods and services, it must devote more of its resources to producing capital goods (factories and equipment) and fewer resources to producing consumer goods. In other words, society must consume less *now* to be able to produce and consume more *later*. Because the central authority has the power to dictate the fraction of the society's resources that will be devoted to capital goods production, in effect, it can force the society to make the sacrifices necessary to increase the rate of economic growth.

You probably recognize that the power to bring about rapid economic changes is not necessarily a good thing. The major shortcoming of command socialism, in fact, is the possibility that the central planning board may pursue goals that do not reflect the needs or desires of the majority. If the socialist government is not democratically elected, its goals may bear no relationship to the wants of the general population.

A second weakness in the model of command socialism is its inefficient information network. The system we have described needs more information than it can reasonably expect to acquire and process to ensure efficient use of the economy's resources. The system must not only have a substantial organizational network to acquire information about consumer preferences and production capabilities, but it must also use that network to transmit the decisions of central planners to millions of economic units. Moreover, the central planners have to be able to process all the acquired information and return it in the form of a consistent plan—a staggering task, considering that the output of one industry is often the production input required by some other industry. Finally, they must see that each product is produced efficiently. This complex and cumbersome process is bound to result in breakdowns in communication and decision making. When these occur, the wrong products may be produced or the right ones produced using the wrong combinations of resources. In either case, inefficiency means that the society does not achieve maximum benefit from its limited resources.

MIXED ECONOMIES: THE REAL-WORLD SOLUTION

No existing economic system adheres strictly to either pure capitalism or pure command socialism. All real-world economies are **mixed economies**; they represent a blending of the two models. To illustrate this point, we look next at the U.S. economy. Then we highlight the diversity of economic systems by taking a brief tour of several of the world's economies.

The U.S. Economic System

Because the U.S. economic system is marked by such a high degree of private ownership and individual decision making, American children learn early from their teachers, the news media, and others that they live in a capitalist economy. And certainly there is ample evidence to support that viewpoint. Most U.S. businesses, from industrial giants like Ford Motor Company and General Electric to small firms like your neighborhood barbershop or hair salon, are private operations, not government-owned enterprises. The U.S. economy is coordinated and directed largely by the market mechanism, the interaction of buyers and sellers in thousands of interdependent markets. Each of those buyers and sellers is guided by self-interest, which among producers takes the form of profit seeking. Fortunately for consumers, the drive for profits is usually kept in check by another feature of pure capitalism: competition. In most American industries, competition, though not pure, is adequate to keep prices reasonable and to ensure that consumers receive fair treatment.

Given these elements of pure capitalism, why do we call the United States a *mixed economy*? In part, that label stems from the degree of public ownership that exists in our economy. A second, perhaps more important, reason is the extent to which the government makes or influences the fundamental economic choices. Let's briefly consider each of these reasons.

Public Ownership of the Means of Production

Pure capitalism requires private ownership of the means of production. The U.S. economy does not fully meet that requirement. Although most American businesses are privately owned, some very important and visible producers are publicly owned enterprises. For example, the electricity on which we rely to heat and cool our homes and to run our appliances is supplied in part by municipal, state, or county power companies. The vast majority of our schoolchildren—almost 90 percent—attend public elementary and secondary schools. When we apply for admission to college, we mail those applications via the U.S. Postal Service, often to state universities. Moreover, the extent of public ownership is not a static concept. During the recent financial crisis, the federal government took partial ownership stakes in hundreds of banks in return for providing aid to these troubled institutions. There were even calls to nationalize such well-known firms as Bank of America and General Motors, rather than allowing them to fail. Although these steps were never taken, the federal government was clearly viewed as the owner of last resort.

Government Decision Making

Although government decision making is the hallmark of a socialist command economy, some government intervention is unavoidable, even in a capitalist economy. The most basic function of government is to establish a *legal framework*—the rules by which citizens must deal with one another. A capitalist economy requires rules to protect private property—from theft, damage, etc. These rules must be maintained and enforced by legal institutions—police and a court system. Without these institutions, the

A capitalist economy requires rules to protect private property.

concept of private property has little meaning, and a capitalist economy could not exist. The U.S. economy has a highly developed legal system, with well-established principles of law.

Government's role in establishing a legal framework clearly is consistent with the model of pure capitalism. But government does much more than this in the U.S. economy. Consider the following functions of government and decide for yourself which are consistent with pure capitalism and which are not.

1. *Maintaining competition.* Competition helps to channel the profit-seeking motives of producers into socially desirable outcomes. When competition is inadequate, consumers may be forced to pay higher prices or accept inferior products. In the U.S. economy, the federal government uses *antitrust laws* to discourage anticompetitive behavior and to promote competition. In one recent use of the antitrust laws, three leading flat-screen producers—LG Display of Korea, Sharp of Japan, and Chunghwa Picture Tubes of Taiwan— were prosecuted for their role in a price-fixing cartel that drove up the price of liquid-crystal display panels used in flat-screen televisions, computers, and cell phones. In essence, these firms illegally agreed among themselves to set prices rather than allowing prices to be established by competition in the marketplace. In 2008, the three firms pled guilty and agreed to pay criminal fines totaling $585 million. The case was the result of the coordinated efforts of enforcement agencies in Europe, Asia, and the United States.

2. *Correcting for externalities.* Buyers and sellers make decisions based on costs and benefits. If an individual judges that the benefits of an action exceed the costs incurred, he or she will perform that action. If, on the other hand, the person determines the costs of the action exceed its benefits, he or she will refrain from that action. This behavior commonly leads to an efficient use of society's scarce resources. But when an action creates *externalities*— costs or benefits that spill over into third parties—the resulting decision may not be optimal for society. For instance, the managers of electricity-generating power plants may use more high-sulfur coal than is socially desirable because they ignore the damage that this variety of coal inflicts on the environment. And dog owners may opt *not* to have their pets inoculated against rabies because they ignore the benefits that this protection provides to others. The U.S. government attempts to adjust for these and other externalities by establishing laws—laws requiring rabies inoculations and limiting waste emissions, for example—and by using taxes and subsidies to alter the behavior of firms and individuals.

3. *Providing public goods.* Some important products cannot be profitably produced by private businesses; they must be provided by government if they are to be available. In the United States, government uses its taxing authority to pay for public goods such as national defense, flood-control dams, and tornado-warning systems. A wide variety of quasi-public goods such as fire and police protection are also financed in this manner.

4. *Redistributing income.* As we saw earlier, total reliance on the market mechanism can produce substantial income inequality. In the United States, government has assumed responsibility for reducing income inequality. This is accomplished in a variety of ways. The federal income tax is somewhat "progressive"—that is, it is intended to take a greater proportion of the incomes of the rich than the poor. Those with very low incomes qualify for an "earned income tax credit." In effect, rather than receiving taxes from them, the government pays these people. Some government programs attempt to bolster the incomes of the poor by providing them with subsidized job training. Other programs attempt to reduce poverty directly. For example, Social Security provides financial assistance to the old, the disabled, and those who are experiencing financial distress due to the death of a breadwinner. In addition, state unemployment compensation provides financial assistance to workers who are temporarily unemployed. Despite these efforts, however, there is still substantial income inequality in the U.S. economy.

5. *Stabilizing the economy.* Many economists argue that capitalist economies are inherently unstable—subject to periodic bouts of unemployment or inflation. The Employment Act of 1946 requires Congress to pursue policies aimed at achieving high employment, economic growth, and price stability. In addition, the Federal Reserve—the governmental agency that regulates

the nation's money supply—attempts to guide the economy's overall performance.

6. *Regulating health and safety*. In addition to the preceding functions, government regulates businesses to ensure product quality and the safety of working conditions. It bans certain goods and services (fully automatic weapons, prostitution, illicit drugs, and child pornography, for example) and certain ingredients (lead in gasoline, for instance, and red dye number two). Government also mandates the purchase of certain products such as seatbelts and airbags in automobiles, smoke detectors in apartments, and lifejackets on boats. Clearly, government's role in attempting to maintain health and safety is not insignificant.

As you can see, there are many decisions that the United States does not leave to the impersonal dictates of the market. And even this relatively lengthy list is not exhaustive! Is all this government intervention a good thing? Does it allow markets to function more efficiently or more humanely? Does it succeed in making our economy more stable? This is open to debate.

The Rest of the World

As we've seen, the U.S. economy does not conform to the model of pure capitalism. A number of important enterprises are publicly owned, and the visible hand of government influences many of our economic decisions. Yet the U.S. economy is probably as close to pure capitalism as any economy in existence. The rest of the world's economies represent an even more thorough blending of public and private ownership, of market and government decision making.

Consider some of the major European countries. **France** has a history of extensive state ownership of the means of production, substantial government regulation, and reliance on "indicative" planning to influence business decisions. (Under indicative planning, the planning agency collects and disseminates information but does not command that specific production targets be achieved. Instead, it uses indirect means, such as tax incentives, to influence business decisions.) In the early 1990s, France turned away from planning and began to convert some public enterprises to private enterprises. It has now fully or partially privatized many large companies, including banks, insurance companies, and such visible firms as Air France, France Telecom, and Renault, the French auto manufacturer. Despite these privatization efforts, the French government continues to maintain a strong presence in certain sectors including power production, railroads, aircraft, and defense industries. Moreover, the French economy remains highly regulated with extensive protections for workers (safety, working conditions, and hours). In addition, government tax policies and social spending are used to moderate income inequality rather than accepting the dictates of the market. As you can see, the French are clearly seeking their own middle-way between pure capitalism and command socialism.

Great Britain, prior to the long Conservative rule of Margaret Thatcher and John Major (1979–1997), was often described as a socialist economic system. This description stemmed from the size of the government's budget, the extent of publicly owned enterprises, and the nation's reliance on economic planning. The socialist label was never completely accurate, but is clearly inaccurate today. The British government has now privatized most state-owned companies—British Steel, British Coal, and British Airways, for instance—and has pursued partial privatization in the few that remain—the London Underground (subway), for instance. Economic planning, which was never practiced to the same extent as in France, has been largely abandoned. Social spending—government spending to aid the elderly, unemployed, poor, and disabled—absorbs about 21% of the U.K.'s output. That's well above the United States (16%), but substantially less than France (29%). In summary, Great Britain is clearly a mixed economy, though one with a somewhat larger role for government than the U.S. economy.

The **German** economy is the third largest in the world (behind the United States and Japan) and the largest in Europe. Privately owned enterprises dominate German industry, but the state intervenes by owning some segments of the economy—part of the banking system, for instance—by subsidizing selected industries, and by extensive rules regarding workplace safety, environmental protection, and the like. There is a state-run system of health insurance, extensive public housing for the poor, and relatively generous unemployment compensation. As a consequence, social spending in Germany accounts for about 27% of the economy's output, only slightly less than France. (In recent years, the government has attempted to cut back on some social programs largely because the high payroll taxes needed to support them have made it increasingly difficult for German firms to compete internationally.) Another distinguishing feature of the Germany economy is a government policy known as "codetermination." Codetermination means that corporations must have worker representatives on their boards of directors. In effect, this forces corporations to consider worker interest when formulating business policy. As you can see, the German economic system blends capitalism with a significant dose of government intervention intended to soften market outcomes. The Germans describe their economic system as a "social market economy."

The **Swedish** economy is similar, in many respects, to the German economy. Private ownership is the norm, and markets dictate most outcomes. The state, however, goes to great lengths to maintain an egalitarian income distribution. For instance, it provides very generous benefits for retirement, medical care, education, and the like. These programs, coupled with higher taxes on those earning higher incomes, lead to a substantial redistribution of income. This may be at least part of the reason that the income distribution in Sweden is significantly more equal than that found in the United States.

When we consider Eastern Europe and Asia, we find a number of economic systems in transition. For most of the last century, the **Soviet Union** was held up as a nearly perfect example of command socialism. Most factories, farms, and other enterprises were owned and operated by the state, and the fundamental choices about what, how, and for whom to produce were made by the State Planning Committee (GOSPLAN). When Mikhail Gorbachev became supreme leader of the Soviet Union in 1985, he was very critical of the Soviet economy, calling it rigid and inefficient. Gorbachev instituted some market reforms, but his own ambivalence about capitalism led to conflicting policy moves. The result was chaos for producers and a substantial disruption in the supplies of goods and services. As the Soviet economy disintegrated, the Communist party collapsed, and most of the Soviet republics declared their independence. Russian president Boris Yeltsin, who had advocated more rapid economic reform, moved to center stage. In December 1991, the Soviet Union was officially dissolved and replaced with the Commonwealth of Independent States, a loose federation of former Soviet republics.

In the period since the breakup, the countries of the former Soviet Union have taken very different paths. **Belarus**, **Uzbekistan**, and **Turkmenistan**, for example, have done very little to change their economic systems. On the other hand, **Russia** began introducing market reforms immediately after the breakup and is now a very different economy. Central planning has been largely abandoned, state ownership has been dramatically reduced, and free-market prices now play a much more important role in the economy. Living standards, which dropped for several years after the breakup, have been rising since 1998. The rate of poverty is falling, and there is an emerging entrepreneurial class, not too unlike that in the United States.

The Russian economy retains a certain Soviet flavor, however, and its future path is hard to predict. Although many industries have been privatized, many others remain state owned or state controlled. In fact, there has been significant expansion of government ownership since 2004, focused particularly on the oil, gas, and mining sectors. This expansion has caused some observers to wonder about a return to greater state control. Critics of the Putin/Medvedev regime argue that the selective and capricious interpretation of tax and licensing laws also seems intended to deter the emergence of private businesses and protect the power of the state. And, intentional or not, the nation's legal system clearly provides inadequate protections for private property, the foundation of capitalism. What direction is the Russian economy moving; toward freer markets or back toward more state control? We'll have to wait to see.

China, long considered the *other* major planned economy of the world, has taken a more gradual and cautious approach to economic reform than that pursued by Russia. The Chinese leadership began introducing modest market reforms in the late 1970s. Peasants who produced more than their production targets were allowed to sell the additional agricultural output at free-market prices, and small private businesses were allowed to develop outside the central plan. As these reforms met with success, additional modest reforms were introduced. In 1992, Deng Xiaoping, head of the Communist party, encouraged entrepreneurs to develop the nonstate sector, providing official sanctioning for this sector.[5]

Although the private sector has expanded significantly since 1992, many key industries—utilities, mining, and heavy manufacturing—remain state owned,[6] and the state continues to regulate some prices—gasoline, farm products, and cooking oil, for instance. As the private sector has grown, China's leaders have shown an increased willingness to shrink, or at least reform, state-owned enterprises (SOEs), many of which are poorly run and highly inefficient. Some SOEs have been closed or converted into private (or quasi-private) businesses. Other SOEs have been exposed to competition with foreign businesses or private businesses in an attempt to make the SOEs more efficient. One consequence of these changes has been the displacement of workers—workers who believed they had a job for life—as state enterprises shed jobs. As you might expect, this change has met with resistance. Another source of resistance has been the growing inequality in the country. Those fortunate enough to live in industrialized coastal cities (which produce products for export) have seen their incomes rise substantially, while those living in rural areas have been unaffected or even harmed. This growth in inequality has led to protests about the fairness of market reforms and the wisdom of proceeding further.

If we venture farther east, we encounter mixed economies that appear to have a strong capitalist flavor. In the **Japanese** economy, there is little public ownership, and most decisions are market driven. But Japan pursues an "industrial policy" in which state bureaucrats attempt to promote what they deem to be key sectors of the economy and phase out other, less-promising sectors. Some have described this approach as midway between planning and free markets. Similar approaches appear to characterize the economies of **South Korea and Taiwan**. In these nations, the government has routinely targeted specific industries (and specific companies) for assistance.

There are obviously many more economies in the world, but it should be clear by now that all real-world economies combine elements of both

---

[5] Robert Solomon, *The Transformation of the World Economy*, 2nd ed. (New York: St. Martin's Press, 1999), pp. 124–133.
[6] The State-Owned Assets Supervision and Administration Commission of China lists 150 SOEs, most with a number of subsidiary firms.

capitalism and socialism. The economies of the United States and **Hong Kong**, which rely heavily on markets, reserve some role for government. And markets are evident even in the most highly regulated of the world's economies—the Chinese economy, for example. But although all real-world economies combine elements of capitalism and socialism, they each blend the capitalist and socialist model in their own unique way—a blend that reflects that nation's history and traditions.

The preceding section provided some appreciation of the diversity of existing economic systems. But our primary interest is in the U.S. economy. To better understand our economy, we need to know more about how markets work and how government influences economic choices in our system.

SUMMARY

An *economic system* is a set of institutions and mechanisms for answering the three fundamental questions of economics—what, how, and for whom to produce. In describing economic systems, it is helpful to ask two questions: (1) Who owns the means of production? (2) Who makes the economic decisions?

Economists commonly use theoretical models to explain the operation of economic systems. *Capitalism* describes an economic system in which the *means of production* are privately owned, and fundamental economic choices are made by individual buyers and sellers interacting in markets. The principal features of pure capitalism include private property and freedom of choice, with self-interest as the driving force (held in check by *pure competition*); price determination through markets; and a minimum of government intervention—a *laissez-faire economy*.

In a capitalist economy, *consumer sovereignty* dictates which goods and services will be produced. If consumers want more of a particular product, its price will tend to rise, encouraging profit-seeking businesses to produce more of it. To produce these products, businesses buy economic resources (e.g., labor) from *households*, thereby providing households with the money needed to purchase the output of businesses. The circular-flow model of capitalism diagrams this process by showing how the flows of money (money flows) and resources and products (real flows) circulate between the household and business sectors and operate through product and resource markets.

At the other extreme, the model of *command socialism* describes an economic system in which the means of production are owned by the public, or the state, and the fundamental economic choices are made by a central authority.

The principal features of command socialism include public ownership, centralized decision making, economic planning, and allocation by command.

In command socialism the central planning authority gathers information on production capabilities and consumer preferences (if the latter is a concern) and establishes production targets for the producing units, such as factories and farms. These units are required to produce the products dictated by the central authority in the manner specified. Output is then distributed according to the central authority's goals. Command socialism is depicted as a pyramid, with the central planning board at the top and the producing and consuming units below. The producing and consuming units supply information to the central planners, who use this information to develop production targets and decide how the limited output will be distributed among the potential customers.

No existing economic system fits neatly into either model. All real-world economic systems are *mixed economies* because they represent some blending of the two models. For example, the U.S. economy, commonly described as a capitalist system, contains some elements of a socialist economy. Public ownership is not uncommon in the United States, and government influences many of our fundamental economic choices. And markets are important even in economies like those of Russia and China, where a significant government bureaucracy guides many of the fundamental economic choices, and government ownership of the means of production remains extensive.

KEY TERMS

Capitalism	Economic system	Market
Command socialism	Household	Means of production
Common-property resources	Invisible hand	Mixed economies
Consumer sovereignty	Laissez-faire economy	Pure competition

STUDY QUESTIONS

Fill in the Blanks

1. The driving force or engine of capitalism

   is _____.

2. The functioning of a capitalist economy is coordinated and directed through

   _____ in which _____ are determined by the interaction of buyers and sellers.

3. In the model of pure capitalism, the pursuit of self-interest by producers is kept in

   check by _____. The model

   of pure capitalism requires _____, a situation in which there are a large number of buyers and sellers of each product.

4. Because businesspeople in a capitalist economy are motivated by self-interest, they want to produce the goods and services that will allow them to earn the

   highest _____. Those products tend to be the ones that are most de-

   sired by _____.

5. According to Milton Friedman, competitive capitalism promotes

   _____ by separating economic and political power.

6. In pure command socialism, the fundamental economic decisions are made by

   the _____ and implemented

   through _____.

7. In pure command socialism, _____ replaces the market as the method of coordinating the various economic decisions.

8. It is possible to represent a socialist command economy as a(n) _____

   with the _____ at the top and producing and consuming units at the bottom.

9. One weakness of command socialism is its

   inefficient _____ network.

10. The United States and China are both

    examples of _____ economies.

Multiple Choice

1. Which of the following is *not* a characteristic of pure capitalism?
   a) Public ownership of the means of production
   b) The pursuit of self-interest
   c) Markets and prices
   d) Pure competition
   e) Limited government

2. In a market economy the scarcest resources will be used very conservatively because
   a) central planners will allocate such resources only where they are most needed.
   b) the scarcest resources will tend to have the highest prices.
   c) government officials will not permit their use.
   d) the scarcest resources will tend to have the lowest prices.

3. In a capitalist economy
   a) businesses are free to produce whatever products they choose.
   b) consumers are free to utilize their incomes as they see fit.
   c) resource owners have the freedom to sell their resources to whomever they choose.
   d) All of the above
   e) None of the above

4. Consumer sovereignty means that
   a) consumers dictate which goods and services will be produced by the way they spend their money.
   b) central planners allocate a major share of society's resources to the production of consumer goods.
   c) the role of government in the economy is very limited.
   d) all economic resources are used efficiently.

5. According to the "invisible hand" doctrine,
   a) as individuals pursue their own interests, they tend to promote the interests of society as a whole.
   b) the actions of individuals often have unanticipated and undesirable effects on society.

c) individuals should put the interests of society first.

d) when individuals attempt to promote the best interests of the entire society, they also further their own personal interests.

6. Adam Smith recognized that the "invisible hand" would function as he envisioned only if
a) individuals unconsciously considered the welfare of others in making their decisions.
b) government regulations forced businesses to behave in an ethical manner.
c) a high degree of competition existed in the economy.
d) individuals lived in accordance with the golden rule.

7. In a market economy, if consumers suddenly stop buying SUVs and start buying fuel-efficient cars,
a) the price of SUVs will tend to fall, and more of them will be produced.
b) the price of fuel-efficient cars will tend to rise, making them less profitable to produce and encouraging producers to supply more of them.
c) resources will tend to be shifted from the production of SUVs to the production of fuel-efficient cars.
d) the price of SUVs will tend to rise, making them more profitable to produce and encouraging producers to supply more of them.

8. Which of the following best describes command socialism?
a) An economic system where the means of production are privately owned and decision making is highly centralized
b) An economic system where the means of production are publicly owned and decision making is highly decentralized
c) An economic system where the means of production are privately owned and decision making is highly decentralized
d) An economic system where the means of production are publicly owned and decision making is highly centralized

9. Which of the following is correct?
a) In command socialism, the basic economic choices are made by individuals.
b) In pure capitalism, powerful economic units have a substantial impact on the way economic choices are made.
c) In command socialism, producers are required to produce whatever products central planners dictate.
d) In pure capitalism, economic planning ensures that the various production decisions will be consistent with one another.

10. In deciding what products to produce, the central planners in a socialist command economy need not consider
a) the size of the economy's labor force.
b) the production capabilities of the economy's factories.
c) consumer preferences.
d) the economy's stock of raw materials.

11. In order to get the most output from society's limited resources, the scarcest resources must be used only where no other input will suffice.
a) In command socialism this function is performed by planners; in pure capitalism it is performed by the central government.
b) In pure capitalism this function is performed by input prices; in command socialism it is performed by planners.
c) In command socialism this function is performed by the producing units; in pure capitalism it is performed by planners.
d) In pure capitalism this function is performed by government regulations; in command socialism it is performed by output targets.

12. In a comparison of command socialism and pure capitalism, which of the following is true?
a) Prices play a larger role in command socialism than in pure capitalism.
b) Resources are likely to be used more efficiently in command socialism than in pure capitalism.

c) Economic planning plays a larger role in pure capitalism than in command socialism.

d) Decision making is more decentralized in pure capitalism than in command socialism.

13. One function of government in the U.S. economy is to "correct for externalities." Which of the following is an example of government performing that function?
   a) Construction of a flood-control dam
   b) Paying a portion of the cost of a flu vaccination
   c) Reducing the income tax rate on citizens with low incomes
   d) Outlawing the sale of automobiles lacking seatbelts

14. One reason the United States is not an example of pure capitalism is that
   a) most producing units are publicly owned.
   b) commands are used to implement some economic decisions.
   c) the pursuit of self-interest is a powerful force.
   d) markets are used to coordinate most economic decisions.

15. Which of the following is a true statement?
   a) Codetermination is a feature of the Swedish economy.
   b) The Germans describe their economy as a "social market economy."
   c) Industrial policy is a characteristic of the British economy.
   d) Japan's leadership employs "indicative planning" in guiding its economy.

Problems and Questions for Discussion

1. What is an economic system? Why is it valid to say that no two real-world economic systems are exactly alike?

2. List the characteristics or elements of pure capitalism and explain each. Are any of these elements absent from the U.S. economy? Explain.

3. How would a socialist command economy answer the three fundamental questions? What elements of command socialism exist in the U.S. economy?

4. Explain the role of economic planning in command socialism. Who is in charge of economic planning in a capitalist economy?

5. Try to draw the circular-flow diagram without looking back at the diagram in the text. Now, label all the parts of the diagram, and indicate which flows are money flows and which are real flows. Use the diagram to explain how a capitalist economy works.

6. Draw the command pyramid and label the parts. What does the command pyramid tell us about the way a socialist economy functions?

7. Milton Friedman suggests that competitive capitalism promotes political freedom. Explain.

8. What functions does the government perform in the U.S. economy? Which of these functions is consistent with the model of pure capitalism?

9. Why can't capitalism exist without a well-developed legal system?

10. Japan, South Korea, and Taiwan all pursue an "industrial policy." Explain what is meant by an industrial policy and why this policy is inconsistent with pure capitalism.

11. How are the objectives of government intervention in Japan and Taiwan different from the objectives of government intervention in Germany and Sweden?

12. Government intervention in Sweden appears to have a single, overriding focus. Does government intervention in the U.S. economy have a single focus or objective?

13. China has introduced a number of market reforms, but continues to regulate the prices of basic agricultural commodities, cooking oil, and gasoline. Why do you believe policymakers have chosen to regulate those particular prices, rather than allowing them to be determined by market forces?

ANSWER KEY

Fill in the Blanks

1. self-interest
2. markets, prices
3. competition, pure competition
4. profits, consumers
5. political freedom
6. central authority, commands
7. economic planning
8. pyramid, planning board
9. information
10. mixed

Multiple Choice

1. a	4. a	7. c	10. c	13. b
2. b	5. a	8. d	11. b	14. b
3. d	6. c	9. c	12. d	15. b

The Key Principles of Economics

From Chapter 2 of *Survey of Economics: Principles, Applications, and Tools*, 5/e. Arthur O'Sullivan. Steven M. Sheffrin. Stephen J. Perez. Copyright © 2012 by Pearson Education. Published by Prentice Hall. All rights reserved.

The Key Principles of Economics

Szefei wong/Alamy

What do we sacrifice by preserving tropical rainforests rather than mining or logging the land? Recent experiences in Guyana and other tropical countries suggest that in some places, the answer is "not much"—only $1 per hectare per year ($0.40 per acre per year).[1] Conservation groups have a new strategy for conserving rain forests—bidding against loggers and miners for the use of the land. When the payoff from developing tropical forest land is relatively low, conservation groups can outbid developers at a price as low as $1 per hectare. When we add the cost of hiring locals to manage the ecosystems, the total cost of preservation is as low as $2 per hectare per year. A conservation group based in Amherst, New Hampshire started by leasing 81,000 hectares of pristine forest in Guyana, and since then has leased land in Peru, Sierra Leone, Papua New Guinea, Fiji, and Mexico.

APPLYING THE CONCEPTS

1 What is the opportunity cost of running a business?
   Don't Forget the Costs of Time and Invested Funds

2 How do people think at the margin?
   Why Not Walk up an Escalator?

3 What is the rationale for specialization and exchange?
   Jasper Johns and Housepainting

4 Do farmers experience diminishing returns?
   Fertilizer and Crop Yields

5 How does inflation affect the real minimum wage?
   The Declining Real Minimum Wage

6 How does inflation affect lenders and borrowers?
   Repaying Student Loans

 n this chapter, we introduce five key principles that provide a foundation for economic analysis. A *principle* is a self-evident truth that most people readily understand and accept. For example, most people readily accept the principle of gravity. You will see the five key principles of economics again and again as you do your own economic analysis.

1 THE PRINCIPLE OF OPPORTUNITY COST

Economics is all about making choices, and to make good choices we must compare the benefit of something to its cost. **Opportunity cost** incorporates the notion of scarcity: No matter what we do, there is always a trade-off. We must trade off one thing for another because resources are limited and can be used in different ways. By acquiring something, we use up resources that could have been used to acquire something else. The notion of opportunity cost allows us to measure this trade-off.

opportunity cost
What you sacrifice to get something.

PRINCIPLE OF OPPORTUNITY COST

The opportunity cost of something is what you sacrifice to get it.

In most decisions we choose from several alternatives. For example, if you spend an hour studying for an economics exam, you have one less hour to pursue other activities. To determine the opportunity cost of an activity, we look at what you consider the best of these "other" activities. For example, suppose the alternatives to studying economics are studying for a history exam or working in a job that pays $10 per hour. If you consider studying for history a better use of your time than working, then the opportunity cost of studying economics is the four extra points you could have received on a history exam if you studied history instead of economics. Alternatively, if working is the best alternative, the opportunity cost of studying economics is the $10 you could have earned instead.

We can also apply the principle of opportunity cost to decisions about how to spend money from a fixed budget. For example, suppose that you have a fixed budget to spend on music. You can buy your music either at a local music store for $15 per CD or online for $1 per song. The opportunity cost of 1 CD is 15 one-dollar online songs. A hospital with a fixed salary budget can increase the number of doctors only at the expense of nurses or physician's assistants. If a doctor costs five times as much as a nurse, the opportunity cost of a doctor is five nurses.

In some cases, a product that appears to be free actually has a cost. That's why economists are fond of saying, "There's no such thing as a free lunch." Suppose someone offers to buy you lunch if you agree to listen to a sales pitch for a time-share condominium. Although you don't pay any money for the lunch, there is an opportunity cost because you could spend that time in another way—such as studying for your economics or history exam. The lunch isn't free because you sacrifice an hour of your time to get it.

The Cost of College

What is the opportunity cost of a college degree? Consider a student who spends a total of $40,000 for tuition and books. Instead of going to college, the student could have spent this money on a wide variety of goods, including housing, electronic devices, and world travel. Part of the opportunity cost of college is the $40,000 worth of other goods the student sacrifices to pay for tuition and books. Also, instead of going to college, the student could have worked as a bank clerk for $20,000 per year and earned $80,000 over four years. That makes the total opportunity cost of this student's college degree $120,000:

Opportunity cost of money spent on tuition and books	$ 40,000
Opportunity cost of college time (four years working for $20,000 per year)	80,000
Economic cost or total opportunity cost	$120,000

We haven't included the costs of food or housing in our computations of opportunity cost. That's because a student must eat and live somewhere even if he or she doesn't go to college. But if housing and food are more expensive in college, then we would include the extra costs of housing and food in our calculations.

There are other things to consider in a person's decision to attend college. As we'll see later, a college degree can increase a person's earning power, so there are benefits from a college degree. In addition, college offers the thrill of learning and the pleasure of meeting new people. To make an informed decision about whether to attend college, we must compare the benefits to the opportunity costs.

The Cost of Military Spending

We can use the principle of opportunity cost to explore the cost of military spending.[2] In 1992, Malaysia bought two warships. For the price of the warships, the country could have built a system to provide safe drinking water for 5 million citizens who lacked it. In other words, the opportunity cost of the warships was safe drinking water for 5 million people. The policy question is whether the benefits of the warships exceed their opportunity cost.

In the United States, economists have estimated that the cost of the war in Iraq will be at least $1 trillion. The economists' calculations go beyond the simple budgetary costs and quantify the opportunity cost of the war. For example, the resources used in the war could have been used in various government programs for children—to enroll more children in preschool programs, to hire more science and math teachers to reduce class sizes, or to immunize more children in poor countries. For example, each $100 billion spent on the war could instead support one of the following programs:

- Enroll 13 million preschool children in the Head Start program for one year.
- Hire 1.8 million additional teachers for one year.
- Immunize all the children in less-developed countries for the next 33 years.

The fact that the war has a large opportunity cost does not necessarily mean that it is unwise. The policy question is whether the benefits from the war exceed its opportunity cost. Taking another perspective, we can measure the opportunity cost of war in terms of its implications for domestic security. The resources used in the war in Iraq could have been used to improve domestic security by securing ports and cargo facilities, hiring more police officers, improving the screening of airline passengers and baggage, improving fire departments and other first responders, upgrading the Coast Guard fleet, and securing our railroad and highway systems. The cost of implementing the domestic-security recommendations of various government commissions would be about $31 billion, a small fraction of the cost of the war. The question for policymakers is whether money spent on domestic security would be more beneficial than money spent on the war.

Opportunity Cost and the Production Possibilities Curve

Just as individuals face limits, so do entire economies. The ability of an economy to produce goods and services is determined by its factors of production, including labor, natural resources, physical capital, human capital, and entrepreneurship.

Figure 1 shows a production possibilities graph for an economy that produces wheat and steel. The horizontal axis shows the quantity of wheat produced by the economy, and the vertical axis shows the quantity of steel produced. The shaded area shows all the possible combinations of the two goods the economy can produce. At point *a*, for example, the economy can produce 700 tons of steel and 10 tons of wheat. In contrast, at point *e*, the economy can produce 300 tons of steel and 20 tons of wheat. The set of points on the border between the shaded and unshaded area is called the **production possibilities curve** (or *production possibilities frontier*) because it separates the combinations that are attainable from those that are not. The attainable combinations are shown by the shaded area within the curve and the curve itself. The unattainable combinations are shown by the unshaded area outside the curve. The points on the curve show the combinations that are possible if the economy's resources are fully employed.

The production possibilities curve illustrates the notion of opportunity cost. If an economy is fully utilizing its resources, it can produce more of one product only if it produces less of another product. For example, to produce more wheat, we must take resources away from steel. As we move resources out of steel, the quantity of steel produced will decrease. For example, if we move from point *a* to point *b* along the

production possibilities curve

A curve that shows the possible combinations of products that an economy can produce, given that its productive resources are fully employed and efficiently used.

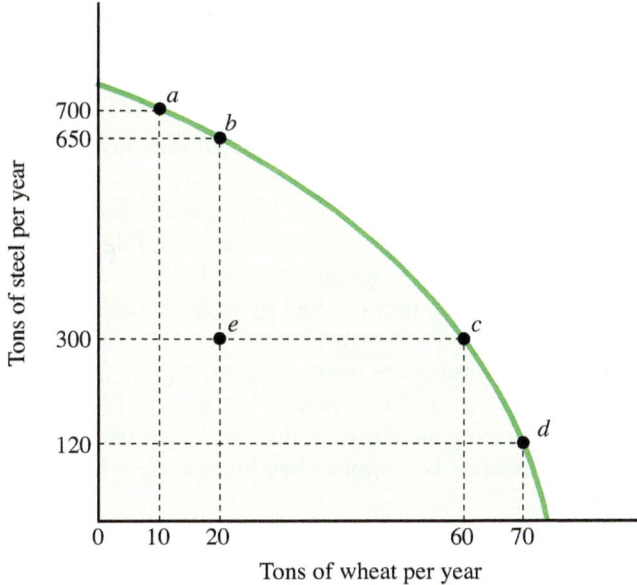

▲ **FIGURE 1**

Scarcity and the Production Possibilities Curve

The production possibilities curve illustrates the principle of opportunity cost for an entire economy. An economy has a fixed amount of resources. If these resources are fully employed, an increase in the production of wheat comes at the expense of steel.

APPLICATION 1

DON'T FORGET THE COSTS OF TIME AND INVESTED FUNDS

APPLYING THE CONCEPTS #1: What is the opportunity cost of running a business?

Betty has a degree in fine arts, and makes a unique product—decorative bottle-cap pins. She paints recycled bottle caps with attractive images, and attaches a pin so the bottle caps can be displayed on sweaters or jackets. She has asked you to compute the annual cost of her business. She uses machines and tools that have a current market value of $10,000. The annual cost of her raw materials (bottle caps, paint, pins) is $2,000. She could be earning $30,000 in another job.

We can use the principle of opportunity cost to compute Betty's costs. In addition to the $2,000 cost of raw materials, we must include two other sorts of costs:

- **Opportunity cost of funds invested.** Betty could have invested the $10,000 in a bank account. If the interest rate on a bank account is 8 percent, the annual cost of her capital (machines and tools) is the $800 she could have earned in a bank account during the year.

- **Opportunity cost of her time.** The opportunity cost of Betty's time is the $30,000 salary she sacrifices by being her own boss.

Adding the $800 cost of funds and the $30,000 cost of her time to the $2,000 materials cost, we find Betty's cost of doing business is $32,800 per year.

---

production possibilities curve in Figure 1, we sacrifice 50 tons of steel (700 tons – 650 tons) to get 10 more tons of wheat (20 tons – 10 tons). Further down the curve, if we move from point *c* to point *d*, we sacrifice 180 tons of steel to get the same 10-ton increase in wheat.

Why is the production possibilities curve bowed outward, with the opportunity cost of wheat increasing as we move down the curve? The reason is that resources are not perfectly adaptable for the production of both goods. Some resources are more suitable for steel production, while others are more suitable for wheat production. Starting at point *a*, the economy uses its most fertile land to produce wheat. A 10-ton increase in wheat reduces the quantity of steel by only 50 tons, because plenty of fertile land is available for conversion to wheat farming. As the economy moves downward along the production possibilities curve, farmers will be forced to use land that is progressively less fertile, so to increase wheat output by 10 tons, more and more resources must be diverted from steel production. In the move from point *c* to point *d*, the land converted to farming is so poor that increasing wheat output by 10 tons decreases steel output by 180 tons.

The production possibilities curve shows the production options for a given set of resources. As shown in Figure 2, an increase in the amount of resources available to the economy shifts the production possibilities outward. For example, if we start at point *f*, and the economy's resources increase, we can produce more steel (point *g*), more wheat (point *h*), or more of both goods (points between *g* and *h*). The curve will also shift outward as a result of technological innovations that enable us to produce more output with a given quantity of resources.

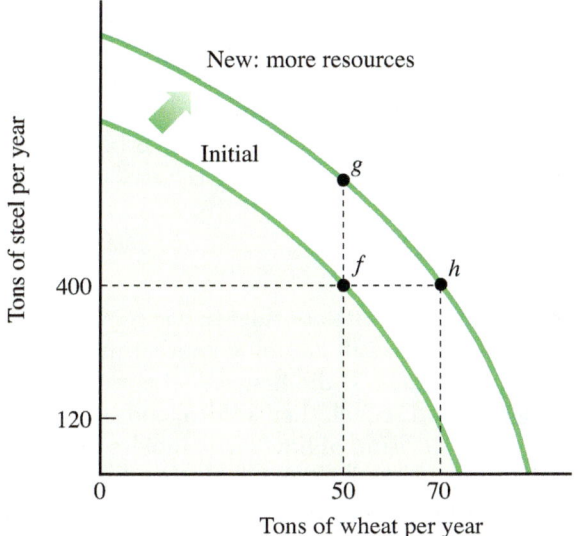

▲ FIGURE 2

Shifting the Production Possibilities Curve

An increase in the quantity of resources or technological innovation in an economy shifts the production possibilities curve outward. Starting from point *f*, a nation could produce more steel (point *g*), more wheat (point *h*), or more of both goods (points between *g* and *h*).

2 THE MARGINAL PRINCIPLE

Economics is about making choices, and we rarely make all-or-nothing choices. For example, if you sit down to read a book, you don't read the entire book in a single sitting, but instead decide how many pages or chapters to read. Economists think in marginal terms, considering how a one-unit change in one variable affects the value of another variable and people's decisions. When we say *marginal*, we're looking at the effect of a small, or incremental, change.

The marginal principle is based on a comparison of the marginal benefits and marginal costs of a particular activity. The **marginal benefit** of an activity is the additional benefit resulting from a small increase in the activity. For example, the marginal benefit of keeping a bookstore open for one more hour equals the additional revenue from book sales. Similarly, the **marginal cost** is the additional cost resulting from a small increase in the activity. For example, the marginal cost of keeping a bookstore open for one more hour equals the additional expenses for workers and utilities for that hour. Applying the marginal principle, the bookstore should stay open for one more hour if the marginal benefit (the additional revenue) is at least as large as the marginal cost (the additional cost). For example, if the marginal benefit is $80 of additional revenue and the marginal cost is $30 of additional expense for workers and utilities, staying open for the additional hour increases the bookstore's profit by $50.

marginal benefit
The additional benefit resulting from a small increase in some activity.

marginal cost
The additional cost resulting from a small increase in some activity.

MARGINAL PRINCIPLE

Increase the level of an activity as long as its marginal benefit exceeds its marginal cost. Choose the level at which the marginal benefit equals the marginal cost.

Thinking at the margin enables us to fine-tune our decisions. We can use the marginal principle to determine whether a one-unit increase in a variable would make us better off. Just as a bookstore owner could decide whether to stay open for one more hour, you could decide whether to study one more hour for a psychology midterm. When we reach the level where the marginal benefit equals the marginal cost, we cannot do any better, and the fine-tuning is done.

How Many Movie Sequels?

To illustrate the marginal principle, let's consider movie sequels. When a movie is successful, its producer naturally thinks about doing another movie, continuing the story line with the same set of characters. If the first sequel is successful too, the producer thinks about producing a second sequel, then a third, and so on. We can use the marginal principle to explore the decision of how many movies to produce.

Figure 3 shows the marginal benefits and marginal costs for movies. On the benefit side, a movie sequel typically generates about 30 percent less revenue than the original movie, and revenue continues to drop for additional movies. In the second column of the table, the first movie generates $300 million in revenue, the second generates $210 million, and the third generates $135 million. This is shown in the graph as a negatively sloped marginal-benefit curve, with the

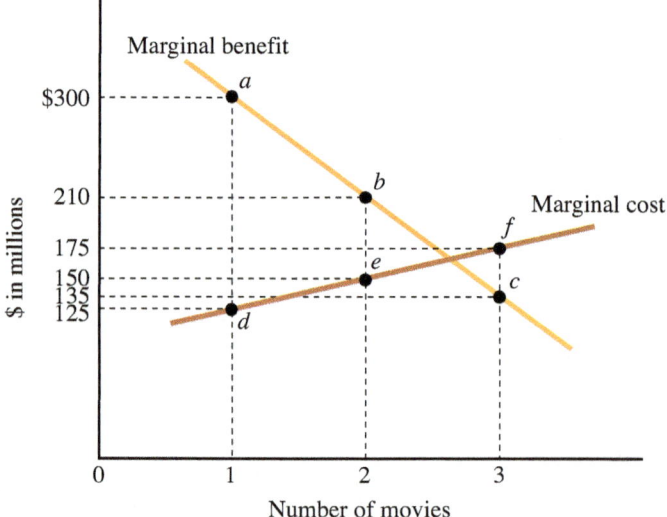

Number of Movies	Marginal Benefit ($ millions)	Marginal Cost ($ millions)
1	$300	$125
2	210	150
3	135	175

▲ **FIGURE 3**

The Marginal Principle and Movie Sequels

The marginal benefit of movies in a series decreases because revenue falls off with each additional movie, while the marginal cost increases because actors demand higher salaries. The marginal benefit exceeds the marginal cost for the first two movies, so it is sensible to produce two, but not three, movies.

marginal benefit decreasing from $300 for the first movie (point *a*), to $210 (point *b*), and then to $135 (point *c*). On the cost side, the typical movie in the United States costs about $50 million to produce and about $75 million to promote.[3] In the third column of the table, the cost of the first movie (the original) is $125 million. In the graph, this is shown as point *d* on the marginal-cost curve. The marginal cost increases with the number of movies because film stars typically demand higher salaries to appear in sequels. In the table and the graph, the marginal cost increases to $150 million for the second movie (point *e*) and to $175 million for the third (point *f*).

In this example, the first two movies are profitable, but the third is not. For the original movie, the marginal benefit ($300 million at point *a*) exceeds the marginal cost ($125 million at point *d*), generating a profit of $175 million. Although the second movie has a higher cost and a lower benefit, it is profitable because the marginal benefit still exceeds the marginal cost, so the profit on the second movie is $60 million ($210 million – $150 million). In contrast, the marginal cost of the third movie of $175 million exceeds its marginal benefit of only $135 million, so the third movie *loses* $40 million. In this example, the movie producer should stop after the second movie.

Although this example shows that only two movies are profitable, other outcomes are possible. If the revenue for the third movie were larger, making the marginal benefit greater than the marginal cost, it would be sensible to produce the third movie. Similarly, if the marginal cost of the third movie were lower—if the actors didn't demand such high salaries—the third movie could be profitable. Many movies have had multiple sequels, such as *Harry Potter and the Sorcerer's Stone* and *Star Wars*. Conversely, many profitable movies, such as *Wedding Crashers* and *Groundhog Day*, didn't result in any sequels. In these cases, the expected drop-off in revenues and run-up in costs for the second movie were large enough to make a sequel unprofitable.

Renting College Facilities

Suppose that your student film society is looking for an auditorium to use for an all-day Hitchcock film program and is willing to pay up to $200. Your college has a new auditorium that has a daily rent of $450, an amount that includes $300 to help pay for the cost of building the auditorium, $50 to help pay for insurance, and $100 to cover the extra costs of electricity and janitorial services for a one-day event. If your film society offers to pay $150 for using the auditorium, should the college accept the offer? The college could use the marginal principle to make the decision.

To decide whether to accept your group's offer, the college should determine the marginal cost of renting out the auditorium. The marginal cost equals the extra costs the college incurs by allowing the student group to use an otherwise vacant auditorium. In our example, the extra cost is $100 for additional electricity and janitorial services. It would be sensible for the college to rent the auditorium, because the marginal benefit ($150 offered by the student group) exceeds the marginal cost ($100). In fact, the college should be willing to rent the facility for any amount greater than $100. If the students and the college split the difference between the $200 the students are willing to pay and the $100 marginal cost, they would agree on a price of $150, leaving both parties better off by $50.

Most colleges do not use this sort of logic. Instead, they use complex formulas to compute the perceived cost of renting out a facility. In most cases, the perceived cost includes some costs that the university bears even if it doesn't rent out the facility for the day. In our example, the facility manager included $300 worth of construction costs and $50 worth of insurance, for a total cost of $450 instead of just $100. Because many colleges include costs that aren't affected by the use of a facility, they overestimate the actual cost of renting out their facilities, missing opportunities to serve student groups and make some money at the same time.

Automobile Emissions Standards

We can use the marginal principle to analyze emissions standards for automobiles. The U.S. government specifies how much carbon monoxide a new car is allowed to emit per mile. The marginal question is "Should the standard be stricter, with fewer units of carbon monoxide allowed?" On the benefit side, a stricter standard reduces health-care costs resulting from pollution: If the air is cleaner, people with respiratory ailments will make fewer visits to doctors and hospitals, have lower medication costs, and lose fewer work days. On the cost side, a stricter standard requires more expensive control equipment on cars and may also reduce fuel efficiency. Using the marginal principle, the government should make the emissions standard stricter as long as the marginal benefit (savings in health-care costs and work time lost) exceeds the marginal cost (the cost of additional equipment and extra fuel used).

> ### APPLICATION 2

Sculpies/Dreamstime

WHY NOT WALK UP AN ESCALATOR?

APPLYING THE CONCEPTS #2: How do people think at the margin?

Why do people walk up stairs, but do not walk up escalators? The rationale for walking up stairs is obvious—if you just stand still, you won't get anywhere. If the benefit of getting to the top of the stairs exceeds the cost (the walking effort), you'll walk up the stairs. So why do most people stand still on escalators? This is a bit of a puzzle because the cost of walking is the same whether you're on a staircase or an escalator, and in both cases, walking allows you to arrive sooner and spend more time at your destination.

We can use the marginal principle to solve this puzzle. Suppose you're on the way to listen to a free concert, and you'd be willing to pay $10 to hear the music. Suppose your cost of walking up a long staircase is $3—that's how much you'd be willing to pay to avoid the staircase. Walking the staircase generates a net benefit of $7 = $10 – $3, so climbing the stairs is sensible. Suppose that the following week you have the same music opportunity, but there is an escalator instead of a staircase. If you stand still on the escalator, you'll get the $10 benefit without any walking cost, so your net benefit would be $10. If you walk up the escalator, you will arrive at your destination sooner and get to listen to more music, but there would be a $3 walking cost. Should you walk or stand still? It depends on the *marginal* benefit of the extra music you will hear if you walk up the escalator instead of standing still, compared to the $3 *marginal* cost. If arriving sooner generates an extra benefit less than $3, it will be sensible for you to stand still, like most people.

SOURCE: Based on Steven E. Landsburg, "One Small Step for Man . . . And One Giant Leap for Economists: How We Figured Out Why People Walk Up Stairs but Not Up Escalators, *Slate.com*, August 28, 2002.

Driving Speed and Safety

Consider the decision about how fast to drive on a highway. The marginal benefit of going one mile per hour faster is the travel time you'll save. On the cost side, an increase in speed increases your chances of colliding with another car, and also increases the severity of injuries suffered in a collision. A rational person will pick the speed at which the marginal benefit of speed equals the marginal cost.

In the 1960s and 1970s, the federal government required automakers to include a number of safety features, including seat belts and collapsible steering columns. These new regulations had two puzzling effects. Although deaths from automobile collisions decreased, the reduction was much lower than expected. In addition, more bicyclists were hit by cars and injured or killed.

We can use the marginal principle to explain why seat belts and other safety features made bicycling more hazardous. The mandated safety features decreased the marginal cost of speed: People who wear seat belts suffer less severe injuries in a collision, so every additional unit of speed is less costly. Drivers felt more secure because they were better insulated from harm in the event of a collision, and so they drove faster. As a result, the number of collisions between cars and bicycles increased, meaning that the safer environment for drivers led to a more hazardous environment for bicyclists.

 **THE PRINCIPLE OF VOLUNTARY EXCHANGE**

The principle of voluntary exchange is based on the notion that people act in their own self-interest. Self-interested people won't exchange one thing for another unless the trade makes them better off.

PRINCIPLE OF VOLUNTARY EXCHANGE

A voluntary exchange between two people makes both people better off.

Here are some examples.

- If you voluntarily exchange money for a college education, you must expect you'll be better off with a college education. The college voluntarily provides an education in exchange for your money, so the college must be better off, too.

- If you have a job, you voluntarily exchange your time for money, and your employer exchanges money for your labor services. Both you and your employer are better off as a result.

Exchange and Markets

Adam Smith stressed the importance of voluntary exchange as a distinctly human trait. He noticed[4]

a propensity in human nature . . . to truck, barter, and exchange one thing for another . . . It is common to all men, and to be found in no other . . . animals . . . Nobody ever saw a dog make a fair and deliberate exchange of one bone for another with another dog.

A market is an institution or arrangement that enables people to exchange goods and services. If participation in a market is voluntary and

APPLICATION 3

JASPER JOHNS AND HOUSEPAINTING

APPLYING THE CONCEPTS #3: What is the rationale for specialization and exchange?

Jasper Johns is a contemporary American artist whose painting *False Start* sold for $80 million, the largest sum paid for a painting of a living artist. According to Skate's Art Market Research, Mr. Johns is among the top 30 artists in terms of the monetary value of art produced. Mr. Johns appears as a guest star in a 1999 episode of *The Simpsons* in which Homer uses a mangled barbeque to launch a career as a contemporary artist.

Mr. Johns is a very productive painter, and his painting skills presumably translate into house painting. If Mr. Johns is ten times more productive at house painting than a professional house painter, should he paint his own house? For example, suppose Mr. Johns can paint his house in one day, compared to 10 days for a professional. Should he take a day to paint his house, or hire someone who will take 10 days to complete the same task?

We can use the principle of voluntary exchange to explain why Mr. Johns should hire the less productive house painter to paint his house. If Mr. Johns can earn $5,000 per day painting works of art, the opportunity cost of house painting is $5,000—the income he sacrifices by spending a day painting the house rather than producing works of art. If the housepainter charges $150 per day, Mr. Johns could hire him to paint the house for only $1,500. By switching one day from house painting to art production, Mr. Johns earns $5,000 and incurs a cost of only $1,500, so he is better off by $3,500. Mr. Johns specializes in what he does best, and then buys goods and services from other people.

people are well informed, both people in a transaction—buyer and seller—will be better off. The next time you see a market transaction, listen to what people say after money changes hands. If both people say "thank you," that's the principle of voluntary exchange in action: The double "thank you" reveals that both people are better off.

The alternative to exchange is *self-sufficiency*: Each of us could produce everything for him- or herself. It is more sensible to specialize, doing what we do best and then buying products from other people, who in turn are doing what they do best. For example, if you are good with numbers but an awful carpenter, you could specialize in accounting and buy furniture from Woody, who could specialize in making furniture and pay someone to do his bookkeeping. In general, exchange allows us to take advantage of differences in people's talents and skills.

Online Games and Market Exchange

As another illustration of the power of exchange, consider the virtual world of online games. Role-playing games such as *World of Warcraft* and *EverQuest* allow thousands of people to interact online, moving their characters through a landscape of survival challenges. Each player constructs a character—called an *avatar*—by choosing some initial traits for it. The player then navigates the avatar through the game's challenges, where it acquires skills and accumulates assets, including clothing, weapons, armor, and even magic spells.

The curious part about these role-playing games is that players use real-life auction sites, including eBay and Yahoo! Auctions, to buy products normally acquired in the game.[5] Byron, who wants a piece of armor for his avatar (say, a Rubicite girdle), can use eBay to buy one for $50 from Selma. The two players then enter the online game, and Selma's avatar transfers the armor to Byron's avatar. It is even possible to buy another player's avatar, with all its skills and assets. Given the time required to acquire various objects such as Rubicite girdles in the game and the prices paid for them on eBay, the implicit wage earned by the typical online player auctioning them off is $3.42 per hour: That's how much the player could earn by first taking the time to acquire the assets in the game and then selling them on eBay.

4 THE PRINCIPLE OF DIMINISHING RETURNS

Xena has a small copy shop, with one copying machine and one worker. When the backlog of orders piled up, she decided to hire a second worker, expecting that doubling her workforce would double the output of her copy shop from 500 pages per

---

APPLICATION 4

FERTILIZER AND CROP YIELDS

APPLYING THE CONCEPTS #4: Do farmers experience diminishing returns?

Navarone/Dreamstime

The notion of diminishing returns applies to all inputs to the production process. For example, one of the inputs in the production of corn is nitrogen fertilizer. Suppose a farmer has a fixed amount of land (an acre) and must decide how much fertilizer to apply. The first 50-pound bag of fertilizer will increase the crop yield by a relatively large amount, but the second bag is likely to increase the yield by a smaller amount, and the third bag is likely to have an even smaller effect. Because the farmer is changing just one of the inputs, the output will increase, but at a decreasing rate. Eventually, additional fertilizer will actually decrease output as the other nutrients in the soil are overwhelmed by the fertilizer.

Table 1 shows the relationship between the amount of fertilizer and the corn output. The first 50-pound bag of fertilizer increases the crop yield from 85 to 120 bushels per acre, a gain of 35 bushels. The next bag of fertilizer increases the yield by only 15 bushels (from 120 to 135), followed by a gain of 9 bushels (from 135 to 144) and then a gain of only 3 bushels (from 144 to 147). The farmer experienced diminishing returns because the other inputs to the production process are fixed.

TABLE 1 FERTILIZER AND CORN YIELD	
Bags of Nitrogen Fertilizer	Bushels of Corn Per Acre
0	85
1	120
2	135
3	144
4	147

hour to 1,000. Xena was surprised when output increased to only 800 pages per hour. If she had known about the principle of diminishing returns, she would not have been surprised.

PRINCIPLE OF DIMINISHING RETURNS

Suppose output is produced with two or more inputs, and we increase one input while holding the other input or inputs fixed. Beyond some point—called the *point of diminishing returns*—output will increase at a decreasing rate.

Xena added a worker (one input) while holding the number of copying machines (the other input) fixed. Because the two workers must share a single copying machine, each worker spent some time waiting for the machine to be available. As a result, adding the second worker increased the number of copies, but did not double the output. With a single worker and a single copy machine, Xena has already reached the point of diminishing returns: As she increases the number of workers, output increases, but at a decreasing rate. The first worker increases output by 500 pages (from 0 to 500), but the second worker increases output by only 300 pages (from 500 to 800).

Diminishing Returns from Sharing a Production Facility

This principle of diminishing returns is relevant when we try to produce more output in an existing production facility (a factory, a store, an office, or a farm) by increasing the number of workers sharing the facility. When we add a worker to the facility, each worker becomes less productive because he or she works with a smaller piece of the facility: More workers share the same machinery, equipment, and factory space. As we pack more and more workers into the factory, total output increases, but at a decreasing rate.

It's important to emphasize that diminishing returns occurs because one of the inputs to the production process is fixed. When a firm can vary all its inputs, including the size of the production facility, the principle of diminishing returns is not relevant. For example, if a firm doubled all its inputs, building a second factory and hiring a second workforce, we would expect the total output of the firm to at least double. The principle of diminishing returns does not apply when a firm is flexible in choosing all its inputs.

 **THE REAL-NOMINAL PRINCIPLE**

One of the key ideas in economics is that people are interested not just in the amount of money they have but also in how much their money will buy.

REAL-NOMINAL PRINCIPLE

What matters to people is the real value of money or income—its purchasing power—not its "face" value.

442

APPLICATION 5 ——————————————————————

THE DECLINING REAL MINIMUM WAGE

APPLYING THE CONCEPTS #5: How does inflation affect the real minimum wage?

Between 1974 and 2007, the federal minimum wage increased from $2.00 to $5.85. Was the typical minimum-wage worker better or worse off in 2007? We can apply the real-nominal principle to see what's happened over time to the real value of the federal minimum wage.

As shown in the first row of Table 2, the minimum wage was $2.00 per hour in 1974, and by 2007 it had risen to $5.85. These are nominal figures, indicating the face value of the minimum wage. By working 40 hours per week, a minimum-wage worker could earn $80 in 1974 and $234 in 2007. The third row of Table 2 shows the cost of a standard basket of consumer goods, which includes a standard mix of housing, food, clothing, and transportation. In 1974, consumer prices were relatively low, and the cost of buying all the goods in the standard basket was only $47. Between 1974 and 2007, consumer prices increased, and the cost of this standard basket of goods increased to $202.

The last row in Table 2 shows the purchasing power of the minimum wage in 1974 and 2007. In 1974, the $80 in weekly income could buy 1.70 standard baskets of goods. Between 1974 and 2007, the weekly income nearly tripled, but the cost of the standard basket of goods more than quadrupled, from $47 to $202. As a result, the weekly income of $234 in 2007 could buy only 1.16 baskets of goods. Because prices increased faster than the nominal wage, the real value of the minimum wage actually decreased over this period.

The minimum wage increased to $6.55 in July 2008 and $7.25 one year later. These wage hikes are not large enough to restore the 1974 purchasing power of the minimum wage. For that to happen, the minimum wage in July of 2008 would have to be about $8.84.

TABLE 2 THE REAL VALUE OF THE MINIMUM WAGE, 1974–2007

	1974	2007
Minimum wage per hour	$ 2.00	$ 5.85
Weekly income from minimum wage	80.00	234.00
Cost of a standard basket of goods	47.00	202.00
Number of baskets per week	1.70	1.16

To illustrate this principle, suppose you work in your college bookstore to earn extra money for movies and snacks. If your take-home pay is $10 per hour, is this a high wage or a low wage? The answer depends on the prices of the goods you buy. If a movie costs $4 and a snack costs $1, with one hour of work you could afford to see two movies and buy two snacks. The wage may seem high enough for you. But if a movie costs $8 and a snack costs $2, an hour of work would buy only one movie and one snack, and the same $10 wage doesn't seem so high. This is the real-nominal principle in action: What matters is not how many dollars you earn, but what those dollars will purchase.

APPLICATION 6

REPAYING STUDENT LOANS

APPLYING THE CONCEPTS #6: How does inflation affect lenders and borrowers?

Suppose you finish college with $20,000 in student loans and start a job that pays a salary of $40,000 in the first year. In 10 years, you must repay your college loans. Which would you prefer: stable prices, rising prices, or falling prices?

We can use the real-nominal principle to compute the real cost of repaying your loans. The first row of Table 3 shows the cost of the loan when all prices in the economy are stable—including the price of labor, your salary. In this case, your nominal salary in 10 years is $40,000, and the real cost of repaying your loan is the half year of work you must do to earn the $20,000 you owe. However, if all prices double over the 10-year period, your nominal salary will double to $80,000, and, as shown in the second row of Table 3, it will take you only a quarter of a year to earn $20,000 to repay the loan. In other words, a general increase in prices lowers the real cost of your loan. In contrast, if all prices decrease and your annual salary drops to $20,000, it will take you a full year to earn the money to repay the loan. In general, people who owe money prefer inflation (a general rise in prices) to deflation (a general drop in prices).

TABLE 3 EFFECT OF INFLATION AND DEFLATION ON LOAN REPAYMENT		
Change in Prices and Wages	Annual Salary	Years of Work to Repay $20,000 Loan
Stable	$40,000	1/2 year
Inflation: Salary doubles	80,000	1/4 year
Deflation: Salary cut in half	20,000	1 year

nominal value
The face value of an amount of money.

real value
The value of an amount of money in terms of what it can buy.

Economists use special terms to express the ideas behind the real-nominal principle:

- The **nominal value** of an amount of money is simply its face value. For example, the nominal wage paid by the bookstore is $10 per hour.
- The **real value** of an amount of money is measured in terms of the quantity of goods the money can buy. For example, the real value of your bookstore wage would fall as the prices of movies and snacks increase, even though your nominal wage stayed the same.

The real-nominal principle can explain how people choose the amount of money to carry around with them. Suppose you typically withdraw $40 per week from an ATM to cover your normal expenses. If the prices of all the goods you purchase during the week double, you would have to withdraw $80 per week to make the same purchases. The amount of money people carry around depends on the prices of the goods and services they buy.

Government officials use the real-nominal principle when they design public programs. For example, Social Security payments are increased each year to ensure that the checks received by the elderly and other recipients will purchase the same amount of goods and services, even if prices have increased. The government also uses this principle when it publishes statistics about the economy. For example, its reports about changes in "real wages" in the economy over time take into account the prices of the goods workers purchase. Therefore, the real wage is stated in terms of its buying power, rather than its face value or nominal value.

SUMMARY

Szefei wong/Alamy

This chapter covers five key principles of economics, the simple, self-evident truths that most people readily accept.

1 Principle of opportunity cost. The opportunity cost of something is what you sacrifice to get it.

2 Marginal principle. Increase the level of an activity as long as its marginal benefit exceeds its marginal cost. Choose the level at which the marginal benefit equals the marginal cost.

3 Principle of voluntary exchange. A voluntary exchange between two people makes both people better off.

4 Principle of diminishing returns. Suppose that output is produced with two or more inputs, and we increase one input while holding the other inputs fixed. Beyond some point—called the *point of diminishing returns*—output will increase at a decreasing rate.

5 Real-nominal principle. What matters to people is the real value of money or income—its purchasing power—not the face value of money or income.

KEY TERMS

marginal benefit

marginal cost

nominal value

opportunity cost

production possibilities curve

real value

EXERCISES

Visit www.myeconlab.com to complete these exercises online and get instant feedback.

1   The Principle of Opportunity Cost

1.1 Consider Figure 1. Between points *c* and *d*, the opportunity cost of _____ tons of wheat is _____ tons of steel.

1.2 Arrow up or down: An increase in the wage for high-school graduates _____ the opportunity cost of college.

1.3 Arrow up or down: An increase in the market interest rate _____ the economic cost of holding a $500 collectible for a year.

1.4 You just inherited a house with a market value of $300,000, and do not expect the market value to change. Each year, you will pay $1,000 for utilities and $3,000 in taxes. You can earn 6 percent interest on money in a bank account. Your cost of living in the house for a year is $_____.

1.5 What is the cost of a pair of warships purchased by Malaysia?

1.6 Conservationists have a new strategy for preserving rainforests: _____ loggers and other developers for the land, paying as little as $_____ per hectare per year.

1.7 **The Cost of a Flower Business.** Jen left a job paying $40,000 per year to start her own florist shop in a building she owns. The market value of the building is $200,000. She pays $30,000 per year for flowers and other supplies, and has a bank account that pays 8 percent interest. The annual economic cost of Jen's business is _____. (Related to Application 1.)

1.8 The Opportunity Cost of a Mission to Mars. The United States has plans to spend billions of dollars on a mission to Mars. List some of the possible opportunity costs of the mission. What resources will be used to execute the mission, and what do we sacrifice by using these resources in a mission to Mars?

1.9 Interest Rates and ATM Trips. Carlos, who lives in a country where interest rates are very high, goes to an ATM every day to get $10 of spending money. Art, who lives in a country with relatively low interest rates, goes to the ATM once a month to get $300 of spending money. Why does Carlos use the ATM more frequently?

1.10 Correct the Cost Statements. Consider the following statements about cost. For each incorrect statement, provide a correct statement about the relevant cost.
   a. One year ago, I loaned a friend $100, and she just paid me back the whole $100. The loan didn't cost me anything.
   b. An oil refinery bought a million barrels of oil a month ago, when the price was only $75 per barrel, compared to $120 today. The cost of using a barrel of oil to produce gasoline is $75.
   c. Our new football stadium was built on land donated to the university by a wealthy alum. The cost of the stadium equals the $50 million construction cost.
   d. If a commuter rides a bus to work and the bus fare is $2, the cost of commuting by bus is $2.

1.11 Production Possibilities Curve. Consider a nation that produces baseball mitts and soccer balls. The following table shows the possible combinations of the two products.

Baseball mitts (millions)	0	2	4	6	8
Soccer balls (millions)	30	24	18	10	0

   a. Draw a production possibilities curve with mitts on the horizontal axis and balls on the vertical axis.
   b. Suppose the technology for producing mitts improves, meaning that fewer resources are needed for each mitt. In contrast, the technology for producing soccer balls does not change. Draw a new production possibilities curve.
   c. The opportunity cost of the first two million mitts is _____ million soccer balls and the opportunity cost of the last two million mitts is _____ million soccer balls.

1.12 Cost of Antique Furniture. Colleen owns antique furniture that she bought for $5,000 ten years ago.

Your job is to compute Colleen's cost of owning the furniture for the next year. To compute the cost, you need two bits of information: _____ and _____.

2 The Marginal Principle

2.1 A taxi company currently has nine cabs in its fleet, and its total daily cost is $4,000. If the company added a tenth cab, its daily total cost would be $4,200, or $420 per cab. Adding the tenth cab will increase the daily total revenue by $300. Should the company add the tenth cab? _____ (Yes/No)

2.2 In Figure 3, suppose the marginal cost of movies is constant at $125 million. Is it sensible to produce the third movie? _____ (Yes/No)

2.3 Suppose that stricter emissions standards would reduce health-care costs by $50 million but increase the costs of fuel and emissions equipment by $30 million. Is it sensible to tighten the emissions standards? _____ (Yes/No)

2.4 Arrows up or down: The decision about whether to walk up an escalator is based on the _____ benefit and the _____ cost. (Related to Application 2.)

2.5 How Fast to Drive? Suppose Duke is driving to a nearby town to attend a dance party, and must decide how fast to drive. The marginal benefit of speed is the extra dance time he will get by driving faster, and the marginal cost is the additional risk of a collision. The marginal-benefit curve is negatively sloped, and the marginal-cost curve is positively sloped.
   a. Draw a pair of curves that suggest Duke will drive 40 mph.
   b. Suppose the normal country band is replaced by Adam Smith and the Invisible Hands, Duke's favorite punk band. Duke's utility from slam dancing is twice his utility from the two-step. Use your curves to show how Duke's chosen speed will change.
   c. Suppose Duke's favorite dance partner, Daisy, is grounded for makeup violations. Use your curves to show how Duke's chosen speed will change.
   d. Suppose the legal speed limit is set at 35 mph, and there is a 50 percent chance that Duke will be caught if he speeds. Use your curves to show how Duke's chosen speed will change.

2.6 Continental Airlines Goes Marginal. In the 1960s, Continental Airlines puzzled observers of the airline industry and dismayed its stockholders by running flights with up to half the seats empty. The average cost of running a flight was $4,000, a figure that includes fixed costs such as airport fees and the cost of running the reservation system. A half-full aircraft generated only $3,100 of revenue.

a. Use the marginal principle to explain why Continental ran half-empty flights.

b. It will be sensible to run a half-empty flight if the marginal _____ of flight is _____ than $_____ .

2.7 Marginal Airlines. Marginal Airlines runs 10 flights per day at a total cost of $50,000, including $30,000 in fixed costs for airport fees and the reservation system and $20,000 for flight crews and food service.

a. If an 11th flight would have 25 passengers, each paying $100, would it be sensible to run the flight?

b. If the 11th flight would have only 15 passengers, would it be sensible to run the flight?

2.8 How Many Police Officers? In your city, each police officer has a budgetary cost of $40,000 per year. The property loss from each burglary is $4,000. The first officer hired will reduce crime by 40 burglaries, and each additional officer will reduce crime by half as much as the previous one. How many officers should the city hire? Illustrate with a graph with a marginal-benefit curve and a marginal-cost curve.

2.9 How Many Hours at the Barber Shop? The opportunity cost of your time spent cutting hair at your barbershop is $20 per hour. Electricity costs $6 per hour, and your weekly rent is $250. You normally stay open nine hours per day.

a. What is the marginal cost of staying open for one more hour?

b. If you expect to give two haircuts in the 10th hour and you charge $15 per haircut, is it sensible to stay open for the extra hour?

2.10 How Many Pints of Blackberries? The pleasure you get from each pint of freshly picked blackberries is $2.00. It takes you 12 minutes to pick the first pint, and each additional pint takes an additional 2 minutes (14 minutes for the second pint, 16 minutes for the third pint, and so on). The opportunity cost of your time is $0.10 per minute.

a. How many pints of blackberries should you pick? Illustrate with a complete graph.

b. How would your answer to (a) change if your pleasure decreased by $0.20 for each additional pint ($1.80 for the second, $1.60 for the third, and so on)? Illustrate with a complete graph.

3 The Principle of Voluntary Exchange

3.1 When two people involved in an exchange say "thank you" afterwards, they are merely being polite. _____ (True/False)

3.2 Consider a transaction in which a consumer buys a book for $15. The value of the book to the buyer is at least $_____, and the cost of producing the book is no more than $_____ .

3.3 Arrow up or down: Andy buys and eats one apple per day, and smacks his lips in appreciation as he eats it. The greater his satisfaction with the exchange of money for an apple, the larger the number of smacks. If the price of apples decreases, the number of smacks per apple will _____ .

3.4 Sally sells one apple per day to Andy, and says "ca-ching" to show her satisfaction with the transaction. The greater her satisfaction with the exchange, the louder her "ca-ching." If the price of apples decreases, her "ca-ching" will become _____ (louder/softer).

3.5 Should a Heart Surgeon Do Her Own Plumbing? A heart surgeon is skillful at unplugging arteries and rerouting the flow of blood, and these skills also make her a very skillful plumber. She can clear a clogged drain in six minutes, about 10 times faster than the most skillful plumber in town. (Related to Application 3.)

a. Should the surgeon clear her own clogged drains? Explain.

b. Suppose the surgeon earns $20 per minute in heart surgery, and the best plumber in town charges $50 per hour. How much does the surgeon gain by hiring the plumber to clear a clogged drain?

3.6 Fishing versus Boat Building. Half the members of a fishing tribe catch two fish per day and half catch eight fish per day. A group of 10 members could build a boat for another tribe in one day and receive a payment of 40 fish for the boat.

a. Suppose the boat builders are drawn at random from the tribe. From the tribe's perspective, what is the expected cost of building the boat?

b. How could the tribe decrease the cost of building the boat, thus making it worthwhile?

3.7 Solving a Tree Cutting Problem. Consider a hilly neighborhood where large trees provide shade but also block views. When a resident announces plans to cut down several trees to improve her view, her neighbors object and announce plans to block the tree cutting. One week later, the trees are gone, but everyone is happy. Use the principle of voluntary exchange to explain what happened.

4 The Principle of Diminishing Returns

4.1 Consider the example of Xena's copy shop. Adding a second worker increased output by 300 pages. If she added a third worker, her output would increase by fewer than _____ pages.

4.2 If a firm is subject to diminishing marginal returns, an increase in the number of workers decreases the quantity produced. _____ (True/False)

4.3 Fill in the blanks with "at least" or "less than": If a firm doubles one input but holds the other inputs fixed, we normally expect output to _____ double; if a firm doubles all inputs, we expect output to _____ double.

4.4 Fill in the blanks with "flexible" or "inflexible": Diminishing returns is applicable when a firm is _____ in choosing inputs, but does not apply when a firm is _____ in choosing its inputs.

4.5 Arrows up or down: As a farmer adds more and more fertilizer to the soil, the crop yield _____, but at a _____ rate. (Related to Application 4.)

4.6 **Feeding the World from a Flowerpot?** Comment on the following statement: "If agriculture did not experience diminishing returns, we could feed the world using the soil from a small flowerpot." (Related to Application 4.)

4.7 **When to Use the Principle of Diminishing Returns?** You are the manager of a firm that produces memory chips for mobile phones.
  a. In your decision about how much output to produce this week, would you use the principle of diminishing returns? Explain.
  b. In your decision about how much output to produce two years from now, would you use the principle of diminishing returns? Explain.

4.8 **Diminishing Returns in Microbrewing?** Your microbrewery produces craft beer, using a single vat, various ingredients, and workers.
  a. If you double the number of workers and ingredients, but don't add a second vat, would you expect your output (gallons per hour) to double? Explain.
  b. If you double the number of workers and ingredients and add a second vat, would you expect your output (gallons per hour) to double? Explain.

4.9 **Diminishing Returns and the Marginal Principle.** Molly's Espresso Shop has become busy, and the more hours Ted works, the more espressos Molly can sell.

The price of espressos is $2 and Ted's hourly wage is $11. Complete the following table:

Hours for Ted	Espressos Sold	Marginal Benefit from Additional Hour	Marginal Cost from Additional Hour
0	100	—	—
1	130	$60 = $2 × 30 additional espressos	$11 = hourly wage
2	154		
3	172		
4	184		
5	190		
6	193		

If Molly applies the marginal principle, how many hours should Ted work?

5 The Real-Nominal Principle

5.1 Your savings account pays 4 percent per year: Each $100 in the bank grows to $104 over a one-year period. If prices increase by 3 percent per year, by keeping $100 in the bank for a year you actually gain $_____.

5.2 You earn 5 percent interest on funds in your money-market account. If consumer prices increase by 7 percent per year, your earnings on $1,000 in the money-market account is $_____ per year.

5.3 Suppose that over a one-year period, the nominal wage increases by 2 percent and consumer prices increase by 5 percent. Fill in the blanks: The real wage _____ by _____ percent.

5.4 Suppose you currently live and work in Cleveland, earning a salary of $60,000 per year and spending $10,000 for housing. You just heard that you will be transferred to a city in California where housing is 50 percent more expensive. In negotiating a new salary, your objective is to keep your real income constant. Your new target salary is $_____.

5.5 Between 1974 and 2005, the federal minimum wage increased from $2.00 to $5.15. Was the typical minimum-wage worker better off in 2005? _____ (Yes/No) (Related to Application 5.)

5.6 Suppose you graduate with $20,000 in student loans and repay the loans 10 years later. Which is better for you, inflation (rising prices) or deflation (falling prices)? _____ (Related to Application 6.)

5.7 Changes in Welfare Payments. Between 1970 and 1988, the average monthly welfare payment to single mothers increased from $160 to $360. Over the same period, the cost of a standard basket of consumer goods (a standard bundle of food, housing, and other goods and services) increased from $39 to $118. Fill the blanks in the following table. Did the real value of welfare payments increase or decrease over this period? (Related to Application 5.)

	1970	1988
Monthly welfare payment	$160	$360
Cost of a standard basket of goods	39	118
Number of baskets per week		

5.8 Changes in Wages and Consumer Prices. The following table shows for 1980 and 2004 the cost of a standard basket of consumer goods (a standard bundle of food, housing, and other goods and services) and the nominal average wage (hourly earnings) for workers in several sectors of the economy.

Year	Cost of Consumer Basket	Nominal Wage: Manufacturing	Nominal Wage: Professional Services	Nominal Wage: Leisure and Hospitality	Nominal Wage: Information
1980	$ 82	$ 7.52	$ 7.48	$4.05	$ 9.83
2004	189	16.34	17.69	9.01	21.70
Percent change from 1980 to 2004					

a. Complete the table by computing the percentage changes of the cost of the basket of consumer goods and the nominal wages.

b. How do the percentage changes in nominal wages compare to the percentage change in the cost of consumer goods?

c. Which sectors experienced an increase in real wages, and which sectors experienced a decrease in real wages?

5.9 Repaying a Car Loan. Suppose you borrow money to buy a car and must repay $20,000 in interest and principal in five years. Your current monthly salary is $4,000. (Related to Application 6.)

a. Complete the following table.

b. Which environment has the lowest real cost of repaying the loan?

Change in Prices and Wages	Monthly Salary	Months of Work to Repay $20,000 Loan
Stable	$4,000	
Inflation: Prices rise by 25%		
Deflation: Prices drop by 50%		

5.10 Inflation and Interest Rates. Len buys MP3 music at $1 per tune, and prefers music now to music later. He is willing to sacrifice 10 tunes today as long as he gets at least 11 tunes in a year. When Len loans $50 to Barb for a one-year period, he cuts back his music purchases by 50 tunes.

a. To make Len indifferent about making the loan, Barb must repay him _____ tunes or $_____. The implied interest rate is _____ percent.

b. Suppose that over the one-year period of the loan, all prices (including the price of MP3 tunes) increase by 20 percent, and Len and Barb anticipate the price changes. To make Len indifferent about making the loan, Barb must repay him _____ tunes or $_____. The implied interest rate is _____ percent.

ECONOMIC EXPERIMENT

Producing Fold-Its

Here is a simple economic experiment that takes about 15 minutes to run. The instructor places a stapler and a stack of paper on a table. Students produce "fold-its" by folding a page of paper in thirds and stapling both ends of the folded page. One student is assigned to inspect each fold-it to be sure that it is produced correctly. The experiment starts with a single student, or worker, who has one minute to produce as many fold-its as possible. After the instructor records the number of fold-its produced, the process is repeated with two students, three students, four students, and so on. How does the number of fold-its change as the number of workers increases?

 For additional economic experiments, please visit *www.myeconlab.com*.

NOTES

1. "Rent a Tree," *The Economist*, March 3, 2008.

2. United Nations Development Program, *Human Development Report 1994* (New York: Oxford University Press, 1994); Linda Blimes and Joseph Stiglitz, "The Economic Costs of the Iraq War: An Appraisal Three Years After the Beginning of the Conflict," *Faculty Research Working Papers*, Harvard University, January 2006; Center for American Progress, "The Opportunity Costs of the Iraq War," August 25, 2004; Scott Wallsten and Katrina Kosec, "The Economic Costs of the War in Iraq," AEI-Brookings Joint Center for Regulatory Studies, September 2005; Joseph Stiglitz and Linda Bilmes, *The Three Trillion Dollar War* (New York: WW Norton, 2008).

3. Colin Kennedy, "Lord of the Screens," in *Economist: The World in 2003* (London, 2003), 29.

4. Adam Smith, *An Inquiry into the Nature and Causes of the Wealth of Nations* (1776), Book 1, Chapter 2.

5. Edward Castronova, *Synthetic Worlds: The Business and Culture of Online Games* (Chicago: University of Chicago Press, 2005).

Demand, Supply, and Market Equilibrium

Earthquake and the Price of Paper. A powerful earthquake in February 2010 damaged many of Chile's wood-pulp mills and the infrastructure (roads, water systems, and ports) required to produce and export wood pulp to the United States, Europe, and China. Chile is responsible for 8 percent of the world supply of wood pulp, and the decrease in the supply of pulp increased the world price by $40 per ton, to $950. Pulp producers in Canada and the United States responded to the higher price by increasing their output, hiring more workers and earning more profit in the process.

The decrease in the supply of wood pulp affected the market for paper. Wood pulp is the main raw material for paper, and the increase in the pulp price increased the cost of producing paper and its price. In other words, part of the cost of the earthquake was borne by paper consumers.

Alex Segre/Alamy

APPLYING THE CONCEPTS

1 How do changes in demand affect prices?
Hurricane Katrina and Baton Rouge Housing Prices

2 How do changes in supply in one market affect other markets?
Honeybees and the Price of Ice Cream

3 How do simultaneous changes in supply and demand affect the equilibrium price?
The Supply and Demand for Cruise Ship Berths

4 How do changes in supply affect prices?
The Bouncing Price of Vanilla Beans

5 How do producers respond to higher prices?
Drought in Australia and the Price of Rice

From Chapter 3 of *Survey of Economics: Principles, Applications, and Tools*, 5/e. Arthur O'Sullivan. Steven M. Sheffrin. Stephen J. Perez. Copyright © 2012 by Pearson Education. Published by Prentice Hall. All rights reserved.

In this chapter we use the model of demand and supply—the most important tool of economic analysis—to see how markets work. We'll see how the prices of goods and services are affected by all sorts of changes in the economy, including bad weather, higher income, technological innovation, bad publicity, and changes in consumer preferences. This chapter will prepare you for the applications of demand and supply.

The model of demand and supply explains how a perfectly competitive market operates. A **perfectly competitive market** has many buyers and sellers of a product, so no single buyer or seller can affect the market price. The classic example of a perfectly competitive firm is a wheat farmer who produces a tiny fraction of the total supply of wheat. No matter how much wheat an individual farmer produces, the farmer can't change the market price of wheat.

perfectly competitive market

A market with many sellers and buyers of a homogeneous product and no barriers to entry.

1 THE DEMAND CURVE

On the demand side of a market, consumers buy products from firms. We have one main question about this side of the market: How much of a particular product are consumers willing to buy during a particular period? Notice that we define *demand* for a particular period, for example, a day, a month, or a year.

We'll start our discussion of demand with the individual consumer. A consumer who is willing to buy a particular product is willing to sacrifice enough money to purchase it. The consumer doesn't merely have a desire to buy the good, but is also willing and able to sacrifice something to get it. How much of a product is an individual willing to buy? It depends on a number of variables. Here is a list of the variables that affect an individual consumer's decision, using the pizza market as an example:

- The price of the product (for example, the price of a pizza)
- The consumer's income
- The price of substitute goods (for example, the prices of tacos or sandwiches or other goods that can be consumed instead of pizza)
- The price of complementary goods (for example, the price of lemonade or other goods consumed with pizza)
- The consumer's preferences or tastes and advertising that may influence preferences
- The consumer's expectations about future prices

Together, these variables determine how much of a particular product an individual consumer is willing and able to buy, the **quantity demanded**. We'll start our discussion of demand with the relationship between price and quantity demanded, a relationship we represented graphically by the demand curve. Later in the chapter, we will discuss the other variables that affect the individual consumer's decision about how much of a product to buy.

quantity demanded

The amount of a product that consumers are willing and able to buy.

The Individual Demand Curve and the Law of Demand

The starting point f or a discussion of individual demand is a **demand schedule**, which is a table of numbers showing the relationship between the price of a particular product and the quantity that an individual consumer is willing to buy. The demand schedule shows how the quantity demanded by an individual changes with the price, *ceteris paribus* (everything else held fixed). The variables that are held fixed in the demand schedule are the consumer's income, the prices of substitutes

demand schedule

A table that shows the relationship between the price of a product and the quantity demanded, *ceteris paribus*.

and complements, the consumer's tastes, and the consumer's expectations about future prices.

The table in Figure 1 shows Al's demand schedule for pizza. At a price of $2, Al buys 13 pizzas per month. As the price rises, he buys fewer pizzas: 10 pizzas at a price of $4, 7 pizzas at a price of $6, and so on, down to only 1 pizza at a price of $10. Remember that in a demand schedule, any change in quantity results from a change in price alone.

The **individual demand curve** is a graphical representation of the demand schedule. By plotting the numbers in Al's demand schedule—various combinations of price and quantity—we can draw his demand curve for pizza. The demand curve shows the relationship between the price and the quantity demanded by an individual consumer, *ceteris paribus*. To get the data for a single demand curve, we change only the price of pizza and observe how a consumer responds to the price change. In Figure 1, Al's demand curve shows the quantity of pizzas he is willing to buy at each price.

Notice that Al's demand curve is negatively sloped, reflecting the **law of demand**. This law applies to all consumers:

There is a negative relationship between price and quantity demanded, *ceteris paribus*.

The words *ceteris paribus* remind us that in order to isolate the relationship between price and quantity demanded, we *must* assume that income, the prices of related goods

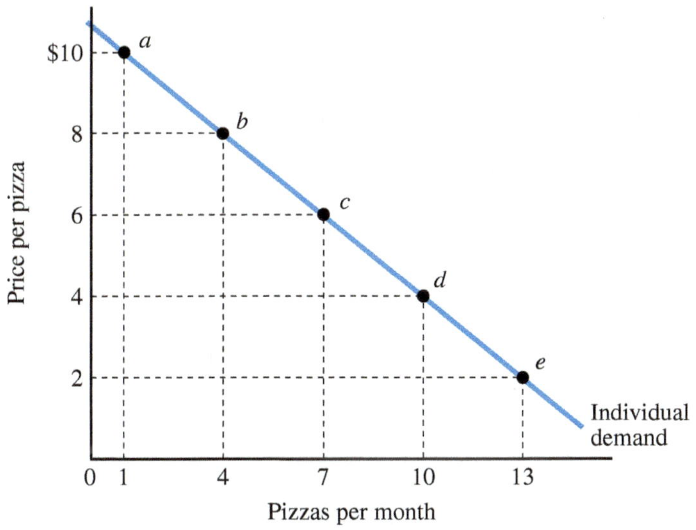

individual demand curve

A curve that shows the relationship between the price of a good and quantity demanded by an individual consumer, *ceteris paribus*.

law of demand

There is a negative relationship between price and quantity demanded, *ceteris paribus*.

AL'S DEMAND SCHEDULE FOR PIZZAS		
Point	Price	Quantity of Pizzas per Month
a	$10	1
b	8	4
c	6	7
d	4	10
e	2	13

▲ **FIGURE 1**

The Individual Demand Curve

According to the law of demand, the higher the price, the smaller the quantity demanded, everything else being equal. Therefore, the demand curve is negatively sloped: When the price increases from $6 to $8, the quantity demanded decreases from seven pizzas per month (point c) to four pizzas per month (point b).

such as substitutes and complements, and tastes are unchanged. As the price of pizza increases and nothing else changes, Al moves upward along his demand curve and buys a smaller quantity of pizza. For example, if the price increases from $8 to $10, Al moves upward along his demand curve from point *b* to point *a*, and buys only one pizza per month, down from four pizzas at the lower price. A movement along a single demand curve is called a **change in quantity demanded**, a change in the quantity a consumer is willing to buy when the price changes.

change in quantity demanded

A change in the quantity consumers are willing and able to buy when the price changes; represented graphically by movement along the demand curve.

market demand curve

A curve showing the relationship between price and quantity demanded by all consumers, *ceteris paribus.*

From Individual Demand to Market Demand

The **market demand curve** shows the relationship between the price of the good and the quantity demanded by *all* consumers, *ceteris paribus.* As in the case of the individual demand curve, when we draw the market demand curve we assume that the other variables that affect individual demand (income, the prices of substitute and complementary goods, tastes, and price expectations) are fixed. In addition, we assume the number of consumers is fixed.

Figure 2 shows how to derive the market demand curve when there are only two consumers. Panel A shows Al's demand curve for pizza, and Panel B shows Bea's demand curve. At a price of $8, Al will buy 4 pizzas (point *a*) and Bea will buy 2 pizzas (point *b*), so the total quantity demanded at this price is 6 pizzas. In Panel C, point *c* shows the point on the market demand curve associated with a price of $8. At this price, the market quantity demanded is 6 pizzas. If the price drops to $4, Al will buy

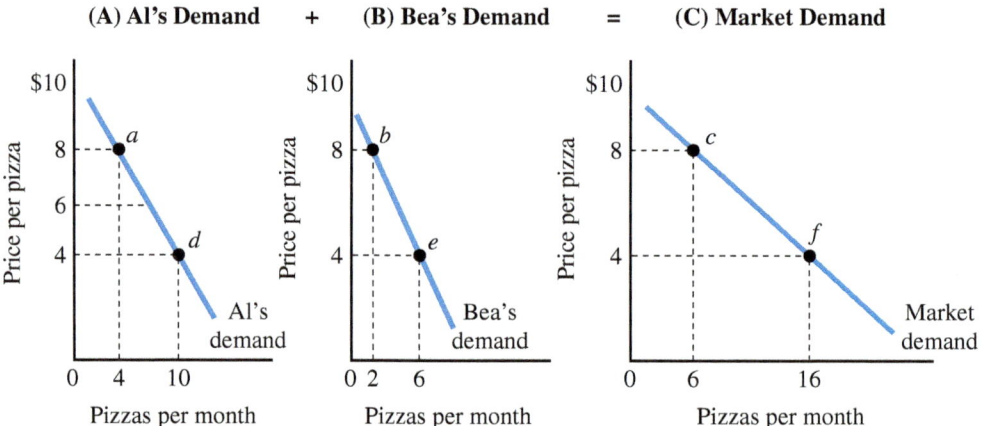

QUANTITY OF PIZZA DEMANDED			
Price	Al +	Bea =	Market Demand
$8	4	2	6
6	7	4	11
4	10	6	16
2	13	8	21

▲ **FIGURE 2**

From Individual to Market Demand

The market demand equals the sum of the demands of all consumers. In this case, there are only two consumers, so at each price the market quantity demanded equals the quantity demanded by Al plus the quantity demanded by Bea. At a price of $8, Al's quantity is four pizzas (point *a*) and Bea's quantity is two pizzas (point *b*), so the market quantity demanded is six pizzas (point *c*). Each consumer obeys the law of demand, so the market demand curve is negatively sloped.

10 pizzas (point *d*) and Bea will buy 6 pizzas (point *e*), for a total of 16 pizzas (shown by point *f* on the market demand curve). The market demand curve is the horizontal sum of the individual demand curves.

The market demand is negatively sloped, reflecting the law of demand. This is sensible, because if each consumer obeys the law of demand, consumers as a group will too. When the price increases from $4 to $8, there is a change in quantity demanded as we move along the demand curve from point *f* to point *c*. The movement along the demand curve occurs if the price of pizza is the only variable that has changed.

2   THE SUPPLY CURVE

On the supply side of a market, firms sell their products to consumers. Suppose you ask the manager of a firm, "How much of your product are you willing to produce and sell?" The answer is likely to be "it depends." The manager's decision about how much to produce depends on many variables, including the following, using pizza as an example:

- The price of the product (for example, the price per pizza)
- The wage paid to workers
- The price of materials (for example, the price of dough and cheese)
- The cost of capital (for example, the cost of a pizza oven)
- The state of production technology (for example, the knowledge used in making pizza)
- Producers' expectations about future prices
- Taxes paid to the government or *subsidies* (payments from the government to firms to produce a product)

Together, these variables determine how much of a product firms are willing to produce and sell, the **quantity supplied**. We'll start our discussion of market supply with the relationship between the price of a good and the quantity of that good supplied, a relationship we represent graphically by the supply curve. Later in the chapter we will discuss the other variables that affect the individual firm's decision about how much of a product to produce and sell.

quantity supplied
The amount of a product that firms are willing and able to sell.

The Individual Supply Curve and the Law of Supply

Consider the decision of an individual producer. The starting point for a discussion of individual supply is a **supply schedule**, a table that shows the relationship between the price of a particular product and the quantity that an individual producer is willing to sell. The supply schedule shows how the quantity supplied by an individual producer changes with the price, *ceteris paribus*. The variables we hold fixed in the supply schedule are input costs, technology, price expectations, and government taxes or subsidies.

The table in Figure 3 shows the supply schedule for pizza at Lola's Pizza Shop. At a price of $2, Lola doesn't produce any pizzas, indicating that a $2 price is not high enough to cover her cost of producing a pizza. In contrast, at a price of $4 she supplies 100 pizzas. In this example, each $2 increase in price increases the quantity supplied by 100 pizzas to 200 at a price of $6, 300 at a price of $8, and so on. Remember that in a supply schedule, a change in quantity results from a change in price alone.

supply schedule
A table that shows the relationship between the price of a product and quantity supplied, *ceteris paribus*.

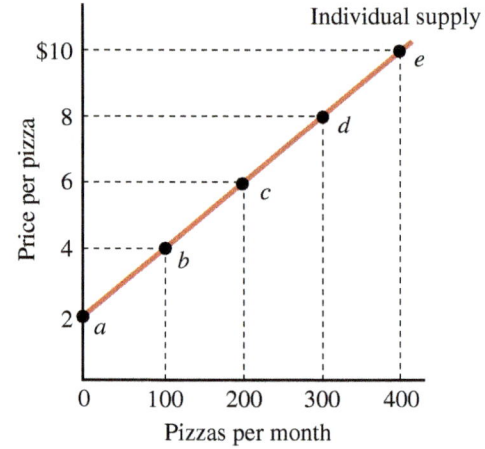

INDIVIDUAL SUPPLY SCHEDULE FOR PIZZA		
Point	Price	Quantity of Pizzas per Month
a	$ 2	0
b	4	100
c	6	200
d	8	300
e	10	400

▲ **FIGURE 3**

The Individual Supply Curve

The supply curve of an individual supplier is positively sloped, reflecting the law of supply. As shown by point a, the quantity supplied is zero at a price of $2, indicating that the minimum supply price is just above $2. An increase in price increases the quantity supplied to 100 pizzas at a price of $4, 200 pizzas at a price of $6, and so on.

individual supply curve

A curve showing the relationship between price and quantity supplied by a single firm, *ceteris paribus*.

 The **individual supply curve** is a graphical representation of the supply schedule. By plotting the numbers in Lola's supply schedule—different combinations of price and quantity—we can draw her supply curve for pizza. The individual supply curve shows the relationship between the price of a product and the quantity supplied by a single firm, *ceteris paribus*. To get the data for a supply curve, we change only the price of pizza and observe how a producer responds to the price change.

 Figure 3 shows Lola's supply curve for pizza, which shows the quantity of pizzas she is willing to sell at each price. The individual supply curve is positively sloped, reflecting the **law of supply**, a pattern of behavior that we observe in producers:

law of supply

There is a positive relationship between price and quantity supplied, *ceteris paribus*.

There is a positive relationship between price and quantity supplied, *ceteris paribus*.

The words *ceteris paribus* remind us that to isolate the relationship between price and quantity supplied we assume the other factors that influence producers are unchanged. As the price of pizza increases and nothing else changes, Lola moves upward along her individual supply curve and produces a larger quantity of pizza. For example, if the price increases from $6 to $8, Lola moves upward along her supply curve from point *c* to point *d*, and the quantity supplied increases from 200 to 300. A movement along a single supply curve is called a **change in quantity supplied**, a change in the quantity a producer is willing and able to sell when the price changes.

change in quantity supplied

A change in the quantity firms are willing and able to sell when the price changes; represented graphically by movement along the supply curve.

The **minimum supply price** is the lowest price at which a product is supplied. A firm won't produce a product unless the price is high enough to cover the marginal cost of producing it. As shown in Figure 3, a price of $2 is not high enough to cover the cost of producing the first pizza, so Lola's quantity supplied is zero (point *a*). But when the price rises above $2, she produces some pizzas, indicating that her minimum supply price is just above $2.

minimum supply price

The lowest price at which a product will be supplied.

Why Is the Individual Supply Curve Positively Sloped?

The individual supply curve is positively sloped, consistent with the law of supply. To explain the positive slope, consider how Lola responds to an increase in price. A higher price encourages a firm to increase its output by purchasing more materials and hiring more workers. To increase her workforce, Lola might be forced to pay overtime or hire workers who are more costly or less productive than the original workers. But the higher price of pizza makes it worthwhile to incur these higher costs.

The supply curve shows the marginal cost of production for different quantities produced. We can use the marginal principle to explain this.

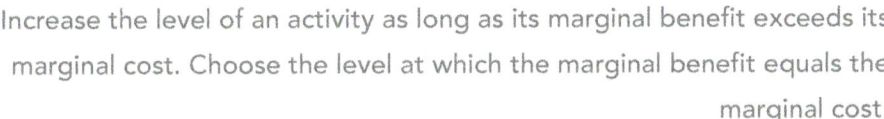

MARGINAL PRINCIPLE

Increase the level of an activity as long as its marginal benefit exceeds its marginal cost. Choose the level at which the marginal benefit equals the marginal cost.

For Lola, the marginal benefit of producing a pizza is the price she gets for it. When the price is only $2.00, she doesn't produce any pizza, which tells us that the marginal cost of the first pizza must be greater than $2.00; otherwise, she would have produced it. But when the price rises to $2.01, she produces the first pizza because now the marginal benefit (the $2.01 price) exceeds the marginal cost. This tells us that the marginal cost of the first pizza is less than $2.01; otherwise, she wouldn't produce it at a price of $2.01. To summarize, the marginal cost of the first pizza is between $2.00 and $2.01, or just over $2.00. Similarly, point *b* on the supply curve in Figure 3 shows that Lola won't produce her 100th pizza at a price of $3.99, but will produce at a price of $4.00, indicating that her marginal cost of producing that pizza is between $3.99 and $4.00, or just under $4.00. In general, the supply curve shows the marginal cost of production.

From Individual Supply to Market Supply

The **market supply curve** for a particular good shows the relationship between the price of the good and the quantity that all producers together are willing to sell, *ceteris paribus*. To draw the market supply curve, we assume the other variables that affect individual supply are fixed. The market quantity supplied is simply the sum of the quantities supplied by all the firms in the market. To show how to draw the market supply curve, we'll assume there are only two firms in the market. Of course, a perfectly competitive market has a large number of firms, but the lessons from the two-firm case generalize to a case of many firms.

Figure 4 shows how to derive a market supply curve from individual supply curves. In Panel A, Lola has relatively low production costs, as reflected in her relatively low minimum supply price ($2 at point *a*). In Panel B, Hiram has higher production costs, so he has a higher minimum price ($6 at point *f*). As a result, his supply curve lies above Lola's. To draw the market supply curve, we add the

market supply curve

A curve showing the relationship between the market price and quantity supplied by all firms, *ceteris paribus*.

457

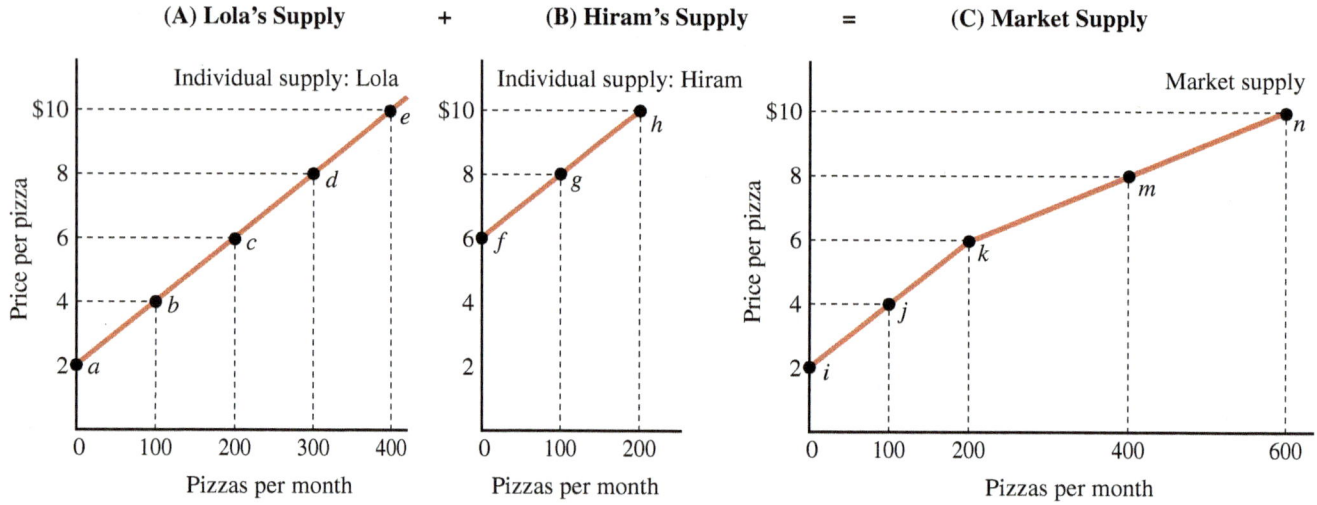

QUANTITY OF PIZZA SUPPLIED			
Price	Lola +	Hiram =	Market Supply
2	0	0	0
4	100	0	100
6	200	0	200
8	300	100	400
10	400	200	600

▲ **FIGURE 4**

From Individual to Market Supply

The market supply is the sum of the supplies of all firms. In Panel A, Lola is a low-cost producer who produces the first pizza once the price rises above $2 (shown by point a). In Panel B, Hiram is a high-cost producer who doesn't produce pizza until the price rises above $6 (shown by point f). To draw the market supply curve, we sum the individual supply curves horizontally. At a price of $8, market supply is 400 pizzas (point m), equal to 300 from Lola (point d) plus 100 from Hiram (point g).

individual supply curves horizontally. This gives us two segments for the market supply curve:

- **Prices between $2 and $6:** Segment connecting points *i* and *k*. Hiram's high-cost firm doesn't supply any output, so the market supply is the same as the individual supply from Lola. For example, at a price of $4 Lola supplies 100 pizzas (point *b*) and Hiram does not produce any, so the market supply is 100 pizzas (point *j*).

- **Prices above $6:** Segment above point *k*. At higher prices, the high-cost firm produces some output, and the market supply is the sum of the quantities supplied by the two firms. For example, at a price of $8 Lola produces 300 pizzas (point *d*) and Hiram produces 100 pizzas (point *g*), so the market quantity supplied is 400 pizzas (point *m*).

A perfectly competitive market has hundreds of firms rather than just two, but the process of going from individual supply curves to the market supply curve is the same. We add the individual supply curves horizontally by picking a price and adding up the quantities supplied by all the firms in the market. In the more realistic case of many firms, the supply curve will be smooth rather than kinked. This smooth line is shown in Figure 5. In this case, we assume that there are 100 firms identical to Lola's firm.

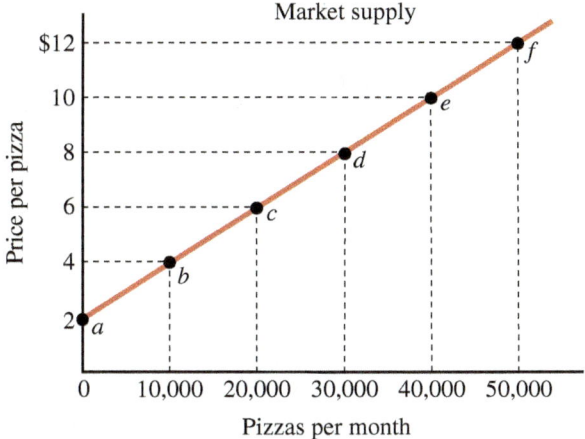

▲ **FIGURE 5**

The Market Supply Curve with Many Firms

The market supply is the sum of the supplies of all firms. The minimum supply price is $2 (point *a*), and the quantity supplied increases by 10,000 for each $2 increase in price to 10,000 at a price of $4 (point *b*), 20,000 at a price of $6 (point *c*), and so on.

The minimum supply price is $2, and for each $2 increase in price, the quantity supplied increases by 10,000 pizzas.

Why Is the Market Supply Curve Positively Sloped?

The market supply curve is positively sloped, consistent with the law of supply. To explain the positive slope, consider the two responses by firms to an increase in price:

- **Individual firm.** As we saw earlier, a higher price encourages a firm to increase its output by purchasing more materials and hiring more workers.
- **New firms.** In the long run, new firms can enter the market and existing firms can expand their production facilities to produce more output. The new firms may have higher production costs than the original firms, but the higher output price makes it worthwhile to enter the market, even with higher costs.

Like the individual supply curve, the market supply curve shows the marginal cost of production for different quantities produced. In Figure 5, the marginal cost of the first pizza is the minimum supply price for the firm with the lowest cost (just over $2.00). Similarly, point *d* on the supply curve shows that the 30,000th pizza won't be produced at a price of $7.99, but will be produced at a price of $8.00. This indicates that the marginal cost of producing the 30,000th pizza is just under $8.00. Like the individual supply curve, the market supply curve shows the marginal cost of production.

 **MARKET EQUILIBRIUM: BRINGING DEMAND AND SUPPLY TOGETHER**

A market is an arrangement that brings buyers and sellers together. So far in this chapter we've seen how the two sides of a market—demand and supply—work. Now we bring the two sides of the market together to show how prices and quantities are determined.

market equilibrium

A situation in which the quantity demanded equals the quantity supplied at the prevailing market price.

When the quantity of a product demanded equals the quantity supplied at the prevailing market price, we have reached a **market equilibrium**. When a market reaches an equilibrium, there is no pressure to change the price. If pizza firms produce exactly the quantity of pizza that consumers are willing to buy, each consumer will get a pizza at the prevailing price, and each producer will sell all its pizza. In Figure 6, the equilibrium price is shown by the intersection of the demand and supply curves. At a price of $8, the supply curve shows that firms will produce 30,000 pizzas, which is exactly the quantity that consumers are willing to buy at that price.

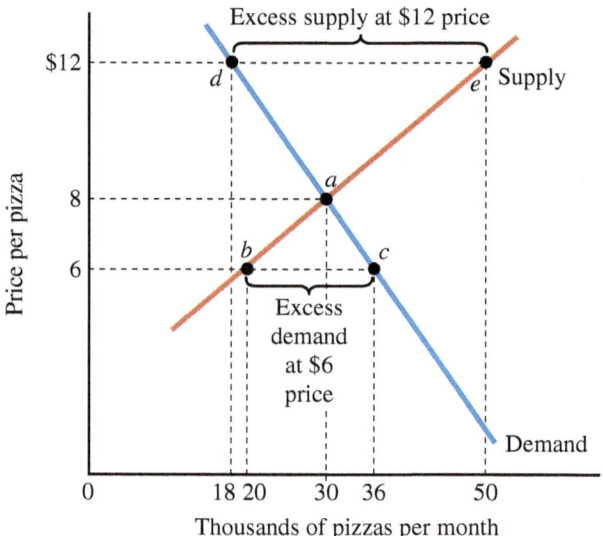

▲ **FIGURE 6**

Market Equilibrium

At the market equilibrium (point a, with price = $8 and quantity = 30,000), the quantity supplied equals the quantity demanded. At a price below the equilibrium price ($6), there is excess demand—the quantity demanded at point c exceeds the quantity supplied at point b. At a price above the equilibrium price ($12), there is excess supply—the quantity supplied at point e exceeds the quantity demanded at point d.

Excess Demand Causes the Price to Rise

If the price is below the equilibrium price, there will be excess demand for the product. **Excess demand** (sometimes called a *shortage*) occurs when, at the prevailing market price, the quantity demanded exceeds the quantity supplied, meaning that consumers are willing to buy more than producers are willing to sell. In Figure 6, at a price of $6, there is an excess demand equal to 16,000 pizzas: Consumers are willing to buy 36,000 pizzas (point c), but producers are willing to sell only 20,000 pizzas (point b) because the price is less than the marginal cost of producing pizza number 20,001 and beyond. This mismatch between demand and supply will cause the price of pizza to rise. Firms will increase the price they charge for their limited supply of pizza, and anxious consumers will pay the higher price to get one of the few pizzas available.

An increase in price eliminates excess demand by changing both the quantity demanded and quantity supplied. As the price increases, the excess demand shrinks for two reasons:

excess demand

A situation in which, at the prevailing price, the quantity demanded exceeds the quantity supplied.

- The market moves upward along the demand curve (from point *c* toward point *a*), decreasing the quantity demanded.
- The market moves upward along the supply curve (from point *b* toward point *a*), increasing the quantity supplied.

Because the quantity demanded decreases while the quantity supplied increases, the gap between the quantity demanded and the quantity supplied narrows. The price will continue to rise until excess demand is eliminated. In Figure 6, at a price of $8 the quantity supplied equals the quantity demanded, as shown by point *a*.

In some cases, government creates an excess demand for a good by setting a maximum price (sometimes called a *price ceiling*). If the government sets a maximum price that is less than the equilibrium price, the result is a permanent excess demand for the good. We will explore the market effects of such policies.

Excess Supply Causes the Price to Drop

What happens if the price is *above* the equilibrium price? **Excess supply** (sometimes called a *surplus*) occurs when the quantity supplied exceeds the quantity demanded, meaning that producers are willing to sell more than consumers are willing to buy. This is shown by points *d* and *e* in Figure 6. At a price of $12, the excess supply is 32,000 pizzas: Producers are willing to sell 50,000 pizzas (point *e*), but consumers are willing to buy only 18,000 (point *d*). This mismatch will cause the price of pizzas to fall as firms cut the price to sell them. As the price drops, the excess supply will shrink for two reasons:

- The market moves downward along the demand curve from point *d* toward point *a*, increasing the quantity demanded.
- The market moves downward along the supply curve from point *e* toward point *a*, decreasing the quantity supplied.

Because the quantity demanded increases while the quantity supplied decreases, the gap between the quantity supplied and the quantity demanded narrows. The price will continue to drop until excess supply is eliminated. In Figure 6, at a price of $8, the quantity supplied equals the quantity demanded, as shown by point *a*.

The government sometimes creates an excess supply of a good by setting a minimum price (sometimes called a *price floor*). If the government sets a minimum price that is greater than the equilibrium price, the result is a permanent excess supply. We'll discuss the market effects of minimum prices later in the text.

excess supply
A situation in which the quantity supplied exceeds the quantity demanded at the prevailing price.

4 MARKET EFFECTS OF CHANGES IN DEMAND

We've seen that market equilibrium occurs when the quantity supplied equals the quantity demanded, shown graphically by the intersection of the supply curve and the demand curve. In this part of the chapter, we'll see how changes on the demand side of the market affect the equilibrium price and equilibrium quantity.

Change in Quantity Demanded versus Change in Demand

Earlier in the chapter we listed the variables that determine how much of a particular product consumers are willing to buy. The first variable is the price of the product. The demand curve shows the negative relationship between price and quantity demanded, *ceteris paribus*. In Panel A of Figure 7, when the price decreases from $8 to $6, we move downward along the demand curve from point *a* to point *b*, and the quantity demanded increases. As noted earlier in the chapter, this is called a *change in quantity demanded*. Now we're ready to take a closer look at the other variables that affect demand besides price—income, the prices of related goods, tastes, advertising, and the number of consumers—and see how changes in these variables affect the demand for the product and the market equilibrium.

If any of these other variables change, the relationship between the product's price and quantity—shown numerically in the demand schedule and graphically in the

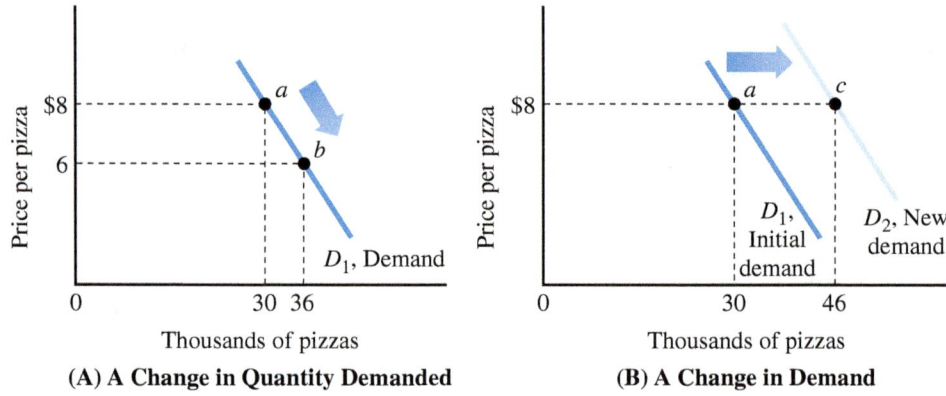

(A) A Change in Quantity Demanded   **(B) A Change in Demand**

▲ **FIGURE 7**

Change in Quantity Demanded versus Change in Demand

(**A**) A change in price causes a change in quantity demanded, a movement along a single demand curve. For example, a decrease in price causes a move from point *a* to point *b*, increasing the quantity demanded.

(**B**) A change in demand caused by changes in a variable other than the price of the good shifts the entire demand curve. For example, an increase in demand shifts the demand curve from D_1 to D_2.

demand curve—will change. That means we will have an entirely different demand schedule and an entirely different demand curve. In Panel B of Figure 7, we show this result as a *shift* of the entire demand curve from D_1 to D_2. This particular shift means that at any price consumers are willing to buy a larger quantity of the product. For example, at a price of $8 consumers are willing to buy 46,000 pizzas (point *c*), up from 30,000 with the initial demand curve. To convey the idea that changes in these other variables change the demand schedule and the demand curve, we say that a change in any of these variables causes a **change in demand**.

Increases in Demand Shift the Demand Curve

What types of changes will increase the demand and shift the demand curve to the right, as shown in Figure 7? An increase in demand like the one represented in Figure 7 can occur for several reasons, listed in Table 1:

- **Increase in income.** Consumers use their income to buy products, and the more money they have, the more money they spend. For a **normal good**, there is a positive relationship between consumer income and the quantity consumed. When income increases, a consumer buys a larger quantity of a normal good. Most goods fall into this category—including new clothes, movies, and pizza.

change in demand

A shift of the demand curve caused by a change in a variable other than the price of the product.

normal good

A good for which an increase in income increases demand.

TABLE 1 INCREASES IN DEMAND SHIFT THE DEMAND CURVE TO THE RIGHT

When this variable...	increases or decreases...	the demand curve shifts in this direction...
Income, with normal good	↑	
Income, with inferior good	↓	
Price of a substitute good	↑	
Price of complementary good	↓	
Population	↑	
Consumer preferences for good	↑	
Expected future price	↑	

- **Decrease in income.** An **inferior good** is the opposite of a normal good. Consumers buy larger quantities of inferior goods when their income *decreases*. For example, if you lose your job you might make your own coffee instead of buying it in a coffee shop, rent DVDs instead of going to the theater, and eat more macaroni and cheese. In this case, homemade coffee, DVDs, and macaroni and cheese are examples of inferior goods.

- **Increase in price of a substitute good.** When two goods are **substitutes**, an increase in the price of the first good causes some consumers to switch to the second good. Tacos and pizzas are substitutes, so an increase in the price of tacos increases the demand for pizzas as some consumers substitute pizza for tacos, which are now more expensive relative to pizza.

- **Decrease in price of a complementary good.** When two goods are **complements**, they are consumed together as a package, and a decrease in the price of one good decreases the cost of the entire package. As a result, consumers buy more of both goods. Pizza and lemonade are complementary goods, so a decrease in the price of lemonade decreases the total cost of a lemonade-and-pizza meal, increasing the demand for pizza.

- **Increase in population.** An increase in the number of people means there are more potential pizza consumers—more individual demand curves to add up to get the market demand curve—so market demand increases.

- **Shift in consumer preferences.** Consumers' preferences or tastes can change over time. If consumers' preferences shift in favor of pizza, the demand for pizza increases. One purpose of advertising is to change consumers' preferences, and a successful pizza advertising campaign will increase demand.

- **Expectations of higher future prices.** If consumers think next month's pizza price will be higher than they had initially expected, they may buy a larger quantity today and a smaller quantity next month. That means the demand for pizza today will increase.

We can use Figure 8 to show how an increase in demand affects the equilibrium price and equilibrium quantity. An increase in the demand for pizza resulting from

inferior good

A good for which an increase in income decreases demand.

substitutes

Two goods for which an increase in the price of one good increases the demand for the other good.

complements

Two goods for which a decrease in the price of one good increases the demand for the other good.

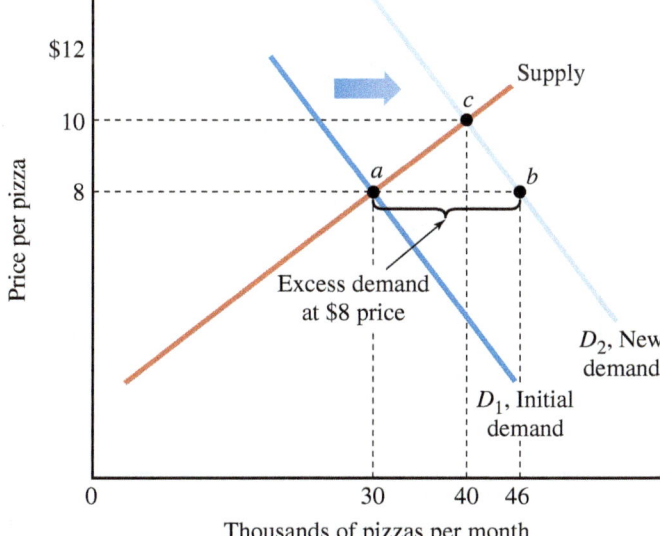

▲ **FIGURE 8**

An Increase in Demand Increases the Equilibrium Price

An increase in demand shifts the demand curve to the right: At each price, the quantity demanded increases. At the initial price ($8), there is excess demand, with the quantity demanded (point *b*) exceeding the quantity supplied (point *a*). The excess demand causes the price to rise, and equilibrium is restored at point *c*. To summarize, the increase in demand increases the equilibrium price to $10 and increases the equilibrium quantity to 40,000 pizzas.

one or more of the factors listed in Table 1 shifts the demand curve to the right, from D_1 to D_2. At the initial price of $8, there will be excess demand, as indicated by points *a* and *b*: Consumers are willing to buy 46,000 pizzas (point *b*), but producers are willing to sell only 30,000 (point *a*). Consumers want to buy 16,000 more pizzas than producers are willing to supply, and the excess demand causes upward pressure on the price. As the price rises, the excess demand shrinks because the quantity demanded decreases while the quantity supplied increases. The supply curve intersects the new demand curve at point *c*, so the new equilibrium price is $10 (up from $8), and the new equilibrium quantity is 40,000 pizzas (up from 30,000).

Decreases in Demand Shift the Demand Curve

What types of changes in the pizza market will decrease the demand for pizza? A decrease in demand means that at each price consumers are willing to buy a smaller quantity. In Figure 9, a decrease in demand shifts the market demand curve from D_1 to D_0. At the initial price of $8, the quantity demanded decreases from 30,000 pizzas (point *a*) to 14,000 pizzas (point *b*). A decrease in demand like the one represented in Figure 9 can occur for several reasons, listed in Table 2:

- **Decrease in income.** A decrease in income means that consumers have less to spend, so they buy a smaller quantity of each normal good.
- **Increase in income.** Consumers buy smaller quantities of an inferior good when their income increases.
- **Decrease in the price of a substitute good.** A decrease in the price of a substitute good such as tacos makes pizza more expensive relative to tacos, causing consumers to demand less pizza.
- **Increase in the price of a complementary good.** An increase in the price of a complementary good such as lemonade increases the cost of a lemonade-and-pizza meal, decreasing the demand for pizza.

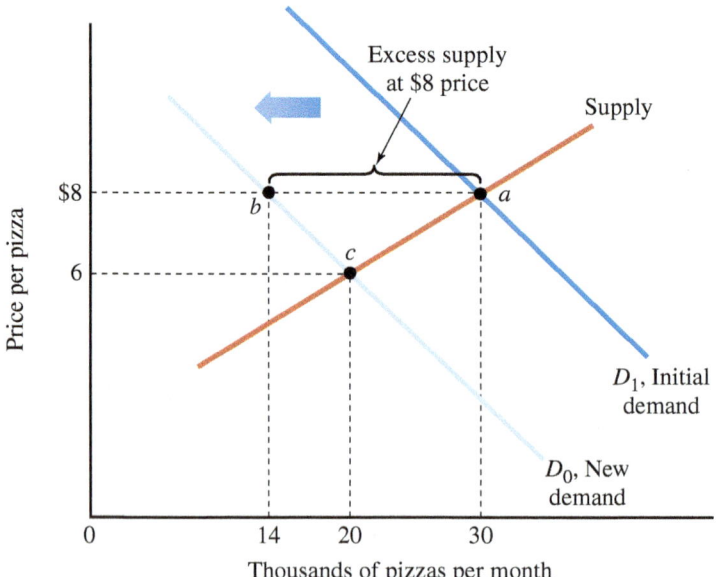

▲ **FIGURE 9**

A Decrease in Demand Decreases the Equilibrium Price

A decrease in demand shifts the demand curve to the left: At each price, the quantity demanded decreases. At the initial price ($8), there is excess supply, with the quantity supplied (point *a*) exceeding the quantity demanded (point *b*). The excess supply causes the price to drop, and equilibrium is restored at point *c*. To summarize, the decrease in demand decreases the equilibrium price to $6 and decreases the equilibrium quantity to 20,000 pizzas.

TABLE 2 DECREASES IN DEMAND SHIFT THE DEMAND CURVE TO THE LEFT

When this variable...	increases or decreases...	the demand curve shifts in this direction...
Income, with normal good	↓	
Income, with inferior good	↑	
Price of a substitute good	↓	
Price of complementary good	↑	
Population	↓	
Consumer preferences for good	↓	
Expected future price	↓	

D_1, Initial demand
D_0, New demand
Price
Quantity

- **Decrease in population.** A decrease in the number of people means that there are fewer pizza consumers, so the market demand for pizza decreases.
- **Shift in consumer tastes.** When consumers' preferences shift away from pizza in favor of other products, the demand for pizza decreases.
- **Expectations of lower future prices.** If consumers think next month's pizza price will be lower than they had initially expected, they may buy a smaller quantity today, meaning the demand for pizza today will decrease.

A Decrease in Demand Decreases the Equilibrium Price

We can use Figure 9 to show how a decrease in demand affects the equilibrium price and equilibrium quantity. The decrease in the demand for pizza shifts the demand curve to the left, from D_1 to D_0. At the initial price of $8, there will be an excess supply, as indicated by points *a* and *b*: Producers are willing to sell 30,000 pizzas (point *a*), but given the lower demand consumers are willing to buy only 14,000 pizzas (point *b*). Producers want to sell 16,000 more pizzas than consumers are willing to buy, and the excess supply causes downward pressure on the price. As the price falls, the excess supply shrinks because the quantity demanded increases while the quantity supplied decreases. The supply curve intersects the new demand curve at point *c*, so the new equilibrium price is $6 (down from $8), and the new equilibrium quantity is 20,000 pizzas (down from 30,000).

5   MARKET EFFECTS OF CHANGES IN SUPPLY

We've seen that changes in demand shift the demand curve and change the equilibrium price and quantity. In this part of the chapter, we'll see how changes on the supply side of the market affect the equilibrium price and equilibrium quantity.

Change in Quantity Supplied versus Change in Supply

Earlier in the chapter we listed the variables that determine how much of a product firms are willing to sell. Of course, one of these variables is the price of the product. The supply curve shows the positive relationship between price and quantity, *ceteris paribus*. In Panel A of Figure 10, when the price increases from $6 to $8 we move along the supply curve from point *a* to point *b*, and the quantity of the product supplied increases. As noted earlier in the chapter, this is called a *change in quantity supplied*. Now we're ready to take a closer look at the other variables that

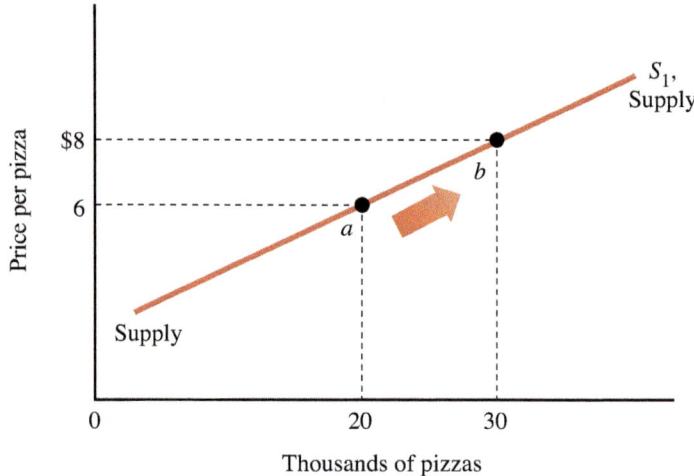

(A) Change in Quantity Supplied

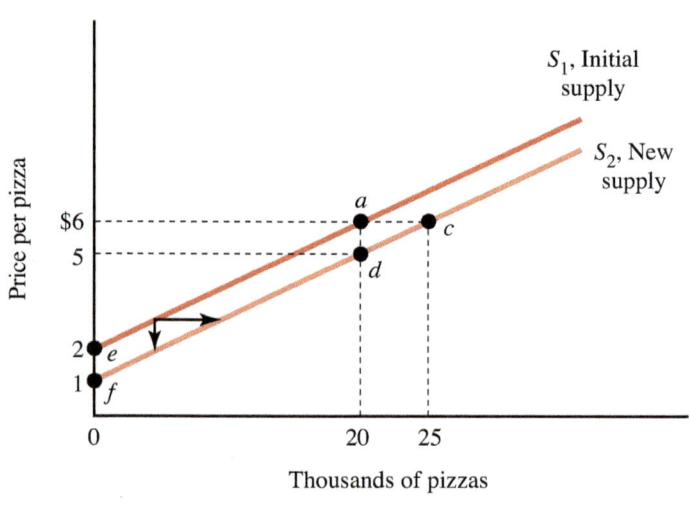

(B) Change in Supply

▲ **FIGURE 10**

Change in Quantity Supplied versus Change in Supply

(**A**) A change in price causes a change in quantity supplied, a movement along a single supply curve. For example, an increase in price causes a move from point *a* to point *b*.

(**B**) A change in supply (caused by a change in something other than the price of the product) shifts the entire supply curve. For example, an increase in supply shifts the supply curve from S_1 to S_2. For any given price (for example, $6), a larger quantity is supplied (25,000 pizzas at point *c* instead of 20,000 at point *a*). The price required to generate any given quantity decreases. For example, the price required to generate 20,000 pizzas drops from $6 (point *a*) to $5 (point *d*).

affect supply—including wages, material prices, and technology—and see how changes in these variables affect the supply curve and the market equilibrium.

If any of these other variables change, the relationship between price and quantity—shown numerically in the supply schedule and graphically in the supply curve—will change. That means that we will have an entirely different supply schedule and a different supply curve. In Panel B of Figure 10, this is shown as a shift of the entire supply curve from S_1 to S_2. In this case, the supply curve shifts downward and to the right:

- The shift to the right means that at any given price (for example, $6), a larger quantity is produced (25,000 pizzas at point c, up from 20,000 at point a).
- The shift downward means that the price required to generate a particular quantity of output is lower. For example, the new minimum supply price is just over $1 (point f), down from just over $2 (point e). Similarly, the price required to generate 20,000 pizzas is $5 (point d), down from $6 (point a).

To convey the idea that changes in these other variables change the supply curve, we say that a change in any of these variables causes a **change in supply**.

Increases in Supply Shift the Supply Curve

What types of changes increase the supply of a product, shifting the supply curve downward and to the right? Consider first the effect of a decrease in the wage paid to pizza workers. A decrease in the wage will decrease the cost of producing pizza and shift the supply curve:

- **Downward shift.** When the cost of production decreases, the price required to generate any given quantity of pizza will decrease. In general, a lower wage means a lower marginal cost of production, so each firm needs a lower price to cover its production cost. In other words, the supply curve shifts downward.
- **Rightward shift.** The decrease in production costs makes pizza production more profitable at a given price, so producers will supply more at each price. In other words, the supply curve shifts to the right.

A decrease in the wage is just one example of a decrease in production costs that shifts the supply curve downward and to the right. These supply shifters are listed in Table 3. A reduction in the costs of materials (dough, cheese) or capital (pizza oven) decreases production costs, decreasing the price required to generate any particular quantity (downward shift) and increasing the quantity supplied at any particular price (rightward shift). An improvement in technology that allows the firm to economize on labor or material inputs cuts production costs and shifts the supply curve in a similar fashion. The technological improvement could be a new machine or a new way of doing business—a new layout for a factory or store, or a more efficient system of ordering inputs and distributing output. Finally, if a government subsidizes production by paying the firm some amount for each unit produced, the net cost to the firm is lowered by the amount of the subsidy, and the supply curve shifts downward and to the right.

Two other possible sources of increases in supply are listed in Table 3. First, if firms believe that next month's price will be lower than they had initially expected, they may try to sell more output now at this month's relatively high price, increasing supply this month. Second, because the market supply is the sum of the quantities supplied by all producers, an increase in the number of producers will increase market supply.

As summarized in Table 3, the language of shifting supply is a bit tricky. An increase in supply is represented graphically by a shift to the right (a larger quantity supplied at each price) and down (a lower price required to generate a particular quantity). The best way to remember this is to recognize that the *increase* in "increase in supply" refers to the increase in quantity supplied at a particular price—the horizontal shift of the supply curve to the right.

change in supply
A shift of the supply curve caused by a change in a variable other than the price of the product.

TABLE 3	CHANGES IN SUPPLY SHIFT THE SUPPLY CURVE DOWNWARD AND TO THE RIGHT	
When this variable...	increases or decreases...	the supply curve shifts in this direction...
Wage	↓	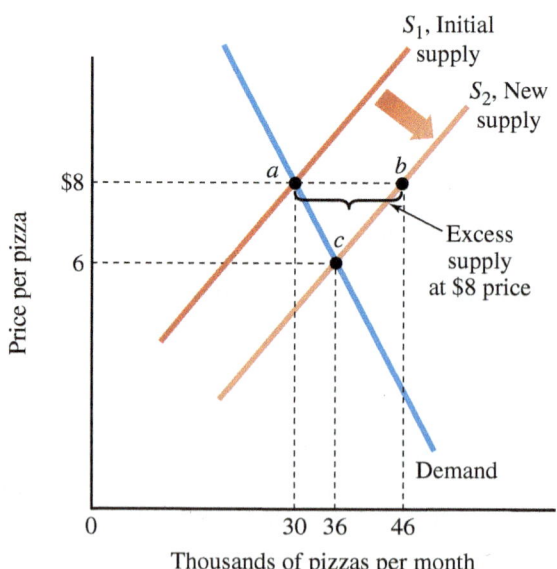
Price of materials or capital	↓	
Technological advance	↑	
Government subsidy	↑	
Expected future price	↓	
Number of producers	↑	

An Increase in Supply Decreases the Equilibrium Price

We can use Figure 11 to show the effects of an increase in supply on the equilibrium price and equilibrium quantity. An increase in the supply of pizza shifts the supply curve to the right, from S_1 to S_2. At the initial price of $8, the quantity supplied increases from 30,000 pizzas (point a) to 46,000 (point b).

The shift of the supply curve causes excess supply that eventually decreases the equilibrium price. At the initial price of $8 (the equilibrium price with the initial supply curve), there will be an excess supply, as indicated by points a and b: Producers are

▲ **FIGURE 11**

An Increase in Supply Decreases the Equilibrium Price

An increase in supply shifts the supply curve to the right: At each price, the quantity supplied increases. At the initial price ($8), there is excess supply, with the quantity supplied (point b) exceeding the quantity demanded (point a). The excess supply causes the price to drop, and equilibrium is restored at point c. To summarize, the increase in supply decreases the equilibrium price to $6 and increases the equilibrium quantity to 36,000 pizzas.

willing to sell 46,000 pizzas (point *b*), but consumers are willing to buy only 30,000 (point *a*). Producers want to sell 16,000 more pizzas than consumers are willing to buy, and the excess supply causes pressure to decrease the price. As the price decreases, the excess supply shrinks, because the quantity supplied decreases while the quantity demanded increases. The new supply curve intersects the demand curve at point *c*, so the new equilibrium price is $6 (down from $8) and the new equilibrium quantity is 36,000 pizzas (up from 30,000).

Decreases in Supply Shift the Supply Curve

Consider next the changes that cause a decrease in supply. As shown in Table 4, anything that increases a firm's production costs will decrease supply. An increase in production cost increases the price required to generate a particular quantity (an upward shift of the supply curve) and decreases the quantity supplied at each price (a leftward shift). Production costs will increase as a result of an increase in the wage, an increase in the price of materials or capital, or a tax on each unit produced. As we saw earlier, the language linking changes in supply and the shifts of the supply curve is tricky. In the case of a decrease in supply, the *decrease* refers to the change in quantity at a particular price—the horizontal shift of the supply curve to the left.

TABLE 4 CHANGES IN SUPPLY SHIFT THE SUPPLY CURVE UPWARD AND TO THE LEFT		
When this variable...	increases or decreases...	the supply curve shifts in this direction...
Wage	↑	
Price of materials or capital	↑	
Tax	↑	
Expected future price	↑	
Number of producers	↓	

A decrease in supply could occur for two other reasons. First, if firms believe next month's pizza price will be higher than they had initially expected, they may be willing to sell a smaller quantity today and a larger quantity next month. That means that the supply of pizza today will decrease. Second, because the market supply is the sum of the quantities supplied by all producers, a decrease in the number of producers will decrease market supply, shifting the supply curve to the left.

A Decrease in Supply Increases the Equilibrium Price

We can use Figure 12 to show the effects of a decrease in supply on the equilibrium price and equilibrium quantity. A decrease in the supply of pizza shifts the supply curve to the left, from S_1 to S_0. At the initial price of $8 (the equilibrium price with the initial supply curve), there will be an excess demand, as indicated by

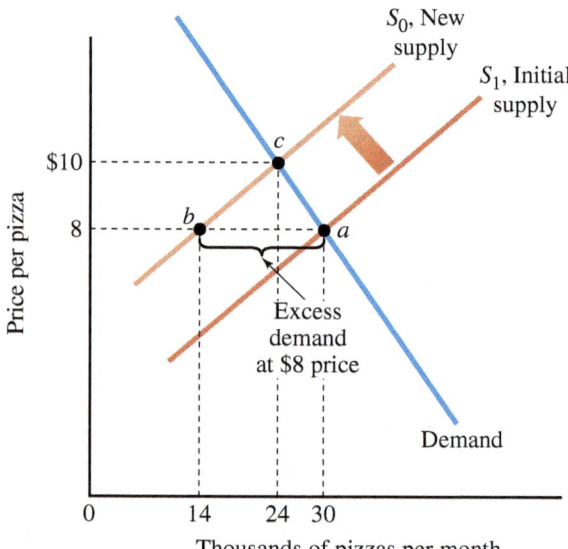

▲ **FIGURE 12**

A Decrease in Supply Increases the Equilibrium Price
A decrease in supply shifts the supply curve to the left. At each price, the quantity supplied decreases. At the initial price ($8), there is excess demand, with the quantity demanded (point *a*) exceeding the quantity supplied (point *b*). The excess demand causes the price to rise, and equilibrium is restored at point *c*. To summarize, the decrease in supply increases the equilibrium price to $10 and decreases the equilibrium quantity to 24,000 pizzas.

points *a* and *b*: Consumers are willing to buy 30,000 pizzas (point *a*), but producers are willing to sell only 14,000 pizzas (point *b*). Consumers want to buy 16,000 more pizzas than producers are willing to sell, and the excess demand causes upward pressure on the price. As the price increases, the excess demand shrinks because the quantity demanded decreases while the quantity supplied increases. The new supply curve intersects the demand curve at point *c*, so the new equilibrium price is $10 (up from $8), and the new equilibrium quantity is 24,000 pizzas (down from 30,000).

Simultaneous Changes in Demand and Supply

What happens to the equilibrium price and quantity when both demand and supply increase? It depends on which change is larger. In Panel A of Figure 13, the increase in demand is larger than the increase in supply, meaning the demand curve shifts by a larger amount than the supply curve. The market equilibrium moves from point *a* to point *b*, and the equilibrium price increases from $8 to $9. This is sensible because an increase in demand tends to pull the price up, while an increase in supply tends to push the price down. If demand increases by a larger amount, the upward pull will be stronger than the downward push, and the price will rise.

We can be certain that when demand and supply both increase, the equilibrium quantity will increase. That's because both changes tend to increase the equilibrium quantity. In Panel A of Figure 13, the equilibrium quantity increases from 30,000 to 44,000 pizzas.

Panel B of Figure 13 shows what happens when the increase in supply is larger than the increase in demand. The equilibrium moves from point *a* to point *c*, meaning that the price falls from $8 to $7. This is sensible because the downward pull on the price resulting from the increase in supply is stronger than the upward pull from

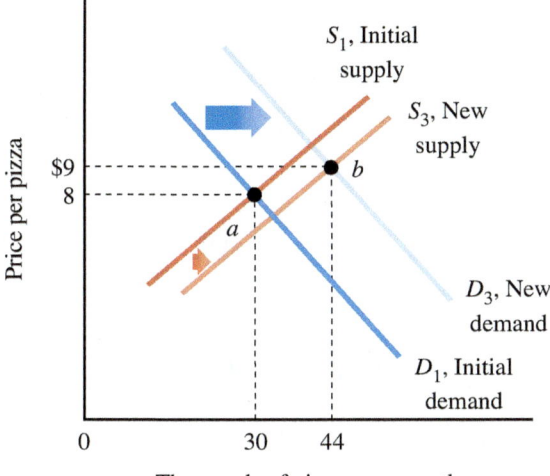

(A) Larger Increase in Demand

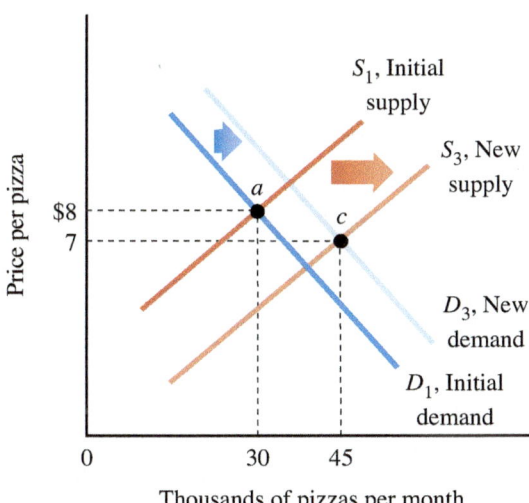

(B) Larger Increase in Supply

▲ **FIGURE 13**

Market Effects of Simultaneous Changes in Demand and Supply

(**A**) Larger increase in demand. If the increase in demand is larger than the increase in supply (if the shift of the demand curve is larger than the shift of the supply curve), both the equilibrium price and the equilibrium quantity will increase.

(**B**) Larger increase in supply. If the increase in supply is larger than the increase in demand (if the shift of the supply curve is larger than the shift of the demand curve), the equilibrium price will decrease and the equilibrium quantity will increase.

the increase in demand. As expected, the equilibrium quantity rises from 30,000 to 45,000 pizzas.

What about simultaneous *decreases* in demand and supply? In this case, the equilibrium quantity will certainly fall because both changes tend to decrease the equilibrium quantity. The effect on the equilibrium price depends on which change is larger, the decrease in demand, which pushes the price downward, or the decrease in supply, which pulls the price upward. If the decrease in demand is larger, the price will fall because the force pushing the price down will be stronger than the force pulling it up. In contrast, if the decrease in supply is larger, the price will rise because the force pulling the price up will be stronger than the force pushing it down.

6 PREDICTING AND EXPLAINING MARKET CHANGES

We've used the model of demand and supply to show how equilibrium prices are determined and how changes in demand and supply affect equilibrium prices and quantities. Table 5 summarizes what we've learned about how changes in demand and supply affect equilibrium prices and quantities:

- When demand changes and the demand curve shifts, price and quantity change in the *same* direction: When demand increases, both price and quantity increase; when demand decreases, both price and quantity decrease.
- When supply changes and the supply curve shifts, price and quantity change in *opposite* directions: When supply increases, the price decreases but the quantity increases; when supply decreases, the price increases but the quantity decreases.

TABLE 5 MARKET EFFECTS OF CHANGES IN DEMAND OR SUPPLY

Change in Demand Supply	How does the equilibrium price change?	How does the equilibrium quantity change?
Increase in demand	↑	↑
Decrease in demand	↓	↓
Increase in supply	↓	↑
Decrease in supply	↑	↓

We can use these lessons about demand and supply to predict the effects of various events on the equilibrium price and equilibrium quantity of a product.

We can also use the lessons listed in Table 5 to explain the reasons for changes in prices or quantities. Suppose we observe changes in the equilibrium price and quantity of a particular good, but we don't know what caused these changes. Perhaps it was a change in demand, or maybe it was a change in supply. We can use the information in Table 5 to work backward, using what we've observed about changes in prices and quantities to determine which side of the market—demand or supply—caused the changes:

- If the equilibrium price and quantity move in the same direction, the changes were caused by a change in demand.
- If the equilibrium price and quantity move in opposite directions, the changes were caused by a change in supply.

7 APPLICATIONS OF DEMAND AND SUPPLY

We can apply what we've learned about demand and supply to real markets. We can use the model of demand and supply to *predict* the effects of various events on equilibrium prices and quantities. We can also *explain* some observed changes in equilibrium prices and quantities.

APPLICATION 1

HURRICANE KATRINA AND BATON ROUGE HOUSING PRICES

APPLYING THE CONCEPTS #1: How do changes in demand affect prices?

In the late summer of 2005, Hurricane Katrina caused a storm surge and levee breaks that flooded much of New Orleans and destroyed a large fraction of the city's housing. Hundreds of thousands of residents were displaced, and about 250,000 relocated to nearby Baton Rouge. The increase in population was so large that Baton Rouge became the largest city in the state, and many people started calling the city "New Baton Rouge."

Figure 14 shows the effects of Hurricane Katrina on the housing market in Baton Rouge. Before Katrina, the average price of a single-family home was $130,000, as shown by point *a*. The increase in the city's population shifted the demand curve to the right, causing excess demand for housing at the original price. Just before the hurricane, there were 3,600 homes listed for sale in the city, but a week after the storm, there were only 500. The excess demand caused fierce competition among buyers for the limited supply of homes, increasing the price. Six months later, the average price had risen to $156,000 as shown by point *b*.

SOURCE: Based on Federal Deposit Insurance Corporation, *Louisiana State Profile—Fall 2005*.

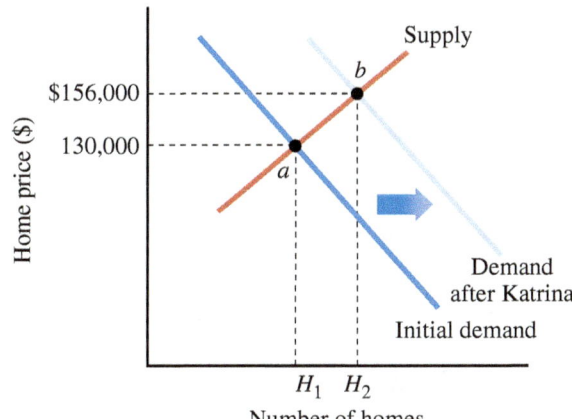

▲ **FIGURE 14**
Hurricane Katrina and Housing in Baton Rouge
An increase in the population of Baton Rouge increases the demand for housing, shifting the demand curve to right. The equilibrium price increases from $130,000 (point *a*) to $156,000 (point *b*).

APPLICATION 2

HONEYBEES AND THE PRICE OF ICE CREAM

APPLYING THE CONCEPTS #2: How do changes in supply in one market affect other markets?

In the last few years thousands of honeybee colonies have vanished, a result of bee colony collapse disorder (CCD). Roughly one-third of the U.S. food supply—including a wide variety of fruits, vegetables, and nuts—depends on pollination from bees. The decline of honeybees threatens $15 billion worth of crops in the United States. The decrease in pollination by bees has decreased the supply of strawberries, raspberries, and almonds, leading to higher prices for these ingredients for ice cream. The higher prices for berries and nuts have increased the cost of producing food products, such as ice cream, increasing their prices as well.

Figure 15 shows the effects of the decline of the bee population on the market for ice cream. Increases in the prices of ingredients (berries and nuts) increase the cost of producing ice cream, shifting the supply curve upward. As a result, the equilibrium price of ice cream increases.

The collapsing of bee colonies is a mystery. The ice cream maker Häagen-Dazs donated money to Pennsylvania State University and the University of California, Davis to support research exploring the causes of CCD and possible solutions. To increase consumer awareness of the problem, Häagen Dazs launched a new flavor, Vanilla Honey Bee.

SOURCE: Based on Parija Kavilanz, "Disappearing Bees Threaten Ice Cream Sellers," *CNNMoney.com*, February 20, 2008.

▶ **FIGURE 15**

Honeybees and the Price of Ice Cream

A decrease in pollination by bees decreases the output of fruit and nuts, increasing the prices of some ingredients for ice cream. The resulting increase in the cost of producing ice cream shifts the supply curve upward, increasing the equilibrium price and decreasing the equilibrium quantity.

APPLICATION 3

THE SUPPLY AND DEMAND FOR CRUISE SHIP BERTHS

APPLYING THE CONCEPT #3: How do simultaneous changes in supply and demand affect the equilibrium price?

What happens when an increase in supply is combined with a decrease in demand? In 2009 the cruise industry invested $4.7 billion on 14 new ships, and in 2010 the industry launched 12 additional new ships. While the supply of cruise berths increased, the demand for cruises decreased, a result of a recession and lower real income. As shown in Figure 16, the simultaneous increase in supply and decrease in demand decreased the equilibrium price. To entice consumers, some cruise lines cut prices by as much as 40 percent. Although consumers responded by purchasing more cruises (about 3 percent more in 2009 than in 2008), the cruise lines' revenues decreased. For Carnival Corporation, the world's largest cruise line, total revenue decreased by 10 percent.

SOURCE: Based on "Dam the Torpedoes: Cruise Lines in the Recession," *Economist*, February 13, 2010, 67.

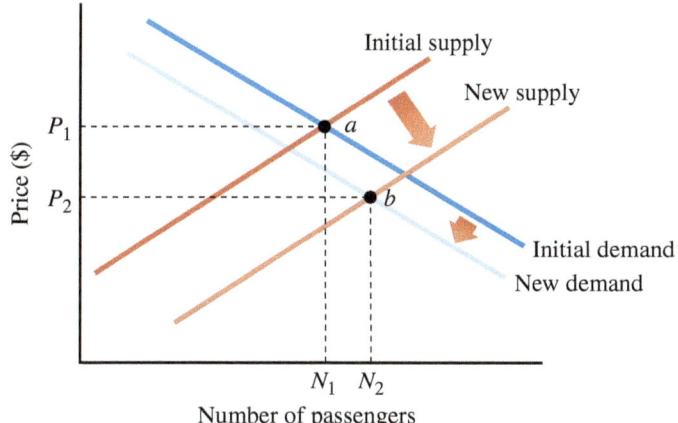

▲ **FIGURE 16**
Increase in Supply and Decrease in Demand for Cruise Ship Berths
An increase in the number of cruise ships increases the supply of berths on cruise ships, while a decrease in income reduces the demand for berths. The increase in supply and decrease in demand combine to decrease the equilibrium price (from P_1 to P_2) and increase the equilibrium quantity (from N_1 to N_2).

APPLICATION 4

THE BOUNCING PRICE OF VANILLA BEANS

APPLYING THE CONCEPTS #4: How do changes in supply affect prices?

The price of vanilla beans has been bouncing around a lot. The price was $50 per kilogram (2.2 pounds) in 2000, then rose to $500 in 2003, then dropped to $25 in 2006. We can use the model of demand and supply to explain the bouncing price.

Figure 17 shows the changes in the vanilla market in recent years. Point *a* shows the initial equilibrium in 2000, with a price of $50 per kilogram. The 2000 cyclone that hit Madagascar, the world's leading vanilla producer, destroyed that year's crop and a large share of the vines that produce vanilla beans. Although the vines were replanted, new plants don't bear usable beans for three to five years, so the supply effects of the cyclone lasted several years. In Figure 17, the cyclone shifted the supply curve upward and to the left, generating a new equilibrium at point *b*, with a higher price and a smaller quantity.

In Figure 17, the changes between 2003 and 2006 are shown by a shift of the supply curve downward and to the right. In 2006, the vines replanted in Madagascar in 2001 started to produce vanilla beans. In addition, other countries, including India, Papua New Guinea, Uganda, and Costa Rica, entered the vanilla market. The vines planted in these other countries started to produce beans in 2006, so the world supply curve for 2006 lies below and to the right of the original supply curve (in 2000). Given the larger supply of vanilla beans in 2006, the price dropped to about half of its 2000 level, to $25 per kilogram. The increase in supply from other countries was facilitated by the development of a sun-tolerant variety of the vanilla plant that allows it to be grown as a plantation crop. The new variety is an example of technological progress.

SOURCES: Based on Rhett Butler, "Collapsing Vanilla Prices Will Affect Madagascar," *mongabay.com*, May 9, 2005; Noel Paul, "Vanilla Sky High," *Christian Science Monitor*, August 11, 2003, http://www.csmonitor.com; G.K. Nair, "Vanilla Prices Fall on Undercutting," *Hindu Business Line*, April 3, 2006, http://www.thehindubusinessline.com.

Reinhard Eisele/Corbis

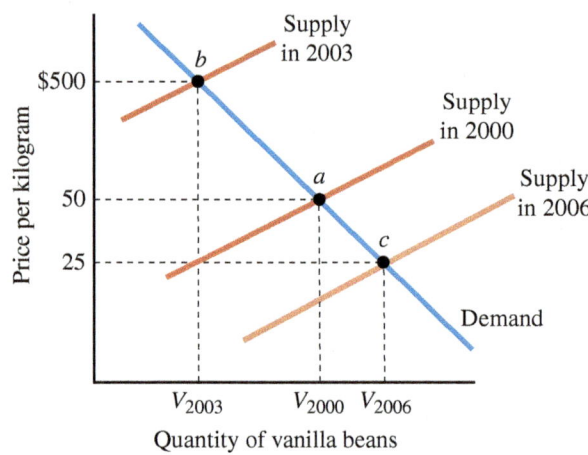

▲ **FIGURE 17**

The Bouncing Price of Vanilla Beans

A cyclone destroyed much of Madagascar's crop in 2000, shifting the supply curve upward and to the left. The equilibrium price increased from $50 per kilogram (point *a*) to $500 per kilogram (point *b*). By 2005, the vines replanted in Madagascar—along with new vines planted in other countries—started producing vanilla beans, and the supply curve shifted downward and to the right, beyond the supply curve for 2000. The price dropped to $25 per kilogram (point *c*), half the price that prevailed in 2000. (To represent the large changes in price and quantity, the graph is not drawn to scale.)

William West/Getty Images

APPLICATION 5

DROUGHT IN AUSTRALIA AND THE PRICE OF RICE

APPLYING THE CONCEPTS #5: How do producers respond to higher prices?

In 2008, the continuation of a six-year drought in Australia reduced the amount of water available to irrigate Australia's rice crop. Farmers responded by reducing the amount of land devoted to rice. The drought was a major factor in a near doubling of rice prices, which led to violent protests in Cameroon, Egypt, Ethiopia, Haiti, Indonesia, Italy, the Ivory Coast, Mauritania, and the Philippines.

The increase in the price of rice generated a number of responses that could eventually increase the quantity of rice produced. Farmers in Australia are experimenting with different varieties and growing techniques that require less water. The more costly techniques do not make economic sense when the price of rice is low, but are sensible when the price is high. In Thailand, farmers are investing in generators to irrigate their fields, allowing a second harvest each year. If the price of rice stays high, the farmers will reap a large profit, but if the price falls, the costs of adding a second crop will exceed the benefits, and farmers will lose money.

SOURCES: Based on David Streitfeld and Keith Bradsher, "Worries Mount as Farmers Push for Big Harvest," *New York Times*, June 10, 2008; Keith Bradsher, "A Drought in Australia, a Global Shortage of Rice," *New York Times*, April 17, 2008.

SUMMARY

Alex Segre/Alamy

In this chapter, we've seen how demand and supply determine prices. We also learned how to predict the effects of changes in demand or supply on prices and quantities. Here are the main points of the chapter:

1 A *market demand curve* shows the relationship between the quantity demanded and price, *ceteris paribus*.

2 A *market supply curve* shows the relationship between the quantity supplied and price, *ceteris paribus*.

3 *Equilibrium* in a market is shown by the intersection of the demand curve and the supply curve. When a market reaches equilibrium, there is no pressure to change the price.

4 A *change in demand* changes price and quantity in the same direction: An increase in demand increases the equilibrium price and quantity; a decrease in demand decreases the equilibrium price and quantity.

5 A *change in supply* changes price and quantity in opposite directions: An increase in supply decreases price and increases quantity; a decrease in supply increases price and decreases quantity.

KEY TERMS

change in demand	individual demand curve	minimum supply price
change in quantity demanded	individual supply curve	normal good
change in quantity supplied	inferior good	perfectly competitive market
change in supply	law of demand	quantity demanded
complements	law of supply	quantity supplied
demand schedule	market demand curve	substitutes
excess demand (shortage)	market equilibrium	supply schedule
excess supply (surplus)	market supply curve	

EXERCISES

Visit www.myeconlab.com to complete these exercises online and get instant feedback.

1 The Demand Curve

1.1 Arrow up or down: According to the law of demand, an increase in price _____ the quantity demanded.

1.2 From the following list, choose the variables that are held fixed in drawing a market demand curve:
- The price of the product
- Consumer income
- The price of other related goods
- Consumer expectations about future prices
- The quantity of the product purchased

1.3 From the following list, choose the variables that change as we draw a market demand curve:
- The price of the product
- Consumer income
- The price of other related goods
- Consumer expectations about future prices
- The quantity of the product purchased

1.4 The market demand curve is the _____ (horizontal/vertical) sum of the individual demand curves.

1.5 A change in price causes movement along a demand curve and a change in _____.

1.6 **Draw a Demand Curve.** Your state has decided to offer its citizens vanity license plates for their cars and wants to predict how many vanity plates it will sell at different prices. The price of the state's regular license plates is $20 per year, and the state's per-capita income is $30,000. A recent survey of other states with approximately the same population (3 million people) generated the following data on incomes, prices, and vanity plates:

State	B	C	D	E
Price of vanity plate	$ 60	$ 55	$ 50	$ 40
Price of regular plates	20	20	35	20
Income	30,000	25,000	30,000	30,000
Quantity of vanity plates	6,000	6,000	16,000	16,000

a. Use the available data to identify some points on the demand curve for vanity plates and connect the points to draw a demand curve. Don't forget *ceteris paribus*.

b. Suppose the demand curve is linear. If your state set a price of $50, how many vanity plates would be purchased?

2   The Supply Curve

2.1 Arrow up or down: According to the law of supply, an increase in price _____ the quantity supplied.

2.2 From the following list, choose the variables that are held fixed when drawing a market supply curve:
- The price of the product
- Wages paid to workers
- The price of materials used in production
- Taxes paid by producers
- The quantity of the product purchased

2.3 The minimum supply price is the _____ price at which a product is supplied.

2.4 The market supply curve is the _____ (horizontal/vertical) sum of the individual supply curves.

2.5 A change in price causes movement along a supply curve and a change in _____.

2.6 **Marginal Cost of Housing.** When the price of a standard three-bedroom house increases from $150,000 to $160,000, a building company increases its output from 20 houses per year to 21 houses per year. What does the increase in the quantity of housing reveal about the cost of producing housing?

2.7 **Imports and Market Supply.** Two nations supply sugar to the world market. Lowland has a minimum supply price of 10 cents per pound, while Highland has a minimum supply price of 24 cents per pound. For each nation, the slope of the supply curve is 1 cent per million pounds.

a. Draw the individual supply curves and the market supply curve. At what price and quantity is the supply curve kinked?

b. The market quantity supplied at a price of 15 cents is _____ million pounds. The market quantity supplied at a price of 30 cents is _____ million pounds.

2.8 **Responses to Higher Soybean Prices.** Suppose that in initial equilibrium in the soybean market, each of the 1,000 farmers produces 50 units, for a total of 50,000 units of soybeans. Suppose the price of soybeans increases, and everyone expects the price to stay at the higher level for many years.

a. Arrows up or down: Over a period of several years, we expect the quantity of soybeans

supplied to _____ as the number of soybean farmers _____ and the output per farmer _____.

b. A farmer who enters the market is likely to have a _____ (higher/lower) marginal cost of production than an original firm.

3   Market Equilibrium: Bringing Demand and Supply Together

3.1 The market equilibrium is shown by the intersection of the _____ curve and the _____ curve.

3.2 Excess demand occurs when the price is (less/greater) than the equilibrium price; excess supply occurs when the price is _____ (less/greater) than the equilibrium price.

3.3 Arrow up or down: An excess demand for a product will cause the price to _____. As a consequence of the price change, the quantity demanded will _____ and the quantity supplied will _____.

3.4 Arrow up or down: An excess supply of a product will cause the price to _____. As a consequence of the price change, the quantity demanded will _____, and the quantity supplied will _____.

3.5 **Interpreting the Graph.** The following graph shows the demand and supply curves for CD players. Complete the following statements.

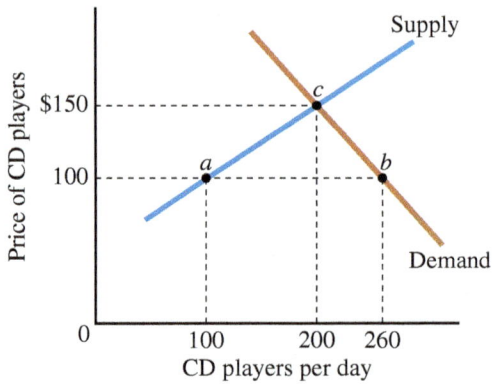

a. At the market equilibrium (shown by point _____), the price of CD players is _____ and the quantity of CD players is _____.

b. At a price of $100, there would be excess _____, so we would expect the price to _____.

c. At a price exceeding the equilibrium price, there would be excess _____, so we would expect the price to _____.

3.6 **Draw and Find the Equilibrium.** The following table shows the quantities of corn supplied and demanded at different prices.

Price per Ton	Quantity Supplied	Quantity Demanded
$ 80	600	1,200
90	800	1,100
100	1,000	1,000
110	1,200	900

a. Draw the demand curve and the supply curve.

b. The equilibrium price of corn is _____, and the equilibrium quantity is _____.

c. At a price of $110, there is excess _____ (supply/demand) equal to _____.

4 Market Effects of Changes in Demand

4.1 A change in demand causes a _____ (movement along/shift of) the demand curve. A change in quantity demanded causes a _____ (movement along/shift of) the demand curve.

4.2 Circle the variables that change as we move along the demand curve for pencils and cross out those that are assumed to be fixed.

- Quantity of pencils demanded
- Number of consumers
- Price of pencils
- Price of pens
- Consumer income

4.3 **Online Movies.** Consider the effects of online distribution of movies. A decrease in the price of online movies shifts the demand for DVD movies to the _____ (left, right). A decrease in downloading time shifts the demand for DVD movies to the _____ (left, right).

4.4 Arrow up or down: The market demand curve for a product will shift to the right when the price of a substitute good _____, the price of a complementary good _____, consumer income _____, and the population _____.

4.5 Arrow up or down: An increase in demand for a product _____ the equilibrium price and _____ the equilibrium quantity.

4.6 **Market Effects of Increased Income.** Consider the market for restaurant meals. Use a demand and supply graph to predict the market effects of an increase in consumer income. Arrow up or down: The equilibrium price of restaurant meals will _____, and the equilibrium quantity of restaurant meals will _____.

4.7 **Public versus Private Colleges.** Consider the market for private college education. Use a demand and supply graph to predict the market effects of an increase in the tuition charged by public colleges.

Arrow up or down: The equilibrium price of a private college education will _____, and the equilibrium quantity will _____.

4.8 **Gas Prices and New Gas Guzzlers.** Use a demand and supply graph to predict the implications for the market for new full-size SUVs. Arrow up or down: The equilibrium price of a full-size SUV will _____, and the equilibrium quantity will _____.

5 Market Effects of Changes in Supply

5.1 A change in supply causes a _____ (movement along/shift of) the supply curve. A change in quantity supplied causes a _____ (movement along/shift of) the supply curve.

5.2 Circle the variables that change as we move along the supply curve for pencils and cross out those that are assumed to be fixed:

- Quantity of pencils supplied
- Price of wood
- Price of pencils
- Production technology

5.3 Arrow up or down: An increase in the price of wood shifts the supply curve for pencils _____; an improvement in pencil-production technology shifts the supply curve for pencils _____; a tax on pencil production shifts the supply curve for pencils _____.

5.4 Arrow up or down: An increase in the supply of a product _____ the equilibrium price and _____ the equilibrium quantity.

5.5 If both demand and supply increase simultaneously, the equilibrium price will increase if the change in _____ is relatively large.

5.6 Arrow up or down: If supply increases while demand decreases, the equilibrium price will _____.

5.7 If supply increases while demand decreases, the equilibrium quantity will decrease if the change in _____ (supply/demand) is relatively large.

5.8 **Effect of Weather on Prices.** Suppose a freeze in Florida wipes out 20 percent of the orange crop. How will this affect the equilibrium price and quantity of Florida oranges? Illustrate your answer with a graph.

5.9 **Immigration Control and Prices.** Consider the market for raspberries. Suppose a new law outlaws the use of foreign farm workers on raspberry farms, and the wages paid to farm workers increase as a result. Use a demand and supply graph to predict the effects of the higher wage on the equilibrium price and quantity of raspberries. Arrow up or down: The equilibrium price of raspberries will _____, and the equilibrium quantity of raspberries will _____ .

5.10 Market Effects of Import Ban. Consider the market for shoes in a nation that initially imports half the shoes it consumes. Use a demand and supply graph to predict the market effect of a ban on shoe imports. Arrow up or down: The equilibrium price will _____ , and the equilibrium quantity will _____ .

5.11 Market Effects of a Tax. Consider the market for fish. Use a demand and supply graph to predict the effect of a tax paid by fish producers of $1 per pound of fish. Use a demand and supply graph to predict the market effect of the tax. Arrow up or down: The equilibrium price will _____, and the equilibrium quantity will _____ .

5.12 Innovation and the Price of Mobile Phones. Suppose that the initial price of a mobile phone is $100 and that the initial quantity demanded is 500 phones per day. Use a graph to show the effects of a technological innovation that decreases the cost of producing mobile phones. Label the starting point with "*a*" and the new equilibrium with "*b*."

5.13 Used Cars: Gas Guzzlers versus Gas Sippers. Consider the market for used cars. In 2008, the price of gas rose while the price of used full-size SUVs dropped and the price of used compact cars increased.
  a. Use a supply–demand graph to show the effects of a higher gasoline price on the market for used full-size SUVs.
  b. Use a supply–demand graph to show the effects of a higher gasoline price on the market for used compact cars.

6 Predicting and Explaining Market Changes

6.1 Fill in the blanks in the following table. Note that the ordering of the first column has been scrambled.

Change in Demand or Supply	How does the equilibrium price change?	How does the equilibrium quantity change?
Increase in supply		
Decrease in demand		
Decrease in supply		
Increase in demand		

6.2 When _____ (supply/demand) changes, the equilibrium price and the equilibrium quantity change in the same direction. When _____ (supply/demand) changes, the equilibrium price and the equilibrium quantity change in opposite directions.

6.3 Suppose the equilibrium price of accordions recently increased while the equilibrium quantity decreased. These changes were caused by a(n) _____ (increase/decrease) in _____ (supply/demand).

6.4 Suppose the equilibrium price of housing recently increased, and the equilibrium quantity increased as well. These changes were caused by a(n) _____ (increase/decrease) in _____ (supply/demand).

6.5 What Caused the Higher Gasoline Price? In the last month, the price of gasoline increased by 20 percent. Your job is to determine what caused the increase in price: a change in demand or a change in supply. Ms. Info has all the numbers associated with the gasoline market, and she can answer a single factual question. (She cannot answer the question "Was the higher price caused by a change in demand or a change in supply?")
  a. What single question would you ask?
  b. Provide an answer to your question that implies that the higher price was caused by a change in demand. Illustrate with a complete graph.
  c. Provide an answer to your question that implies that the higher price was caused by a change in supply. Illustrate with a complete graph.

6.6 Rising Price of Milk. In 2007, the price of milk increased by roughly 10 percent while the quantity consumed decreased. Use a supply–demand graph to explain the changes in price and quantity.

6.7 Rising Price of Used Organs. Over the last few years, the price of transplantable human organs (livers, kidneys, hearts) has increased dramatically. Why? What additional information about the market for used organs would allow you to prove that your explanation is the correct one?

6.8 The Price of Summer Cabins. As summer approaches, the equilibrium price of rental cabins increases and the equilibrium quantity of cabins rented increases. Draw a demand and supply graph that explains these changes.

6.9 Simplest Possible Graph. Consider the market for juice oranges. Draw the simplest possible demand and supply graph consistent with the following observations. You should be able to draw a graph with no more than four curves. Label each of your curves as "supply" or "demand" and indicate the year (1, 2, or 3).

Year	1	2	3
Price	$5	$7	$4
Quantity	100	80	110

6.10 Zero Price for Used Newspapers. In 1987 you could sell a ton of used newspaper for $60. Five years later, you couldn't sell them at any price. In other words, the price of used newspapers dropped from $60 to zero in just five years. Over this period, the quantity of used newspapers bought and sold increased. What caused the drop in price? Illustrate your answer with a complete graph.

6.11 Decrease in the Price of Heroin. Between 1990 and 2003, the price of heroin decreased from $235 per gram to $76. Over the same period, the quantity of heroin consumed increased from 376 metric tons to 482 metric tons. Use a demand and supply graph to explain these changes in price and quantity.

7 Applications of Demand and Supply

7.1 Arrow up or down: Hurricane Katrina _____ the demand for housing in Baton Rouge, so the price of housing _____ and the quantity of housing _____. (Related to Application 1.)

7.2 Arrows up or down: The decrease in the number of bee colonies _____ the supply of fruits and berries, _____ the cost of producing ice cream, and _____ the equilibrium price of ice cream. (Related to Application 2.)

7.3 Between 2008 and 2009, the equilibrium price of cruises _____ because _____ and demand _____. (Related to Application 3.)

7.4 Arrow up or down: The development of a sun-tolerant variety of the vanilla plant _____ the supply of vanilla and its price. (Related to Application 4.)

7.5 Arrow up or down: The drought in Australia _____ the supply of rice and _____ its price. (Related to Application 5.)

7.6 Katrina Victims Move Back. Suppose that five years after Hurricane Katrina, half the people who had relocated to Baton Rouge move back to a rebuilt New Orleans. Use a demand and supply graph of the Baton Rouge housing market to show the market effects of the return of people to New Orleans. (Related to Application 1.)

7.7 Honeybees and Ice Cream. Suppose the decline of bee colonies increases the prices of some ingredients used to produce ice cream. Consider two flavors of ice cream, strawberry and vanilla. The cost of producing strawberry ice cream increases by 20 percent, while the cost of producing vanilla ice cream increases by only 5 percent. Use a supply–demand graph to show the implications for the equilibrium prices and quantities of the two flavors of ice cream. (Related to Application 2.)

7.8 Cruise Ship Berths. Consider the change in the equilibrium quantity shown in Figure 16. Draw a new graph (with a decrease in demand and an increase in supply) such that the equilibrium quantity (the number of passengers) decreases. What is the fundamental difference between your graph and Figure 16? (Related to Application 3.)

7.9 Artificial versus Natural Vanilla. An artificial alternative to natural vanilla is cheaper to produce but doesn't taste as good. Suppose the makers of artificial vanilla discover a new recipe that improves its taste. Use a demand and supply graph to show the effects on the equilibrium price and quantity of natural vanilla. (Related to Application 4.)

7.10 Drought and Rice Prices. Consider the market for rice. Use a demand and supply graph to illustrate the following statement: "The drought was a major factor in a near doubling of rice prices." (Related to Application 5.)

ECONOMIC EXPERIMENT

Market Equilibrium

This simple experiment takes about 20 minutes. We start by dividing the class into two equal groups: consumers and producers.

- The instructor provides each consumer with a number indicating the maximum amount he or she is willing to pay (WTP) for a bushel of apples: The WTP is a number between $1 and $100. Each consumer has the opportunity to buy one bushel of apples per trading period. The consumer's score for a single trading period equals the gap between the WTP and the price actually paid for

apples. For example, if the consumer's WTP is $80 and he or she pays only $30 for apples, the consumer's score is $50. Each consumer has the option of not buying apples. This will be sensible if the best price the consumer can get exceeds the WTP. If the consumer does not buy apples, his or her score will be zero.

- The instructor provides each producer with a number indicating the cost of producing a bushel of apples (a number between $1 and $100). Each producer has the opportunity to sell one bushel per trading period. The producer's score for a single trading period equals the gap between the selling prices and the cost of producing apples. So if a producer sells apples for $20, and the cost is only $15, the producer's score is $5. Producers have the option of not selling apples, which is sensible if the best price the producer can get is less than the cost. If the producer does not sell apples, his or her score is zero.

Once everyone understands the rules, consumers and producers meet in a trading area to arrange transactions. A consumer may announce how much he or she is willing to pay for apples and wait for a producer to agree to sell apples at that price. Alternatively, a producer may announce how much he or she is willing accept for apples and wait for a consumer to agree to buy apples at that price. Once a transaction has been arranged, the consumer and producer inform the instructor of the trade, record the transaction, and leave the trading area.

Several trading periods are conducted, each of which lasts a few minutes. After the end of each trading period, the instructor lists the prices at which apples sold during the period. Then another trading period starts, providing consumers and producers another opportunity to buy or sell apples. After all the trading periods have been completed, each participant computes his or her score by adding the scores from the trading periods.

 For additional economic experiments, please visit *www.myeconlab.com*.

Measuring a Nation's Production and Income

During the deep economic downturn in 2009 and 2010, economists, business writers, and politicians anxiously awaited the news from the government about the latest economic developments. They pored over the data to determine if the economy was beginning to recover from its doldrums and when more robust economic activity would resume.

At the same time, a distinguished group of economists, led by Nobel Laureates Joseph Stiglitz and Amartya Sen and French economist Jean-Paul Fitoussi, issued a report calling for major revision in the way we measure economic performance. They suggested that our government statisticians focus more on how much we consume and how much leisure we enjoy, and not solely on what we produce. They also suggested that we should be more concerned about whether our current activities are sustainable over the long run, perhaps recognizing environmental constraints.

But perhaps their most radical suggestion was that we switch our focus away from economic production to measuring people's economic well-being. This could include examining the diets and living conditions of the poorest people. For residents of developed countries, this might involve analyzing surveys of people's reported happiness with their own lives.

Fancy/Alamy

These changes, however, may be far in the future. Economists and businesses will still rely for some time on the traditional measures of economic activity that we study in this chapter.

APPLYING THE CONCEPTS

1 How can we use economic analysis to compare the size of a major corporation to the size of a country?
   Using Value Added to Measure the True Size of Wal-Mart

2 How severe was the most recent recession for the United States?
   Comparing the Severity of Recessions

3 Do increases in gross domestic product necessarily translate into improvements in the welfare of citizens?
   The Links between Self-Reported Happiness and GDP

From Chapter 11 of *Survey of Economics: Principles, Applications, and Tools*, 5/e. Arthur O'Sullivan. Steven M. Sheffrin. Stephen J. Perez. Copyright © 2012 by Pearson Education. Published by Prentice Hall. All rights reserved.

macroeconomics

The study of the nation's economy as a whole; focuses on the issues of inflation, unemployment, and economic growth.

This chapter begins your study of **macroeconomics**: the branch of economics that deals with a nation's economy as a whole. Macroeconomics focuses on the economic issues—unemployment, inflation, growth, trade, and the gross domestic product—that are most often discussed in newspapers, on the radio and television, and on the Internet.

Macroeconomic issues lie at the heart of political debates. In fact, all presidential candidates learn a quick lesson in macroeconomics. Namely, their prospects for reelection will depend on how well the economy performs during their term in office. If voters believe the economy has performed well, the president will be reelected. Democrat Jimmy Carter as well as Republican George H. W. Bush failed in their bids for reelection in 1980 and 1992, respectively, partly because of voters' macroeconomic concerns. Both Republican Ronald Reagan in 1984 and Democrat Bill Clinton in 1996 won reelection easily because voters believed the economy was performing well in their first terms. Public opinion polling shows that presidential popularity rises and falls with the performance of the economy.

Macroeconomic events profoundly affect our everyday lives. For example, if the economy fails to create enough jobs, workers will become unemployed throughout the country, and millions of lives will be disrupted. Similarly, slow economic growth means that living standards will not increase rapidly. If prices for goods begin rising rapidly, some people will find it difficult to maintain their lifestyles.

This chapter will introduce you to the concepts you need to understand what macroeconomics is all about. In this chapter, we'll focus on a nation's production and income. We'll learn how economists measure the income and production for an entire country and how they use these measures. We will explain the terms the media often uses when reporting economic information.

Macroeconomics focuses on two basic issues: long-run economic growth and economic fluctuations. We need to understand what happens during the long run to understand the factors behind the rise in living standards in modern economies. Today, living standards are much higher in the United States than they were for our grandparents. Living standards are also much higher than those of millions of people throughout the globe. Although living standards have improved over time, the economy has not always grown smoothly. Economic performance has fluctuated over time. During periods of slow economic growth, not enough jobs are created, and large numbers of workers become unemployed. Both the public and policymakers become concerned about the lack of jobs and the increase in unemployment.

At other times, unemployment may not be a problem, but we become concerned that the prices of everything that we buy seem to increase rapidly. Sustained increases in prices are called **inflation**.

inflation

Sustained increases in the average prices of all goods and services.

1 THE "FLIP" SIDES OF MACROECONOMIC ACTIVITY: PRODUCTION AND INCOME

Before we can study growth and fluctuations, we need to have a basic vocabulary and understanding of some key concepts. We begin with the terms *production* and *income* because these are the "flip" sides of the macroeconomic "coin," so to speak. Every day, men and women go off to work, where they produce or sell merchandise or provide services. At the end of the week or month, they return home with their paychecks or "income." They spend some of that money on other products and services, which are produced by other people. In other words, production leads to income, and income leads to production.

But this chapter really isn't about production and income of individuals in markets. That's what a microeconomist studies. On the contrary, this chapter is about the production and income of the economy *as a whole*. From a "big picture" perspective, we will look at certain measures that will tell us how much the economy is producing and how well it is growing. We will also be able to measure the total income generated in the economy and how this income flows back to workers and investors. These two measures—a country's production and income—are critical to a nation's economic health. Macroeconomists collect and analyze production and income data to understand how many people will find jobs and whether their living standards are rising or falling. Government officials use the data and analysis to develop economic policies.

The Circular Flow of Production and Income

Let's begin with a simple diagram known as the *circular flow*, shown in Figure 1. We'll start with a very simple economy that does not have a government or a foreign sector. Households and firms make transactions in two markets known as *factor markets* and *product markets*. In factor, or input, markets, households supply labor to firms. Households are also the ultimate owners of firms, as well as of all the resources firms use in their production, which we call *capital*. Consequently, we can think of households as providing capital to firms—land, buildings, and equipment—to produce output. Product, or output, markets are markets in which firms sell goods and services to consumers.

The point of the circular flow diagram is simple and fundamental: Production generates income. In factor markets, when households supply labor and capital to firms they are compensated by the firms. They earn wages for their work, and they earn interest, dividends, and rents on the capital they supply to the firms. The households then use their income to purchase goods and services in the product markets. The firm uses the revenues it receives from the sale of its products to pay for the factors of production (land, labor, and capital).

When goods and services are produced, income flows throughout the economy. For example, consider a manufacturer of computers. At the same time the computer manufacturer produces and sells new computers, it also generates income through its production. The computer manufacturer pays wages to workers, perhaps pays rent on offices and factory buildings, and pays interest on money it borrowed from a bank. Whatever is left over after paying for the cost of production is the firm's profit, which is income to the owners of the firm. Wages, rents, interest, and profits are all different forms of income.

In an example with a government, your taxes pay for a school district to hire principals, teachers, and other staff to provide educational services to the students in your community. These educational services are an important part of production in our modern economy that produces both goods and services. At the same time, the principals, teachers, and staff all earn income through their employment with the school district. The school district may also rent buildings where classes are held and pay interest on borrowed funds.

Our goal is to understand both sides of this macroeconomic "coin"—the production in the economy and the generation of income in the economy. In the United

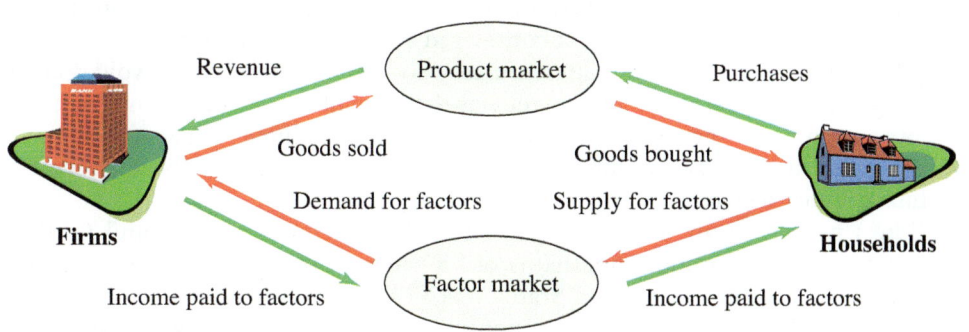

◄ **FIGURE 1**

The Circular Flow of Production and Income

The circular flow shows how the production of goods and services generates income for households and how households purchase goods and services produced by firms.

States, the national income and product accounts, published by the Department of Commerce, are the source for the key data on production and income in the economy. As we will see, we can measure the value of output produced in the economy by looking at either the production or income side of the economy. Let's begin by learning how to measure the production for the entire economy.

2 THE PRODUCTION APPROACH: MEASURING A NATION'S MACROECONOMIC ACTIVITY USING GROSS DOMESTIC PRODUCT

To measure the production of the entire economy, we need to combine an enormous array of goods and services—everything from new computers to NBA and WNBA basketball games. We can actually add computers to basketball games, as we could add apples and oranges if we were trying to determine the total monetary value of a fruit harvest. Our goal is to summarize the total production of an entire economy into a single number, which we call the **gross domestic product (GDP)**. Gross domestic product is the total market value of all the final goods and services produced within an economy in a given year. GDP is also the most common measure of an economy's total output. All the words in the GDP definition are important, so let's analyze them.

"Total market value" means we take the quantity of goods produced, multiply them by their respective prices, and then add up the totals. If an economy produced two cars at $25,000 per car and three computers at $2,000 per computer, the total value of these goods will be

$$2 \text{ cars} \times \$25,000 \text{ per car} = \$50,000$$
$$+$$
$$3 \text{ computers} \times \$2,000 \text{ per computer} = \$6,000$$
$$= \$56,000$$

The reason we multiply the goods by their prices is that we cannot simply add together the number of cars and the number of computers. Using prices allows us to express the value of everything in a common unit of measurement—in this case, dollars. (In countries other than the United States, we express the value in terms of the local currency.) We add apples and oranges together by finding out the value of both the apples and the oranges, as measured by what you would pay for them, and adding them up in terms of their prices.

"Final goods and services" in the definition of GDP means those goods and services that are sold to ultimate, or final, purchasers. For example, the two cars that were produced would be final goods if they were sold to households or to a business. However, to produce the cars the automobile manufacturer bought steel that went into the body of the cars, and we do not count this steel as a final good or service in GDP. Steel is an example of an **intermediate good**, one that is used in the production process. An intermediate good is not considered a final good or service.

The reason we do not count intermediate goods as final goods is to avoid double-counting. The price of the car already reflects the price of the steel contained in it. We do not want to count the steel twice. Similarly, the large volumes of paper a commercial printing firm uses also are intermediate goods, because the paper becomes part of the final product delivered by the printing firm to its clients.

The final words in our definition of GDP are "in a given year." GDP is expressed as a rate of production, that is, as "X" amount of dollars per year. In 2008, for example, GDP in the United States was $14,196 billion. Goods produced in prior years, such as cars or houses, are not included in GDP for a given year, even if

gross domestic product (GDP)
The total market value of final goods and services produced within an economy in a given year.

intermediate goods
Goods used in the production process that are not final goods and services.

one consumer sells a house or car to another in that year. Only *newly produced* products are included in GDP.

Because we measure GDP using the current prices for goods and services, GDP will increase if prices increase, even if the physical amount of goods that are produced remains the same. Suppose that next year the economy again produces two cars and three computers, but all the prices in the economy double: The price of cars is $50,000, and the price of computers is $4,000. GDP will also be twice as high, or $112,000, even though the quantity produced is the same as during the prior year:

$$2 \text{ cars} \times \$50,000 \text{ per car} = \$100,000$$

$$+$$

$$3 \text{ computers} \times \$4,000 \text{ per computer} = \$ 12,000$$

$$= \$112,000$$

But to say that GDP has doubled would be misleading, because exactly the same goods were produced. To avoid this problem, let's apply the real-nominal principle, one of our five basic principles of economics.

REAL-NOMINAL PRINCIPLE

What matters to people is the real value of money or income—its purchasing power—not the face value of money or income.

What we need is another measure of total output that doesn't increase just because prices increase. For this reason, economists have developed the concept of **real GDP**, a measure that controls for changes in prices. Later in this chapter, we explain how real GDP is calculated. The basic idea is simple. When we use current prices to measure GDP, we are using **nominal GDP**. Nominal GDP can increase for one of two reasons: Either the production of goods and services has increased, or the prices of those goods and services have increased.

To explain the concept of real GDP, we first need to look at a simple example. Suppose an economy produces a single good: computers. In year 1, 10 computers were produced, and each sold for $2,000. In year 2, 12 computers were produced, and each sold for $2,100. Nominal GDP is $20,000 in year 1 and $25,200 in year 2; it has increased by a factor of 1.26 or 26 percent. However, we can also measure real GDP by using year 1 prices as a measure of what was produced in year 1 *and* what was produced in year 2. In year 1, real GDP is

$$10 \text{ computers} \times \$2,000 \text{ per computer} = \$20,000$$

In year 2, real GDP (in year 1 terms) is

$$12 \text{ computers} \times \$2,000 \text{ per computer} = \$24,000$$

Real GDP in year 2 is still greater than real GDP in year 1, now by a factor of 1.2, or 20 percent. The key idea is that we construct a measure using the same prices for both years and thereby take price changes into account.

Figure 2 plots real GDP for the U.S. economy for the years 1930 through 2009. The graph shows that real GDP has grown substantially over this period. This is what economists call **economic growth**—sustained increases in the real GDP of an economy over a long period of time. Later in this chapter, we'll look carefully at the behavior of real GDP over shorter periods, during which time it can rise and fall. Decreases in real GDP disrupt the economy greatly and lead to unemployment.

real GDP
A measure of GDP that controls for changes in prices.

nominal GDP
The value of GDP in current dollars.

economic growth
Sustained increases in the real GDP of an economy over a long period of time.

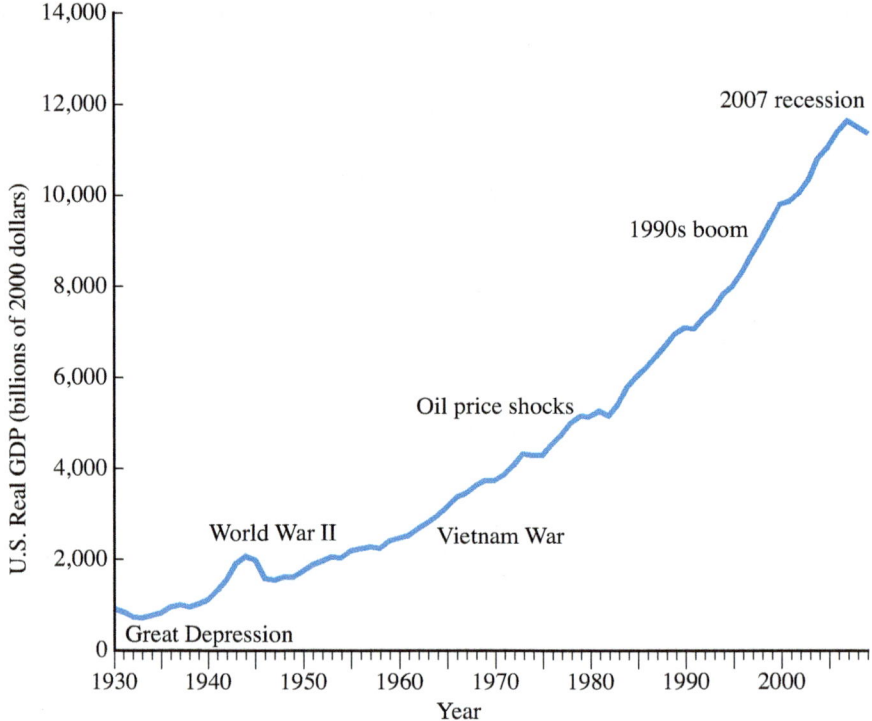

▲ **FIGURE 2**

U.S. Real GDP, 1930–2009

During the Great Depression in the 1930s, GDP initially fell and then was relatively flat. The economy was not growing much. However, the economy began growing rapidly in the 1940s during Word War II and has grown substantially since then.

SOURCE: U.S. Department of Commerce.

The Components of GDP

Economists divide GDP into four broad categories, each corresponding to different types of purchases represented in GDP:

1 *Consumption expenditures:* purchases by consumers

2 *Private investment expenditures:* purchases by firms

3 *Government purchases:* purchases by federal, state, and local governments

4 *Net exports:* net purchases by the foreign sector (domestic exports minus domestic imports)

Before discussing these categories, let's look at some data for the U.S. economy to get a sense of the size of each of these four components. Table 1 shows the figures for GDP for the fourth quarter of 2009. (A quarter is a three-month period; the first quarter runs from January through March, while the fourth quarter runs from October through December. Quarterly GDP expressed at annual rates is GDP for a year if the entire year were the same as the measured quarter.) In the fourth quarter of 2009, GDP was $14,461 billion, or approximately $14.4 trillion. To get a sense of the magnitude, consider that the U.S. population is approximately 300 million people, making GDP per person

TABLE 1 COMPOSITION OF U.S. GDP, FOURTH QUARTER 2009 (BILLIONS OF DOLLARS EXPRESSED AT ANNUAL RATES)				
GDP	Consumption Expenditures	Private Investment Expenditures	Government Purchases	Net Exports
$14,461	$10,234	$1,716	$2,960	–$449

SOURCE: U.S. Department of Commerce.

approximately $48,203. (This does not mean every man, woman, and child actually spends $48,203, but it is a useful indicator of the productive strength of the economy.)

CONSUMPTION EXPENDITURES **Consumption expenditures** are purchases by consumers of currently produced goods and services, either domestic or foreign. These purchases include flat-screen TVs, smart phones, automobiles, clothing, hair-styling services, jewelry, movie or basketball tickets, food, and all other consumer items. We can break down consumption into durable goods, nondurable goods, and services. *Durable goods*, such as automobiles or refrigerators, last for a long time. *Nondurable goods*, such as food, last for a short time. *Services* are work in which people play a prominent role in delivery (such as a dentist filling a cavity). They range from haircutting to health care and are the fastest-growing component of consumption in the United States. Overall, consumption spending is the most important component of GDP, constituting about 70 percent of total purchases.

PRIVATE INVESTMENT EXPENDITURES **Private investment expenditures** in GDP consist of three components:

1 First, there is spending on new plants and equipment during the year. If a firm builds a new factory or purchases a new machine, the new factory or new machine is included in the year's GDP. Purchasing an existing building or buying a used machine does not count in GDP, because the goods were not produced during the current year.

2 Second, newly produced housing is included in investment spending. The sale of an existing home to a new owner is not counted, because the house was not built in the current year.

3 Finally, if firms add to their stock of inventories, the increase in inventories during the current year is included in GDP. If a hardware store had $1,000 worth of nuts and bolts on its shelves at the beginning of the year and $1,100 at the year's end, its inventory investment is $100 ($1,100 − $1,000). This $100 increase in inventory investment is included in GDP.

We call the total of new investment expenditures **gross investment**. During the year, some of the existing plant, equipment, and housing will deteriorate or wear out. This wear and tear is called **depreciation**, or sometimes a *capital consumption allowance*. If we subtract depreciation from gross investment, we obtain net investment. **Net investment** is the true addition to the stock of plant, equipment, and housing in a given year.

Make sure you understand this distinction between gross investment and net investment. Consider the $1,716 billion in total investment spending for the fourth quarter of 2009, a period in which there was $1,525 billion in depreciation in the private sector. That means there was only $191 billion ($1,716 − $1,525) in net investment by firms in that year; 88 percent of gross investment went to make up for depreciation of existing capital.

Warning: When we discuss measuring production in the GDP accounts, we use *investment* in a different way than that with which you may be accustomed. For an economist, investment in the GDP accounts means purchases of new final goods and services by firms. In everyday conversation, we may talk about investing in the stock market or investing in gold. Buying stock for $1,800 on the stock market is a purchase of an existing financial asset; it is not the purchase of new goods and services by firms. Therefore, that $1,800 does not appear anywhere in GDP. The same is true of purchasing a gold bar. In GDP accounting, *investment* denotes the purchase of new capital. Be careful not to confuse the common usage of *investment* with the definition of *investment* as we use it in the GDP accounts.

GOVERNMENT PURCHASES **Government purchases** are the purchases of newly produced goods and services by federal, state, and local governments. They include any goods that the government purchases plus the wages and benefits of all

---

consumption expenditures
Purchases of newly produced goods and services by households.

private investment expenditures
Purchases of newly produced goods and services by firms.

gross investment
Total new investment expenditures.

depreciation
Reduction in the value of capital goods over a one-year period due to physical wear and tear and also to obsolescence; also called *capital consumption allowance*.

net investment
Gross investment minus depreciation.

government purchases
Purchases of newly produced goods and services by local, state, and federal governments.

government workers (paid when the government purchases their services as employ-ees). Investment spending by government is also included. The majority of spending in this category comes from state and local governments: $1,790 billion of the total $2,960 billion in 2009. Government purchases affect our lives very directly. For exam-ple, all salaries of U.S. postal employees and federal airport security personnel are counted as government purchases.

transfer payments
Payments from governments to individuals that do not correspond to the production of goods and services.

This category does not include all spending by governments. It excludes **transfer payments**, payments to individuals that are not associated with the production of goods and services. For example, payments for Social Security, welfare, and interest on government debt are all considered transfer payments and thus are not included in government purchases in GDP. Nothing is being produced by the recipients in return for money being paid, or "transferred," to them. But wage payments to the police, postal workers, and the staff of the Internal Revenue Service are all included, because they do correspond to services these workers are currently producing.

Because transfer payments are excluded from GDP, a vast portion of the budget of the federal government is not part of GDP. In 2008, the federal government spent approximately $3,454 billion, of which only $1,170 billion (about 33 percent) was counted as federal government purchases. Transfer payments are important, however, because they affect both the income of individuals and their consumption and savings behavior. Transfer payments also affect the size of the federal budget deficit. At this point, keep in mind the distinction between government purchases—which are included in GDP—and total government spending or expenditure—which may *not* be included.

import
A good or service produced in a foreign country and purchased by residents of the home country (for example, the United States).

export
A good or service produced in the home country (for example, the United States) and sold in another country.

net exports
Exports minus imports.

NET EXPORTS   To understand the role of the foreign sector, we first need to define three terms. **Imports** are goods and services we buy from other countries. **Exports** are goods and services made here and sold to other countries. **Net exports** are total exports minus total imports. In Table 1, we see that net exports in the first quarter of 2009 were –$449 billion. Net exports were negative because our imports exceeded our exports.

Consumption, investment, and government purchases include all purchases by consumers, firms, and the government, whether or not the goods were produced in the United States. However, GDP is supposed to measure the goods produced in the United States. Consequently, we subtract purchases of foreign goods by consumers, firms, or the government when we calculate GDP, because these goods were not pro-duced in the United States. At the same time, we add to GDP any goods produced here and sold abroad, for example, airplanes made in the United States and sold in Europe. By including net exports as a component of GDP, we correctly measure U.S. production by adding exports and subtracting imports.

Suppose someone in the United States buys a $25,000 car made in Japan. If we look at final purchases, we will see that consumption spending rose by $25,000 because a consumer made a purchase of a consumption good. Net exports fell by $25,000, how-ever, because we subtracted the value of the import (the car) from total exports. Notice that total GDP did not change with the purchase of the car. This is exactly what we want in this case, because the car wasn't produced in the United States.

Now suppose the United States sells a car for $22,000 to a resident of Spain. In this case, net exports increase by $22,000 because the car was a U.S. export. GDP will also be a corresponding $22,000 higher because this sale represents U.S. production.

trade deficit
The excess of imports over exports.

trade surplus
The excess of exports over imports.

Recall that for the United States in the fourth quarter of 2009 net exports were –$449 billion dollars. In other words, in that quarter the United States bought $449 billion more goods from abroad than it sold abroad. When we buy more goods from abroad than we sell, we have a **trade deficit**. A **trade surplus** occurs when our exports exceed our imports. Figure 3 shows the U.S. trade surplus as a share of GDP from 1960 to 2009. Although at times the United States has had a small trade surplus, it has generally run a trade deficit. In recent years, the trade deficit has increased and has fluctuated between 3 and 6 percent of GDP.

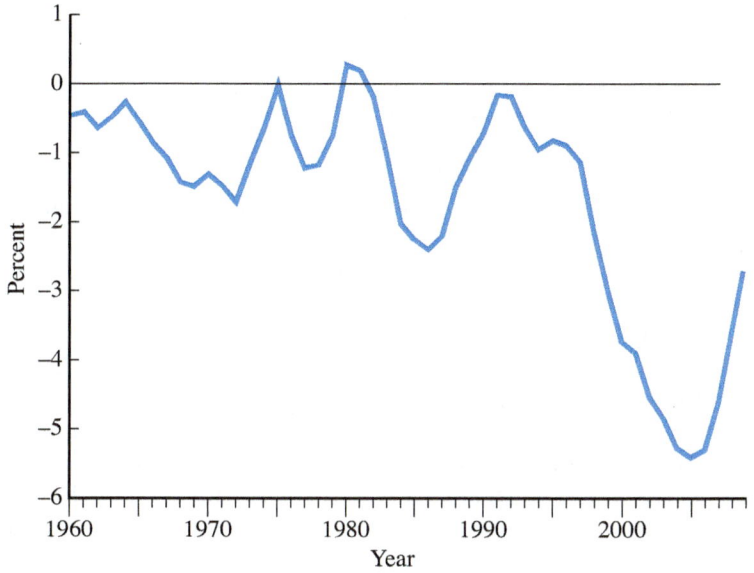

◄ **FIGURE 3**

U.S. Trade Balance as a Share of GDP, 1960–2009
In the early 1980s, the United States ran a trade surplus (when the line on the graph is above zero, this indicates a surplus). However, in other years the United States has run a trade deficit. In 2004 through 2006, the trade deficit exceeded 5 percent of GDP, although it most recently is near 3 percent of GDP. *SOURCE: Department of Commerce.*

Putting It All Together: The GDP Equation

We can summarize our discussion of who purchases GDP with a simple equation that combines the four components of GDP:

$$Y = C + I + G + NX$$

where

$$Y = \text{GDP}$$

$$C = \text{Consumption}$$

$$I = \text{Investment}$$

$$G = \text{Government purchases}$$

$$NX = \text{Net exports}$$

In other words,

GDP = consumption + investment + government purchases + net exports

This equation is an *identity*, which means it is always true no matter what the values of the variables are. In any economy, GDP consists of the sum of its four components.

3 THE INCOME APPROACH: MEASURING A NATION'S MACROECONOMIC ACTIVITY USING NATIONAL INCOME

Recall from the circular flow that one person's production ends up being another person's income. Income is the flip side of our macroeconomic "coin." As a result, in addition to measuring a nation's activity by measuring production, we can also gauge it by measuring a nation's income. The total income earned by U.S. residents working in the United States and abroad is called **national income**.

Measuring National Income

To measure national income, economists first make two primary adjustments to GDP.

First, we add to GDP the net income earned by U.S. firms and residents abroad. To make this calculation, we add to GDP any income earned abroad by U.S. firms or residents and subtract any income earned in the United States by foreign firms or

national income

The total income earned by a nation's residents both domestically and abroad in the production of goods and services.

residents. For example, we add the profits earned by U.S. multinational corporations that are sent back to the United States but subtract the profits from multinational corporations operating in the United States that are sent back to their home countries. The profits Wal-Mart sends back to the United States from its stores in Mexico are added to GDP. The profits Toyota earns in the United States that it sends back to Japan are subtracted from GDP. The result of these adjustments is the total income earned worldwide by U.S. firms and residents. This is the **gross national product (GNP)**.

gross national product
GDP plus net income earned abroad.

The distinction between what they produce within their borders, GDP, and what their citizens earn, GNP, is not that important to most countries. For the United States, the difference between GDP and GNP is typically just 1 percent. In some countries, however, the differences are much larger. The country of Kuwait, for example, earned vast amounts of income from its oil riches, which it invested abroad in stocks, bonds, and other types of investments. These earnings comprised approximately 9 percent of Kuwait's 2006 GNP. Foreigners have traditionally made large investments in Australia. As they sent their profits back to their home countries, Australia's net income from abroad was negative in 2006, and Australian GDP in that year exceeded Australian GNP by 4.1 percent.

The second adjustment we make when calculating national income is to subtract depreciation from GNP. Recall that depreciation is the wear and tear on plant and equipment that occurred during the year. In a sense, our income is reduced because our buildings and machines are wearing out. When we subtract depreciation from GNP, we reach *net national product (NNP)*, where *net* means "after depreciation."

After making these adjustments and taking into account statistical discrepancies, we reach *national income*. (Statistical discrepancies arise when government statisticians make their calculations using different sources of the same data.) Table 2 shows the effects of these adjustments for the fourth quarter of 2009.

TABLE 2 FROM GDP TO NATIONAL INCOME, FOURTH QUARTER 2009 (BILLIONS OF DOLLARS)	
Gross domestic product	$14,242
Gross national product	14,363
Net national product	12,513
National income	12,259

In turn, national income is divided among six basic categories: compensation of employees (wages and benefits), corporate profits, rental income, proprietors' income (income of unincorporated business), net interest (interest payments received by households from business and from abroad), and other items. Approximately 65 percent of all national income goes to workers in the form of wages and benefits. For most of the countries in the world, wages and benefits are the largest part of national income.

personal income
Income, including transfer payments, received by households.

In addition to national income, which measures the income earned in a given year by the entire private sector, we are sometimes interested in determining the total payments that flow directly into households, a concept known as **personal income**. To calculate personal income, we begin with national income and subtract any corporate profits that are retained by the corporation and not paid out as dividends to households. We also subtract all taxes on production and imports and social insurance taxes, which are payments for Social Security and Medicare. We then add any personal interest income received from the government and consumers and all transfer payments. The result is the total income available to households, or personal income. The amount of personal income that households retain after paying income taxes is called **personal disposable income**.

personal disposable income
Personal income that households retain after paying income taxes.

Measuring National Income through Value Added

Another way to measure national income is to look at the **value added** of each firm in the economy. For a firm, we can measure its value added by the dollar value of the firm's sales minus the dollar value of the goods and services purchased from other firms. What remains is the sum of all the income—wages, profits, rents, and interest—that the firm generates. By adding up the value added for all the firms in the economy (plus nonprofit and governmental organizations), we can calculate national income. Let's consider a simple example illustrated in Table 3.

value added

The sum of all the income—wages, interest, profits, and rent—generated by an organization. For a firm, we can measure value added by the dollar value of the firm's sales minus the dollar value of the goods and services purchased from other firms.

TABLE 3 CALCULATING VALUE ADDED IN A SIMPLE ECONOMY			
	Automobile Firm	Steel Firm	Total Economy
Total sales	$16,000	$6,000	$22,000
Less purchases from other firms	6,000	0	6,000
Equals value added: the sum of all wages, interest, profits, and rents	10,000	6,000	16,000

Suppose an economy consists of two firms: an automobile firm that sells its cars to consumers and a steel firm that sells only to the automobile firm. If the automobile company sells a car for $16,000 to consumers and purchases $6,000 worth of steel from the steel firm, the auto firm has $10,000 remaining—its value added—which it can then distribute as wages, rents, interest, and profits. If the steel firm sells $6,000 worth of steel but does not purchase any inputs from other firms, its value added is $6,000, which it pays out in the form of wages, rents, interest, and profits. Total value added in the economy from both firms is $16,000 ($10,000 + $6,000), which is the sum of wages, rents, interest, and profits for the entire economy (consisting of these two firms).

As this example illustrates, we measure the value added for a typical firm by starting with the value of its total sales and subtracting the value of any inputs it purchases from other firms. The amount of income that remains is the firm's value added, which is then distributed as wages, rents, interest, and profits. In calculating national income, we need to include all the firms in the economy, even the firms that produce intermediate goods.

APPLICATION 1

USING VALUE ADDED TO MEASURE THE TRUE SIZE OF WAL-MART

APPLYING THE CONCEPTS #1: How can we use economic analysis to compare the size of a major corporation to the size of a country?

During 2008, Wal-Mart's sales were approximately $374 billion, nearly 2.6 percent of U.S. GDP. Some social commentators might want to measure the impact of Wal-Mart just through its sales. But to produce those sales, Wal-Mart had to buy goods from many other companies. Wal-Mart's value added was substantially less than its total sales. Based on Wal-Mart's annual reports, its cost of sales was $286 billion, leaving approximately $88 billion in value added. This is a very large number, as might be expected from the world's largest retailer, but it is much smaller than its total sales. If we used Wal-Mart's sales to compare it to a country, it would have a GDP similar to that of Belgium, which is ranked 28th in the world. However, using the more appropriate measure of value added, Wal-Mart's size is closer to Bulgaria, ranked 56th in the world.

SOURCE: Based on Wal-Mart Annual Report, 2008, http://walmartstores.com/sites/AnnualReport/2008/docs/finrep_00.pdf (accessed July, 2008).

An Expanded Circular Flow

Now that we have examined both production and income, including both the government and the foreign sector, let's take another look at a slightly more realistic circular flow. Figure 4 depicts a circular flow that includes both the government and the foreign sector. Both households and firms pay taxes to the government. The government, in turn, supplies goods and services in the product market and also purchases inputs—labor and capital—in the factor markets, just like private-sector firms do. Net exports, which can be positive or negative, are shown entering or leaving the product market.

In summary, we can look at GDP from two sides: We can ask who buys the output that is produced, or we can ask how the income that is created through the production process is divided between workers and investors. From the spending side, we saw that nearly 70 percent of GDP consists of consumer expenditures. From the income side, we saw that nearly 65 percent of national income is paid in wages and benefits. Macroeconomists may use data based either on the production that occurs in the economy or on its flip side, the income that is generated, depending on whether they are more focused on current production or on current income.

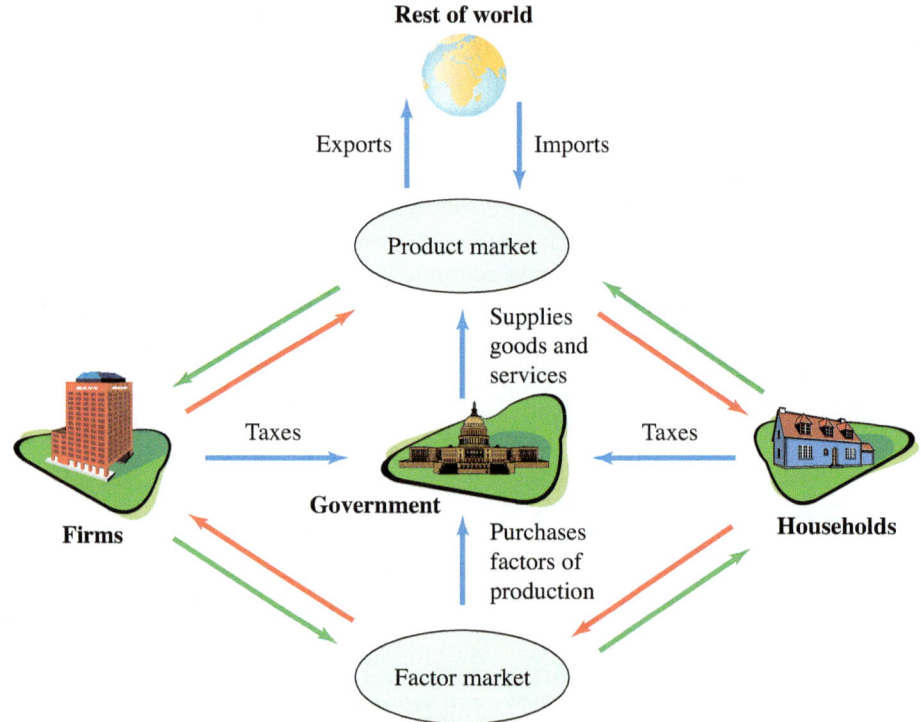

▲ **FIGURE 4**

The Circular Flow with Government and the Foreign Sector

The new linkages (in blue) demonstrate the roles that the government and the foreign sector (imports and exports) play in the circular flow.

4   A CLOSER EXAMINATION OF NOMINAL AND REAL GDP

We have discussed different ways to measure the production of an economy, looking at both who purchases goods and services and the income it generates. Of all the measures we have discussed, GDP is the one most commonly used both by the public and by economists. Let's take a closer look at it.

Measuring Real versus Nominal GDP

Output in the economy can increase from one year to the next. And prices can rise from one year to the next. Recall that we defined nominal GDP as GDP measured in current prices, and we defined real GDP as GDP adjusted for price changes.

Now we take a closer look at how real GDP is measured in modern economies. Let's start with a simple economy in which there are only two goods—cars and computers—produced in the years 2011 and 2012. The data for this economy—the prices and quantities produced for each year—are shown in Table 4. The production of cars and the production of computers increased, but the production of computers increased more rapidly. The price of cars rose, while the price of computers remained the same.

TABLE 4 GDP DATA FOR A SIMPLE ECONOMY

	Quantity Produced		Price	
Year	Cars	Computers	Cars	Computers
2011	4	1	$10,000	$5,000
2012	5	3	12,000	5,000

Let's first calculate nominal GDP for this economy in each year. Nominal GDP is the total market value of goods and services produced in each year. Using the data in the table, we can see that nominal GDP for the year 2011 is

$$(4 \text{ cars} \times \$10,000) + (1 \text{ computer} \times \$5,000) = \$45,000$$

Similarly, nominal GDP for the year 2012 is

$$(5 \text{ cars} \times \$12,000) + (3 \text{ computers} \times \$5,000) = \$75,000$$

Now we'll find real GDP. To compute real GDP, we calculate GDP using constant prices. What prices should we use? For the moment, let's use the prices for the year 2011. Because we are using 2011 prices, real GDP and nominal GDP for 2011 are both equal to $45,000. But for 2012, they are different. In 2012, real GDP is

$$(5 \text{ cars} \times \$10,000) + (3 \text{ computers} \times \$5,000) = \$65,000$$

Note that real GDP for 2012, which is $65,000, is less than nominal GDP for 2012, which is $75,000. The reason real GDP is less than nominal GDP here is that prices of cars rose by $2,000 between 2011 and 2012, and we are measuring GDP using 2011 prices. We can measure real GDP for any other year simply by calculating GDP using constant prices.

We now calculate the growth in real GDP for this economy between 2011 and 2012. Because real GDP was $45,000 in 2011 and $65,000 in 2012, real GDP grew by $20,000. In percentage terms, this is a $20,000 increase from the initial level of $45,000 or

$$\text{Percentage growth in real GDP} = \frac{\$20,000}{\$45,000} = .444$$

which equals 44.4 percent. This percentage is an average of the growth rates for both goods—cars and computers.

Figure 5 depicts real and nominal GDP for the United States from 1950 to 2009. Real GDP is measured in 2000 dollars, so the curves cross in 2000. Before 2000, nominal GDP is less than real GDP because prices in earlier years were lower than they were in 2000. After 2000, nominal GDP exceeds real GDP because prices in later years were higher than they were in 2000.

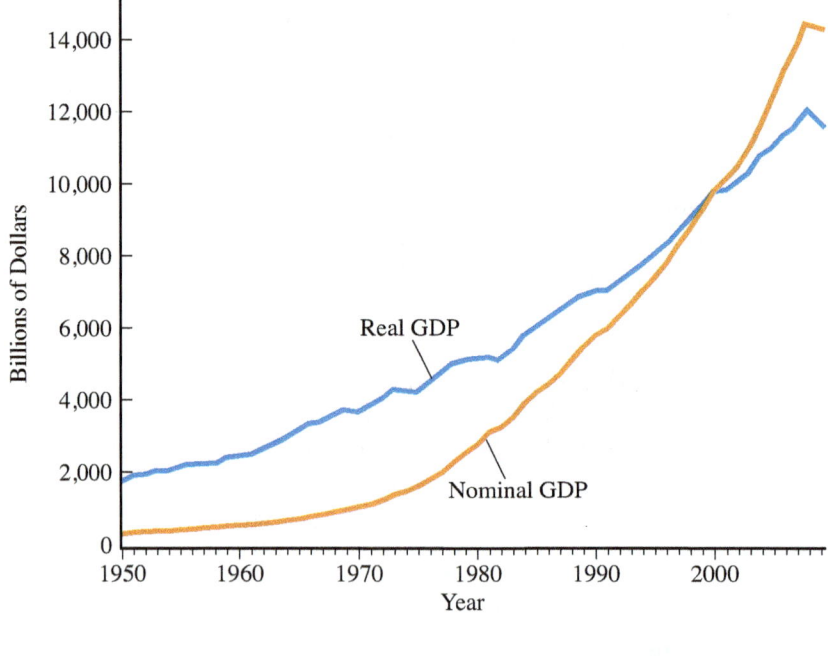

How to Use the GDP Deflator

GDP deflator

An index that measures how the prices of goods and services included in GDP change over time.

We can also use the data in Table 4 to measure the changes in prices for this economy of cars and computers. The basic idea is that the differences between nominal GDP and real GDP for any year arise only because of changes in prices. So by comparing real GDP and nominal GDP, we can measure the changes in prices for the economy. In practice, we do this by creating an index, called the **GDP deflator**, that measures how prices of goods and services change over time. Because we are calculating real GDP using year 2011 prices, we will set the value of this index equal to 100 in the year 2011, which we call the base year. To find the value of the GDP deflator for the year 2012 (or other years), we use the following formula:

$$\text{GDP Deflator} = \frac{\text{Nominal GDP}}{\text{Real GDP}} \times 100$$

Using this formula, we find that the value of the GDP deflator for 2012 is

$$\frac{\$75,000}{\$65,000} \times 100 = 1.15 \times 100 = 115$$

Because the value of the GDP deflator is 115 in 2012 and was 100 in the base year of 2011, this means prices rose by 15 percent between the two years:

$$\frac{115 - 100}{100} = \frac{15}{100} = 0.15$$

Note that this 15 percent is a weighted average of the price changes for the two goods—cars and computers.

Until 1996, the Commerce Department, which produces the GDP figures, used these formulas to calculate real GDP and measure changes in prices. Economists at the department chose a base year and measured real GDP by using the prices in that base year. They also calculated the GDP deflator, just as we did, by taking the ratio of nominal GDP to real GDP. Today, the Commerce Department calculates real GDP and the price index for real GDP using a more complicated method. In our example, we measured real GDP using 2011 prices. But we could have also measured real GDP using prices from 2012. If we did, we would have come up with slightly different numbers both for the increase in prices between the two years and for the increase in real GDP. To avoid this problem, the Commerce Department now uses a **chain-weighted index**, which is a method for calculating price changes that takes an average of price changes using base years from consecutive years (that is, 2011 and 2012 in our example). If you look online or at the data produced by the Commerce Department, you will see real GDP measured in chained dollars and a chain-type price index for GDP.

chain-weighted index
A method for calculating changes in prices that uses an average of base years from neighboring years.

5 FLUCTUATIONS IN GDP

As we have discussed, real GDP does not always grow smoothly—sometimes it collapses suddenly, and the result is an economic downturn. We call such fluctuations *business cycles*. Let's look at an example of a business cycle from the late 1980s and early 1990s. Figure 6 plots real GDP for the United States from 1988 to 1992. Notice that in mid-1990, real GDP begins to fall. A **recession** is a period when real GDP falls for six or more consecutive months. Economists talk more in terms of quarters of the year—consecutive three-month periods—than in terms of months. So they would say that a recession occurs when real GDP falls for two consecutive quarters. The date at which the recession starts—that is, when output starts to decline—is called the **peak**. The date at which it ends—that is, when output starts to increase again—is called the **trough**. In Figure 6, we see the peak and trough of the recession. After a trough, the economy enters a recovery period, or period of **expansion**.

From World War II through 2010, the United States experienced 11 recessions. Table 5 contains the dates of the peaks and troughs of each recession, the percent decline in real GDP from each peak to each trough, and the length of the recessions in months. Complete information is not yet available for the most recent recession, which began in December 2007. Aside from the most recent recession, which was very severe, the sharpest decline in output occurred during the recession from 1973 to 1975, which started as a result of a sharp rise in world oil prices. This was also one of the longest recessions, although the most recent recession will most likely be the longest.

In the last three decades, there have been four recessions, three of them starting near the beginning of each of the decades: 1981, 1990, and 2001. In the 2001 recession, employment began to fall in March 2001, before the terrorist attack on the United States on September 11, 2001. The attack further disrupted economic activity and damaged producer and consumer confidence, and the economy tumbled through a recession. The recession that began in December 2007 followed a sharp decline in the housing sector and the financial difficulties associated with this decline. It deepened during the financial crisis that hit in September and October of 2008. As credit

recession
Commonly defined as six consecutive months of declining real GDP.

peak
The date at which a recession starts.

trough
The date at which output stops falling in a recession.

expansion
The period after a trough in the business cycle during which the economy recovers.

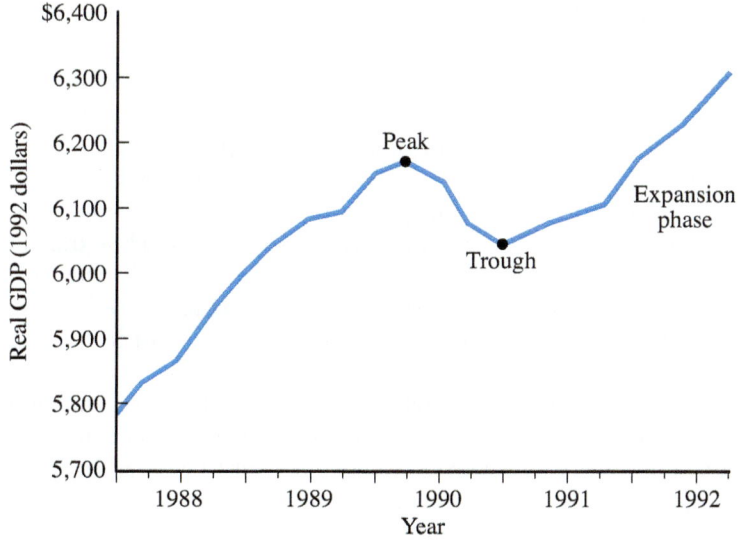

◄ **FIGURE 6**
The 1990 Recession
Recessions can be illustrated by peaks, troughs, and an expansion phase. The date at which the recession starts and output begins to fall is called the peak. The date at which the recession ends and output begins to rise is called the trough. The expansion phase begins after the trough.
SOURCE: U.S. Department of Commerce.

TABLE 5 ELEVEN POSTWAR RECESSIONS

Peak	Trough	Percent Decline in Real GDP	Length of Recession (months)
November 1948	October 1949	−1.5	11
July 1953	May 1954	−3.2	10
August 1957	April 1958	−3.3	8
April 1960	February 1961	−1.2	10
December 1969	November 1970	−1.0	11
November 1973	March 1975	−4.1	16
January 1980	July 1980	−2.5	6
July 1981	November 1982	−3.0	16
July 1990	March 1991	−1.4	8
March 2001	November 2001	−0.6	8
December 2007	June 2009	−4.1	18

SOURCE: National Bureau of Economic Research, "Business Cycle Expansions and Contractions," http://wwwdev
.nber.org/cycles/cyclesmain.html.

became less available to both businesses and consumers, the effects of the financial crisis began to show up in reduced consumer spending for durable goods such as automobiles and reduced business investment.

Throughout the broader sweep of U.S. history, other downturns have occurred—20 of them from 1860 up to World War II. Not all were particularly severe, and in some unemployment hardly changed. However, some economic downturns, such as those in 1893 and 1929, were severe.

Although we used the common definition of a recession as a period when real GDP falls for six months, in practice, a committee of economists at the National Bureau of Economics Research (NBER), a private research group in Cambridge,

APPLICATION 2

Corbis RF/Alamy

COMPARING THE SEVERITY OF RECESSIONS

APPLYING THE CONCEPTS #2: How severe was the most recent recession for the United States?

Was the most recent recession the most severe economic downturn since the Great Depression? With the data now in, it appears that the recession starting in December 2007 will rival the recession starting in November 1973, which was caused by a sharp and unexpected rise in oil prices. From Table 5, we see that the fall in output from peak to trough was 4.1 percent. A similar calculation based on available quarterly data for the recent recession from the fourth quarter of 2007 to the second quarter of 2009 reveals a fall of approximately 4.1%. On this measure, the 2007 recession was equally severe as measured by the decline in GDP.

However, along other important dimensions, the 2007 recession was more damaging to the economy. The 1973 recession lasted 16 months, while the 2007 recession lasted 18 months, the longest in the postwar era. Additionally, the toll on workers appears greater in the most recent recession. Unemployment rose from 4.9 percent to 8.5 percent in the earlier recession as compared to 4.6 percent to 10.0 percent in the most recent recession.

Of course, governments can offset some of these effects on individuals through social programs such as payments to those individuals who become unemployed or welfare payments. For a complete analysis, we would want to look at the incomes of those who lost their jobs as well as those who kept their jobs.

Massachusetts, of primarily academic economists, officially proclaims the beginning and end of recessions in the United States using a broader set of criteria than just GDP. The NBER's formal definition is "a significant decline in economic activity, spread across the economy, lasting more than a few months, normally visible in production, employment, real income, and other indicators." As you can see, it uses a wide variety of indicators to determine whether a recession has occurred and its length.

Depression is the common term for a severe recession. In the United States, the Great Depression refers to the years 1929 through 1933, the period when real GDP fell by over 33 percent. This drop in GDP created the most severe disruptions to ordinary economic life in the United States during the twentieth century. Throughout the country and in much of the world, banks closed, businesses failed, and many people lost their jobs and their life savings. Unemployment rose sharply. In 1933, over 25 percent of people who were looking for work failed to find jobs.

depression
The common name for a severe recession.

Although the United States has not experienced a depression since that time, other countries have. In the last 20 years, several Asian countries (for example, Thailand) and Latin American countries (for example, Argentina) suffered severe economic disruptions that were true depressions.

6 GDP AS A MEASURE OF WELFARE

GDP is our best measure of the value of output produced by an economy. As we have seen, we can use GDP and related indicators to measure economic growth within a country. We will use GDP to compare the value of output across countries as well. Economists use GDP and related measures to determine if an economy has fallen into a recession or has entered into a depression. But while GDP is a very valuable measure of the health of an economy, it is not a perfect measure.

Shortcomings of GDP as a Measure of Welfare

There are several recognized flaws in the construction of GDP. We should thus be cautious in interpreting GDP as a measure of our economic well-being, because it does not take into account housework and childcare, leisure, the underground economy, or pollution.

HOUSEWORK AND CHILDCARE   First, GDP ignores transactions that do not take place in organized markets. The most important example is services, such as cleaning, cooking, and providing free childcare, that people do for themselves in their own homes. Because these services are not transferred through markets, GDP statisticians cannot measure them. If we included household production in GDP, measured GDP would be considerably higher than currently reported.

LEISURE   Second, leisure time is not included in GDP because GDP is designed to be a measure of the production that occurs in the economy. To the extent that households value leisure, increases in leisure time will lead to higher social welfare, but not to higher GDP.

UNDERGROUND ECONOMY   Third, GDP ignores the underground economy, where transactions are not reported to official authorities. These transactions can be legal, but people don't report the income they have generated because they want to avoid paying taxes on it. For example, wait staff may not report all their tips and owners of flea markets may make under-the-table cash transactions with their customers. Illegal transactions, such as profits from the illegal drug trade, also result in unreported income. In the United States in 2005, the Internal Revenue Service estimated (based on tax returns from 2001) that about $310 billion in federal income taxes from the underground economy was not collected each year. If the federal income tax rate that applies to income evaded from taxes was about 20 percent, approximately $1.5 trillion ($310 billion ÷ 0.20) in income from the underground economy escaped the GDP accountants that year, or about 15 percent of GDP at the time.

APPLICATION 3

THE LINKS BETWEEN SELF-REPORTED HAPPINESS AND GDP

APPLYING THE CONCEPTS #3: Do increases in gross domestic product necessarily translate into improvements in the welfare of citizens?

Two economists, David Blanchflower of Dartmouth College and Andrew Oswald of Warwick University in the United Kingdom, have systematically analyzed surveys over a nearly 30-year period that ask individuals to describe themselves as "happy, pretty happy, or not too happy." The results of their work are provocative. Over the last 30 years, reported levels of happiness have declined slightly in the United States and remained relatively flat in the United Kingdom despite very large increases in per capita income in both countries. Could it be the increased stress of everyday life has taken its toll on our happiness despite the increase in income?

At any point in time, however, money does appear to buy happiness. Holding other factors constant, individuals with higher incomes do report higher levels of personal satisfaction. But these "other factors" are quite important. Unemployment and divorce lead to sharply lower levels of satisfaction. Blanchflower and Oswald calculate that a stable marriage is worth $100,000 per year in terms of equivalent reported satisfaction.

Perhaps most interesting are their findings about trends in the relative happiness of different groups in our society. While whites report higher levels of happiness than African Americans, the gap has decreased over the last 30 years, as the happiness of African Americans has risen faster than that of whites. Men's happiness has risen relative to that of women over the last 30 years.

Finally, in recent work Blanchflower and Oswald looked at how happiness varies over the life cycle. Controlling for income, education, and other personal factors, they found that in the United States, happiness among men and women reaches a minimum at the ages of 49 and 45, respectively. Since these are also the years in which earnings are usually the highest, it does suggest that work takes its toll on happiness.

SOURCE: David Blanchflower and Andrew Oswald, "Well-Being Over Time in Britain and the USA," (working paper 7847, National Bureau of Economic Research, January 2000) and "Is Well-being U-Shaped over the Life Cycle," (working paper 12935, February 2007).

Economists have used a variety of methods to estimate the extent of the underground economy throughout the world. They typically find that the size of the underground economy is much larger in developing countries than in developed countries. For example, in the highly developed countries, estimates of the underground economy are between 15 and 20 percent of reported or official GDP. However, in developing countries, estimates are closer to 40 percent of reported GDP. Table 6 contains

TABLE 6 THE WORLD UNDERGROUND ECONOMY, 2002–2003	
Region of the World	Underground Economy as Percent of Reported GDP
Africa	41%
Central and South America	41
Asia	30
Transition Economies	38
Europe, United States, and Japan	17
Unweighted Average over 145 Countries	35

SOURCE: Based on estimates by Friedrich Schneider in "The Size of Shadow Economies in 145 Countries from 1999 to 2003," unpublished paper, 2005.

estimates of the underground economy as a percent of reported GDP for different regions of the world.

POLLUTION   Fourth, GDP does not value changes in the environment that occur in the production of output. Suppose a factory produces $1,000 of output but pollutes a river and lowers its value by $2,000. Instead of recording a loss to society of $1,000, GDP will show a $1,000 increase. This is an important limitation of GDP accounting as a measure of our economic well-being, because changes in the environment affect our daily lives. Previous attempts by the Commerce Department to measure the effects of changes in environment by adding positive or subtracting negative changes to the environment from national income did not yield major results. But they were limited and looked only at a very select part of the environment. Has our environment improved or deteriorated as we experienced economic growth? Finding the answer to this question will pose a real challenge for the next generation of economic statisticians.

Most of us would prefer to live in a country with a high standard of living, and few of us would want to experience poverty up close. But does a higher level of GDP really lead to more satisfaction?

SUMMARY

In this chapter, we learned how economists and government statisticians measure the income and production for an entire country and what these measures are used for. Developing meaningful statistics for an entire economy is difficult. As we have seen, statistics can convey useful information—if they are used with care. Here are some of the main points to remember in this chapter:

1 The circular flow diagram shows how the production of goods and services generates income for households and how households purchase goods and services by firms. The expanded circular flow diagram includes government and the foreign sector.

2 *Gross domestic product* (GDP) is the market value of all final goods and services produced in a given year.

3 GDP consists of four components: consumption, investment, government purchases, and net exports. The following equation combines these components:

$$Y = C + I + G + NX$$

The *GDP deflator* is an index that measures how the prices of goods and services included in GDP change over time. The following equation helps us find the GDP deflator:

$$\text{GDP Deflator} = \frac{\text{Nominal GDP}}{\text{Real GDP}} \times 100$$

4 *National income* is obtained from GDP by adding the net income U.S. individuals and firms earn from abroad, then subtracting depreciation.

5 *Real GDP* is calculated by using constant prices. The Commerce Department now uses methods that take an average using base years from neighboring years.

6 *A recession* is commonly defined as a six-month consecutive period of negative growth. However, in the United States, the National Bureau of Economic Research uses a broader definition.

7 GDP does not include nonmarket transactions, leisure time, the underground economy, or changes to the environment.

KEY TERMS

chain-weighted index	government purchases	national income
consumption expenditures	gross domestic product (GDP)	net exports
depreciation	gross investment	net investment
depression	gross national product (GNP)	nominal GDP
economic growth	import	peak
expansion	inflation	personal disposable income
export	intermediate good	personal income
GDP deflator	macroeconomics	

private investment expenditures	recession	transfer payments
real GDP	trade deficit	trough
	trade surplus	value added

EXERCISES

Visit www.myeconlab.com to complete these exercises online and get instant feedback.

1 The "Flip" Sides of Macroeconomic Activity: Production and Income

1.1 The circular flow describes the process by which GDP generates _____, which is spent on goods and services.

1.2 Labor and capital are exchanged in _____ markets.

1.3 Which government department produces the National Income and Product Accounts?
  a. The Department of Education
  b. The Department of Commerce
  c. The Congressional Budget Office
  d. The Council of Economic Advisors

1.4 The provision of educational services is not counted as output in modern economies. _____ (True/False)

1.5 **Understanding the Circular Flow Diagram.** In the circular flow diagram, why do the arrows corresponding to the flow of dollars and the arrows corresponding to the flow of goods go in the opposite direction?

1.6 **Types of Income.** Sometimes economists distinguish between wages on the one hand, and rents, interest, and profits on the other. What is the basis of that distinction?

2 The Production Approach: Measuring a Nation's Macroeconomic Activity Using Gross Domestic Product

2.1 Which of the following is not a component of GDP?
  a. Consumption
  b. Investment
  c. Producer Price Index
  d. Government purchases
  e. Net exports

2.2 What part of government spending is excluded from GDP because it does not correspond to goods and services currently being produced?
  a. National defense
  b. Transfer payments
  c. Education
  d. Purchases of police cars

2.3 If depreciation exceeds gross investment, net investment will be _____.

2.4 A trade deficit occurs when _____ exceeds _____.

2.5 **GDP Statistics and Unemployed Workers.** In Economy A, the government puts workers on the payroll who cannot find jobs for long periods, but these "employees" do no work. In Economy B, the government does not hire any long-term unemployed workers but gives them cash grants. Comparing the GDP statistics between the two otherwise identical economies, what can you determine about measured GDP and the actual level of output in each economy?

2.6 **Health Care Subsidies.** If the federal government provides subsidies for individuals to buy health-care insurance, is this included in the federal budget? Is it included in GDP?

2.7 **The Upside and Downside of Trade Deficits.** A student once said, "Trade deficits are bad because we are buying goods from abroad and not making them here." What is an upside to trade deficits?

2.8 **Depreciation and Consumer Durables.** Consumer durables depreciate just like investment goods. Suppose you purchase a refrigerator for $1000 and, at the same time, four new designer dresses worth $1,000. After one year, has the refrigerator or the designer dresses depreciated more? Why?

2.9 **Investment Spending versus Intermediate Goods.** A publisher buys paper, ink, and computers to produce textbooks. Which of these purchases is included in investment spending? Which are intermediate goods?

3 The Income Approach: Measuring a Nation's Macroeconomic Activity Using National Income

3.1 What do we add to GDP to reach GNP?
  a. Net income earned abroad by U.S. households
  b. Personal income
  c. Depreciation
  d. Net exports

3.2 What is the largest component of national income?

    a. Compensation of employees (wages and benefits)

    b. Corporate profits

    c. Rental income

    d. Proprietors' income (income of unincorporated business)

    e. Net interest

3.3 Personal income and personal disposable income refer to payments ultimately flowing to _____ (households/firms).

3.4 The difference between gross national product and net national product is _____ .

3.5 **Measuring Value Added for a Charity.** The United Way is a nonprofit charity and does not sell products. Explain one way you could measure its value added.

3.6 **Understanding Why GNP and GDP May Differ.** If a country discovered vast amounts of oil, sold it abroad, and invested the proceeds throughout the world, how would its GDP and GNP compare?

3.7 **Transfer Payments, National Income, and Personal Income.** Taking into account the role of transfer payments, explain why national income could fall more than personal income during a recession.

3.8 **Philippine Immigrants Abroad.** Every year, the Philippines sends many workers abroad including nurses, health professionals, and oil workers. How do you think GNP and GDP in the Philippines compare?

3.9 **Sales versus Value Added.** Explain carefully why value added may be a better measure than total sales in comparing a country to a corporation. Hint: If we measured total sales in a country, would this exceed GDP? (Related to Application 1.)

---

4 A Closer Examination of Nominal and Real GDP

4.1 The GDP deflator is calculated for any given year by dividing nominal GDP by _____ GDP and multiplying by 100.

4.2 If the base year is 2010, then real and nominal GDP in 2010 will be equal. _____ (True/False)

4.3 Measured price changes do not depend on the particular base year chosen when calculating

    a. the traditional GDP deflator.

    b. the chain-weighted GDP deflator.

    c. real GDP.

4.4 To compute nominal GDP, it is important to use an accurate price index. _____ (True/False)

4.5 **Calculating Real GDP, Price Indices, and Inflation.** Using data from the following table, answer the following questions:

    a. Calculate real GDP using prices from 2011. By what percent did real GDP grow?

    b. Calculate the value of the price index for GDP for 2012 using 2011 as the base year. By what percent did prices increase?

	Quantities Produced		Prices	
	CDs	Tennis Rackets	Price per CD	Price per Tennis Racket
2011	100	200	$20	$110
2012	120	210	22	120

4.6 **Using a New Base Year to Calculate Real GDP and Inflation.** Repeat Exercise 4.5 but use prices from 2012.

4.7 **Understanding the Relationship between Real and Nominal GDP in a Figure.** In Figure 5 the base year is 2000. Explain why the line for nominal GDP lies below the line for real GDP in the years prior to 2000. If the base year was 2005, where would the two lines cross?

4.8 **Using U.S. Economic Data to Measure the Economy.** Go to the Web site for the Federal Reserve Bank of St. Louis (www.research.stlouisfed.org/fred2). Find the data for nominal GDP, real GDP in chained dollars, and the chain price index for GDP.

    a. Calculate the percentage growth for nominal GDP since 2000 until the most recent year.

    b. Calculate the percentage growth in real GDP since 2000 until the most recent year.

    c. Finally, calculate the percentage growth in the chain price index for GDP over this same period and compare it to the difference between your answers to (a) and (b).

---

5 Fluctuations in GDP

5.1 The date that a recession begins is called the _____ .

5.2 Since World War II, the United States has experienced seven recessions. _____ (True/False)

5.3 The _____ marks the date that ends a recession and output starts to increase again.

5.4 The organization that officially dates recessions in the United States is the

a. Congressional Budget Office.
b. Department of Commerce.
c. National Bureau of Economic Research.
d. Council of Economic Advisors.

5.5 Counting Recessions. Consider the data for the fictitious economy of Euronet:

Year and Quarter	2003: 1	2003: 2	2003: 3	2003: 4	2004: 1	2004: 2	2004: 3
Real GDP	195	193	195	196	195	194	198

How many recessions occurred in the economy over the time indicated?

5.6 Alternative Methods of Measuring Recessions. To compare how deeply recessions affected the economies of two different countries, we might use the following measures:

a. The number of recessions
b. The proportion of time each economy was in a recession
c. The magnitude of the worst recession

Here are data from three hypothetical economies. According to each of the measures listed, which economy was affected most deeply by recessions? (Related to Application 2.)

Year and Quarter	Country 1	Country 2	Country 3
2010.1	100.0	100.0	100.0
2010.2	103.0	103.0	103.0
2010.3	100.9	106.1	106.1
2010.4	95.9	102.9	109.3
2011.1	91.1	99.8	87.4
2011.2	86.5	96.8	69.9
2011.3	90.9	93.9	72.0
2011.4	95.4	91.1	74.2
2012.1	100.2	88.4	76.4
2012.2	105.2	85.7	78.7
2012.3	99.9	83.1	81.1
2012.4	94.9	85.6	83.5
2013.1	90.2	88.2	86.0
2013.2	85.7	90.9	88.6
2013.3	90.0	93.6	91.2
2013.4	94.5	96.4	94.0

5.7 Most Severe Recession? Using the data in Table 5, identify the two most severe recessions since World War II. What other information might you want to know about these and other recessionary periods to judge their severity? (Related to Application 2.)

6 GDP as a Measure of Welfare

6.1 Which of the following are not included in GDP?

a. Leisure time
b. Sales of new cars
c. Strawberries sold in a grocery store
d. Economics textbooks sold in the bookstore

6.2 Men's reported happiness has increased relative to women's reported happiness in the last several decades. _____ (True/False) (Related to Application 3.)

6.3 The approximate percentage of GDP in the United States that goes unreported because of the underground economy is _____.

6.4 Illegal activities are not computed as part of measured GDP because they are not

a. legal.
b. production.
c. reported.
d. big enough to worry about.

6.5 Does Spending Measure Welfare? Suppose a community spends $1 million on salaries and equipment for its police department. Because it believes that citizens are now more law abiding, the community decides to cut back on the number of police it employs. As a result, the community now spends $800,000 less on the police officers. The crime rate remains the same.

a. What happens to measured GDP?
b. Does GDP accurately reflect welfare in this case? Discuss the underlying issue that this example poses.

6.6 Disappearing Trees and National Income. Suppose you were worried that national income does not adequately take into account the extraction of trees that provide shade and help stem global warming. How would you advise the Commerce Department to include this factor in its calculations?

6.7 Air Quality and Measured GDP. Air quality in Los Angeles deteriorated in the 1950s through the 1970s and then improved in the 1980s and 1990s. Can a change in air quality such as this be incorporated into our measures of national income? Discuss.

6.8 **Comparing Welfare across Countries.** Suppose Country A and Country B have exactly the same measured real GDP, but in Country A, the average worker spends more time at home, either doing housework or on vacation. Which country has a higher level of welfare and why?

6.9 **Does Money Buy Happiness?** Although people with high incomes appear to be happier than those with low incomes, people in the United States in general have become less happy over the last 30 years even though real GDP has risen. What are some of the reasons why the increase in real GDP does not always imply greater happiness? (Related to Application 3.)

6.10 **Measuring Happiness across States.** Suppose statisticians find from survey data that the residents of California and Louisiana report that they are equally happy. However, incomes in California are higher, on average, than those in Louisiana. Could you make a case that living in Louisiana actually makes you happier than living in California?

Index

Page references followed by "f" indicate illustrated figures or photographs; followed by "t" indicates a table.